ENTREPRENEURSHIP MANAGEMENT

PASSION WORKS WONDERS

- ENTREPRENEURSHIP
- OPPORTUNITIES
- IDENTIFICATION
- ROLE
- MANAGEMENT
- MARKETING
- SOLUTION

VASANT DESAI

Himalaya Publishing House
ISO 9001:2015 CERTIFIED

First Edition : 2011
Reprint : 2015
Reprint : 2018
Reprint : 2023
Reprint : 2024
Reprint : 2026

Published by : Mrs. Meena Pandey
for **HIMALAYA PUBLISHING HOUSE PVT. LTD.,**
Vishal Industrial Estate, 1st Floor, Office No. 63/64,
Bhandup Village Road, Subhash Nagar (Opp. CEAT Tyres),
Nahur (W), Mumbai - 400 078. **Phone:** 022-35131464/65/66/67
E-mail: himpub@bharatmail.co.in; **Website:** www.himpub.com

Branch Offices :

New Delhi : "Pooja Apartments", 4-B, Murari Lal Street, Ansari Road, Darya Ganj, New Delhi - 110 002.
Phone: 011-23270392, 23278631; Fax: 011-23256286

Nagpur : Kundanlal Chandak Industrial Estate, Ghat Road, Nagpur - 440 018.
Mobile: 09325409992, 09325908881

Bengaluru : Plot No. 91-33, 2nd Main Road, Seshadripuram, Behind Nataraja Theatre,
Bengaluru - 560 020. Phone: 080-41138821; Mobile: 09379847017, 09379847005

Hyderabad : No. 3-4-184, Lingampally, Besides Raghavendra Swamy Matham, Kachiguda,
Hyderabad - 500 027. Phone: 040-27560041, 27550139

Chennai : No. 34/44, Motilal Street, T. Nagar, Chennai - 600 017. Mobile: 09380460419

Pune : "Laksha" Apartment, First Floor, No. 527, Mehunpura,
Shaniwarpeth (Near Prabhat Theatre), Pune - 411 030.
Phone: 020-24496323, 24496333; Mobile: 09370579333

Cuttack : Plot No. 5F-755/4, Sector-9, CDA Markat Nagar, Cuttack - 753 014,
Odisha. Mobile: 09338746007

Kolkata : 3, S.M. Bose Road, Near Gate No. 5, Agarpara Railway Station,
North 24 Parganas, West Bengal - 700 109. Mobile: 09674536325

DTP by : Prerana Enterprises, Mumbai.

Printed at : Geetanjali Press Pvt. Ltd., Nagpur. On behalf of HPH (P).

IN RECOGNITION OF ENTREPRENEURIAL SPIRIT

BILL GATES

This "Entrepreneurship Management" study is dedicated to the infotech icon, Bill Gates for his entrepreneurial spirit in founding and nurturing Microsoft, the biggest software company in the world. Microsoft had revenues of $39.79 billion for the fiscal year ending June 2005, and employs more than 61,000 people in 102 countries and regions and opening up windows to revolutionise information technology, fostering entrepreneurship and philanthropic efforts.

PERSONAL FOLDER

Name : William Henry Gates III

Born : October 28, 1955

Parents : Gates' father, William H. Gates II, is a seating the attorny. His late mother, Mary Gates, was a schoolteacher, University of Washington regent, and chairwoman of United Way International.

Education : Dropped out of Harvard University during his junior year.

Work Experience: Founded Microsoft Corp with childhood friend Paul Allen, 1975; served as chief executive until 2000, chief software architect 2000-2006; remains chairman; founded the Bill and Melinda Gates Foundation, 2000.

Family : Wife, Melinda; three children.

Gates married Melinda French, a Microsoft employee, on 1st January, 1994. The couple have three children: daughters Jennifer Katharine (b. 1996) and Phonebe Adele (b. 2002) and son Rory John (b. 1999).

Personal Wealth: \$50 bn (Forbes estimate), making him the world's richest man. (Approx Rs. 2,30,000 crore)

Trivia about Gates

- In 1968, when the first computers were installed at his school, Gates' grades fell because he would spend days and nights learning the new device.
- Bill Gates bought the Codex Leicester in 1995 for \$30 million. This manuscript, the only one not held in Europe, includes Leonardo da Vinci's studies on hydraulics and the movement of water.
- If you presume that Bill Gates has worked 14 hours a day on every business day of the year since he started Microsoft, then he's been making money at a staggering million dollars per hour, around \$300 per second. Which means if Gates found a \$1,000 note on the street, it wouldn't be worth his while to pick it up.
- If Gates gave away Rs. 1 crore every day, he would have to live for another 653 years to give it all away.
- If Gates liked making expensive movies, he could make Titanic — the most expensive film ever made — 2884 times.
- If all of Gates' wealth was distributed equally to everyone on the earth, each person — including Bill Gates — would get \$15.

PREFACE

Entrepreneurship is a dynamic process of creating incremental wealth. It is an applied seience. In the twenty-first century entrepreneurship has received a big push with the information technology revolution sweeping all over the globe.

Entrepreneurship is a multi-disciplinary subject and has been rightly introduced in various universities and management schools in India.

To be successful, an entrepreneur needs expertise in various allied fields like production, finance, marketing, organisation, human resources, administration, taxation, labour laws, etc., in addition to possessing distinct entrepreneurial qualities. In fact an entrepreneur is a leader motivator with a passion to excel in the activities he undertakes.

Entrepreneurship management forms the core of a business venture. The success depends on the core values, management techniques and their implementation.

Entrepreneurship management is basically concerned with the issues concerning development, growth and organization of enterprises. The very purpose of an enterprise is to carry out business in a smooth and effective manner. It is the prime objective of an entrepreneur to ensure that his basic urge for enterprising abilities be satisfied and that the business earn reasonable returns on the investment.

The purpose of the text is to enrich students, entrepreneurs with an understanding of the entrepreneurial process as well as entrepreneurship management practice. In the process to help them to be better prepared for transforming dreams into realities. consequently. The book is organised to explore the nature of entrepreneurship management and help to succeed.

DISTINGUISHING FEATURES

The book is organised to provide a systematic presentation in founding a new venture, nurture it to grow and manage it with great success. Chapters are organised to help students to learn about entrepreneurship management.

Cultivating entrepreneurship often involves changing and sustaining a new set of social values. The challenge of this process is perhaps most clearly discerned in the transitional economies of Central and Eastern Europe, but in fact many emerging democracies around the world have equally daunting obstacles to overcome. For this reason Allan Gibb's article on building a culture of entrepreneurship in Central and Eastern Europe provides insights that are applicable to most developing countries.

A big part of cultivating entrepreneurship involves establishing an environment where business can flourish.

Organization of the Text

There are 30 chapters in the text. This mumber was chosen to provide a sequence of topics that could be presented in a normal semester.

In particular Chapters 22-30 explore a few of the modern entrepreneurial solutions which will enhance the effeciency of the organisations and make it globally competitive.

A CREATIVE STUDY

Entrepreneurship and management is not only creative but also cohesive and interesting. It offers to entrepreneurs, intrapreneurs a rich fare of stimulating ideas, a new vision challenging insights, right management and entrepreneurial solutions. All people engaged in entrepreneurial activities will find the study assisting in accelerating and steering the process of economic growth in the right direction.

The book would not only be useful to the students of M.Com., M.B.A. and other related entrepreneurial courses, but also to administrators, planners, educationists, bankers, project officers, industrial consultants, financial institutions, industrialists and more importantly, to the new entrepreneurs. It is the new entrepreneurs who have the onerous responsibility of shaping the destiny of the nation. They are the catalytic agents of change, progress and performance.

In the preparation of this book, I have drawn heavily from the published works in the sphere of entrepreneurial development programmes.

I look forward to receiving suggestions from students, entrepreneurs, managers and readers for improving the contents and presentation of this book.

ACKNOWLEDGEMENT

Many people — students, business executives, entrepreneurs, professors, and publishing staff have made this book possible.

My debt to those who have helped me in one way or the other is heavy indeed. While I take this opportunity to thank all of them — they are too numerous to be mentioned in this brief preface — I would like to acknowledge my deep sense of gratitude to Dr. Narendra Kumar for his ungrudging help at all stages, and to the many veteran professional entrepreneurs and consultant economists for their precise guidance. Thanks are also due to K.N. Pandey, Shri Anuj Pandey, Shri Neeraj Pandey, Ms. Pratibha Chowdhary, Phalguni Ravi and M.V. Desai for their suggestions for affecting a number of stylistic improvements.

Lastly, no words can adequately express my debt of gratitude to my late father, Shri Ranganath Balwant Mutalik Desai, and my late mother, Smt. Laxmidevi, for generating in me a perennial interest in higher studies. I will be failing in my duty if I do not mention here the tremendous co-operation I received from my wife and my daughter in the completion of this voluminous work, in particular, whose patience, support, encouragement, understanding and love helped to bring this effort to fruition.

Vasant Desai

Contents

UNIT – I
ENTREPRENEURSHIP

1. Entrepreneurship: A Conceptual Framework
2. Entrepreneurship: An Indian Scenario
3. Entrepreneurial Personality

Azim Premji
Chairman, WIPRO

Premji's Advice to Startups

- If you want something hard, you can make it happen
- There is no substitute for action
- You should be driven by a deeply captivating challenge
- Strategy achieves little without hardwork and passion
- Have a deep and unflinching commitment to values

Entrepreneurship

The words entrepreneur and entrepreneurship have acquired special significance in the context of economic growth in a rapidly changing socio-economic and socio-cultural climates, particularly in industry, both in developed and developing countries. The experience in the industrialised countries like the United States of America, Germany, Japan and the United Kingdom are authoritatively cited in support of this claim. An in-depth study of the subject thus, becomes not only relevant but also necessary.

Entrepreneurial development is a complex phenomenon. Productive activity undertaken by him and constant endeavour to sustain and improve it are the outward expression of this process of development of his personality. Such process is crystallisation of social milieu from which he comes, family imbibes, make-up of his mind, personal attitudes, caste system, educational level, parental occupation, and so on.

An entrepreneur is one of the important segments of economic growth. Basically he is a person responsible for setting up a business or an enterprise. In fact, he is one who has the initiative, skill for innovation and who looks for high achievements. He is a catalytic agent of change and works for the good of people. He puts up new greenfield projects that create wealth, open up many employment opportunities and leads to the growth of other sectors.

Who is an Entrepreneur?

The entrepreneur as a person brings in overall change through innovation for the maximum social good. Human values remain sacred and inspire him to serve society. He has firm belief in social betterment and he carries out this responsibility with conviction. In this process, he accelerates personal, economic as well as human development. The entrepreneur is a visionary and an integrated man with outstanding leadership qualities. With a desire to excel, he gives top priority to Research and Development. He always works for the well-being of the society. More importantly, entrepreneurial activities encompass all fields / sectors and fosters a spirit of enterprise for the welfare of mankind.

Urges of an Entrepreneur

An urge to exercise power over things and objects persists among all human beings. The urge may vary in degree from person to person. This urge is an intrinsic quality of an entrepreneur. Sociologists consider him as a sensitive energiser – in the modernisation of societies. The psychologists look upon him as an entrepreneurial man, his motivations and aspirations as conducive to development. Political scientists regard him as a leader of the system. To economists, he is a harbinger of economic growth. In all he combines entrepreneurial drive with leadership and innovativeness.

The entrepreneur is a critical factor in the socio-economic change. He is the key person who envisages new opportunities, new techniques, new lines of production, new products and coordinates all other activities.

Importance of an Entrepreneur

The Entrepreneur is one of the most important inputs in the economic development of a country or of regions within the country. Entrepreneurial competence makes all the difference in the rate of economic growth. In India, state and private entrepreneurship co-exist. The small-scale industrial sector and business are left completely to private entrepreneurs. It is in this context that an increasingly important role has been assigned to the identification and promotion of entrepreneurs for this sector.

The need for a broad-based entrepreneurial class in India arises from the need to speed up the process of activating the factors of production, leading to a higher rate of economic growth, dispersal of economic activities, development of backward and tribal areas, creation of employment opportunities, improvement in the standard of living of the weaker sections of the society and involvement of all sections of the society in the process of growth.

Several factors go into the making of an entrepreneur. Individuals who initiate, establish, maintain and expand new enterprises constitute the entrepreneurial class. The socio-political and economic conditions, the availability of industrial technology and know-how, state of art and culture of business and trading, existence of markets for products and services and the incentives and facilities available for starting an industry or business, all have a bearing on the growth of entrepreneurship. A conducive environment is created through the policies and interest of the government in economic and industrial development.

Entrepreneurial Behaviours

- *grasping opportunity*
- *taking initiative*
- *solving problems creatively*
- *managing autonomously*
- *taking responsibility for, and ownership of, things*
- *seeing things through*
- *networking effectively to manage interdependence*
- *putting things together creatively*
- *using judgement to take calculated risk*

Enterpreneurial Attributes

- *achievement orientation and ambition*
- *self-confidence and self-esteem*
- *perseverance*
- *high internal locus of control (autonomy)*
- *action orientation*
- *preference for learning by doing*
- *hard-working*
- *determination*
- *creativity*

Enterpreneurial Skills

- *creative problem-solving*
- *persuading*
- *negotiating*
- *selling*
- *proposing*
- *holistically managing business/projects/ situations*
- *strategic thinking*
- *intuitive decision making under uncertainty*
- *networking*

Logistics will not operate on operational efficiency, but will also demand a strategy aligned to one's business objectives.

Strategic logistics will look beyond its own parish to check for optimisation at the other nodes on your value chain. After all, with linkages to most of the other activities in your company, logistics is more likely to deliver better results if it can operate in those areas as well. The involvements, usually, tactical, being the result of on-the-spot innovations rather than of established principles. The only rule: do what it takes.

Laws of Logistics:

(1) Hone your operations
(2) Channel your resources
(3) Serve the end-user
(4) Attack the inventories
(5) Apply tactical solutions

1

ENTREPRENEURSHIP: A CONCEPTUAL FRAMEWORK

Introduction

Entrepreneurship is a process undertaken by an entrepreneur to augment his business interests. It is an exercise involving innovation and creativity that will go towards establishing his/her enterprise. It is one of the four mainstream economic factors: land, labour, capital and entrepreneurship.

In this chapter, the concept of entrepreneurship and of its related issues are analysed, discussed and deliberated.

Development of the Concept of Entrepreneurship

The word 'Entrepreneurship' appeared first, in French according to Encyclopedia Britannica. In the early 16th Century, it was applied to those who were engaged in Military expeditions. In the 17th Century, it was extended to cover civil engineering activities such as construction fortification. The word itself derived from 17th Century French entrepreprendre, refers to individuals who were 'undertakers' meaning those who "undertook" the risk of new enterprise. They were "contractors" who bore the risks of profit or loss.

Oxford English Dictionary (1897) defined entrepreneur simply as "the director or manager, of a public musical institution; one who 'gets up' entertainments, especially musical performance." Not until its supplement appeared in 1933, did the dictionary recognise that the word has a place in business, and would mean "One who undertakes an enterprise especially contractor... acting as intermediary between capital and labour." Joseph Schumpeter noted that the fifteenth century thinkers had established ideas about the businessman and his functions. But it is not a profession or a permanent occupation and, therefore, it cannot formulate a social class like that of capitalists or wage earners. Psychologically, entrepreneurs are not solely motivated by profit. Schumpeterian 'innovation' is a creative response to a situation.

Entrepreneurship was a common to prime economic essays for much of the 18th and 19th centuries. Notable early French and Austrian economists wrote enthusiastically as well as exhaustively about entrepreneurs as the preservative economists.

One of the qualities of entrepreneurship is the ability to discover an investment opportunity and to organise an enterprise, thereby contributing to real economic growth. It involves taking of risks and making the necessary investments under conditions of uncertainty and innovating, planning, and taking decisions so as to increase production in agriculture, business, industry etc.

Entrepreneurship is a composite skill, the resultant of a mix of many qualities and traits — these include tangible factors as imagination, readiness to take risks, ability to bring together and put to use other factors of production, capital, labour, land, as also intangible factors such as the ability to mobilise scientific and technological advances.

A Practical approach is necessary to implement and manage a project by securing the required licences, approvals and finance from governmental and financial agencies. The personal incentive is to make profits from the successful management of the project. A sense of cost consciousness is even more necessary for the long-term success of the enterprise. However, both are different sides of the same coin. Entrepreneurship lies more in the ability to minimise the use of resources and to put them to maximum advantage. Without an awareness of quality and desire for excellence, consumer acceptance cannot be achieved and sustained. Above all, entrepreneurship today is the product of team work and the ability to create, build and work as a team. The entrepreneur is the maestro of the business orchestra, wielding his baton to which the band is played.

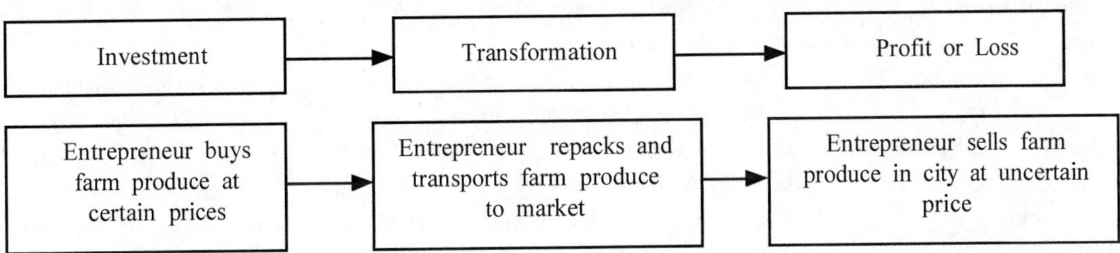

Fig. 1.1: *Cantillon's Early View of Entrepreneurs and Behaviour*

What is Entrepreneurship?

Entepreneurship is the propensity of mind to take calculated risks with confidence to achieve a pre-determined business or industrial objective. In substance, it is the risk-taking ability of the individual, broadly coupled with correct decision-making. When one witnesses a relatively larger number of individuals and that too, generation after generation in a particular community, who engage themselves in the industrial or commercial pursuits and appear to take risks and show enterprise, it is acknowledged to be a commercial class. The commercial class is a myth just like that of the so-called martial race. There are neither, for all time, martial races nor commercial classes. Communities which in the course history once appeared to be martial in spirit have in later period emerged as mercantile societies. Those who were once concerned with and relished in trade, later in history seem to have taken to the profession of these word. Today, it is quite evident to anyone that national communities which have developed world-wide industrial and consequent commercial interests are militarily powerful; nay, great industrial powers have today become super-military powers as well. An enterprise finds manifestation in different ways. The capacity to take risk independently and individually with a view to making profits and seizing an opportunity to make more earnings in the market-oriented economy is the dominant characteristic of modern entrepreneurship. An enterprise, ready for the pursuit of business and responsive to profit by way of producing and/or marketing goods and commodities to meet the expanding and diversifying actual and potential needs and demands of the customers is what constitutes the entrepreneurial stuff. But this category of enterprising citizens throws up a species of entrepreneurs who are mostly mercantile in outlook and performance. In countries like India, a new species of entrepreneurs is desirable because here the economic progress has to be brought about along with social justice.

Entrepreneurship in India therefore, has to sub-serve the national objectives. The apparent conflict between social objectives and economic imperatives has to be resolved first by the individual entrepreneur in his own mind and initiate economic growth which includes industrial development as one of the instruments of attaining the social objectives. A high sense of social responsibility is thus an essential attribute of the emerging entrepreneurship in India.

Table 1.1

Entrepreneurship : Some Important Definitions

Joseph Alois Schumpeter : (1883-1957)	Schumpeter described entrepreneurship as a process to shatter the *status quo* through new combinations of resources and new methods of commerce.
Richard Cantillon :	Entrepreneurship is a matter of foresight and willingness to assume risks, which is not necessarily connected with the employment of labour in some productive process.
Leon Walrus :	Entrepreneurship is not itself a factor of production, but rather a function that can be carried on.
William Diamond :	Entrepreneurship is equivalent to enterprise which involves the willingness to assume risks in undertaking an economic activity particularly a new one.
Jaffrey J.A. Timmons :	Entrepreneurship is the ability to create and build something from practically nothing. A human creative activity.
Janil and Howard Stevenson :	Entrepreneurship is a process by which individuals — either on their on or inside organisation — pursue opportunities without regard to the sources they currently control.
Isrel Kirzner :	Entrepreneurship means alertness towards profit opportunities.
Arthur H. Cole :	Entrepreneurship is the purposeful activity of an individual or a group of associated individuals, undertaken to initiate, maintain or aggrandise profit by production or distribution of foods and services.
Everett E. Hessins :	Entrepreneurship meant the function of seeking investment and production opportunity, organising an enterprise to undertake a new production process, raising labour, arranging the supply of raw materials, finding site, introducing a new technique, discovering sources of raw materials and selecting top managers of day operations of the enterprise.
Peter F. Drucker : (1909-2005)	Entrepreneurship is neither a science nor an art. It is a practice. It has knowledge, base knowledge in entrepreneurship is a means to an end, it is not just about making money. It is about imagination, flexibility, creativity, willingness to think continuously, readiness to take risks, affiliate to moguls, agents of proton action and cape city to see change as an apportunity. It is also about marrying passion and process with a good dose of perseverance.
M. Low and J. Mac Millan :	Entrepreneurship is the creation of an innovative economic organisation. Core network of organisations for the purpose of gain or growth under conditions of risk and uncertainty.

H. Aldrich and C. Zimmer:	The definition of entrepreneurship includes more than the mere creation of a business, it also includes the generation and implementation of an idea.
Robert Ronstadt :	Entrepreneurship is the dynamic process of creating incremented wealth. The wealth is created by individuals who assume the major risks in terms of equity, time and /or career commitment or provide unlike for some produce or service.
Robert D. Hisrich :	Entrepreneurship is the process of creating something new with value by devoting. The necessary time and effort assuming the accompanying financial, psychic, and bold risks and receiving. The resulting rewards of monetary and personal satisfaction and independence.
John J. Kao :	Entrepreneurship is the attempt to create volume through regulation of business opportunity, the management of risk-taking appropriate to the opportunity and through the communicative and management skills to mobilise human, financial and scattered resources necessary to bring a project to functioning.
Robert K. Lamb:	Entrepreneurship is that form of social decision which is performed by economic innovators.
V. R. Gaikwad :	Entrepreneurship connotes innovativeness, an urge to take risk in face of uncertainties and an intuition.
Musscleman and Jackson :	Entrepreneurship is the investing and risking of time, money, and effort to start a business and make it successful.
H. N. Pathak :	Entrepreneurship involves, *(i)* Perception of an opportunity *(ii)* Organisms a industrial unit, and *(iii)* Running the industrial unit as a profitable going and growing concern.
The Global Entrepreneurship Monitor :	Entrepreneurship the process of planning, organising, operating, and assuming the risk of a business venture is now a mainstream activity. The culture of entrepreneurship is deeply rooted: Entrepreneurs are celebrated role models, failure is seen as a learning experience, and the entrepreneurial career option is regarded as attractive. In today's economic environment, entrepreneurship is a key employment of globalisation.

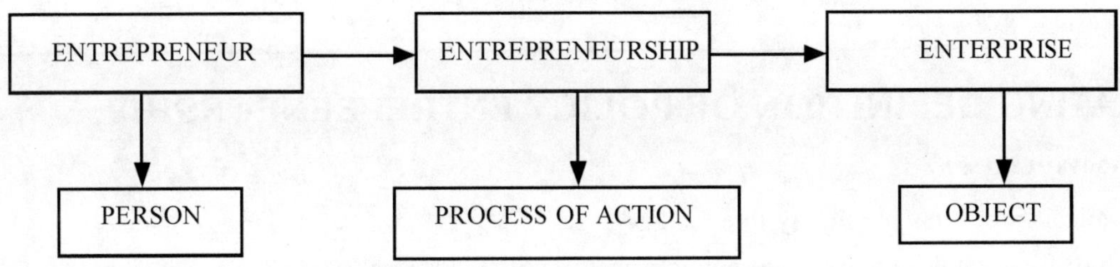

Fig. 1.2: *Concept of Entrepreneurship*

Stimulation of Entrepreneurship

Entrepreneurship development is probably one of the most elusive, complicated and perplexing issues in the promotion and growth of small enterprises. Recently, a number of development agencies have been involved. However, in spite of all these efforts there have been only a few partially successful programmes, and there are many Instances of colossal failures in this field.

The stimulation of entrepreneurship is a function of both internal and external variables. The presence of certain personal qualities in an individual is a requisite. Some of the findings about entrepreneurs in Nepal are as follows:

(a) Mainly there are two types of entrepreneurs: the Government and private individuals.

(b) In a family-run business the entrepreneur is owner as well as manager. Entrepreneurs are frequently found to have parents who were engaged in business-related occupations. Membership in certain types of communities (Newars, Marwadis, Gurung etc.) is highly correlated with entrepreneurship.

(c) Many people who migrated from the hills to the southern part of the country (Terai), and returned have become entrepreneurs.

(d) In the family, a change is taking place. Now the educated young members are becoming entrepreneurs rather than head of the family who generally is old.

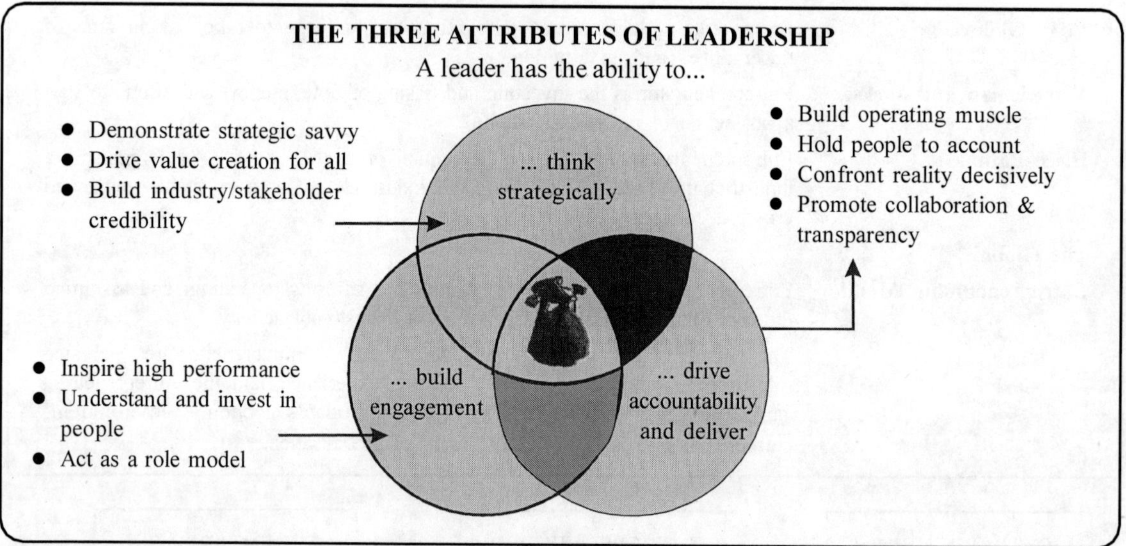

OPERATING DEFINITION OF POLICY ENTREPRENEURSHIP

Policy Innovativeness

Availability of Equity or Equity-like funds.

Efforts to assemble public or joint public-private equity funds locally.

Willingness of local developers to risk some of their resources on small or new firms.

Creation-of Incubator Facilities for new or young firms.

Availability and nature of small business technical assistance.

Small Business Targeting

Presence of an explicit small business component in the local development organisation.

Amount of staff resources devoted to small firm concerns.

Percentage of capital funds channeled through development organisations into young ventures less than 3 years old.

Policy Commitment

Support of local governmental bodies for economic development

— public monies channeled into loan programs

— public monies supporting local development organisations

Characteristics of Public Support

— level of funding

— stability and trends in public monies going to development matters

— year in which programs first used locally

Cooperation of country and municipal officials on economic development.

Working relations between economic developers and elected officials.

Working relations among economic developers.

Entrepreneurship as a Process

Joseph Schumpeter (1883-1950) specifically addressed entrepreneurship as a process. Schumpeter described entrepreneurship as a force to 'create destruction' wearily established ways of new and better ways to get things done. Sehumpeter describes entrepreneurship as a process and entrepreneurs as innovators. Who use the process to shatter the status quo through new method of commerce. The phenomenon has been particularly strong in some countries through several generations of explosive economic activity. It is no accident that every fortune 500 enterprise that exists today was the result of an entrepreneur who took a simple idea and preserved.

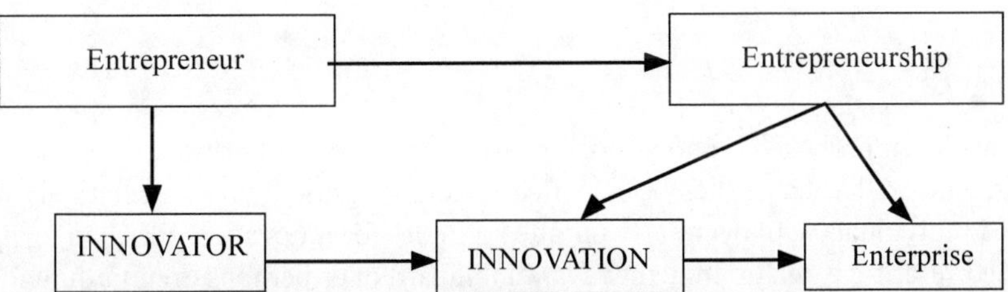

Fig.1.3: Entrepreneurship Process

In Schumpeter's words, the entrepreneur seeks to reform or revolutionize. The pattern of production by exploring an invention or, more generally an untried technological possibility an old one in a new way, by opening up a new source of supply of materials or a new outlet for products – entrepreneurship products. Entrepreneurship as defined is essentially consists in decamp things that are not generally done in the ordinary course of business routine.

Robert Ronstadt cappers the essence of Entrepreneurship:

Entrepreneurship is the dynamic process of creating incremental wealth. This wealth is created by individuals who assume the major risks in terms of quality time and/or career commitment of providing volume for some product or service. The product or service-itself may or may not be new or unique but volume must somehow be induced by the entrepreneur by securing and allowing the necessary service and resources.

The critical point is that enterprisers disrupt the status quo putting economic development and society on a new course. They create new means of production and new systems of services. Today, these inspired thinkers are well-educated, experienced and independent thinkers who can transform society through innovation.

Early Survey of Entrepreneurship

From the classical economists to the post-Keynesian analysts, the topic of the entrepreneur has been surveyed and observations, theories and pronouncements advanced. Not only were pure economists involved in this endeavour but also prominent social theorists such as Marx, Weber, Sombard and Veblen.

In general, contemporary economists agree that the entrepreneur is a business leader and that his role in fostering economic growth and development is a pivotal one. At present, however there is no consensus at to what constitutes the essential activity which makes the entrepreneur a crucial figure. While some economists have identified the basic entrepreneurial function as risk-taking, others have emphasised the coordination of production resources, the provision of capital or the introduction of production resources, the provision of capital or the introduction of innovations. Professor James R. Omps of the International Institute of Entreprenology, Honolulu, Hawaii, in his paper entitled “Entreprenology, the Critical Factor in National Development”, has this to say: ‘in all crisis situation, there is one critical factor. There is one factor in each situation that can be cited as being the straw that broke the camel’s back! In listing some of today’s possible critical factors, such familiar words and phrases limited natural resources... food... energy all would emerge. A question may phrased thus: What is the critical factor?’

Over-population?

Food shortage?

National resources shortage?

Energy shortage?

Lack of technology?

“Many factors have been proposed... and yet is it possible that the most critical factor has not been recognised? What is this factor that has either been stifled or totally ignored? It is a relatively untapped source... that of qualified individuals with peculiarly unique aptitudes for innovation, for change, aptitudes, in other words, for using present-day technology in ways yet unheard of or perhaps even unthought of. The critical factor is a dire shortage of the appropriate economic innovator and implementor... the Entreprenologists.”

In the words of A. H. Cole, entrepreneurship is the purposeful activity of an individual or a group of associated individuals undertaken to initiate, maintain or organise a profit-oriented business unit for the production or distribution of economic goods and services.

McClelland describes the innovative characteristics of entrepreneurial role. Entrepreneurial role, by definition involves doing things in a new and better way. A businessman who simply behaves in a traditional way is not an entrepreneur. Moreover, entrepreneurial role calls for decision-making under uncertainty. If there is no significant uncertainty and the action involves applying known and predictable results, then entrepreneurship is not at all involved.

McClelland, like others, identified two characteristics of entrepreneurship. First, doing things in a “new and better way.” This is synonymous with the innovative characteristics given by Schumpeter, and secondly, decision-making under uncertainty, i.e., risk as identified by Cantillon McClelland more explicitly emphasised the need for achievement orientation as the most directly relevant factor for explaining economic behaviour. This motive is defined as a tendency to strive for success in situations involved and of one's performance in relation to the same standard of excellence.

In other words, entrepreneurship means the function of creating something new, organising and coordinating and undertaking risk and handling economic uncertainty. Higgins defines the term, "Entrepreneurship" as the function of seeing investment and production opportunity, organising an enterprise to undertake and new production process, raising capital, hiring labour, arranging for the supply of raw materials and selecting top managers for the day-to-day operation of the enterprise.

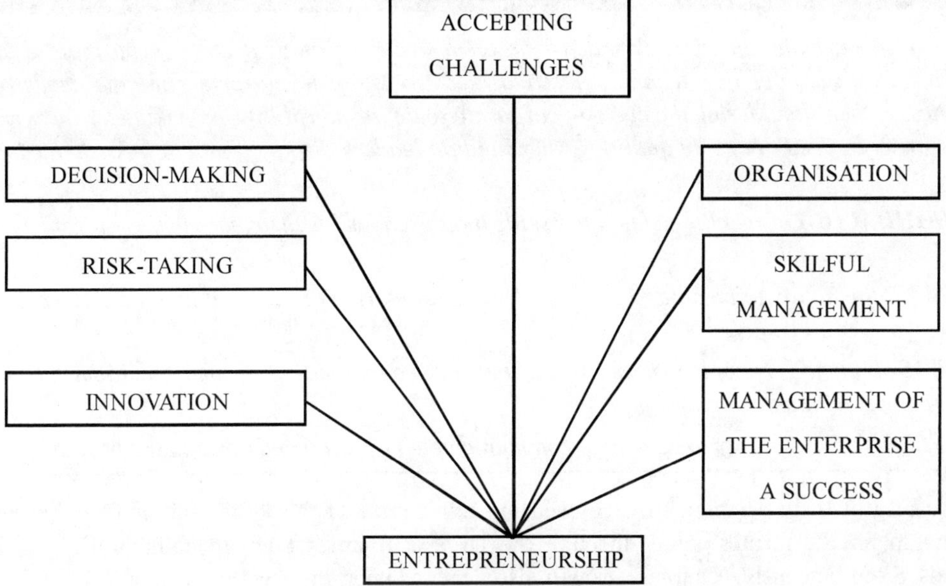

Fig. 1.4: *Characteristics of Entrepreneurship*

According to Peter Drucker, "Entrepreneurship is neither a science nor an art. It is a practice. It has a knowledge base. Knowledge in entrepreneurship is a means to an end. Indeed, what constitutes knowledge in practice is largely defined by the ends, that is, by the practice."

Innovation and entrepreneurship are thus needed in society as much as in the economy, in public-service institutions as much as in business. It is precisely because innovation and entrepreneurship are not "root and branch" but "one step at a time", a product here, a policy there, a public service yonder; because they are not planned but focused on this opportunity and that need; because they are tentative and will disappear if they do not produce the expected and needed results. In other words, they are pragmatic rather than dogmatic and modest rather than grandiose — that they promise to keep any society, economy, industry, public service, or business flexible and self-renewing.

Thus, entrepreneurship is a complex phenomenon. "Some think of entrepreneurs primarily as innovators, some chiefly as managers of enterprise, some as bearers of risks, and others place major emphasis on their function as mobilisers and allocators of capital." In the Indian context, however, an entrepreneur may at best be defined as a person (or a group of persons) responsible for the existence of a new business enterprise.

Entrepreneurship is an attitude of mind which calls for calculated risks; a true entrepreneur is one who can see possibilities in a given situation where others see none and has the patience to work out the idea into a scheme to which financial support can be provided. The stimulation of entrepreneurship is a function of both internal and external variables. In developing countries, there is no dearth of ideas but there is a real scarcity of men with the right blend of vision and practical sense to become successful entrepreneurs. The objective of the programme is to identify such people and to provide them with the support needed to make them a success. They then become "demonstration models" to the community; and once a right climate is generated, entrepreneurship becomes a way of life.

What are their Strengths?

Indian leaders maintain a single minded focus on innovation, growth, people and business results, as we voraciously seek out new technologies and ideas to adapt to customers unique needs and opportunities. Father, shouldering the needs of corporate social responsibility and taking business risks to address society's need are some qualities where Indian leaders display a more altruistic business philosophy.

NIKHIL MAINI *also enlists a few other skills Indian leaders need to learn to be 'relevant' in the modern business environment:*

POWER *the ability to be able to generate and sustain formal power and in quite a few cases – even political power is critical.*

IDEAS *ability to get people to think outside the box, and in some constrained environments, even generate creativity within the box.*

INFLUENCE *the ability to be able to communicate your vision and goals to the people.*

Industrial growth in a country is achieved through a mix of the large and small industry; the entrepreneurship for the former comes through the large companies often in collaboration with the multinationals. Simultaneously, economic growth also depends upon the level of development and use of information system in the country.

In fact, the small-scale industry sector is considered as an ideal nursery for the rapid growth and development of entrepreneurship. But alas, there are only a handful of entrepreneurs in the true sense of the term in this sector. The men who will set up small industry units have to come from within the country and the community; they are "locals" in a true sense and their success, therefore, has a much greater impact on generating the right climate for successful entrepreneurship.

Programmes for developing entrepreneurship must recognise that, ultimately, the change they seek to induce is attitudinal — it is more than just providing information, land or money. It is to provide new goals so that a motivated young person is no longer content to take up a secure job which will assure him a modest income but seeks bigger challenges in setting up and running his own business. The risks are greater but so are the rewards both in monetary sense and psychologically, in the feeling of confidence and pride it generates in the person. It is through the efforts of such persons that a small industry can become a dynamic sector of the economy and hence, the effort made to develop such persons is well worth the investment in terms of labour and cash. The need of the hour is the growth of entrepreneurship to accelerate the process of economic growth. In a way, the society needs innovation and entrepreneurship in a normal, steady and on ongoing basis. Just as management has become the specific organ of all contemporary institutions and the integrating organ of our society of organisations, so innovation and entrepreneurship have to become an integral life sustaining activity in our organisations, our economy, our society.

This requires of executives in all institutions to make innovation and entrepreneurship a normal, ongoing, everyday activity, a practice in their own work and in that Dynamics of Entrepreneurial Development of their organisation. Entrepreneurship is the cornerstone of the emerging economic scene in the world.

The entrepreneur usually lacks managerial and technical know-how, as well as marketing, production and personnel management skills. These are needed so that even if the entrepreneur can operate on only a small-scale basis, the operation will be economically viable.

Technological advances in the environment create new needs for the entrepreneur as far as adaptation and adjustment are concerned. The entrepreneur may need to learn how to adjust to the new technological environment, or to take a set of advance technologies and bring this to his own level in this sector. Either way, constant reexamination is needed for possible utilization and improvement of existing technologies.

Finally, the socio-cultural environment also creates a very important climate for the survival of this sector. Small enterprises need the following conditions to keep them alive.

(1) tolerance for changes in the society and culture; (2) social mobility; (3) tolerance of profit making; and (4) tolerance of private ownership.

Japanese Experience

The Japanese have very successfully integrated their culture with their business and have achieved great success. Some of the values they have brought into their management are life long employment, worker participation, quality circles, loyalty and pride in the organisation. Similarly, whatever is good in Indian culture should he reflected and reinforced in the business culture also. In the absence of this, India cannot design its own unique form of management, suitable for its values, and achieve excellence.

Some of these values could be mutual respect among the management and workers, commitment to nation building similar to the spirt it shown during the Independence movement and pride in whatever one does. A sense of equity and pride in one's own profession will be an antidote for the old caste based professions and their unequal values. Similarly, the ancient philosophical tenets like equality before God could be extended to mutual consideration and respect in the Workplace also. This requires a conscious acceptance of these values by the managers and its constant practice. Strong corporate culture suitable for one's own traditional values like strong family cultures have to come from within or be cultivated by individual leaders to maximise the achievements.

Culture building is achieved by selecting the ideals, motivating through retaining and encouraging such ideals in employees. It requires refining of the human resources development tools and consistency in recognising the achievements.

Strategy and culture — each contribute to the success of any organinsation. Brilliant strategies bring great business successes and strong cultures survive great upheavals. In the absence of one, the other is useless. The Indian situation badly needs both.

Indian Leadership

In the first four decades of independence, India's annual economic growth was sluggish at about 3.5 percent. The focus for organisational leaders then was on consolidation of resources. At the same time, the government's top priorities were to protect and nurture indigenous industries to help them grow. But when the floodgates were flung wide open post-liberalisation, leaders found themselves confronted by several competitive challenges. In recent times, with employable talent becoming scarce, recruitment and retention have assumed prime importance in the priority-lists of business leaders. Not only that, new management mantras have evolved and the focus has shifted towards innovation, communication and risk-taking. The Indian environment today is highly competitive and the constantly increasing global pressure of optimisation puts leaders through constraints which are new and did not exist in a strong way within the old economy. Leaders today have to deal with the increasing factors of the new economy, and at the same time manage growth.

The Hay group study says that Indian leaders seem to excel in entrepreneurial drive, adaptive thinking and networking, while they need to strengthen their understanding of organisational politics, exert influence in 'complex and sophisticated ways', and assess individual aptitude and strengths and leverage them or business benefit.

Mere financial success is not a sure-fire indicator of a great leadership at the helm. Also, leadership is as much an individual quality as an organisational one. This makes it much harder to distinguish between a good leader and a bad one. The best leaders, irrespective of where they are, know that greatness comes from sharing power instead of hoarding it. Sometimes leadership is about the vision and translating into a mission action to each the self good amidst globalisation and growing competition.

An Ideal Entrepreneur

An ideal entrepreneur is one who combines values in the market economy; that profits do not somehow preclude ethical behaviour; that growth is possible even if political patronage is not used to bend rules and cut corners, and quite simply that pursuit of wealth can be a mannerly one. He takes with him the interest of his people, his country, his natural resources, the ecology and sees that his enterprise becomes a catalytic agent of development. There is thus a need of true entrepreneurs, who do not need incentives, infrastructure, government support; but build their enterprises, harness the resources and develop. They adopt a responsible value-driven corporate philosophy for their enterprises and/or business activities. As such, there is no dispute among economists and social thinkers about the urgent need for the emergence of an entrepreneurial society as a forerunner of accelerated development of the economy in an integrated manner. The success of an entrepreneur in any enterprise depends on the degree of his vision, leadership, competitiveness, talent, self-reliance, connections/communication and resourcefulness.

Box 1.2 : The Best Entrepreneurs are in China

The most promising entrepreneurs are to be found in China today. China has had a long history of entrepreneurship and capitalism. They have been terrible at it during certain periods in their history, like in the 18th and 19th century, but have been brilliant during other times. Now China has unleashed entrepreneurship once again and they seem to be on the rise.

But entrepreneurship has nothing to do with race but may have something to do with genetic pool. if you tour the world you'll find many entrepreneurs of every race. You'll also find some countries at particular times in their history which have more entrepreneurs than others. in fact, there're many promising entrepreneurs in today but they don't accumulate capital for some reason and haven't built successful organisations.

Entrepreneurship is not confined to industry and is needed in all activities. Its flowering in agriculture among the cultivators, small and large, is seen by all today. The. smiling farm of today in many parts of the country is a proof of such entrepreneurship. The need for entrepreneurship is even greater in management of government, more so as it is the largest entrepreneur.

India has a proud record of entrepreneurship. Its present status in the industrial world is its proof. It has now to prepare itself for entrepreneurship of a different order. Tremendous advances of science and technology will have to be harnessed, requiring on the part of the people and the government a more mature and finer approach to match the level reached in the advanced countries. Philips, Sony, Honda, Ford provide the signposts of entrepreneurship today for all to emulate. Some of these have come up only in recent years and from small beginnings. In India, too, one sees glimpses of such entrepreneurship. ICICI's experience tells a great deal about entrepreneurship — good as well as not so good.

Conclusion

Entrepreneurship is an attitude of mind which can take risks but calculated ones; a true entrepreneur is one who can see possibilities in a given situation where other see none and has the patience to work out the idea into a scheme to which financial support can be provided. It is one of the catalytic activities fostering initiative, promoting and maintaining economic activities fostering initiative, and distribution of wealth. The stimulation of entrepreneurship is a function of both internal and external variables. In developing countries, there is no dearth of ideas but there is a real scarcity of men with the right blend of vision and practical sense to become successful entrepreneurs. The objective of the programme is to identify such people and to provide them with the support needed to make them a success. They then become "demonstration models" to the community; and once a right climate is generated, entrepreneurship becomes a way of life.

Industrial growth in a country is achieved through a "mix" of the large and small industry; the entrepreneurship for the former comes through the large companies often in collaboration with the multinationals. Simultaneously, economic growth also depends upon the level of development and use of information system in the country.

In fact, the small-scale industry sector is considered as an ideal nursery — for the rapid growth and development of entrepreneurship. But, alas, there are only a handful of entrepreneurs in the true sense of the term in this sector. The men who will set up small industry units have to come from within the country and the community; they are "locals" in a true sense and their success, therefore, has a much greater impact on generating the right climate for successful entrepreneurship.

Programmes for developing entrepreneurship must recognise that ultimately, the change they seek to include is attitudinal; it is more than just providing information, land or money. It is to provide new goals so that a motivated young person is no longer content to take up a secure job which will assure him a modest income but seeks bigger challenges in setting up and running his own business. The risks are greater but so are the rewards, both in monetary sense and psychologically, in the feeling of confidence and pride it generates in the person. It is through the efforts of such persons that a small industry can become such dynamic sector of the economy and, hence, the effort made to develop such persons is well worth the money and labour. The need of the hour is the growth of entrepreneurship in the country to accelerate the process of economic growth. According to Peter Drucker, the entrepreneurial strategy is as important as purposeful innovation and entrepreneurial management. In a way, the society needs innovation and entrepreneurship in a normal, steady and an ongoing basis. Just as management has become the specific organ of all contemporary institutions, and the integrating organ of our society of organisations, so innovation and entrepreneurship have to become an integral life-sustaining activity in our organisations, our economy, our society.

This requires of executives in all institutions to make innovation and entrepreneurship a normal, ongoing everyday activity, a practice in their own work and in that of their organisation. Entrepreneurship is the cornerstone of the emerging economic scene in the world.

ANNEXURE 1

Code of Business Principles

Standard of Conduct

We conduct our operations with honesty, integrity and openness, and with respect for the human rights and interests of our employees. We shall similarly respect the legitimate interests of those with whom we have relationships.

Obeying the Law

Companies and employees are required to comply with the laws and regulations of the countries in which we operate.

Employees

The Enterprise is committed to diversity in a working environment where there is mutual trust and respect and where everyone feels responsible for the performance and reputation of our company. We will recruit, employ and promote employees on the sole basis of the qualifications and abilities needed for the work to be performed. We are committed to safe and healthy working conditions for all employees. We will not use any form of forced, compulsory or child labour. We are committed to working with employees to develop and enhance each individual's skills and capabilities. We respect the dignity of the individual and the right of employees to freedom of association. We will maintain good communications with employees through company based information and consultation procedures.

Consumers

The Enterprise is committed to providing branded products and services which consistently offer value in terms of price and quality, and which are safe for their intended use. Products and services will be accurately and properly labelled, advertised and communicated.

Shareholders

The Enterprise will conduct its operations in accordance with internationally accepted principles of good corporate governance. We will provide timely, regular and reliable information on our activities, structure, financial situation and performance to all shareholders.

Business Partners

The Enterprise is committed to establishing mutually beneficial relations with our suppliers, customers and business partners. In our business dealings we expect our partners to adhere to business principles consistent with our own.

Community Involvement

The Enterprise strives to be a trusted corporate citizen and, as an integral part of society, to fulfill our responsibilities to the societies and communities in which we operate.

Public Activities

The Enterprise is encouraged to promote and defend their legitimate business interests. Unilever will cooperate with governments and other organisations, both directly and through bodies such as trade associations, in the development of proposed legislation and other regulations which may affect legitimate business interests. Unilever neither supports political parties nor contributes to the funds of groups whose activities are calculated to promote party interests.

The Environment

The Entrepreneur is committed to making continuous improvements in the management of our environmental impact and to the longer-term goal of developing a sustainable business. Unilever will work in partnership with others to promote environmental care, increase understanding of environmental issues and disseminate good practice.

✸ ✸ ✸

2

Entrepreneurship: An Indian Scenario

Growth comes with a vision to change.

But perfection comes with experience.

Introduction

Entrepreneurs are considered as the change agents in the socio-economic development of the country. They are innovators, risk-takers, decision-makers and people with a definite vision. They are the dreamers, passion for achievement and good achievers. They are the people always strived for economic development. In the process the entrepreneurs have set up enterprises in manufacturing, retail trade and service sectors. There they created ample employment opportunities, raised the income level standard of living and generated profits for the stakeholders.

The Process of Socio-economic Change

Economic development in every economy is a continuous activity. The process of socio-economic change is an intrinsic part of human activity. Man continuously works for utilising the gift of nature and make his living comfortable. He always thinks of and works for maximising economic growth. This is what is happening in every economy. The governments evolve effective programmes to co-ordinate social, economic, technological and cultural factors for the balanced and sustained rate of economic growth. Economic planning is increasingly becoming an effective instrument of socio-economic transformation. The political system also influences the economic growth. In a democratic country, planning is evolved at every level of economy and people are made to be involved in economic growth. In a closed or controlled economy, the economic programmes are designed by few people and is imposed on the general public. So, the planning in each country differs in its design and action. However, planning under different political systems do not deviate from basic laws that motivate economic development. There are certain laws of dynamics of economic development. One such law clearly indicates that MAN is a key factor in economic development.

"Economic development originates and fosters in relation to the strength and health of the local entrepreneurship and depends on the rate of its generation and equality to the intensity of its sense of social responsibility, its index of managerial capabilities." This is one such law of dynamics of economic development which clearly states that human being is the key factor in economic development and "Entrepreneur" is the driving force. The growth of an economy depends upon the strength of entrepreneurs who work for the growth. "The higher the birth rate of genuine industrial and innovative entrepreneurship, the faster is the rate of economic growth. Entrepreneurship must also acquire new management skills. Entrepreneurial density, innovative propensity and management capability in the society in a particular period determine the character and future of economic development." From this statement it is clear that individual human beings play a vital role in the economic development of a nation. Industrial history reveals that in almost all countries, the industrial development has started with individual enterprises. Many multinational and national corporations have mostly received their inspiration from one or few individuals. While promoting any enterprise, quality of entrepreneurship becomes a major resource. The skill and creativity of an individual can convert a sick business unit into a viable unit. Small business houses give scope for the development of entrepreneurs. Without entrepreneurship, industrialisation process cannot take place. Entrepreneurs can be developed through well designed entrepreneurship development programmes.

On the Indian scene, there is an impressive growth of entrepreneurs particularly in the small scale business sector. Small business houses today are producing wide variety of sophisticated goods in different product lines requiring high degree of skill and precision. Small-scale business sector has become a breeding centre for entrepreneurs who are contributing toward a better quality of life for millions of people. In India, small-scale sector has become a dynamic sector. The entrepreneur is a critical factor for socio-economic change. He is the key man who envisages new opportunities, new techniques, new lines of production, new products and co-ordinate all other activities.

The term "entrepreneur" is defined in a variety of ways. Yet, no consensus has been arrived at on the precise skills and abilities that make a person a successful entrepreneur.

The term "entrepreneur" is derived from the French word "ENTERPRENDRE." Its meaning is to "undertake." The simple meaning of an "entrepreneur" is "a person who is responsible for setting up a business or an enterprise." He possesses skill, initiative and innovative ideas and aspires for high achievements in business. He promotes projects for the welfare of people and creates wealth for the society. In the process of implementing new projects, he creates employment.

Many qualities are attributed to him. "Sensitive energiser," "Entrepreneurial man," "Leader of the system," "Harbinger of economic growth" are some of the creative qualities an entrepreneur possesses. He is influenced by human values and works for people and their welfare. He is a firm believer in the development of society and works with strong conviction. His innovative character makes him to take up research. Individuals who initiate, establish, maintain and expand new enterprises constitute the entrepreneurial class.

Historical Development of the Concept Entrepreneur

In the early 16th century, the Frenchmen who organized and led military expeditions were referred to as "entrepreneurs." Around 1700 A.D. the term was used for architects and contractors of public works. Quesnay regarded the rich farmer as an entrepreneur who manages and makes his business profitable by his intelligence, skill and wealth.

In many countries, the entrepreneur is often associated with a person who starts his own, new and small business. Business encompasses manufacturing, transport, trade and all other self-employed vocations in the service sector. But not every new small business is entrepreneurial or represents entrepreneurship.

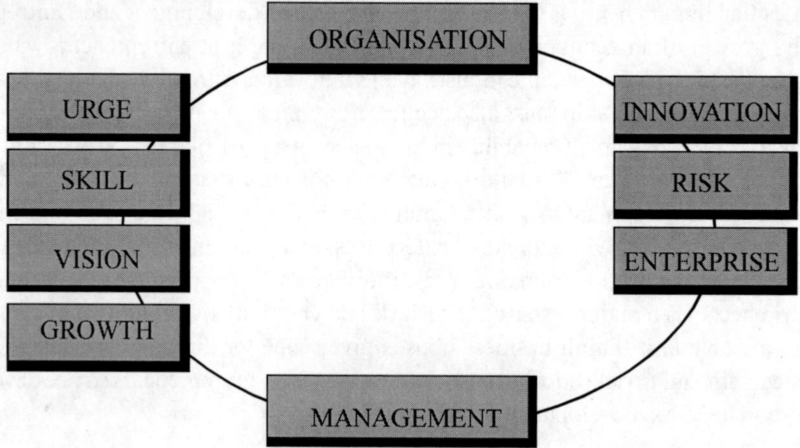

Fig. 2.1: Basis of an Entrepreneur

The term "entrepreneur" was applied to business initially by the French economist, Cantillon, in 1811, to designate a dealer who purchases the means of production for combining them into marketable products. Another Frenchman, J.B. Say, expanded Cantillon's ideas and conceptualized the entrepreneur as a organizer of business firm, central to its distributive and production functions. Beyond stressing the entrepreneur's importance to the business, Say did little with his entrepreneurial analysis.

According to J.B. Say, "an entrepreneur is the economic agent who unites all means of production, the labour force of the one and the capital or land of the others and who finds in the value of the products which results from their employment, the reconstitution of the entire capital that he utilizes and the value of the wages, the interest and the rent which he pays as well as profit belonging to himself." He emphasized the functions of co-ordination, organization and supervision. Further, it can be said that the entrepreneur is an organizer and speculator of a business enterprise. The entrepreneur lifts economic resources out of an area of lower into an area of higher productivity and greater yield.

Innovation and Entrepreneur

Innovation is based on knowledge, ingenuity, diligence, persistence and commitment and it must be built on its strength. Innovation should be market-driven.

Innovation, the chief character of an entrepreneur, is monitored by internal and external activities of the organisation. Change in population, change in understanding and new knowledge also influence innovation and entrepreneur is motivated by these factors. Being an innovator he becomes a leader, his actions will be simple and effective, opportunities that come in his way are analysed and best course of action is designed and implemented.

Peter Drucker, Management Guru

"The purpose of a company is to create a customer. A business... is defined by the want the customer satisfies when he or she buys a product or a service. To satisfy the customer is the mission and purpose of every business."

"Knowledge workers cannot be controlled; they must be motivated. Such employees must see a purpose more meaningful than personal profit."

Innovative concept was evolved in 18th Century in England, when the Industrial Revolution took place. Many innovations came in the limelight during and after this period. Many entrepreneurs of international repute emerged on the industrial scene. Hundreds of consumer and industrial products were flooded in the market. Latest innovation in telecommunication systems and computers has brought the world close and the concept of "Global village" has come into being. All this was possible due to innovative character of entrepreneurs.

Thus, the concept of entrepreneurship according to current thinking is the "ability of a person who detects and evaluates a new situation in his environment and directs the making of such adjustments in the economic systems as he deems necessary." The entrepreneur conceives an idea and implements his idea into action with grit and determination. In the process of implementation, he understands profitable investments, examines in detail the investment opportunities, mobilises capital, completes statutory proceedings, adopts required technology and faces threats which come in the way of promoting his idea.

Now the term "entrepreneur" covers individuals who have vision and skill and are capable of converting vision into action for the good of the society. People also imitate the ideas and a way of viewing the constraints embodied in the process of creating a new business or manufacturing operation.

Box 2.1 : Innovation and Entrepreneurship

The entrepreneur, said the French economist J B Say around 1800, "Shifts economic resources out of an area of lower and into an area of higher productivity and greater yield." But Say's definition does not tell us who this "entrepreneur" is and since Say coined the term almost two hundred years ago, there has been total confusion over the definitions of "entrepreneur" and "entrepreneurship." The entrepreneur is often defined as one who starts his own, new and small business. But not every new small business is entrepreneurial or represents entrepreneurship. Admittedly, all new small businesses have many factors in common. But to be entrepreneurial, an entreprise has to have special characteristics over and above being new and small.

Indeed, entrepreneurs are a minority among new businesses. They create something new, something different; they change or transmute values. An enterprise aslo does not need to be small and new to be an entrepreneur. Indeed, entrepreneurship is being practised by large and often old enterprises.... Finally, entrepreneurship is by no means confined solely to economic institutions. The modern university as we know it started out as the invention of a German diplomat and civil servant, Wilhelm von Humboldt, who in 1809 conceived and founded the University of Berlin.... Sixty years later, around 1870, when the German university itself had peaked, Humboldt's idea of the university as a change agent was picked up across the Atlantic, in the United States.

The Entrepreneur: Other Definitions

Quesnay recognised a rich farmer as an entrepreneur who manages and makes his business profitable by his intelligence and wealth.

Adam Smith described entrepreneur as a person who only provides capital without taking active part in the leading role in enterprise.

Karl Marx regarded entrepreneur as a social parasite.

Richard Cantillon considered all persons engaged in economic activity as entrepreneurs.

Jean Baptiste Say opined that the entrepreneur was a person endowed with the qualities of judgement, perseverance and a knowledge of the world as well as of business. The entrepreneurships economise resources out of an area of lower and into an area of higher productivity and greater yield. The definition included the concept of bringing together the factors of production.

French tradition regarded an entrepreneur as a person translating a profitable idea into a productive activity.

Joseph A. Schumpeter (1883-1950) recognised person who introduces innovation changes is an entrepreneur. He treated entrepreneur as an integral part of economic growth. The fundamental source of equilibrium was the entrepreneur.

Frank Young describes entrepreneur as a change agent.

Noah Webster thinks entrepreneur is one who assumes the responsibility of the risk and management of business.

Francis A. Walter observes that the true entrepreneur is one who is endowed with more than average capacities in the risk of organising and coordinating the various other factors of production.

Peter F. Drucker defines an entrepreneur as one who always searches for change, respond to it and exploits it as an opportunity. Innovation is the specific tool of entrepreneurs, the means by which they exploit change as an opportunity for a different business or service.

Arthur Dewing conceptualised the function of the entrepreneur as one that promotes ideas into business.

Clarence H. Dantrof considers entrepreneur as a person who makes decision under alternative courses of action.

Entrepreneur has become the focal point in economic activities. He is viewed as an initiator of action, a stimulant of socio-economic change and development.

Robert D. Hisrich says, "The person who is going to establish a successful new business venture must also be a visionary leader — a person who dreams great dreams. Although there are many definitions of leadership, the one that best describes the needed intrapreneurial leadership is: A leader is like a gardener. When you want a tomato, you take a seed, put it in fertile soil, and carefully water under tender care. You don't manufacture tomatoes, you grow them."

Martin Luther King said, "I have a dream, and thousands followed in spite of overwhelming obstacles. In order to establish a successful new business venture the intrapreneurial leader must have a dream and work against all obstacles to achieve it."

Entrepreneur is one who distinguishes as a person who undertakes to organise, manage and assume the risk of running a factory and/or a business or an enterprise.

Entrepreneurship is neither a science nor an art. It is a practice. It has a knowledge base. Knowledge in entrepreneurship is a mean to an end. Indeed, what constitutes knowledge in practice is largely defined by the ends, that is by practice.

According to Everett E. Haggen, an entrepreneur is an economic man who tries to maximise his profits by innovations. Innovations involve problem-solving and the entrepreneur gets satisfaction from using his capabilities in attacking problems.

According to *David McClelland:* "An entrepreneur is someone who exercises some control over the means of production and produces more than what he can consume in order to sell (or exchange) it for individual (or household) income."

An entreprenur, as defined by *Robert E. Nelson*, is a person who is able to look at the environment, identify opportunities to improve the environment, marshall resources and implement action to maximize those opportunities.

According to *J.K. Galbraith:* "An entrepreneur must accept the challange and should be willing hard to achieve something."

Akhouri, M.M.P, describes entrepreneur as a character who contributes innovativeness, readiness to take risk, sensing opportunities, identifying and mobilising potential resources, concern for excellence, and who is persistent in achieving the goal. The term entrepreneur contain notions of newness innovation, vision, organising, creating wealth, mobilising resources, risk-taking and achievement. A driving force of economic development.

Not every new small business is entrepreneurial or represents entrepreneurship. To be entrepreneurial, an enterprise has to have special characteristics. Over and above doing new things entrepreneurs create, something different, they change the value.

Laura Parkin entrepreneurs are both born and made. While some people are born with natural talent and risk tolerance. Entrepreneurship is a discipline and entrepreneurship skills can be learned by every one.

Albert Shapero observes that the entrepreneur takes initiative, organises some social and economic mechanism and accepts risks of failure.

Karl Vesper affirms that the entrepreneur is seen differently by economists, psychologists, business persons and politicians. Robert C. Ronstadt considers that the wealth is crated by individuals who assume the mayor risks in terms of equity time, commitment, and value for some products service.

According to *David Ricardo*, the foremost motive of a risk taker is to amass capital and capital accumulation is the sine quinine of economic development.

John Stuart Mill viewed the world entrepreneur as organiser who is paid for his non-manual type of work.

Leonwalrus pointed out that entrepreneur is the coordinator of basic factors of production. He treated 'entrepreneur as the fourth factar of production who combines other factors such as land, lalour and capital.

Carl Menger (1840-1921) considers the entrepreneur as the change agent who transforms resources into useful goods and service, often creating the circumstances that lead to industrial growth.

Frank H. Kright points out that entrepreneurs are a specialised group of persons who bear risk and deals with uncertainty.

Mark Cassons points that an entrepreneur is a person who specialises in taking sound mental decision about the co-ordination of scarce resources.

Max Weber states that the entrepreneurs are a product of particular social condition in which they are brought up and it is the society which shapes individuals as entrepreneurs.

A. Daurid Silver described the entrepreneur as energetic, single minded, and having a mission and clear vision. Here she intends to create vision, a product or service in such a manner to improve the lives of millions.

Henry Ford created the manufacturing miracle that launched a modern era in industry.

Entrepreneur can do anything with passion and enthusiasm. Enthusiasm is the yeast that makes his hopes rise to the stars. Enthusiasm is the spark in his eye, the swing in his gait, the grip of his hand, the irresistible surge of his will and energy to execute his ideas. Enthusiasts are fighters, they have fortitude, they have strong qualities. Enthusiasn is at the bottom of all progress. With it there is accomplishment. Without it there are only alibis.

The slow pace of the propensity to enterprise is mainly due to the existence of a tangible set of barriers prohibiting the process of entry into, continuity in and an eventual exit from a business venture of a would be entrepreneur is a function of forces that one may view as barriers limiting a fully-fledged business performance. There may be entry barriers, survival barriers and exit barriers.

Importance of an Entrepreneur

Entrepreneur is one of the most important inputs in the economic development of a country or of regions within the country. Entrepreneurial competence makes all the difference in the rate of economic growth. In India, state and private entrepreneurship co-exist. The small-scale industrial sector and business are left completely to private entrepreneurs. It is, therefore, in this context that an increasingly important role has been assigned to the identification and promotion of entrepreneurs for this sector.

The need for a board-based entrepreneurial class in India arises from the need to speed up the process of activating the factors of production, leading to a higher rate of economic growth, dispersal of economic activities, development of backward and tribal areas, creation of employment opportunities, improvement in the standard of living of weaker sections of the society and involvement of all sections of the society in the process of growth.

Several factors go into the making of an entrepreneur. Individuals who initiate, establish, maintain and expand new enterprises constitute the entrepreneurial class. The socio-political and economic conditions, the availability of industrial technology and know-how, the state-of-art and culture of business and trading, existence of markets for products and services and incentives and facilities available for starting an industry or business, all have a bearing on the growth of entrepreneurship. A conducive environment is created through the policies and interest of the government in economic and industrial development.

It is now well recognised that entrepreneurs can be developed through appropriately designed entrepreneurship development programmes. These programmes broadly envisage a three-tiered approach: developing achievement motivation and sharpening of entrepreneurial traits and behaviour, project planning and development and guidance on industrial opportunities, incentives and facilities and rules and regulations and developing managerial and operational capabilities. Various techniques and approaches have been developed and adopted to achieve these objectives, keeping in view the target groups and /or target areas. The structuring of the programmes and training methodology also necessitate consideration of the specific target groups and target areas. Methodology for selection of the prospective entrepreneurs as well as support services after training have a significant impact on the success of the entrepreneurs' development programmes.

Relevance of Entrepreneur

In any economic system government has to play two types of roles, viz., "Promotional role" and "Regulatory role." In playing both the roles, government needs certain amount of skill and knowledge to promote various economic activities. Few individuals directly associated with government activities cannot promote all activities. Therefore, the subjects of economy should also participate in all the activities of the government to have an all sided development of the economy. Here comes the relevance of an entrepreneur. Every citizen of the society, having entrepreneurial skills will be allowed to play, his/her role and contribute for the growth of the economy. The government in this context has to play the promotional role to tap the entrepreneurial skills of the people in that society or economy. Entrepreneural skills being vital for the growth of the economy, it is more relevant that skill of each individual to promote business activities of the economy has to be tapped. As business activities anywhere in the world comprise more of small business, it is implied that entrepreneural skills are availed to the possible extent in all economies. Today controlled economic systems are also opening up for market economy to utilise the entrepreneural skills of human resources of such economies. Therefore, whether it is a controlled economy or an open economy, entrepreneurial skills of the citizens of such economy has to be utilized for economic growth and they should be allowed to play independently. Government should play the promotional role to assist the small business people to contribute their mite to develop the economy. This is the relevance of entrepreneur in an economy.

Entrepreneurship and Economic Growth

Economic development of any region is an outcome of purposeful human activity. Men assume various roles in the development process, namely, as organizer of human capital, natural material resources, worker and consumer. He stands at the center of the whole process of economic development. According to Schumpeter, economic development consists of "employing resources in a different way" in doing a new combination of means of production, The entrepreneur locates ideas and puts them into effect in the process of economic development.

Entrepreneur versus Entrepreneurship

Y. C. Deveshwar *(ITC)*

The term 'entrepreneur' is often used interchangeably with 'entrepreneurship.' But conceptually, they are different, yet they are just like the two sides of a coin.

Entrepreneur and entrepreneurship are co-related.

The entrepreneur is the person who bears risks, unites various factors of production and carries out creative innovations. He is an individual or one of a group of individuals who tries to create something new. He always attempts to bring about change in terms of factor proportions which is known as innovation.

On the contrary, entrepreneurship is the set of activities performed by an entrepreneur. It is the process of identifying opportunities in the market place and marshalling the resources required to pursue these opportunities for long-term gains. It is the attempt to create value.

D. S. Brar *(RANBAXY)*

The Single-Most Critical Ingredient that makes a successful entrepreneur is passion. Without passion, entrepreneur might succeed in managing an organisation but he can never succeed in inspiring his people. Unlike in art, where intense individual passion is enough to attain excellence, managing an organisation requires the leader to be able to infuse his whole team with that same passion.

An entrepreneur shares his passion with his term by translating it into a vision for the organisation. He needs to coax, cajole and inspire his people into sharing his vision. Alexander's soldiers grew tired and weary on more than one occasion, but were driven to great achievements by his passionate leadership. On the eve of each charge, Alexander used his communication skills to psyche up his army.

The entrepreneur must also evoke trust among his followers. He should communicate with empathy and yet not deviate from his mission.

Passion also generates courage of conviction, which acts as a source of strength in times of adversity. Mahatma Gandhi was convinced that the British rule in India was unjust and it was his moral duty to fight it. It was this conviction that gave him the courage to take on the might of the Empire.

Organisations need leaders who are passionate institution builders, institutions survive their builders and contribute enormously to the society. Dr. Vikram Sarabhai, the man behind the setting up of India's space research programme, IIM, Ahmedabad, the Physical Research Laboratory, and many other institutions, might not be around today, but his institutions continue to remind us of his contributions to the nation's progress.

Entrepreneurship is about understanding that an organisation will function effectively when it has the right mix of people, backgrounds, and experiences. This entails radical changes in recruitment policies. Entrepreneurship is a Iong journey and not a destination. It presupposes and presumes great preparation. To be an entrepreneur one must have a sound grounding in preparation. It is the art of human relationships (ability to interact with other people). It also calls for growing mastery over the work and long hours of hard work. The status and quality of entrepreneurship directly depends on these ingredient characteristics.

Above all, the entrepreneur should strive at all times to attain transparency in his organisation. Information should be freely given to those who need it. The entrepreneur should send out a message that information is not a source of power for an individual, but a power that contributes to the growth of an organisation.

The relationship between an entrepreneur and entrepreneurship is given in Table 2.2.

Table 2.1

The Relationship between Entrepreneur and Entrepreneurship

Entrepreneur (PERSON)	*Entrepreneurship (ACTION/ACTIVITY)*
Administrator	Administration
Able	Ability
Aimer	Aim
Analyser	Analysis
Adopter	Adopting
Accelerator	Accelerating
Accountant	Accounting
Builder	Building

Balanced	Balancing
Believer	Belief
Brilliant	Brilliance
Bold	Boldness
Creator of value and trust	Creativity
Character	Values
Considerator	Consideration
Courageous	Courage
Communicator	Communication
Competitor	Competitive, Competence
Capitalist	Capital — venture, seed, working, confidence/long-term etc.
Confident cultured	Collaborative culture
Dreamer	Dreams
Designer	Designs
Director	Direction
Decision-maker	Decision-making
Delegator	Delegation
Dominant player	Focussed
Educator	Education
Empowerer	Empowerment
Excellor	Excelling
Ethical	Ethics
Facilitator	Facilitating, Fostering
Foresighter	Foresight
Futurist/Farsighted	Futuristic
Goal-setter	Goal-setting
Growth-Fixer	Growth-oriented
Humble	Humility
Honest	Honesty
Human	Humanity
Initiator	Initiating, Initiative
Investor	Investing/Investment
Innovator	Innovation
Imitator	Imitating
Inspirer	Inspiring
Integrator	Integrity
Ignitor	Igniting
Imaginator	Imagination, Imagining
Intellectual (Driven by values)	Intelligence
Informer	Information
Knowledged	Knowledge
Leader	Leadership
Leverager	Leveraging
Learner	Learning
Mentor	Confidence building/Fostering
Motivator	Motivation
Marketier	Marketing
Net-worker	Net-working
Nurturer	Nurturing
Organiser	Organisation, Organising

Opportunist	Opportunities (Taking advantages of opportunities)
Planner	Planning
Programmer	Programming, Actions
Producer	Production
Performer	Performance
Partner	Partnership
Positioner	Positioning
Packager	Packaging
Promoter	Promotion
Passion-player	Passionate
Risk-bearing	Risk-taking
Responsible	Responsibility
Re-Inventor	Re-Inventing
Re-Engineerer	Re-Engineering
Skilled	Skills
Striver	Striving
Strategist	Strategy
Salesman	Selling
Talented	Talent
Trainer	Training
Trend-setter	Trend-setting
Technologist	Technology
Transformer	Transformation
Venturist	Venturing
Visionary	Vision
Visualiser	Visualisation
Wealth-creator	Wealth creation
Wizard	Specialist, Strategist, Diplomatic

Entrepreneurship management is basically concerned with the development and coordination of entrepreneurial functions. In a way, an entrepreneur precedes entrepreneurship.

Experience shows that entrepreneurship as an economic function is not a single point but rather a varied range of behaviour. There are six critical dimensions that distinguish entrepreneurial behaviour from more administratively-oriented behaviour: (i) strategic orientation; (ii) commitment to opportunity; (iii) the resource commitment process; (iv) the concept of control over resources; (v) the concept of management and (vi) compensation policy.

		Desired future state involves growth or change: Yes	Desired future state involves growth or change: No
Sell-perceived Power to Achieve goals	Yes	Entrepreneur	Satisfied Manager
	No	Frustrated potential entrepreneurs	Bureaucratic functionary

Fig. 2.1.: Manager's Opportunity Matrix

A matrix defining entrepreneurship is shown in Fig. 26.4. One can see how the present position influences whether one is entrepreneurial or not. It also clearly states that the particular skills, talents and attitudes towards risk influence the perception as to whether an outcome is feasible. Training, knowledge and self-confidence contribute to such perceptions.

Role of Entrepreneurs

Entrepreneurs, on the other hand, as Schumpeter and many others have pointed out, are distinct from business owners and managers. They are essentially strategic innovators, seeking profitability with growth. Promoting entrepreneurship, in that sense, is intrinsically different from promoting small-scale industry.

If any small business in the developed countries has received special attention, it is because it has been the fountainhead of innovation and creativity. Studies have brought out that a large number of innovations have come from small, rather than large businesses. As these innovative firms entered the market, they made profits and created jobs. In the U.S. Presidents Jimmy Carter and Gerald Ford emphasised that small businesses created 60 per cent of the new jobs in the United States. And this employment generation was due to its better financial performance. Similarly, the Bolton Committee, 1971, and the Wilson Committee, 1979, also concluded that the small business in the U.K. had higher profitability than any large business.

The studies on entrepreneurship also point out that, "most of the risk in entrepreneurial management lies not in misperception of opportunity, but in trying to pursue opportunity, without adequate resources. One of the fundamental errors of large corporations, on the other hand, is overcommitment of resources."

Managers and Entrepreneurs

Both managers and entrepreneurs are answerable for producing results. The results are, of course, different. In their respective result areas, the buck stops with them. While they can delegate, they are finally accountable.

Both have to produce results through people working with them though they deal with different sets of people. They are not effective in the long-run, if they are loners.

Both are decision-makers but the decisions are different as their tasks vary.

Both have to operate under constraints which are also understandably different.

To be effective in their respective roles, both have to follow sound principles of management like planning, staffing, delegation and control. The focus of these management tools may vary depending upon the ultimate purpose.

Table 2.2 summarises the similarities, focussing on the different perspectives within each similarity.

A successful organisation needs both enterprise and management. The entrepreneurial role may be played by the Chief Executive and his team of top-level executives, the managerial role by the middle-level and joint-level executives.

The entrepreneur differs from the professional manager in that the former undertakes a venture for his personal gratification. As such he cannot live within the framework of occupational behaviour set by others. He may engage a professional manager to perform some of his functions such as setting of objectives, policies, procedures, rules, strategies and formal communication network. However, the entrepreneurial functions of innovation, assumption of business risk cannot be delegated to the manager. Failure to the professional executive may mean a little more than locating a new job perhaps even at a higher salary, whereas failure of an entrepreneur in his efforts would mean a devastating loss to his career. The professional manager has to work within the framework of policy guidelines laid down by the entrepreneur.

Table 2.2
Similarities Between Managers and Entrepreneurs

Area of Similarity	Differing focus	
	Managers	*Entrepreneurs*
To produce results	Results of today, this month, this year. Short-term and medium-term.	Result of tomorrow, next year and coming five years. Long-term and very long-term.
To produce results through people	Have usually to handle people-oriented to day-to-day management of nitty-gritty and nuts and bolts type — Men of details.	Have to deal with people who can conceptualise with aggregate perspectives — Strategists.
To take decisions	Operational and administrative decisions, which have a bearing on short-term and medium-term results.	Mostly strategic decisions, involving growth through expansion, diversification, takeovers and mergers.
To co-operate under constraints	The constraints are usually organisational, i.e., those within an organisation like machine capacity, labour productivity, routing and scheduling, information availability, financial limitations etc.	The constraints are usually environmental which lie outside an organisation like the policy of financial institutions, import policy, licencing policy, infrastructure constraints etc.
To follow sound principles of management	The principles are more oriented towards internal administration and controls like delegation, accountability, responsibility, planning, budgeting, reporting and information system.	The principles are with reference to macro-social aspects like social responsibility, equal opportunity, employment, ethical advertisement practices, adherence to government policies etc.

Distinctive Features of Traditional Managers and the Entrepreneurs

	Managers	*Entrepreneurs*
Primary motives	Wants promotion and traditional corporate rewards. Power motivated.	Wants freedom, goal-oriented, self-reliant and self-motivated.
Time orientation	Responds to quotas and budgets, weekly, monthly, quarterly, annual planning horizons, the next promotion or transfer.	End goals of 5-10 year growth of business in view as guides. Takes action now to move the next step along the way.
Action	Delegates action. Supervising and reporting take most of energy.	Gets hands dirty. May upset employees by suddenly doing their work.
Skills	Professional management. Often business-school trained. Abstract analytical tools, people-management, and political skills.	Knows business intimately. More business acumen than managerial or political skill. Often technically trained if in technical business. May have had former P&L responsibility in corporation.
Courage and Destiny	Sees others in charge of his or her destiny. Forceful and ambitious, but may be fearful of other's ability.	Self-confident, optimistic, courageous.
Attention	Primarily on events inside the corporation.	Primarily on technology and market place.

	Managers	*Entrepreneurs*
Risk	Careful	Likes moderate risk. Invests heavily, but expects to succeed.
Market Research	Has market studies done to discover needs and guide product conceptualization.	Creates needs. Creates products that often can't be tested with market research — potential customers don't yet understand them. Talks to customers and forms own opinions.
Status	Cares about status symbols (corner office, etc.)	Happy sitting on an orange crate if job is getting done.
Failure and mistakes	Strives to avoid mistakes and surprises. Postpones recognising failure.	Deals with mistakes and failures as learning experiences.
Decisions	Agrees with those in power. Delays decision until hegets a feel of what bosses want.	Follows private vision. Decisive and action oriented.
Who serves	Please others.	Pleases self and customers.
Attitude Towards the system	Sees system as nurturing and protective, seeks position within it.	May rapidly advance in a system, then, when frustrated, reject the system and form his or her own.
Problem-solving Style	Works out problem within the system.	Escapes problem in large and formal structures by leaving and starting over on his own.
Family history	Family members worked for large organisations.	Entrepreneurial small-business, professional or farming background.
Relationship with parents	Independent of mother, good relations with father, but slightly dependent.	Absent father or poor relations with father.
Socio-economic background	Middle-class background.	Lower-class background in some early studies, middle-class in more recent ones.
Educational level	Highly educated.	Less well educated in earlier studies, some graduate work but not Ph.D. in later ones.
Relationship with others	Hierarchy as basic relationship.	Transactions and deal making as basic relationship.

The story of business in India is the history of the business families. They are the proudest institution, symbolising courage, innovation, commonsense, energy and enterprise, aspiration and adventurousness. The seeds of entrepreneurship were sown in the 1860s — when the First Cotton mill came up in Mumbai. Over the years, entrepreneurship multiplied in all directions manufacturing to service, trade to export, health to care, knowledge to information, technology to bio-technology.

The entrepreneurs have indulged in asset-building, wealth creation and creating mega-empires.

History of Entrepreneurship in India

In the historical past Indian communities consists of four main castes, viz., the Brahmins, the Kshatriyas, the Vaishyas and the Shoodras. The caste groups were rigidly separated on a functional basis. The Brahmins were the learned men who assisted the Kshatriyas (rulers) in administration and the Shoodras were involved in agricultural occupation. The Vaishya community were engaging in Trade and Commerce and Industrial Productive activities. The brief description of entrepreneurship during the past is as follows:

1. The industrial activity was influenced by the caste system.
2. The skill for any enterprise was inherited from ancestors.
3. The Trading/merchantile class use to take care of providing forward and backward linkage to craftsmen and skilled artisans.
4. There were no formal organisational units. All family members used to associate themselves in production process of an enterprise.
5. Supply of a product was mainly on the basis of demand for the same. The mercantile class used to help in getting orders from buyer and communicate it to the producer.

Pre-medieval and Medieval Times

The people were organised in a very simple type of economic and social system. The village was the unit. The entrepreneur was known as artisan. They were divided mainly on the basis of castes. The Arthashastra of Kautilya gives the account of industrial activity, manufacture of textiles (separate factories for weaving different types of cloth, cotton, linen, silk etc.), armours, ropes, thongs and straps. Useful for carts, chariots manufacture of chariots, coins etc. Artisans were engaged in varied gold, silver and part jewellery, wine manufacturing and agricultural related commercial activities. Later, the study gives an account of the tradesmen. Other industries flourished were woollen industry, metal industry, apparel industry etc.

Entrepreneurship in Pre-british India

The artisans, craftsmen and balutedars used to produce various products and provide necessary services. They reprehended the entrepreneurs. Indian handicrafts, marble carvings, wooden articles, woollens garments, jewellery and textiles attracted the world market. In fact, entrepreneurial culture flourished during the British Rule.

India, the land of gold received a setback in the early period of the British rule. The artisans were mercilessly crushed. The flooding of the Indian market with the British goods caused a complete destruction of Indian handicrafts and village industries, The introduction of a new system of education negated the value of labour and entrepreneurial activities.

In the process, people developed the employment oriented mentality. Entrepreneurial culture was submerged. Risk-teaning ability and confidence were substituted by complete obedience, creativity and innovativeness were substituted by submissiveness and a blind imitation of the British – India remained an underdeveloped country.

At the last quarter of the 19th century, the Parsis, the Gujaratis and Marwaris initiated in various industrial activities. In the beginning, the Parsis initiated in cotton textiles, steelmaking, the Marwaris in bicycle and automobiles and the Gujaratis in textiles and finance.

They are the proudest entrepreneurial communities in India, symbolising courage and commonsense, energy and enterprise, aspiration and adventures. They revived the entrepreneurial culture and sowed the seeds of entrepreneurship. A transformation from trade to manufacturing and service sectors. The seeds of entrepreneurship were sown in the early 1860s.

The industrial activity consisting small and cottage industries in India received a blow during the British regime. But Trade and Commerce prevailed in India especially in Western parts. There were instances in which the entrepreneurs achieved success in opening Textile Mills at Bombay (Cowasjee Davar 1854) and Ahmedabad (Ranchodlal Chotalal 1861). During 1850-1880 Indian entrepreneurship was extended to textiles, shipping, Iron & Steel and Hydro Electric systems.

Present Scene

Over the last 60 years, India has seen the entrepreneur evolve in different roles. The modern entrepreneurs are wealth creators, communicators, entertainers etc. The third millennium rightly belongs to Indian entrepreneurs.

With liberalisation setting in, it was bound to be sooner, rather than later, that a new business class would emerge. Never could we have predicted that Azim Premji, who inherited a vegetable oil company, could beat traditional industrialists in becoming the richest Indian. And that a school teacher's son, Narayana Murthy, would own the most valued company in the country, Infosys. Such twists of fate, possible only in today's India, were a far cry a decade ago.

Late Shri G.D. Birla (1894-1983)

Late Shri J.R.D. Tata (1904-1993)

That it has been possible for these transformations to occur is largely on account of the fact that there has been a shift in the way of conducting business over the last 50 years. Using Alvin Toffler's terminology, one of the main aspects of change has been that India has moved from essentially being a primary economy through a secondary phase to a tertiary one. In other words, it has moved from an agricultural economy to an industrial one to a service-driven one. This shift is reflected in the country's GDP figures as well. According to the Statistical Outline of India, 1999-2000, agriculture contributed 55.8 per cent and in 1950-51, industry 15.2 per cent, and services 29 per cent. Today the figures tell another story — the contribution from agriculture has halved to 25.3 per cent, that from industry a has doubled to 30.1 per cent, and the share of services has gone up to 44.6 per cent.

The Past Indian Business Scene

Before 1943, the Indian business scene was completely dominated by British companies. Apart from a few Parsi families, notably the Tatas in steel and the Wadias in shipbuilding, and scattered Gujarati and Bohri Muslim businessmen, Indians had to be content with the crumbs. Manufacturing was closed to all but a handful of Indian business houses with large financial resources and a working relationship with British companies. Trading was the only viable option, with jute and cottonbroking in Calcutta another possible alternative.

Late Ashok Birla

Aditya Birla was the first Indian industrialist with a global vision

In such a bleak scenario, the Birla Jute Mill, which was started in 1919, marked the entry of the Birla family, essentially traders, into industrial manufacturing. More business opportunities surfaced when World War II ended in 1945. Reconstruction after the war required cement, steel, and other infrastructure industries. However, it was only after Independence in 1947 that the Indian industry began to expand in the core sector.

N.R. Narayana Murthy

Sabeer Bhatia

In 1947, India had inherited a shrivelled industrial economy after nearly 200 years of British rule. If anything was available, it was shortage. The government's idea was that a rationing of resources might work and hence it adopted socialist policies. Through the 1960s, the Indian government was in the throes of the licence raj, also known as the Industrial Development and Regulation Act, and business houses were hostage to the Monopolies and Restrictive Trade Practices (MRTP) Act. Indira Gandhi's retrograde policies sent the Indian industry into a tailspin for nearly 20 years. There were problems aplenty — licences, red tapes, quotas. Indian business was characterized by high taxes, low productivity, strict licensing and a parallel economy called the black market.

Box 2.2 : Leadership Secrets

Entrepreneurial spirit: A leader senses, targets and accomplishes his goals with unswerving faith and resolve. Hurdles the road to entrepreneurial initiative need to be steadfastly surmounted through self-belief, conviction and a never-die attitude.

Innovation: The very quality that makes a team deliver successfully over time is innovation. A leader realises that the timeless adage 'change is the only constant' holds true throughout the life of an organisation.

Empowerment of people: This is the cornerstone of management thinking at every successful organisation, A good leader encourages his people to participate in decision-making and is open to their ideas and suggestions.

Simplicity: This ensures that the ideas of the leader will reach and be understood by each member of his team. The virtue of simplicity, coupled with assertiveness, determines the effectiveness of a leader.

Quality: Maintaining quality at work is an infallible way of ensuring an organisation's success. Demanding perfection while realising each team member's limitations is the essence of good leadership.

Risks: Leaders always take risks. They never hesitate to take decisions. The key to success is the ability of a leader to take unambiguous decisions, right or wrong. The need to act and implement practical initiatives quickly should take precedence over intellectual debutes.

Contextual: Leadership is contextual. There is no single leadership style that works everywhere. A successful leader adapts his or her style to the organisation and uses it lot the company's and employees' benefit. A good leader, therefore, is one who understands the organisation and its employees, creates goals accordingly and executes them effectively.

Success Mantras: Successful leaders have had their success mantras analysed, dissected and, if proven effective, adopted. A lot of effort has been made by experts and researchers to unravel the qualities and secrets of leadership. Others have diligently worked towards emulating them. Nevertheless, good leaders arc as rare today as ever.

Common sense: Success as a leader, therefore, does not come from specialised training or education. It comes from common sense and from the ability to learn from others. Examples of successful leadership are visible in plenty all around us — in different situations, in different social groups, as also in different organisations. The trick is to comprehend the behavioural.patterns of these people that lead them to be exceptionally brilliant as leaders.

Ethics: Leadership is built on trust, Leaders need to ensure that their conduct inspires the confidence of the people they lead. They must consistently espouse and act upon their values, standards and principles in their public as well as private lives.

Knowledge: Knowledge helps develop perspective. It also opens up the mind and removes biases. And it is this that helps leaders to see the big picture and develop an agenda that is aligned not only to the present but also to the future.

The ability to listen: Almost everyone can hear. But few really listen, especially when they are at the top. Good leaders need to be patient listeners — they must listen to their colleagues and collaborators, to markets and constituencies. and ultimately, to themselves, This feedback is vital to their staying on course to success.

Decisiveness: Good leaders listen to all but do what they think is best for their companies. Leaders must rely on their intuition while making key decisions.

Communication: Through communication, leaders inform, convince, unite, motivate, and direct their flock. The power to inform and persuade is critical to winning the hearts and minds of employees — something that is essential to leading organisations effectively.

Exemplification: Credibility comes from walking the talk. Stepping back while others take risks simply doesn't work for leaders. They must be where they are expected to be — ahead. in front, leading the charge.

The ability to think differently: For instance, a leader who's able to ask "What can I get out of my team?" instead of a "What does my team want from me?", is the one whose team members go out of their way to help him realise his vision. The key, therefore, is to think differently and be innovative in one's approach to handling people in an organisation.

Trusting by delegation: Allocating tasks to team members with complete empowerment earns their trust. Once that is done, a sense of belonging sets hi. Delegation is not just about assigning tasks. If team members believe that the leader trusts them, they go out of their way to do the tasks they are set with greater efficiency. A leader must be liberal in appreciating such extra effort — this goes a long way in acting as a morale-booster for the team members and, in turn, helps increase the productivity and efficiency of the organisation.

Decision making: Decisiveness is one of the key traits a leader must possess. Indecision is the biggest risk in business and a leader cannot afford to be fickle-minded.

Faith: Great leaders display unwavering faith in their dreams and remain focused with a strong will to pursue those dreams. They give due credit for success to their co-workers while taking responsibility for failures. Good leaders are also those who remain humble in their disposition because humility allows them to learn even from subordinates. Also may have a few good lessons to teach.

Finally, as a Chinese proverb goes: "All things come to the person who is modest and kind at a high position." A team will support a leader only if he is modest and kind. A humane leader undispuledly command more respect from his team than a merely proud one.

However, while the world, and particularly the economies of East Asia, spurred themselves on with free market regimes, India sank deeper into socialism. Business houses were prevented from developing global production capacities and vertical expansion by MRTP. A high tax bracket of 99 per cent constrained capital formation. Foreign investment was largely banned and hard currency shortages made even foreign travel a rare luxury. And then there was a long waiting period to obtain approval from the government to set up a new business, with the added risk of the idea being given away to the small-scale sector. Setting up new industries required licences, which were nearly impossible for new entrepreneurs to get. A licence was the first step to a fortune in an economy governed by controlled production, controlled markets and controlled competition. Some of the dominant business groups of the 1960s were Tata, Mafatlal, Sarabhai and Walchand Hirachand.

The decade beginning 1970 was the most politically turbulent in India's post-independence history. It was during this period that the Foreign Exchange Regulation Act (FERA) and MRTP came into force. In fact, MRTP crippled the nascent attempt of the Indian industry to build plants of global size with large economies of scale. In spite of the odds, G. D. Birla and J. R. D. Tata have gone down in Indian corporate history as the men who created the country's two largest industrial empires, comprising companies such as Grasim, Hindalco, Tata Steel and Telco, This period also witnessed the emergence of a new entrepreneur class — those who started their business with small-scale licences and grew to become large corporates. Karsanbhai Patel and his soap manufacturing company Nirma would be worth a mention. Hence, though growth did occur it was rather slow as all industries were asset-based, the main inputs coming from raw materials, finance and asset-creation.

Azim Premji

It was only in the 1980s that things began to change. The new leaders began to forge a laissez-faire economic policy. But four decades of Nehruvian socialism had built a steel grid of bureaucratic control over the private sector that could hardly be dismantled overnight. But the seeds were planted by him in two things; he wanted to modernise India and he introduced computerisation in the public sector, irrespective of whether the computers were being used or not.

Raising finance was essential. The two main areas that were available for financing were the capital market and savings. With a high tax bracket, starting a business from savings was essentially ruled out. Government financial institutions, banks and mutual funds on an average held 35-40 percent of the equity of blue chip companies. Dhirubhai Ambani and Aditya Birla realised the importance of raising money from the public. In 1977, Reliance had its first IPO. In 1990 Hindalco was the first company to raise capital at a premium of Rs. 100 per share in the domestic market.

Emergence of New Breed of Entrepreneurs

Finance Minister V.P. Singh's 1985 budget was a benchmark for economic liberalization. Manmohan Singh's sweeping reforms in 1991 was the precursor. Till the latter's 1991 budget, there was still too much government involvement in business activities. Foreign equity participation was still limited to 40 per cent. The system of seeking permits and licences had to be discontinued if India wanted to integrate with the global economy. However, globalisation and privatization appeared on the government's agenda only in 1992.

Economic liberalization was a mixed blessing for most big Indian business houses. It was between 1991 and 1995 that the Indian economy entered a new orbit of high growth. Liberalisation kickstarted the stock market, drew foreign investment, all but abolished industrial licensing, and gave groups like Tata, Birla and Reliance more room to grow. With Indian companies allowed to tap foreign equity and debt funds, Grasim floated a $90-million global depository receipt issue in late 1992. It became the second Indian company to do so after Reliance Industries. Hindalco followed shortly after with a $110-million Euro issue. With foreign direct investment pouring in, Indian companies without deep pockets were vulnerable. The takeover of Parle by Coca-Cola was the first warning signal that a market economy could cut both ways.

The second aspect of change is that today there are many avenues of finance that are available to the entrepreneur. It is not just the family unit that is used to raise funds. Now even someone with a bunch of ideas can get funding. Institutions such as HDFC and ICICI change of heart towards financing. By 1997 it was possible for the professionals to look towards entrepreneurship. Ashok Wadhwa left his secure job at Arthur Andersen to set up his own outfit, Ambit.

With the consumer today dictating terms, the change that we are seeing is taking place a lot faster. The move away from asset based towards knowledge based industries is quite obvious.

Some Observations

The term "entrepreneur" has now been attributed to all small industries, small business, traders and industrialists. All people who are gainfully engaged in work — manufacturing, distribution or service and other sectors — are called entrepreneurs. Again, even the founder, creator and risk-taker are called entrepreneurs. Each of these terms focus on some aspect of some entrepreneurs. They have some attributes, but they are not entrepreneurs in the strict sense. Many successful people have been good at copying and/or imitating others. For example, the first commercial producer of two-wheelers is to be called an entrepreneur, who has visualized the importance in modern times for the benefit of the maximum risk taken in manufacturing, marketing etc. And, all subsequent scores of people engaged in manufacturing, distribution, financing etc., are just imitators. Likewise, a brothel-keeper or a call-girl business organizer cannot be an entrepreneur, though he takes risks, creates a market and gets a reward more than visualized. So also a bootlegger, drug peddler, blackmarketeer etc. These occupations are not for the social good. They violate business ethics. The "term entrepreneur" is to be understood in its totality and. not in fabricated manner. Innovation precedes entrepreneur and runs parallel with entrepreneurship. The term "entrepreneur" can only be understood with a bearing on economic, psychological, social and cultural bearings. The social responsibility is essentially a part of entrepreneurial outlook on life.

A Classic Example

Since the dawn of civilization, there have appeared, at periodic intervals, men who have led mankind, shaping the future out of the lessons of the past and the experiences of the present. Visionaries, builders, thinkers, scientists were those who saw ahead of their times: whose presence benefited not only the country of their birth, but all mankind. In this illustrious company of uncommon people, a special place is occupied by an Indian who was born one hundred and fifty years ago — Jamshedji Nusserwanji Tata. His inspired vision of modern industrialized India was to sustain economic growth to support freedom.

To breath life into his dream, he set about to create steel, electric power and scientific-cum-technical education — the vital ingredients of economic growth. Today, the Tata organization covers a bright landscape in Indian economy. To this day, Jamshedji Tata's industrial philosophy, including his firm belief in the principle of trusteeship, his insistence on absolute standards of integrity, and realization that to survive and prosper free enterprise must serve the needs of society, were all remarkably in tune with modern thinking and the ethical and social standards of the most advanced societies of today.

Jamshedji Tata, Jamnalal Bajaj, Laxmanrao Kirloskar, Ganshyamdas Birla, Karsan Bhai Patel (Nirma), N.R. Narayana Murthy (Infosys), Azim Premji. (Wipro) are some of the entrepreneurs in their truest sense.

Entrepreneurship is not just a way to increase the level of innovation and productivity of organizations, although it will do that. More importantly, it is a way of organizing vast businesses so that work becomes a joyful expression of one's contribution to society.

The concept of entrepreneur and entrepreneurship incorporates basic qualities of leadership, innovation, enterprise, hard work, vision and maximization of profits. He is an able motivator and brings in change for the betterment of the society. All his socio-economic, organizational and managerial qualities are always directed towards the well-being of the society/community. He is committed to progress. He is a catalytic agent of development and change. Personal satisfaction and monetary rewards are blended with social betterment and welfare of mankind.

The concepts of entrepreneur and entrepreneurship have been investigated from economic, social, political, cultural and managerial points. Essential ingredients of entrepreneurship are entrepreneurs and the spirit they possess and the bold ventures they embark upon. Keeping these aspects in the backdrop, issues such as characters, required skills of entrepreneurs, role of small business in developing entrepreneurs, institutional support to develop them, promotional role of government and other related issues are discussed in detail in the following chapters.

Entrepreneurs are found in every economic system and in every form of economic activity as well as in other social and cultural activities. They are found amongst artisans, labourers, artists, importers, exporters, engineers, supervisors, bankers, industry, professional etc. They are also found among farmers, fishermen, forest workers, tribals and so on. Some writers have also identified entrepreneurs among politicians, theologists, philosophers, bureaucrats. In modern times stress has been laid on entrepreneur. It is the thrust area of development planners, economic thinkers and policy makers considering the importance of the presence of entrepreneurs, it is essential to know the type of entrepreneurs prevail in an economy, their characteristic features, competencies and awareness of self-competencies.

Types of Entrepreneurs

The entrepreneurs are broadly classified according to the types of business, use of professional skill, motivation, growth and stages of development. The various types of entrepreneurs are exhibited in the following chart:

The above Classification of entrepreneurs is not exhaustive, for it aims at highlighting the broad range of entrepreneurs found in business and profession. We shall now discuss in brief, each type of entrepreneurs. Entrepreneurs are found in various types of business occupations of varying size.

Women Entrepreneurs

Economic, social, religious, cultural and psychological factors influence entrepreneurs to emerge in a society. In this context the role of women entrepreneurs in building the nation cannot be ignored. In the advanced countries of the world there is a phenomenal increase in the number of self-employed women after the world war. In the United States, women own 25 percent of all business, even though their sales on an average are less than two-fifths of those of other small businesses. In Canada one-third of small businesses are owned by women and in France it is one-fifth. In the UK, the number of self-employed women is growing year by year and they have outnumbered male entrepreneurs. In other parts of the world also, there is considerable increase in the role of women entrepreneurs in nation building activities.

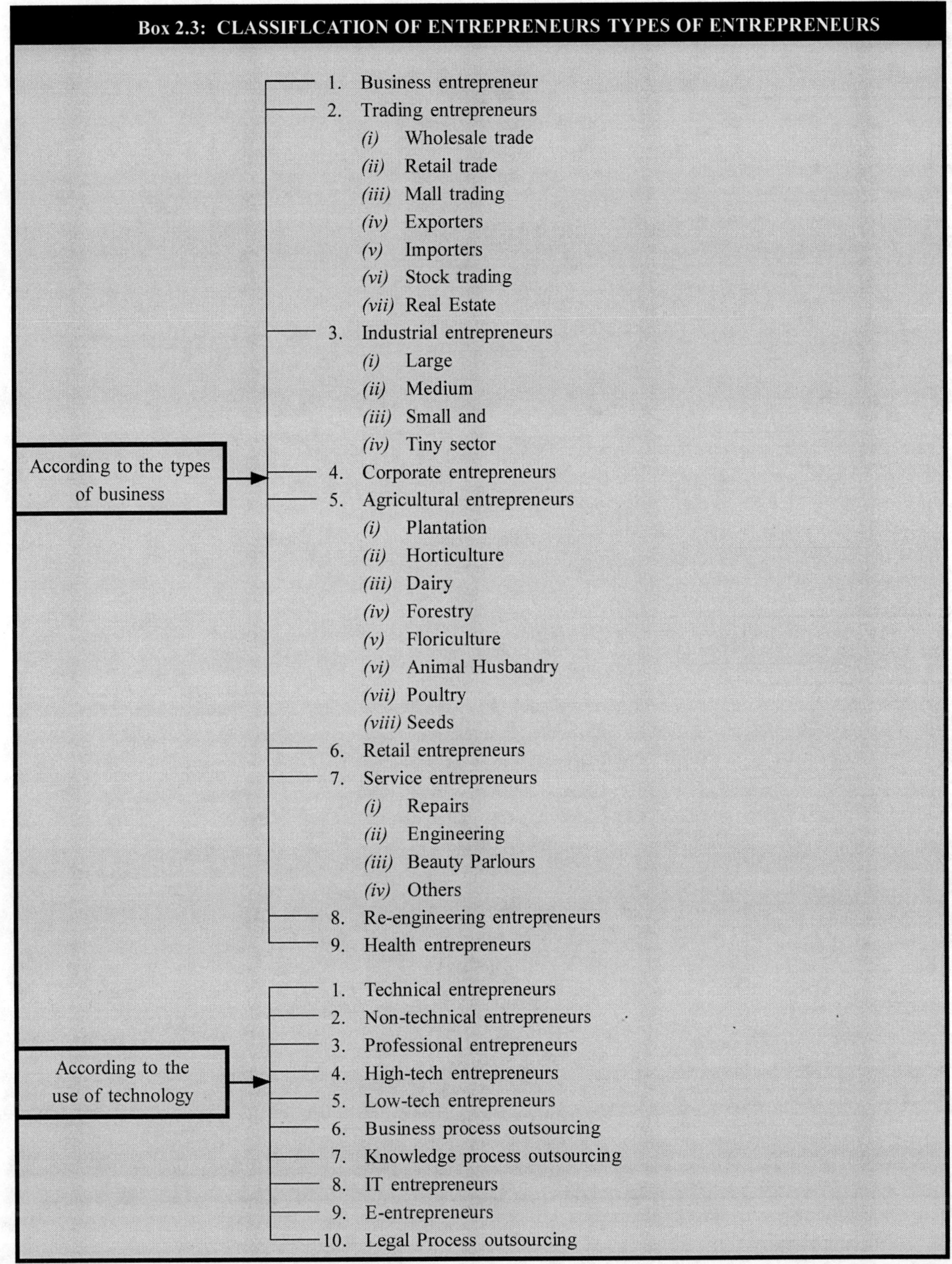
Box 2.3: CLASSIFLCATION OF ENTREPRENEURS TYPES OF ENTREPRENEURS
According to the types of business
1. Business entrepreneur
2. Trading entrepreneurs
(i) Wholesale trade
(ii) Retail trade
(iii) Mall trading
(iv) Exporters
(v) Importers
(vi) Stock trading
(vii) Real Estate
3. Industrial entrepreneurs
(i) Large
(ii) Medium
(iii) Small and
(iv) Tiny sector
4. Corporate entrepreneurs
5. Agricultural entrepreneurs
(i) Plantation
(ii) Horticulture
(iii) Dairy
(iv) Forestry
(v) Floriculture
(vi) Animal Husbandry
(vii) Poultry
(viii) Seeds
6. Retail entrepreneurs
7. Service entrepreneurs
(i) Repairs
(ii) Engineering
(iii) Beauty Parlours
(iv) Others
8. Re-engineering entrepreneurs
9. Health entrepreneurs
According to the use of technology
1. Technical entrepreneurs
2. Non-technical entrepreneurs
3. Professional entrepreneurs
4. High-tech entrepreneurs
5. Low-tech entrepreneurs
6. Business process outsourcing
7. Knowledge process outsourcing
8. IT entrepreneurs
9. E-entrepreneurs
10. Legal Process outsourcing

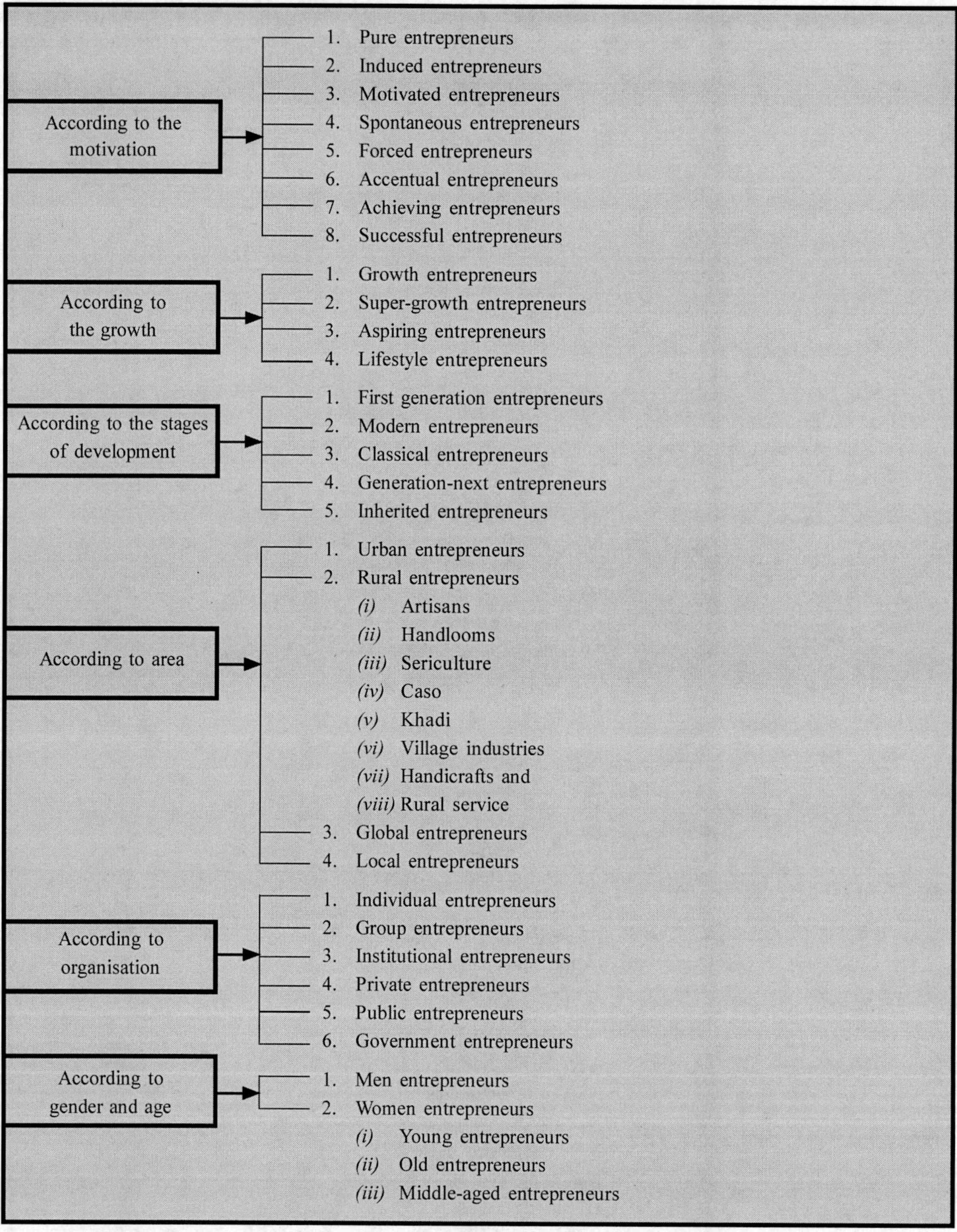
According to the motivation
1. Pure entrepreneurs
2. Induced entrepreneurs
3. Motivated entrepreneurs
4. Spontaneous entrepreneurs
5. Forced entrepreneurs
6. Accentual entrepreneurs
7. Achieving entrepreneurs
8. Successful entrepreneurs
According to the growth
1. Growth entrepreneurs
2. Super-growth entrepreneurs
3. Aspiring entrepreneurs
4. Lifestyle entrepreneurs
According to the stages of development
1. First generation entrepreneurs
2. Modern entrepreneurs
3. Classical entrepreneurs
4. Generation-next entrepreneurs
5. Inherited entrepreneurs
According to area
1. Urban entrepreneurs
2. Rural entrepreneurs
(i) Artisans
(ii) Handlooms
(iii) Sericulture
(iv) Caso
(v) Khadi
(vi) Village industries
(vii) Handicrafts and
(viii) Rural service
3. Global entrepreneurs
4. Local entrepreneurs
According to organisation
1. Individual entrepreneurs
2. Group entrepreneurs
3. Institutional entrepreneurs
4. Private entrepreneurs
5. Public entrepreneurs
6. Government entrepreneurs
According to gender and age
1. Men entrepreneurs
2. Women entrepreneurs
(i) Young entrepreneurs
(ii) Old entrepreneurs
(iii) Middle-aged entrepreneurs

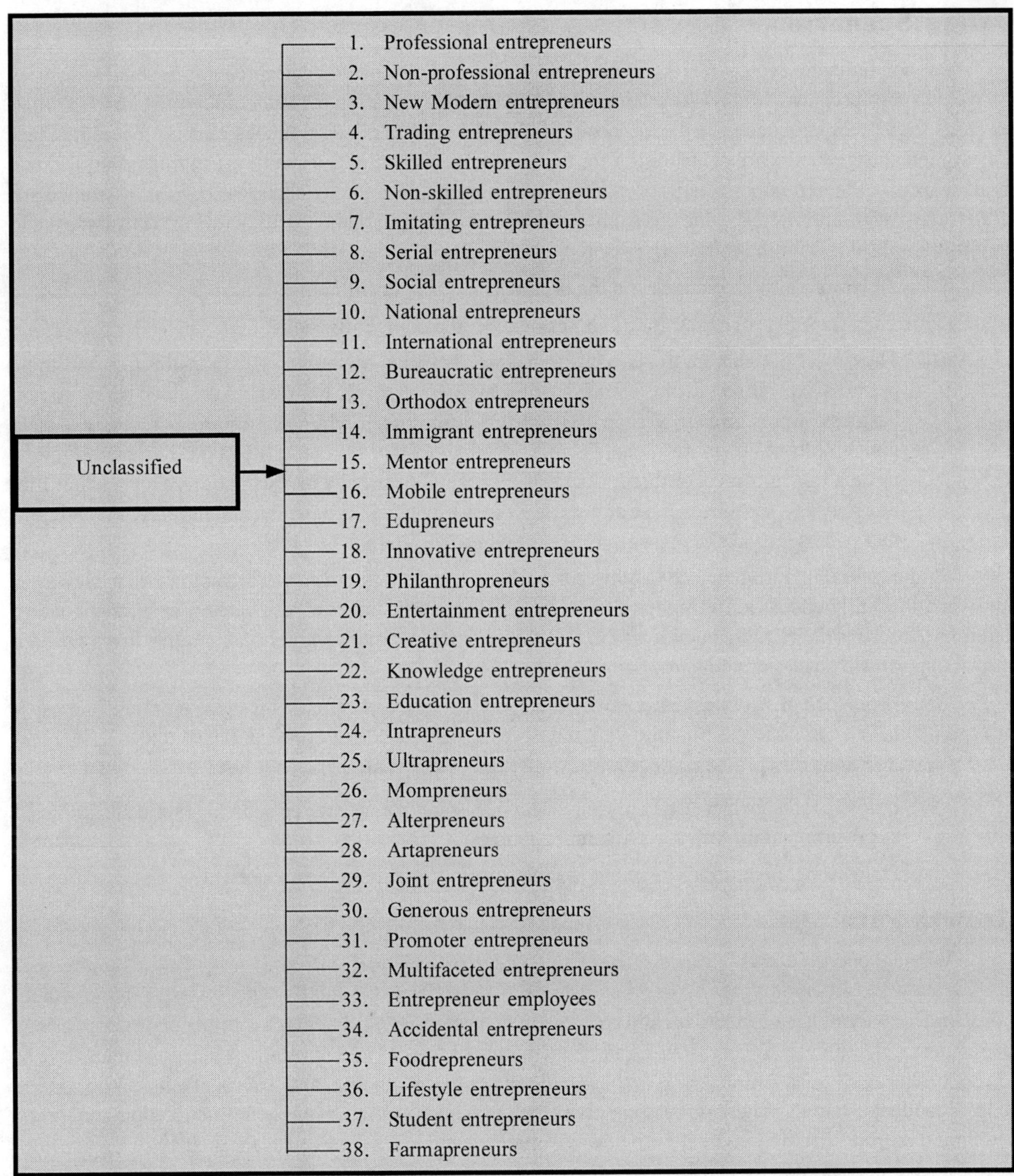

Fig. 2.2: Classification of Entrepreneurs

Indian Scenario

Even in India their role is no less significant. Nearly 9 percent of total entrepreneurs in small industries are women entrepreneurs. State-wise distribution shows a wide variation between different states. If Punjab accounts for 3%, Gujarat occupies the top position with 15%. As in other countries, this is an accepted fact that women entrepreneurs are contributing for the economic growth of the country. But this group forms a small segment of total number of entrepreneurs functioning in the country. The areas chosen by women are retail trade, restaurants, hotels, education, cultural, cleaning, insurance and manufacturing. They have made their mark in business for the following reasons:

(i) They want new challenges and opportunities for self-fulfillment.

(ii) They want to prove their mettle in innovative and competitive jobs.

(iii) They want the change to control the balance between their family responsibilities and their business lives. Dina Lavoie, a professor of Entrepreneurship, Montreal has observed "that, women business owners hire an average of two to three employees, whereas men are more likely to have nine employees or more. Often, a micro-business fits a woman's life-style. Expansion might mean a loss of control or disruption in the amount of time she invests in other facets of her life. She may also want to oversee and control every aspect of her business and may feel she will lose that opportunity if she grows to the point where she cannot."

Studies reveal that women face tough security requirement on their lines of credit than men. However, other identified differences such as higher interest rates, lower credit approval rates and espousal co-signature requirements are primarily attributable to the fact that women operate younger and smaller firms that are known to meet with such financing problems.

On taking stock of voluntary efforts which are exclusively concerned with the promotion of women entrepreneurs, one comes across the following measures which have taken roots in the country:

- Associations are exclusively concentrating on women entrepreneurship.
- Entrepreneurship Development Cells are concentrating on women entrepreneurs and are promoted by governmental/semi-governmental agencies.
- Educational institutions have put in their efforts to augment these efforts.

Growth Path

Women, one time in this world, were not considered to become entrepreneurs. It took hundreds of years to show the different types of roles that a women can perform. Gradually role of women in the society took to different forms, shapes and sizes and are moving in these different channels assuming bigger dimensions in each form. But the pace is very slow. Even today in many societies and in different places women "live in a bygone century chained and shackled to the social structures and coding, and wishes of others who carve a code of conduct on stone. Whereas there are other locales where women struggle to find freedom and space to define their roles in a new context with new occupations and forge a new path for their lives."

Indian women play very many roles. They may be pure, supreme or virtue to vice or downtrodden. Constantly, the role is also undergoing several changes. While playing their role, Indian women are confronted with contradictions. Because of these contradictions, they are unable to identify themselves with the society. The attitude, perceptions, roles etc. of Indian women look like an assembly of diverse fragments. One cannot have a logical look at all these aspects. Every advantage is having a disadvantage. This perplexed situation of Indian women has made it very difficult to define their roles and they cannot identify their roles for themselves.

Because of this plain truth, assuming the role of entrepreneur and leadership for an Indian women was a difficult task. But still times have changed. The present society is freeing the Indian women from the chains and shackles of centuries. This slow but definite shift over is happening for the following reasons:

(i) The concept of globalisation is accepted in a big way.

(ii) The sudden emerging trend in information technology and its percolation to every segment of life.

(iii) Adoption of diversified culture in the Indian society due to globalisation and other inherent ethoes of Indian society.

(iv) Unexpected happenings around the world and their impact on Indian society.

(v) Change in socio-cultural context due to increased education for women since independence.

(vi) Change in political ideology and governance of the country.'

Vital Statistics

Description	*Data*
1. Total population	1080 million
2. Women population	460 million
3. Percentage to total population	46.5
4. Women workforce	140 million
5. Percentage of female population	32.9
6. Women Entrepreneurs	9 per cent of total entrepreneurs
7. Rural-Urban divide	90 per cent (Rural) 10 per cent (Urban)

In nineteen seventies, women entrepreneurship began in its real sense. By this time, the first generation after independence had completed their education. Educated women to fulfill their aspirations and ambitions, began opting for self-employment. This was an active step not taken out of compulsions or helplessness, but with zeal to make a better life. In this decade, women were in transition period. They could not come out fully from traditional activities of looking after home, their in-laws, parents, husbands and children. At the same time, they had to get into autonomous economic activities. This was a challenge.

Eighties and Nineties saw a sea change in women entrepreneurship domain. These were the decades of the breakthrough for women to become entrepreneurs in many fields. They developed courage to make new beginnings. Parents also developed a new thinking. The traditional practice of making only male progeny as a business partner in family owned businesses (law of Inheritance supporting this). Parents started taking their female children as partners in their businesses. Governments also supported this new thinking by making amendments to Succession Act.

Legislations said that both male and female have equal rights in the inherited property. This coupled with professional education made young ladies to get into self-employment. Many became partners in their family owned business. Good number of lady doctors opened their own clinics. Engineering graduates started their own consultancy houses, providing different types of technical services. They also got into service areas like chartered accountants, advocates, hospitality business and good number opened secretarial offices. Good percentage of women took to small business activities. Today we can see many women entrepreneurs in small business.

In earlier Five Year Plans, women entrepreneurship concept was not significantly considered. Only in recent plans, particularly after Eighth Five Year Plan, "Women Empowerment" concept came to limelight. From this plan onwards, women started working on new frontiers. The new generation of women did not think on the lines of their mothers. They started developing independent activities. They had aspirations and ambitions. Taking to self-employment was not out of compulsion or helplessness. It became a desired choice of many ladies to design and develop their own enterprises. Women started thinking that self-employment is an integral aspect of their life. They stated thinking on the lines of selecting their own careers. Adapting own occupation for income generation without deviating much from the social system is becoming a key factor in a woman's life. Besides having home and children, women have started thinking to have an independent occupation. While accepting the traditional role behaviour, from older generation, women today expect understanding and support from their husbands and children to have their occupational choice. As entrepreneurs, women want their voice to be heard as leaders, as they are capable of contributing to the growth and success of their enterprise.

Women Entrepreneurs in Several Industries

Today we find women in different types of industries, traditional as well as non-traditional, such as engineering, electronic, readymade garments, fabrics, toy making, printing, dairy, canning, knitting, jewellery design, solar cooker etc. What motivates women to aspire for career in business is an interesting thing to explore and analyse. According to Mclelland and Winter, motivation is a critical factor that leads one towards entrepreneurship. This apart, the challenge and adventure to do something new, liking for business and wanting to have an independent occupation are some of the attractive leverage for women. These factors indicate a relatively deeper commitment to entrepreneurial profession on the part of entrepreneur. Responsibility thrust, due to death or incapacitation of a near relation, tax benefit for self and for relations are the push factors. In addition, special qualification attained for running a concern, identifying the demand from the market, external motivation, employment to needy and destitutes to setup an ancillary unit, business already in the family, are some of the factors which gave stimulus to women entrepreneurs to start business.

Profile of a Woman Entrepreneur

Who is this Woman entrepreneur? What are her qualities?

She is a woman of commitment, who is relevant, independently employed, she has close relationship with her father and, after obtaining an undergraduate and subsequently graduate degree in some area of liberal arts, marries, has children and starts her first significant entrepreneurial venture in the service area in her late 30s or early 40s. Her biggest problems at start-up and later in the venture, reflect a lack of business training and generally are in the financial area.

Profile of a Woman Entrepreneur and her Business

First-born child of middle class parents

Father and/or mother in independent business

College educated

Married

Early 30s for the first significant venture

Previous experience in new venture

Desires independence

Motivated by desire for independence and job satisfaction

Small and young business

Self-confident

Moderate risk-taker

High tolerance for ambiguity

High energy level

Biggest Problems in Start-up:

- Lack of business training
- Obtaining credit
- Availability of information
- Obtaining seed capital
- Marketing
- Personnel management

Biggest Problems in Current Operations:

- Lack of experience in financial planning
- Weak collateral position
- Cash flow management
- Taxation

With education and training, women have gained confidence to do all work, which was the prerogative of man and do it excellently, rather better than men. Over the years, the educated women have become ambitious, acquired experience and basic skills of competency and self-assurance.

Psycho-social Barriers

Although some women entrepreneurs have excelled in their enterprise, the fear of success haunt women in general. Some psycho-social factors impeding the growth of woman entrepreneurship are as follows:

1. Poor self-image of women
2. Inadequate motivation
3. Discriminating treatment
4. Faulty socialization
5. Role conflict
6. Cultural values
7. Lack of courage and self-confidence
8. Inadequate encouragement
9. Lack of social acceptance
10. Unjust social-economic and cultural system
11. Lack of freedom of expression
12. Afraid of failures and criticism
13. Susceptible to negative attitudes

14. Non-persistent attitude
15. Low dignity of labour
16. Lacking in leadership qualities, i.e., planning, organizing, controlling, coordinating and directing.

Leadership Qualities

Some of the outstanding qualities of women entrepreneurs are as follows:

Accept Challenges	Adventurous
Ambitious	Conscious
Drive	Educated
Enthusiastic	Determination to excel
Hard work	Keenness to learn and imbibe new ideas
Patience	Experienced
Industrious	Intelligent
Motivator	Perseverance
Skilful	Studious
Unquenchable optimism	

The New Thrust

Earlier researches conducted indicate that several women are now willing to become entrepreneurs due to various factors. These factors can be broadly classified under two headings, namely, "Pull factors" and "Push factors." Under the first category, the women entrepreneurs choose a profession as a challenge and adventure with an urge to do something new, liking for business and to have an independent occupation. The other category is the ones who take up business enterprises to get over financial difficulties and responsibility that is thrust on them due to family circumstances. However, the later category forms a negligible percentage of the total women entrepreneurs.

The new thrust given to the process of economic development of the country by the new dynamic leadership has created an all-round enthusiasm and the new slogan of "March in the twenty-first century" had gained popularity. But in this new enthusiasm a very vital sector of the society which can contribute substantially towards the economic development of the country is not given enough attention to women entrepreneurs. This comes naturally to women. Therefore they feel that successful managers will be those who combine this feminist attribute of nurturing and futuristic planning with male aggressiveness. But this inherent management talent of woman and her entrepreneurial skill go unrecognized and unaccounted as it does not show profit or loss in monetary terms.

With the spread of education and new approaches/awareness, women entrepreneurs are achieving higher level of 3Es, namely, engineering, electronics and energy, though the number of such units is not as large as it should be. But the very fact that women are putting up units to manufacture solar cookers as in Gujarat, small foundries in Maharashtra and T.V. capacitors in the industrially backward area of Orissa, IT and Bio-technology units (Kiran Majumdor Shaw) in Karnataka show that women if trained and given opportunities can venture in non-traditional industries. Even the so-called socially tabooed industrial activity of wine-making and selling is being done by women entrepreneurs in Mumbai. So today no field is unapproachable to the trained and determined modern Indian women.

Basic Problems of Women Entrepreneurs

The basic problem or difficulty of a woman entrepreneur is that she is a woman. This pertains to her responsibility towards facility, society and work. With joint families breaking up, many women simply don't have the support of elders. Women have been confronted by such dilemmas ever since they started leaving home for the work place. On the other hand, the attitude of the society towards her and constraints in which she has to live and work are not very conducive.

The problems faced by women entrepreneurs are briefly analysed below:

(i) Start up finance
(ii) Working capital management
(iii) Marketing skills
(iv) Access to technology
(v) Regulatory requirements
(vi) Management skills
(vii) Lack of confidence.

(i) Access to start-up finance is the greatest single issue faced by women entrepreneurs. It is observed that women entrepreneurs face greater problems in this regard than small business in general. As family members are not in favour of supporting their ladies to take up the business in which they have skills, naturally they will be unwilling to support with the finance required for starting a business unit. Men are not willing to stand as surety to the loan granted by financial agencies. Women are not in a position to start the business with own capital. External finance is not so easily coming forward, and self-financing is very meager. This is the greatest hurdle for the development of women entrepreneurs.

(ii) Another key disturbing factor is managing the working capital, required for maintaining finished stock to meet the market demand, for production, and for meeting marketing and other administrative expenses. It will be very difficult for women entrepreneurs to avail such loan facilities from financial institutions as they are unable to provide security. Although financial institutions have liberalized lending schemes, women entrepreneurs are not in a position to avail required finance, as family members in most of the cases do not support to raise heavy capital.

(iii) Regarding marketing skills, women entrepreneurs have the problem of access to markets as their marketing skills are weak compared to male entrepreneurs. This is a major barrier for them to expand business or enter into business. Maintaining existing business and access to fresh business requires strategic marketing skills. This is the most commonly repeated problem faced by women entrepreneurs after finance. Therefore, marketing skills, management skills and technology skills have to be improved in female owned businesses. This encourages other women to enter into self-employment.

(iv) Access to technology and adopt it in production process, poses certain problems. Coordinating factors of production is really a challenge to women entrepreneurs. To compete with producers, they need guts. Women entrepreneurs cannot easily co-ordinate the production process particularly with the ever changing technology. Very few women can sustain such production onslaughts. Women who aspire to become entrepreneurs cannot keep pace with technology advancement. This puts down their initiative to become entrepreneurs. Even they feel that women are discriminated by finance providers to a greater or significantly greater extent to upgrade the technology. Whilst many small businesses face difficulties for the finance that they need, organizations specialising in providing support for female entrepreneurs clearly feel that this is one area where their clients face greater difficulties than their male counterparts.

(v) Regarding administrative and regulatory requirements, many feel that this is a significantly greater problem for women entrepreneurs than their male counterparts. Micro enterprises of every type experience these problems. It is because of the disproportionate effect of compliance costs on small companies compared with large firms. In spite of this, women entrepreneurs do not feel that it is a major issue. But still this is a factor to reckon with.

(vi) Another vital problem encountered by women entrepreneurs is lack of management skills in majority of the cases, although this is common to all entrepreneurs, women are particularly disadvantaged in this respect. Because they have lower propensity of previous business experience. Besides this, support providers discriminate against women entrepreneurs to a greater extent in providing these skills. Skills are concerned with and ranged from day-to-day management to long-term strategic development. As external support to develop managerial skills is not that encouraging, women entrepreneurs have to develop their own seminars and workshops to equip in this area.

(vii) Other problems like society's attitude towards women entrepreneurs, unequal opportunities between men and women and very important amongst all the *"Lack of Confidence"* in women are also haunting women entrepreneurs.

Women in this society have a subordinate status. This has made them constantly to have a sort of inferiority complex and do not have courage and confidence to take up the activities on their own. Though they have the competence to become entrepreneurs, the family members having not much faith in women are not allowing them to become independent business persons. Lack of confidence and less support from family members are also the problems that are preventing women to become successful entrepreneurs.

Promotion of Women Entrepreneurs

The problems of women entrepreneurs discussed so far, provides some direction in which the supporting agencies, family and government have to work to solve their problems and promote them as successful entrepreneurs. All these supports have come out with their (supporting agencies) programmes and policies to support and promote women entrepreneurs.

As already stated, 48 percent of the total population of the country are women. Of this, only 34 percent are employed in some form or the other. Women entrepreneurs also fall in this percentage and it is very meager and marginal. As in other parts of the world, women have not achieved equality with men. People believe that men are only the breadwinners in every family which is not correct. But every one now understands that women in the families can only move their families forward. The "Gender And Development (GAD)" approach, in 1980s clearly identified the role of women as entrepreneurs. Today people believe that women should be brought to the central stage from marginality in entrepreneurial development. The concept of woman entrepreneur development is not merely to initiate a process of economic growth but also a process which will improve the lives of people.

In this backdrop, certain measures have to be taken to strengthen the women entrepreneurship development. The women entrepreneurship movement has taken off the ground and it is felt that the movement has crossed the stage of transition. It is only during the last 20 years women have started becoming entrepreneurs. They are yet to go a long way to be on par with men. Women activities are influenced by occupational background of the families, and educational attainments of their husbands. Besides, she has to play a dual role as housewife and income-earner. As a woman, and as a manager of most complicated social institution — family, she has learnt the art of managing many human interfaces between the sexes, different age groups and different stakeholders. Women have learnt over the centuries the art of negotiation and reconciliation and qualities of patience and understanding, along with an inherent quality of emotional intelligence. All these skills can be used in her business, she chooses.

Since service sector is growing at a very faster rate in our country and still large majority of women live in semi-urban and rural areas, measures to be adopted to promote and continue women as entrepreneurs are:

(i) Establishing only small units

(ii) Deciding the correct time of establishment

(iii) Providing adequate financial assistance

(iv) Solving the problem of gender inequality. Gender and Development approach — GAD in 1980s has done something in this direction

(v) Coordinating the dual role of family and business

(vi) Imparting necessary training in financial management, quality concept, availing proper technology etc. and

(vii) Training to have patience and tolerance.

Training is also necessary in *(i)* Core Competence and *(ii)* Facility for IT Enabled Services.

(i) **Core Competence:** Women can establish their business units in which they have core competence. Today, many a woman are trained in Information Technology, Management, other Engineering areas, Bio-Technology, Hospitality Services, Tourism, Secretaryship, Health care services, Personal care services, Educational services, Financial services and other need-based areas. This type of educational facility has provided greater opportunity to select an area for availing professional training in which she has inherent skills. She becomes a successful entrepreneur in a business she has core competence. Family and society should motivate women having core competence to start their business units.

(ii) **Facilities for IT Enabled Services:** Today, Information Technology, Management and Bio-Technology areas are opened up like anything. Women are having umpteen number of opportunities to start and run their own units successfully in these sectors. Even the financial requirements for start up in IT and Management sectors are not prohibitive but affordable. The position is well within the reach of less affluent and economically weaker sections of the society. But they should have profound marketable skills. New areas like web designing, database management, multi-media services sector, HR training areas, advertising etc. are very fertile fields to take to entrepreneurship. Facilities for training in these areas are to be further extended.

With this brief analysis of problems and promotion of women entrepreneurs, some measures are listed here as to how to motivate women to become entrepreneurs in large numbers.

- To collect information on specific actions and support measures prompting female entrepreneurship. (Many government and private associations have taken up counseling women to make them as entrepreneurs).
- To identify good practices in the promotion of female entrepreneurship.
- To develop a methodology for assessing member's actions, and support measures for promoting female entrepreneurship overtime.

- Promoting measures should cover, start-up facilities, information and advice, funding (identification of sources and help prospects in availing the funds without any hassle) training facilities, mentoring and networking.

These measures would attract more and more women to become entrepreneurs. Today the doors are wide open with unimaginable facilities in new domains, besides the traditional business. Only the number of female entrepreneurs should increase.

Opportunities for Women Entrepreneurs

Considering the flow of women entrepreneurs in the traditional: and conventional industries and product lines, it is often criticised that the women entrepreneurship in India is caught up in "3 Ps," (papads and pickles, food industry, petticoats, readymade garment industry, paintings and handicrafts). The entry of women entrepreneurs in the conventional product is justified on the grounds that they have acquired the skills required for these products traditionally. If they could manage these product lines, let them excel. But many all-India level surveys have proved that in present years, women entrepreneurs have entered all fields of business and industry in the last decade, there has been a remarkable shift in emphasis from the manufacturing which are identified for industry to the service industry. Considering this, some important opportunities for women in urban areas:

1. Computer services and information dissemination
2. Trading in computer stationery
3. Computer training at various levels
4. Computer maintenance
5. Travel and tourism
6. Quality testing, quality control laboratories
7. Sub-assemblies of electronic products
8. Nutrition clubs in schools and offices
9. Poster and indoor plant library
10. Recreation centres for old people
11. Culture centres
12. Screen printing, photography, and video shooting
13. Stuffed soft toys, wooden toys
14. Mini laundry, community eating centres
15. Community kitchens
16. Distribution and trading of household provision as well as saris, dress materials, etc.
17. Job contracts for packaging of goods
18. Photocopying, typing centres
19. Beauty parlours
20. Communications centres like STD booths, cyber cafes, etc.
21. Creches

ANNEXURE - 1

The Ideal Entrepreneur

Not a workaholic. Sure, you should be prepared to work long — and irregular — hours, but the freedom to choose and prioritize free time is always at hand. If you cannot sleep at night, as long as there is single file left unperused, a memo unread, a number uncrunched, back off right now. Entrepreneurship isn't onedayer. You must have the self-control to play for a long innings instead of burning yourself out.

Be warned, therefore, even when you are your own boss, long-term sustainability demands that you balance your professional and personal life. Only then can you truly make your own business sustainable in the long-term.

To Morph into an Entrepreneur:

- Managers must translate their career ambitions into specific business goals.
- They must use their people management skills to motivate and inspire their employees.
- Managers must capitalize on their skills to manage the financial aspects personally.
- They must turn their aggression in the workplace into a risk-taking approach.
- They must leverage their functional expertise when choosing their line of business.
- Managers must develop leadership qualities on the job before venturing out on their own.

  Prepare, therefore, a mental checklist of the other side to the entrepreneur's job. Sure, your once-in-a-lifetime innovative idea will convert customers immediately, but are you as prudent as a penny-pinching CEO? – has the diplomacy of the personnel manager? – has the doggedness of the door-to-door salesman? You will need them all, in addition to that gem of an idea.

The entrepreneurship audit will judge an individual's capabilities, be it an entrepreneur or not. Just try it.

The Entrepreneurship Audit

Do you measure upto the tough task of being your boss? Assess yourself impartially and objectively your positive and negative points in becoming your own boss. If need be, negative points might be corrected by training and education. Take this test to find out:

	Yes	No
1. Do you enjoy taking big, even unwarranted risks?	☐	☐
2. Do you plan ahead on most things you do?	☐	☐
3. Do you have a head for numbers and finances?	☐	☐
4. Do you make it a point to complete what you start?	☐	☐
5. Can you survive a drop in your standard of living?	☐	☐
6. Are you able to take decisions without dithering?	☐	☐
7. Are you free of major financial commitments?	☐	☐
8. Can you get along with different kinds of people?	☐	☐
9. Is your career path in your company flattering out?	☐	☐

10.	Do you enjoy travelling on work?	☐	☐
11.	Are you capable of leading people?	☐	☐
12.	Do you have a clear vision about your dreams?	☐	☐
13.	Do you have innovative ideas about projects and services?	☐	☐
14.	Have you acquired specific skills to run the new venture?	☐	☐
15.	Do you plan your work methodically?	☐	☐
16.	Are you adaptable and flexible?	☐	☐
17.	Do you prefer working alone or in teams?	☐	☐
18.	Do you find yourself envying entrepreneurs?	☐	☐
19.	Can you cope with punishing work schedules?	☐	☐
20.	Does your spouse support your plans?	☐	☐

The Scoring

Give yourself 5 points for every YES, and 0 for every NO.

Total

The Rating

0-35	You won't get far with I Inc. Be satisfied with what you already have in hand.
40-60	The passion as a self-starter is weak. You seek the status quo rather than a crisis.
65-100	All systems go. Greener pastures and challenges await you.

ANNEXURE – 2

The New Credo at Levi's Strauss Behavioural Change

Management must exemplify directness, openness to influence, commitment to the success of others, and willingness to acknowledge our own contributions to problems.

Diversity: Levi's 'values a diverse workforce (age, sex, ethnic group, etc.) at all levels of the organisation .... Differing points of view will be sought; diversity will be valued and honestly rewarded, not suppressed.'

Recognition: Levi's will "provide greater recognition — both financial and psychic — for individuals and teams that contribute to our success... those who create and innovate and those who continually support day-to-day business requirements."

Ethical Management Practices: Management should epitomise the stated standards of ethical behaviour. We must provide clarity about our expectations and must enforce these standards through the corporation.

Communications: Management must be "clear about company, unit and individual goals and performance. People must know what is expected of them and receive timely, honest feedback...."

Empowerment: Management must 'increase the authority and responsibility of those closest to our products and customers. By actively pushing the responsibility, trust, and recognition into the organization, we can harness and release the capabilities of all our people.'

The Motivation Audit

Do you cultivate a positive environment for your team and bolster everyone's spirits? Take this audit to find out:

1. Do you rally your workers by treating them to special food, prizes, and cook-outs? Yes No
2. Do you prod people to express their appreciation for others through spoken praise or notices? Yes No
3. Do you look for ways to make jobs rewarding, such as training and friendly competitions? Yes No
4. Do you help your people laugh and bear adversity by giving them something to smile about? Yes No
5. Do you take advantage of scheduling flexibility by giving deserving workers extra time off? Yes No
6. Do you describe your group's achievements whenever you have a chance? Yes No
7. Do you support other groups within you company, and let them know about it? Yes No
8. Do you invest your group's time in being helpful to your customers, both internal and external? Yes No
9. Do you tell your team that you are committed to help it get the recognition it deserves? Yes No
10. Do you ask your team members what they need from you to get through the crunch? Yes No

The Scoring

Give yourself 10 points for every YES and 0 for every NO

Total

The Rating

0-30	You are a miserable motivator. Learn to utilise your greatest asset: your people.
40-70	You are a mediocre motivator. Strive to improve your communication skills.
80-100	You are a master motivator. You know how to get the best of your people..

ANNEXURE – 3

Analysis of Activities of Entrepreneurs into Knowledge Skills and Attitude Requirements

Activities	*Knowledge*	*Skills*	*Attitudes*
1. Perceiving the need and analysing own self in relation to ones life goals.	– Human needs hierarchy – Strengths, weaknesses and resources – Entrepreneurial traits – Process of goal setting	– Proper self concept – Analysis of strengths and weaknesses – Internalising entrepreneurial traits – Goal setting attitudes	– Positive self concept – Willing to change – Proactive – Entrepreneurial
2. Scanning the environment for opportunities	– Economic scene – Business environment – Facilities, incentives and procedures – Emerging trends – Information collection technique – Opportunities available	– Information gathering skills – Analytical skills – Decision making – Communication skills	– Decisive – Flexibility
3. Identification of product/project	– Knowledge of products and services – Manufacturing practices – Service skills – Business environment	– Analytical skills – Creativity – Communication – Reasoning skills	– Decisive – Flexibility – Hard working – Persistent

	– Demand potential – Resource requirement		
4. Conducting market survey	– Market survey techniques – Agencies and organisations to be contacted – Uses of product – Suppliers of plant, equipment and raw material	– Information – Analytical skills – Report writing – Communication	– Optimistic gathering
5. Identification of technology, plant and equipment	– Production design – Product design – Existing seeker – Consideration for choice of technology, plant and equipment – Facility layout and process planning – Legal provisions – Sources of raw materials plant and equipment	– Production – Manufacturing skills – Communication – Planning	– Decisive – Risk taking – Opportunity
6. Determination of sources of finance	– Financial institutions – Commercial banks – Development corporations – Norms of financing	– Analytical skills – Business acumenship – Planning – Working under stress	– Risk taking – Calculative – Optimistic

	– Procedures of financing – Total financial requirement		
7. Preparation of project report Business plan	– Structure of project report – Purpose of project report – Working and fixed capital – Utilities requirement – Feasibility criteria – Break-even analysis – Accounting ratios – Cash inflow and outflow – Men, material and machine requirement	– Report writing – Analytical abilities – Communication judgement – Accounting and financial skills – Forecasting skill	– Clear thinking – Decisive – Good
8. Arranging finance infra-structure and utilities	– Source – Requirement – Specification criteria – Procedures relations – Environment – Legal requirement – Municipal by-laws – Safety considerations	– Communication – Negotiating – Forecasting – Public	– influencing – Pleasing – Assertive
9. Project implementation	– Planning skills – Resource requirement	– Management – Planning	– Hard working – Goal setting

	– Time management – Legal formalities – Plant layout – Commissioning of plant and equipment – Trial production and quality assurance	– Communication	
10. Market and sales management	– Elements of sales management – Marketing management – Costing and pricing – Marketing practices – Distribution channels – Advertising packaging	– Public relations – Salesmanship – Demonstration skills – Negotiating skills – Forecasting	– Persuasive – Foresightedness – Optimistic
11. Management enterprise	– Forms of business organisations – Human behaviour – Personnel management – Management of resources	– Management skills – Public relations – Problem solving	– Leadership – Creative – Innovative

Source: *Report for Institutionalising Entrepreneurship Development and Management Course in Selected Institutions. T.T.T.I., Chandigarh.*

3

ENTREPRENEURIAL PERSONALITY

Every small dream of yours became the vision of our future.
Every little action of yours became the seeds of our prosperity.
Every adversity you faced with courage has paved the path for us.
Every brave step you took became a leap for our growth.
In everything we do, you live in our souls forever.

Introduction

The entrepreneur is a human being. But, he is distinct from others on account of his personality. The entrepreneur is a motivated person and at the same time a motivator.

The theories of motivation are based on the fact that behaviour is essentially purposeful and directed towards the attainment of a goal. Essentially, motivation is a process of stimulating action sustaining the activity. David McClellan advocated the Theory of Achievement Motivation.

Achievement Motivation is represented by

- An urge to excel.
- Desire to achieve success in competition with self and with others (Role model)
- Long-term goals and long-term involvement
- Unique accomplishment
- Perfection and excellence

Thus, entrepreneurial personality is a cruciel factor in entrepreneurship, entrepreneurism, economic development and sustained growth.

Nature of Personality

Personality is one of the psychological factors that influences individual behaviour.

Understanding personalities is important because personality affects behaviour, as well as perception and attitudes. Personality types also affect human relations and retaliation. People with similar personality types tend to get along well at work, while opposites do not, though there are exceptions.

Personality profiles are used to categorize people as a means of predicting job performance. Some personality characteristics are more productive than others. Conscientiousness is a good indicator of performance, though it is not the only dimension. Many organizations administer personality tests to ensure a proper match between the worker and the job.

The concept of personality is not to be understood in an organizational context only. The need for understanding human characteristics, in general, is more significant than comprehending personality in the context of organizations. Despite serious attempts, experts have not been able to comprehend the real nature of personality. Of all the problems that have confronted human beings since the beginning of recorded history, perhaps the most significant has been the riddle of their own nature.

Generally, personality refers to the set of traits and behaviours that characterise an individual. A more comprehensive meaning of personality is that it refers to the relatively stable pattern of behaviour and consistent internal state and explains a person's behavioural tendencies.

The following elements should form the meaning of personality:

1. Personality has both internal and external elements. The external traits are the observable behaviours that we notice in an individual's personality, for example, sociability. The internal states represent the thoughts, values and genetic characteristics that we infer from the observable behaviours.
2. An individual's personality is relatively stable. If it changes at all, it is only after a very long time or as the result of traumatic events.
3. An individual's personality is both inherited as well as shaped by the environment. Our personality is partly inherited genetically from our parents. However, these genetic personality characteristics are altered somewhat by life experiences.
4. Each individual is unique in behaviour. There are striking differences among individuals.

Determinants of Personality

What determinants go into the development of personality? Of all the complexities and unanswered questions in the study of human behaviour, this question may be the most difficult one. The problem lies in the fact that the cognitive and physiological processes, and many other variables, all contribute to personality. However, for convenience of study, the determinants of personality can be grouped into the five broad categories: heredity, environmental, family, social, and situational. (See Fig. 3.1).

Entrepreneurial Capabilities

An entrepreneur who has a high level of administrative capability, flair and ability for decision-making, computational skill, delegation skill, organisational skill, good at communication and has a sound technical knowledge stands a much better chance of success than his counterpart who possesses none or a low level of these basic qualities. It is the possession of these scarce qualities which confers an advantage on some people in becoming an entrepreneur. Besides these qualities, however, the entrepreneur also needs either to be himself a generalist so that he can discharge his function without delegation, or to process delegation and organisational skills.

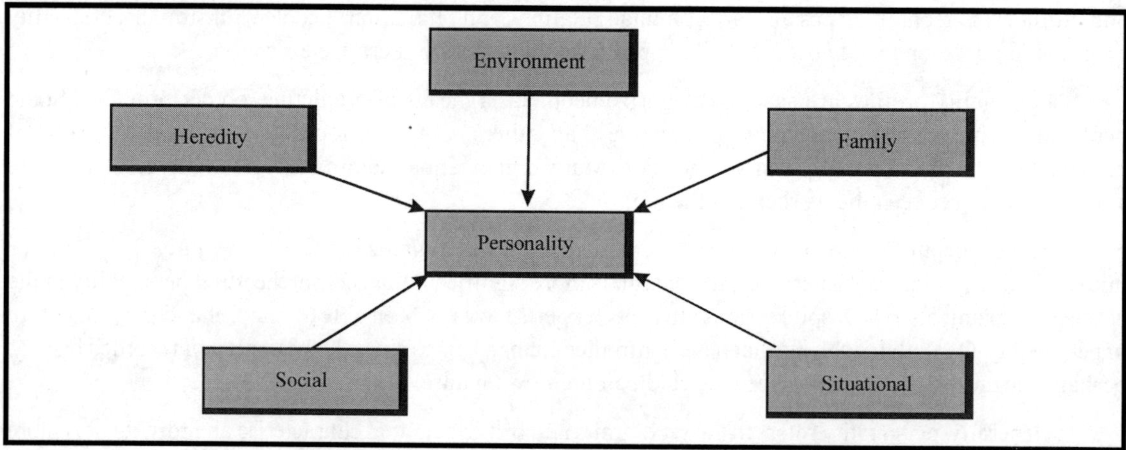

Fig. 3.1: Determinants of Personality

The entrepreneurial qualities are to some extent innate. But not all of them are entirely innate. Some can be enhanced by training, or simply by experience. For example, analytical ability and computational skills can be enhanced by education at school and university, while practical knowledge and foresight skills can be enhanced by the general experience of everyday life. Entrepreneurial careers will be strongly influenced by the desire to enhance qualities which are scarce, yet difficult to obtain through delegation because of the problems involved in screening for them. Of the two indispensable qualities of the entrepreneur, imagination is almost entirely innate, while foresight, though to some extent innate, can be enhanced by a varied experience. Imagination and foresight are the scarce qualities which are difficult to analyse and quantify. Delegation skill and organisation skill, though to some extent innate, can be enhanced by a varied experience. Imagination and foresight are the scarce qualities which are difficult to analyse and quantify. Delegation skill and organisation skill, though not essential, are highly desirable whenever large-scale decision-making is contemplated. These too are qualities which can be enhanced through experience.

Box 3.1 : How to be a Great Manager

Management consultant Peter Stark suggested the following if you want to make it to the top in management:

- Develop positive vision: See success before it arrives. Example: Successful managers — when visualising themselves walking across a high wire — see themselves walking to the other side. Managers who struggle usually have their focus on not falling off the rope.
- Think big. Look for ideas that will be contagious and excite people.
- Encourage others to do their best. Successful managers believe that people do want to make a significant contribution. Coach, Counsel and develop people to live up to their potential.
- Set and maintain high expectations for all who work with you. Mediocrity does not generate a highly motivated work force.
- Overuse polite phrases. Unsuccessful managers don't seem to find the time to say "please" and "thank you."

[***Source:*** *The Manager's Advisor, Peter Barron Stark & Associates. (Communication Briefinas)*]

Characteristics of Entrepreneurs

The characteristics of an entrepreneur that contribute to success are the result of his achievement motivation. The characteristics of achievement motivated persons as identified by McClelland have been discussed in the chapter on "Future of Entrepreneurship in India.' A successful entrepreneur must be a person with technical competence, initiative, good judgement, intelligence, leadership qualities, self-confidence, energy, attitude, creativeness, fairness, honesty, tactfulness and emotional stability.

1. Mental ability: Mental ability consists of intelligence and creative thinking. An entrepreneur must be reasonably intelligent, and should have creative thinking and must be able to engage in the analysis of various problems and situations in order to deal with them. The entrepreneur should anticipate changes and must be able to study the various situations under which decisions have to be made.

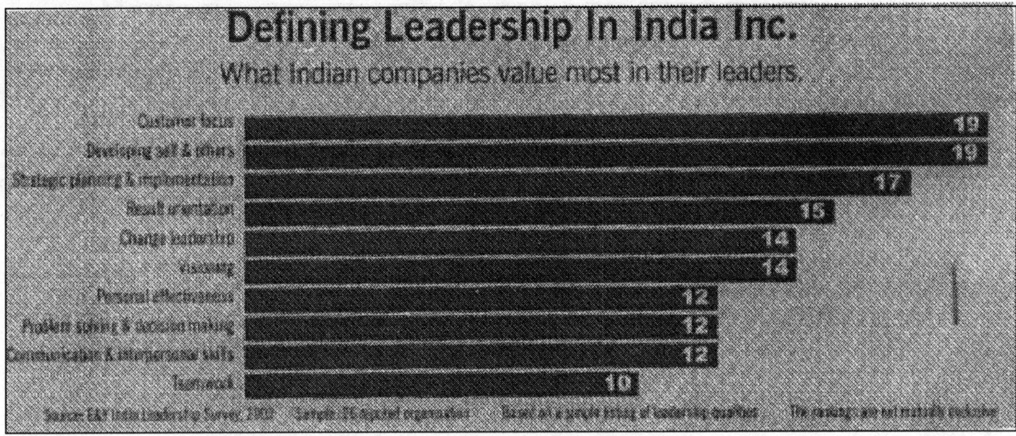

Fig. 3.2: *Defining Leadership in India Inc.*

2. Clear objectives: An entrepreneur should have a clear objective as to the exact nature of the business, the nature of the goods to be produced and subsidiary activities to be undertaken. A successful entrepreneur may have the objective to establish the product, to make profit or to render social service.

3. Business secrecy: An entrepreneur must be able to guard business secrets. Leakage of business secrets to trade competitions is a serious matter which should be carefully guarded against by an entrepreneur. An entrepreneur should be able to make a proper selection of his assistants.

4. Human relation ability: The most important personality factors contributing to the success of an entrepreneur are emotional stability, personal relations, consideration and tactfulness. An entrepreneur must maintain good relation with his customers if he is to establish relations that will encourage them to continue to patronise his business. He must also maintain good relations with his employees if he is to motivate them to perform their jobs at a high level of efficiency. An entrepreneur who maintains good relations with customers, employees, suppliers, creditors and the community is much more likely to succeed in his business than the individual who does not invest in maintaining these relations.

5. Communication ability: This ability pertains to communicate effectively. Good communication also means that both the sender and the receiver understand each other and are being understood. An entrepreneur who can effectively communicate with customers, employees, suppliers and creditors will be more likely to succeed than the entrepreneur who does not.

6. Technical knowledge: An entrepreneur must have a reasonable level of technical knowledge. This is the one ability that most people are able to acquire if they try hard enough.

An entrepreneur who has a high level of administrative ability, Mental ability, human relations ability, communication ability and technical knowledge stands a much better chance of success than his counterpart who possesses low levels of these basis qualities. Brilliant men with first class degrees from university hesitate becoming entrepreneurs because the one thing they cannot be taught is coping with human emotions.

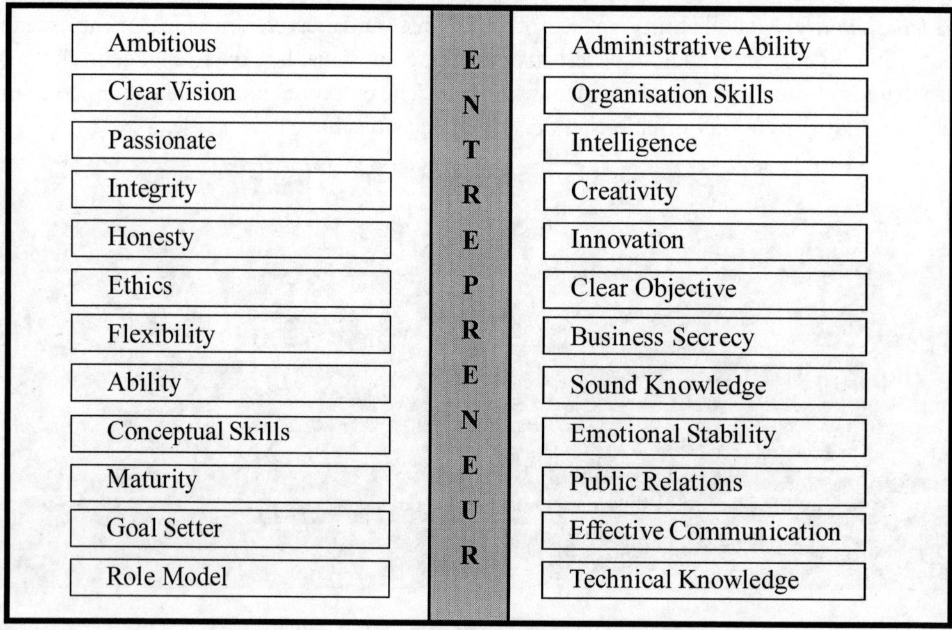

Fig. 3.3: *Characteristics of an Entrepreneur*

The Mark of A Leader

What separates wining organisations from the also-rans? Winning organisations share certain financial attributes. Companies consistently ranked in the top quartile of the S&P 500 maintain annual revenues — growth of 12 per cent and 16 per cent operating returns on assets. Gains achieved by simply slashing payroll and expenses are seldom sustained in the long-run. Likewise, erstwhile winners who fail to keep pace with change, and thereby destroy billions of dollars in shareholder value, are severely punished.

Companies such as General Electric, Allied Signal, PepsiCo, Intel, and others are led by people who personally and methodically nurture the development of other leaders at all levels of the organisation. Even if you, as a leader, are smart enough to anticipate and prepare for massive economic and social shifts, you cannot response to the ground-level demands of the moment without the energy, commitment, and ability of people throughout the organisation. Effective leaders recognise that the ultimate test of leadership is sustained success, which demands the constant cultivation of future leaders.

Three Keys for Leading: The ability to develop the leadership of others needs 3 things: a teachable point of view, a story for your organisation, and a well defined teaching methodology.

To succeed as a leader, you must be able to talk clearly and convincingly about who you are, why you exist, and how you operate. This means you need to have ideas on products, services, distribution-channels, customers and growth. But you also need something I call e^3: emotional energy and edge. Winning leaders seem naturally to generate positive emotional energy in others. They also have the edge to face reality, and take tough decisions. All 3 components of leadership — good ideas, appropriate values, and positive energy and edge — are part of the package you resent to those you hope to develop. How you apply these essential elements of leadership has changed in important ways in recent years.

The basic cognitive form in which people organise their thinking is the narrative story. There are 3 kind of stories that leaders can tell. There's the 'who I am' story, in which leaders describe themselves. There's the 'who we are' story, in which you articulate for your constituents what their identity is. But the most important leadership tale is the "where we are going' story. To be a great teacher, you have to be a great learner. Most effective teachers and leaders will tell you that they grow as much as those they teach and lead. The process of teaching can be quite simple; it starts with having a conscious system for interacting with people.

Learning to Teach: The current conventional wisdom in leadership — development programmes is to develop a set of competencies for what a good leader is, and then, to figure out a way to develop people around those competencies. At the end of the day, the competencies developed in these programmes look similar: integrity, trust, knowing how to overcome resistance. What's missing is the leaders themselves teaching their colleagues — not leaving to others, or talking about somebody else's values.

Practice What You Teach: The military has understood this for years. You need someone who has hands on expertise, credibility, and a teachable point of view about how to develop others' capabilities. To compete in the 21st Century, leaders need to build not just a learning organisation, but a teaching organisation — one with the capacity to build leaders.

Making Training Pay: Most leadership-training springs from the question, Are leaders born or made? and is designed to prove that the latter is correct. It's an age-old, pointless debate. The answer is, obviously, both. Any organisation that takes the time to get more leadership out of people is going to be ahead of its competitors. Are all managers candidates for the top job? Of course not. But can they be a lot better than they are now? Absolutely.

Leaders who invest personally in the process of developing future leaders are also building the most precious of organisational assets. The long-term success of leaders cannot be measured by whether they win today or tomorrow. The measure will be whether or not their company is still winning 15 years from now, when a new generation of leaders has taken over.

Noel Tichy

Robert D. Hisrich has identified a few more capabilities or personal characteristics that an entrepreneur should possess. According to him, the entrepreneur must have an adequate commitment, motivation and skills to start and build a business. The entrepreneur must determine if the management team has the necessary complementary skills to succeed. Some key characteristics of a successful entrepreneur are:

Motivator: An entrepreneur must build a team, keep it motivated and provide an environment for individual growth and career development.

Self-confidence: Entrepreneurs must have belief in themselves and the ability to achieve their goals.

Long-term Involvement: An entrepreneur must be committed to the project with a time horizon of five to seven years. No ninety-day wonders are allowed.

High energy level: Success of an entrepreneur demands the ability to work long hours for sustained periods of time.

Persistent problem-solver: An entrepreneur must have an intense desire to complete a task or solve a problem. Creativity is an essential ingredient.

Box 3.2 : Entrepreneurial Traits

- You need to have a dream. But it should be teamed with venture and action.
- Following your dream is the toughest thing on earth. Doubts will always linger around the corner but you've to have a single-minded vision.
- Always try to see the light. Never get overwhelmed by the shadows. Your focus should be so overpowering that it overshadows all fears.
- Be ready to put in 100 per cent in your venture. It may be your property of life saving — you should be ready to go bankrupt if the need arises.
- Cynicism has never worked in entrepreneurship. An entrepreneur should be the agent for change and be a part of that change.
- Once the entrepreneur phase ends, you need funds to continue the show. The abillity to convince people to buy your dream comes from the firm belief in your venture.
- You need to have nose for right people; after all, however great a business idea may be, you need the right people to kick-start it.
- Once you choose your people, allow them to make mistakes, and learn from the mistakes. Remember, you've picked the best and you need to make them feel challenged, constanty.
- Speed is very important — speed to market and speed in deployment.
- You need an intuitive understanding of the market. Be in touch with ground realities and your frontline employees.

Initiative: An entrepreneur must be able to set challenging but realistic goals.

Moderate risk-taker: An entrepreneur must be a moderate risk-taker and learn from failures. These personal traits go a long way in making an entrepreneur successful. However, no entrepreneur possesses total strength. In such cases, he acquires and/or associates and thus strengthens his enterprise.

Success Depends on...

Building value propositions for customer groups

Dealing with competitors as business partners

Tracking and analysing customer database for trends

Setting up strong front-end solution units

Potential Pitfalls are...

The absence of product specific sales teams

Managing culturally diverse alliance partners

Focusing on volumes rather than profits

Keeping up the pace of new product launches

Personality of A Leader : Some Traits

Leadership is about building winning chracteristics into the organisation so that achievement levels exceed normal expectations.

- **Purpose:** Every leader has a vision. The most important characteristic of a winning company is that all employees should share this vision and understand the purpose behind every organisational goal.
- **Pride:** Every employee should take pride in his or her company. Pride gives the employees of a company a sense of motivation and energy to strive for success. A leader should create an environment that instills this attitude in each employee. This adds to the brand equity of a company and customers like to deal with such companies.
- **Patience:** Leaders should be patient. Impatience leads to unnecessary tension and creates an uncomfortable work, environment. Patience also helps a person think straight and think right in pressure situations and brings the right balance to work-styles.
- **Persistence:** Leaders need to make sure that their teams understand that persistence is not about trying — but about the determination to achieve definite objective.
- **Perspective:** Employees need to reflect on how they can help their company achieve its objectives. Proper communication helps build the right perspective among employees.
- **Transparency:** To be transparent, and to be seen as being so, in all his dealings is both a challenge and a necessity for the leader if he wants to earn and retain the respect of his team. A transparent leader, by the power of his convictions, will act as a beacon for his team.
- **Integrity:** This is key to building a team that reflects all the core values of the organisation. Every leader should be an epitome of integrity. Integrity is the cornerstone of transparency.
- **Fair play:** For a leader to get unequivocal support from his team, he needs to ensure fair play. Fair play is a characteristic of a top-notch leadership. Only a leader who employs fair play can be successful in building and retaining a strong pool of talent for his company.
- **Participatory style:** History has taught us that a hands-on leader is what every team member desires and such a leader is more likely to have the loyalty of his team members.
- **Make every day count:** This is the mantra every leader should live by. A leader should be a learner all his life and look forward to learning something new every day, even as he passes on the knowledge he has acquired. He must make every day count by making a difference.
- **Vision:** A compelling Vision creates and forges corporate identity. It imparts a larger purpose and meaning to individual endeavour. It is aspirational, unifying and motivational.

- **Communication:** Leadership is all about communicating with your subordinates and inspiring every single person who works with you. Leadership is about making the work environment less authoritative and more friendly. It's about talking to people and making them think you and think with you. Leadership is about having a vision and convincing people around you to have the same vision.
- **Involvement:** Leadership is about involving every member of the organisation, especially during a crisis. An ideal leader is one who can convince the management to include the entire team to collectively take a decision. In fact, the new name of our company – Accenture – was adopted after suggestions from 5,000 employees across the globe. An exercise of this kind brings a sense of belonging to the entire team.
- **Values:** Leadership is about living the values – if vision gives direction, values set the boundaries. Values demand that leaders be completely transparent. Values transmit trust, which is the cementing force that holds an organisation together during challanging times. Values refer to the institutional standards of behaviour that strengthen commitment to the Vision, and guide strategy formulation and purposive action. The core Values of your Company are shaped around the belief that enterprises exist to serve society. In terms of this belief, profit is a means rather than an end in itself, a compensation to owners of capital linked to the effectiveness of contribution to society and the essential ingredient to sustain such enlarged societal contribution.
- **Energy:** Leader should exude energy while working hard. This creates an enthusiastic atmosphere in the organisation. They should be articulate while dealing with others and be able to communicate effectively to influence them.
- **Innovation:** Leaders should support and strive for continuous innovation in the functional system of the organisation. Innovation is applying creativity. Leaders should delegate authority to fuel innovation.
- **Ethical:** A major responsibility that lies with a good leader is to make ethical decisions and behave accordingly, and make sure that the organisation understands and practices this code of conduct. A leader must be able to guide and mentor his organisation into achieving the goals in an integrated and harmonious manner.
- **Knowledge: A** leader must know himself. Knowledge of one's own strengths and weaknesses is an essential prerequisite towards building a great team. A leader must be open to the best of what everyone, everywhere has to offer and must constantly seek to learn from his peers and subordinates.
- **Leading:** A good leader always leads from the front. Frontline leadership is the most inspiring, probably because it is the most enduring. Words can be forgotten, but words translated into actions and practiced diligently are remembered forever. There is no substitute for leading by example.
- **Nurturing:** The leader's role is to nurture the attitude of constant learning by providing open opportunities for learning throughout the organisation, with an unrelenting focus on the customer. The customer is central to our business, and customer loyalty is not won by technology alone. The leader should be aware that today's customer has no tolerance for inconsistency and mediocrity, as he has the means to compare the quality of services in real time, all the time. The leader's role is to harness technology as a means to build and deliver consistently superior customer experience.

- **Motivation:** Leadership means communicating a vision that motivates and inspires others. A great leader should be able to transform and energise the people working in his organisation. He should have the ability to ignite passions and connect with his team. To go with this, he must also have strategic vision. His team should know where exactly it is headed and how it can translate that vision into reality.
- **New Opportunities:** A leader must constantly be on the lookout for new opportunities and challenges. My belief is firmly rooted in the 3S philosophy – systems, speed, and spirit. When combined with transparency, result-orientation, and empowerment, these three catalyse the organisation towards accelerated growth and create greater value for stakeholders.
- **Flexibility:** Leadership is about being Flexible. A successful leader is one who is willing to learn and follow when needed. In these times of business change, it is important for a leader to be adaptive – be open to change and influence change and be an effective decision maker at the same time.
- **Dynamism:** Today's leader needs to have a broader portfolio of skills and experience to tackle challenging business situations. Today's business is characterised as global, dynamic and customer-driven. The global nature of business requires leaders to transcend boundaries, adapt to cultures, develop efficient processes and integrate teams. A dynamic leader requires to keep himself abreast of developments and keep the team informed. He must possess an innate ability to foresee changes as well.
- **Clear Vision:** A leader must have a clear vision; maintain strategic agility, build and maintain a strong organisation that is performance oriented, execute better than the competitor, and at the same time maintain the highest business code of conduct. This is a formidable challenge, but can be overcome by following a systematic approach of building great teams, fostering teamwork and striving for excellence.
- **Clear Focus:** Successful teams are those that have a clear focus on the larger goals of the organisation, have a strong culture and identity, strive for clear and open communication, and maintain a learning environment.
- **Teamwork:** The team makes the leader. The ability to get a team to work cohesively and effectively is the primary defining trait of a successful leader. A team that does well usually has a successful leader behind it, as does a successful leader, a strong team behind him.
- **Purpose:** Leadership is about finding a purpose and then charging others into pursuing that purpose with a collective sense of enthusiasm. Leadership is also about creating, sustaining and directing the collective charge for a shared purpose.
- **Clarity:** Another key attribute is clarity of thought. Effective leaders use this clarity to establish well-defined targets, to set clear performance expectations, and to devise a systematic execution strategy. They create an environment where each employee feels accountable towards his targets and motivated to attain them.
- **Trusting:** Leadership is about trusting. A leader must have faith in his people. It is not possible for anyone, no matter how competent, to do any task single-handedly. Therefore, he should give responsibilities to the other members of the teams. This not only makes people more confident and responsible but contributes towards creating leaders of tomorrow.

- **Positive Attitude:** Maintaining a positive attitude is critical to good leadership. A leader should always lead by example and be prepared to show the way. Only by doing so can he or she ensure employee participation that is so essential for an organisation's continued survival in a highly competitive environment.
- **Customer Focus:** The most important factor for being a successful leader is customer focus. For every vision, there is an end-beneficiary. The customer is the biggest gainer from a corporate culture of excellence. Link each outcome to the needs of the customer and ask whether that is really going to add value. Any outcome that fails this test has to be relegated to the dustbin and the cycle repeated anew.
- **An Art:** Leadership is an art and a true leader is one who has the ability to understand what motivates people and who channelises their strengths to achieve positive results. A sense of self-worth is more often than not what drives people to work harder. A good leader is one who understands this and exploits it to the hilt.

The traits are not exhaustive, but indicative to shape the leaders'/entrepreneurs' personality.

Table 3.1

Characteristics of Entrepreneurs

Small-Scale Entrepreneurs	*Large-Scale Entrepreneurs*
1. Youngmen	1. Middle-aged Professionals
2. Ambitious	2. Professional Specialists
3. Intelligent	3. Shareholders contribute venture Capital
4. Energetic	4. Energetic
5. Enthusiastic	5. Outsourcing
6. Minimum education	6. Net-workers
7. Hard-working	7. Ability to get along with people
8. Confident	8. Tolerant
9. Passionate	9. Risk Takers
10. Dedicated	10. Large Assets controlled
11. Practical	11. Engaged in Diversified Activities
12. Goal-oriented	12. Diversified products
13. Mobile	13. Multiple activities
14. Adaptable	14. Easy access to institutional finance
15. Able	15. Leverages
16. Aggressive	16. Well connected with Politics/Bureacrats
17. Innovative	17. Trend setters
18. Well-mannered	18. Demand creators
19. Self-made person	19. Value-driven
20. Disciplined	20. Corporate Philosophy
21. Zealous	21. Ambitious
22. Flexible	22. Drive to go ahead
23. Courageous	23. Self-confident
24. Skilful	24. Innovative/immitative

25.	Creative	25.	Adaptable
26.	Experienced	26.	Trained
27.	Meager capital	27.	Large capital
28.	Small operation	28.	Large operation
29.	Employ few people	29.	Skilled manpower
30.	Small turnover	30.	Large turnover/sales/profit
31.	Honest	31.	Honest
32.	Progressive	32.	Progressive
33.	Patient	33.	Pragmatic
34.	Perseverance	34.	Perseverance
35.	Self-reliant	35.	Self-Reliant
36.	Common sense	36.	Abundant common sense
37.	Adaptive	37.	Competitive
38.	Ability to strive	38.	Versatile
39.	Compassionate	39.	Quality conscious
40.	Dreamer	40.	Visionaries
41.	Conscious	41.	Focussed
42.	Intuitive	42.	Singleness of purpose
43.	Practical	43.	Ability to change
44.	Imaginative	44.	Educated
45.	Achiever	45.	A strong need to achieve
46.	Hopefull	46.	Passionate
47.	Independent	47.	Analytical
48.	Self-starter	48.	Optimistic
49.	Individualist	49.	Organisation man
50.	Sensitive	50.	Loyal
51.	Perceptive	51.	Pleasing personality
52.	Quality conscious	52.	Dynamic
53.	Desire to share experience	53.	Tolerant
54.	Ability to change	54.	Active
55.	Money oriented	55.	Contributor
56.	Driven by values	56.	Knowledgeable
57.	Intrapreneurial	57.	Motivator
58.	Facilitator	58.	Strategist
59.	Learner	59.	Goal conscious
60.	Opportunist	60.	Compassionate
61.	Ability to strive	61.	Leader
62.	Task master	62.	Scanner — Looking for opportunities
63.	Striving Richness	63.	Planner
64.	Gut-Feeler	64.	Thinker
65.	Dictator	65.	People Manager

Entrepreneurial Initiative

Recent data on entrepreneurial initiative and self-employment reveal a few problems. To overcome these problems it is essential to develop entrepreneurial skills for which the entrepreneur has to initiate the process of development. This is a challenging task. This unprecedented, perpetual change with unlimited barriers makes entrepreneurial initiative in the future more significant and more dynamic.

This means that entrepreneurial initiative is a strategic process which embodies calculated strategic choices. There are strategies open to the entrepreneur himself in terms of industry choice and individual and resource-task fit, and there are strategies open to the regulators and support agencies in terms of industrial policy tools, incentive and explicit stimulation of industrial sector or branches. A conceptual framework that contains both dimensions will provide a convenient base for analysis and possible policy action.

Encouraging entrepreneurial initiative is an issue applicable to both developed and developing countries and the search for effective means is proceeding in earnest. The analysis has dealt with a way of viewing the constraints embodied in the process of creating a new business or manufacturing operation.

The slow pace of the propensity to enterprise is mainly due to the existence of a tangible set of barriers prohibiting the process of entry into, continuity in, and an eventual exit from a business venture of a would-be entrepreneur if it is a function of forces that one may view as barriers limiting full-fledged business performance. There may be entry barriers, survival barriers and exit barriers.

Entry barriers are those forces limiting access to identified business opportunities and capitalisation on these opportunities. Survival barriers are constraints on the conditions essential for the small business entity. Exit barriers are constraints limiting the termination of small industrial ventures that have outlived their business viability or the growth of such ventures to a different size category.

The existing entry barriers are:

1. A cultural bias in identifying and managing the entrepreneurial development process.
2. Limited industry-specific data and insufficient market information.
3. Limited effectiveness of the infrastructural base.
4. Existence of visible and invisible obstacles to entry of a specific societal group (e.g., women) into business.
5. Unorganised capital market and traditional feasibility assessment processes.
6. Unsympathetic and cumbersome government attitude.
7. Hostile environment.
8. Limited access to technology.

Observed survival barriers include the following:

1. A behavioural pattern that could impair basic managerial practices.
2. Constraining practices within the capital market,. The threatening shadow of changing technology.
3. The threatening shadow of changing technology.
4. Limited learning.
5. The cultural management of resources.

6. Failure of guidance agencies to guide.
7. Scarce information and limited dissemination of that information.

Identified exit barriers include:

1. The emotional commitment of the entrepreneur to his venture.
2. Specialised assets, sunk funds.
3. The increasing demand for managerial skills.
4. Fear of failure.

Barriers, single or combined are said to have an impact on to strategic and long-term planning perspective of the small entrepreneur and could, equally, have an impact on the government's promotional policies within the sector. Low entry and low survival industries (or industrial branches) could provide policyrnakers with an area for quick and intensive intervention. At the other extreme, industries with high entry barriers and high survival barriers, can probably be regarded as low priority areas that deserve a different kind of attention, i.e., barrier adjustment instead of enterprise development. The relationship between entry and exit barriers could lead to a similar set of conclusions. One of those conclusions is the advisability of the management of enterprise flow and the early identification of the potential for switching (a form of exit), or planned divestment. Again this can prove valuable for government policies for small industry promotion at the national and regional levels.

Progress in economic development and technological diversification does not happen accidentally or haphazardly. In a hyper competitive environment, the economic renaissance of an area depends on a city's or region's ability to address critical needs. To sustain the momentum of positive economic growth, communities must establish programmes for investment in a viable public private infrastructure. This includes not only meeting the other essential infrastructure needs such as roads, water, and services but also providing for educational needs and diversified cultural amenities.

A vibrant financial environment is essential for continued economic development. This includes sophisticated banking community that understands the unique problems and needs of emerging companies, especially technologically based companies, and an expanding venture capital industry that can address the requirements of high-risk ventures. Only in this way can an area ensure diversified opportunities for entrepreneurs.

A pool of capable people hold the responsibility for economic development. A community, therefore, has to find ways to ensure a locally-trained workforce with a minimum reliance on imported services. As needs are supplied locally there are more opportunities for entrepreneurs. By responding to a rapidly changing environment, it engenders a dynamic entrepreneurial spirit.

Motivation

Motivation is an indispensable function of management. When man is at work, he cannot be forced to work like a machine. He is a human being who has his dignity, self-respect, values, sentiments and aspirations apart from the economic status. Under such circumstances the efficiency of the enterprise is related not merely to the efficiency of sophisticated machines installed but more importantly upon the satisfaction and the spontaneous desire of man to put his mind and heart into the work. This spontaneous urge to involve in work is not merely relate to monetary awards or assignment of position or the direction to perform the duty or even the fear of punishment but to the mechanics and system of motivation.

Motivation encompasses complex aspects of human behaviour to which contribution has been made by sociologists, social anthropologists, psychologists and business executives. This concept has its roots in motives within a person which induce him to behave in a particular manner. Generally speaking, the concept of motivation is by and large psychological which "relates to those forces operating within the individual employee or subordinate which impel him to act or not to act in certain ways"—

'Motivation refers to the way in *which* urges, drives, desires, aspirations, strivings or needs direct, control or explain the *behaviour of* human beings.'

This is a deep-seated definition of Motivation. It includes three things:

(i) The urges, drives, desires, aspirations, strivings or needs of human beings influence human behaviour.

(ii) The factors which influence human behaviour — psychological, sociological, economic or managerial.

(iii) The efficiency of such behaviour — this may be tested by the resultant action. Whether this behaviour has directed, controlled or implemented the desired action.

If the entrepreneur feels motivated his behaviour will bring about the desired action.

Here, one reaches the most crucial point in the Regional or District Development Strategy of the under-developed regions. The development agency with all the institutions concerned, will have to formulate a motivation programme and by continuous and ingenious methods, involve people in the process of development so that they acquire new attitudes and confidence to enter into new activities and to show the propensity of enterprise. Appropriate values will have to be inculcated and risking capacity be cultivated. Unless this aspect is given its due weightage in the Development Plan, in spite of all the incentives, most of the projects will hardly make much progress. Development is the consequence of motivated people.

Motivational factors constitute the inner urge present in an individual which continuously demands from him to do something new and unique as also to perform better than others. The motivational factors again are compressed of three basic elements — entrepreneurial motivation, personal efficiency and coping capability. The achievement motivation is also termed efficiency motivation. McClelland and Winter have made considerable studies and concluded that what motivates a person to do something new or something to seek better is the inner urge which directs him towards such ends. This urge also force a person to use the resources efficiently than to be negligent of it. Also important is the power of motivation which is really the urge to have control over others and to direct their course of activities towards the end which one seeks to attain. These motivational factors induce the person to undertake entrepreneurial activities which relate to creating a new business where there was none. This also means to excel the performance in carrying out any activity by striving through persistent efforts unlike others who do not have sufficient capacity for hard work.

What Makes Entrepreneurs?: A Survey

Access to capital, positive attitude, and favourable regulations, says an Accenture survey.

THIS SHOULD COME AS NO SURPRISE: The US is perceived as the most enterprising country. And neither should this: India is seen as the most enterprise-unfriendly nation. So what accounts for this huge disparity in entrepreneurial success? According to a survey done by Accenture on entrepreneurship, no matter where in the world a company is located or does business, certain basic aspects must be in place for an entrepreneurial climate to evolve, these include: access to capital, the right regulatory and tax environment, and positive social and cultural attitudes towards entrepreneurship.

The survey — which spanned 18 months and 22 countries, including India — reveals that the US is overwhelmingly seen as the most entrepreneurial country, with Japan coming a clear, albeit distant, second. Interestingly, while executives in the US chose their country as the most entrepreneurial nation, very few Japanese executives thought likewise of their country, and virtually no other executives of other countries chose their own country.

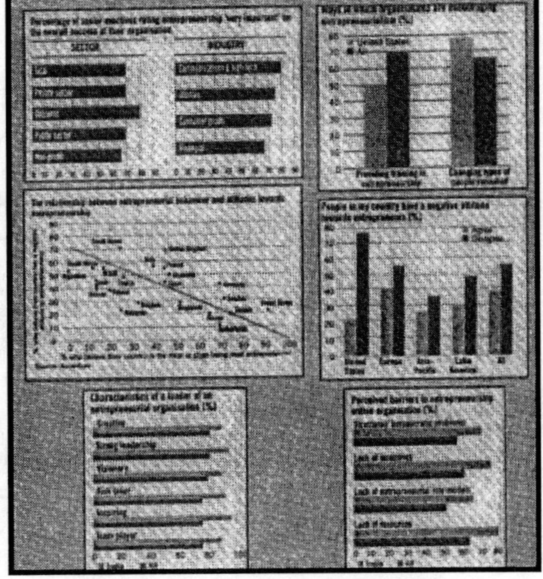

Fig. 3.4

Countries that stand out as having positive social attitudes to entrepreneurship include the US, Canada, Singapore, Taiwan and Netherlands. Art of the social acceptability of entrepreneurs is tied up with cultural attitudes to wealth and success. For instance, in India, when talking about entrepreneurs and their will to succeed, the chairman of Triveni Engineering, Dhruv Sawhney, says: 'As a society we tend to suspect motives rather than encourage them.'

According to the survey, most executives in Indian do not perceive their country to be highly entrepreneurial. Only 5 per cent mentioned India as the most entrepreneurial country, with half citing the US, while over four-fifths thought that India was far behind the country they regarded as the most entrepreneurial.

Bureaucratic problems are seen by three-quarters of Indian executives as one of the impediments to progress, with 78 per cent citing a lack of incentives against a global average of 63 per cent. Also, in India, entrepreneurship seems to be associated above all with leadership. Top executives see entrepreneurial organisations as those driven by strong leaders with propensity for risk taking. The survey doesn't say this, but give India another decade for entrepreneurship to take risk.

What Makes an Entrepreneur?

What makes an entrepreneur is the combination of various factors that have enabled the personality formation right from the childhood as also the psychological urge that exists intensively in the person. These psychological processes which lead men to set up on their own a successful business enterprise beginning the very early life and have cumulative effect. The influence of early childhood and other social roles are determinate factors for the formation of that personality which motivates an individual towards becoming an independent businessman or entrepreneur.

In the case of persons who take up jobs, it has always been found that they have secured success in the established organisations. These people do not have a rejection towards the established institutions and neither do they attempt to rebel against the traditional path to success. On the other hand, an entrepreneur fails to achieve educational success through the established organisations and this is because of the general rejection of the established organisations at all levels. People who tend to like security and not uncertainty gets more satisfied by taking up jobs which are less risk-oriented and hence are not motivated towards building up their own industrial enterprise.

Men who establish new business are men who have right from the childhood faced a different set of environment in their family, school and other social situations. Research studies have indicated that successful entrepreneurs identify a crisis before they venture into new entrepreneurial activities. Even in their childhood most of them had threatening non-supportive and disgusting adult figures who had much say in their social and economic life. Most of these have a childhood of imperverishment and stress. Economic deprivation also works as a motivational factor towards creating something on their own and free oneself from the clutches of oppressing forces which attempt to kill their spirit of individualism. Thus it has been found that creating a successful new business is not due to an isolated incidence in the life of an individual but it has been as a result of learned response to their total social, emotional and economic environment.

The family background plays an important role in, building up personality necessary for turning into an entrepreneur later in life. In family situations where security and non-risk bearing activities are encouraged right from childhood, the individual likes to be more security-oriented rather than attempt on his own in areas where adventures and uncertainty conditions prevail. Also in families where deep attachments and emotional relationships are encouraged, it has been found that the child growing under such situations tends to take up activities which are more security-oriented than risk-oriented. Since in most of the middle class families, attachment and security-oriented activities are encouraged despite seeking academic excellence, it itself does not help the person to develop a deep urge to be independent and create a framework required for enjoying autonomy.

As a result of this attitude building, many bright graduates shy away from placing themselves in open positions but instead choose to stay in the established organisations because they have developed a favourable attitude towards the establishment. On the other hand, the entrepreneurial personality would rather face the impersonal forces of the economy than cope with inter-personal relations of the established organisations. Due to this characteristic of an entrepreneur, they tend to shift from job to job till they have finally found a field of activity in which they will ultimately have a say and also enjoy the happenings of events by their sheer will, determination and efforts.

While people who take up jobs prefer to see success in the traditional and highly structured roles in the established undertakings, entrepreneurs, on the other hand, prefer to have a different approach toward success and be unique in their own way. They find more satisfaction in their creative faculties getting an opportunity to express themselves fully rather than submitting themselves to forces which are already structured and rigid. The bright graduates may very often lack creativity and are not in a position to break through the undifferentiated mask of circumstances and make something of their own.

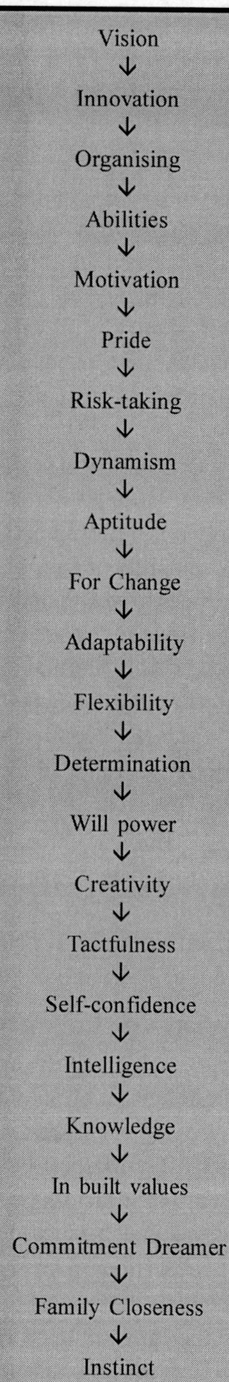

Fig. 3.5: Qualities of a Successful Entrepreneur

The entrepreneur, on the other hand, find such situations extraordinarily challenging and attempt with determination and persistence to come out of this web of oppressing factors, which tend to keep him in the rigid framework. Thus we find entrepreneurial characteristics are formed through a combination of various social, economic and psychological factors to which the person becomes subjected right from childhood. These factors reinforce in him the urge to excel others and seek satisfaction in creating on his own a new enterprise instead of seeking a security-oriented job, in the absence of these reinforcing elements which go into the formation of the entrepreneurial personality, however bright a person may be in the academic life, it is not a guarantee that he would also become a successful entrepreneur. Something more than mere academic excellence is a pre-requisite for becoming an entrepreneur of success and repute. These requisites are embodied in the various qualities that the entrepreneur must have basically within himself in order to establish himself as a successful entrepreneur. But many graduates do lack in these qualities.

Qualities of an Entrepreneur

A true entrepreneur besides possessing functional qualities, must also possess a broad personality which help in developing initiative and drive to accomplish great tasks and face challenges squarely.

James J. Berne has stressed the following qualities of a good entrepreneur:

1. He is an enterprising individual, is energetic, hardworking, resourceful, aware of new opportunities and able to adjust himself to changing conditions with ease and willing to assume risks involved in change.
2. He is interested in a advancing technologically and in improving the quality of his product or service.
3. He is interested in expanding the scale of his operations by reinvesting his earnings.
4. He visualizes changes and adapts to changing conditions.
5. He is a firm believer in planning and systematic work.
6. He works for the society at large and for the good of his fellow-beings.

These qualities sum up, what is usually implied from the phrase, the "spirit of enterprise." It is difficult to conceive a first-rate industrial entrepreneur who is not adaptable to change, anxious to grow large and improve technologically.

Entrepreneurship appears as a personal quality which enables certain individuals to make decision with far-reaching consequences. The personal qualities that contribute to the success of an entrepreneur are as follows:

1. Motivation Towards Achievement: A successful entrepreneur should be a good administrator. He should know the art of getting things done by other people without hurting their feelings or self-respect. He should have a strong motivation towards the achievement of a task and must be able to exert considerable efforts in getting things done by others.

2. Creativity: Mental ability consists of intelligence, an analytical approach and creative things. An entrepreneur should have creative thinking and be able to engage in the analysis of various problems and situations in order to deal with them. The entrepreneur should anticipate changes and must be able to study various situations in which decisions may have to be made.

3. Clarity: An entrepreneur should have clear objective as to the exact nature of the business, the nature of the goods to be produced and the subsidiary activities to be undertaken.

The qualities of an entrepreneur are given in Fig. 3.6.

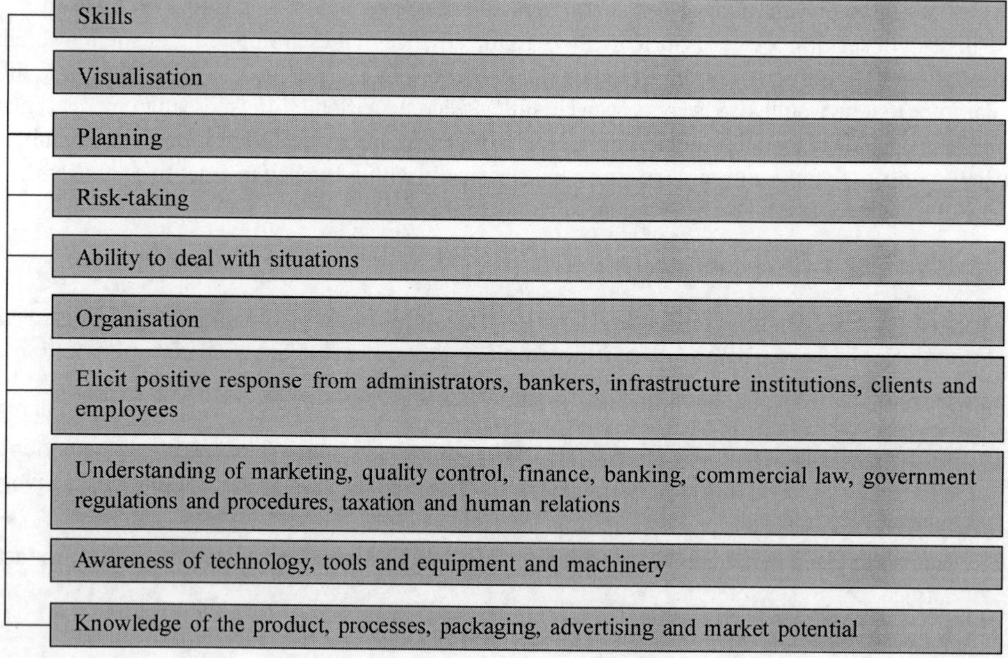

Fig. 3.6: *Entrepreneurial Skills*

Kilby has rightly numerated the following activities for a successful entrepreneur in an underdeveloped economy:

1. Perception of market opportunities (novel or imitative).
2. Gaining command over scarce resources.
3. Purchasing of inputs.
4. Marketing of the product and responding effectively to competition.
5. Dealing with public bureaucracy as regards concessions, licences, taxes, etc. provided through the various fiscal policies of the government.
6. Management of the human relations within the enterprise.
7. Management of customer and supplier relations.
8. Financial management.
9. Production management, including control through written records, supervision, coordinating input flows with orders, maintenance.
10. Acquiring and overseeing assembly of the plant.
11. Taking care for minimising inputs for a given production process.
12. Maintaining the production process and improving the quality of the product.
13. Introduction of new production techniques and product lines.

From the above discussion and definitions, it can be stated that entrepreneurial activities encompass those factors right from the perception of the profitable opportunity to its translation into reality through establishing a successful enterprise and further leading to its growth and development. Especially in an underdeveloped economy, the expectations from entrepreneurial units are much more varied and related to many dimensions, including socio-economic objectives. This is because this type of economy is characterised by a majority of low income strata than the developed economy characterised by high income.

Entrepreneurial Skills

To deal with entrepreneurial skills is to concern oneself with a wide coverage of aspects of setting up an enterprise and its management. It is not confined to visualization, planning, setting-up and risk-taking. The skills which an entrepreneur includes are his ability to deal with view situations, organisations and social and economic forces as they emerge from time to time. The skills to deal with a situation forevisualised or suddenly emerging must be an essential characteristic of an entrepreneur.

The small entrepreneur must have skills to positive response from administrators, bankers, infrastructure institutions, clients and employees.

The entrepreneur is rarely a master of the management skills, and yet is usually directly responsible for all aspects of business. Often he or she has to be the general manager, production manager, purchasing manager, personnel manager, controller and research organiser for the business all rolled into at least during its early years. The entrepreneur therefore has to have an understanding of marketing, quality control, finance, banking, commercial law, government regulations and procedures, and human relation as each of them has a vital bearing on the health of the enterprise.

Need for Skills

We often talk of transfer of technology. As a matter of fact, the whole world is talking about it. There is hardly any international event at the global and regional level where this subject does not come up for discussion. The poor nations demand technology and resources from industrialised and rich countries and rightly so. The developing countries would rather export semi-finished and finished products which are value added than export raw materials. The development of entrepreneurial skill must precede transfer of technology if we do not desire to keep such technologies and equipment serving such technologies idle. One has also to realise that technologies are developing very fast and the skills are to match with this dynamic growth.

Attributes of Entrepreneurs

The attempts to discover the secret of entrepreneurs' success has pre-occupied writers and analysts from a variety of disciples. Biographies of successful entrepreneurs and businessmen, for example, frequently reflect the tendencies of the subject of such studies in term of simple virtues of thrift, hard work, and clean living. As an alternative to the biographical models are those studies that turn the entrepreneur into a superman, manipulating the complexities of an uncertain world with a sure and omnipotent touch. Thus, emerges the notion of the "genuis entrepreneur" whose success is in large measure caused by his unswerving dedication to setting high goals and to reaching for them. He has vision which he bases on his own objectives and sets his own goals, And he does this not simply on the basis of last year's results plus some growth factor, but on the basis of his own perception, of his own capabilities and to satisfy his own needs.

Among other distinguishing attributes of entrepreneurship are a willingness to assume risks; a sense of acquisitiveness or unceasing curiosity; insight into the relationship between concepts, objectives, needs. and needs satisfaction; sound judgement as to what is central and peripheral to attaining his objectives;

initiative and creativity, problem-solving ability; ability to Marshall resources needed to achieve his objectives and goals; and the administrative ability to organise those resource to accomplish his goals and satisfy his minor needs.

The Role Model

Entrepreneurs play an important role in the development of society. For example, the use of Jeans in America has created the demand for it throughout the world. Similarly, Coca Cola has been accepted as a social drink. The introduction of colour T.V. has provided the society a means of information and entertainment. The society has accepted the innovations of such entrepreneurs as Gillet, Wright Brothers, and Henry Ford. The inventions of these great entrepreneurs of the history has revolutionised the lifestyle of men in the society.

- PERCEPTIONS
- DEDICATION
- VISION
- HIGH GOALS/OBJECTIVES
- THRIFT
- VIGOROUS ENERGY
- HARD WORK
- CLEAN LIVING
- QUEST FOR NEW IDEAS
- WILLINGNESS TO ASSUME RISKS
- UNCEASING CURIOSITY
- RESTLESS URGE TO GET GOING
- SENSE OF ACQUISITIVENESS TO GET THINGS DONE
- INSIGHT
- GAMBLER'S INSTINCT
- INITIATIVE
- CREATIVITY
- ZEST TO EXPLORE THE UNEXPLORED
- PROBLEM-SOLVING ABILITY
- ABILITY TO MARSHALL RESOURCES
- TO ACHIEVE ONE'S OBJECTIVES AND GOALS
- ADMINISTRATIVE ABILITY

Fig. 3.7: *Attributes of an Entrepreneur*

The role of entrepreneurs in economic development varies from economy to economy, country to country, depending upon its material resources industrial climate and more importantly, the responsiveness of the political system to the growth of entrepreneurs. By and large, the entrepreneurs' contribution to development and growth is relatively higher in favourable opportunity conditions than in less favourable situation. The growth of an entrepreneurial society will bear fruitful results in a shortspan.

Entrepreneurship, the *de facto* barometer of overall economic, social and industrial growth has brought revolutionary changes in the society. It is the *sine quo* non of an nation's progress. It has facilitated large-scale production and distribution. It has widened the area and scope of the marketing of goods and services. Perhaps it is for these reasons that the small business sector has been given priority in our national development programmes for entrepreneurship flourishes when the size of business remains relatively small and viable.

Modern business studies have a distinct entrepreneurial disicipline. The approach to the study of entrepreneurship is multi-disciplinary. It images on such areas as demography, economic anthropology, business history, politics, sociology, psychology, marketing and finance. That is why entrepreneurship development becomes an integral part of the overall economic, social and industrial development of a country. This is what makes the identification and management of entrepreneurial functions a highly complex exercise.

Conclusion

A number of entrepreneurial managers have attempted to identify the true nature of entrepreneurs and entrepreneurship in the post-industrial revaluation. The definition has, therefore, undergone changes with the changes in the socio-economic environment and will continue to undergo changes with the changing times. However, some basic concepts of innovation, risk-taking, vision and organising skills continue to be the four pillars on which the edifice of entrepreneurial concept has to be perceived from time to time.

An ideal entrepreneur is one who confines values in the market economy, that profits do not somehow preclude ethical behaviour, that growth is possible even if political patronage is not used to bend rules and cut corners, and quite simply that pursuit of wealth can be grateful and mannerly one. He takes with him the interest of his people, his country, his natural resources, the ecology and see that his enterprise becomes a catalytic agent of development. There is thus a need of true entrepreneurs, who do not opt for incentives, infrastructure, government support: but build his enterprises, harness the available resources and develop. They adopt a responsible value-driven corporate philosophy for their enterprises and/or business activities. As such, there is no dispute among economists and social thinkers about the urgent need for the emergence of an entrepreneurial society as a forerunner of accelerated development of the economy in an integrated manner.

ANNEXURE – 1

Characteristics of a Successful Entrepreneur

A successful entrepreneur is a person who has started the business where there was none before. A successful entrepreneur is essentially an enterprising individual who is able to recognise the potential profitable opportunity and who initiates to produce marketable products by combining the various technologies and through organising together the people, finance, material resources marketing tools, in order to ultimately translate the idea in the minds to physical realities. In short, entrepreneur is a person who initiates, establishes, maintains and expands a new enterprise. He is basically an innovator, creator and accomplisher.

According to research studies, there are more than 50 personality traits and all these traits and attitudes constitute the characteristic of a successful entrepreneur. Though all the characteristics cannot be found in a single entrepreneur yet the presence of greater number of these characteristics in an individual makes him an entrepreneur and only then it is possible for him to be successful to achieve the goals of entrepreneurship.

Some of the characteristics or qualities of an entrepreneur are discussed below:

(1) Need for achievement, (2) Risk taking, (3) Need for Independence, (4) Sense of effectiveness, (5) Social consciousness, (6) Need for extension, (7) Optimistic, (8) Open minded, (9) Non-fatalist, (10) Low Affiliation, (11) Pragmatist, (12) Aggressive, (13) Persistent, (14) Commitment and conviction, (15) Capacity to analyse, (16) Initiative, (17) Hopeful and (18) Efficiency.

(1) Need for achievement: The urge to achieve or the urge to excel others is the forceful psychological factor which is an essential characteristic found in almost all the individuals with enterprising qualities. McCelland Winter have through their research studies indicated that this is the single critical factor present in the entrepreneurs. Entrepreneurs belong to that category of people who are willing to work hard and to achieve something excellent despite the challenges and threats in the environment. Under such challenging and threatening forces, many people would lose or give up and would not care at all for achieving something better. But the high need of achievement present in the entrepreneurs drive them to excel others. This trait also indicates the urge to be different from others and strive to achieve the goals which are difficult to be achieved by other ordinary people. At the same time these people do not aim at practically impossible goals. The goals set are achievable in reality. The high need of achievement urge results in a high drive in individuals and as a result high activity levels are present in these persons. As a consequence of this driving force, thought processes are always linked with the problems of doing things better than the others. Unless the persons possesses this urge to accomplish, excel or achieve through a balanced sense autonomy and tolerance, it is difficult to be a successful entrepreneur.

(2) Risk taking: Risk taking is another attribute of entrepreneurs. Entrepreneurs like to take risks which are calculated and not extreme ones. They undertake challenging risks which are difficult to overcome but are not impossible. They do not have the attitude of depending upon chance factors to get the expected results, instead they would like their own efforts to give the desired results. By this way of influencing the results by their own efforts, they like to enjoy the sense of having accomplished the tasks by their own efforts. In this process, the risks involved are calculated risks. To ensure success in the accomplishment of the goals entrepreneurs see to it that they spend lot of time in planning their enterprises and ensure success before actually launching the project. This is done by studying in detail the various interfering forces and obstacles and keeping ready the solutions to overcome these interferences. Moderate risk taking and safeguarding against anticipated difficulties are the qualities that can be found in successful entrepreneurs.

(3) Need for Independence and Autonomy: The strong need to be an independent or autonomous individual is another driving force associated with the entrepreneurs. The entrepreneurs dislike controls from outsiders as a result, conformations to set ideas and standards are not, their forte to appreciate. This non-conformative attitude is also responsible for their starting a new enterprise based on new ideas of their own. Autonomy coupled with a sense of determination is an essential characteristic of entrepreneurs.

(4) Sense of Effectiveness: Entrepreneurs like to see the problem solved through their involved efforts. They do not like to avoid the problems but like to be effective and instrumental in solving problems rather than avoiding them. Their attitudes towards a problem is always one of directing the efforts and finding ways and means to give solutions to such problems. Since they are full of confidence in their own capacities they tend to be action-oriented, rather than being passive conformists.

(5) Social Consciousness: Rightful entrepreneurs tend not to take undue advantage of social and economic conditions of the society in general. Instead there is a universal urge among the entrepreneurs for social change and economic development. As a result entrepreneurs are always on the lookout for new methods of producing or developing new products that would create jobs for many. Hence the pursuit of such business activities are directed to achieve social goals on larger interest than personal goals of individual interest.

Entrepreneurs in the real sense do not patronage or indulge in anti-social activities like black-marketing, hoarding, profiteering and such other malpractices which causes considerable damages to interests of the consumers as a whole. They dislike economic backwardness of the society which is the result of such antisocial and unfair business practices. Instead they direct their energies in the eradication of the underside implications by finding new suitable opportunities of business and by providing the services at prices, the community can afford. An entrepreneur hence is socially concerned and respects labour. They spread the message of dignity of manual labour through their own example. They have very low resistance towards doing a work manually. They are ever ready to get the work done through their own hands if the situation demands without any hesitation. This kind of respecting labour enables them to work in cooperation with the people by generating high morale among the people with whom they work. Persons who hesitate to do the work with their own hands will find it difficult to succeed as an entrepreneur. Hence this quality of respecting labour is also a driving force which enables them to be successful by setting examples of doing the work manually. The examples set by them enable others to learn and follow suit. Co-operation therefore becomes easy and effective under such situations.

(6) Need for Extension: An entrepreneur though likely to be self-centred in the pursuit of his goals so that his urge for achievement is satisfied, yet in the true sense he is not so. Many entrepreneurs understand the importance of industrialisation and faster economic development through rapid growth and expansion of the industries, hence they tend to share their experiences with others who have similar attributes and accomplish the task through joining hands with the suitable persons. But the degree of such participations by entrepreneurs in the developing economy is very low, hence by giving appropriate training the entrepreneurs should be motivated towards this goal of expansion through joint ventures. In a country like India, the need of the entrepreneurs for the rapid development in every field for the economy is more a necessity and therefore government efforts should be directed towards this end.

(7) Optimistic: The entrepreneurs have the quality of being optimistic and hoping to succeed rather than experiencing failure. This hope to succeed would enable a sense of determination which will boost their confidence in carrying out the task successfully. Hence this quality of being optimistic is nonetheless important. As a consequence of their self-confidence, they are more successful in their efforts than those with pessimistic attributes.

Thus pessimistic approach or fear of failure does not find place in their mind and they undertake all the tasks after careful planning and with the hope of succeeding with their efforts.

(8) Non-Fatalist: Entrepreneurs, though they have faith in God or in the power of nature, yet disapprove the belief that outside forces will change the environment towards the desired needs. They would like to be instrumental through their own efforts rather than to be dependent upon chance factors or luck or those forces which are beyond their control, for attaining desired goals. Man's destiny can be changed by man himself by his own efforts is their strong belief. Psychologically this type of an attribute is called internal locus of control. This drives them to do things with extra vigour and help them to change the happenings by their own efforts and enjoy the feeling of making things to happen. This nature helps them to accept the mistaken efforts in any case and to attempt to bring about improvements in their approaches in future actions.

(9) Open Minded: Entrepreneurs develop the habit of learning from experience the limitations of achievements. They modify the goals according to the environmental challenges and threats. This modification does not mean avoiding the problems or the tasks, instead they like to face it. The modification is done in order to make it possible to achieve the goal within the given environmental conditions. They always like to get the feedback of their efforts and effectiveness of the programmes modified so that changes or modifications if needed can be effected as and when required. Entrepreneurs in a sense, therefore, always test their capabilities and for that purpose they tend to keep their mind open to receive information on their abilities or otherwise to achieve the desired goals.

(10) Low Affiliation: Entrepreneurs do not get attached emotionally with the people with whom they work. They know that if they do get into emotional involvement with the people they would be working more for the people with whom they are working rather than for the institutions which they intend to build. But even with this attribute they can show concern for their employees by checking, or restraining the behaviour that tends to show obviously their true reactions.

(11) Need for power and influencing: Entrepreneurs always feel the need to influence people and implement the ideas so that the organisation takes the shape in actuality. Excellence is no doubt a criteria for the entrepreneurs but leading others and influencing them to a great extent through the effective dealing is not secondary to an entrepreneur. Since they have a strong belief in their own capacity, they tend to a very high sense of morale which ultimately help to influence others to their. own way of thinking and action. Here the entrepreneur takes the role of a successful manager and influencing others in the accomplishment of the goals.

(12) Aggressive and persistent: These are also the characteristics which help the entrepreneurs to continue with the drive till the goals are achieved. Aggressiveness indicates the presence of a driving force which enables the efforts to come out with full vigour through persistent attempts. This quality, therefore, indicates that entrepreneurs are not problem avoiders. They pursue the goals till they are achieved by modifying the same as and when required as also by removing the obstacles in the way so that the goals are finally achieved. With every failure, the entrepreneur learns to improve the method of approach rather than being passive in the face of frustrating experiences.

(13) Pragmatists: Another attribute of an entrepreneur is to be concerned with the present than the past or future. Though he learns from the past and intends to change the future through his visions and dreams yet he is downright a practical person living in the present. He is a pragmatist who lives in the present effectively. He is not a man of merely day dreams or one who is overhelmed by the past achievements or failures. Though entrepreneurs may at times give the impression of past oriented personalities by narrating their pasts profusely, yet really speaking they are pragmatists who cannot easily be overwhelmed by either the past or the future orientations.

Other characteristics of a successful entrepreneur are high expectations from their employees, pleasing personality, dynamic opportunity seeker, self starter, individualist, sensitive and perceptive of the environment, high tolerance towards ambiguities and uncertain happenings, Materialist tendencies, always hoping and believing in the existence of a better way of doing things, many interests, mentally very active, courageous, etc.

(14) Commitment and Conviction:

- Fully commits himself to the project and rests only when achieved.
- Leaves no effort to complete the task in time.

(15) Capacity to analyse:

- Knows the need for information, its relevance, where and how to find it.

– Has a thought process for diagnosing problems, conceiving and comparing alternative courses of action and approaches in that direction to solve rather than avoid.

(16) Initiative:

– Takes initiative and does not wait for the other to do first.

– Likes to lead rather than being led.

– Likes to act on his own rather than follow others' directions.

(17) Hopeful about future and search for good business environment:

– Reasonably optimistic and tends to look at future with hope.

– Tends to search the environment in order to seek answers to questions.

– Sets goal and plans his line of operations.

– Perceives opportunities.

(18) High personal efficiency:

– Has a sense of effectiveness and

– Presents himself with ability to do things with higher degree of efficiency.

There could be a long series of characteristics, but in my opinion, these are some of the very important and essential ones which should fit into the profile of a successful entrepreneur. It is actually not necessary that he may have high degree of all these traits but a fairly good combination of these is required to be reasonably available. The level of degrees could, however be increased by motivation and proper training through entrepreneurship development programmes.

ANNEXURE – 2

The Success Audit

Take the success audit for enterprise success:

1. Do you contribute creatively to any business function other than your own? Yes No
2. Do you consciously attempt to network with other professionals in your field? Yes No
3. Do you have an overall perspective of the industry you are in? Yes No
4. Do you understand your company's business goals, and how your job fits into them? Yes No
5. Do you understand the needs and constraints of the different business functions? Yes No
6. Can you cope with upgraded software packages without professional help? Yes No
7. Would you volunteer for a challenging long-term overseas assignment? Yes No
8. Do you make a conscious effort to keep abreast of international trends in your field? Yes No
9. At a pinch, can you take over for a colleague in the event of his sudden illness? Yes No
10. Do you often enroll for courses that deal with subjects that are supplementary to yours? Yes No

The Scoring

Give yourself 10 points for every YES, and 0 for every No.

Total

The Rating:

0-30	Take those blinkers off. Else, you could get left behind in the career-stakes.
40-70	Wishy-washy. You have the potential, just get more focused.
80-100	Congrats! You're in a pole position in the corporate grand prix.

ANNEXURE – 3

Business Skills Inventory

The following inventory will help you to assess your strengths and weaknesses as a future small business owner. In this exercise, you need to identify how much knowledge and/or experience you have in relation to each of the skills listed in the inventory. These are the most important skills that you will need to start and run your future contracting business. They have been grouped under various management functions representing the key roles that you will have to play as a business owner.

It is important to realistically examine your background knowledge and your experience in these key roles. The success of your business depends on how well you are prepared to assume these roles.

Rate yourself on a four-point scale and circle the figure that you feel most accurately represents your explanation of each category:

- No knowledge, no experience
- Some knowledge, but no experience
- Some experience and
- Much experience

Question: How much knowledge or experience do you have in relation to each skill listed in the inventory?

I. Marketing the Construction Firm	Your Rating
• Identify the Construction Firm.	1 2 3 4
• Determine the territory within which you will operate.	1 2 3 4
• Determine the types of customers you will serve.	1 2 3 4
• Use Statistics of India as information to assess the size of the target market.	1 2 3 4
• Design a questionnaire to identify potential customers and their needs.	1 2 3 4
• Choose a location for the business.	1 2 3 4
• Give yourself an overall rating reflecting your level of competency in identifying your target markets.	1 2 3 4
II. Competing with Others	
• Find our how well your competitors are doing.	1 2 3 4
• Analyse how the competitors obtain their contracts.	1 2 3 4
• Determine how your firm will be different from the competitors.	1 2 3 4
• Give yourself an overall rating reflecting your level of competency in competing with others.	1 2 3 4
III. Pricing Your Service	
• Set a competitive hourly labour rate.	1 2 3 4
• Prepare an estimate of the costs for providing your services.	1 2 3 4
• Submit bids with/without cost-escalating clauses.	1 2 3 4
• Negotiate contracts with other parties.	1 2 3 4
Give yourself an overall rating reflecting your level of competency in properly pricing your services.	1 2 3 4

IV. Promoting Your Business

- Develop a promotional strategy. 1 2 3 4
- Design promotional materials. 1 2 3 4
- Prepare a budget for advertising. 1 2 3 4
- Use quality of workmanship and customer service as a promotional tool. 1 2 3 4

Give yourself an overall rating reflecting your level of competency in promoting your future construction firm. 1 2 3 4

V. Managing Finances

1. Borrowing Money

- Determine how much money is needed to start and run your business. 1 2 3 4
- Forecast the need for additional capital or cash. 1 2 3 4
- Identify appropriate sources for short-term/long-term financing. 1 2 3 4
- Negotiate loans. 1 2 3 4

Give yourself an overall rating reflecting your level of competency in borrowing money. 1 2 3 4

2. Managing Money

- Do book-keeping. 1 2 3 4
- Establish and use financial controls. 1 2 3 4
- Set up a cost control system for separate jobs or contracts. 1 2 3 4
- Analyse overhead costs. 1 2 3 4
- Prepare profit and loss statements and balance sheets. 1 2 3 4
- Prepare budgets. 1 2 3 4

Give yourself an overall rating reflecting your level of competency in managing money. 1 2 3 4

3. Analysing Financial Statements

- Prepare a cash flow analysis. 1 2 3 4
- Prepare a break-even analysis. 1 2 3 4
- Understand profit and loss statements and balance sheets 1 2 3 4

Give yourself an overall rating reflecting your level of competency in analysing financial statements. 1 2 3 4

4. Handling Credit and Collection

- Understand current credit policies in the construction industry set by sub-contractors, general contractors and developers. 1 2 3 4
- Design accounts payable and receivable ageing systems. 1 2 3 4
- Use various collection techniques. 1 2 3 4
- Know how and when to commence legal action, file a lien, go to Small Claim Court. 1 2 3 4

Give yourself an overall rating reflecting your level of competency in handling credit and collection. 1 2 3 4

VI. Organising the Business

1. Handling Legal Issues

- Choose the appropriate: proprietorship, partnership, incorporation. 1 2 3 4

- Write a partnership agreement. 1 2 3 4
- Write a valid contract with general contractors, sub-contractors and/or clients. 1 2 3 4
- Determine appropriate terms for a leasing agreement. 1 2 3 4
- Use the litigation process or other alternatives to resolve construction disputes. 1 2 3 4
- Choose a lawyer who can understand your legal problems. 1 2 3 4

  Give yourself an overall rating reflecting your level of competency in handling legal issues. 1 2 3 4

2. Complying with Government Regulations

- Obtain appropriate business licences and permits. 1 2 3 4
- Comply with federal, provincial and municipal tax laws. 1 2 3 4
- Comply with the Labour Code: minimum wage, payment of wages, holidays, hours of work, Human Rights code, Worker's Compensation Board. 1 2 3 4

  Give yourself an overall rating reflecting your level of competency in complying with government regulations. 1 2 3 4

3. Insuring Your Business

- Purchase proper insurance coverage for important business risks. 1 2 3 4
- Select an insurance broker or company. 1 2 3 4
- Obtain performance bonds. 1 2 3 4
- Give yourself an overall rating reflecting your level of competency in insuring your business. 1 2 3 4

VII. Managing Business Operations

- Buy supplies from the best sources at the best price possible (including discount). 1 2 3 4
- Buy reliable equipment with adequate warranties. 1 2 3 4
- Negotiate contracts with suppliers. 1 2 3 4
- Use techniques for controlling material inventories. 1 2 3 4
- Set up quality control procedure to ensure quality of workmanship. 1 2 3 4
- Coordinate own work schedule with the schedule of other trade people on the same project. 1 2 3 4
- Set up a system for recording work orders.

  Give yourself an overall rating reflecting your level of competency in managing your business operations. 1 2 3 4

VIII. Managing People

- Develop a job description. 1 2 3 4
- Interview applicants for jobs available. 1 2 3 4
- Provide employees with feedback on their performance. 1 2 3 4
- Supervise and motivate employees. 1 2 3 4
- Train employees. 1 2 3 4
- Schedule workers on a daily or weekly basis 1 2 3 4

- Work effectively with other trades on a construction job. 1 2 3 4
  Give yourself an overall rating reflecting your level of competency in managing people. 1 2 3 4

The skills for which you have rated yourself as 1 or 2 represent your weaknesses. Before you start your business, you should plan on acquiring these skills or find a partner who has such an expertise. You must also plan to improve those skills which are rated 3.

In any case, attempting to develop or improve your skills as you run your business may be very costly and lead to bankruptcy. There will be numerous tasks to accomplish and they will put high demands on your ability to make your business profitable. If you are not sufficiently prepared and organised to have them done, you will soon fall behind and the problems will rapidly pile up with no relief in sight.

The skills which you rated as 4 represent the strengths that will contribute to the success of your future contracting business.

You should not expect to be equally strong in all the functions necessary for operating a business. However, knowing your weaknesses will allow you to see assistance for solving problems requiring those skills.

Consult the overall rates you have assigned to the main functions listed in the inventory (there are 13 overall rates). List your four strongest management functions and your four weakest management functions.

Strongest management functions: ____________________

____

Weakest management functions: ____________________

____

ANNEXURE – 4

Ranking Entrepreneurial Traits Centre

No single entrepreneur possesses all the traits or characteristics described earlier, nor are all those characteristics needed to be successful. But which of the traits and characteristics are most commonly shared and most important for success?

In order to assess what you believe to be important entrepreneurial abilities, complete the following quiz. Rate the characteristics on a scale of 1 to 5. A rating of 1 indicates little importance, and a rating of 5 indicates great importance.

Characteristics	***Little importance***			***Great importance***	
	1	2	3	4	5
1. A strong need to achieve					
2. A visionary					
3. A need to associate closely with others					
4. Ability to focus on people and process					

5. An ability to get along with employees
6. Ability to motivate and build relationship
7. A willingness to tolerate uncertainty
8. Good physical health
9. A high level of energy
10. Singleness of purpose
11. A willingness to take risks
12. Drive to be ahead of others
13. Ambitious
14. Self-confidence
15. Innovation
16. Ability to chart a course of direction
17. Ability to lead effectively
18. Patience
19. Ability to strive
20. A strong desire for money
21. Being well-organised
22. Thirst for knowledge and adequate reading habits
23. A desire to create
24. A desire to adopt active attitudes towards goals
25. A need for power
26. Perseverance
27. Commitment and hard work
28. Self-reliance
29. Abundant commonsense
30. Desire and willingness to take the initiative
31. Competitiveness
32. Versatility
33. Desire to share knowledge/experience
34. Quality conscious
35. Desire to add value
36. Honesty
37. Progressive
38. Flexibility
39. Ability to change and
40. Uniqueness.

Now that you have rated the various entrepreneurial characteristics, rank the characteristics in order of importance in your opinion under one of the following three categories:

(a) Most important for success (include those characteristics that you numbered 4 and 5)

(b) Important for success (include those characteristics that you gave a rating of 3)

(c) Least important for success (include those characteristics that you rated as 1 and 2)

Most Important	Important	Least Important
____________	____________	____________
____________	____________	____________
____________	____________	____________
____________	____________	____________
____________	____________	____________
____________	____________	____________
____________	____________	____________

The idea is not just work to finish a task but rather to work well and to savour each step you take up the mountain you've chosen. Then, when you reach the top, you won't feel spent from all the effort. In fact you won't even feel you've arrived. Instead, you'll feel refreshed and invigorated by what you've accomplished, and you'll find yourself looking for the next peak to conquer.

Taken together, mission, vision and a set of unique traits forms the bedrock of entrepreneurship. They allow them to help shape their future. Mastering the discipline of innovation will require organisations to learn from one another.

Ranking entrepreneurial traits will definitely guide the entrepreneurs, particularly the first generation entrepreneurs to build up their deficiencies and move ahead with speed in this competitive entrepreneurial environment.

Leadership

Leadership isn't about what leaders do; it's about what they are. It's about what their underlying belief system is. What separates the best leaders from others is the nuances, the subtleties. It is these little things that companies need to pay attention to in order to build a leadership culture.

There is an essential by product of these reciprocal relationships: the "social network" that is formed by the consistent movement of people across geographies and functions and by the efforts of leaders to spend time nurturing and growing new talent. The organisational power of these networks should not be underestimated. These networks pave the way for the belief systems, the communication, the risk taking and the reciprocity and help the organisation stay 'connected.'

Ultimately, these little things are the really big things. They form patterns in organisations and become institutionalised. Leaders experience what was done for them, they observe and then perpetuate a system that is powerful and enduring. They ingrain their belief systems into the next generation, enabling leadership culture to continue indefinitely. The combination of little things amounts to a very big difference in organisational life. Great leadership is based on personal values and belief system. Values envisages the vision, mission and strategy.

The Entrepreneurship Ecosystem

Early Customers
- Early adopters for proof-of-concept
- Expertise in productizing
- Reference customer
- First reviews
- Distribution channels

Leadership
- Unequivocal support
- Social legitimacy
- Open door for advocate
- Entrepreneurship strategy
- Urgency, crisis and challenge

Government
- Institutions
  e.g. investment, support
- Financial support
  e.g. for R & D, jump start funds
- Regulatory framework incentives
  e.g. Tax benefits
- Research institutes
- Venture-friendly legislation
- e.g. Bankruptcy, contract enforcement, property rights, and labor

Support Services
- Legal
- Accounting
- Investment bankers
- Technical experts, advisors
- board members

Culture
- Tolerance of risk
- Innovation, creativity, experimentation
- Social status
- Ambition, drive, hunger

Network
- Entrepreneur's networks
- Diaspora networks
- Multinational corporations

Success Stories
- Visible successes
- Wealth generation for founders
- International reputation

Economic Clusters
- Critical masses of companies
- Country specific reputation
- Doman-specific skills
- Technology

Human Capital
- Skilled and unskilled
- Series entrepreneurs
- Later generation family

Infrastructure
- Telecommunications
- Transportation & logistics
- Energy

Financial Capital
- Micro-loans
- Angel investors, friends and family
- Zero-stage venture capital
- Venture capital funds
- Private equity
- Public capital markets
- Debt

Educational Institutions
- General degrees (professional and academic)
- Specific entrepreneurship training

Non-Government Institutions
- Entrepreneurship promotion in non-profits
- Business plan contests
- Conferences
- Entrepreneur-friendly associations

Entrepreneurship

Ealry Customers
Leadership
Government
Culture
Success stories
Human capital
Financial Capital
Enterpreneurship organisation
Educational
Infrastructure
Economic customers
Networks
Support Services

There is now enough evidence out there that proves entrepreneurship is the sure way to development. It contributes disproportionately to rapid job creation, GDP growth, and long-term productivity and a lot of the things that societies are struggling to get right. So, launch an entrepreneurship revolution.

❋ ❋ ❋

Co-ordinating x and y

"There is a whole wealth of knowledge being generated from problem-based learning. The problems in the 21st century will not be just engineering problems, they will be more complex business problems. How do you think horizontally and not just vertically." – ***Nick Donofrio, senior V-P, IBM***

Unit – II

Entrepreneurial Development

4. Entrepreneurial Development
5. Institutions in Aid of Entrepreneurship Development

Many governments in developing countries recognise that small and medium-scale industries continue to play an important role in their socio-economic development. There is growing interest in developing programmes for stimulating and encouraging entrepreneurship development in these countries with this the entrepreneur becomes the focal point in economic activities, especially in developing countries.

The most commonly adopted approach to entrepreneurship development is training.

Approaches to Entrepreneurship Development

There are various approaches to entrepreneurship development which policy makers, planners, trainers and other officials involved in development may choose. This development could be achieved within the conceptual framework in which the various strategies and policies of an entrepreneurship development programme are evolved or formulated. There is need for a thorough discussion of the various theories and their implications for the organisations' resources and capabilities. But however it is approached, entrepreneurship development should be viewed in the total perspective and should integrate entrepreneurial training, provision of incentives, consultancy services, sectoral development and other essential strategies of intervention. There are at least four major approaches:

1. *Develop and arrange the course content by analysing needs and stating outcomes.*
2. *Choose the appropriate training methods.*
3. *Consider the subject area, the nature of learning, the trainee populations, the trainers themselves and time and material factors.*
4. *Achieve training objectives.*

Training

Achievement motivation training is designed to increase the achievement orientation of the trainees with the idea that positive behaviour, such as striving for excellence, learning from feedback and moderate risk-taking, is initiated. Likewise, it strengthens the ability of an individual to generate alternatives as well as to solve problems creatively. It also develops the ability to define and set goals in life. As such, entrepreneurship development is viewed as behaviour-oriented. One of the factors contributing to the success of this training intervention in entrepreneurship development is that it is based on experience. In entrepreneurship training, learning by discovery is usually preferred. Here, one is able to learn from one's actions and behaviour in training, learning by discovery is usually preferred. Here, one is able to learn from one's actions and behaviour in training. Thus, the learning process becomes a positive reinforcement.

Although there are some variations of and/or models for this intervention, the overall objective of this aspect of training is making the entrepreneur more professional, the training intervention may also take the form of management skills development. Most entrepreneurs lack managerial skills and techniques needed to deal with the management problems of the enterprise. Therefore, for any entrepreneurship development programme to succeed, it is important not only to motivate the trainees but also to provide them with all the skills necessary to run their business successfully.

Designing an Entrepreneurship Training Programme

As mentioned earlier, designing the training programme involves setting training objectives, developing the course content and choosing appropriate training methods. The programme design is prescribed by the training needs of the target clientele. These objectives should be stated dearly, be trainee-centered, employ practically and be concerned with ends rather than means. When objectives are set, the course content can be developed. The elements of content are knowledge, habits, skills and control of emotion, The material to be included should be accorded priority according to the goal to be achieved.

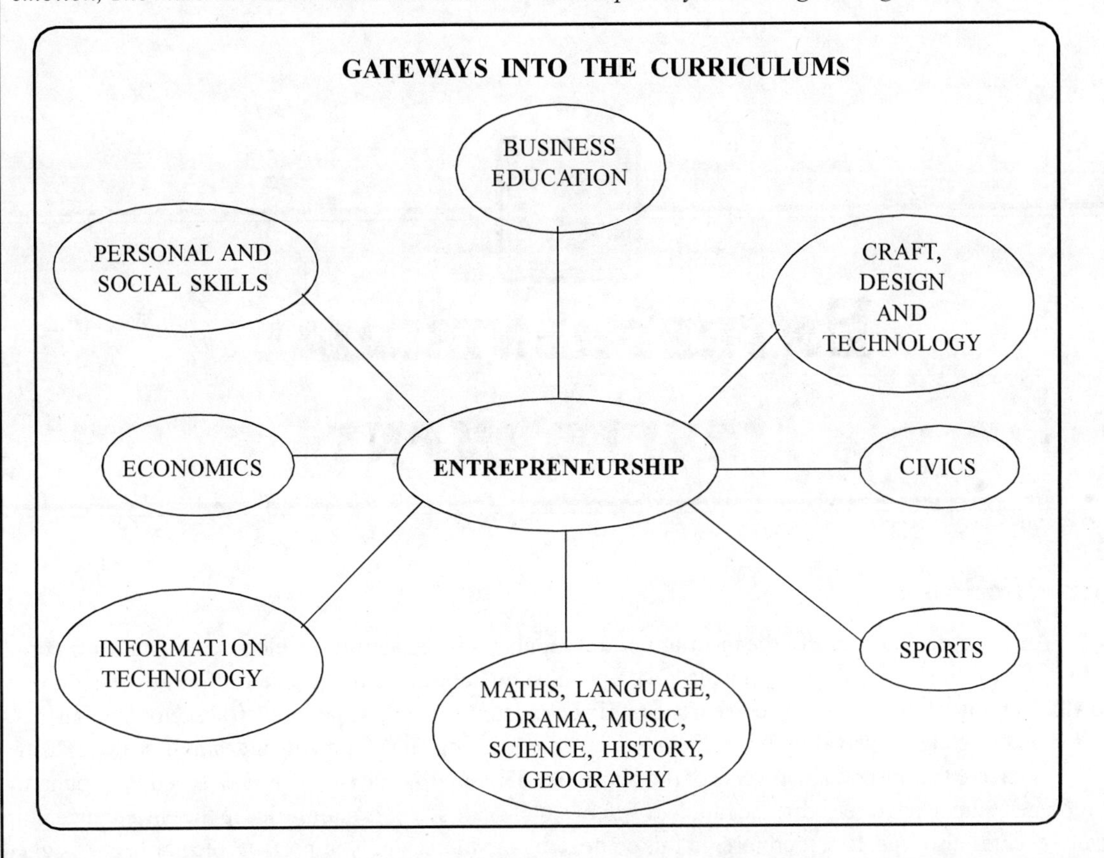

4

ENTREPRENEURIAL DEVELOPMENT

Introduction

An entrepreneur is one of the most important inputs in the economic development of a country or of regions within the country. Entrepreneurial competence makes all the difference to the rate of economic growth. In India, state and private entrepreneurship co-exist. The small-scale industrial sector and business are left completely to private entrepreneurs. Entrepreneurship development and small-scale industry development are the obverse and reverse of the same coin. The small-scale enterprise is a breeding ground for entrepreneurship. Conversely, that the rapid growth of small-scale sector is mainly due to the entrepreneurship development is also true. It is, therefore, in this context that an increasingly important role has been assigned for the identification and promotion of entrepreneurs to this sector.

Peter Drucker, the well-known management expert, defines an entrepreneur as one who always searches for change, responds to it and exploits it as an opportunity. Entrepreneurs innovate and innovation is a specific instrument of entreprenruship, according to one definition that has emerged very recently, and an entrepreneur is a person who senses opportunity for economic gains in the socio-economic spheres around him and initiates activity leading to production/distribution/service, through interaction of men and materials. Entrepreneurship involves taking risks or making investment under conditions of uncertainty and to innovate, plan and take decisions so as to increase production, productivity and profits. Growth-oriented development is the cornerstone of entrepreneurs.

Approaches to Entrepreneurship Development

There are various approaches to entrepreneurship development which policy makers, planners, trainers and other officials involved in development may choose. Such development could be achieved within the conceptual framework in which the various strategies and policies of an entrepreneurship development programme are evolved or formulated. There is need for a thorough discussion of the various theories and their implications for the organisation's resources and capabilities. But however it is approached, entrepreneurship development should be viewed in the total perspective and should integrate entrepreneurial training, provision of incentives, consultancy services, sectoral development and other essential strategies of intervention. There are atleast four major approaches.

Box 4.1 : STARTING FROM SCRATCH

All successful programmes and initiatives for developing leadership talent within an organisation are created for one single purpose: to support important business needs. These programmes are an integral part of running the day-to-day business of the company. They fuel growth while fulfilling the needs of human capital and leadership.

Most companies are not sure where to begin, others don't believe they can build leadership from scratch. Yet others start from scratch, launch costly initatives with a variety of programmes, but with no real plan to build a system that will sustain good leadership.

The truth is great leadership programmes are not programmes at all. They are essential processes for driving the business.

Everything in leadership begins and ends with business. A leadership strategy needs to define how you will support your business strategy. It is a fundamental part of running the business, and needs to run across selecting, developing, assessing and compensating your leaders.

Identifying Critical Capabilities

First, you need to identify the critical capabilities you will need in your leaders so that you realise your long-term business goals. Each organisation is different and these differences will dictate a different and unique competency model. However, while good processes allow executive teams to assess their needs and rethink their stretegy, they need to be kept in perspective.

A good competency model is a starting place for a dialogue and discussion of what's required, and its sole function should be to add clarity to expectations. You need to choose the critical behaviours that will define the success of your leaders, which will create clarity of what's really important for your business and industry.

Two factors decide how well a leader fits with his or her role: the business strategy and the amount of change in the environment.

Business Strategy

There is no universal best-leader model that describes ideal leadership characteristics and strategies. Business strategy can be broadly classified into two – growth strategy and return strategy. Having a growth strategy means you propose profits primarily by expanding sales, while having a return strategy means you will compete on the basis of having a more efficient organisation than your competitors. Both these strategies require different sets of skills and capabilities from the leadership team.

Starting from scratch isn't easy, but it can be done. Sometimes, it's easier to start from scratch than to dismantle bad processes and then work out a new strategy.

Finding and developing leaders will become more challenging in the future than it is today. The future poses new challenges and greater speed and complexity, but also opportunities to develop leadership capability more effectively.

The great companies of the future will be those that recognise the new challenges early and respond aggressively with the help of a strong senior team, a focus on their best talent and doing the right programmes the right way.

Source: *The Economic Times,* 28 November, 2003.

Human Resources Development

The issue of human resources development is very important in small-scale industries. Since it is people-oriented and labour-intensive, developing the human resource is a *sine qua non* in the development.

Human resources development as defined by Harbison and Myer, 'is the process of increasing the knowledge, the skills and the capacities of all the people in society. In economic terms, it could be described as the accumulation of human capital and its effective investment in the development of an economy.' It is achieved more effectively through training, education, information and scholastic exchange, but also as the supply and demand of manpower, with a view to improving employment generation and income distribution and supporting the expanded socio-economic development activities of the country. Human resources development is the key to the growth of small-scale industries.

The Meaning

Entrepreneurial Development Programme (EDP) means programme designed to help a person in strengthening his entrepreneurial motive and in acquiring skills and capabilities necessary for playing his entrepreneurial role effectively. Towards this end, it is necessary to promote his understanding of motives, motivation pattern, their impact on behaviour and entrepreneurial value. A programme which seeks to do this can qualify to be called an EDP. This has to be stressed here, because there are a number of programmes which aim at providing informational or managerial inputs or focus on preparation of a project. Although all these inputs are required by a new entrepreneur, a programme not touching entrepreneurial motivation and behaviour cannot be called an EDP.

The Need

The need for a broad-based entrepreneurial class in India arises from the need to speed up the process of activating the factors of production, leading to a higher rate of economic growth, dispersal of economic activities, development of backward and tribal areas, creation of employment opportunities, improvement in the standard of living of the weaker sections of the society and involvement of all sections of the society in the process of economic growth.

In India, some of the management schools at the top end of the ladder do have some courses for SSE promotion in their regular MBA programmes. But taken together, they are doing pretty little for the development of entrepreneurship.

In advanced countries like the United States or Britain, small business study forms a significant part of management education.

Generally small business studies are offered as optional in the second half of the programme. During the course of the study, not only various aspects of small business management are discussed, but the students prepare their business plans (project reports) and make tie-ups with financial institutions.

Thus the MBA course offers him a sound education in general management with special orientation in small business enterprises. Recognising the importance of SSEs, it was only recently that the National Westminster Bank instituted a chair for a Small Business Professor at the Cornfield School of Management in Britain.

Though EDP has been recognised as an effective human resource development tool, many a time there are very many expectations from a single programme, like removing unemployment, enhancing industrial development, promoting small-scale industries, developing industrially underdeveloped regions, etc.

EDP is primarily meant for developing those first-generation entrepreneurs, who on their own cannot become successful entrepreneurs. It covers three major variables: location, target group and enterprise (entrepreneurial activities). Any of these can become the focus or starting point for initiating and implementing an EDP. The remaining two then will follow by making proper synthesis with the first. As for example, if the objective is to promote women entrepreneurs, suitable location and proper entrepreneurial activities must match or if the objective is to develop North-East region, then the potential target group and feasible entrepreneurial ventures must follow.

EDP by itself therefore aims at achieving the specific objectives of the programmes and therefore cannot create any magical result. It is a continuous process of training and motivating then to set up profitable enterprises in large measure.

Appropriate Design

It is now well recognised that entrepreneurs can be developed through appropriately designed entrepreneurship development programmes. These programmes broadly envisage a three-tiered approach: developing achievement motivation and sharpening of entrepreneurial traits and behaviour, project planning and development and guidance on industrial opportunities, incentives and facilities and rules and regulations, and developing managerial and operational capabilities. Various techniques and approaches have been developed and adopted to achieve these objectives, keeping in view the target groups and/or target areas. The structuring of the programmes and training methodology also necessitate the consideration of the specific target groups and target areas. Methodology for selection of the prospective entrepreneurs as well as support services after the training have a significant impact on the success of the entrepreneur development programmes.

Combined Courses May Help

In our management schools too, full-time courses in small business management should be offered in the MBA programme. These courses should focus on manufacturing and service sectors. Management schools can also help existing SSEs through part time courses. As many of the management schools are located near the technological institutions, it is possible to have combined programmes for both technological and managerial areas. This will also enable technology students intending to start ventures to have adequate management education.

Possibly, in the long-run, association with SSEs can lead to short courses and consultancy, not only to bridge the gap between theory and practice, but also as a source of revenue it is not claimed here that all the problems of SSE development can be solved by the introduction of small business studies in management schools. Far from it, the idea is to remove as many constraints as possible for industrial development. These programmes oriented to entrepreneurship. Creativity and innovation can help sustain a healthy growth of small business,

Entrepreneurship Development Programme

Past endurance has shown that industrial promotion by provision of facilities, technical assistance, management training and consultancy, industrial information and other services alone are not sufficient to develop entrepreneurs. It was concluded that the focal point should be aimed at the overlooked entrepreneurial spirit and entrepreneurial characteristics of the people to be developed. The EDP package was therefore launched.

1. Entrepreneurial Education
2. Planned Publicity for entrepreneurial opportunities
3. Identification of potential entrepreneurs through scientific methods
4. Motivational Training to new entrepreneurs
5. Help and guidance in selecting products and preparing project reports
6. Making available techno-economic information and product profits
7. Evolving locally suitable new products and processes
8. Availability of local agencies with trained personnel for entrepreneurial counselling and promotions
9. Creating entrepreneurial forum
10. Recognition of entrepreneurs

Simulatory — Support — Sustaining

Entrepreneurial Cycle

1. Registration of unit
2. Arranging finance
3. Providing land, shed, power, water etc.
4. Guidance for selecting and obtaining machinery
5. Supply of scarce raw materials
6. Getting licence/import licences
7. Providing common facilities
8. Granting tax relief or other subsidies
9. Offering management consultancy
10. Help marketing products
11. Providing information

1. Help modernization
2. Help diversification/expansion/substitute production
3. Additional financing for full capacity utilization
4. Deferring repayment/interest
5. Diagnostic industrial extension/consultancy source
6. Production units legislation/policy change
7. Product reservation/creating new avenues for marketing
8. Quality testing and improvident services and
9. Need-based common facilities centre

Fig. 4.1: Entrepreneurial Development Cycle

A Complex Phenomenon

Entrepreneurial development is a complex phenomenon. Entrepreneurs play a key role in the economic development of a country. Importance of the development of entrepreneurship as an ingredient of economic development has been recognised a long time back. It was as early as 1950 that the need for entrepreneurial development was first felt and since then a substantial amount of research has gone into this sphere. It is a well-known fact that entrepreneurs are not born and can be made in the sense that the quality can be improved. In our country where human resources are to be found in plenty, we can identify individuals in all segments of the population who have the requisite entrepreneurial skills. But it requires to mould them, motivate them and train them through proper, Entrepreneurial Development, Programmes (EDPs) for undertaking risk-bearing ventures. Thus the EDPs become a vital approach for harnessing the vast untapped human skills, to channelise them into accelerating industrialization in general and growth of the small-scale sector in particular. It is also observed by several scientists like McClelland, that with proper training provided to the right kind of persons, entrepreneurship could be developed.

Of late, entrepreneurship development has become extremely important in achieving the goals of allaround development in the country. Consequently, many entrepreneurial opportunities are emerging in various fields. Be it electronic, medicine, engineering, agriculture, communication, atomic energy, telecommunication, food technology and packaging, entrepreneurial opportunities have surfaced at rapid pace in all these and many other areas. Such opportunities, however, become more perceptible to entrepreneurs if they are exposed to the latest development in the respective fields either in terms of technology, use or style of living. Accessibility and understanding of such information widens the base of opportunity sensing by potential entrepreneurs.

Different Perceptions, Different Needs

Qualities of governments and corporations value	*Vs*	*Qualities of entrepreneurial organisations*
order		untidiness
formality		informality
accountability		trusting
information		personal observation
clear demarcation		overlapping
planning		intuitive
corporate strategy		"tactically strategic"
control measures		"I do it my way"
formal standards		personal monitoring
transparency		ambiguous
functional expertise		holistic
systems		"feely"
positional authority		owner managed
formal performance appraisal		customer/network exposed

Objectives of the Programme

In line with the national programme for the promotion and development of small and medium industries in the countryside, the Industrial Service Institute (ISI) under the Department of Industrial Promotion (DIP) launched the EDP to give substance to the government's policies of stimulation of economic growth, dispersing industries to rural areas and promoting the processing of local raw materials. The EDP was considered a part of the industrial development policy articulated in the present Five-Year National Economic and Social Development Plan.

The Programme sought to develop entrepreneurial activities in the rural areas of Thailand as a vehicle for economic growth and also had the following objectives:

(a) To promote the development of small and medium enterprises that would encourage self-employment among potential entrepreneurs;

(b) To provide, in the rural areas, special programmes designed to stimulate new ventures and encourage expansion of existing activities of small and medium industries;

(c) To generate employment and self-employment in the processing of indigenous raw materials for local consumption and for export;

(d) To develop entrepreneurial capabilities for potential entrepreneurs and upgrade managerial skills of existing entrepreneurs.

From a sound training programme for entrepreneurship development in India, the expert group constituted by the NIESBUD accepted that it must be able to help selected entrepreneurs to:

(a) Develop and strengthen their entrepreneurial quality/ motivation;

(b) Analyse environment related to both small industry and small business;

(c) Select project/product;

(d) Formulate projects;

(e) Understand the process and procedure of setting up of small enterprise;

(f) Know and influence the source of help/support needed for launching the enterprise.

(g) Acquire the basic management skills;

(h) Know the pros and cons of being an entrepreneur and

(i) Acquaint and appreciate the needed social responsibility/entrepreneurial disciplines.

Some of the other important aspects of entrepreneurial training are:

(i) To let him set or reset the objectives of his business and work individually and along with his group for their realisation.

(ii) To prepare him for accepting totally unforeseen risks of business for a long time after such training.

(iii) To enable him to take strategic decisions.

(iv) To enable him to build an integrated team equal to the demands of tomorrow.

(v) To communicate fast, clearly and effectively.

(vi) To develop a broad vision to see the business as a whole and to integrate his function with it.

(vii) To enable him to relate his product and industry to the total environment; to find what is significant in it and to take it into account in his decisions and actions.

(viii) To enable him to cope with and coordinate the different types of paper work, most of which is statutorily obligatory.

(ix) To make him subscribe to industrial democracy, that is, accepting workers as partners in enterprise and

(x) To strengthen his passion for integrity, honesty and compliance with law which is the key to success in the long run.

Entrepreneurial Behaviours

- grasping opportunity
- taking initiative

- solving problems creatively
- managing autonomously
- taking responsibility for, and ownership of, things
- seeing things through
- networking effectively to manage interdependence
- puffing things together creatively
- using judgement to take calculated risk.

Entrepreneurial Attributes

- achievement orientation and ambition
- self-confidence and self-esteem
- perseverance
- high internal locus of control (autonomy)
- action orientation
- preference for learning by doing
- hardworking
- determination
- creativity

Entrepreneurial Skills

- creative problem solving
- persuading
- negotiating
- selling
- proposing
- holistically managing business/projects/situations
- strategic thinking
- intuitive decision making under uncertainty
- networking.

Structuring Entrepreneurial Development Programmes

The above case studies bring out certain features important for the success of entrepreneurial development programmes. The training programme aims at identification and careful selection of entrepreneurs (using advanced series of psychological tests), developing the motivation and entrepreneurial capabilities of the trainees, equipping the trainees to identify viable industrial projects and to prepare project profiles or brief project reports, equipping the trainees with basic enterprise-building skills, imparting basic managerial skills required for the successful management of the unit and helping the trainees to secure the necessary financial, infrastructural and related assistance during the implementation of the project. Skill training formed a vital and major component of this programme.

Entrepreneurship development model/promotion are pre-requisites for entrepreneurial development programme training.

The entire infrastructure of an area should be reviewed. Entrepreneurs require various levels of assistance and support in arranging finance, plant and machinery, land, readymade sheds, power, raw materials and finally information relating to the industry. The support activities provide nurturing and help entrepreneurship to grow and survive. The inadequacy of the support system may impede provision of timely help to entrepreneurs. The coordinator of the entrepreneurial training programme may convene a meeting of various developmental agencies to elicit their cooperation.

Survey of Entrepreneurial Opportunities

It consists of identifying viable industrial activities and enterprises based on demand and resources and the extent of competition. Although the emphasis is to be given to demand of an area, the adjoining areas having linkages and the requirement of a region should also be considered. The objective of a survey is to identify opportunities in industries and other activities which offer a promising future for entrepreneurs.

Selection of Entrepreneurs

Selection methodology is a critical input in the entrepreneurship development scheme. If the entrepreneurs are not properly selected, the entire programme can be affected; and this has a direct bearing on the success rate to stand guarantee for the young entrepreneurs. Continuous and sustained follow-up action was undertaken. This was the responsibility of the project officer and the assistant project officer. A success rate of 60 per cent was attained. The State Government later gave assistance to the institutes for conducting entrepreneurial development programmes for unemployment engineers, diploma holders, graduates and ITI trained boys and the institute has done fairly well.

Experiences in EDPs Abroad

It will not be out of place to touch upon the experiences of some foreign countries in the area of entrepreneurship development. In a recent workshop organised by the East-West Centre Technology Institute, Hawaii, the EDP experiences of various countries were discussed which revealed that training made positive contributions in the performance of entrepreneurs. The non-entrepreneurial participants were motivated to start a business. The general conclusion was that EDPs could be developed as a valid substitute for natural institutions (i.e., business families). The experiences of other institutions like Development Technology Centre, Institute of Technology, Bandung Institute of Psychology, University of Indonesia, Jakarta also reiterate that EDPs have a great scope in increasing the number of new entrepreneurs to accelerate the process of industrialisation.

The basic features of the EDP programme has gone through several modifications over time as:

(a) Identification and careful selection of entrepreneurs for training;

(b) Developing the entrepreneurial capabilities of the trainee;

(c) Equipping the trainee with the basic managerial understanding and strategies;

(d) Ensuring a viable industrial project for each potential entrepreneur;

(e) Helping him to secure the necessary financial, infrastructural and related assistance; and

(f) Training cost is highly subsidised and only token fee is charged. A deposit is, however, taken to ensure commitment of participants.

Entrepreneurial Discipline

Entrepreneurs who are developed and promoted at social cost have a certain responsibility to the society that promotes and supports them. The society expects adequate returns from these people. Towards this end, entrepreneurs are expected to follow a certain discipline which is essential for entrepreneurial career. This covers subjects like:

1. Repayment behaviour – financial management.
2. Response to tax and statutory requirement – Law and compliances.
3. Progressive outlook towards labour – labour management.
4. Care for ecology and environment – environment management.

Issues of Entrepreneurial Development Programmes

The present stage of development of EDP as a factor continuation to the industrialisation of backward and other areas needs a proper direction and organisation for making it more effective and purposeful. The contribution of EDP is very uneven among regions and definite programmes need to be chalked out to bring about some degree of uniformity and upgradation. Before this is tackled, some important issues need immediate attention. They are detailed below for consideration:

1. Structure and Composition of EDPs: The structure and content of EDPs, taking into account the regional variations, need to be streamlined. The programme should have a practical content and needs a lot of inter-institutional organisational arrangement to make it a success. The successful EDPs have, at their base, the inter-institutional co-operation or an institution such as Gujarat Centre of the State Bank of India, which besides conducting the programmes also arranges for finance and other input for the entrepreneurs. The EDPs conducted in isolation would dissipate resources and talents. The issue, therefore, for effective functioning of EDPs is to have financial agency strongly backing up efforts of the Entrepreneurial Development. The place and role of Technical Consistency Organisations (TCOs) need to be reviewed and their activities suitably accelerated. Who should conduct an EDP is an important issue.

2. Areas of Operation: As has been stated earlier, in the North-Eastern Area, entrepreneurial development activities are lacking the support activities of the financial institutions. In these areas, programmes have to be linked with support activities.

3. Fixing Priorities: Another area of fixing the priorities of EDPs is to consider their working in terms of efficiency and social need (justice) criteria. Evaluation of EDPs have revealed that those who have business experience, education and skills are proving successful entrepreneurs. This source should be tapped first and then go to the stratum to cover *entrepreneurs from the non-traditional class, i.e., without business and industrial experience, but having the potential of becoming successful entrepreneurs. Next come the entrepreneurs belonging to backward and other communities who have to overcome many additional handicaps to become successful entrepreneurs. A proper course counter of EDPs has to be developed to meet the specific requirements of each of these three strata of entrepreneurs in proper balance, without sacrificing the efficiency criteria.

4. Lack of Specialists' Support: Entrepreneurship is a comparatively new area of study requiring inter-disciplinary efforts by people from different disciplines. A large number of organisations/agencies engaged in entrepreneurship development in India do not have in-house specialists required and have to depend upon external faculty. The number of specialists available in the country for developing small-scale industries is not very large. As a result, many a time organisations are unable to locate/avail services of experts. On the other hand, there are specialists who have time to spare in which they can render their services to the organisations.

This apart, the ED programmes in India are afflicted with a number of operational problems. As such, though there are many institutions to train entrepreneurs, the growth of entrepreneurs is inhibited by these problems. The operational problems of EDP are as follows:

(a) Inherent inability,
(b) Diverse opinions,
(c) No proper strategy,
(d) Low institutional commitment,
(e) No local support,
(f) Non-availability of inputs,
(g) Poor follow-up,
(h) No adequate research facilities,
(i) Ill-planned training methodology,
(j) Inconsistent programme design,
(k) Perpetual ambiguity,
(l) No clear-cut objective,
(m) Lack of clarity in approach and
(n) Lack of creativity and commitment.

- There appears to be inherent inability to identify the need of the institution and differences of opinion prevailing amongst the practitioners and also amongst the trainers.
- There seems to be low institutional commitment for local support to entrepreneurs and there is low involvement of marketing, voluntary and financial institutions in the programme, except for a few.
- Non-availability of various inputs, i.e., raw materials, power etc. and infrastructural support entwined with poor follow-up by the primary monitoring institution, results in the failure of EDP.
- There seems to be ill-planned training methodology, inconsistency in programme design, its content, sequence and themes and focus of the programme is not clear.
- Training institutions do not show much concern for objective identification and selection of entrepreneurs and the follow-up training.
- Some of the institutions seem to be still debating whether to look for proper identification and selection of entrepreneurs for making successful entrepreneurs.
- Those involved and concerned with the 'selection and follow-up' activities have either limited manpower support or a narrow linkage with other support agencies.
- There does not appear to be standard course curricula even in terms of broad module being adopted by such institutions.

- Majority of the institutions engaged in EDP are themselves not convinced of what they are doing as a task delegated. by the Government of helping the policy in attaining its social objectives.
- Perceptual ambiguity of the EDP objective seems to have percolated to grassroot level with a significant distortion both in terms of content and intent.

To conclude, it can be stated that many of the issues related to an EDP are conceptual in nature, many are practical and operational and many are in the borderline between concept and practice. Research and studies, building sophisticated skills and expertise, coordinating, collaborating, corroboration of ideas and actions are necessary strategies that should be continuously pursued to confront these issues.

In the post-independence period, the nation laid stress and put its faith in science and technology. The country has made tremendous investments in scientific institutions and scientific and technical manpower. These investments need to be harvested. We have learnt that the managerial skills necessary to harvest businesses are different from the skills required to create businesses. Similarly, to create technology enterprises we may also require a different breed of managers in our institutions. Development of technical entrepreneurship and the management of science and technology cannot be dealt with in mutual exclusion.

Strategy for Entrepreneurship Development

Keeping this background in view, the following strategies of entrepreneurship development in India may be suggested:

(i) Public entrepreneurship should remain confined only to those industries and sectors where private enterprise, individual or corporate, is generally not attracted. Existing public entrepreneurship should be improved through better management and by putting relatively greater emphasis on research and development. There is need to streamline the R&D wing of public sector enterprises.

(ii) All possible efforts be made very seriously for the development of an industrial culture. It should be realised that the central core of entrepreneurship is the motive force since an appropriate, entrepreneurship implies positive action and initiative. Motivated individuals with combination of abilities and attributes can pursue their goal with enthusiasm. One can easily give examples of men like J.N. Tata or Ranchodlal Chhotalal who established their enterprises against heavy odds in the country under British rule. Without motivation, an individual cannot become a successful entrepreneur even though he may have access to finance. Individual qualities of vision, vigour, leadership and enterprise need to be inculcated.

(iii) There is need to develop management education and industrial training. In modern times, management education is being viewed as an effective supplement to the development of entrepreneurship since entrepreneurial decisions have to be effectively supported by managerial decisions. Quite often, the entrepreneur functions a manager especially in small-scale industries where the entrepreneur is his own technician and manager. This fact justifies the route of formal education and necessitates the establishment of business schools and management institutes in the country, where relevant courses may be introduced. Happily, some such institutions have come up but they should further be strengthened and developed into first-class institutions comparable with their counterparts in developed countries. In addition, facilities should be provided on an increasing scale for sending talented young men and women to business schools abroad. But, strategies should be chalked out to give a conducive environment for them to come back to India and apply this knowledge in a suitable manner. Besides, industrial training

programmes should be frequently organised. This will help in widening the mental horizon toward practical business and industrial problems. New industrial training centres well equipped may as well be established. Education and training will very much help in developing and augmenting a race of new entrepreneurs needed to harness and utilise the scarce resources for economic development.

(iv) The development of backward regions/areas constitutes a new challenge. Programmes for their development be drawn up and should be effectively implemented. Such programmes await new entrepreneurs whose technical expertise and managerial competence would bring about the desired development and fulfil social needs.

(v) Adequate measures are a must for mobilising and fostering entrepreneurial talent in the country. In this context, it should be realised that entrepreneurs are not the gift of a particular class. For instance, in Japan, innovators came from the underprivileged classes as the affluent classes had hardly any incentive to innovate. "Innovating entrepreneurs have frequently come from those classes of people normally barred from advancement to status-bearing positions."

(vi) Economic administration by the State should be improved and made more effective so that objectives of economic policies may be fully achieved in the overall interest of the country's economy. Better economic administration would go a long way in ensuring and increasing entrepreneurship. Monopoly benefits to a few big entrepreneurs is an evil and must be checked. The general policy of encouraging the small entrepreneur will go a long way in activating and broadening the leadership potential. Improvement in business climate by the state through its well-designed economic policies, be it fiscal, commercial, industrial or agricultural will benefit the entrepreneurs in a changing technological society and thus facilitate healthy development of entrepreneurship.

(vii) Institutional framework should work towards meeting major industrial or economic needs or goals. Such framework, in addition to its several facets, must place entrepreneurial development and its objectives in a proper and meaningful perspective following which entrepreneurs may plan their business activities within the bounds of such a framework for the desired coordinated development.

(viii) Greater emphasis should be put on research relating to processes and enhancement of the value of indigenous techniques. This would have an encouraging impact on entrepreneurship and technology at the domestic level. As a general rule, Indianisation of entrepreneurship should be effected in place of foreign collaboration. However, general guidelines should be stated for* cases in which foreign collaboration with well-known foreign companies may be allowed.

(ix) Financial institutions should provide adequate and timely credit and technical assistance, especially to small and medium-sized enterprises. They should also impart knowledge about the needs of the economy and they should file their massive data in terms of growth of new entrants or entrepreneurs in the field of industry. These may as well be dwelt upon at length in their reports and other publications. All this will go a long way in inculcating and sustaining entrepreneurial spirit in the newly-emerging classes.

(x) Now, special categories of entrepreneurs, viz., women, retired army personnel, handicapped persons, educated youths, Non-Resident Indians (NRIs), displaced persons etc., have appeared on the economic scene. Their emergence is more directly conditioned by economic and industrial factors and not only by social factors of caste, community and social approval or disapproval.

Factors like access to capital, business experience, opportunity to acquire technical and managerial competence have played a crucial role. For instance, in the case of light engineering products, electronics, computers and in several other new products, the entrepreneurial source is generally not traceable to any specific caste or community background. The entrepreneurs in such fields are usually technologists and in their endeavour to establish manufacturing units, they reveal a multiple basis of entrepreneurship, viz., foreign collaboration, diversification, etc. Conducive working environment should be ensured for the healthy development of such entrepreneurs in future. It is only then that their qualities of vision, vigour, leadership and enterprise can be well utilised for the industrial development of the country.

Entrepreneurship is not confined to industry and is needed in all activities. Its existence in agriculture among the cultivators, small and large, is seen by all today. The growing farm of today in many parts of the country is a proof of such entrepreneurship. The need for entrepreneurship is even greater in management of the Government, more so as it is the largest entrepreneur.

Table 4.1

EDP at a Glance

No.	Topics/Subjects
1.	Entrepreneurship motivation training
2.	Business opportunity guidance and product selection
3.	Government infrastructure and role of support institutions
4.	Steps in setting up an enterprise
5.	Market survey
6.	Cost of production, determination of price and break-even point analysis
7.	Production management
8.	Financial management
9.	Human resource management
10.	Marketing management
11.	Business administration
12.	Entrepreneurial planning
13.	Taxation
14.	Labour laws
15.	Opportunities, policy and problems
16.	Interaction with bank officials
17.	Preliminary project report preparation
18.	Interaction with successful entrepreneurs
19.	Field visits
20.	Final project report preparation
21.	Demonstrations (if any)
22.	Self-practice sessions (if applicable)

Duration of the EDP: Usually, the duration of the EDP is considered to be 13 weeks. But, the duration can vary from 15 days to 3 months also, depending on the objectives.

India has a proud record of entrepreneurship. Its present growing status in the industrial world is its proof. It has now to prepare itself for entrepreneurships of a different order. Tremendous advances of science and technology will have to be harnessed and incorporated requiring on the part of the people and the Government a more mature approach to be on par with advanced countries. Philips, Sony, Honda, Ford are the signposts of entrepreneurship today for all to emulate. Some of these have come up only in recent years and from small beginnings. In India, too, one sees glimpses of such entrepreneurship.

Conclusion

It is now well recognised that entrepreneurs can be developed through appropriately designed entrepreneurship development programmes. These programmes broadly envisage a three-tiered approach: developing achievement motivation and sharpening of entrepreneurial traits and behaviour, project planning and development and guidance on industrial opportunities, incentives and facilities and rules and regulations, and developing managerial and operational capabilities. Various techniques and approaches have been developed and adopted to achieve these objectives, keeping in view the targetgroups and/or target areas. The structuring of the programmes and training methodology also necessitate consideration of the specific target-groups and target areas. Methodology for selection of the prospective entrepreneurs as well as support services after the training have significant impact on the success of the entrepreneur development programmes.

More importantly, the Government and the financial institutions are in forefront in entrepreneurial development. However, it is said that various training programmes of these institutions work at training people for self-employment to acquire gainful employment. Thus the very purpose of developing entrepreneurial talent among the youths is defeated. This calls for a critical evaluation of EDPs and of personnel with conviction and commitment to undertake the task of planning, designing and implementing programmes in this area. More importantly, entrepreneurial programmes must be attuned to Indian economic environment and be made available in regional languages. The need of the hour is to develop genuine and not imitative entrepreneurs to accelerate the process of industrialisation. The need of the hour is for stimulating innovation and the entrepreneurial spirit to support the. development of new ideas through new and mature enterprises.

The entrepreneurs themselves constitute the human factors and their needs as a human being must, therefore, not be overlooked. Being the kingpin in the whole small enterprise development game, the human factors involved in the small and medium-scale industry must be analysed, assisted to grow and develop.

The success of small industries depends upon the entrepreneurial and managerial capabilities of those involved in the business. Because of its size and unique operation characteristics, a small industry requires a management approach which is also unique. In general, small industries are managed in a personalized fashion. Their managers or entrepreneurs tend to know all the employees personally. They participate in all aspects of managing the business and there is usually no sharing in the decision-making process. As far as the scope and scale of operations are concerned, small industries, generally serve a local or regional market rather than a national or international one. They also tend to have a very limited share of any given market. These special characteristics must, therefore, be taken into account in the planning of small industries development on a national scale.

The human factor or the entrepreneur should also be considered. The entrepreneurial spirit, as mentioned earlier, involves not only a desire to gain monetary benefits but also an admixture of the characteristics of a high achiever, and social, family and service motives. Long-term involvement with a goal. which the entrepreneur has set for himself creates the need to persist with an undertaking even in the face of difficulties.

Management and entrepreneurial skill must, therefore be blended in the small industry owner's total make-up as these will spell the difference between success and failure. The ideal would be to find a person who is both efficient and effective. Without the latter capabilities, a person may simply be a good manager. He still has to be developed into an effective manager by inculcating the entrepreneurial spirit in him. A small enterprise development programme, therefore, must take into consideration upgrading the managerial and entrepreneurial skills in the whole country in order to create a pool of enlightened entrepreneurs who can form a strong small industry sector in the business community of the country concerned.

The ability of an enterprise to wield influence to change the status quo would be an appropriate definition of power. The enterprises that enjoy the greatest influence are those that lead in their industry sectors, by making the biggest impact on consumers through innovative ideas, winning strategies and bold tactics.

Sunil Bharti Mittal

In the corporate world, we don't see the sense of power that people outside think of us as having. Every one of my customers has more power than me, since he can take away my business with the stroke of a pen.

Nr Narayana Murthy

Power is a double-edged sword and hence should be managed very carefully. It is imprudent to be reckless when you are in the driver's seat. Judge the situation exhaustively and discreetly before charting your course of action and be brave enough to face the consequences of your decision.

Deepak Parekh

Power is generally measured by the authority to allocate resources or used to demonstrate how many people you have in your organisation. To me, power is about influence. It is about how much influence your ideas have. That is a more effective way of measuring power.

CK Prahalad

❋ ❋ ❋

5

Institutions in Aid of Entrepreneurship Development

Introduction

Since 1950, a substantial volume of study has gone into the different facets of entrepreneurial development in India to accelerate the process of industrialisation. The study showed that entrepreneurs are born and can also be made – their skills sharpened, quality of an enterprise improved and generated in good number. It is possible to identify individuals in all communities, in rural and urban areas, among men and women with entrepreneurial talent, to motivate and train them through properly organised programmes undertaking risk-bearing innovative activities for raising the growth rate in agriculture, in industry as well as in the service sector.

The Entrepreneurial Development Programmes (EDPs) thus became a new concept for harnessing the vast untapped human resources. The EDPs are presently one of the most talked about social development activities which many organisations have taken up in right earnest. It strikes a welcome note in respect of change in perception and recognition of the critical role the entrepreneurs play in industrial development by creating potential avenues for self-employment.

Focus of EDPs

While organising EDPs, it should be remembered that entrepreneurs cannot be created like degreeholders in a university and that it would be necessary to eliminate those who do not possess the basic capabilities for entering into business ventures, weed out such persons and help develop latent facilities of those who possess the potential for becoming entrepreneurs.

As the quality of entrepreneurship differs from region to region, the type of inputs that a particular group of entrepreneurs would require should be understood clearly and the training programmes tailored accordingly. Training should be not only to set up an industrial venture but also to enable the trainee to run it successfully. The focus of EDP should be on the person rather than on the project and this calls for proper counselling facilities available to the trainees. These programmes should be conducted in places where necessary infrastructure for training is available and proximity of the support agencies is assured. This would underline the need for proper selection of the trainees. It should be ensured that the trainees show interest in setting up industries and that they do not treat the ED as a stop Ps gap arrangement for taking up a job subsequently. For this purpose, we should think new techniques to make the process of selection more appropriate. Poor involvement on the part of the institutions as also trainees and an incorrect selection of target groups contribute largely to the failure of a number of EDPs. One of the objects of training should be on changing the attitude and set of mind of young people from security-oriented activities to risktaking through entrepreneurship development.

Entrepreneurship Development Programme Organisations

There are several organisations engaged in conducting entrepreneurship development programmes in India. The lead in the matter was given by Small Industries Development Organisation through its Small Industries Service Centres.

In the area of creation of the institutional infrastructure for entrepreneurship development, the first step of Indian financial institutions including IFCI was the establishment of Entrepreneurship Development Institute of India (EDII) in March, 1983, at Ahmedabad as a resource organisation at the national level. The Central Government also established in the same year the National Institute for Entrepreneurship and Small Business Development (NIESBUD) at New Delhi, with the objective of coordinating activities related to entrepreneurship and small business development. Both these organisations are working hand in hand for giving a fillip to the entrepreneurship development movement.

In addition, institutions established by the government are: Rural Entrepreneurship Development Institute (RED) at Ranchi in 1983, Rural Management and Management Centres (RMEDC) at Maharashtra and Training cum Development Centres (RDCS) aim increasing interaction between entrepreneurs and enterprise.

This apart, a host of management institutions, various universities have included entrepreneurship development in their Curriculum.

Other organisations that have been actively conducting entrepreneurship development programmes are State Bank of India; financial institutions such as IDBI; Entrepreneurial Motivation Training Centre in Northern-Eastern Region; Xavier Institute of Social Services, Ranchi; industrial consultancy organisations in various states; Centre for Entrepreneurship Development, Ahmedabad; state financial corporations; the Centre for Entrepreneurship Development, Hubli; Small Industries Extension Training Institute, Hyderabad; National Science and Technology Entrepreneurship Development Board etc.

For institutionalising the entrepreneurship development activities at the state level, Institutes of Entrepreneurship Development (IEDs) in Uttar Pradesh, Bihar and Orissa have already come into existence with the support of India's financial institutions, concerned State Governments and banks, and are carrying on their activities on a full-fledged basis. During the period under review, a Centre for Entrepreneurship Development (CED) was registered in Madhya Pradesh on 17th November, 1988, taken up later by IFCI. An Institute for Entrepreneurship Development was also set up at Goa under DB on the same pattern as other IEDs. A proposal to set up an IED for North-Eastern Region was also under consideration by the North Eastern Council. A few State Governments of Karnataka, Andhra Pradesh, Rajasthan, etc., have also expressed the desire to set up CEDs in their respective States. The proposals of these State Governments to be considered on their merits by the financial institutions in due course, while the focus of the national organisations like

EDII, NIESBUD etc., continued to be on *(a)* institutional entrepreneurship activities, *(b)* generating, sharpening and sharing knowledge through research documentation and publication, *(c)* creating and developing professionals in the discipline of 'entrepreneurship' to emerge and flourish, and *(e)* developing new products and pursuing market segments for carrying the entrepreneurship development in priority areas and sections of the people. The State-level Institutes/ CEDs endeavoured to carry out at the grass-root level to provide the support of human resources to various State and district EDPs level organisations engaged in entrepreneurship. The State-level organisations also continued to provide industrial extension motivation services, business opportunities guidance, project counselling, etc., and helped in initiating entrepreneurship at school level in the career planning of the younger generation. For this these organisations conducted, during the period under review, a number of workshops, seminars, conferences brought out well researched publications, for training of entrepreneurs. The organisations also produced a number of video films as audio visual aids for training the entrepreneurs and motivating them towards enterprise setting and operating the same on sound and healthier lines.

Management Development Institute (MDI)

For developing and improving the quality of day-to-day management, which is so crucial for the success of any industrial venture, as also, with a view to encouraging professionalisation in management, IFCI had sponsored in 1973, the Management Development Institute (MDI) at Gurgaon (Haryana) near Delhi. MDI is now a cornucopia of management training, research and consultancy, its prime goal being to improve managerial effectiveness in the industry/government and banking sectors of the economy. Research studies undertaken by MD are in both macro areas of economic and industrial development as also in micro areas relevant to a specific industry or economic activity.

A mention was made in the last year's Annual Report about MD having been chosen by the Government of India, Department of Personnel and Training as an agency for conducting the first-ever intensive 15 month National Management Programme (NMP) for Government Officers belonging to IAS/ Group 'A' Services as well as executives from public and private sector organisations having potential to acquire top positions.

MDI conduct Management Development Programmes in various disciplines. These programmes included the programmes for officers of the Indian Economic Service (IES), Indian Administrative Service (IAS) and for the executives of a number of PSUs of, like Oil & Natural Gas Commission (ONGC), Bharat Heavy Electrical Ltd. (BHEL), Bharat Aluminiurn Co. Ltd. (BALCO), Export Credit Guarantee Corporation of India (ECGC), Bureau of Indian Standards (BIS), Hindustan Zinc Ltd. (HZL), Hindustan Machine Tools Ltd, (HMT), Indian Drugs & Pharmaceuticals Ltd. (IDPL), Uttar Pradesh State Industrial Development Corporation Ltd. (UPSIDC), Madhya Pradesh Financial Corporation (MPFC), etc.

MDI also had conducted in Karnataka a programme on Identification, Promotion and Implementation of Industrial Projects (IPIIP), special catering to the needs of officers of District Industries Centres (DICs), State-level Promotional and Financial Institutions, Commercial Banks, etc. In addition, a number of programmes, particularly in concerning strategic planning, marketing of new products, strengthening of cooperative short-term credit system, marketing and sales, management consultancy, development banking, labour-management relations, human resources development, of small industries financing performance evaluation, role of directors, merchant banking, leasing, working capital financing, technology transfer, management, documentation and recovery practices of Development Financing Institutions, etc., were carried out by MDI and its subsidiary Development Banking Centre (DBC). As many as 23 workshops were conducted by MDI under the Planning Commission International Labour Organisation United Nations Development Programme, In-house Management Consultancy Development Project (Phase II).

A major effort was also made by MDI during the period in the area of consultancy and research – focus was not only on developing management consultancy through training programmes and workshops but also undertaking process consultancy assignments in large complex organisations and directing efforts to develop in-house management consultancy teams in public utilities. The Consultancy and Research Wings of MDI have done extensive work in areas like corporate planning, evaluation of appraisal systems, feasibility studies, job structuring, management information systems, manpower planning, marketing appraisal, capital markets, offshore banking, inter-firm comparison, seed capital, technology – its relevance, assessment and diffusion etc.

The National Institute for Entrepreneurship and Small Business Development (NIESBUD)

The need for a national organisation to serve as an apex body to co-ordinate the training programmes of various centres and organisations in the country, to train a larger number of trainers and motivators in entrepreneurship development, to prepare model syllabuses of training for various target groups and target areas, etc. was felt for further accelerating training in entrepreneurship.

The Delhi-based National Institute for Entrepreneurship and Small Business Development (NIESBUD), established by the Government of India, is an apex body for coordinating and overseeing the activities of various institutions and agencies engaged in entrepreneurship development particularly in the area of small industry and small business. The Institute, registered as a Society under Government of India Societies Act XXI of 1860, started functioning from 6 July, 1983.

Over the years, the Institute stands devoted to evolving model syllabi for training various target groups by effective training strategies, methodology, manuals and tools; facilitating and supporting Central/State governments and other agencies in executing programmes of entrepreneurship and small business development; maximising benefit and accelerating entrepreneurship development; conducting programmes for motivators, trainers and entrepreneurs which are commonly not undertaken by other agencies. Above all organising those that help in developing entrepreneurial culture is worth appreciation in society. The Institute is also the secretariat of the National Entrepreneurship Development Board (NEDB), the apex body which determines policy for entrepreneurship development in the country. The Institute, therefore, performs the task of processing the recommendations made by the Board.

Objectives

The main objectives of the Institute are:

- To accelerate the process of entrepreneurship development ensuring its impact throughout the country and among all segments of the society.
- To help/support institutions/agencies in carrying out activities relating to entrepreneurship development with greater success.
- To evolve standardised process of selection, training support and sustenance to potential entrepreneurs enabling them to set up and run their enterprise successfully.

— To provide vital information support to trainers, promoters and entrepreneurs by organising documentation and research work relevant to entrepreneurship development.

— To provide functional forums for interaction and exchange of experiences helpful for policy formulation and modification at various levels.

Since development of entrepreneurship and self-employment is basically a promotional and industrial extension activity, the programmes organised by the Institute are mostly by the founded government. However, the institute's training activities are restricted to areas in which either demand for programmes is very great or there is absence of such training programmes. For organisations directly or indirectly engaged in promoting entrepreneurship and self-employment in the country, the NIESBUD's role is that of a catalyst as it helps in developing the effectiveness of all these organisations. Programmmes initiated/sponsored by the NIESBUD are constantly evaluated and revised to suit the changing needs in the area of entrepreneurship and small business development. The institute is engaged in creating a climate conducive for entrepreneurship and in developing favourable attitude amongst the general public in support of those who opt for entrepreneurial career.

Activities

The activities of the Institute include evolving effective training strategies and methodology; standardising model syllabi for training various target groups; formulating scientific selection procedures; developing training aids, manuals and tools; facilitating and supporting Central/ State/other agencies in executing entrepreneurship development programmes; maximising the benefits and accelerating the process of entrepreneurship development.

The various functions which the National Institute has been called upon to perform are as follows:

- To serve as an apex national level institute.;
- To organise and conduct training programmes;
- To co-ordinate the training activities of various institutes and organisations in the country imparting training in entrepreneurship;
- To affiliate institutes and organisations conducting entrepreneurship training;
- To identify, train and assist potential entrepreneurs amongst technical and non-technical personnel in setting up self-employment ventures in small industries including service industries;
- To hold examinations and tests and confer certificates and diplomas on the trainers as well as trainees;
- To undertake documentation and research in the field of entrepreneurship and small business development;
- To conduct workshops, seminars and conferences, etc. for promotion and development of entrepreneurship in small scale industries and small business;
- To publish literature for furtherance of entrepreneurship and small business development;
- To provide a forum for interaction and exchange of view with agencies engaged in various aspect of entrepreneurship in small industries and small business development.
- To assist in setting up of regional and state level training institutes for entrepreneurship and small business development.

The Institute interacts with all other organisation centres engaged in conducting entrepreneurship development programmes in the country and provides them support in various areas including funding of programmes wherever necessary and feasible. The Institute addresses itself to working with them in enhancing the efficiency and utility of entrepreneurship development programmes bringing about co-ordination.

With the setting up of this Institute, entrepreneurship development in India through organised training has assumed added significance particularly for training educated unemployed youth for taking up self-employment ventures.

Entrepreneurship Development Institute of India (EDII)

Entrepreneurship Development Institute of India (EDII). Ahemdabad, is an autonomous non-profit institution, set up in 1983, sponsored by financial institutions such as Industrial Development.

Industrial Development Bank of India (IDBI), Industrial Finance Corporation of India (IFCI), Industrial Credit and Investment Corporation of India (ICICI) and the State Bank of India (SBI). The Government of Gujarat has also provided assistance for the setting up of EDII.

EDII has been spearheading an entrepreneurship movement throughout the nation with a belief that entrepreneurs need not necessarily be born; they can be developed through well-conceived and well-directed activities.

In consonance with this belief, the objectives of the EDII are to:

- augment the supply of trained entrepreneurs through training;
- generate a multiplier effect on opportunities for self-employment;
- improve managerial capabilities of small-scale industries;
- contribute to the dispersal of business ownership and thus expand the social base of Indian entrepreneurial class;
- contribute to the creation and dissemination of new knowledge and insight into entrepreneurial theory and practice through research;
- augment the supply of trainer-motivators for entrepreneurship development;
- participate in institution-building efforts;
- sensitise the support environment to facilitate potential as well as existing entrepreneurs to establish and manage their enterprises;
- promote micro-enterprises at the rural level;
- inculcate the spirit of 'Entrepreneurship' amongst youth and
- collaborate with similar organisations in India and other developing countries to accomplish the above objectives.

Training Programmes

The training programmes of the Institute are grouped under four heads:

- Entrepreneurship in education;

- Micro-finance and micro-enterprise development;
- Performance and growth of existing entrepreneurs and
- Performance improvement of ED institutions and ED programmes.

The educational environment and policy framework offer opportunities for sustainable self-employment to ensure the contribution of the workforce to the industrial economy. Entrepreneurship, self-employment and enterprise creation thus provide a solution to the crisis of both unemployment and disguised unemployment. With this in view, the EDII has designed and successfully implemented several national and international training programmes and workshops for the academic community and for the youth.

EDII organises training programmes on Informal Micro Credit Delivery Systems (IMCDS) and management for strengthening the participating NGOs in the area of informal credit. To strengthen NGOs through building their managerial capabilities, the EDII has launched a programme on the sustainability of NGOs through better management. It also provides a platform to NGOs and bankers with the objective of facilitating the access of the poor to credit.

The small industry sector is required to gear up to face the challenges of liberalisation and globalisation. The EDII in 1984 initiated Performance Improvement Programmes in anticipation of the need of management strategy and growth-oriented awareness and competencies. These programmes focus on functional management inputs and strategic techniques, thereby channelising entrepreneurial competencies to rejuvenate enterprises.

The Institute conceptualises and designs several strategic programmes through innovative training techniques and updated information and documentation. It regularly organises trainers' meets and chief executives' meets to foster linkages among trainers and chief executives of ED organisations to facilitate and experience sharing.

EDII has supported the creation of Centres for Entrepreneurship Development and Institutes of Entrepreneurship Development in various states of the country to achieve institutionalisation of ED activities.

Institutes for Entrepreneurship Development

As part of a strategy of giving special attention to entrepreneurship development needs of the more backward states, IDBI had announced the proposal to set up Institutes for Entrepreneurship Development (IEDs) in association with other financial institutions and banks and the State Governments. IEDs set up in Uttar Pradesh, Bihar and Orissa have become operational and the proposed IED in Madhya Pradesh has already been registered.

IED in the UP had conducted 16 EDPs covering 664 trainees, besides training state level trainers. It also has conducted programmes on industrial extension motivation, business opportunity guidance and project counselling for women, entrepreneurial awareness workshop for ex servicemen, state level meet of EDP conducting agencies, studies on "Factors inhibiting and facilitating turnaround possibilities in small sector' and "Relevance of hill wool scheme.' IED in Orissa had conducted 11 EDPs which benefited 307 trainees. It also conducted four Management Development programmmes, four entrepreneurship awareness camps and lecture-cum-discussion session on 'Problems and Prospects of Indo-US Trade and Investment." IED in Bihar conducted two EDPs and organised an entrepreneurs' meet during the period under review.

Science and Technology Entrepreneurship Parks (STEPs)

As part of the programme for supporting the setting up of 15 STEPs jointly with other institutions, IDBI over the years has assisted seven STEPs, viz., those sponsored by the Birla Institute of Technology (BIT), Ranchi, National Entrepreneurs Chemical Park (NECP), Regional Engineering College (TREC), Trichy, Harcourt Butler Technological Institute (HBTI), Kanpur, Sri Jayachamarajendra College of Engineering (SJCE), Mysore, Guru Nanak Engineering College, Ludhiana and Maulana Azad College of Technology, Bhopal with the aggregate assistance of Rs. 6.2 crore. While the first five STEPs were sanctioned assistance prior or 1988-89, the last two were sanctioned assistance during the reporting period. STEPs proposed by Guru Nanak Engineering College will specialise in machine tools and electro-mechanical control equipment while the STEP sponsored by the Maulana Azad College of Technology will be specialising in electronics and power engineering.

BIT-STEP has developed a unique technology for automatic wire length measurement system and import substitutive stainless steel wedge wire screen, besides other technologies for industrial applications. NECP is engaged in the preparation of project profiles of selected imported drugs.

TREC-STEP has developed technology for hi-tech paints for nuclear applications, besides other hi-tech and import-substitutive products. Commercial production had already been started by seven TREC-STEP entrepreneurs. Student entrepreneurs of HBTI-STEP are working on projects which include fibre reinforced concrete and plastic components. SJCE-STEP has already transferred technology of liquid level pump controller to one of its entrepreneurs for commercial exploitation and eight of the STEP entrepreneurs have established their units.

The Centre for Entrepreneurship Development

Development of entrepreneurs on a systematic basis started in 1970. A number of specialised institutions came up to provide training to various target groups – educated unemployed persons, women, technicians, foremen, rural artisans, physically handicapped persons, etc. The Centre for Entrepreneurship Development (CED), Ahmedabad was sponsored by the State government and public sector corporations concerned with industrial development in the State. This Centre conducts entrepreneurship development programmes. Persons were selected from amongst the employees, workers, merchants and graduates and training was imparted at six centres. The following are some of the significant features of the programme of training:

(a) Before conducting the programme of training, a survey of investment opportunity was made for identifying industries having good scope in the area;

(b) Appropriate linkage was developed with various agencies which provide support and service to entrepreneurs in getting finance, readymade sheds, raw materials and other inputs;

(c) Entrepreneurs were selected through bahavioural tests. Due weightage on experience was given rather than education or unemployment;

(d) Programmes of training included theoretical and practical coverage, including visits to industrial units consistent with the items identified by the entrepreneurs;

(e) Follow-up action was taken by the full-time project leader and individual attention was given to each entrepreneur trainee.

The success rate of CED programmes is reported to be of the order of 66 per cent.

The Entrepreneurial Motivation Centre, set up in Assam in the north-eastern region of India, conducts entrepreneurial development programmes. In the earlier stages 28 officers drawn from various departments of the state government were given training in entrepreneurial motivation, economic investigation and survey, management of small enterprise etc. in the Small Industries Extension training Institute in Hyderabad. These officers then joined the various branches of the Entrepreneurial Motivation Training Centre in six districts.

The Entrepreneurial Motivation Training Centre gave wide publicity to the entrepreneurial development programmes and invited applications from educated unemployed persons. Selection was made based on psychological tests and personal interviews. Selected entrepreneurs were given preliminary motivation training of two weeks for developing or strengthening the motivation for self-employment, managerial and economic aspects of entrepreneurial development. The entrepreneurs were further assisted in selecting enterprises for themselves, conducting guided market surveys and preparing economically viable and feasible projects reports. The Centre acted as link agency and helped the entrepreneurs in obtaining finance from banks and other institutions, and readymade sheds as working space. The Centre further provided 10 per cent of the sanctioned amount as seed money wherever necessary. An evaluation revealed that by March 1975, the number of entrepreneurs trained came to 1,550, of which 1,053 entrepreneurs (68 per cent) completed their project reports and 581 were given in-plant training. Among those who completed the project reports, 310 entrepreneurs were assisted in obtaining sanction of financial assistance. Of these 310 entrepreneurs, 279 (90 per cent) actually established their enterprises and started functioning.

Central Manufacturing Technology Institute, Bangalore

The Xavier Institute of Social Service in Ranchi was involved with tribals and people from the villages in training to become entrepreneurs. A group of young tribal youths constituted into a local organisation for promotion of socio-economic and health schemes (known as Vikas Maitry) received some funds from the Indo-German Social Service Society in New Delhi in 1975. They desired that an entrepreneurship development programme be run for them. A project leader who himself was a tribal was appointed. The programme was organised and 20 candidates were selected, all belonging to tribal areas. In selecting, little importance was given to academic qualifications. Clarity of presentation of goals and determination to reach that goal were the important considerations. Four months full-time training was arranged. During the day the entrepreneurs worked as apprentices in shops of the type they intended to set up themselves. In the evening, they got a grounding in the basis of achievements, motivation, leadership and communication, management, finances, costing, laws and taxation, marketing and project preparation. After completion of the training course, the entrepreneurs went back to their respective villages and made mini-market surveys. They brought back the field data and worked these into a project proposal for financing by the bank. The financing was undertaken through the intermediacy of Vikas Maitri Kalyan Sangh and the organisation undertook to stand guarantee for the young entrepreneurs. Continuous and sustained follow-up action was undertaken. This was the responsibility of the project officer and assistant project officer. A success rate of 60 per cent was attained. The State government later gave assistance to the Institute for conducting entrepreneurial development programmes for unemployed engineers, diploma holders, graduates and ITI trained boys and the Institute has done well.

Role of Development Banks

Various development banks in India have introduced "special capital' and "seed capital' schemes to provide equity of assistance to new and technically-skilled entrepreneurs who lack financial resources of their own. In view of the long-term benefits to society from the emergence of a new class of entrepreneurs, development banks have been actively involved in entrepreneurship development programmes and in establishing a set of institutions which identify and train potential entrepreneurs. The promotional activities like carrying out industrial potential surveys, identification of potential entrepreneurs, conducting entrepreneurship development programmes and providing technical consultancy services have contributed in a significant manner to the process of industrialisation and effective utilisation of institutional finance by industry. In recent years, the development banks have initiated special measures for the creation of specialised institutions for the training of entrepreneurs and research in this field.

Role of Business Schools

Can any B-school actually teach ENTREPRENEURSHIP?

To the would-be MBA entrepreneur, 'O' no longer spells opportunity as much as opportunity cost. Yet, interest in entrepreneurship as a subject is growing steadily in Indian B-school campuses.

They have entrepreneurship cells, business plan contests, elective courses and, in some cases, fullfledged entrepreneurship centres, some going so far as to provide 'incubation support.' The question remains: can entrepreneurship really be 'taught'? And the case study method answer is: it depends.

Originally, entrepreneurship courses were meant to literally 'produce entrepreneurs.' In 1947, Harvard Business School (HBS) developed an elective titled 'Management of Small Enterprises' for students eager to start their own businesses after World War II. The real thrust into teaching and research in the area came in the early 1980s when HBS graduate and pioneering venture capitalist Arthur Rock funded the first professorship in the field of entrepreneurship at HBS.

Under legendary Professor Howard H. Stevenson, entrepreneurship came to be defined not just as an 'innate trait' but a particular type of managerial behaviour available to virtually all managers in organisations of all kinds and sizes. Today HBS requires its 900 first-year students to take a course called 'The Entrepreneurial Manager', and offers almost 20 elective courses in the area to its second year students. American B-schools, including the likes of Wharton, offer entrepreneurial management as a major, 'preparing students for careers as autonomous entrepreneurs, family business entrepreneurs, or entrepreneurs in. corporate setting. Entrepreneurship centres have also become an integral feature at campuses in the US, thanks to corporates and individuals who are keen to fund them. The University of Michigan, for example, got $10 million to set up such a centre in 1999.

In contrast, Indian B-schools have made a more modest foray into entrepreneurship education. Every self-respecting B-school offers at least one elective in the area as part of the second year of the postgraduate programme (PGP). And interest from students is high. At IIM Lucknow, the 'New Venture Planning' (NVP) course has seen an enrolment as high as 70 per cent in some years. The course gives perspectives from all functional areas like marketing, finance, operations, strategy and also preparation of business plans. IIM Bangalore offers as many as four electives covering the entire gamut – from the regulation 'Managing New Ventures' to the gung-ho 'Entrepreneurship from the Trenches: A Real World Perspective.' Further, a course in 'Social Entrepreneurship' is being introduced. In March 2002, IIM-B set up the Nadathur S. Raghavan Centre for Entrepreneurial Learning (NSRCEL) with a generous grant from N.S. Raghavan, one of the co-founders of Infosys Technologies (See 'Incubation, The New Buzzword').

In addition to supporting teaching and research, NSRCEL has a state-of-the-art incubator "to help entrepreneurs launch their business plans into commercially viable products and services." The problem is, students of the PGP seem to be showing little interest (so far) in utilising its facilities. "Most of the entrepreneurship courses are not taken seriously as they are taught in the fifth and sixth term when marks are not counted for placements," a second-year student points out. "There is a 'Start-up Club' as well in the campus, but its activities are infrequent and limited to a few VC lectures and games."

While the NSRCEL incubator can house about 10 teams of up to six members each, it currently supports just two – education BPO Meta-i Technologies and software company EmbedX. Neither boasts any IIM-B students or alumni. There are some practical issues adding to the problem. For instance, the NSRCEL board meets only once in six months to evaluate new entrepreneurial ideas. But at the heart of the matter lies the same old argument: IIMs are a platform to get lucrative jobs, which you won't get once you are out of this place.

This very attitude is being attacked head on – with remarkable success – with 'Laboratory in Entrepreneurial Motivation' (LEM), an elective course at IIM Ahmedabad. Taught since 1992 by IIM-A alumnus and entrepreneur Sunil Handa, the course has no textbook, no readings, no quizzes, no test, no exams. No fundas on how to apply for loans or make project reports – students can always figure that out later. LEM simply targets the 'fear factor' involved in spurning or giving up a job to start out on your own.

EDPs OF SIDBI

The aim of SIDBI's EDPs is to build and nurture a reservoir of enterpreneurs. Such EDPs are conducted through the specialised agencies in Entrepreneurship Development Institute of India, Institutes of Entrepreneurship Development (IEDs), Centre for Entrepreneurship Development (CEDs), Technical Consultancy Organisation (TCOs) and Non-Governmental Organisations (NGOs).

Management deficiency and a low level of skills and technology have been some of the major weaknesses of small industries. SIDBI is constantly endeavouring to address these problems by bringing reputed management and technical institutions close to the small scale industries and arranging specially designed programmes, viz., Small Industries Management Assistants' Programme (SIMAP) and skill-cum-Technology Upgradation Programme (STUP). The objective of SIMAP is to develop a cadre of industrieal managers specifically trained to assist the SSI entrepreneurs in their multiple responsibilities. STUP is structured to improve the performance of the existing SSI units by developing/strengthening managerial skills and the technical competence of the entrereneurs and senior executives of the small enterprises.

The Institutes of Entrepreneurship Development (IEDs) set up with Bank's support in Bihar, Orissa, Madhya Pradesh and Uttar Pradesh, continued to make good progress.

Box 5.1: Incubation, The New Buzzword

In sync with the global trends, Indian B-schools are jumping onto the wealth creation bandwagon. Entrepreneurship centres offering research, training and incubation facilities are coming up all over the place.

IIM-A set up the Centre for Innovation, Incubation and Entrepreneurship (CIIE) in 2001 through grants from the Gujarat government and National Innovation Foundation, and its own funds.

IIM-C set up a Centre for Entrepreneurship and Innovation to spearhead activities to promote, train and incubate entrepreneurial ventures, especially in high-tech areas.

Member's K.J. Somaiya Institute of Management Studies and Research is setting up the Centre of Excellence in Entrepreneurship with Strathclyde University's Hunter Centre for Entrepreneurship.

The ICFAI Centre for Enterpreneurship Development at Hyderabad offers training as well as incubation facilities (It presently supports one company).

Mudra Institute of Communications, Ahmedabad (Mica) has set up an entrepreneurship development centre (EDC).

ISB Hyderabad's Wadhwani Centre for Entrepreneurial Development aims to "inspire the next generation of entrepreneurs to create 1,000 new businesses over the next 10 years." It is funded and chaired by Romesh Wadhwani, former vice-chairman, 12 Technologies.

On paper, everything looks great. Most of the centres plan to the in-house student community, as well as offer services and training to outsiders. IIM-C hopes to network with other top educational institutions in the eastern region, and all the incubators are open to evaluating proposals from 'anyone with a viable business plan'. However, the centres haven't been able to enthuse their students – not even those with entrepreneurial ambitions.

But that might be changing. At Mica, Raunica Sethi, a 2004 graduate, is the first student whose dream is being supported by the centre on campus. Sethi plans to set up a 'Career Exploration, Training and Counselling' centre to guide students. She is spending a year as a project associate at Mica's EDC-time that she is using to put her ideas into practice. And for the very first time, Anveshan, a national search for innovation by IIM-A's CIIE, has thrown up a second-year student from the campus as a winner. 'Biosynthesis of Nanomaterials', a project submitted by Kunal Upadhyaya (IIM-A) and Dr. Murali Sastry (National Chemical Laboratory, Pune) bagged third place in the 'Innovation/Prototype in search of an enterprise' category.

CIIE is offering incubation support to Upadhyaya as well as team from IIIT Gwalior which won gold in the 'business plan' category. This means not just working space and computers, but mentoring as well as networking to see the idea through to the commercialisation stage. Says CIIE co-ordinator Somnath Chatterjee: "The dream is that one day we will have not just banks and consultants, but VCs chasing our students on Day 1." Amen.

SIDBI's strategy for entrepreneurship development involves support to specially designed programmes covering the target groups like rural poor, women, Scheduled Castes/Tribes, ex servicemen, etc. In tune with the renewed policy initiatives on rural development, the Bank has given thrust to promote rural entrepreneurs. This is evident from the fact that of 102 EDPs supported, during the 1994-95 for various target groups, 66 were exclusively targeted at rural entrepreneurs. Besides rural EDPs conducted during the current year, SIDBI supported 30 EDPs for women and 8 for other groups having special focus on North Eastern and other backward areas. A few specialised technical institutes like Central Institute of Plastic Engineering & Technology at Bhopal, Patna, Lucknow and Madras; Rural Technology Institute, Ahmedabad and UP Electronics Corporation, Lucknow were extended assistance for conduct of product specific EDPs. To back up the EDP efforts, the Bank has been compiling project profiles on viable project ideas suitable for tiny and rural entrepreneurs. A compendium of Profiles on Food Processing and Agrobased Industries, prepared by Central Food Technological Research Institute, Mysore, on behalf of SIDBI, was brought out during the year. Two more compendia – one on new hi-tech projects prepared by various CSR laboratories in collaboration with National Research Development Corporation and the other on location neutral projects (Volume - 11), prepared by Gujarat Industrial and Technical Consultancy Organisation Ltd. have been Published.

Role of Commercial Banks

The State Bank of India at that time was the only bank amongst commercial banks to come out with a comprehensive programme for entrepreneurship development. From the orthodox role of commercial banks, the State Bank of India pioneered as a premier banking institution in India by assuming the role of a development bank. The sixties and early seventies saw many important strides towards the fulfilment of this objective. The bank recognised the importance of small-scale industries in industrial development and started financing small-scale industries on a large scale. To cater to he specific needs of this sector a package of schemes and programmes was formulated by the bank. These are in (i) Liberalised scheme of financing small-scale industries wherein 75 per cent of the project cost is met as bank loan; (ii) Entrepreneur scheme for financing technically-qualified persons where the entire project cost could be financed by way of term loan; and (iii) Equity Fund Scheme for providing interest-free loan to meet the equity gap up to Rs. 1 lakh.

Approach Modifications

Looking to the characteristics of the small-scale industries, it must be realised that these are basically owner-manager oriented and need special attention and support. The norms for financing such industries were, therefore, liberalised and a need-based approach was evolved – a major departure from earlier security-oriented approach.

Non-financial Support

In spite of liberalisation in financing policy and government incentives, the progress in industrialisation was not so rapid. Realising that mere provision of financial support was not sufficient for bringing about that desired change, the need was felt for evolving a policy of providing for non-financial assistance. A number of measures were thereafter initiated – development of management skills of the SSI borrowers through Management Development Programmes and Management Appreciation Programmes. The bank went to the extent of conducting training programmes for development of entrepreneurial attitude and financing such entrepreneurs. It was indeed the beginning of a new banking era.

To set up an industry, the ability to meet the margin money requirements of the small-scale project itself is not enough, but entrepreneurial characteristics have to be identified and reinforced in the entrepreneur of that industry. Thus the important characteristics of the entrepreneur, namely, psychological, economic, social and managerial characteristics, have to be learnt, understood and digested by every prospective entrepreneur. For the success of the industry, the man behind the project is more important than its fixed assets; the entrepreneur has to be trained well. Industrial and Technical Consultancy Organisation Limited (ITCO), as subsidiary of Industrial Development Bank of India, having a professional experience in counselling the entrepreneurs, identifying the project ideas and preparing detailed project reports, conducting EDPs with the following objectives:

(1) Assess and develop entrepreneurial abilities required to become a successful industrialist.

(2) Dissemination of information on the formalities and procedures to be followed for starting small-scale industries.

(3) Dissemination of information on the facilities and incentives available for starting small-scale industries.

(4) Guidance in selecting projects suitable for different trainees based on their investment, educational background, technical expertise, proficiency, aptitude, etc.

(5) Acting as a liaison between the various officers/organisation engaged in industrial promotional activities in the State and trainees for availing of necessary facilities available in their projects.

(6) Dissemination of information on how to plan and manage a small-scale industry successfully.

These programmes cover all educated unemployed youths —

(1) Having a strong desire to set up an industry and having the confidence of its success.

(2) With basic technical qualification of S.S.C. with 5 years' industrial experience.

(3) In the age group of 21 to 35 years.

(4) Able to invest the required share capital (25 per cent of project cost) to the selected project.

(5) With independent thinking and decision-making status.

(6) Claiming nativity of the district.

This course is intended to give a working knowledge of industrial promotional agencies, project report preparation, general management of small-scale industries, besides transforming the prospective entrepreneurs by achievement motivation. These programmes include the academic inputs necessary for the purpose.

SBI's Programmes

The State Bank of India formulated an elaborate plan to conduct the EDPs, particularly in the backward areas and started conducting such programmes since 1978. As per the Bank's model, the EDPs consist of one month's intensive training in Behavioural Sciences, aspects of Management and field training. During this period, the entire cost of boarding and lodging is borne by the Bank. In this year, the bank had conducted 7 EDPs covering 11 districts in Madhya Pradesh (7 lead districts plus Surguja, Bhind, Morena, and Gwalior districts) and a total of 156 candidates were trained under these programmes. A total loan of Rs. 121 lakhs has been sanctioned to 44 such trained persons.

Phases of Entrepreneurship Development

In broad terms, the EDP consists of three basic phases:

(i) *Initiation Phase:* For creating awareness about the entrepreneurial opportunities.

(ii) *Development Phase:* Through training programmes in developing motivation and management skills.

(iii) *Support Phase:* Counselling, encouragement and infrastructural support for establishing and running an enterprise.

In the initiation phase, it is aimed at identifying persons with a potential for development of entrepreneurial disposition. The development phase aims at infusing motivation through achievement motivation training, supported with adequate management and technical knowledge. But finally, the most important is the support phase as from the entrepreneurial point of view, the most crucial stage is the start-up period.

The development of entrepreneurship depends very much on organisation, education, stimulation and motivation of the clientele through a concerted and systematic approach, focusing on individuals and groups. Entrepreneurial development, is essential not only to solve the problem of industrial development but also to solve the long existing problems of unemployment, unbalanced area development concentration of economic power, and diversion of profits from traditional avenues of investment. Therefore, one can notice some attempts made by the Government's agencies and other institutions to undertake the task of entrepreneurial promotion. Most of the promotional activities are directed towards the financial and physical facilities with a strong belief that there will be a conglomeration of entrepreneurs if such facilities are created in the a conglomeration economically backward states of India. Financial and physical facilities are not the only crucial inputs in the development of entrepreneurship. There are other inputs also which one has to consider in any model for entrepreneurial development. In this study, a quantitative survey of entrepreneurship development India has been presented. The study says that in spite of abundant natural resources, the pace of industrial and entrepreneurial development is slow not only because of lack of basic facilities and financial institutions, but due to untapped entrepreneurial talent in the country and suggests that timely action by the Government and other agencies should be taken for the entrepreneurship development in the country.

Role of Naye (National Alliance of Young Entrepreneurs)

NAYE has been a pioneer in promotion and development of entrepreneurship among women. In keeping with the emerging trends, then NAYE had set up a Women's Wing in 1975, the internationally acknowledged Women's Year. NAYE convened a Conference of Women Entrepreneurs in November 1975 in New Delhi to discuss at length steps to be taken to make women self-reliant and to raise their status in the society. Since then three International Conferences and eight National Conventions of Women Entrepreneurs have been organised in different cities in the country.

Women's wing of NAYE assists women entrepreneurs in:

(a) getting better access to capital, infrastructure and markets;

(b) development of management and production capabilities;

(c) identifying investment opportunities;

(d) attending to problems by taking up individual cases with appropriate authorities;

(e) sponsoring delegations, participation in trade fairs, exhibitions, buyer-seller, specialised conferences, etc.;

(f) organising seminars, workshops and training programmes for giving them wider exposure to available facilities and developing their entrepreneurial capabilities;

(g) lobbying for them in Press, Parliament, State legislatures and other forums;

(h) advocating effectively for securing their rightful place in the Indian economy.

In addition, the Association of Women Entrepreneurs of Karnataka (AWAKE), Women Entrepreneurs Association of Maharashtra (WIMA) and Self-Employed Women's Association (SWWA) are not only fighting for their rights but also striving to promote entrepreneurship among women.

Set up in May 1985, WIMA – the Association of Women Industrialists/Entrepreneurs of Maharashtra has 400 members all over Maharashtra, with its head office in Pune, and branches at Mumbai, Aurangabad, Nasik and Dhulia. NAYE of which WIMA forms a part, presented the organisation with a national award in 1988 for promoting entrepreneurship among women. WIMA aims to help 1,000 women all over Maharashtra.

WIMA's main objective has been to provide a forum for members and to help them sell their products. But making is their main problem. WIMA also has training programmes.

There should be a curriculum change along with proper career guidance in women's polytechnics, which will shape the students to become capable entrepreneurs in future. There should also be some reservation for admission of women to disciplines like engineering, medicine, law, agriculture and architecture, with some concessions in regard to the qualification marks. It will be worthwhile to consider the institution of special scholarship schemes for meritorious women students. As far as the State and Central Governments are concerned, a scheme could be evolved for extending additional concessions for women entrepreneurs for setting up industrial units. As in the case of weaker sections of society, the financial institutions and banks should consider feasibility of waiving collateral security, because women do not possess any land or other property. Women should also be given property rights and an equal share in their fathers' property.

Although the rate of interest then charged by banks on loans extended to women entrepreneurs slightly lower than that charged on the normal loans, what is more important is further reduction and the reorientation by the Reserve Bank of India. In order to ensure that there was adequate credit flow to women entrepreneurs, a sub-goal was considered under the priority sector advances by the banks as is being done presently for advances to weaker sections and other special sectors. More importantly, the condition of a guarantor in the case of women entrepreneurs should be waived by the banks.

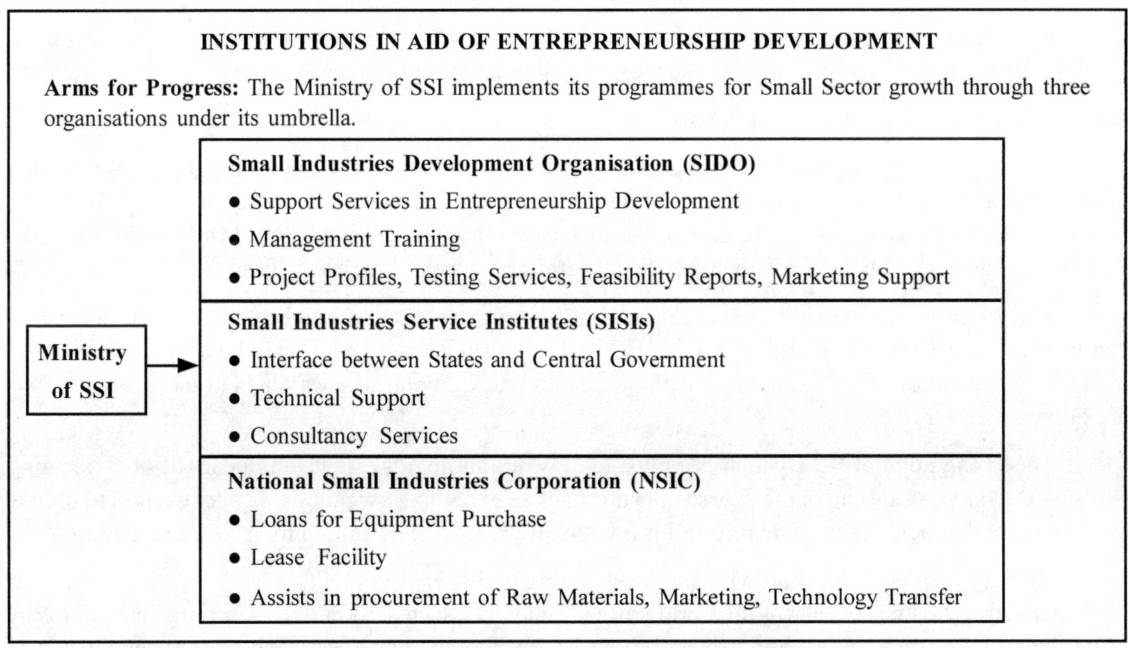

In order to ensure that development of women entrepreneurship takes place, as fast as possible, there is a case for setting up apex bodies at the State capital level and organisations at district levels which could be affiliated to the apex body. Separate industrial cooperative estates for women in different cities may be set up. And 15% to 20% of the purchases of the state governments should be made from women entrepreneurs.

Women entrepreneurs in rural and backward regions need special assistance and incentives from the Government and other associate agencies. What is more, training of lakhs of women entrepreneurs in the coming decade is a Herculean task for various agencies.

Although it is still in the growing stage, there is unquestionably a business revolution in the works across the nation – and women are a major part of it. Whether they opt to remain on a micro level, or move to expand on a major scale, they are making their impact felt on the society.

Indian Institute of Management, Ahmedabad

Established in 1961, it was one of the first three management education centres to be established across the country. Starting modestly with support help and guidance from the Harvard Business School, today IIMA is considered to be the best of all other centres.

IIMA pioneered management education by first introducing its executive development programmes for working managers and following it up with its graduate diploma programme a year later in 1962. Following the case study method of teaching, over the years, it has in its collection, more than 2000 Indian cases developed by its own faculty.

In 1991, IIMA introduced student exchange programmes. This cross-cultural approach is desirable especially when students are vying for overseas placement after graduation.

Even though it falls under the Ministry of Education, IIMA enjoys functional and academic autonomy, Although there is a common admission test for all IIM centres, each centre applies different selection criterion and IIMA's selection procedure is totally internal, i.e., IIMA faculty do the evaluation at all stages.

Besides a two-year post-graduate programme, IIMA also offers a fellow programme in management, faculty development programme and its executive development programmes are considered to be the best.

National Institute of Design, Ahmedabad

Like IIMA, NID was started in 1961 as a part of post-independence government initiative of establishing educational institutions across the country. Today, NID is most recognised for its quality – quality of its professionals as well as training. It functions autonomously as a part and parcel of the Ministry of Commerce and Industry and as an institute of excellence in education, research, service and training.

The primary focus is on design education encompassing a number of fields such as industrial design, communication design, textile and apparel design and exhibition design, making it the only one offering so many disciplines under a single umbrella. All these are the broad disciplines under which further specialisations are offered.

The strong point of NID, which is a must for any design institute, is its unique mode of inculcating learning by doing. At the end of the course, it is this bank of experience accumulated over the period of five, or more years that helps each student form his own set of views, beliefs and opinions of a good design.

NID does not work in isolation from the changing global environment. Its collaboration with other prestigious design institutions across the world prove ideal for its students. As part of its information technology initiatives, it has already entered into strategic alliance with other institutes as a mechanism to reinforce IT in its design curriculum.

Indian Institute of Technology, Kharagpur

The first in a chain of six IITs, it was established in 1950 following the recommendations of the Sarkar Committee, to cater to the need for skilled manpower in the country. From a modest start in the dilapidated Hijli jail building, in an idyllic, sylvan setting IIT Kharagpur has been engaged in a virtually continuous process of development to let the creative edges of the budding engineers run free. Maulana Abul Kalam Azad adopted the present name 'Indian Institute of Technology' before the formal inauguration of the institute on August 18, 1951. The handsome main building with its majestic tower was inaugurated in 1956. It was aptly described by Pundit Jawaharlal Nehru at the first convocation address that, "Hijli detention camp stands this fit monument of India, representing India's urges, India's future in the making.' IIT Kharagpur started its journey in the old Hijli Detention Camp where some of our great freedom fighters toiled and sacrificed their lives for the independence of our country. This is possibly one of the very few institutions all over the world which started life in a prison house. A large amount of financial help was available for procuring a number of machine tools from the Ministry of Industry and Supply. The institute workshop was supposed to be one of the best in the country. Today, IIT Kharagpur has come a long way to its present position of preeminence with eighteen academic departments, eight multidisciplinary centers, a school of management, a school of telecommunications and several sophisticated central facilities. It is the largest and most diversified among all the IITs. In a study sponsored by the Department of Science and Technology, Government of India, it was found to have the highest relative employment productivity index among the IITs and is the top supplier of fresh engineers and technologists to the public and private sector industries. It also ranked first among the IITs in the production of science and engineering PhDs. From this modest start in 1950, IIT Kharagpur has been engaged in a steady process of development with about 18 academic departments, five centres of excellence. IIT Kharagpur, the premier institute of technology in the country, promotes the pursuance of academic excellence in disciplines ranging from Aerospace Engineering to Biotechnology; Computer Science Engineering to Agriculture and Food Engineering through its various departments, centres and central facilities and special R&D Cells which offer 22 undergraduate and 50 postgraduate courses. Over the last four decades of its existence, IIT Kharagpur has redefined its aims, broadened its objectives, and introduced major changes in its programmes and priorities. The syllabi and the curricula are constantly updated and modified keeping in pace with technological developments. Consoliclation and diversification of academic effort to relate the entire educational endeavour to the larger context of the national development process, constitute the focus of its dynamic educational philosophy. A special Cell for Sponsored Research and Industrial Consultancy (SRIC) was set up in the institute more than two decades ago to promote sponsored and industrial R&D. The activities have grown phenomenally during the last decade. With the surging of the international collaborative projects, both the students and faculty are looking up to horizons of new possibilities that still await the optimum technological excellence.

Structuring Entrepreneurial Development Programmes

The above case studies bring out certain features important for the success of entrepreneurial development programmes. The training programme aims at identification and careful selection of entrepreneurs (using advanced series of psychological tests), developing the motivation and entrepreneurial capabilities of the trainees, equipping the trainees to identify viable industrial projects and to prepare project profiles or brief project reports, equipping the trainees with basic enterprise-building skills, imparting basic managerial skills required for the successful management of the unit and helping the trainees to secure the necessary financial, infrastructural and related assistance during the implementation of the project. Skill training formed a vital and major component of this programme.

Conclusion

Economic activities could be directly linked with the entrepreneurial level of a nation and, therefore, entrepreneurship development be considered as a critical input for industrial and business development efforts of a country. In this process, institutions play a catalytic role in entrepreneurship development.

Entrepreneurial development in India has now been conducted for a long-time, and sophisticated selection techniques and training methodology have been developed. The programme integrates identification and training of potential entrepreneurs, identification of viable industrial projects and developing managerial capabilities. Institutional support in the areas of finance, infrastructure, etc. is also linked with the programme.

The role of EDPs in accelerating industrialisation of a state or a region can hardly be over-emphasised. All those who are engaged in the administration of this programme must fully realise the enormous responsibility entailed in seeking to assist those without much influence, managerial ability or capability to bear risks. No tangible results can, therefore, be expected unless all the agencies involved in the task work with determination, zeal and a sense of dedication and commitment. Entrepreneur development is to be attuned to economic needs. It is, therefore, necessary to recognise the importance of entrepreneurship as an aspect of social life. Similarly, entrepreneurship education should be made more socially utilitarian. It is, nevertheless, imperative to restructure the entire curriculum – should identify the area of entrepreneurship and to motivate young people to start their own business at an early age in their chosen field of interest, for entrepreneurship exists in every profession, irrespective of its size. This will generate self-employment, which is always more satisfying than working for others.

A great leader is one who is not only good in creating a vision, creating the big picture, but also ensuring that he goes into the nitty-gritty, into the details of making sure that the vision is actually translated into reality through excellence of execution. In other words, great leaders have great vision, great imagination, great ideas, but they also implement those ideas through hard work, commitment and flawless execution. In doing so, they motivate thousands of people.

ANNEXURE – 1

Syllabus for Entrepreneurship Development Programme

Duration: 3 months

Specific subjects

I. Micro Laboratory

(1) Tests – achievement successful experience

— Ring toss game

— Individual

— Group

— Group with stake

(2) Scoring achievement stories

Interpretation of results of achievement and ring toss

(3) Interpretation of stories and games

Problem solving game

Boat building game

Block building game

(4) Group discussions

Life goal exercises

II. (1) Role of small-scale industries, need for small industries, problems and prospects.

III. (1) Development programme for small industries and selected small industries having prospects for development.

- *(a)* Engineering industries
- *(b)* Chemicals
- *(c)* Rubber and plastics
- *(d)* Electrical and electronics
- *(e)* Leather
- *(f)* Ceramics
- *(g)* Ancillaries

IV. Financial and physical facilities for small industries.

(1) Risk capital – long-term and short-term loans, financing of entrepreneurs by banks, other agencies/corporations (filling out application forms, etc.)

(2) Role of industrial estates/industrial areas, availability of built-up sheds, developed areas in the state, procedure and formalities required.

(3) Assistance provided by state industries development corporations.

(4) *(a)* Procedures and formalities in obtaining raw materials (indigenous/imported).

(b) Availability of power, water, municipal licence, etc.

(c) Marketing assistance programme etc.

(d) Export possibilities and assistance.

V. Project selection and preparation of project report, preliminary report, technical consultancy discussions with officers, institutions etc. Library consultations.

(1) Experience of successful entrepreneurs drawn from mechanical, chemical and other trades in small-scale sector.

VI. Study visits to industrial units and in-plant training.

(1) This tour is mainly intended to broaden the outlook of entrepreneurs by actual observations and discussions with small industrialists regarding managerial and technical problems.

(2) Trainees should also visit industrial units of their own choice relating to the lines chosen by them. The participants in the course should be taken in a group to a few well-organised large and small-scale industrial units with a view to exposing them to modern techniques of management etc. and training. As far as possible, arrangements may be made for in-plant training in industrial units or production centres of importance.

VII. Industrial and other Tax Acts regulating:

- *(a)* Working hours
- *(b)* Minimum wages
- *(c)* Employees' insurance
- *(d)* Industrial disputes
- *(e)* Income tax

(f) Sales tax

(g) Other aspects.

VIII. Practice of management.

(1) Functions of management, planning, organisation, co-ordination, direction, control and motivation, definition of organisation, organisation structures, line and staff, functional role of committees etc.

(2) Practice of management, organisation and structure of an enterprise, problem of maintaining team spirit, modern office management, automation and management, research in management techniques and practice etc.

(3) Types of organisations.

(4) Scope and functions of O & M selection and initiation of assignment, method study, design and control of forms, layout, office environment and design of functional furniture etc.

IX. Functional areas of management.

(1) Production, planning and control.

(2) Creative marketing, planning, policies and strategies, etc.

(3) Finance and costing etc.

X. Project finalisation.

(1) To conduct an explorative survey individually by the trainees by contacting dealers, consumers, established agencies and manufacturers in line for collecting factual market data concerning the production lines chosen by them. Efforts should also be made to collect details about the availability of machinery and terms and conditions of their supply etc.

(2) How to create market for the production line chosen, processing and compilation of market data in consultation with the different development agencies and technical officers.

(3) Finalisation of the project report and its presentation.

XI. Evaluation and workshop for project registration and a approval – with DIs/banks etc.

(1) Evaluation of the progress achieved by the trainees during the course.

(2) Workshop and group discussions.

(Management adjustment can be resorted to by the training institute in respect of allotment of number of working hours to each one of the major topics covered, keeping in view that the approach should be conceptual and oriented more towards practical aspects rather than theory).

ANNEXURE – 2

Important Guidelines

(A) Entrepreneurial Quality/Identity Development

(1) Number of sessions range from 20-30 covering 4 sessions a day upto a maximum 6 days.

(2) It varies with the number of participants because EMT Lab demands individual attention.

(3) The above sequence has been largely in a chronological order: however, certain areas need to be spread over a number of days as indicated above.

(4) In the case of rural entrepreneur activity, data may be generated in the beginning at stretches followed with TAT. Analysis need not precede activity exercise.

(5) Sessions on coping mechanization, influencing ability and other aspects of entrepreneurial behaviour can be incorporated during enterprise launching or afterwards fitting it with the language of enterprise.

(6) In order to develop identity of entrepreneur, EMT trainer cannot be just concerned with the first week's input or behaviour input; trainer has to provide a linkage and integrate it with the entire syllabus. Entrepreneurial process integration can emerge with appropriate interventions at various points in different programmes. Trainer has to use his own discretion in this.

(7) Goal-setting and action plan may need more time.

(8) Public statement on proposed action plan may enhance the commitment to entrepreneurial goal.

(B) Enterprise Launching and Resourcing

(1) Each session would be of 90 minutes' duration.

(2) Lecture notes would be based on the lectures delivered.

(3) Reading material would be additional literature.

(4) Wherever available, appropriate films would be shown.

(5) Audio-visual aids to be used wherever necessary.

(6) All exercises related to enterprise launching should be related to the selected enterprise. In case the entrepreneurs have not selected a project during training, a separate one week period may be allotted for preparing actual project report after field visit. Selected References have been indicated separately.

(C) Enterprise Management

(1) Additional sessions can be added, depending on the entrepreneur's background, size and type of enterprise introducing to computer/information management.

(2) Production planning, systematic control etc. can be included accordingly.

(D) Social Responsibility and Entrepreneurial Discipline

(1) The topic indicated under this maybe treated simultaneously with other topics or maybe taken up separately at one place.

This can also be done by discussing pros and cons of entrepreneurial career or in the need and scope of entrepreneurship in the present economic context.

Field Visits/In-plant Study

Depending on the level of enterprises, both the fieId visits and in-plant studies of 4-6 days' duration each can be organised as a part of the EDTP. However, a field study of 4-6 days' duration will always help provide practical experience and is recommended as part of the general entrepreneurship course.

*(**Source:** Model Syllabi for Entrepreneurship Development Training Programmes)*

ANNEXURE – 3

Course code: Entrepreneurship 100

Course title: Entrepreneurship and Economic Development in the Philippines.

Course Description

The first part is concerned with the presentation of a firm. It also presents and discusses the current business outlook in relation to the prevailing social, political and economic conditions of the country.

The second part aims at increasing the level of confidence and achievement orientation among the students, thereby developing in them proper psychological preparation for and mental attitude to business.

Course Outline

Part I

Topic	No. of Hours
1.1 Entrepreneurship defined	1
1.2 Attitudinal Factors in the development of entrepreneurs	3
1.2.1 Psychological	
1.2.2 Social	
1.2.3 Others	
1.3 Environmental factors affecting entrepreneurial performance in the Philippines	6
1.3.1 Social	
1.3.2 Political	
1.3.3 Economic	
1.3.4 International	
1.3.5 Others	
1.4 The Role of Entrepreneurs in Economic Development	9
1.4.1 Starting own Business	
1.4.2 Motivating others to engage in business	
1.4.3 Assisting others in managing business	
1.5 The social responsibilities of an entrepreneur	
2.1 Goal setting	5
2.1.1 Definition of goals	
2.1.2 General and specific objectives	
2.2 Risks in business	8
2.2.1 Definition,	
2.2.2 Kinds of risk	

Rank 1 : Indian Institute of Management, Ahmedabad

Director: Dr. Bakul H. Dholakia

Student Intake: 494

Average Salary: Rs. 9.7 lakh

Website: www.iimahd.emet.in

The IIMS are facing a delicate future with their hard earned brand image under threat, thanks to the populist UPA government's decision to introduce quotas for OBCs. The IIM A being the natural leader of the pack is unfazed and has already declared that it would abide by the law of the land and go in for an aggressive expansion of its infrastructure and faculty numbers, to introduce almost 380 seats in the next three years. That it did not give in without fight speaks volumes about its leadership.

The best corporates of the world have stayed in business through constant reinvention, something IIM A, the unassailed leader of Indian b-schools, has been practising consciously. The school introduced two major programmes – post graduate diploma in public policy (PGP-PMP) and a general management programme for working executives called PGPX. IIM A's greatest strength is its faculty and its business model is based on empowering the faculty and abiding by their decisions – something many of the up-and-coming business schools are emulating for their own good. For IIM A, the road to future would be continuous innovation and leadership.

Rank 2 : Indian Institute of Management, Bangalore

Director: Prakash G. Apte

Student Intake: 486

Average Salary: Rs. 9.00 lakh

Website: www.iimbemet.in

The second most aggressive IIM in the country is restless and is striving for more action, as it realises its sheer strength and acknowledged market presence, as one of the best schools of management from India. Its first forays into international campus at Singapore early last year may have been checkmated by the government, but the school has not given up hope and is working on plans not just for Singapore but for the Gulf and other European destinations too. The string of memorandums of understandings the school signed with global universities is a case in point.

The school has one of the best student and faculty exchange programmes in the country and is well-cued into the IT and ITes segment, giving it a natural edge among the b-schools in the country, for attracting the best student talent and also a large faculty pool. The school was included in the *Wall Street Journal's* annual listing of global schools last year – an endorsement of its super league status among world schools. There is more to this school than what is being seen at present.

Rank 3 : Indian Institute of Management, Kolkata

Director: Dr. Shekar Chaudhry
Student Intake: 322
Average Salary: Rs. 9.81 lakh
Website: www.iimcal.ac.in

The school is known in the industry for its tenacity and perseverance in staying on course and building on its brand image with diversified course offerings, something that it has continued to work over the years. In recent times, the school has gone closer to the society through its Initiative for Community Action programme, largely conducted by the students, suiting its image as a strong player in the b-school education.

The school has been a force to reckon with in executive education. Along with IIM A, it, has introduced a PGPX progamme for working executives last year. The mission of the PGPX programme is to develop experienced and ambitious executives for leadership positions in global organisations. What the future holds for the school would depend upon how aggressive it can get in revisiting its course offering and expanding it to suit the market needs.

Rank 4 : Management Development Institute, Gurgaon

Director: Dr. Pritam Singh
Student Intake: 244
Average Salary: Rs. 9.10 lakh
Website: www.mdi.ac.in

MDI tops the list of high-growth schools in the country on almost all the counts by which our survey was seeking to uncover. And all the IIMS, chiefly the IIM Lucknow, showed that their intellectual capital growth has been not so aggressive as the Gurgaon school, even though by sheer number and presence they have been able to retain their order in our ranking. Be it growth in number of faculty, increase in number of books written by faculty, submission of papers, new case preparation, international student and faculty exchanges, conduct and profile of the management training programmes, *et al*., MDI has been able to score heavily over its peers – an indication that it is within biting distance of dislodging heavyweight IIM Kolkata and not to speak of the other two IIMS – IIM A and IIM B, which seems remote at the moment.

MDI is the first institute in India and the second in Asia to be accredited by AMBA. The accreditation based on South Asian Quality System accredits the graduate programmes of MDI for five years. The institute introduced a programme in public policy, to which it admitted 19 students. It already ran a post-graduate diploma in energy management jointly with NTPC and another in HR with NHRD Network. It is surely on a winning path.

Rank 5 : Indian Institute of Management, Lucknow

Director: Dr. Devi Singh
Student Intake: 287
Average Salary: Rs. 8.74 lakh
Website: www.iiml.ac.in

Indian Institute of Management, Lucknow, has been having a tough time with a drop in intellectual capital measured by way of faculty numbers, their publication track-record, their academic track record, faculty support and such other aspects. However, ironically, the institute is also consolidating itself and reworking on its strength to build an aggressive future.

It is no longer a fringe player among the IIMS and is now an acknowledged leader among business schools. By converting its weakness (of being a relatively new IIM and located in Lucknow, a city not much known for corporate growth), into its strength, the school has been aggressively promoting its in-house training and pushing ahead with its offerings in the area of public policy and governance.

The corporates have acknowledged the maturity and market presence of IIM L and has been flocking to pick up talent. The school should have no difficulty in building its future, based on its present strength of possessing one of the largest infrastructure and well-developed real estate and sees no difficulty in acceding to the government demand for expanding its seats to provide reservation to OBCs.

Rank 6 : Indian School of Business, Hyderabad

Director: M. Rammohan Rao
Student Intake: 345
Average Salary: Rs. 9.89 lakh
Website: www.isb.edu

It is a rollicking time for Indian School of Business, Hyderabad, with its record number of placements, high-profile management development programmes and a massive surge in demand for the highest priced one-year management programme it offers. The first truly international business school – promoted by a consortium of Indian business houses and three top of the line International b-schools (Wharton, Kellogg and London School of Business) – the school has not just blazed a hot trail in the somewhat laid-back Indian b-school arena, but also set the scene for an aggressive competition, which in turn is feeding its own growth. The school might still be losing money owing to its rather ambitious investment of close to $200 million in its infrastructure, but the capacity usage is going up; so are the admission numbers and their price tag too.

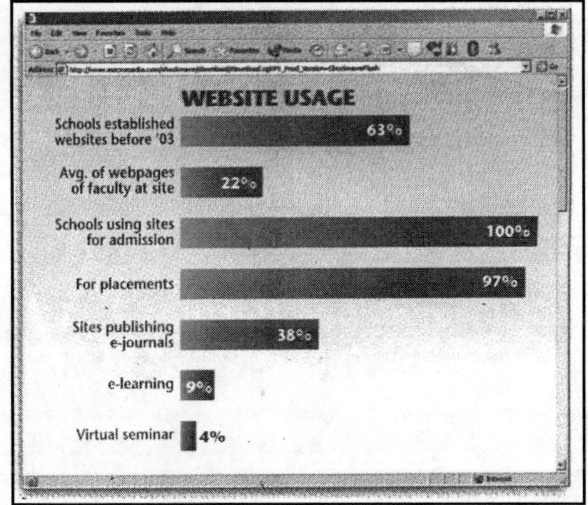

The business model the school has adopted is to balance the fee income with that of management training, which by hindsight has proved to be a paying strategy. The school is also constantly evolving its academics and delivery and changing the profile of its students, bringing in the standards that has made and sustained its alma mater schools as global b-school brands. If there is one school – that would pose a serious challenge to the decade old supremacy of IIM Ahmedabad, it could easily be ISB, provided the school introduces a larger basket of course offering and go in for a larger pool of resident faculty and also look to spread to other cities and geographies, all of which is now in the school's scanner.

Rank 7 : XLRI, Jamshedpur

Director: Fr. N. Casimir Raj, S.J.

Student Intake: 381

Average Salary: Rs. 8.40 lakh

Website: www.xlri.ac.in

The number one HR institute in the country still remains as such and perhaps will remain in that position for a long time to come. Its homestead is under serious threat, with aggressive new players including Symbiosis Centre for Management and HRD from our Next Ten stable, and MDI from the Top Ten list nipping at its heel, offering industry savvy HR courses. The reason XLRI can remain complacent is that its sheer presence in the field of HR, savvy market orientation and conscious linkages with its alumni who support the institute at every move.

The school has also been constantly evolving with technology and was one of the first to recognise the potential of e-learning and its programme in this sphere has been doing well. The school has also expanded its academic offering in tune with the industry demand and tried consciously to underplay its positioning as an HR school and perhaps even been successful in its efforts in the recent times. The institute has opened a study centre at Singapore after its successful run in Dubai, being the first b-school to set shop in the Gulf region.

✹ ✹ ✹

SUCCESS MANTRA

"To succeed you need perseverance, patience and passion. You also need good luck, but you have to do your bit to position yourself for receiving it." – ***Ashok Soota, Chairman, MindTree Consulting.***

UNIT – III
IDENTIFICATION

6. Opportunity Identification

7. Product Selection

8. Enterprise Launching Formalities

11 tips to grow beyond the start-up phase

HIRE PEOPLE WHO ARE BETTER AT THE JOB THAN YOU ARE

It's a fact that companies are built by people, and the best people build the best and most profitable companies. Put simply, great employees may cost you 20 to 30% more in wages, but they can be twice as productive as mediocre employees. Invest in good people.

PLACE HIGH URGENCY IN EVERYTHING YOU DO

Always do everything you can today. Too many people treat their businesses as 9- 5 jobs. Never put something off until tomorrow if you can do it right now.

GET CUSTOMERS COMING BACK

The road to profitability is through repeat business. Too few business owners set themselves up for long-term success. Your business grows when you add regular new customers on top of existing regular customers. Think of it this way: What if every customer you ever got stayed for life? How many regular buyers would you have?

MAKE DECISIONS QUICKLY

New companies don't have the time or resources to stand still. General H Norman Schwarzkopf once said, "When placed in command, take charge." It's better to make a decision and move than to stand still.

DELIVER MORE THAN YOU PROMISE

If you tell a customer it'll be three days, deliver in two. If you think it'll be two hours, say three hours and surprise them. This is the best form of marketing ever.

PRICE YOURSELF FOR PROFIT

Don't ever be the cheapest. You're the little guy; you don't have economies of scale. Big companies can make up in volume what they lack in margin. You can't.

NEVER SPEND A RUPEE YOU DON'T HAVE TO

You don't need a new desk, you need a cheap desk. Too many new business owners go and buy the best stuff because they think image is important. Listen, when you get profitable, you can have a big mahogany desk. Right now, just get a desk.

SET A BIG VISION

Start Small, Finish Big should be the title of your book. Don't aim to be the best dog trainer in your city – aim to be the best in the country. Remember, building a business is a 10 - year plan, not a one -year plan.

MARKETING IS MATHS

Don't ever let an advertising sales representative teach you anything about marketing. They will say dumb things like, "Half your advertising works and half doesn't – and you'll never know which half." Rubbish. if an ad that costs Rs. 100 gets you Rs. 100 back in profit, it's a good ad. One other tip: image advertising doesn't make sense when you're not yet profitable.

LEARN TO SELL

There's nothing worse than a business owner who isn't willing to sell – or even learn to sell. No company makes money unless someone sells something, and you can't just rely on people you hire to do the selling for you. If you want to grow a profitable business, you've got to learn to sell yourself.

IT'S SIMPLER THAN YOU THINK

Before most people even go into business, they work it up to be far more complex than it really is. Business is very simple: Sell at a profit and keep at it. Overcomplicating the process won't help anyone. If your business seems too complex it probably is, so make it simple and watch yourself succeed.

(Adapted from entrepreneur.com)

A product belonging to licensed category or de-licensed category also is considered before selecting the product. (i) Many products enjoy specific advantages in regard to the scale of manufacture or carry locational advantage, e.g., if protected in a free trade zone or in the backward areas with special incentives and concessions which are made available for manufacturing such a product. Selection of a product therefore also depends upon these factors. (ii) If a product belongs to an ancillary unit and serves as a major component for the parent industry, it provides a ready demand, hence selection of this type of product entails easy marketability.

Finally, at this stage, the selection of product would also be weighed in favour or against depending upon whether or not the machinery and the raw materials required would be imported or indigenous. Similarly, the selection would also be based upon the skill and unskilled labour position as well as the technical know-how which is available indigenously or would require a foreign collaboration.

The study of the project idea is the starting point of the feasibility analysis. The study is undertaken to identify the logic of the project, the tasks which must be performed for achieving the objectives, and the inputs, outputs and process involved in each activity. The ultimate aim is to identify the characteristics of the project. A project idea poses a problem, on the one hand and seeks a solution of the problem, on the other. In order that the solution may be an appropriate one, it is necessary to examine and appreciate the nature and extent of the problem and to clearly identify its dimensions.

CHECKLIST FOR CHOOSING IDEAS

Fit with your skills and experience

- *Do you believe in the product or service?*
- *Does the need it fits means something to you personally?*
- *Do you like and understand the potential customers?*
- *Do you have experience in this type of business?*
- *Do the basic success factors of this business fit your skills?*
- *Are the tasks of the enterprise ones you will enjoy doing yourself?*

6

Opportunity Identification

Introduction

Industrialisation is widely recognised not only as one of the important means to usher in socio-economic transformations and achieving industrial self-sufficiency but also for the accelerated development of agriculture, transport, trade, services and other potential sectors through the forward and backward linkages. It is a process which accelerates economic growth; effects structural changes in the economy, particularly in respect of resource utilisation, production functions, income generation, occupational pattern, population distribution and foreign trade; and induces social change. Jawaharlal Nehru had emphasised that "Real progress must ultimately depend on industrialisation. Throughout the world, industrialisation has indeed become the magic word of the mid-twentieth country."

Industrialisation is brought about by well-trained entrepreneurs. Entrepreneurship is one of the most important factors of industrialisation in the process of economic growth.

Project identification is the first step of a new venture. A right direction may take an entrepreneur to new heights. Otherwise, he has to undergo a number of hurdles in his way. It is therefore, very crucial to entrepreneurs. We have made an attempt in this chapter to analyse the various aspects of project identification.

Theoretically, an entrepreneur has an infinitely wide choice with respect to his project. The important dimensions of choice are: Project, service, market, technology, equipment, scale of production, location, incentives and time phasing. The task of identifying a feasible and promising project is somewhat difficult. Moreover it is interrelated with the government policies, infrastructure development and skills of people.

The Power of Imagination

Studies show that winning requires intense desire, relentless focus and flawless execution. Winning big requires dreaming big and taking bold steps to fulfill these dreams. Out of dreams a vision emerges and an idea takes shape. In other words creativity leads to innovation.

We need to start imagining about a new opportunity. This turns into a dream and a goal. In a way vision captures the worth of business, integrating the goals, strategies and action plans.

Mission provides an orientation — not a check-list of accomplishments. It defines a direction not a destination. It tells the members of an organisation why they are working together, how they intend to contribute to the work. But there is a big difference between having a mission statement and being mission-based. To be mission-based means that people can, and should object to edicts that they do not see as connected to the mission. It means that thinking about, and continually taken together, mission, vision, and assessment create an ecology, a set of fundamental relationships forming the bedrock of real leadership. They allow people, regardless to their designations, to help shape their future. Mastering the discipline of innovation will require organisation to learn from one another.

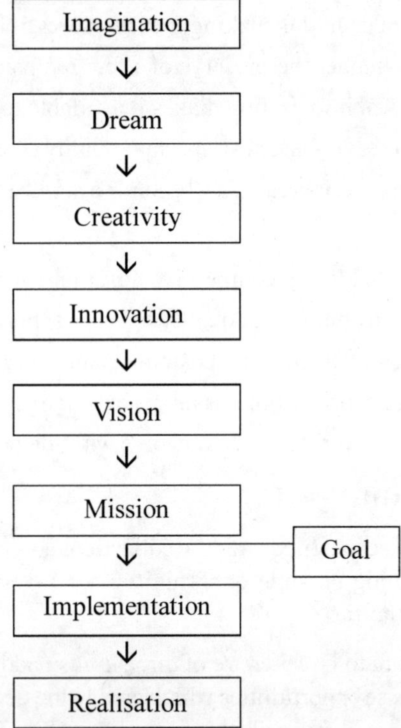

The lessons from success-stories are similar. They are:

(1) Imagination is a pre-requisite for coping with apparent resource-constraints. We have to think outside the box, breaking both the conventional wisdom in India as well as the existing business models elsewhere. Strategy here is about discovery and innovation.

(2) The business models that work in India are indigenously-developed.

(3) Strong leadership, knowledge, persistence, belief and commitment pays.

(4) Entrepreneurship is well and alive among the poorest. Government intervention, subsidies, and policies cannot accomplish what millions of entrepreneurs can.

(5) The appropriate technology was state-of-the-art technology that was creatively adapted to Indian conditions. The task of deployment of the technology required as much innovation as the technology *per se*.

(6) New organisational models are critical for India's development.

(7) All transactions must be based on commercial considerations.

(8) Accountability and transparency in performance is a pre-requisite.

(9) Indian operations can be world class; in fact, it must strive to set global standards.

(10) All useful initiatives will upset the power structure. Leaders must recognise that major innovations will meet with enormous resistance up-front.

The success of these efforts provides us with an understanding of how to transform the problem of the poor in India to the opportunity of a mass market.

Major Changes in Business

- Free movement of capital is making it easily accessible
- Technology is no longer the preserve of a few companies
- Unrestricted flow of information makes it available to all
- Globalisation is creating one all-important quality standard
- The world economy is increasingly becoming service-oriented.

And its Main Advantages are

- It uses only knowledge as a competitive advantage for survival
- It constantly tries to attain total quality in every sphere
- It builds evolutionary bonds with customers and vendors
- It is best-suited to cope with incessant global change
- It creates energised workforces that evolve with the organisation

Project Identification

Project identification is concerned with the collection, compilation and analysis of economic data for the eventual purpose of locating possible opportunities for investment and with the development of the characteristics of such opportunities.

Opportunities according to Drucker are of three kinds : additive, complementary and breakthrough. Additive opportunities are those opportunities which enable the decision-maker to better utilise the existing resources without in any way involving a change in the character of business. Complementary opportunities involve the introduction of new ideas and as such do lead to a certain amount of change in the existing structure. Breakthrough opportunities, on the other hand involve fundamental changes in both the structure and character of business. Additive opportunities involve the least amount of disturbance to the existing state of affairs and hence the least amount of risk. The element of risk is greater in the case of complementary opportunities but is the greatest in the case of breakthrough opportunities. As the element of risk increases, it becomes more and more important to precisely define the scope and nature of the project idea, to develop alternative solutions for achieving the project objectives and to select the best possible approach so as to minimise both resource consumption and risks and to optimise returns or gains.

The human mind had an infinite capacity to observe, to deduct and to innovate. Observation is one of the most important sources of project ideas. The observant mind continuously comes across situations which can be utilised to develop investment opportunities. The observation may be made during the course of one's routine occupation or otherwise. The dearth of a particular article or service may for instance lead to the development of an industry which can provide the article or service in short supply. The availability of a specified type of raw material or skill may lead to yet another type of industrial activity. The observant mind is always on the look-out for opportunities which can form the existing processes which can sometimes lead to new opportunities and project ideas.

Box 6.1 – Global Opportunities

There are several things Indian that helped me succeed. The work ethic inherent in India's Culture provided a solid foundation: its philosophical roots, a sense of balance. There is also a new advantage to being an immigrant because new opportunities can be, created only when one changes something in the system: it is sometimes easier to do that when you are an immigrant. Then, there's thrift. In India, most of us grew up with few resources and learnt to do with them. The ability to manage with little gives one the leverage to explore new opportunities and take risks. The pay-off is that if you win, you win big. Business in the US is, and has always been, a meritocracy.

Gururaj 'Desh' Deshpande

Co-Founder & Chairman of Sycamore Networks Inc.

If You look at people like me who moved to either the US or Canada in the 1970s you'll find several similarities. In the 1970s , we excelled in universities as graduate students. In the 1980s, we made a name for ourselves in universities, as distinguished researchers, and in industry, as technical leaders. In the early 1990s, we proved we could be technical managers, and by the end of the decade we had arrived: Indians were accepted as managers in sales, and business and general, as CEOs, as entrepreneurs, and as founders of companies.

What I have listed is a broad trend and several of us participated in it. It would have been very difficult to get a similar trend going in India. That it isn't impossible has been proved by the likes of Narayana Murthy. The result is that it is now possible to build profitable global companies in India.

Today, there isn't very much of a technology gap between India and the rest of the world, Advances in telecommunications have created a global economy and we are rapidly getting to a point where something has the same value anywhere in the world irrespective of where the value been added.

Over the last 10 years, India's success in software has proved that it can compete with the wolrd's best in the knowledge based service sector. As is evident from hectic industrial activity, this can he extended to call centers, business process outsourcing outfits, financial services back offices, and biotech research centers, India, can continue to position itself as a low-cost provider of highly-skilied knowledge-based services. This will create huge opportunities for all kinds of business activity in India. I see several great entrepreneurs and great companies coming out of India in the next 10 years. There is an opportunity for India to become the world leader by applying advanced technology to solve problems vital to the global economy, The government, entrepreneurs, venture capitalists and scientists need to work to harness this opportunity.

This would for instance be the case when a processing unit decides to go in for the manufacture of the machines which it has so far been using for processing purpose only. The process of deduction is on many occasions used to supplement and rationalise the project ideas based on pure observations. In Innovative units, it often becomes necessary to depend upon the deductive process for the development of new approaches to the solution of existing problems.

Trade and professional magazines proved a very fertile source of project ideas. The statistics and information thrown up by these magazines and reports and records of professional bodies often reveal opportunities which can be eventually developed into investment propositions. It is very important for every person who is involved in the process of development of new investment opportunities to remain in touch with the latest developments in his own field of specialization. It is also necessary for him to keep in touch with developments in other field which may be horizontally or even vertically linked with his own line of specialization. Study of technical and professional literature, besides keeping a person all *constant* also stimulates and helps in the process of development of new project ideas.

Bulletins of Research Institutes are also a very fertile source of information for the development of new project ideas. These bulletins generally give broad outlines of the new processes or products developed by research institutions and are very useful in identification of new opportunities. The information made available in the Research Bulletin may not be adequate for concretisation of ideas. Further correspondence with the Research Institute may become necessary.

In most developing countries where planned development has been accepted as an approach towards the removal of proverty, the plan document published by the Government provides a very useful source of project ideas. The plan document generally analyses the existing economic situation in a country and also

The Art of Spotting Opportunities:

India is like a blank canvas to the entrepreneur. Painting requires the ability to visualise the picture and the colours, gather the paints and apply the brushstrokes. With the big picture increasingly clear to many, the opportunities will be snapped up like never before.

pinpoints the investment opportunities which fit into the overall planning effort. Considerable information can, therefore, be gathered from the plan document.

Departmental publication of various departments of the Government also provides useful information which can help in the development of new project ideas. These publications are either periodical in character or are issued on special occasions. The census document which a periodical publication is a very useful source of information about the economic structure of the society and various trends in the growth of economy and purchasing power can be used to develop new ideas.

The project ideas is the user's concept of what a project should be like. It is the raw expression of the desire of the project sponsoring body to achieve something. The exact form in which the project idea is expressed is immaterial. In order to avoid unnecessary communications between the project sponsoring body and the project formulation team, the project idea should indicate the broad objectives of the sponsor and limit these in time, space, function and structure. In case no limitations are envisaged, the sponsoring body should state so and leave the project formulation team in no doubt about it.

The business ideas may be generated from internal and external sources.

Internal sources of Business Ideas:

Internal sources refer to the storehouse of knowledge built by a person over the years. These are as follows:

(a) Analysis of concepts in the fight of existing problems and their solutions

(b) Search from memory to identify similarities and elements related to the concept

(c) Recombining the available elements in new and better ways

(d) Personal interests and hobbies of the individual

(e) Thinking of novel uses of existing product, e.g., use of rice husk for making hard boards, use of fly ash in making concrete and bricks, etc.

(f) Conceiving improvements in existing products

(g) Examining possibilities of anciliarisation to large scale industry

(h) Knowledge of the potential customer needs

External Sources of Ideas for New Products

These are as under:

(i) List of items reserved by the Government for exclusive production in the small sector

(ii) Items reserved for exclusive purchase from small-scale industries under the Central Store Purchase Programme of the Government

(iii) Professional journals, trade journals, etc. catering to particular interests such as electronics, components, oils and vanaspati

(iv) Success stories of friends and relatives

(v) Trade fairs and exhibitions displaying new products

(vi) Government agencies like SIDO, NSIC, etc.

(vii) Market surveys to know trends in fashions

(viii) Technical and management consultants

(ix) Project profiles for various industries

Generation of business ideas or opportunities is also known as 'opportunity scanning and identification' (OSI). After generating ideas, it is necessary to evaluate them so as to identify the most appropriate idea/ opportunity. This process is called "zeroing in process." Following factors should be considered while selecting the product to be manufactured:

(i) Market potential

(ii) Degree of competition

(iii) An innovative idea which has greater profit potential than an existing product

(iv) Availability of raw material and technology

(v) Resources and experience of the entrepreneur in the line

(vi) Government policies and regulations

(vii) Suitability of the product to market requirements

To Every Operation

- Product design is an outcome of sustained personal innovation
- Manufacturing is the result of teamwork applied to technology
- Marketing is the sum of people-devised service added to products
- Restructuring is the redeployment of people and their knowledge
- TQM is the application of human intelligence to improve processes

Project Ideas — Scanning of Business Environs and Identifying A Project

Project ideas could originate from various sources or due to different reasons like the success story of a friend/relative, experience of others in manufacture/sale of product, demand for certain products, changes of producing a substitute of an article imported for which there is good demand etc. and of course, the motivation, background and skills of the entrepreneur and his associates.

One major aspect while choosing a project idea should be to ascertain the extent of the marketing of the product proposed to be manufactured, its general use, industries which use it, its end-use and its buyers. You should, therefore, study the demand and supply of the product over the last few years to estimate its future demand based on the past trends. While doing so, it would be necessary to take into consideration the anticipated changes in fashions, technology and levels of income of the people. If the product proposed to be manufactured has a market throughout the country, the study should take into account the demand and supply of the product for the whole country. However if the market for the product would be confined to one /two states/ or a particular region, the study may be confined to the concerned states/region. Many units function as ancillaries to major industries. In such a case, their fortunes being very closely dependent and linked to that of the 'parent unit', it is very important that detailed analyses are made on various areas before the decision to become an ancillary is made, i.e., areas like, will, the unit be totally dependent on the parent unit, the potential for reasonable profit and future growth, the experience of similar ancillary units, whether there are any problems in obtaining payments or supportive know-how, whether the investment in fixed assets will be such as to facilitate easy branching off into a new product line in case the ancillary arrangement does not yield anticipated benefits etc.

It will be equally important to judge market demand even when you are setting up a 'general purpose' workshop or service industry. In such cases, it will be necessary to have a clear idea of the industrial environment, the type of job orders you may obtain, whether they will be repeated, who will be giving them local competition, whether there are any large projects/establishments which promise potential for assured orders, whether your unit will have specialization in a particular type of work which will give an edge over competitors etc.

Box 6.2 – Innovate or Perish

Innovation is so critical to Wipro that the management articulated it in its promise statement in 1998, as one of its four values. The groundwork for the initiative, however, started only in January 2000 because other big initiatives such as Six Sigma, brand building arid SEI initiatives had to stabilise.

The initial days were spent studying the concept of innovation from book and the internet. The firm entrusted with starting the initiative did its survey among selected employees to understand their perception arid understanding of innovation, they also listed Wipro's past successes and failures.

The project was taken so seriously that the team travelled to study organisations such as 3M, Home Depot, Nike arid Nokia which are known for their innovations. The team also met academicians and consultants who specialise the subject.

In the end, these were the findings:

- All uccessful organisations are Innovative.
- You cannot copy an organisation. Each organisation has its own culture, processes and customer relationship. You can certainly learn from them.
- Organisations who have succeeded in innovations are those who had a strong driver or a need to innovate. The innovation initiative is linked to the business.
- Top management commitment to the initiative is the starting point of the journey.
- Mistakes are part of the innovation journey. We must learn to accept and learn from them. We need the ability to take risk and kill fear of failure. There has to be a culture of forgiveness.
- You need to build a learning organisation.
- You need to have a lot of organisational support arid most importantly perseverance in order to succeed.
- You need to have stability of people, High turnover hits innovation.
- Innovation as an initiative cannot have one framework or methodology that could be readily deployed.
- We need to develop our own framework and methodology that suits our organisation in order to succeed.
- Only when innovation is valued by the customer will it give returns, Customer validation of the idea at various stages could be most essential.
- Walls and silos in the organisation kills innovation. Communication network is essential. Proximity of teams helps.
- The need to understand the unstated needs of the customer is its necessity for innovation.
- Idea implementation is far more challenging than idea generation.

Finally, Wipro came up with its definition of innovation: "implementation of new idea resulting in marketable product or service."

An import-substitute product, basically, should have a good market in view of the general policy to encourage indigenous production. It would, however, be necessary to have a clear idea of the government's import policy, present demand, the landed price of the imported item and how your price will compare with its, quality differences etc.

In order to arrive at reasonable estimates of the future demand for and supply of a product, information relating to the capacity of existing units manufacturing that product, the extent of its utilisation, the capacity of the units that have already been granted licences but are in the process of being established, import and export potentiality of the product etc. should be taken into consideration.

Although it is a difficult exercise to arrive at a precise forecast for demand and supply of a particular product, specially since reliable and up-to-date information is difficult to obtain on the basis of the available data, it should be possible to decide on the future prospects of the item proposed to be selected by you. Towards this, capacity utilisation of the existing units could be taken as a broad indication of market for the product. Similarly, under utilisation of the exiting capacity could be taken as a single for little or no scope for setting up a new unit.

An SSI unit generally enters the market which is localised and already had existing manufacturers. The success of the new unit in competing with the existing manufacturers would depend on a combination of its capability to identify and approach its targeted customer group and its marketing features like price, quality, delivery schedule, sales promotion etc.

Box 6.3 – Big Business

Chances are that you have never seen at all Sula wines. Ritu Beri or Rohit Bal couture and for the Athena or Olive restaurants. But most people have heard of them: The wine and couture industries and designer restaurants have all been built by the page 3 culture. Take wine: The industry had been virtually non-existent a few years back. The modus operandi has been simple: celebrities endorsing hitherto unheard of wines, lengthy articles on the history of wine, extensive coverage of new launches and wine tasting sessions all brought to you courtesy of page 3. The industry is valued at a cool Rs. 50 crore today.

It is difficult to value the industries that are a creation of page 3 but if one were to take the three above-mentioned businesses alone it would probably be in the range of Rs. 300-400 crore. This is not including a number of retail stores, fragrance brands, Swiss watches and the burgeoning Feng Sui business. Look at the hair colour business, while the cosmetics majors may advertise their products, the barrier to hair colouring was broken down by page 3 which showed Indian celebrities with constantly changing hair colour.

Most of these brands are aspirational and reaching their audience through advertising is expensive. It's aspirant to associate themselves with celebrities and make sure that they find enough mention in page 3 to reach out to the top end of Gen P 3. After all the celebrities are not the ones who bring in the money, it's Gen P 3 patronage which makes them success or failure. A favourable mention on page 3 can make these unknown brands/restaurants/designers talking points. It works for a circle of art impresarios and gallery owners — Naresh Kapuria's efforts are minutely here — as well. Restaurants are constantly holding theme night and sending out invitations to the press with the hope that they will make it to page 3. Wine sellers try and ensure that the brand name is mentioned in the copy about the celebrity and his drink. Fashion designers try and make sure that they point out all the people at a party who are wearing their creations.

It's difficult to estimate to what extent the economy is impacted by page 3, but it's hard to argue that there are few brands that wouldn't give an arm and a leg to be seen there.

Key Performance Areas	Key Areas and Variables
Market standing	Sales
	Production margin
	New orders
	Lost orders
	Lost customers
Innovation	Number of new: products
	New markets
Productivity	Capacity utilisation
	Backlogs
	Back orders
	Manufacturing costs
	Yields
Physical and financial resources	Number of idle equipment
	Number of obsolete inventory items
	Accounts receivable turnover:
	Inventory turnover
	Cash flow
	Working Capital turnover
	Return on investment
Motivation and organisation	Absenteeism trend
development	Number of personnel problems going to arbitrations
	Number of personnel attending training programmmes
	Labour turnover
Public responsibility	Number of employees involved in community programmes
	Expenditure, oil pollution control
	Contribution to charitable organisations.

Importance of Project Identification

Project identification is often of great importance for the following reasons:

(1) They become the catalytic agents of economic development.

(2) They initiate the process of development – production, employment, income generation and so on.

(3) They have consequences which are long-term in nature.

(4) Projects provide the framework of the future activities of the enterprises.

(5) They also shape the future pattern of services.

(6) Projects usually involve substantial financial outlays.

(7) They also initiate development of basic infrastructure and environment.

(8) Project commitments cannot be easily reversed.

(9) Project identification brings necessary changes in society in course of time and

(10) Projects accelerate the process of socio-cultural development.

Criteria for Selecting a Particular Project

After gathering a large number of project profiles, the entrepreneur should consider the following criteria for selecting a particular project:

Investment Size: Professional managers, who have worked in multinational companies or large Indian companies, should think of starting medium-sized or large-sized units only. The investment size (project cost) should be at least Rs. 3 to 5 crore. They should not commit the common mistake of restricting the project size to less that Rs. 2 crore so that they need not go to all financial institutions. In fact, under the present circumstances, it will be much easier to get projects cleared by all-India institutions, requiring even lesser promoter's contribution.

Location: *A* new entrepreneur should locate his project to the extent possible, in and around a state headquarters. There are many backward areas around such cities. It is necessary to have such a location to attract competent managers. This will also facilitate liaison with the State Electricity Board, State Industrial Development Corporation and various other agencies.

Technology: The first project should not be for a product which requires high technology, necessitating foreign technical collaboration. It is better to go in for a product with a proven technology that is indigenously available. It makes life easier to begin with.

Equipment: The entrepreneur should select the best equipment based on the advice of experienced technical consultants. He should not compromise on the quality of the equipment. Many entrepreneurs enter into some sort of a deal with the equipment manufacture for a 'kick back' and in the process sacrifice quality. Industry is a goose that lays golden eggs. One should not be shortsighted and come to grief by going in for poor quality equipment.

Marketing: It is not advisable to get into a project particularly the first, which would mean survival amidst cut-throat competition involving direct selling to the ultimate consumer. One should go in for products with a limited number (say 10 to 20) of industrial customers.

Project Profile

Ceiling Fan

1. General

(i) Profile. New

(ii) Whether reserved for manufacture in small-scale sector. No

(iii) Whether reserved for purchase from small scale sector. No

2. Product and its Uses

Ceiling fan is a household appliance and is used for circulating of air in the room.

3. Market Potential

With the increase in housing activity and construction of multi-storied building, the demand of ceiling fans will increase considerably.

4. Production Targets and Range

Ceiling fans (900 min to 1,500 mm) 4000 Nos. per Installed Capacity. Annum per shift.

5. Basis and Presumption

No of working days	300 days per Annum
No of working hours	6 hrs per day
Size of fan taken for calculations	1,200 mm
Annual production	3,000 Nos. per annum per shift.

6. Process of Manufacture and Production Details

The manufacturing process of the ceiling fans involves the following operations:

(i) The casting of the body are purchased and turned to the required size.

(ii) Core is assembled

(iii) Coil winding is done on the automatic coil winding machines.

(iv) Shaft is turned to the required size

(v) Fan body and the blades are painted

(vi) All the parts/components are assembled.

(vii) The assembled fan is tested to IS specifications

7. Pollution Control

The pollution control is not applicable.

8. Quality Control and Standardization

IS: 347-1979	Specifications for Electric Ceiling Type Fans and Regulators.
IS: 1709 - 1960	Fans - Fixed Capacitors for
IS; 648-1970	Specifications for Steel Sheet and Magnetic Circuits of Power Electrical Apparatus.
IS: 302-1979	General & Safety Requirements for Household Electrical Appliances.

9. Land and Building

	Rs.
(a) Land	
500sq. metres @ Rs. 60/- per sq. metre.	30,000.00
(b) Building	
(i) Workshed 15M x 20M = 300 sq M. @ Rs. 1,000/- per sq. metre.	3,00,000.00
(ii) Office 4M x 5m - 20 sq. metre @ Rs. 1,200/- per sq. metre.	24,000.00
(iii) Laboratory 4M x 5m - 20 sq. metre @ Rs. 1,200/- per sq. metre	24,000.00
(iv) Room for air delivery test 8M x 8M @ Rs. 100 per sq. metre	64,000.00
(v) Cycle Stand, Lavatory Block and Boundary wall	20,000.00
	4,32,000.00

10. Machinery and Equipments

(a) Machinery

1. Lathe Machine 6'	Two	48,000.00
2. Automatic Coil Winding Machine for Fan Rotar	Two	40,000.00
3. Drill Machine Pedestal I" cap	Two	6,000.00
4. Bench Grinder D.E.	One	2,000.00
5. Fly Press no. 4 4' x 4' x 6'	Two	2,000.00
6. Hand Presses	Two	2,000.00
7. Electric Oven 4' x 2' x 2	One	6,000.00
8. Electric Oven	One	4,000.00
9. Air Compressor	One	5,000.00
10. Hand Tools	—	2,500.00
		1,17,500.00

(b) Testing Equipments

1. AC High Voltage Test Set 0-5000V.	One	6,000.00
2. A.C. Variac Transformer 0-300 V 5 Amp	One	2,000.00
3. Meggar 500 V	One	1,500.00
4. Watt meter	One	1,200.00
5. Wheat-Stone Bridge	One	10,000.00
6. Test Panel Complete with Amp. Meter volt meter, watt meter.	One	7,800.00
7. Avo meter	One	2,000.00
8. Anemometer	One	5,000.00
9. Air Delivery Test Chamber	One	25,000.00
		61,000.00

(c) Office Equipment and Furniture	10,000,00
(d) Installation and Electrification @ 10%	17,850.0
(e) Transportation, Packing, Forwarding and Sales tax @ 10%.	17,850.00
	2,24,200.00

11. Total Fixed Cost **Rs.**

Land and Building	4,62,000.00
Machinery and Equipment	2,24,200.00

12. Raw Materials per month

1. Stampings CRGO 250 kg @ Rs. 65/- per kg	16,250.00
2. C.I.Body 250 Sets @ Rs. 40/- per set.	10,000.00
3. Ball Bearing 250 sets @ Rs. 45/- per set.	11,250.00
4. S.E.Copper wire 75 kg @ Rs. 110/- per kg	8,250.00
5. M.S.Rod 100 kg @ Rs. 10/- per kg	1,000.00
6. Blade Assembly 250 sets @ Rs. 25/- per set	6,250.00
7. Hanger 250 Nos. @ Rs. 6/- each	1,500.00
8. Canopy 250 sets @ Rs. 6/- per set	1,500.00
9. Condensers 2.5 MFD 250 Nos. @ Rs. 12/- each	3,000.00
10. Regulators 250 Nos. @ Rs. 10/- each	2,500.00
11. Black pipe 250 ft. @ Rs. 2/- per foot	500.00
12. Insulating materials @ Rs. 5/- per Fan	1,250.00
13. Paint /Varnish @ Rs. 5/- per Fan	11,250.00
14. Hardware @ Rs. 4/- per Fan	1,000.00
15. Packing Materials @ Rs.	1,000.00
	66,500.00

13. Staff and Labour per month **Rs.**

(a) Administrative and Supervisory

1. Manager-cum-production Engineer	One	1,000.00
2. Salesman	One	750.00
3. Clerk-cum-store-keeper	One	750.00
4. Chowkidar	One	500.00
		3,000.00

(b) Technical

1. Skilled workers @ Rs. 750/- each	3	2,250.00
2. Semi-skilled workers @ Rs. 600/- each	4	2,400.00
3. Helpers @ Rs. 500/-	3	1,500.00
		6,150.00
perquisites @ 15% of total Salaries		1,350.00
		10,500.00

14. Utilities per month

1. Power 30 HP @ Rs. 28/- per H.P.	840.00
2. Water	200.00
	1,040.00

15. Other Expenses per month

1. Postage, Stationery & Printing etc.	250.00
2. Advertisement & Publicity	500.00
3. Consumable Stores	100.00
4. Transport Charges	250.00
5. Telephone	500.00
6. Repair and Maintenance	350.00
7. Sales Expenses	750.00
8. Miscellaneous Expenses	100.00
	2,800.00

16. Working Capital

(a) Per Month (12) + (13) + (14) + (15)	80,860.00
(b) For 3 months 16(a) x 3	2,42,580.00

17. Total Capital Investment

(a) Fixed Investment	6,86,200.00
(b) Working Capital for 3 Months	2,42,580.00
	9,28,780.00

18. Cost of Production per annum

1. Raw Materials	7,98,000.00
2. Staff & Labour	1,26,240.00
3. Utilities	12,480.00
4. Other Expenses	33,600.00
5. Depreciation on Building @ 50%	21,600.00
6. Depreciation on Machinery @ 10%	17,850.00
7. Depreciation on Office Equipment @ 20%	2,000.00
8. Interest on total investment @ 15%	1,39,317.00
	11,51,087.00

19. Sales Proceeds per annum

By sales of 3,00 ceiling fans @ Rs. 450/- each	13,50,000.00

20. Profitability per annum **Rs.**

Profit	1,98,913.00
(a) Percentage of profit on sales	14.7%
(b) Percentage of Profit on Total Investment	21.42%

21. Break-even analysis **Rs.**

Fixed Cost

Depreciation on Building	21,600.00
Depreciation on Machinery	17,830.00
Interest on Capital	1,39,317.00
40% of Salary	50,496.00
40% of other Expenses	13,440.00
	2,29,263.00

$$\text{BEP} = \frac{\text{Annual Fixed Cost} \times 100}{\text{Annual Fixed Cost} \times \text{Profit}}$$

$$\frac{2,29,263 \times 100}{2,29,263 + 1,98,913} = \frac{2,29,263.00}{4,28,176} = 535\%$$

22. Addresses of Machinery and Equipment Suppliers

1. M/s. Batli Boi & Co. Ltd., M.I. Road, Jaipur- 302 001. — General Machines
2. M/s Sri Ram Lathe House, Anba-bari, Jaipur- 302 002 — – do –
3. M/s. Perfect Machine Tools Co. Bell building, Sir P.M. Road, Bombay - 400 001 — – do –
4. M/s. Atlas Engineering Co., G.T. Road, Batala-143,505
5. M/s BMP & Equipment Co., Block 16-B, Kurla Ind, Estate, Agra Road, Ghatkopar, Mumbai- 400 077. — Coil winding Machine
6. M/s. Choudhary Trading Co. Bhagirath Place, Delhi- 110 006 — – do –
7. M/s Gyro Laboratories Pvt. Ltd., — Testing
8. Gazdar Street, Thakurdwar, Mumbai-400002 — Equipments
8. M/s. Toshniwal Bros. Pvt Ltd., M.G. Road, Ajmer- 305 007 — – do –
9. M/s BHS India Pvt. Ltd., 304, Ashok Bhawan, Nehru Place, New Delhi - 110 024. — – do –

23. Addresses of Raw Material Suppliers

1. G.K.W. (Stamping Division), Gopi Nath Marg, Jaipur- 302 001. — Stampings
2. M/s. Golden Pressing Factory, 104, Ind. Area, Jhotwara, Jaipur - 302 012 — – do –
3. M/s National Engineering Industries, Khatipura Road, Jaipur- 302 006. — Ball bearing
4. M/s Indian Cable Company Ltd., Ind. Assurance Building Chor Rasta, Gandhi Road, P.O. Box 33, Ahmedabad - 380 001. — Enameled wire
5. M/s National Insulated Co. of India Ltd., Nicoo House, Hare street, Kolkata-700 001. — – do –
6. M/s National Casting & Industries, Sudershanpura Ind. Area, Jaipur - 302 006. — C.I. Castings
7. M/s. Agarwal Engge. Works, 125, Ind Area, Jhotwara, Jaipur - 302 012. — – do –

Note:

1. Casting can be procured for any C.1 Foundry.
2. SE Copper wire, Bearings, Insulating materials etc. are available in open market.

(Prepared by SISI Jaipur)

Many innovative ideas are needed to find one good idea worth for commercialisation and many new ideas fail to pass the screening stage. Few ideas are compatible with the corporate resources and goals. Finally, five ideas are eliminated for lack of profit potential. Finally, having profitability, only one new product idea becomes eligible for market introduction and officially enters its life cycle.

Revolutions for the Future

1. Healthcare: Biotechnology has opened up a world of endless possibilities to mankind. Diseases that traumatise and kill people today will become a thing of the past. Surgery may be replaced with non-intrusive techniques that don't just repair, but grow new cells to heal. That in turn will have a dramatic impact on productivity and efficiency of workforce. But increasing longevity will create a market for new kinds of healthcare.

2. Environment: Population growth in developed countries will begin to taper off, while that of Third World countries will continue to clip. Basic natural resources such as air, water, fuel will become big issues. Innovations aimed at squeezing more out of dwindling resources will hit the market. Increasing global incomes would increase the consumption of energy. Therefore, new ways of tapping green and renewable sources of fuel will be developed.

3. Education: In the new age, labour will increasingly be replaced by knowledge. Mechanical jobs will either be eliminated or entrusted to machines. Personal progress would be linked to education. With more people seeking education, the need will be for the service providers to reach out to them inexpensively but ubiquitously.

4. Communications: The demand for information and connectivity will grow exponentially. Media will converge with greater force, and more versatile communication devices will see the light of day. Geographical distance would become meaningless, and the cost of communication ape the trend in information technology.

5. Artificial Intelligence: Robots built to think like humans will be everywhere: at road crossings, shop counters, offices, restaurants, and even in the cockpit of an aircraft. Highly developed user interface will allow such robots to talk to human beings and build their knowledge dynamically. In the short term, artificial intelligence will potentially endanger all low-skill tasks currently carried out by human beings. In the long run, it may play God.

The Golden Age of Biotech

Alzheimer's, Cancer, AIDS, Down's Syndrome, disease-free plants, regenerative body parts and, perhaps, human immortality. All these and much more would be on the radar of biotech scientists, now that they've constructed the human genome map. But to make repairs at cell level, scientists will have to understand how proteins in our genes work. Proteomics (the study of proteins) will create the next big wave in biotech. Once the protein mystery is solved, medicines will be able to do almost anything. Repair damaged neurons in an Alzheimer's patient, rebuild the immune system in an AIDS-sufferer, or grow a new layer of skins for a burn victim.

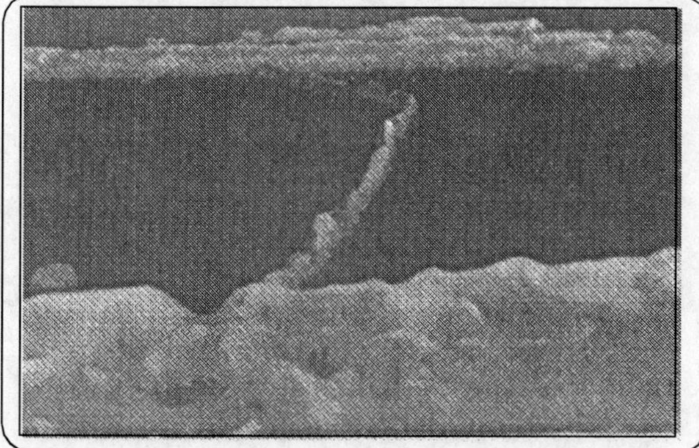

Circuits of the future: nanotubes draped across electrodes

Another revolution will be in terms of regrowing body parts. Scientists are battling ethical issues to experiment with stem cells – cells responsible for growing blood, muscles, and tissues – to find ways to regrow body parts. A breakthrough would mean amputees, deformity, and handicaps become a thing of the past.

Nanotechnology, which explores activities at sub-atomic level, is another exciting area. The premise is simple: since everything – human beings, potatoes, and diamonds – is made of atoms, it is theoretically possible to produce copies of them inexpensively and rapidly, if their chemical structures were replicated. So, sitting in a laboratory one could grow potatoes and diamonds.

Nanotechnology would also make it possible to make 'machines' that work at the sub-atomic level. In March this year, IBM researchers announced that they had succeeded in creating " a network of tiny transistors from nanotubes only a few atoms wide." Although its commercial application may be several years away, what it means is that Moore's Law will not only hold true in the future, but it may actually be bettered.

Conclusion

During the past two decades, advance information and computer technologies have interconnected world economies. The globalisation of national economies has brought considerable benefits, and also thrown open plenty of opportunities to entrepreneurs at all levels. What is more important is that the service sector, IT sector and knowledge sectors are growing at a greater speed.

In an environment of wide range of opportunities, the search for a business idea and converting it into a successful venture is a continuous process. The responsibility of the entrepreneur is to build winning characteristics into the organisation so that achievement levels exceed normal expectations. Towards this end, 'our dreams have to be bigger, our ambitions higher, our commitment deeper, and our efforts greater."

In short, India is a land of opportunity, where the economy is fast becoming global and the empowerment of ordinary people a reality. There is abundant scope to entrepreneurs to set up new ventures, open up new services, generate employment and create wealth. It is time for all of India's entrepreneurs, new and old, to shrug off the chains and play a leading role by grabing the opportunities by converting into enterprises, services etc.

CHANGE AGENTS 1

The power of ideas Convocation 2010 on October 30 will see a high powered panel discussion on 'Entrepreneurs as Change Agents'. Today, we announce the names of a few such change agents – young entrepreneurs who are all set to rock India with their ideas and who have got cash grants of ` 5 lakh each as part of the programme. Below are just the first set of names, with more to follow tomorrow:

Sr. No.	Name	Sector	City	Impact of India
1	Aaditeshwar Seth	Mobile/Telecom	New Delhi	Information services to rural India using mass media.
2	Amit Jain	IT/Web	Mumbai	Web-based application server providing asset tracking solutions for all movable assets to prevent transit theft.
3	Aniruddha Gupta	Media & Enter	Pune	Technology based service using practically unbreakable copy-protection and flexible payment system, making content distribution easier
4	Ankit Sabharwal	IT/Web	New Delhi	Online/offline application enabling online exploration of locations in 360 degree form thus replacing photo galleries and video tours
5	Ankur Tripathi	Logistics/ Transportation	Mumbai	Electronic pan-India road transportation exchange encompassing all stakeholders, reducing lead tome of transportation requirements and improving reach and efficiency
6	Annu Grover	Retail	Noida	Retail chain selling green gifts and lifestyle to those who seek to flaunt the same also giving employment to poor artisans
7	Arpita Ganesh	Retail	Hyderabad	High and lingerie boutique offering women a variety of exclusive brands and products, as well as consultation to choose the most suitable innerwear
8	Ashok Jagatia	Cleantech/Energy	Mumbai	Energy efficient hardware and software for outdoor & indoor lighting reducing carbon footprint
9	Ashok Mittal	Healthcare/ Life Sciences	New Delhi	An all encompassing dental health service under one roof with extended working hours to serve patients better
10	Ashutosh Khurana	Education	New Delhi	Curriculum on Thinking Development to develop cognitive, social and emotional thinking skills among children

❋ ❋ ❋

7

Product Selection

Introduction

Industrialisation is widely recognised not only as one of the important means to usher in socio-economic transformations and achieving industrial self-sufficiency but also for the accelerated development of agriculture, transport, trade, services and other potential sectors through the forward and backward linkages. It is a process which accelerates economic growth; effects structural changes in the economy, particularly in respect of resource utilisation, production functions, income generation, occupational pattern, population distribution and foreign trade; and induces social change. Jawaharlal Nehru had emphasised that "Real progress must ultimately depend on industrialisation. Throughout the world, industrialisation has indeed become the magic word of the mid-twentieth century."

Industralisation is brought about by well trained entrepreneurs. Entrepreneurship is one of the most important factors of industrialisation in the process of economic growth.

Choosing an Idea

Establishing yourself as a successful entrepreneur depends, in part, upon choosing a good idea. That idea must not only be good for the market, but good for the project and good for the entrepreneurs. It should also be manageable by you without much dependence on others. Importantly, the idea should give satisfacting results to you.

As an entrepreneur, when you are searching for an idea worthy of your commitment, don't pursue one idea at a time. Develop five or ten in parallel until one emerges so appropriate that it begins to dominate your thoughts and fantasies. To adopt one idea at a time has several disadvantages. First, because you are constantly receiving random information from what you read and from people you talk to, having a number of back burner ideas gives you a greater likelihood of finding uses for information you pick up. Secondly, if you are pursuing a single idea by feigning commitment before you feel it, you may put yourself into a tight corner. It is very hard to be objective when you are down to your last idea.

Choosing an idea is quite difficult and the entrepreneur has to weigh objectively his intrinsic capabilities in finalising an idea.

In the idea stage, suggestions for new products are obtained from all possible sources: customers, competitors, R & D, distributors, and company employees. Frequently, one of the creative problem solving techniques discussed below are used to develop marketable ideas. The suggested ideas need to be carefully screened to determine which are good enough to qualify for a more detailed investigation. Established objectives and defined growth areas provide a basis for developing these criteria.

PRODUCT IDEA

It had been an exhausting day. Mansukhbhai had spent all morning cycling to and fro, hawking his home made goods in the lanes and bylanes of the crowded city. Now he sat outside a pan shop, trying to snatch a few minutes' rest before starting another round.

As he sat there, he noticed how the customers at the pan shop kept growing, in number and impatience. Mansukhbhai saw the time it took to make each pan, the panwallah trying to attend to a dozen people at the same time. It occurred to him that if pan could be packaged and sold, it would instantly find a ready market

And an idea was born. A man of the masses, with only his native shrewdness to guide him, had hit upon a marketing idea in a million. The kind that takes a genius to think of. That man was Mansukhbhai Mahadevbhai Kothari. The man behind Pan Parag Pan Masala.

An Illustration: Choice of a Product

Sanitary Napkin

The product was first introduced in the late 60s, and the concept of a sanitary napkin was popularised through the 70s while the 80s introduced new variations like the beltless napkin and tampons.

Since the very concept of a sanitary napkin was so new to India, one realised that conventional retailing alone was not enough to sell the product. What was important was educating women about the product and about personal hygiene, so the manufacturers started schools, screening firms on menstruation and how to cope with it. This was followed up by free sampling.

The market leaders and pioneer in the field is undoubtedly Johnson and Johnson with Carefree, Stayfree, OB tampons and now, Freshday, Pantyliners. As things stand, the consumer does not yet have a real choice in terms of wide price variations, for instance. But the market is poised for a boom and even smaller manufacturers who admit that they earn 50 per cent of their income from his one product category alone are doing well, though they are not advertising or retailing their product.

Starting with the base, which is still the belted napkin, the pyramid narrows to the apex consisting of products like tampons (3 per cent of the market share) and pantyliners. There is still a tremendous potential for expansion even at the base. The women population needing sanitary napkins is estimated to be around 20 crores, of which 5 crore lives in urban centres. There is thus scope for (Rs. 840 crore industry) 500 crore pieces alone in urban centres.. At that time, big cities were prime targets for expansion and the huge rural market remained untapped. Given this scenario, the 21st century will see many new brands and consequently more brand wars, hopefully resulting in the ideal napkin at the right price, for the consumer. And this is what is happening in this industry.

Observations

With the constant awareness campaign, the entrepreneurs have targeted the consumers and made an impact on them. The product has a ready market. Technology is available. Raw material is in plenty. With the widenings of the market the demand for the product has increased manyfold. It is profitable. It is healthier, comfortable and socially accepted. Market is vast but tricky. The product is tempting entrepreneurs/manufacturers to step into this field.

Selection of Product

At this stage, the entrepreneur is concerned with identifying a particular product that he hopes to market successfully at a reasonable profit. Therefore, the selection of the right product is very essential for being successful in the business venture. The right product here means that which can be marketed at a reasonable profit which will go towards growth business. Various factors influence the entrepreneur in selecting the right product. These decisive factors are *(i)* whether import restrictions or the items selected are banned items would considerably weigh favourably or otherwise in the selection of the products. This is because in the case of banned items the domestic market offers considerable scope for selling as the demand for such a product would not be met by import.

Thus, if the item selected fall in the category of banned import items, the entrepreneur would favour the category of banned import items, the entrepreneur would favour it and in the case of unrestricted import of the items, he would definitely not show his favour for selecting such a product. *(ii)* If the entrepreneur himself or his partners have gathered, substantial amount of experience in the manufacture and marketing of certain products, then the selection of such a product would be to their advantage. Therefore, most often the items selected are of those lines of products in which the entrepreneur or his colleagues have gathered enough experience. The line in which they are not experienced obviously would not be favoured much as it will entail uncertain situations very often. *(iii)* The selection of the product will also be based upon the degree of profitability that generally rules in the market. Such information. can be obtained from the banks or the financial corporations or the market itself. The selection, therefore, will depend upon the information compiled for the particular line of product for its profitability. *(iv)* Many concessions are available from the government for producing a product which serves as an import substitute or even essential item, hence if a particular product enjoys a substantial amount of incentives, concessions, liberal taxation policies, obviously the entrepreneur will select that item to enjoy these advantages conferred on the production of this particular type of product. *(v)* Many products belong to the priority industries or small scale sector also; certain products are listed by the Government for purchasing exclusively from the small scale sector. As a result if a particular product belongs to this category, the selection of such a product would be advantageous for the entrepreneur; therefore, these factors also must receive due consideration before the selection of a product. *(vi)* The market for the product also plays a significant role in the selection of the product. If the product also has an export market, it widens the scope of marketing, hence such a product has its own advantages in the success of the enterprise. *(vii)* Certain products are permitted for production only if the licence is obtained from the appropriate authority while others belong to the delicensed category. In the case of a licensed product, obtaining a licence would be a difficult proposition or the capacity required for the entire industry may also have been created fully by the government. As a consequence, impossibility of seeking further permission for the production of such a product. A product belonging to licensed category or de-licensed category also is considered before selecting the product. *(viii)* Many products enjoy specific advantages in regard to the scale of manufacture or carry locational advantages, e.g., if produced in a free trade zone or in the backward areas with special incentives and concessions which are made available for manufacturing such a product. Selection of a product therefore depends upon these factors. *(ix)* If a product belongs to an ancillary unit and serves as a major component for the parent industry, it provides a ready demand, hence selection of this type of product entails easy marketability.

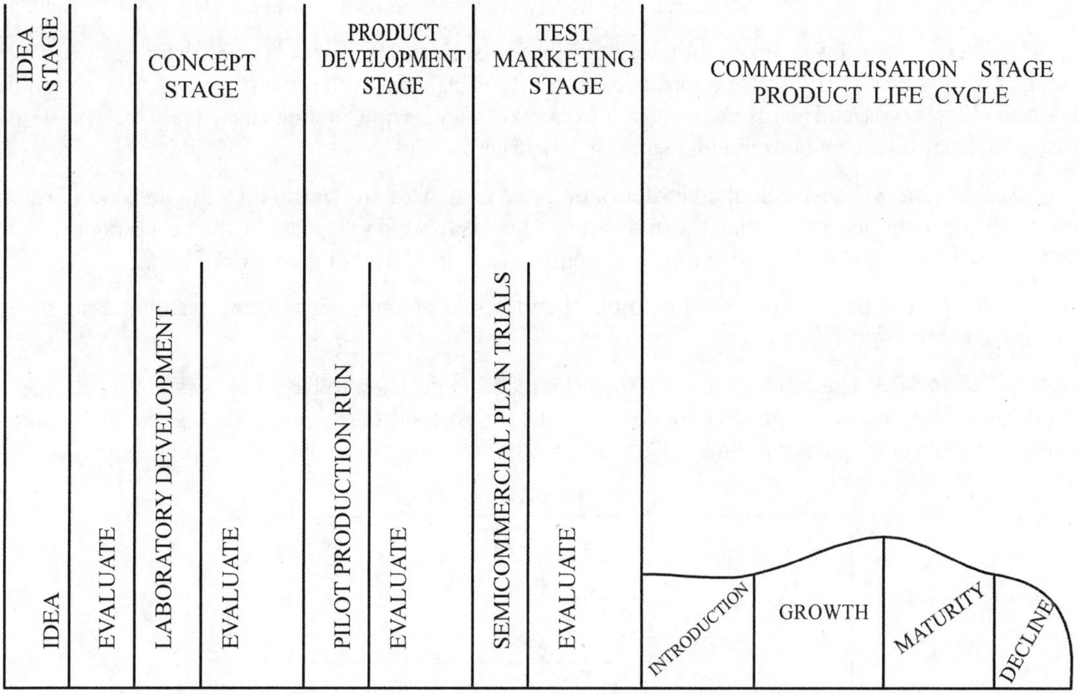

Fig. 7.1: Product Planning and Development Process

Source: *Adapted from Robert D, Hisrich and Michael P. Peters, Marketing Deceptions for New and Mature Products (Columbus, Ohio: Charles E. Merrill Publishing Co., 1984).*

Finally, at this stage, the selection of product would also be weighed in favour or against depending upon whether or not the machinery and the raw materials required would be imported or indigenous. Similarly, the section would also be based upon the skill and unskilled labour position as well as the technical know-how which is available indigenously or would require foreign collaboration.

The study of the project idea is the starting point of the feasibility analysis. The study is undertaken to identify the logic of the project, the tasks which must be performed for achieving the objectives, and the inputs, outputs and process involved in each activity. The ultimate aim is to identify the characteristics of the project. A project idea poses a problem, on the one hand and seeks a solution of the problem, on the other. In order that the solution may be an appropriate one, it is necessary to examine and appreciate the nature and extent of the problem and to clearly identify its dimensions.

The Adoption Process

The adoption of an innovation demands planned management of change (overcoming the resistance to change). An adoption process is a process bringing about a change in a buyer's attitudes and perception. Consumer adoption process covers the steps that a consumer usually goes through in determining the feasibility of buying new products: (1) Awareness, (2) Interest, (3) Evaluation or mental trial, (4) Trial (physical), (5) Adoption.

(1) Awareness: A person learns about a new idea, product or practice. He has general information about it, e.g., through advertisement. He has, however, limited knowledge about special qualities, usefulness, performance, etc., regarding the innovation. He merely knows about its existence.

(2) Interest: He now develops an interest in the innovation. He demands more detailed information about the new product, its utility, its performance, and so on. He listens with interest to Jingles on the radio or TV ads, reads press ads, and learns more about it from others, and is now inclined to actively seek the desired information from sales persons, opinion leaders, peers, friends, etc.

(3) Evaluation: The accumulated information and evidences are weighed by the person in order to assess the basic soundness or worth of the innovation. He tries to weigh the value of the new product and the extent to which it is good for him. In a sense, he conducts a mental trial of the new product.

(4) Trial: The person now is ready to put the idea into practice. Competent personal assistance is necessary to put the innovation to use.

(5) Adoption: It is the final stage in which he makes a decision to buy. The person now decides to adopt the new idea, product or practice for continued use. If postpurchase experience is good, he becomes a repeat buyer and a talking advertisement of the innovation.

Product Development

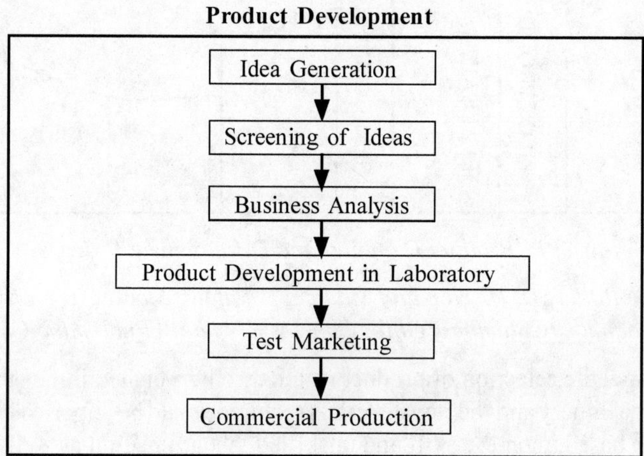

Fig. 7.2: Stages of Product Development

Product Innovation

The innovation attitude of the marketer is expressed in the watch word "innovate or die." Such an attitude must be an integral part of the marketing concept. P. Drucker recognised the equal importance of innovative attitude and marketing concept. He said, "Because it is its purpose to create a customer, any business enterprise must have only two basic functions: *marketing* and *innovation.* All growth industries have an important role for innovation in their marketing and market penetration plans. Innovation alone assures growth and survival while customer orientation assures survival. The evolution of new products is a practical business function and it is described as a process product management. The new product programme must be organised and controlled if it is to be effectively managed. The process of product planning and development is always adopted for product innovation. Product development is a general term covering the search for new products and new innovations as well as the improvement of existing products.

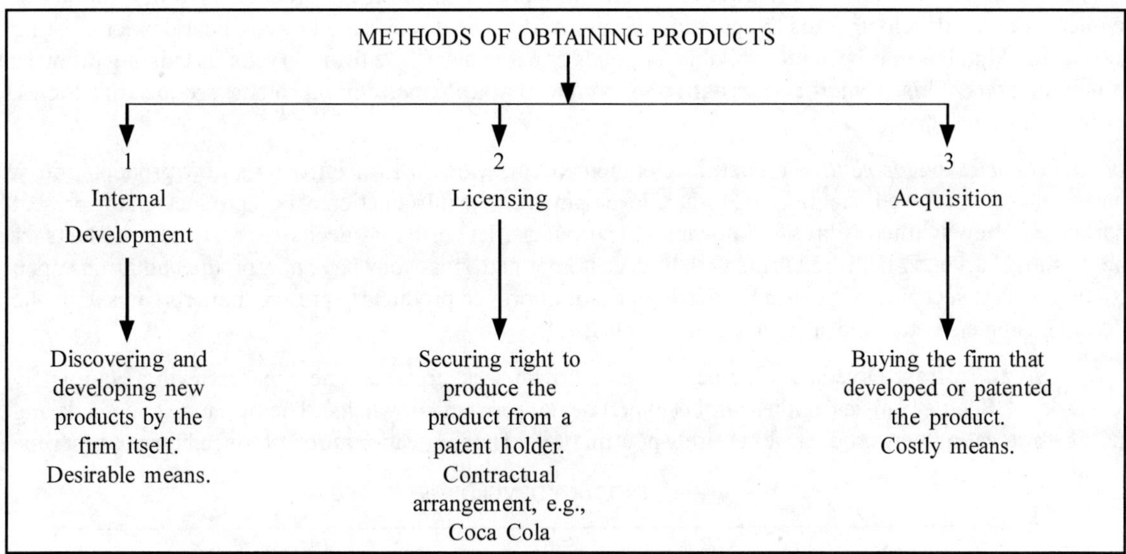

Note:
1. Internal product innovation implies no payment of profits to inventor or developer.
2. Licensing obviates the possibility of internal discovery and may inevitable or preferable, e.g., complex products like electronics.
3. Acquisition is very costly but gives exclusive rights.

Fig. 7.3

Product Planning and Development Strategy

Marketers have four alternative ways of bringing about an increase in sales and profits: (1) market penetration, (2) market development, product development, and product diversification.

	EXISTING MARKETS	NEW MARKETS
EXISTING PRODUCTS	EXISTING PENETRATION A	MARKET DEVELOPMENT B
NEW PRODUCTS	PRODUCT DEVELOPMENT C	DIVERSIFICATION D

Fig. 7.4: Four Basic Types of Opportunities for Sales Growth

Market Penetration: It involves the expansion of sales of the existing products in the existing markets by selling more to present customers or gaining new customers in the existing markets. The firm can market its present products to existing markets. This is done through a more aggressive marketing mix. Customers from rivals or potential buyers can also be attracted. Existing buyers may be induced to increase their rate of use. We may have a temporary price cut to raise the volume of sales and penetrate the market in a big way.

Market Development: In market development, a present product is introduced to a new market or segment. Market development is the creation of new markets by discovering new applications for existing goods, e.g., Mini bus may be made available for goods or passengers. The firm can offer its existing products to new markets. This is another alternative to expand market opportunity, prolong product life cycles, profitability and survival.

Product Development: Product development occurs when a firm introduces new products into a market in which it is well established. Product development is the introduction of new products in the present market, e.g., new synthetic fibres for known textile products. The firm may decide to create new products for the existing market. Established firms with high customer patronage may have new product additions upon existing market successes. The firm by offering new or improved products to present markets can satisfy the present customers better and stand assured of their loyalty.

Diversification: Diversification occurs when a firm seeks to enter a new market with a completely new product. Such a firm has neither market expertise nor product knowledge. The firm may adopt a daring strategy by creating new products for entirely new markets. The innovations are introduced for the first time

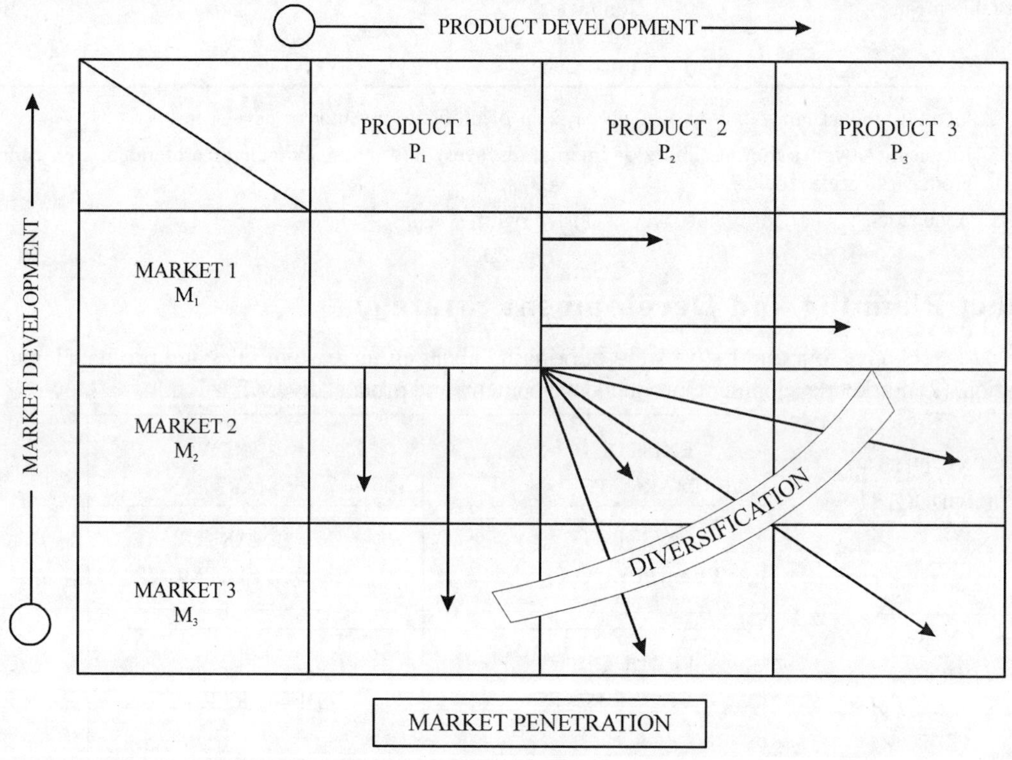

Fig. 7.5: Relationship between Various Marketing Strategies

Note: 1 We have four marketing strategies to achieve growth: (1) Market Penetration, (2) Product Development, (3) Market Development, and (4) Diversification.

2. Market penetration, i.e., penetrating the current market for higher usage rate is a conservative choice.
3. Diversification by entering a new market with brand new product is the most radical choice. It is the most difficult strategy as the firm has no market expertise and no product knowledge. Many firms fail in their diversification strategies.

in the new markets. Only innovation marketers venture to go in for diversification of products. The strategy is risky but the innovator can have spectacular results. In 1960, polaroid camera and television were in this category in many countries. Microwave ovens and digital watches are novelties even today in many countries. We have entirely an unfamiliar product for an unfamiliar market. Factors rating for a new product introduction are: (1) marketability, (2) durability, (3) productive ability, and (4) growth potential. Philips is an example of diversification or lateral integration: light bulbs, radio lamps, television tubes, radio sets, taperecorders and a wide range of luminaries or lamp shades.

New Product Idea

Excluding the continual search for new ideas, the time and costs involved in the activities relating to product planning and development process, from experience in the U.S.A., is as follows:

Stage	*Time*	*Money cost*	*Ideas reduced from original 60* to
1. Screening	3 p.c.	2 p.c.	12
2. Business Research	12 p.c.	7 p.c.	7
3. Development	40 p.c.	31 p.c.	3
4. Testing	20 p.c.	15 P.C.	2
5. Commercialisation	25 p.c.	45 p.c.	1 (One successful new product)

Note: 1. Development, testing and launching are the most expensive stages.
2. They take more than 50 per cent of total time involved in the process.

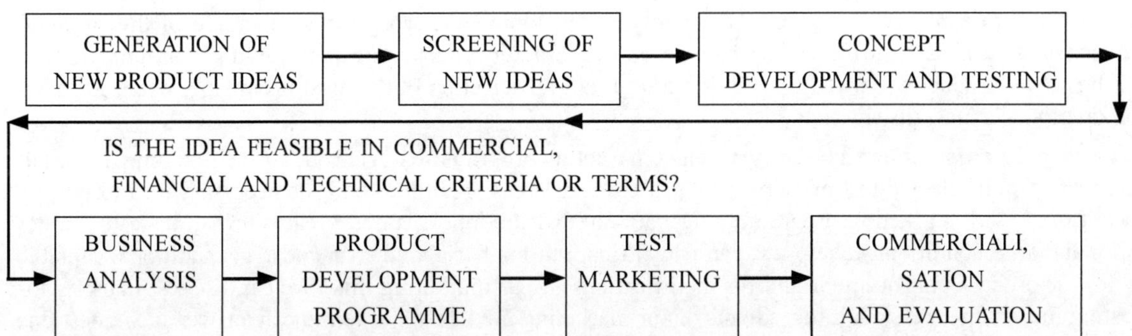

Fig. 7.6: New Product Development Process (Innovation Management)

Note: 1. Product life cycle requires the product development programme for new products and new profit opportunities.
2. New product development must be carefully planned and managed.
3. Special organisational wing is necessary to stimulate, collect, screen, evaluate, develop, test, and commercialise new product ideas.
4. Business analysis is the crucial stage. It concentrates on demand analysis, cost analysis and profitability analysis. It also considers social responsibilities of marketing new product.

Many innovative ideas are needed to find one good idea worth for commercialisation and many new ideas fail to pass the screening stage. Few ideas are compatible with the corporate resources and goals. Finally, five ideas are eliminated for lack of profit potential. Finally, having profitability, only one new product idea becomes eligible for market introduction and officially enters its life cycle.

Product Planning and Development Process

There are seven steps in the planning and development of a new product:

(1) New Product Ideas: We visualise the detailed features of a model product. Ideas may be contributed by scientists, professional designers, rivals, customers, sales force, top management, dealers, etc. We may need sixty new ideas to get one commercially viable product.

(2) Idea Screening: We have to.evaluate all ideas and inventions. Poor or bad ideas are dropped and through the process of elimination, only the most promising and profitable ideas are picked up for further detailed investigation and research.

(3) Concept Development and Testing: All ideas that survive the process of screening (preliminary investigation) will be studied in detail. They will be developed into mature product concepts. We will have a precise description of the ideas and features of the proposed product. At this stage, we can incorporate consumer preference into our agenda for concept development and testing product ideas. For concept testing the company has to choose the best among the alternative product concepts. Consumers are called upon to offer their comments on the precise written description of the product concept, viz., the attributes and expected benefits.

(4) Business Analysis: Once the best product concept is picked up, it will be subjected to rigorous scrutiny to evaluate its market potential, capital investment, rate of return on capital, etc. Business analysis is a combination of marketing research, cost-benefit analysis and assessment of competition. We have demand analysis, cost analysis and profitability analysis. Business analysis will prove the economic prospects of the new product concept. It will also prove the soundness and viability of the selected product concept from a business viewpoint. Now we can proceed to concentrate on product development programme. The proposed product must offer a realistic profit objective.

(5) Product Development Programme: We have three steps in this stage when a paper idea is duly converted into a physical product. *(a)* prototype development, giving a visual image of the product, *(b)* consumer testing of the model or prototype, and *(c)* branding, packaging and labelling. Consumer testing of the model product will provide the ground for the final selection of the most promising model for mass production and mass distribution.

(6) Test Marketing: The entire product marketing programme is tried out for the first time in a small number of well selected test markets, i.e., test cities or areas. Test marketing is necessary to find out the viability of a full marketing programme for national distribution. Customer reactions can be tested under normal market conditions. It helps the company to learn through trial and error and to get additional valuable clues for product improvement and for modifications in our marketing mix. We can use test markets for testing the effectiveness of all ingredients of our marketing mix. Test marketing can answer such questions as: Is the new product labelled and packaged properly? Is the new product liked by the consumer? Is the firm justified in spending large sums on productive capacity? Has the communication (promotion) programme been right? Positive answers will reassure marketers.

(7) Commercialisation: Once the test marketing gives the green signal for the product with or without expected modifications, the company can proceed to finalise all features of the product. Now marketing management can launch a full fledged advertising and promotion campaign for mass distribution. Mass production will start and all distribution channels will be duly organised. The product is now born and will start its life cycle in due course.

Conclusion

The search for a business idea is a continuous process. The entrepreneur will have to undertake constant checking of the new product through its life cycle. And, keep a constant tap on the markets, consumer needs and their changing styles, research and development as an ongoing source of information regarding business idea as well as appropriate technology.

Checklist For Choosing Ideas

Fit with your skills and experience

- Do you believe in the product or service?
- Does the need it fits mean something to you personally?
- Do you like and understand the potential customers?
- Do you have experience in this type of business?
- Do the basic success factors of this business fit your skills?
- Are the tasks of the enterprise the ones you will enjoy doing yourself?
- Are the people the enterprise employ will enjoy working with and supervising?
- Has the idea begun to take over your imagination and spare time?
- Is the idea innovative to the extent of social benefit?
- Are you expecting a good return?

Fit with the Market

- Is there a real customer need?
- Can you get a price that gives you good margins?
- Would customers believe in the product coming from your company?
- Does the product or service you propose produce a clearly perceivable customer benefit which is significantly better than that offered by competing ways to satisfy the same basic need?
- Is there a cost effective way to get the message and the product to the customers?

Fit with the Enterprise

- Is there a reason to believe your enterprise could be very good at the business?
- Does it fit the enterprise culture?
- Can you imagine who might sponsor it?
- Does it look profitable (high margin low investment)?
- Will it look to large markets and growth?

What to Do When Your Idea is Rejected?

Frequently, as an entrepreneur, you will find that your idea has been rejected and /or is not successful as envisaged. There are a few things you can do:

(1) Give up and select a new idea.

(2) Listen carefully, understand what is wrong, improve your idea and your presentation and try again.

(3) Find someone else to whom you can present your idea by considering:

– Who will benefit most if it works and can they be a sponsor?

– Who are the potential customers and will they demand the product?

– How can you get to the people who really care about entrepreneurial ideas?

❋ ❋ ❋

8

Enterprise Launching Formalities

Introduction

The success of a small-scale industry solely depends upon doing the right thing at the right time. In other words, a small-scale industrialist has to be conversant with the varied regulations governing the small-scale industry and the procedures to be followed in order to acquire the necessary assistance and incentives offered by the Government from time to time.

The procedural aspects of the small-scale industry are quite formidable. Each and every entrepreneur is often overwhelmed by the multitude of procedures which help to face at every stage of the development of a small-scale industry. It is therefore, necessary to emphasise here that the student should concentrate more on the purpose and the principles underlying the various procedural formalities than on such routine formalities as filling in various forms, applications etc.

Basic Objectives

The basic objectives underlying the development of small and medium-scale industries are the increase in the supply of manufactured goods, the promotion of capital formation, the development of indigenous entrepreneurial talents and skills and the creation of broader employment opportunities. In addition, they include socio-economic goals such as the decentralisation and dispersal of manufacturing activities from the metropolitan to the non-metropolitan and rural areas, the reduction of regional economic imbalances within a country and the diffusion of entrepreneurial and managerial abilities and skills and technology throughout the country.

In the Indian economy, cottage and small-scale industries have a significant role to play with increasing pace of industrialisation and sophistication of the large-scale industries, a new orientation is inevitable in the relationship of the SSIs with the large and medium industries. This relationship calls for integration of the production methods, upgradation of the qualities of production, ability to meet stringent delivery schedules and very many other problems that arise in a changing environment.

Box 8.1 – Are you Ready for Business?

Some questions to ask yourself before you take the entreneurial leap. *– Udayan Ray (30 Apr. 2001)*

Bitten by the business bug? Remember, it is not easy to shake off the soporific security of a 9-to-5 job and perks to adopt a career that promises huge rewards but is rife with uncertainties. Ask yourself these questions before you make the leap.

Have the personality? You have passion but equally, you have to be a good general. You must attract great talent, and later get the best out of your team and motivate it.

Can you persevere? There will be setbacks: finance, labour, valet downturns. You must have tremendous faith in yourself and your idea to wither these.

Have the big idea? First evaluate your business idea. Is it unique or is it better/cheaper than the rest? It's a good idea to use informal market research to get feedback on the idea's viability.

What's your gameplan? Figure out your scale of operations: will you cater to a niche segment? Chart a road map of your business goals and time frames.

Is it on paper? Make a sound business plan. This process will help you spot planning oversights early. If you're looking for loans, a business plan is mandatory.

Where is the money? Figure out how much you can raise from personal and other sources. Money from the wrong investors can be source of conflict.

Is cash flow in place? Cash flows must see you through contingencies and hidden costs, and help you stay afloat for at least six months after start-off. Don't make optimistic revenue projections.

Will revenues be stable? Get at least one or two another clients, the ones who will provide large, regular orders.

How lean can you get? Keep a tight leash on expenses till opearations stabilise. Cut down on fixed costs, like high rentals, till your venture finds its feet.

Then Act

(1) Eveluate your business idea and ensure your product/service is superior to what's available in the market.

(2) Making a sound business plan will help you spot planning oversights early. Also essential if you want a loan.

(3) How much money can you raise from personal sources? Will your cash flows see you through the initial period?

(4) Attract talent and make the most of your team. And have enough faith in yourself, your idea and your team to wither initial setbacks.

(5) Get at least two anchor clients who can provide large, regular orders. This should keep revenues stable.

Right Thing at the Right Time

In this chapter, the treatment of procedures – right from conceiving a small-scale industry until the repayment of creditors and ploughing back of profits – is based on the personal and practical experience of a small industrialist. In the latter part of the discussion, a reference has been made to the varied regulations that a small-scale industrialist has to abide by. They are mentioned later.

A discussion of the relevant procedures to be followed when setting up a small-scale industry has been dealt with reference to various phases of its development. These phases are:

(i) Selection of a small industry and preparation of feasibility and project reports;

(ii) Accommodation, power and other infrastructural facilities;

(iii) Machinery;

(iv) Raw materials;

(v) Finance;

(vi) Marketing and

(vii) Securing various incentives offered for the development of the small-scale industry.

1. Selection of a Small-Scale Industry

The process of setting up a small-scale industry has been shown in Fig. 8.1, which has been drawn on the basis of practical experience gained in its promotion. It indicated all the important stages in setting up of a small-scale industry.

The objectives of the promotional regulation are to provide an impetus to the growth of a small-scale industry and regulate the supply of machinery, electricity, water, premises, finance, raw materials and markets. The process of production and marketing is governed by set rules and regulations. In a way, these regulations are a boon to the small entrepreneur.

The procedure for setting up a small-scale industrial unit is given below:

(1) Selection of the product and preparation of project report.

(2) Selection of site.

(3) Selection of forms of ownership.

(4) Direct purchase of land or obtaining land/shed in the industrial estates.

(5) Registration in case of company or partnership type of organisation.

(6) Agreement with collaborator, if any.

(7) Obtaining letter of intent or provisional registration of SSI.

(8) Preparation of detailed project feasibility report.

(9) Obtaining import licence, customs, clearance, etc.

(10) Applying for power connection to KSEB.

(11) Sanction by financial institutions.

(12) Start of civil construction work after obtaining clearance from local authority or town planning officer.

(13) Obtaining letter of credit for imported machinery, etc.

(14) Selection of personnel, both administrative and technical.

(15) Completion of civil works.

(16) Delivery of imported and indigenous machinery.

(17) Erection of machinery and equipments.

(18) Obtaining clearance from pollution control board.

(19) Obtain industrial licence or permanent SSI registration.

(20) Arrangement of raw materials and unskilled labour.

(21) Apply for getting grants/subsidies from the government.

(22) Trial run and commissioning of plant.

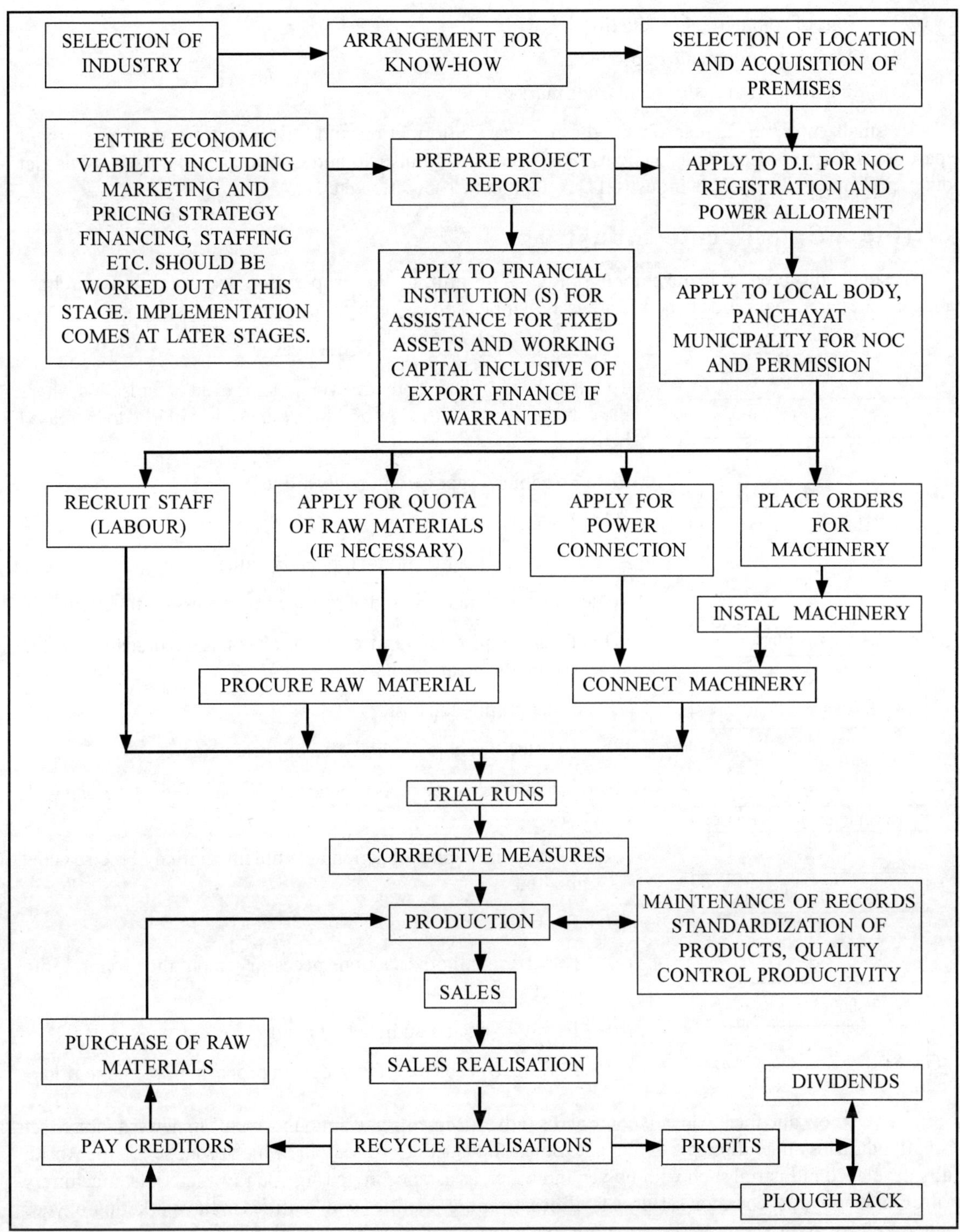

Fig. 8.1: Process of Setting-up a Small-scale Industry

(23) Start of commercial production.

(24) Arrangement for sale of products.

(25) Registration of designs and trade marks.

A small entrepreneur can obtain the necessary information and guidance from the Government Departments, Organisations and Agencies like Director of Industries and Commerce, Manager of District Industries Centres, Kerala State Industrial Development Corporation etc.

Starting a Small-scale Industry

A small entrepreneur is the chief executive of his unit, its floor supervisor, accounts clerk, purchase manager, salesman, legal and economic adviser, planner and visionary – all in one.

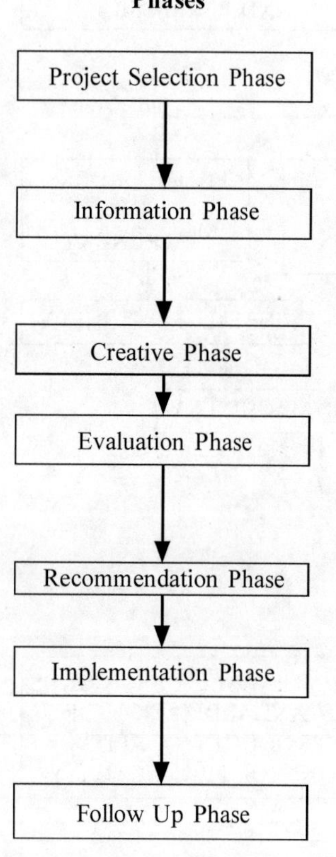

Fig. 8.2: Project Objectives

Objectives

To select those products, processes or systems in an organisation where the value and cost ratio is low and where analysis will lead to increased benefits

(*a*) To gather, organise and analyse data

(*b*) To define functions

(*c*) To establish a functional monetary value

To generate alternate methods for providing necessary functions

(*a*) To develop, refine and evaluate alternate methods generated during the creative phase

(*b*) To determine the cost

(*c*) To select feasible method offering best value

To prepare and present a report containing recommendation along with benefits.

(*a*) To establish a plan of action for implementation of the selected method

(*b*) To obtain approval

(*c*) To perform all other actions necessary to put the proposal into effect

(*a*) To follow-up and audit actual results

(*b*) To resolve problems, if any, during proposal implementation.

Every now and then, you will come across advertisements and announcements in newspapers, to set up small industries under the aegis of the State Small Industries Corporations, which promise you the world: a fully developed industrial shed with power and water, assistance in getting you raw materials, machinery on hire-purchase basis, common services facilities, training facilities and facilities in the marketing of your product. You are assured of term loans on attractive terms and working capital in time and at concessional rates, in backward areas, a number of additional subsidies are available.

An entrepreneur may be a qualified engineer. Even so, he should not dream of becoming a small entrepreneur unless he is confident of meeting the following twelve essential requirements:

(i) The entrepreneur should be fully conversant with the product line. It is not enough that he knows the method of manufacturing; he has to know how to operate the machines etc.

(ii) He should have adequate shop floor experience to guide the machine operators in toolsetting techniques or the die-maker on the specific needs of his press tools.

(iii) He should be familiar with the raw materials he requires, their specifications, how to ensure their quality and where to get them at reasonable prices.

(iv) He should know how to keep accounts, how to maintain stores, how to prepare the balance sheet etc.

(v) He should have knowledge of marketing channels, distribution network, agency practices, transport intricacies and the economics of packaging.

(vi) He should know how to ensure the stipulated quality of his product.

(vii) He should be well versed in taxation and other laws governing small-scale industries.

(viii) He should be willing to control polluted environments and small inconveniences.

(ix) He should be willing to put up with bureaucratic regulations and hurdles, and move with the wind.

(x) He should know how to avail himself of the various benefits available for the small-scale industry.

(xi) He should possess the following qualities – expertise, shrewdness, resourcefulness and most important, perseverance. There is no substitute for hard work.

(xii) He should have the guts to withstand the polluted climate in which he has to build his unit.

Objectives: Any entrepreneur desirous of starting a small-scale industry should have a clear picture of the objective of his project. It is advisable to prepare a comprehensive check list. Such a list, embracing all the important matters, has been given below for the guidance of prospective entrepreneurs. Students will get an insight into the various processes of a small-scale industry.

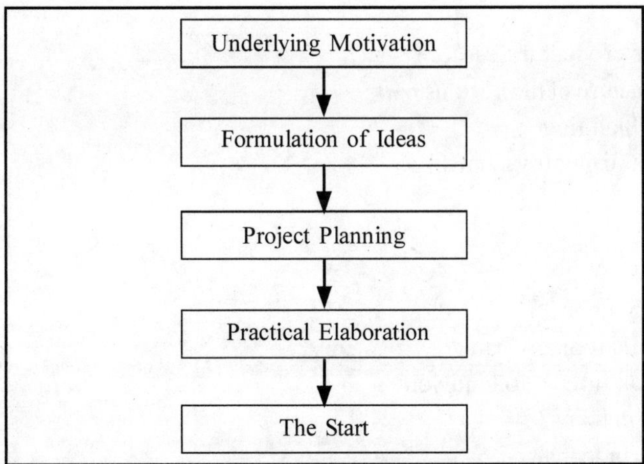

Fig. 8.3: Process of Starting a Small Enterprise

Checklist

Does your industry have scope for development? (Consult Director of Industries)	Yes/No
Is there enough demand for the item you propose to manufacture?	Yes/No
Do you have some experience of	
(a) Manufacturing	Yes/No
(b) Marketing?	Yes/No
Have you studied the viability of your scheme? (Consult the Small Industries Service Institute)	Yes/No
Is factory space available:	
(a) In the Industrial Estate	Yes/No
(b) In an Industrial Area or	Yes/No
(c) In some other approved place?	Yes/No
Have you obtained the necessary licence from the Municipality or the local body?	Yes/No
Are the necessary raw materials available:	
(a) Indigenously	Yes/No
(b) Are they to be imported?	Yes/No
Are facilities available for:	
(a) Tooling	Yes/No
(b) Quality Control?	Yes/No
Is necessary labour available:	
(a) Of skilled workers	Yes/No
(b) Of semi-skilled workers?	Yes/No
Have you the necessary technical background for:	
(a) The manufacture of various parts	Yes/No
(b) Operations?	Yes/No
Have you studied your product in resect of	
(a) The manufacture of the various parts	Yes/No
(b) Production Planning	Yes/No
(c) Inspection and Quality Control	Yes/No
(d) Assembly	Yes/No
(e) Packing	Yes/No
(f) Diversification?	Yes/No
Have you the necessary finance:	
(a) Are you a client of any bank?	Yes/No
(b) Has any bank offered to lend you	
(i) Short-term loans?	Yes/No
(ii) Long-term loans?	Yes/No
(c) Have you any assets?	Yes/No
(d) Are your assets adequate for obtaining the necessary funds?	Yes/No

(e) Have you other sources/ways of raising money? Yes/No

(f) Have you approached the Director of Industries/State Financial Corporation for financial help? Yes/No

(g) Do you propose to approach the NSIC/SSIC for machinery on hire-purchase basis? Yes/No

(h) Have you adequate cash/bank arrangement to furnish the earnest money required by the NSIC? Yes/No

What are your markets?

(a) Local Yes/No

(b) Country-wide Yes/No

(c) Export? Yes/No

How would you market your products(s)? Through

(a) Retailers Yes/No

(b) Wholesalers or Yes/No

(c) Agents? Yes/No

Are necessary transportation facilities available by

(a) Road or Yes/No

(b) Rail? Yes/No

Have you attended a course on

(a) Production, Planning and Control Yes/No

(b) Purchasing and Marketing Yes/No

(c) Finance and Cost Control Yes/No

(d) Personnel Management Yes/No

(e) General Industrial Management? Yes/No

Have you entered into a foreign collaboration agreement for

(a) Technical know-how Yes/No

(b) Royalty/Commission on sales? Yes/No

(c) Has your agreement been approved by the Government? Yes/No

Feasibility Report

Before starting a small-scale industry, one should consult the Director of industries and the Small Industries Service Institute (SISI) located in one's State. The SISI guides entrepreneurs as to the type of industry to start, where to start and how to start it. The SISI helps them to select the various items of manufacture which have scope for development in different areas. It suggests the lines on which a project report for the proposed units should be prepared for the consideration of various financial institutions with a view to securing financial assistance. Similarly, technical help in the selection of proper raw materials and type of machinery is also provided. Apart from this, the SISI gives valuable information of the various incentives available to the small-scale industries from various organisations.

Project Feasibility Analysis

A project feasibility analysis includes market analysis, technical analysis, financial analysis and social profitability analysis. Although each feasibility analysis is different and is tailored to the product, its goal is to identify the strengths and weaknesses of the project.

The starting point of a project analysis is the establishment of the objectives to be attained. The next stage is the pre-selection stage – the advisability of having an indepth study. The analysis stage consists mainly of three factors – market, technical and financial analysis. A market analysis is a method of screening project ideas as well as a means of evaluating a project's feasibility in terms of the market. A market analysis should cover the following areas:

(i) A brief description of the market including the market area, methods of transportation and existing rates of transportation. Channels of distribution and general trade practices are also included.

(ii) An analysis of past and present demands, including the determination of quantity and the value of consumption and identification of the major consumers of the product.

(iii) An analysis of past and present supply, broken down as to source (whether imported or domestic) as well as information which will assist in determining the competitive position of the product such as selling prices, quality and marketing practices of the competitors.

The technical analysis of a project feasibility study establishes whether the project is technically feasible or not, and whether it offers a basis for the estimation of costs. Moreover, it provides an opportunity for a consideration of the effect of various technical alternatives on employment, ecology, infrastructure demands, capital services, support or other industries, balance of payments and other factors. A technical analysis should contain a review of the techniques or processes to be applied and should incorporate:

(i) A description of the product, including specifications relating to its physical, mechanical and chemical properties, as well as uses of the product.

(ii) A description of the selected manufacturing process, showing detailed flow charts and presenting the alternative process which may have been considered and the justification for the adoption of the selected process.

(iii) A determination of the plant size and production schedule, which includes the expected volume for a given time period on the basis of start-up and technical factors.

(iv) Selection of machinery and equipment, including specifications, equipment to be purchased and its origin, quotations from suppliers, delivery dates, terms of payment and a comparative analysis of alternatives in terms of cost, reliability, performance and spare parts availability.

(v) An identification of the plant's location and an assessment of its desirability in terms of its distance from raw material sources and markets. For a new project, this part may include a comparative study of different sites, indicating the advantages and disadvantages of each.

(vi) A design of the plant layout and an estimate of the cost of the erection of the proposed buildings and land improvements.

(vii) A study of the availability of raw materials and liabilities and utilities, including a description of physical and chemical properties, quantities needed, current and prospective costs, terms of payment, locations of sources of supply and continuity of supply.

(viii) An estimate of labour requirements, including a detailed breakdown of direct and indirect labour requirements, and the supervision required for the manufacture of the product.

(ix) A determination of the type and quantity of waste to be disposed off together with a description of the waste disposal method, its costs and the necessary clearance from proper authorities and

(x) An estimate of the production cost of the product.

In the financial analysis of a project feasibility study, emphasis is on the preparation of financial statements, so that the project may be evaluated in terms of the different measures of commercial profitability and the magnitude of financing required may be determined. The financial analysis requires the assembly of the market and technical costs estimated into various proforma statements. If it is necessary to have more information on which to base an investment decision, a sensitivity analysis or possibly, a risk analysis may be conducted. The financial analysis should concentrate on :

(i) Projects that involve new companies, statements of total project cost, initial capital requirements and cash flows relative to the project time-table;

For all projects, financial projections for future time periods including income statements, cash flows and balance sheet are imperative.

(ii) All projects, supporting schedules for financial projection, stating the assumption made as to the collection period of sales, inventory levels, payment period of purchases and expenses, and the element of production cost, selling, administrative and financial expenses.

(iii) All projects, prepare a financial analysis showing returns on investments, returns on equity, break-even volume and price analysis.

(iv) All projects, if necessary, a sensitivity analysis to identify items which have a substantial impact on profitability or possibly a risk analysis.

For the small entrepreneur, the studies conducted during the analysis stage of the project provide the material for an assessment. If positive results are obtained, the entrepreneur, in seeking finance will want to prepare an investment proposal. The planners or government officials, however, having obtained positive conclusion from the economic feasibility study, will want to evaluate the element of social profitability.

The purpose of the investment or loan application is to convince a lender (financial institution) that the project is a desirable investment; that it not only possesses the potential for profit but that the proposed management team has the capability to achieve the potential. The investment proposal normally contains:

(i) General information on the product, company history, the nature of the industry and the reputation and qualifications of the existing or proposed management.

(ii) A description of the period, which usually consists of extracts from economic feasibility studies and includes information on such items as market, production, selected manufacturing methods (with detailed indication of the cost of equipment and operational expenses) and a financial statement and

(iii) Miscellaneous information, such as the steps taken for the implementation of the project and the qualifications of the technical partners envisaged or selected.

Break-even Analysis

Let us first address 'why break-even analysis?' While discussing preparation of a project report of feasibility report, we stated that the level of estimated capacity utilisation, i.e., quantum of production in terms of goods or services as the case may be, needs to be spelled out in advance in the project report. Our business experience tells us that when the enterprise/business is actually started, in other words, the project is actually implemented, the projected or targeted level of capacity is not achieved due to various unforeseen reasons.

Such a situation entails financial implications. Then, the entrepreneur needs to decide to what extent the curtailment in production can be afforded to meet all its liabilities. Steinhoff and Burgess put it as "How much must I sell before I start making profit." The answer-to this question is called the 'break-even analysis' where income exactly equals expenses. Let us now understand 'What is break-even analysis?' In simple words, it is an analysis of production point at which profit starts. This point is where income and expenses are exactly equal and the point is called 'break-even point.' Thus, break-even analysis is used to find the break-even point.

Having understood the concept of break-even analysis, we now intend to expose you to the mechanics involved in finding out break-even point. In carrying out any enterprise, profit comes from sale of goods or services as the case may be and expenses emerge out from the cost involved. Expenses to be incurred refer to cost. Cost is broadly divided into two types, viz.: (1) Fixed cost, and (2) Variable cost. What are these costs?

Fixed Cost: Fixed costs are defined as those that do not change with increase or decrease in production. No matter what the production is, the fixed cost remains the same. Examples of fixed costs could be the monthly rent paid for the factory, interest on long-term loan, administrative expenses, etc. Even if there is zero production, the fixed cost will remain unchanged. Say, if factory rent, i.e., Rs. 10,000 per month is the only cost, it wiIl remain fixed at Rs. 10,000 if there is a production of 500 units or 200 units or even no production at all.

Variable Cost: In short, what is not fixed cost is variable cost. Variable cost is defined as expenses that change with the volume of production. It varies proportionately with changes in production. Thus, if production is zero, variable cost would be zero. The absolute total variable cost increases or decreases along with increases or decrease in production. But the variable cost per unit is constant at any level of production: The following example clears it.

There are some variable costs that do not vary proportionately with the change in production. In fact, these vary in varying degres. As a result such costs are called semi-variable. The popular examples of such costs could be telephone, electricity and gas charges if they are billed on a usage basis. In such cases that proportion of expenses which continue even if production falIs are considered as fixed and expenses which increase or decrease as production increases or decreases are considered as variable cost.

After knowing sales and total cost in terms of fixed cost and variable cost, now the break-even point can be calculated.

According to the simplest method, Profit is the excess of sales over cost, i.e.,

Sales – Cost = Profit. The calculation of break-even point involves four steps. These are:

(1) Segregation of fixed and variable costs

(2) Percentage of variable costs to sales

(3) Calculate the contribution or margin, i.e., the difference between 100 and the percentage of variable cost to sales as worked out above.

(4) Divide the fixed cost by the percentage of contribution or margin as worked out above.

Thus, the calculated figure will be 'break-even point.'

It will be better, at least for those of you who are coming across to the concept of break-even point for the first time, to calculate break-even point with the help of an example.

Once the industry is identified, the SISI prepares a feasibility report and project report, thus giving a comprehensive idea of an industry's prospects and profitability.

Licences: An impression seems to have gained round among some people that there are some restrictions on the setting up of small-scale industrial units and that licences from either the Central or State Government have to be taken out before an entrepreneur can take steps to start a small-scale industrial unit. This impression is not correct. It is open to any entrepreneur to set up an industrial unit in the small-scale sector; no formal permission from the State or Central Government is necessary for this purpose. Also, industries employing less than 100 workers and having fixed assets of less then Rs. 10 lakh need not obtain any licence under the Industries (Development and Regulation) Act.

Small-scale units have, however, to conform to the rules and regulations prescribed by the State or local authority under the Factories Act, the Commercial Establishment Act, the Town Planning Rules made for the issue of quotas of raw materials etc.

However, powerlooms do not come under the purview of the small-scale industries programme. For installing powerlooms, the prior permission of the Textile Commissioner, Government of India, Mumbai, is required.

(1) Registration of Small-scale Industries

In their own interest, all existing small-scale units or intending entrepreneurs employing more than 10 workers should get themselves registered with the Director of Industries in their State. A copy of this application for registration should be sent to the Director of Small Industries Service Institute in the concerned State. Such registration with the Director of Industries and the Small Industries Services Institute will be of considerable help to the small-scale unit in obtaining financial assistance from the Government and for obtaining machinery on hire-purchase basis from the national Small Industries Corporation. Assistance in the supply of controlled raw materials, essentiality certificate for imported raw materials and components and facilities for export promotion, would then be easily made available to small-scale units registered with the State Director of Industries. The registration number is now required to be quoted while submitting import applications. Registration procedures have been substantially simplified. Revised forms of SSI have been introduced from 1.1.1994.

(2) Infrastructure

This pertains to approaching the Director of Industries and/or the SISI in the State to provide you with built-up factory space in an industrial estate or develop the factory site, power etc. After the initial clearance from the State Director of Industries, the Municipality or the Panchayat issues a 'No Objection Certificate'. The procedure for obtaining the basic infrastructure facilities is given below. The mechanics of establishing a new factory in Greater Mumbai are:

(i) Apply to the Industries Commissioner, Industries and Labour Department, Government of Maharashtra, and obtain a 'No Objection Certificate.'

(ii) With a copy of the above NOC, apply, in Factory Form "A" to the Ward Engineer of B.M.C.

(iii) Clarification and submission of further details on the information supplied in Form 'A' may, follow.

(iv) The Sub-Engineer will inspect the premises and submit Form No. '2' to his Assistant Engineer.

(v) The Assistant Engineer will scrutinise and confirm if the applicant's activity conforms to the zone and will intimate to the applicant in Form No. '3' if there is no objection or in Form No. '4' if there is any objection.

(vi) Form 'B' will be received by the applicant if Form No. '3' is issued to him. This form should be filled in and submitted.

(vii) Within 21 days after the submission of Forms "A", 'B" and the factory plans in triplicate, the Assistant Engineer will issue Form Nos. '5' and V in which he will specify:

(a) The electric power sanctioned (thereafter the BEST provides electricity);

(b) Adequate water facilities provided;

(c) The various requirements, requisitions and conditions for operating the factory, including those required by the Chief Inspector of Factories.

Form 'C' 'will also be issued along with these forms. (Upon complying with the stipulation in Form 'B' I the BMC should be informed thereof in writing.)

Thereafter, permission to commence production will be given.

(3) Machinery

The small entrepreneur needs the requisite type of machines for production. He can get the necessary machinery from the National Small Industries Corporation (NSIC) under a hire-purchase scheme.

The scheme for the supply of indigenous and imported machines on hire-purchase basis was launched in March 1956 to enable small entrepreneures without substantial means to avail themselves of assistance. The scheme is different from the credit operations scheme for entrepreneurs. The NSIC has acquired the necessary experience and expertise in the procurement of machines from the right sources. It also takes care of the problems upto the stage of delivery of machineries to the entrepreneurs. Also, while financial institutions look mainly to the creditworthiness of entrepreneurs, the NSIC would look primarily to the motivation of the individual applicant, his capacity, his technical competence and his managerial ability to run the enterprise.

The small entrepreneur should enlist himself as a member with the NSIC. His application form should be accompanied with the Registration Certificate and report of the Director of Industries. The application for obtaining machines under the hire-purchase scheme of the NSIC is quite comprehensive. The small entrepreneur has to provide full details along with the relevant documents.

The application form for hire-purchase machinery calls for information regarding the organisational set-up of a unit, its programme of production and marketability and profitability of the enterprise. It also calls for additional information regarding the cost of production, the infrastructure facilities available for the unit, the technical capability of the entrepreneur etc. The details in the application are self-explanatory.

(4) Raw Materials

The raw materials required by small-scale units may broadly be classified as under:

(i) Raw material components and spares — both indigenous and imported;

(ii) Non-ferrous materials — both indigenous and imported;

(iii) Iron and steel — both indigenous and imported and

(iv) Chemical — indigenous and imported.

Under the liberalised scheme, the actual users are provided with adequate foreign exchange to meet their justifiable requirements of imported items of industrial materials. The 'priority' industries are assured of an adequate supply to the extent of their requirements by way of grant of rotational licences.

Small-scale units should apply directly to the Regional Licensing Authority, and not through the sponsoring authority, for import licences for raw materials, components and spares after utilising the previous set of licences to the extent of 90 per cent by way of opening their own credit or 60 per cent by way of actual import, covering six months' requirements of the unit. New units should submit their applications through their respective sponsoring authority.

The State Director of Industries allocates indigenous non-ferrous metals. Some of the non-ferrous items are canalised through the State Trading Corporation of India (STC). The raw materials imported by the STC are given to the SSI units in accordance with the recommendations of the Director of industries concerned.

Iron and steel raw materials are canalised through the MMTC in accordance with the recommendations of the Director of Industries.

In times of difficulties, the decontrolled chemical raw materials are canalised through the DGTD in accordance with the recommendation of State Director of Industries. Indigenous controlled chemicals are allocated through the State DIS/SICs. Imported raw materials are canalised through the STC.

In short, controlled and imported raw materials are to be obtained through the State DIS, SICs (SSI).

(5) Finance

The financial function in a small-scale industry is similar to the financial function in any other organisation, but with this essential difference — that there are a host of banking and insurance regulations to be strictly adhered to and quite a few precautions to be taken.

The areas where finance would be needed, after the small-scale industrialist fixes the land accommodation are:

- *(i)* Purchase and installation of machinery;
- *(ii)* Procurement of raw materials and components and the manufacture of products;
- *(iii)* Working funds and
- *(iv)* Availability of funds until the realisation of sales.

The State Director of Industries provides loans for block capital under the Industries Act. One should apply through the sponsoring authority. State Financial Corporations provide long-term credit for the purchase of fixed assets. The application should be submitted to the SFCs along with the following documents: *(i)* Project Report; *(ii)* Copy of Registration; *(iii)* Cashflow Statement and *(iv)* Stock Statement.

In some states, the SFCs and the banks have agreed to process the common application for loans. For an amount of Rs. 2 lakh, the commercial bank provides medium-term instalment credit. It also provides loans for meeting needs for working capital for the purchase of raw materials as also for day-to-day requirements.

In order to get a loan from a commercial bank, the entrepreneur has to fill in an application form as per the specimen (Annexure VIII) and submit it to the bank along with the following documents:

- *(i)* Authentic copies of Balance Sheets and Profit and Loss Accounts (if the industrial concern is a limited company or an industrial co-operative society.)
- *(ii)* A statement of assets and liabilities in the prescribed form (Appendix I of Annexure VIII) in the case of partnership and proprietary concerns.
- *(iii)* Proforma statements in all other cases.
- *(iv)* Copies of the affidavit in regard to the size of the unit.
- *(v)* Technical Feasibility Report from the Small Industries Service Institute, the Director of Industries, if obtained, may also be enclosed.

Box 8.2 – Finance – To take or not to take

Indians are known to be entrepreneurs But to be one needs funds. A guide to bank funding for wanna-be entreneurs.

Munira Mohat is an Architect cum interior designer who works for a famous Architect firm. She has had a good stint of three years at the same job and is itching to strike out on her own. But the big question that looms large in her head is how to fund for the office space and expenses till plum projects fall on her lap.

Sudenshu Gupta wants to start an auto ancillary unit. He has done his homework on the manufacturing side of the business as well as built report with a number of Auto Manufacturers who have assured him of regular orders. He knows his idea is sure fire.

FOCAL POINT

- Individuals wish to start off businesses but cannot due to lack of funds.
- Banks provide finance to enterpreneurs under many schemes.
- If your papers are in order it is safe and fast to avail credit from a bank.
- Till you pay off the loan, banks are owners of your property.
- You have to be psychologically strong to be an entrepreneur.

If wishes were horses all of the above would have been riding them as CEOs. But the biggest thorn on their future bed of roses is MONEY... or rather a lack of it.

In an ideal world, all of them would have Sugar Daddies to fund their dreams, if they decide to wait and save up till they shore up all the capital they require the business opportunity may no longer be a viable option. The only other option is of course a rich father in law or the Bank. Banks have lots of schemes for such entrepreneurs.

TERM LOANS: Normally these loans are given to fund property and immovable assets like plant and machinrey. The repayment is 3 to 5 years and the interest is in the range of 11% to 14%.

Working Capital Loans/Cash Credit: Simplistically this loan would finance the day-to-day running of your business. The interest charged is on the actual amount used and falls within the band of 10.5% to 12%.

Bill Discounting Facility: Say you sell goods to X and Co. You raise a bill but give them credit for three months. If you want the money right away, the bank shall deduct some charges, pay you the bill amount and levy interest. After 3 months the bank collects directly from X and Co.

Apart from the above there are many schemes floated by the banks like small-scale liberalized schemes, Entrepreneur's scheme, schemes for Woman Entrepreneurs etc.

A composite tailor made packge can also be devised for suitable customers. What are the pros and cons for availing this kind of a loan?

Pros:

- If you have a dream, this is most certainly the safest way to finance it.

Alternatively, you can find people who also believe in you and finance you in terms of equity or extend a loan to you. In that case you make partners in your business or pay them interest just like a bank. The only hitch is that individuals can decide to pull out of your business at will, which just might leave you in the lurch.

- Banks will clear repayment and interest schedules making cash flow planning easy.
- Banks have technical teams that sometimes help you in assessing the viability of your projects.

Cons:

- There will be tons of administrative work, scores of forms to be filled.
- Normally, banks require the entrepreneur to bring in his own money into the business. This is called margin money.
- Banks will have a first charge on your assets. This means that till you pay the bank off completely, they are the owners of the property they have given a loan for.
- Bank ask for personal guarantee and/or Guarantors. This mens that if your business fails your personal assets like house etc. can be attached and/or your Guarantors will be made to repay your loan.

If you can sleep peacefully at night after taking on a debt and you are such that your business will generate at least that much money to take care of the interest and loan repayment, you have the stomach of an entrepreneur go for it.

Documents Required for Procuring Business Loans

Sole Proprietorship/Partnership Firm

- Proof of identity (Copy of Sales Tax/VAT/Service Tax/PAN ID/IT Return of the Concern/Water/ Electricity/Municipal Tax Bill in the Name of the Concern)
- Proof of individual identity (Copy of Passport/Voter's Identity Card/Photo PAN Card/Driving License/MAPIN Card)
- PAN Number/Form 60 of the Concern Financial Documents (Copy of P&L Account and Balance Sheet for last two years, audited by a CA and Copies of IT returns for the last two years)
- Proof of residence address (Copy of Passport/Voter's Identity Card/Driving License/Ration Card/ Life Insurance Policy/Electricity Bill/Telephone Bill)
- Bank Statements for last 6 months
- Partnership deed (Required only in case of Partnership Firm)
- Two passport size photographs
- Proof of place of business

For Private Limited Company

- Proof of Identity (Copy of Sales Tax/VAT/Service Tax/Excise Registration or Registration under Shops and Establishment Act or PAN ID/IT Return of the Concern or Water/Electricity/ Municipal Tax Bill in the Name of the Concern)
- Memorandum and Articles of Association (Copy of Certificate of Incorporation)
- Board Resolution (Copy of Annual Return establishing the shareholding pattern)
- Proof of Individual Identity for the authorized signatories and 2 directors, including the Managing Director (Copy of Passport/Voter's Identity Card/Photo PAN Card/Driving License/MAPIN Card)
- List of Directors
- Copy of Form 32 filed with ROC
- PAN Card / Form 60 of the Concern
- Financial Documents (Copy of P&L and Balance Sheet for last two years, audited by a CA, and Copies of IT returns for the last two years)
- Bank Statements for last 6 months
- Proof of Place of Business
- Two passport size photographs

Steps to Obtain a Business Loan

(1) **Gather information:** Obtain information on the type of loan you are looking for

(2) **Application and assessment:** Submit the required document, so that the lending institution can evaluate your financial status and your ability to repay

(3) **Approval:** On approval of the loan, you will receive a Facility Offer Letter

(4) **Receiving the money:** The approved amount will be deposited into an agreed bank account

(5) **Making payments:** Installments will be deducted directly from a designated bank account.

According to the Code of Bank's Commitment to Micro and Small Enterprises, once the loan is sanctioned, the Bank has to supply authenticated copies of all the loan documents executed along with a copy each of all enclosed documents quoted in the loan document and the list thereof.

(6) Marketing

The rationale of the Government Purchase Scheme of the Corporation lies in the fact that the Government of India is the largest single buyer; and by channelising these purchases in favour of small-scale units, it gives a tremendous boost to the marketing of their products.

The salient features of the scheme are:

(a) The small-scale units, desiring to avail themselves of assistance, have to enlist themselves with the NSIC;

(b) Instead of purchasing tender sets from the DGS & D, the small units enlisted with the NSIC automatically gets them from it and its branches free of cost;

(c) If their prices are acceptable to the DGS & D, they are not required to pay a security deposit on the issue of a competency certificate by the NSIC;

(d) Price preference upto 15 per cent over the quotations of large-scale units is considered by the Purchasing Agency, depending on the merits of each case;

(e) Wherever they feel that injustice has been done to them, the NSIC takes up their cases with the DGS and D and other government departments such as Defence, the Railways and the P&T Department in order to find out the reasons for non-placement of the contract with the units, and tries to redress their grievances.

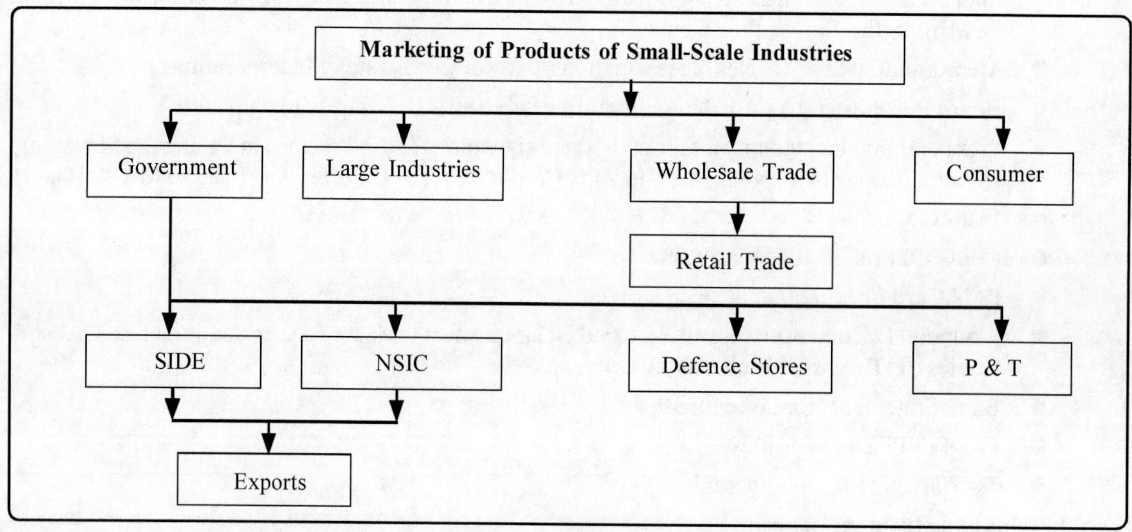

Fig. 8.4: Marketing of Products of SSIs

The Corporation also helps small-scale industries in securing contracts from other government departments such as Railways, Posts and Telegraphs etc.

Hitherto, the purchase programme has been restricted purely to Central purchase houses like DGS & D, the P&T and the Railways. It is proposed to extend the base further to cover state government departments such as the — State Electricity Boards, PWDs etc. and provide liaison offices at each of the principal purchase centres of the State.

(7) Incentives

For availing the various incentives, it is advisable to seek the help of the SISI and/or the Director of Industries.

The Small Industries Development Organisation (SIDO), Ministry of Industry, Nirman Bhavan, New Delhi, co-ordinates policies and programmes at the national level and provides a comprehensive range of extension services through its network of sixteen Small Industries Services Institutes, nineteen Branch Institutes and forty-five Extension Centres.

At the State level, organisations like State Directorates of Industries, Small Industries Development Corporations and Finance Corporations cater to the need of small industries; these needs include land, sheds, credit, power, raw materials etc.

The National Small Industries Corporation (NSIC), Okhla, New Delhi, provides machines and equipment on hire-purchase basis to entrepreneurs, assists units to participate in stores purchase programmes and provides training and prototype development facilities.

Registration with the NSIC entitles the units to obtain facilities from Central or State Government organisations. New units have to apply to the respective State Directors of Industries for provisional registration, which is given within a week. It enables the party to take the necessary steps to bring the unit into existence, i.e., apply for sheds in industrial estates or on developed sites for water and power, connections and for credit facilities. After the party has taken all the steps, it can apply for registration.

SIDO provides technical consultancy on improved technical processes, use of modern machines and equipment and technical assistance on all aspects of production. Each SISI has attached workshops for common facility services, training of workers, demonstration of modern machines and processes, making of tools and dies etc.

The ten components of the National Manufacturing Competitiveness Programme (NMCP) to be implemented by the Ministry of the micro, small and medium enterprises (MSME) during XI Plan are:

(i) Support for entrepreneurial and managerial development of MSMEs through 'Business Incubators.'

(ii) Quality Management Standards (QMS) and Quality Technology Tools (QTT) for MSMEs

(iii) National campaign for investment in Intellectual Property Rights (IPR)

(iv) Marketing support/assistance for MSMEs for adoption of 'Bar Code'

(v) Lean manufacturing

(vi) Setting up of New Mini Tool Rooms (MTR)

(vii) Energy efficiency and quality upgradation support for MSMEs

(viii) Design Clinics

(ix) Promotion of Information and Communication Technology (ICT) in MSMEs

(x) Marketing assistance for MSMEs and technology upgradation activities, called 'Marketing Scheme' in short.

Box 8.3: Start-up Hiring Checklist

RECRUITING IS MARKETING

More often than not, the best employees are the ones that find you, not the ones you go out and look for. The problem a lot of startups have is, how do I get more people to find me? Simple – think of it as a marketing exercise. Just as you would explain the product features to a potential customer, explain to a candidate what it's like to work for you (in real language, no HR platitudes thanks), what you took for in people and then make sure people find out about it. You can even post a Web page on life at your company. It's a small investment to make but an effective tool in getting a vast audience to read about the work experience under your roof.

TRUST YOUR TEAM

You've hired smart people already right? You think your team is the best on the planet. So put them in front of candidates! Don't hide them in a back room. Too many people have their HR people do most of the interviewing. Let the candidates get to know the people they'll be working with, if they join your company.

YOU DON'T WIN WITH MONEY

Many entrepreneurs think that the simple way to hire a good team is to throw money at the problem. In choosing a place to work, people look at the company, the role, the people, the environment and the money. Pretty much in that order, but it's important to keep the balance among all the variables. As long as the money is competitive (and this is key), the other factors should decide the final outcome. Money doesn't win people over, money prevents you from losing them. It gets you in the game. People value their time and while you might be able to 'buy it' with an outrageous salary, that's a temporary measure. They'll eventually realise that doing a boring job 10 hours a day for huge dollars isn't the way they want to spend their life. it's not a way to build a company, it's a short-term band aid strategy. You don't win people with a lot of money and I'd say you don't want to. People who chose a job purely on the larger salary are probably people you don't want on your team anyway. That said, the corollary here is that you can definitely lose people with money. if you're not paying what the market is or your firm just pays really low salaries, people will go elsewhere. it's all about balance.

MAKE SPACE FOR SMART PEOPLE

Sometimes people come along who don't fit into any existing role. You can consider hiring really smart people, even if you don't have a defined role for them. At the same time, don't be afraid to redirect a candidate if you feel they're interviewing for the wrong job. If you have a roadmap for your company's progress, you would have created titles and jobs that you would require in the next two or three years. Many smart people will fit into these roles, current or future, but others create the job profile for themselves. Have the flexibility to include both groups in your team.

TO HIRE OR NOT TO HIRE

The hire-or-don't-hire decision is critical. Why is this decision so important? The damage a wrong choice can do to morale, to your product, to your company should never be overstated. It's a little like poker, the most important and hardest skill to learn is when to fold a hand not when to bet. Not hiring a few good people is far better in the long-term than hiring a few bad ones. Err on the side of caution.

NO KEYWORD HIRING

This mostly applies to software developers, but the principle is important for all. Don't hire based on keywords in a resume. Too many companies look for "JMS", "EJB 3 " and "J2EE" and assume someone is a good developer. Look for people who are good at learning new technologies, rather than stacking up acronyms.

(Adapted from the blog of Atlassian, an Australian software company)

Lessons for Software Bravehearts

Building a software product company is an activity from the ground-up. There is hardly any guidance from an external entity like in the case of software services companies where the customer specifies the requirement, the technology, the platform and the tools. This unique situation makes building a software product company, a wonderful experience on one hand and one that constantly tests your sanity, on the other. This article does not purport to be a 'Guide to Sure Success in Software Products Business since there are many ways to succeed in this business. So, this is only a collection of my experience at Subex.

Identifying the "Product"

Products can be grouped into "absolutely-essential," "need-to-have," 'nice-to-have" and "frill." One of the reasons for the bankrupticies of product companies during the tech downturn was that they were in the last two categories. How does one identify a potential product idea? Look around and choose a few areas in the domain that you are familiar with, apply filters to quality each one of these and arrive at a shortlist. Then meet potential users and apply a generous dose of "gut feel" to choose the product.

Strategy and Funding

Following the selection of a product, the company should formulate a sound strategy with regard to markets to be addressed, sales channel, marketing methodology, product management, support etc. Although a software product company has to invest large amounts in product development, sales and marketing, the outflow can be controlled by employing a well thoughtout strategy. The Indian scene with regard to funding for software product companies is quite bleak. So, costs need to be monitored very closely.

Focus and the Domain Game

Focus on a niche. Superior knowledge of the domain is essential to develop products that will be future proof and to define the road map for the product. While the external environment and a multitude of opportunities might lure the company towards different domains, the management's conviction in themselves, their strategy and products must enable it to continue to be focused.

Personnel

Software product companies need people with certain unique skill-sets not common in India and also with mindsets that are different from those in services companies. Product management is a key function and personnel with that experience are scarce in India. In such a scenario, Indian companies must tap overseas markets or returning Indians for this critical function.

Reference ability

Gone is the adage 'Customer is King.' It now reads, 'Customer is Emperor.' Customers invest considerable amount of time and money in procuring products. The due diligence process is extensive and exhaustive. Unlike services business where customers can change vendors with minimal cost impact, after a trial, software products are tricky even for customers. Companies need to ensure that every customer is a good reference as they can be used as excellent ambassadors with potential customers.

Advantage India

Setting up software product companies in India is an attractive proposition given advantages like low cost of handling marketing, implementation and customer support, availability of high quality technical skill and a large domestic market for most products. A recent example of a Silicon Valley company that managed to get through two years of operations with only about $5 million (by depending on India) instead of about

Box 8.4: Mind Your Business

The entrepreneurial road is paved with risks of every kind. How to anticipate them and risk-proof your small business.

Given the ease with which burglars broke into leather goods exporter Udai Piplani's gift accessories showroom in south Delhi in August 2003 and carted away merchandise worth Rs. 1.3 lakh, they may have felt they were plundering an unguarded fortress. But they would have been wrong.

It's of course true that there were serious breaches in the defence and Piplani's business did suffer a material loss that could have dented it seriously. But the businessman wasn't entirely without a last line of defence. A silent unseen arm held the fort and ensured that the Piplani empire's flag remained flying from its ramparts. It came in the form of a low-cost insurance policy that helped him bear the financial shock of the loss, and ensured that his business was not laid low by a common-enough risk.

"A small business is like a one day cricket innings," says Piplani, with a touch of Sidhuism. "You can't avoid risk altogether – not if you want to score big but there are ways of containing in." It was with this rick containment objective that he secured a shopkeepr's cover for stocks and goods in his showroom which would commpensate him in the event of fire or theft,"For a small price of Rs. 4,500 as premium for Rs. 4.5 lakh of stocks plus about Rs.10 lakh cover for the premises and Rs. 2 lakh worth of fittings-I insulated my business against a big risk and bought myself complete peace of mind," says he.

It was this poilcy that ensured and he got Rs. 1 lakh as compensation for the material loss he suffered.

"Very few small businesses adequately understand the importance of risk management," says L. Ravindran, a Huderabad based risk management consultant "And even those that do, fail to realise that with increasing scale of operations, the risks only get compounded."

And although there are a range of insurance covers that address specific kind of risk, there are other business hazards for which the defences like outside the realm of financial products.

Insurable Risks

The risks that any business is susceptible to depends on the nature of the business. Principally, the "insurable risks" that is risks for which there are defences in the form of insurance covers – relate to theft of or demage to assets, the risk of business interruption or breakdown, the loss of money or goods in transit, employee fraud, and legal liability towards employees or a third party. It's important to identify the specific risks your business may face and then buy appropriate cover for the right amount.

Insurable Risks

- Cover your assets
- Never take a break
- Schedule the business process
- Know your liability
- Ensure high fidelity
- Insure goods in transit
- No-Insurable risks
- Have a plan 'B'
- Manage your cash flows
- Stick to a budget
- Do not borrow blind
- Master the art of businrss

$15 to 20 million that they would've otherwise invested shows that its time we take advantage of this unique situation too.

Building a software product company is actually an exhilarating experience. Herein lies the Opportunity to be truly creative, innovative and be a true generator of value and wealth. India is today at the cross roads of IT revolution. It is upto us to cock a snook at those who have labeled us as "techno coolies." However, we need to tread cautiously to avoid the pitfalls that have resulted in a high rate of mortality – seven out of ten software product companies fail. It is within us, to succeed in a grand scale provided we pay considerable attention to the cardinal principles of a software products business – a 'need to have" product, well-honed strategy, razorsharp focus, motivated and qualified personnel, eminently referenceable customers, tight cost control, commitment and above all, conviction that India can be the thought leader of tomorrow.

The Winning Edge

The opening up of the Indian small industry sector to competition as well as the increase in the need to cater to the global market demands fresh perceptions to respond to the radical changes in the 90s. Consequently, the Indian small industry sector must change first to survive as well as restructure itself to meet the new challenges through a critical evaluation of the forces of free global trade and increased competition. These events demand quantum strategic changes in terms of industry culture, flattening of the organisation structure, employee empowerment as well as team building. Only those organisations which can respond to these changes will be able to survive and retain a winning edge.

Some of the important characteristics that differentiate the successful organisations from the unsuccessful ones are:

(1) The most important aspect of successful business is leadership. It calls for clear vision, goals and objectives, well defined mission, dash and employees' participation.

(2) Adequate but well-orchestrated control. Constant feedback of results as well as setting and adherence of high standards gives an organisation a cutting edge over others. Planning, foresight and analysis are also important qualities.

(3) To able to extract the best from its employees through total involvement, the organisation put a lot of emphasis on proper internal communication and on training employees.

(4) The successful organisation is one which is very close to the market place. The process of systematic market research is used to develop products or processes and to provide value for money to the customers. This helps to gain the market share.

(5) The next most important characteristic of a winning business organisation is 'Zero Basing' or sticking to the last – knowing what business the company is in and swiftly recognising when it has diverted into an unsuitable path.

(6) Another important characteristic for success is commitment to innovation which is vital in keeping ahead of the competition and perhaps the most difficult one to achieve. Yet, most of the organisations just pay lip service to creativity and innovation. They ask for new ideas and then quickly reject them and even when a new idea is accepted, the employee rarely gets a reward proportionate to the idea's worth.

Successful business organisation creates a climate that encourages new ideas as a part of the employee's job. Anything that helps create the innovative culture and a natural curiosity, about how things are done in other companies will add value to the organisation.

The Strategy

It is therefore imperative that the vision of a company be shared across all levels. Effective communication of the vision statement across the organisation is the first step towards designing a focused work environment and a goal-oriented people force.

Translating goals into action calls for synergising individual effort and belief to create a single force. It requires an able team and equally able leaders who invoke a sense of camaraderie and team spirit and vision, both in terms of words and meaning. Simply preaching the vision will not alone achieve it, and this is where people management and the art of motivation becomes paramount. Taking the values of the company and what it seeks to become in the future, beyond the walls of the boardroom is important, but what is vital is for the team members to feel that they are an integral part of this vision. This means involving them in setting goals which is the key to gaining their commitment to achieve and to excel.

One thing is certain that customer service excellence is the true differentiator and the secret of long-term success. Customer service is a passion that transcends all boundaries and is the glue of organisational goals and success.

Customers and their growing demands are at the forefront of our business models, supported by people sharing a common vision. With this combination, performance and success can't be far ahead. The test of true leadership is in executing the perceived future of success. This future will be won by capable people.

Given the ever-changing business situation today, it is indeed a herculean task for entrepreneurs to keep realigning services, products, methods and practices to match needs. They can, however, do it best by empowering their team members to take calculated decisions as and when the need arises, and providing them with space for innovation at every touch point. this, apart from motivating employees to continuously strive for the better, makes them feel a part of each success story that the company can boast of.

A company that creates a customer-oriented culture where it sees every problem as an opportunity to serve the customer better, is the one that will survive the toughest competition today.

To be self-employed one has to be a vision. To entrepreneurs who has it as one of the fundamental characteristics, vision is a vivid, dramatic and complete picture of what the company wants to be, and do. Crucially, this future is not one that can be reached in normal course; it needs a quantum leap.

Vision has been defined as the power of perceiving by imagination or by clear thinking in the organisational context, vision is a picture of the future of the organisation. Vision is the hallmark of a forward looking organisation. It provides the motivation needed to get the best out of an organisation enterprise and people. Vision inspires one to strive for better.

The founder of an organisation needs to paint a picture of the organisation as he sees it in the future. This encompasses primarily its scope as an organisation in terms of areas of business or products; the geographic boundaries and the value system by which it desires to attain the same, and a clarity of the relationships that it will develop with various members associated with the organisation.

It is important for an enterprise to have clarity of vision primarily because the organisation can stay focused and not wander off into any unrelated areas that arise as a result of opportunities or apparent synergies. For instance, a company may feel that it can get into situations of vertical integration to optimise cost/returns, profitability, etc. While it may be profitable in the short run or may appear to be a strategically good move, it may not be optimal in the long-term if it is not in keeping with the corporate vision.

Box 8.5: The Enterprise Manual

Enterprise will never be the same again. The mega dotcom boom saw the intiation of big-ticket venture funding in the country, with an enormous infusion of capital into start-ups covering a whole gamust of industries – ranging from the ubiquitous IT to biotechnology and customer services.

Now the party is over but that does not mean the demise of enterprise. What it does mean is that both funders and entrepreneurs noe play a much more cautious game. As Sanjay Anadaram managing director, Jumpstartup, says: "VCs will fund entrepreneurs who ve failed before if the reasons for failure have nothing to do with issues like ethics and team building skills"

After tha dust has settled, what has emerged is a storehouse of start -up lessons that serve as signposts on the road to successful enterprise. The money is there and so is the opportunity: but before taking the plunge, it help to get a grip on the rules.

The DOs

- **Stay low profile**. Building a start-up from the idea stage to the cash-positive companey is best done away from the mesmeric arc lights. IT reseller veritas software grew from a single-vendor reseller into a Rs. 12 crore outfit in seven years, without ever using mass media, Says Asha Pandey co-founder:You would never have heard of us we never made a noise."
- **Read the fine print.** Make sure you know the finer points of all the contracts signed with investors or customers; this can save.
- **From nesty surprises later.** Particularly if as founder you are facted with the proapect of an abrupt exit from the start, ashappened to parkesh Gurbaxani of 24/7 customer com.
- **Network.** It's vital to keep your contacts intact, both within and outside the entrepreneurial ecosystem. Lovaii Navlakhi sent out afarewell mail to 300 names on his address list on his last day at indya. com; the replies helped convince him of the market for his new venture, Money Matters.
- **Take care of the pennies.** Cash is always at a premium for start-ups; don't be a guzzler. Money Matters is run from a home office; it helps the six month-old outfit cincentrate on building new business instead of meeting needless overhead expenses.
- **Make VCs your last resort.** Asha Pandey's Veritas Software used debt funding from commercial banks for a decade, as there was no significant knowledhe equity that a VC ciuld bring into the reselling space they were in.VC money is valuable only when it brings both intellectual and cash equity.

The DON'TS

- **Follow the herd.** It was e-commerce yesterday and its call centres and business process outsouring today. Following the herd without thinking your gemeplan through can result in your being trampled underfoot by the competition. Gautam Agrawal launched formsindia com at the height of the boom only to cash out in a distress sale seven months later.
- **Calculate just profits.** Instead of eveluating your business idea merely on potential profits calculate the losses too to arrive at the real value of your investment Nisheeth Srivastava signed a sweat-and -chas deal to get on board support but returned to the security of the corporate world after a tumultuous two years without cashing casbing out his equity holding
- **Ignore change.** Although Asha Pandey was running a tight ship at Veritas, as the Internet transformed the business landscape she realised her personal growth had been stunted. She cashed out to launch e-learning start-up onward Education.
- **Focus just on the long term.** It is the short-term goals that build a company paying customers building the management team making cash profits. These need to be in place first before the long-term goal of market expansion. Prakash Gurbaxani had to quit 24/7 customer. comultimately because his long-term goals did not match those of his partners on the board.

Similarly, a firm's long-term interests in terms of developing a well-integrated organisation may not be served if it considers unrelated diversification just because an opportunity comes its way, or because the officials have specific contact with certain officials in the government.

The second important reason why clarity of vision is needed is because it develops a culture of learning within the organisation, in order to fulfill the clarified and stated vision. For instance, if an organisation's vision is to expand and become a global player in the market of the developing world, then the entire organisation could develop an interest in the specific industry sector and the geographic area and would, over a period of time, gain the knowledge to fulfill that vision.

Clarity of vision also enables the entire organisation to develop an inspirational force towards attaining a common goal, thus enhancing the team building process in an organisation since the entire organisation as the team will perform even a simple task.

An organisation (entrepreneur) must develop its vision statement based on where it is today via a thorough analysis of swot.

Building a Vision: Stage I

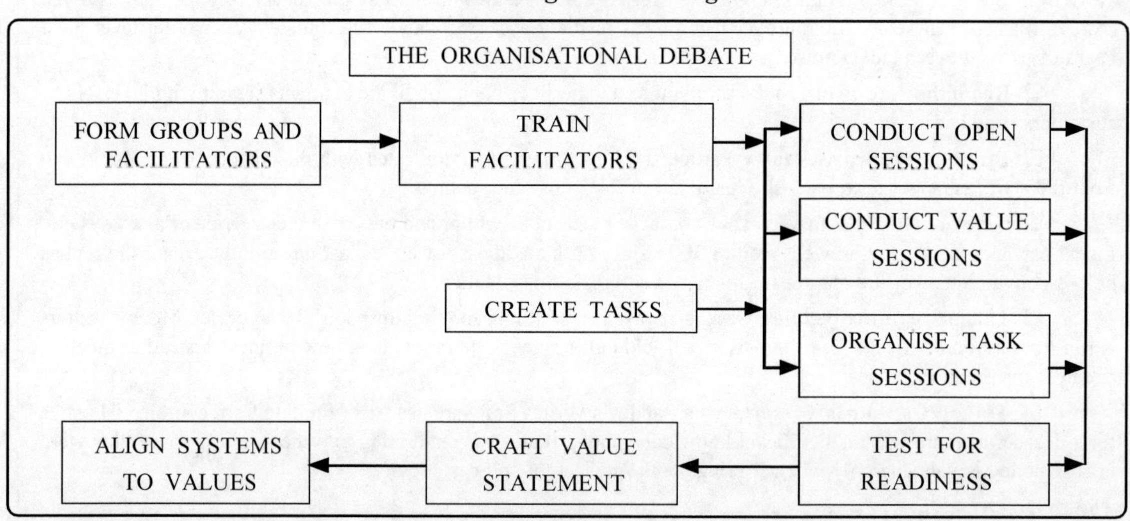

Fig. 8.5.

Box 8.6: Vijay Govindarajan and Chris Trimble on 10 Rules for Strategic Innovators

(1) In all great innovation stories, the great idea is only chapter one.
(2) Sources of institutional memory are powerful.
(3) Large, established companies can beat start-ups.
(4) Strategic experiments face critical unknowns.
(5) The new business must be built from scratch.
(6) Managing tensions is job one for the senior management.
(7) The new business needs its own planning process.
(8) Interest, influence, internal competition, and politics disrupt learning.
(9) Hold the new business accountable for learning, not results.
(10) Companies can build a capacity for breakthrough growth.

Increased Innovation

Innovation will provide the basis for the sustainability of an organisation. Richard Foster in his book *Innovation* has sketched the curve of performance versus effort for technological progress. The result is an S-shaped curve that moves from infancy to explosion and then a gradual maturation. The key to sustainability is the ability to glide through successive such S-curves, in other words, the ability to continually innovate. 3M, on account of its constant innovation (it has something like 60,000 products in its stable) has been able to glide smoothly through many successive S-curves and thus has built an incredible amount of staying power in the market.

Implicit in continuous innovation is the importance of cannibalisation'. Intel is one of the few organisations that has perfected the art of cannibalisation. As the market of a processor begins to mature, Intel launches a superior processor, and tries to make the market graduate to its new offering. This not only pre-empts imitators, but also keeps margins high for Intel. In fact, with its continual innovation and cannibalisation, Intel has been able to create an artificial monopoly for itself.

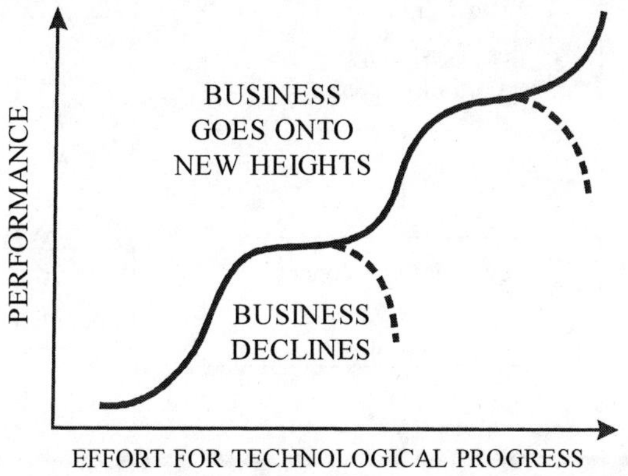

Fig. 8.6. The Successive S-Curve

New Business Concept Generation and Gestation Process

Though there are no set rules, Rosebeth Moss Kanter, a Professor at Harvard University has suggested six characteristics of innovation:

- Uncertain
- Knowledge intensive
- Controversial
- Crosses boundaries
- Changes work relationships and hierarchical arrangements
- Conditions for organisation and innovation are different from those of adoption and diffusion.

Thus, "if innovation is uncertain, fragile, political and imperialistic (reaching out to other territories),' she adds, 'then it is most likely to flourish where conditions allow flexibility, feedback, quick action and intensive care, coalition formation, and connectedness.' Here Kanter also hints at the organisational environment that surrounds the entire process.

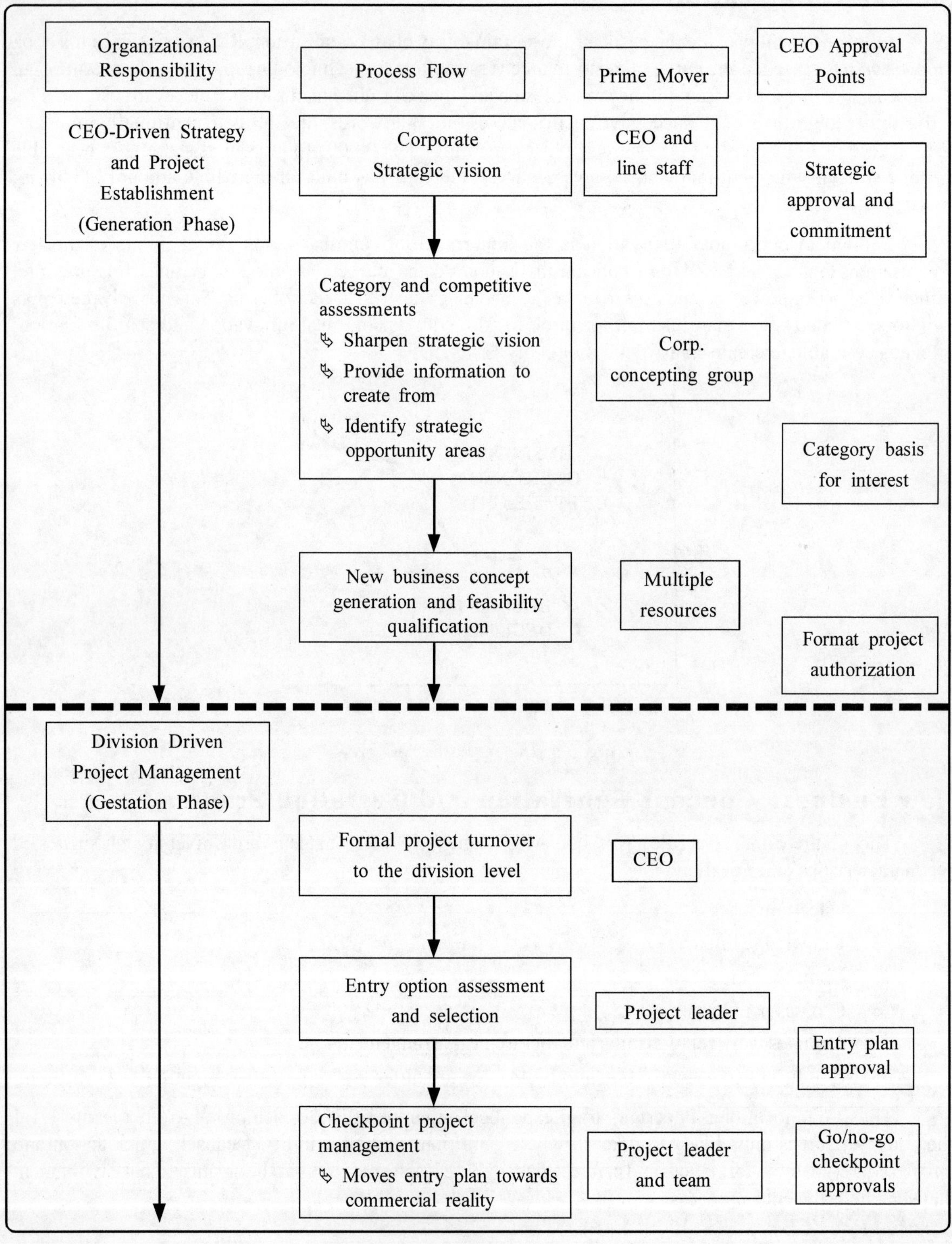

Organizational Responsibility
Process Flow
Prime Mover
CEO Approval Points
CEO-Driven Strategy and Project Establishment (Generation Phase)
Corporate Strategic vision
CEO and line staff
Strategic approval and commitment
Category and competitive assessments
Sharpen strategic vision
Provide information to create from
Identify strategic opportunity areas
Corp. concepting group
Category basis for interest
New business concept generation and feasibility qualification
Multiple resources
Format project authorization
Division Driven Project Management (Gestation Phase)
Formal project turnover to the division level
CEO
Entry option assessment and selection
Project leader
Entry plan approval
Checkpoint project management
Moves entry plan towards commercial reality
Project leader and team
Go/no-go checkpoint approvals

THE STEP THEORY

Attraction of new customers

Innovation of products and services

Innovation of value-delivery system

Acquisition and/or consolidation

Expansion into new geographics

Step outs into new competitive arenas

Current Business

The innovation process involves at least five generic stages:

- Idea generation and concept definition
- Model development
- Limited/test production
- Full production and growth
- Diffusion and adoption

Innovation cannot be divorced from change. A technological innovation may bring a change in the materials, manufacturing process, stop-floor management, product packing and marketing strategies too. This change may be opposed by the people affected by it and this could initiate a debate or opposition which is seldom objective. Often restructuring in an organisation follows a major innovation or break through. It is important to ensure that a minor innovation that could possibly take place at such a time is not ignored.

Peaks of Success

Fuelling ambitions and dreams. Breathing life into promising business ventures. Charting the course of incisive business ideas. Providing foresight with a fine sense of direction. Helping insightful, imaginative business ideas glide smoothly over rough passages. Helping vision and enterprise sight the target and achieve it with pin-point accuracy. Complementing acumen and enterprise with a steady flow of resources. Partnering enterprises on the move, till they reach the Peaks of success.

Steps of the Ladder

For starting an enterprise, an entrepreneur will have to climb the steps narrated on the next page, one by one; and for doing so, he would do well to give careful thought to the following considerations. This thought in advance may help him to avoid some mistakes. So many things must be considered that unless some kind of a check list is followed seriously, there is the danger of important matters being overlooked. And, once the entrepreneur has started the business, his getting busy with the urgency of the day-to-day details reduces the opportunity of thoughtful consideration to important questions.

Obviously, this list does not cover everything. It should be used as a starter. The list is designed with the object of focusing the entrepreneur's thought, on the different steps of the ladder he would have to climb. Carefully consider each one as it applies to your particular problem. Before deciding to ignore any question, completely satisfy yourself that it does not apply to your particular operation.

SUCCESS FACTORS FOR TODAY

- Total quality in manufacture, design and delivery
- Lean organisation
- Focus on core competence (market segments)
- Productivity (new product development)
- Global player
- Total customer satisfaction

SUCCESS FACTORS FOR TOMORROW

- More of all the above
- Risk management
- Survival skills
- New organisation
- Learning organisation
- Creativity

Although the ladder of success an entrepreneur has to climb in setting up an enterprise and run it consists of 34 steps, the ladder may undergo a change with the change in the environment and entrepreneurial climate. For an entrepreneur, work is worship. Leisure is a luxury. There is nothing like hard work. A 14 to 18 hour work is the norm. He should have a killer instinct to push ahead in the competitive environment.

Steps of the Ladder the Entrepreneur has to Climb

It is a continuous process of industrialisation.

(34) ANCILLARY DEVELOPMENT

(33) GROW BIGGER

(32) COMPETE WITH OTHERS

(31) MODERNISATION

(30) DIVERSIFICATION

(29) PLOUGH BACK PROFITS

(28) KEEP UP-TO-DATE

(27) SELL

(26) PRODUCE

(25) PLAN OUT RECORD-KEEPING

(24) ORGANISE MARKETING

(23) DECIDE ON PRICING POLICY
(22) TRIAL RUN
(21) RECRUIT PERSONNEL
(20) PROCURE MATERIALS
(19) INSTAL MACHINERY
(18) PLAN BUYING
(17) APPLY FOR MATERIALS (IF IMPORTED OR CONTROLLED)
(16) PLACE ORDER FOR MACHINERY (PREFERABLY ON HIRE-PURCHASE)
(15) PLAN SOURCES OF MACHINERY
(14) PLAN FINANCE
(13) OBTAIN CLEARANCE FROM CENTRAL, STATE AND LOCAL AUTHORITIES AND SSI REGN. NO.
(12) MAKE SURE WHAT LAWS WILL PARTICULARLY AFFECT YOU
(11) ARRANGE THE WORKSHED WITH FACILITIES (PREFERABLY ON RENT)
(10) DECIDE ON LOCATION AND SITE
(9) OBTAIN THE PROJECT REPORT FROM SISI OR ELSEWHERE OR PREPARE IT YOURSELF
(8) DECIDE WHETHER TO PURCHASE A GOING CONCERN OR TO START A NEW ONE
(7) DECIDE ON FORM OF OWNERSHIP [SOLE-PROPRIETARY/PARTNERSHIP/COOPERATIVE/COMPANY (PRIVATE/PUBLIC)]
(6) CHOOSE A LINE
(5) DATE WITH YOURSELF FOR A DECISION
(4) DISCUSS WITH ALL AROUND YOU AND WITH SISI AND D.I. OFFICE
(3) CONSULT PUBLICATIONS AND AGENCIES
(2) DATE WITH YOURSELF FOR NEWER IDEAS
(1) ANALYSE YOURSELF AND YOUR OBJECTIVES

Emerging Business Models

Competitiveness is not limited by a restricted set of business variables; it is actually the ability to compete at national and international frontier of best practices. It can also be defined as sustained increases in efficiency. With the increasing integration between domestic and global markets, it is essential for firms to be competitive in export markets too. Enhancement of competitiveness through restructuring, upgrading and continuous improvements thus constitutes the foundations for success. MSMEs need to achieve higher productivity through modern management techniques and technologies, and exploit economies of scale or identify targeted niches. Productivity gains are the ultimate gauge of the impact of such interventions. Productivity growth for sustainable economic progress is now based on flexibility and specialisation, with higher inter-firm interaction.

Conclusion

As an entrepreneur you have the pleasure of being in charge of your own business. And it is possible for you to exercise your individuality.

Employment generation, dispersal of industries in rural and semi-urban areas, utilisation of local resources and skills and development and widening of entrepreneurial base figure prominently in our plan priorities. Similarly, maximisation of exports has assumed added importance in the context of current balance of payments position. The prospects for export of non-traditional items such as readymade garments, leather and marine products, processed food, plastics and engineering goods etc. have improved.

As the main thrust of the new economic policy is to encourage competitiveness, characteristic of market driven economy, small-scale units have to increasingly equip themselves to be on their own. Technology, together with quality promotion measures, holds the key to improved factor productivity and strengthening of competitiveness. An enlightened entrepreneurial class, fully conscious of the directions in which changes are taking place, can look forward with confidence to improve its market share, both within and in a global setting in recognition of the opportunities available for further growth.

But you may have to face some problems too. Raw materials may be scarce. Finding a market for your products may not always be easy. Procuring or executing really large orders may be virtually possible.

You would need assistance in such circumstances. And this can best come from organisations that are specially geared to assist small-scale units.

Primarily, it is necessary to decide on what to manufacture, where and how. Then follows the process of establishing a small-scale industry. But, till the dream is realised, there are a number of hurdles, which could be crossed over, if one takes care. Herein, one's perseverance is at least. Let us start the hurdle race. No, before participation in this hurdle as well as marathon race, let us prepare ourselves or be fit for the race.

If you are a novice in the field, the first exercise you should concentrate on is what items you can market either on your own or through a reliable selling agency. Once a product is decided, you can then take up for examination their manufacture, marketing, viability and profitability in the small-scale sector. You are just a pin, a small pin in the huge machine of industry. While exploring the market, please assess the element of competition. Please do not overlook competition to your products as well as the capacity of the competitors to outwit you by underselling. Bear always that the road is not smooth. Even the hurdles are of uneven nature, competition is taken for granted. Even the special institution will suggest to you to manufacture only such item which you can successfully market.

Managing growth itself will be their biggest challenge going forward, followed by rising cost of materials and services and access to funds. Given their aggressive plans, they expect constraint on growth to also come from within, particularly from their human resources. Nothing beats strong entrepreneurship to tackle these constraints and challenges, but government's support can be a powerful vehicle to their empowerment, provided the government acts wisely. Interestingly, these growth-oriented companies do not expect much help from policymakers. They have survived the past and scaled new heights and they plan to continue doing just that in the future.

The age of continuous change has finally arrived. The choice is between two positions; either we can influence the same to the advantage of the firm, or end up as victims of the onslaught caused by the change. Accepting the status quo will directly lead to competitive decline. A better approach would be to shift the managerial and organisational mind-set to the new paradigm stated above and thereby increase the overall capabilities of the firm to take charge of its own destiny.

ANNEXURE – 1

Process of Setting up a Small-Scale Industry — Guidelines

I. Selection of Industry	
Small Industries Service Institutes	They guide entrepreneurs in the selection of industries, areas, suitable raw materials and machinery.
Indian Investment Centre Parliament Street, New Delhi-1	It advises on foreign capital participation and technical collaboration. Provides guidance to entrepreneurs regarding government policies, procedures, available incentives and facilities for investment, economic size of unit and the magnitude of investments required, demand forecast, availability of raw materials etc.
Ministry of Industrial Development and Company Affairs, New Delhi.	It approves the cases of foreign collaboration.
II District Industries Centres	In each district, there would be one agency to deal with all requirements of small and village industries, which would be called the District Industries Centre. Under the single roof of the centre, all the services and support required by small and village entrepreneurs would be provided. The Centre would have a separate wing for looking after the special needs of cottage and household industries as distinct from the small industry. The Rural Industries Project and Rural Artisans Programme would be merged with the programme of the District Industries Centre. Each DIC would have a General Manager and seven managers of different disciplines for looking after planning and economic investigation, credit, marketing etc.
III. Factory Accommodation	
Directors of Industries	They provide built-up factory space in industrial estates or developed factory sites, power, water etc. (The building designs have to be approved by Municipalities or Corporations while power and water connections are sanctioned by State Governments/Undertakings.
IV. Industrial Estates	There are more than 600 industrial estates in India which provide constructed accommodation in developed areas. Main facilities include common facility services, workshops, allotment of sheds on hire-purchase, concessional charges on water and power, exemption from octroi duty on building materials etc.
V. Registration	Although it is not mandatory, it is certainly helpful to obtain the SSI Registration Number from the Director of Industries.
VI. Machinery	
Small Industries Service Institutes	They advise about the kind of machinery and equipment needed for the manufacture of different products.

National Small Industries Corporation, New Delhi	It supplies indigenous as well as imported machinery on hire-purchase basis.
State Small Industries Corporations	They provide indigenous machinery on deferred credit basis.
Chief Controller of Imports Exports, New Delhi	He issues import licences for machinery of foreign origin on the recommendation of the Directors of Industries.
Consultants	Install machinery as per the layout drawn by them.
VII. Raw Materials	
Development Commissioner, Small-Scale Industries, New Delhi	He procures raw materials for the small industry and distributes them among State Governments. He also arranges imports of raw materials through the Minerals and Metals Trading Corporation and the State Trading Corporation of India.
Directors of Industries	They allot quotas of scarce raw materials.
State Small Industries Corporations	They supply raw materials.
Chief Controller Of Imports and Exports and His Port Offices	They issue licences for the import of raw materials.
VIII. Finance	
Small Industries Development	Small Industries Development Bank of India (SIDBI) has started operations through its 25 offices located in different states of the country. The SIDBI has been set up under an Act of Parliament as the principal financial institution for promotion, financing and development of industry in the tiny and the small scale sector. The SIDBI is also expected to coordinate the functions of the institutions engaged in similar activities. The SIDBI is a wholly-owned subsidiary of the Industrial Development Bank of India (IDBI). It has taken over IDBI's financing activities relating to the small-scale sector.
State Financial Corporations	They provide long-term credit for the purchase of fixed assets.
State Directors of Industries	They provide loans under State Aid to Industries Act/Rules for block capital.
State Bank of India and its Subsidiaries	They sanction medium-term and instalment credit loans for the purchase of machinery and the construction of factory buildings. They also provide working capital for the purchase of raw materials and meeting other day-to-day requirements.
Commercial Banks	They sanction loans for working capital needs.

Small Industrial Service Institutes	They furnish technical reports to Institutes, the State Bank of India on the applicant units.
IX. Technical know-how	
Small Industries Service Institutes	They prepare improved designs and Institute's drawings for products. They assist in making tools, dies, jigs and fixtures. They help in the optimum utilisation of men, materials and machinery. They prepare management control charts for the maximisation of profits. They train managers and supervisors in industrial management. They train workers to upgrade their skill. They demonstrate modern technical processes.
National Small Industries Corporation, New Delhi	They give advanced training in their prototype Production-cum-Training Centres in the operation of modern machines.
Council of Scientific and Industrial Research, New Delhi	It develops new technological processes and disseminates the same to the industry.
Productivity Councils Small Industry Extension Training Institute, Hyderabad Central Institute of Tools Designs (CITD) Hyderabad	Train factory-owners to increase productivity. It gives full-time and management training to managers/proprietors in the small industry sector Specialises in provision of technical consultancy and tool facilities, training in design and manufacture of tools.
Institute for Design of Electrical Measuring Instruments (IDEMI), Mumbai	Provides technical know-how and testing, calibration laboratory, workshop and training facilities to electrical measuring instrument manufacturers.
X. Standardisation	
Small Industries Service Institutes	They provide technical guidance in the production of goods according to prescribed standards.
Indian Standards Institution	It prescribes specifications for the products and issues ISI certification.
Directors of Industries	They prescribe standards and give 'Q' Mark to the small industry's products.
Quality Control	Those in charge provide technical guidance in maintaining the quality of products.
XI. Marketing	
Small Industries Service Institutes	They conduct distribution and surveys for the benefit of small industrialists. They enlist the units for participation in the Central Government Stores/Purchase Programme. They issue competency certificates to the units receiving government orders. They promote ancillary relationships with large and medium-scale units in public and private sectors.

National Small Industries Corporation, New Delhi	It secures contracts from the Director General of Supplies and Disposals, Railways, and Defence Departments for supply of manufactured goods by small scale units.
State Small Industries Corporations	They secure orders from the State Government and other semi-government organisations for the supply of stores.
XII. Export	
Small Industries Service Institutes	They enlist small units for participation under the Export Aid to Small Industry Scheme of the State Trading Corporation of India.
	They render technical counselling services for a satisfactory execution of export orders.
	They disseminate information about the items having export markets.
	They maintain a close liaison with specialised agencies like the Export Promotion Councils to have up-to-date knowledge about the products having export markets.
Chief Controller of Imports and Exports, New Delhi	He issues licences for the export of products to foreign countries.
Directorate of Export Promotion, Udyog Bhavan, New Delhi	It collects and supplies information on foreign markets. It carries out market studies for particular products. It publishes Trade Directories, Brochures and Bulletins.
Export Promotion Councils	They organise exhibitions and show-rooms. They maintain a close liaison between Indian exporters and foreign buyers. They settle commercial disputes.
	They frame special export promotion schemes.
State Trading Corporation of India, New Delhi	It registers units for participation under Export Aid to Small Industry Scheme.
	It helps the small-scale units in the preparation of sales leaflets, price lists etc. It secures export orders for small industries.
Trade Fair Authority of India, New Delhi	Organises National Small-Scale Industries Fairs. Conducts publicity work. Project image of the industry and assists in finding potential markets.
XIII. Inventions	
The Inventions Promotion Board, 39 Ring Road, Lajpat Nagar IV, New Delhi-110014	It promotes workable inventions of practical utility through financial assistance and other incentives.
The Central Institute of Tools Design, Hyderabad.	It produces tools, jigs, fixtures, dies and moulds. It trains practicing personnel in the design and manufacture of tools etc.

XIV. *Training*	
Small-Scale Industries Development Organisation	It trains practicing managers and technologists.
Small Industries Service Institutes	They conduct management courses for senior managerial personnel.
Extension Centres	They conduct regular and ad hoc training courses in various technological trades for skilled and semi-skilled workers.
Indian Investment Centre	Conducts regular entrepreneurial development programme courses. Assistance is given to the trainees in the identification of project reports. They are also helped in obtaining the necessary financial assistance from the financial institutions and guidance is also provided upto the stage of trial production.
Small Industry Extension Training Institute (SIET)	Offers training in industrial management and other aspects of small industries development; undertakes feasibility and research studies and collects and disseminates technical information through its Documentation Centre.
	Under assistance to Young Engineers program, training is provided through specified agencies and interest subsidy, i.e., difference between interest rate of 7% per annum and the normal rate charged by the financial institutions is provided subject to a maximum of Rs. 20,000 per annum for a period of five years in backward areas and three years in other areas.
National Institute for Entrepreneurship and Small Business Development (NIESBUD)	NIESBUD is an apex body established in 1983 for coordinating and overseeing the activities of various institutes/agencies engaged in entrepreneurship development in the small industry and related business.
XV. *Problems*	
The Federation of Associations of Small Industries of India, Rohtak Road, New Delhi,	They represent the problems faced by the small industries to the Government.
Chambers of Commerce and Industry	They discuss the problems and represent them to the appropriate authorities.
XVI. *Monitoring*	
The National Alliance of Young Entrepreneurs (NAYE)	It is a national level apex organisation of entrepreneurs. It assists in promoting new enterprises through first-generation entrepreneurs. It also monitors the programmes of entrepreneurial development in India.
XVII. *Other Voluntary* Organisations	Association of Women Entrepreneurs of Karnataks (AWAKE) Women Entrepreneurs Association of Maharashtra (WIMA) Self-Employed Women's Association (SEWA) World Association of Small and Medium Enterprises (WASME)

National Alliance of Young Entrepreneurs (NAYE)
National Association of Software and Service Companies (NASSCO)
Consortium of Women Enterprises of India (CWEI) etc.

IT'S A GREASED POLE: INDIA SLIPS A NOTCH IN DOING BUSINESS RANKINGS

India may be on a high-growth path and embracing economic globalisation, but it is a tough world out there. The country's ranking has slipped by one position to 133 among 183 nations in the 'Doing Business Index' prepared by World Bank and International Finance Corporation.

WHAT THE REPORT MEASURES

World Bank uses 10 indicators including the following:

- Import-export regime
- Tax administration
- Ease in starting and closing businesses

WHAT THEY DON'T MEASURE

- Macroeconomic policy
- Work-force skills
- Crime Rates

WHAT MAKES IT TOUCH FOR INDIA

- Delays in construction permits
- Difficulties in enforcement of contracts
- Availability of credit
- High cost of electricity

UPS AND DOWNS

- India has improved its score in closure of businesses by easing up the resolution of insolvency cases
- India's performance has slipped in factors like starting a business, obtaining credit and protection of investors
- In construction permits, it is one of the worst in the world

GUESS WHO IS AHEAD?

- Only Afghanistan lags India in the South Asian region. Pakistan, Sri Lanka, Bhutan, Nepal and Maldives are ahead

RWANDA JUMPS

- The tiny African nation of Rwanda, which was in the news about 15 years ago for tribal massacres, has jumped 76 spots to 67 by cutting bureaucratic delays.

WHO's WHERE

Country	Rank	
	2009	**2010**
Singapore	**1**	1
US	**4**	4
UK	**6**	5
Pakistan	**85**	85
Bangladesh	**115**	**119**
Brazil	**127**	129
Russia	**118**	120
China	**86**	89
Sri Lanka	**97**	105
India	**132**	133
Japan	**13**	15

Source : World Bank

ANNEXURE – 2

Production Channel and Control

Progressive Condition	Average Condition	Weak Condition
Purchase of all materials through competitive bids, in accordance with specifications, in quantities requisitioned by production control. Effective expediting procedure.	*I. Procurement* Purchasing function generally well handled. Lacks complete coordination with Engineering and Production Control. Fair expediting procedures.	Purchasing not completely centralised. Poorly co-ordinated with Engineering. Production Control and other departments. Poor expediting procedures.
Production completely planned and scheduled in accordance with sales requirements and manufacturing facilities.	*II. Production Control and Scheduling* Production planned, as to principal items. Scheduling of material and labour needs by department heads.	No central production control and scheduling, production often dictated by need to keep men busy, resulting in unbalanced, excess inventories.
Plant location determined by studies of material and labour supply, market location. Plant facilities arranged in accordance with production methods and processes, maintenance and replacement of plant, equipment and facilities well controlled.	*III. Plant Engineering* Plant not located as a result of economic study. Machinery and equipment layout not well correlated to material flow. Maintenance and replacement of plant and equipment loosely controlled.	Plant location determined by available building space. Machinery location and plant layout arranged with little regard to econoical material flow or handling. No facility for replacement programme and production control of maintenance.
Tools developed, designed and tested to yield to lowest feasible manufacturing cost for each product. Tools efficiency maintained and controlled.	*IV. Tool Engineering* Tools well constructed, but not designed to produce lowest manufacturing cost. Fair tool maintenance and control.	Tool engineering not well correlated with manufacturing and processing to produce low production costs. Poor tool maintenance and inventory control.
Head of Methods and Process Engineering capable of developing, improving, standardising and simplifying and manufacturing processes to reduce costs in cooperation with Factory and Engineering Departments.	*V. Methods Engineering* Separate methods and standards department. Full coordination with Manufacturing, Tool and General Engineering Departments not maintained.	Methods worked out by various department heads – improvements low. Poor records and little control of manufacturing and processing.
High quality, low-cost production for all products obtained by use of modern machinery, good plant layout and material flow, with high labour efficiency acquired by the offer of incentive pay and by able supervision.	*VI. Manufacturing* Material flow needs improvement. Machinery up-to-date. Costs not low in field; loose incentive rates for labour. Improved supervision needed.	Manufacturing not well planned or supervised. Machinery old, material flow poor. Production quality fair. No incentive pay rates, supervision indifferent.
Quality control maintained as a separate function. Efficient inspection programme tailored to each product and used as aid to sales and manufacturing.	*VII. Quality Control* Quality control function not centralised. Inspection performed as a manufacturing necessity only, except when quality complaints are made by customers.	No separate quality control function except when complaints force extra precautionary measures. Inspection carried out independently by each department foreman.

*(**Source:** Nau Nihal Singh: Scientific Management of Small-Scale Industries, pp.320-322.)*

ANNEXURE – 3

Case Studies

A Study in Success

Murudeshwar Ceramics Forays into New Areas

Inspiration and Early Beginning

Rama Nagappa Shetty would have been ploughing in his ancestral fields but for his father's inspiration. Today, he heads a multicrore empire, whose flagship company Murudeshwar Ceramics Ltd., is a study in success.

Shetty started off in the late fifties with some money loaned by his father. He ventured into construction and took up minor jobs like metalling and asphalting of roads. By 1961, he had become big enough to undertake construction of three major bridges on the Honnavar-Gerusoppa road in North Kanara district. In 1996, he moved his operating base to Hubli and switched over to irrigation power works. Since then, Shetty has not looked back.

He has, over the years, executed major irrigation works like the Malaprabha, Ghataprabha and Upper Krishna projects. He has even completed the prestigious Varahi hydel power project, the first underground power house in Karnataka. Currently, Shetty has his hand full. He is also involved in the Upper Krishna canal work and the Gerusoppa dam for the Sharavathi project – both financed by the World Bank.

Diversification

A natural offshoot of all this construction activity was the Murudeshwar Tile Factory, set up at Murudeshwar in 1977. Explains Shetty, "in North Kanara, we get a lot of clay suitable for manufacturing Mangalore tiles." Now, this is the biggest Mangalore tile factory in North Kanara district. A decade later, Shetty set up Murudeshwar Ceramics Ltd., a joint-sector undertaking with the Karnataka State Industrial Investment and Development Corporation, for the manufacture of ceramic glazed tiles. 'in 1985, the KSIIDC was looking for a partner for a ceramic tile venture and my father, who showed an interest, was awarded the project.'

Ceramics

A Rs. 13.45 crores project to manufacture 12,500 tonnes per annum of ceramic tiles, the MCL project was financed by an equity capital of Rs. 4.50 crores and loans of Rs. 8.80 crores. The plant was completed in a record 14 months times. MCL is one of the major industries to have come up in the backward North Karnataka region. He selected Hubli for MCL because of its proximity to raw material sources and to the major consuming centres like Mumbai, Bangalore, Pune and Goa.

Turnover

In the first year itself, for a 11-month period in 1988-89, MCL achieved a turnover of Rs. 9.64 crores and posted a net profit of Rs. 42 lakhs. In 1991-92, its sales moved to Rs. 29.66 crores, while the net profit reached Rs. 4.79 crores. The EPS also moved from Rs. 0.94 in 1988-89 to Rs. 9.53 in 1991-92.

Over the years, MCL ceramic tiles marketed under the brand name 'Naveen' have been well accepted in the ceramic tile market in spite of the tough competition from established players like Johnson Tiles, Somany, Pilkington and Spartek. Compared to Spartek, MCL has an edge in quality. It also enjoys an advantage in price since it enjoys a tax holiday between 1990 and 1993. And in spite of a large number of entrants in the market, MCL has managed to survive because of its higher capacity utilisation and cost control measures. Today, 'Naveen' ceramic tiles are available in over 40 colours and shades.

Capacity Utilisation

In 1990 MCL doubled its capacity to 25,000 tpa. By January 1993, this will go up to 40,000 tpa at a cost of Rs. 17 crores. This should help them reach a turnover of Rs. 37 crores in 1992-93. Since the domestic market was growing slowly, MCL decided to concentrate on exports as well. In 1991-92, MCL exported Rs. 45 lakh worth of ceramic tiles to the Middle East. This year, it has so far exported tiles worth Rs. 60 lakhs against a target of Rs. 1 crore.

Marketing

The domestic market has improved this year. And they are tapping the market aggressively with the help of 160 dealers most of whom sell only 'Naveen" ceramic tiles. They have eight marketing offices and they will soon set up marketing offices in Pune, Vizag and Ahmedabad as well.

But it has not always been smooth sailing for MCL. The government has labelled ceramic tiles as a luxury item and clamped a 57.5 per cent excise duty on them. MCL's cost of production is less than mosaic tiles. But then they are bogged down with the excise duty.

In four years, MCL has notched up 9.3 per cent of the market share in ceramic tiles. It has recorded an impressive growth in the net sales (26.8 per cent), gross profit (31.3 per cent) and net profit (45 per cent). Its dividend went up, thanks to its excellent performance, from 16 per cent in 1990-91 to 20 per cent in 1991-92.

New Avenues

During 1971-72, Mr. R.N. Shetty promoted Seshank Sea Foods Ltd. at Bhatkal in North Karnataka for processing and export of sea foods. This year it hopes to achieve an export turnover of Rs. 25 crores. It exports to Japan (which is the major buyer), the US and France.

Mr. Shetty now plans to go in for aquaculture in a big way. For this purpose, he has already acquired 40 hectares of land near Kumta in North Karnataka and negotiations are on for another 60 hectares. This will be a Rs. 10 crore project.

TRANSFORMING DREAMS

Early Beginning

In 1966, a young electrical engineer, R.K. Parasuram, returned to his hometown Madras after working for General Electric Company, U.K. for 10 years. He dreamt of manufacturing world-class electrical transformers and selling them all over the world. Three decades later, his dream is coming true.

The Kappa group of companies (named after his wife Kamala Parasuram) – a bunchy of tiny private limited companies and proprietary firms with a turnover of Rs. 16 crores and an export turnover of Rs. 9 crores – manufacture almost the entire range of transformers. These are low-tech but essential items which require a lot of manual labour.

Having established his products successfully in the domestic market, Parasuram decided to go global. Exports in the early seventies really meant the rupee market. It was not easy to penetrate the European and American markets. So he looked towards South-East Asia which was a relatively easier hard-currency area.

No one had previously attempted to export products like transformers. Right from the outset, Parasuram's emphasis was on quality. The export products were produced to conform to the international standards prescribed by British Standards and International Electro-technical Commission. Due to the availabilty of cheap skilled labour, the cost of Kappa's transformers was very competitive.

First Order

In 1973, the company got its first export order from Dickson Primer, an engineering firm in Singapore, for 300 pieces of transformers worth Rs. 20,000. Singapore and Malaysia were the major markets then. By late 70s, Kappa decided to expand its activities to the Middle East. The focus was on Beirut. However, when the militarisation of Lebanon became complete in the early 80s exports to Beirut came to a grinding halt.

Parasuram was on the constant lookout of a big deal. Kappa's ability to produce transformers as custombuilt original equipment fetched its first order from Siemens, Australia, in 1980. Siemens and EmailWestinghouse became their major buyers in Australia and New Zealand. A bulk of the company's international sales is to Asea Brown Boveri. Worth just Rs. 20,000 in the 80s, business with the SwedishSwiss giant has now grown to Rs. 60 lakhs annually. Says Kamala, "With more and more enquiries from abroad, we opened an export office at Singapore in 1983."

In order to broad base exports, it was decided to trade in a wide range of current technology products not necessarily produced by the group. The relays produced by English Electric, semiconductor fuse and voltage transformer fuse links manufacturered by S&S Power Switchgear Ltd. are some of the well-known products trade by Kappa Exports. Says T.V.G. Menon, general manager, relay division, English Electric, 'We cannot export directly because of our agreement with our parent company. So we make our sales to Kappa who are doing a splendid job.' Kappa has emerged as the biggest exporter of electrical goods from South India. Today 60 per cent of Kappa's export turnover is from trading.

Kappa's exports reached Rs. I crore in 1987. Since then, the annual growth rate has been phenomenal, around 40 per cent now. The main reason for this, according to Kamala, was Kappa's strategic move to become a single-window export house for all electrical engineering equipment. Parasuram is convinced that constant upgradation of technology is the only way for survival. Five per cent of the total turnover is being spent on R&D and another five per cent on technological upgradation. According to Kamala, the neglected but important area in exports is packaging. Says she, "Our special packaging efforts to withstand the wear and tear of the transit costs an additional three per cent."

To ensure quality, Kappa has invested about Rs. 1 crore in various imported testing equipment and this has now proved to be a great advantage as the group is gearing to enter the European market in a big way. Says the founder's daughter Mira Parasuram, an electrical engineer, 'We are working with the Indian Statistical Institute to get the ISO 9000 accreditation. Our production systems already seem to conform to international standards. We have to only effect changes in areas like inventory, billing and accounting. We will get our accredition in the middle of 1993." Kappa wants to reach an export figure of Rs. 100 crores by the turn of the century and hence it is seriously studying the Middle East and African markets.

✸ ✸ ✸

THE AGE OF EXTREMES

"Entrepreneurs should scale up as much as they comfortably can, but at the end of the day, they should be able to identify a speciality. Customers will give the specialist credit for sure. So, the future belongs to either very large global players or small specialist entrepreneurs." – ***Jack Trout, Marketing Guru***

9. Role of Support Institutions to Promote Small Entrepreneurs

10. Preliminary Project Report

Entreprenur plays a significant role in economic development of a country. Economic development greatly depends upon entrepreneurial and industrial development. In western countries, entrepreneurs have contributed a great deal in making their country developed. According to ***Harbison****, entrepreneurs are prime movers of innovation and* ***Sayigh*** *describes entrepreneurship as a dynamic force. Indeed, entrepreneur is the person who perceives business opportunity and converts it into a viable business plan culminating into a business venture ultimately. The entrepreneur, therefore, not only launches a venture but also contributes to the objectives of employment creation, output growth, technological upgradation, inprovement in the quality of production, export promotion. import substitution and supply of goods at reasonable price to the customers.*

Therefore, growth of entrepreneurship and development of entrepreneurial culture in underdeveloped and developing countries are imperatively needed not only for employment generation but also for infusing entrepreneurial culture in the society which is so far exposed to it. Entrepreneurship may also help in skill formation and technological upgradation developing countries. Efforts made by a group of entrepreneurs in motivating the youths to change their attitude for self-employment, thus, may lead to further creation of wealth through enterprise creation.

As an entrepreneur you have the pleasure of being in charge of your own business. And it is possible for you to exercise your individuality.

Employment generation, dispersal of industries in rural and semi-urban areas, utilisation of local resources and skills and development and widening of entrepreneurial base figure prominently in our plan priorities. Similarly, maximisation of exports has assumed added importance in the context of current balance of payments position. The prospects for export of non-traditional items such as readymade garments, leather and marine products, processed food, plastics and engineering goods etc. have improved.

As the main thrust of the new economic policy is to encourage competitiveness, characteristic of market-driven economy, small-scale units have to increasingly equip themselves to be on their own. Technology, together with quality promotion measures, holds the key to improved factor productivity and strengthening of competitiveness. An enlightened entrepreneurial class, fully conscious of the directions in which changes are taking place, can look forward with confidence to improve its market share, both within and in a global setting in recognition of the opportunities available for further growth.

But you may have to face some problems too. Raw materials may be scarce. Finding a market for your products may not always be easy. Procuring or executing really large orders may be virtually impossible.

You would need assistance in such circumstances. And this can, best come from oganisations that are specially geared to assist small-scale units.

Primarily, it is necessary to decide on what to manufacture, where and how. Then follows the process of establishing a small-scale industry. But, till the dream is realised, there are a number of hurdles, which could be crossed over, if one takes care. Herein, one's perseverance is at least. Let us start the hurdle race. No, before participation in this hurdle as well as marathon race, let us prepare ourselves or be fit for the race..

If you are a novice in the field, the first exercise you should concentrate on is what items you can market either on your own or through a reliable selling agency. Once a product is decided, you can then take up for examination their manufacture, marketing, viability and profitability in the small-scale sector. You are just a pin a small pin in the huge machine of industry. While exploring the market, please assess the element of competition. Please do not overlook competition to your products as well as the capacity of the competitors to outwit you by underselling. Bear always that the road is not smooth. Even the hurdles are of uneven nature, competition is taken for granted. Even the special institution will suggest to you to manufacture only such item which you can successfully market.

The age of continuous change has finally arrived. The choice is between two positions; either we can influence the same to the advantage of the firm, or end up as victims of the onslaught caused by the change. Accepting the status quo will directly lead to competitive decline. A better approach would be to shift the managerial and organisational mind-set to the new paradigm stated above and thereby increase the overall capabilities to take charge of its own destiny.

Vision

To be self-employed one has to have a vision. To entrepreneurs who has it as one of their fundamental characteristics, vision is a vivid, dramatic and complete picture of what the company wants to be, and do. Crucially, this future is not one that can be reached in normal course; it needs a quantum leap.

Vision has been defined as the power of perceiving by imagination or by clear thinking. In the organisational context, vision is a picture of the future of the organisation. Vision is the hallmark of a forward looking organisation. It provides the motivation needed to get the best out of an organisation-enterprise and people. Vision inspires one to strive for better.

The founder of an organisation needs to paint a picture of the organisation as he sees it in the future. This encompasses primarily its scope. as an organisation in terms of areas of business or products; the geographic boundaries and the value system by which it desires to attain the same, and a clarity of the relationships that it will develop with various members associated with the organisation.

It is important for an enterprise to have clarity of vision primarily because the organisation can have apparent synergies. For instance, a company may feel that it can get into situations of vertical integration to optimise cost/returns, profitability etc. While it may be profitable in the short run or may appear to be a strategically good move, it may not be optimal in the long-term if it is not in keeping with the corporate vision.

Similarly, a firm's long-term interests in terms of developing a well-integrated organisation may not be served if it considers unrelated diversification. just because an opportunity comes its way, or because the officials have specific contact with certain officials in the government.

The second important reason why clarity of vision is needed is because it develops a culture of learning within the organisation, in order to fulfill the clarified and stated vision. For instance, if an organisation's vision is to expand and become a global player in the market of the developing world, then the entire organisation could develop an interest in the specific industry sector and the geographic area and would, over a period of time, gain the knowledge to fulfill that vision.

Clarity of vision also enables the entire organisation to develop an inspirational force towards attaining a common goal, thus enhancing the team building process in an organisation since the entire organisation as the team will perform even a simple task.

An organisation (entrepreneur) must develop its vision statement based on where it is today via a thorough analysis of swot.

Basic Principles of Business young people must know even before they venture into the work world that there are six basic principles of business etiquette, which have been enunciated by Gary YukI – as the foundation for good human relations in corporations and in society. These six key etiquette rules will improve your business etiquette quotient and help you to get ahead in whatever job you do or aspire to. These rules benefit people at all levels.

(1) Be on time : *Be punctual by sensibly scheduling appointments. It's the little things that add up. Show respect for other people's time and their own pre-occupations.*

(2) Be discreet : *So that you are sensitive to the impact that information might have on those working with it, as well as what the competition might do if they find it.*

(3) Be courteous, pleasant and positive : *And this is irrespective of the pressures on you or your company. Spread joy and cheer to lighten up the environment.*

(4) Be concerned with others, not just yourself : *People's careers are ended, stalled or reversed because they lacked concern for others.*

(5) Dress appropriately : *First impressions are best impressions. You only make one. It is good to look, listen and pick a role model. This always helps.*

(6) Use proper written and spoken language : *Because people who can express themselves clearly are always at a definite advantage.*

If one inculcates these rules in behaviour, even before entering the workforce – it will be a great lead over the others in the race.

9

Role of Support Institutions to Promote Small Entrepreneurs

Introduction

With the quickened pace of economic development under the impetus of the Five-Year Plans, the most striking change in the Indian economy has been the initiation of an industrial revolution and the re-emergence of small-scale industries. Further, during the past decade, there has been a deepening as well as a widening of the small-scale industrial structure. Not only have the established small industries increased their installed capacity and output, but a wide range of new small industries has also come into being. Thus, in the field of capital and goods industries, small units manufacturing such items as machine tools, electrical and engineering equipment, chemicals etc., which provide the foundation for a self-sustained growth of the economy have been set-up; amongst consumer goods industries, small units producing such items as bicycles, sewing machines, plastic products etc., are forging ahead.

These far-reaching developments and the scale and scope of operation of small-scale industries have brought to the fore the importance of provision of administrative and institutional assistance at various levels.

Need for Institutional Support

The success of entrepreneurial development depends solely on the well established institutional set-up. In order to meet the requirements of the rapidly expanding small-scale industries sector in the country, the Government gave adequate institutional support; and it may well claim to have achieved success. in this sphere. 'The role of various institutions set-up specially to promote the growth of small-scale industries is quite unique. In this chapter, an attempt has been made to discuss the role of industrial institutions in the promotion of small-scale industries in India. In other words, the assistance that the small entrepreneur can take from different institutions for varied purposes.

Institutional Support

The scale and scope of operation of entrepreneurs and the far-reaching developments in the economic climate have brought to the fore the importance of institutional assistance at various levels. In fact, the success of entrepreneurship depends solely on the well established institutional set-up.

The institutions fostering entrepreneurial development can be classified into: *(i)* Promotional, *(ii)* Financial, *(iii)* Technical, *(iv)* Marketing, *(v)* Training, *(vi)* Others, and *(vii)* Associations.

These are as follows:

A. Promotional

(1) Directorate of Industries of the State Governments
(2) The Small Industries Development Organisations
(3) State Small Industries Corporations
(4) State Industrial and Investment Corporations
(5) Industrial Development Corporation
(6) Electronic Corporations
(7) Udyog Mitra
(8) State Development Corporations
(9) National Small Industries Corporation
(10) Small-Scale Industries Board
(11) The National Industrial Development Corporation
(12) National Productivity Council
(13) State Electricity Boards
(14) Indian Bureau of Standards
(15) District Industries Centres
(16) State Industrial Development Corporations

B. Financial

(1) State Financial Corporations
(2) Industrial Finance Corporation of India
(3) Commercial Banks
(4) Life Insurance Corporation
(5) General Insurance Corporation
(6) Unit Trust of India
(7) Small Industries Development Bank of India
(8) Mutual Funds
(9) Leasing Companies
(10) Risk Capital Foundation
(11) National Bank for Agriculture and Rural Development

(12) Khadi and Village Industries Commission
(13) Stock Exchange
(14) The Asian Development Bank
(15) Infrastructure and Leasing Finance Corporation
(16) Venture capital
(17) Housing Development Finance Corporation
(18) Housing Finance Companies
(19) Graha Nirman Finance Companies
(20) The World Bank
(21) Infrastructure Development Finance Corporation

C. Technical

(1) Industrial and Technical Consultancy Oganisation
(2) Controller of General Patents, Designs and Trade Marks
(3) Pollution Control Boards
(4) Central Institute of Tool Design
(5) The Institute for Design for Electrical Measuring Instruments
(6) National Institute of Design
(7) Technology Development and Information Company of India Ltd.
(8) The Products and Process Development Centers
(9) Technical Consultancy Organisations

D. Marketing

(1) Indian Investment Centre
(2) Export Promotion Councils
(3) Commodity Boards
(4) Bhandars – Retail Shops
(5) Export Houses
(6) Indian Institute of Packaging
(7) Export Inspection Council
(8) Jute Corporation of India
(9) The State Trading Corporation of India
(10) The Minerals and Metals Trading Corporation of India
(11) Export-Import Bank of India

E. Training

(1) Centre for Entrepreneurship Development
(2) Entrepreurship Development Institute of India
(3) Management Development Institute

(4) Institutes of Management

(5) Institutes of Entrepreneurship Development

(6) National Institute for Entrepreneurship and Small Business Development

(7) Science and Technology Entrepreneurship

(8) Parks National Institute of Small Industry Extension Training

(9) Universities – Commerce Faculty

(10) Integrated Training Centre (Industries)

(11) Industrial Training Institutes

(12) Polytechniques

(13) Training of Rural Youth for Self-Employment

F. Others

(1) Bureau of Industrial Costs and Prices

(2) Indian Council of Arbitration

(3) The Credit Rating Information Services of India Ltd.

(4) The OTC Exchange of India

G. Associations

(1) National Alliance of Young Entrepreneurs

(2) Association of Women Entrepreneurs of Karnataka

(3) Coimbatore District Small-Scale Industries Association

(4) Industrial Associations

(5) Merchant Chambers

(6) Industry,and Trade Associations

Small Industries Development Organisation

The office of the Development Commissioner (Small Scale Industries) also known as Small Industries Development Organisation (SIDO) is an attached office of the Department of SSI, A&RI, SIDO, set up in 1954, functions through a network of 28 Small Industries Service Institutes (SISIs), 30 Branch SISIs, 4 Regional Testing Centres, 8 Field Testing Stations, 10 Tool Rooms, 2 Central Footwear Training Institutes, one Production Centre, 6 Product-cum Process Development Centres, and 3 Training Institutes.

The major activities of SIDO include: *(i)* evolving an all India policy and programme for the development of SSIs; *(ii)* coordinating the policies and programmes of various State Governments; *(iii)* maintaining liaison with different State and Central Ministries, Planning Commission, Reserve Bank of India and Financial Institutions and dissemination of economic information; *(iv)* providing a comprehensive range of extension services through allied institutions; *(v)* providing facilities for technology upgradation, modernisation, quality improvement, etc.; *(vi)* monitoring the Prime Minister's Rozgar Yojana (PMRY) Scheme; and *(vii)* offering services such as consultancy in technical and managerial aspects, training, common facility centres, testing and tool room facilities and marketing assistance for SSI.

Small Industries Service Institutes

Twenty eight Small Industries Service Institutes (SISIs) and 30 Branch SISIs are operational throughout the country and their respective performance is overseen by the office of the DC (SSI). The main functions performed by SISIs are interface between Central and State Governments, dissemination of economic information, technical support services and consultancy services, entrepreneurship development programmes, etc. SISIs prepare reports covering, among others, implementation of programmes on modernisation, energy conservation, quality control/upgradation and pollution control for the benefit of entrepreneurs.

The main functions performed by SISIs are as follows:

- Interface between Central and State Governments
- Technical support services and consultancy services
- Technical training
- Economic data support
- Entrepreneurship Development Programmes
- Development efforts
- Promotional Programmes
- Modernisation
- Quality upgradation.
- Improvement of productivity
- Development of the market
- Exibition of products of small entrepreneurs
- Export promotion and liaison activities
- Ancillary development

Reptorts prepared by SISIs have been emphasising the implementation of programmes on modernisation of programmes, energy conservation, quality control upgradation and pollution control for the benefit of entreneurs.

Product-cum-Process Development Centres (PPDCs)

Six PPDCs have been established and are providing services to SSIs at Firozabad (for glass industry), Kannauj (for essential oils), Meerut (for sports goods), Ramnagar (for electronic industry), Mumbai (for electrical measuring instruments), and Agra (for foundry and forging). In addition, there is SITARC Pump Institute at Coimbatore. The main functions of PPDCs include serving as research and development institutions in areas of industry clusters, looking into specific problems of industry product design and innovation, developing new processes and upgrading the existing level of technology, acting as centres of excellence in the concerned field and rendering technical support services, etc.

The main functions of PPDCs are:

- To serve as research and development institution in areas of dense industry clusters
- To look into the specific problems of industry

- Product design and innovation
- To develop new processcs and upgrade the existing level of technology
- To act as centres of excellence in the concerned field
- To render technical support services
- Manpower development and training

Regional Testing Centres

Four Regional Testing Centres (RTCs) at Chennai, New Delhi, Mumbai and Kolkata have been established for spreading quality awareness amongst industrial units through systematic testing and by rendering technical consultancy services. These centres are equipped with modern sophisticated machinery and equipment for testing mechanical, electrical, chemical and metrological products. They are accredited to the Bureau of Indian Standards, Pollution Control Board, etc. RTCs have been supporting 7 Field Testing Stations that provide testing services to SSI units in different product lines and are located at Bangalore, Bhopal, Changanacherry, Hyderabad, Jaipur, Kolhapur and Pondicherry.

Training Institutes

National Institute of Small Industries Extension &Training (NISIET), Hyderabad, National Institute for Entrepreneurship and Small Business Development (NIESBUD), New Delhi, and Integrated Training Centre (Industries), Nilokheri, are the main training institutes which function under the administrative control of SIDO and organise a variety of training courses for entrepreneurial development.

National Small Industries Corporation

The National Small Industries Corporation Limited (NSIC) is a public sector undertaking set up by the Government of India in February 1955 to promote, aid and foster the growth of small-scale industries in the country. The Corporation provides support to small-scale industries in the form of *(i)* supplying indigenous and imported machines on easy hire-purchase and lease term basis; *(ii)* enlisting competent units and facilitating their participation in Government Stores Purchase Programme and providing diversified marketing support through Marketing Assistance Scheme; *(iii)* assisting in export of small industries products and developing export worthiness of small scale units; *(iv)* developing prototypes of machines, equipment and tools which are subsequently passed on to small-scale units for commercial production; *(v)* providing training in industrial trades; *(vi)* extending assistance to SSIs through financial centres operating at New Delhi, Mumbai, Ahmedabad and Goa for marketing, bills discounting, raw materials purchases and exports; *(vii)* assisting SSIs in technology acquisition, adaption and upgradation through its Technology Transfer Centre at New Delhi.

Khadi and Village Industries Commission

The Khadi and Village Industries Commission (KVIC) is a statutory organisation established in 1957 under an Act of the Parliament. KVIC assists in promotion and development of khadi and village industries. The main objectives of KVIC include rural industrialisation, promotion of self-reliance among the people and to build up strong rural community base, skill development, creation of employment opportunities in rural areas and transfer of technology. For development of khadi and village industries, KVIC plans, promotes, organises and implements programmes and provides financial assistance to the eligible agencies. The corporation arranges training for persons employed in the sector or desirous of seeking employment in khadi

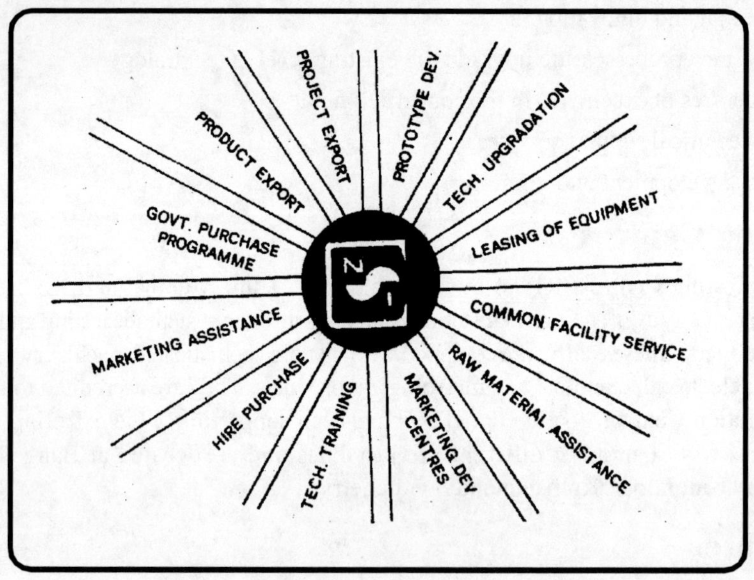

A UNIQUE PACKAGE OF ASSISTANCE FOR SMALL ENTRREPRENEURS

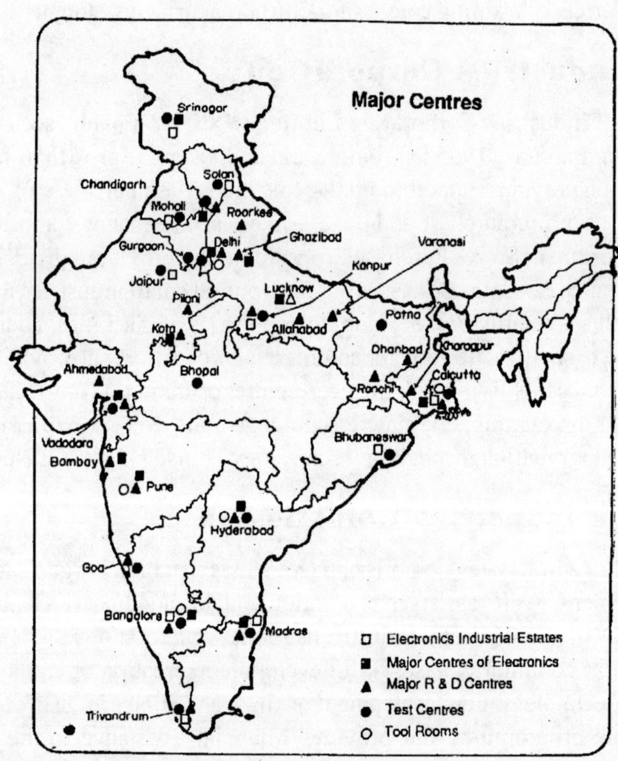

and village industries, besides supervisors and other functionaries. KVIC also holds stocks of raw materials and supplies them at such rates as may be decided from time to time. It undertakes R&D activities in khadi and village industries sector and encourages promotion of cooperative efforts among persons engaged in khadi and village industries.

With a view to giving a fillip to development efforts and to supplement the activities of State Small Industries Corporations and District Industries Service Institutes, the NSIC has opened its offices in some of the States in which the (NSIC) Corporation has been hitherto under-represented. In the western region, offices have been opened in Bhopal and Raipur in Madhya Pradesh. Four development executives and six field inspectors have been recently posted in the backward areas of the western region to serve as "contact points" and work in close co-operation with DICs and other developmental agencies in the area. Of these, three field inspectors have been posted in Raigad, Ratnagiri, Satara, Yeotmal, Chandrapur, Bhandara, Buldhana, Aurangabad, Nanded, Beed, Osmanabad, etc. – all backward districts in Maharashtra.

Objectives of KVIC

(1) To preserve the traditional arts and crafts in India

(2) To equip the artisans and craftsmen to take up the challenges of the modern market

(3) To promote the handicrafts, khadi, village and cottage industry by facilitating them with the necessary inputs like raw materials, equipments, capital, etc.

(4) To develop a market for these products

(5) To introduce the products even in the international market

To achieve these objectives, the following schemes are provided by KVIC

(a) Financial assistance for purchase of land, building, workshop, shed, machinery and equipment at 4% rate interest

(b) Working capital provision

(c) Equity capital

(d) Loan provision for purchase of raw materials

(e) Marketing avenues and selling centres for the products of artisans and craftsmen

(f) Subsidies for the registered societies of artisans and craftsmen belonging to scheduled castes, scheduled tribes, ex-servicemen, women, etc.

In addition to these schemes, KVIC provides various facilities for cottage industry like integrated village development programme, special beneficiary schemes, silk industry development scheme, interest subsidy scheme, artisans employment guarantees etc. The government has defined "Gramodyog" (village industry) as

(1) population of the village should not be more than 10 thousand people

(2) investment in the place of prcducts, machines and equipment should not exceed Rs.15 thousand

(3) manufacturing can be done either with power or without power.

It has approved nearly 96 industries under the preview of the KVIC. These industries are grouped under the following categories:

(1) Material based industriess
(2) Industries based on products from forests
(3) Agro-based industries
(4) Polymer and other chemical based industries
(5) Khadi and textile industry
(6) Service industry

Coir Board

The Coir Board is an autonomous body established by the Government of India under Coir Industry Act, 1953 for overall development of the coir industry. The activities pursued by the Board include undertaking scientific, technological and economic research and development activities, collection of statistics relating to exports and domestic consumption of coir and coir products, development of new products and designs, policy formulation to promote exports and domestic sales, marketing of coir and coir products in India and abroad, preventing unfair competition among producers and exporters, carrying out training for grooming skills, assisting in setting up of factories for manufacture of products, promoting cooperative organisations among producers of husk, coir fibre, coir yarn and manufacturers of coir products and ensuring remunerative returns to producers and manufacturers.

National Productivity Council (NPC)

NPC is an autonomous institution functioning under the overall supervision of the Ministry. Government of India. The primary objective of NPC is to act as a catalyst in enhancing the productivity of all sectors of the economy council (GC) which has equal representation from the Government, the industry and the trade unions. The Council has the Minister for Industry Goverment of India as its ex-officio President and is chaired by the secretary for Industrial Development. The Director General of NPC is the Chief Executive Officer dealing with the day-to-day management of the Council.

NPC is active in the field of consultancy and training and has a number of specialied divisions to provide tailor made solutions to the agriculture and industry. These divisions manned by trained consultants deal with issues related to Industrial Engineering. Plant Engineering, Energy Management. Human Resource Development, Informal Sector, Agriculture, etc. NPC has on its rolls about 200 professionals specialising in various fields.

NPCs head office is in New Delhi and it has Regional Directorates in almost all the state capitals. This kind of a structure makes it possible for the council to take up assignments which have an all India coverage. Because of its tripartite constitution, NPC is called in to take up sensitive assignments like manpower assessments, wage fixation time and motion studies, etc. NPC also co-ordinates the Annual productivity Awards which have been instituted by the Ministry of Industry and the Ministry of Agriculture for various sub-sectors of the economy.

NPC is a member of the Asian Productivity Organisation (APO) Tokyo, an umbrella body of all Productivity Councils in the Asian region. NPC plays host to a number of conferences, seminars and workshops of APO and and also nominates suitable persons from different organisations in India for APO training courses abroad.

In an effort to channelise the expertise of NPC to the small-scale and informal sector SIDBI has entered into a tie-up with the council. The collaboration aims at promoting the concept of productivity in small industry clusters and at enhancing the technology level of small units.

State Government Agencies

The State Governments have their own policies for promotion and development of small-scale, cottage, medium and large scale industries. In each State, the Commissioner/Director of Industries implements the State government policies and directives for promoting industrial development. The Central policies for SSI sector serve as guidelines for framing State level policies and package of incentives. The Commissioner/ Director of Industries also oversees the activities of the field offices, viz., District Industries Centres (DICs), at the district level which are mostly engaged in extension activities, besides administrative and regulatory work.

Functions of the Directorate

(1) Implementation of the industrial policy of the government.

(2) Promotion of the industrial development in the state and accelerate the speed of implementation of various industrial projects.

(3) Establishment of cooperative industrial estates.

(4) Registration for the small-scale units.

(5) Procurement of land, water, electricity for the small-scale sector.

(6) Provision of financial assistance to industries.

(7) Helping the small-scale units in procuring plant and machinery, scarce raw material and machinery.

(8) Training to new entrepreneurs.

(9) Coordination between various government departments and committees established for the promotion and development of small-scale industries.

(10) Implementation of the various financial schemes, subsidies and grants for small-scale industries.

(11) Helping and rehabilitating the sick industries.

(12) Development of rural industries.

(13) Export promotion.

(14) Promotion and development of agro-industries.

(15) Compilation of statistics related to industry, trade and commerce.

(16) Marketing assistance.

Initially, all the functions related to promotion and development of new industries and small entrepreneurs were assigned to the Directorate of Industries. But, to accelerate the speed of implementation of the scheme and enhance efficiency, the government has established separate corporations like SSIDC, IDC, SFC, etc. These corporations function under the directives of the Directorate of Industries.

District Industries Centres

The District Industries Centres (DICs) Programme was initiated in May 1978, as a Centrallysponsored scheme, with the objective of developing small, tiny and cottage industries in the country and to generate more employment opportunities especially among rural and backward areas. The establishment of offices of DICs at district level aimed at providing support facilities/concessions/ services in dispersed rural areas and other small towns. There were 430 centrally approved DICs, which covered almost all parts of the country except the metropolitan cities at the time of the withdrawal of the Central sponsorship in 1993-94.

At present, DICs are being operated under respective State budgetary provisions. The extension services provided by DIC include *(i)* dissemination of information, *(ii)* supply of machinery and equipment, *(iii)* provision of raw materials and quality inputs, *(iv)* arrangements for credit facilities, *(v)* marketing, and *(vi)* consultancy, *(vii)* research, education and training, and *(viii)* Cottage industries.

Objectives of DIC

(1) Accelerate the overall efforts for industrialisation of the district.

(2) Rural industrialisation and development of rural industries and handicrafts.

(3) Attainment of economic equality in various regions of the district.

(4) Providing the benefit of the government schemes to the new entrepreneurs.

(5) Centralisation of procedures required to start a new industrial unit and minimisation of the efforts and time required to obtain various permissions, licences, registrations, subsidies, etc.

Functions of DIC

(1) Acts as the focal point of the industrialisation of the district.

(2) Prepares the industrial profile of the district with respect to:

(a) Statistics and information about existing industrial units in the district in the large, medium, small as well as co-operative sectors

(b) Opportunity guidance

(c) Compilation of information about local sources of raw materials and their availability

(d) Manpower assessment with respect to skilled, semi-skilled workers

(e) Assessment of availability of infrastructure facilities like quality testing, research and development, transport, prototype development, warehouse, etc.

(3) Organises entrepreneurship development training

(4) Provides information about various government schemes, subsidies, grants, and assistance available from the other corporations set up for promotion of industries

(5) Gives SSI registration

(6) Prepares techno-economic feasibility report

(7) Advises the entrepreneurs on investments

(8) Acts as a link between the entrepreneurs and the lead bank of the district

(9) Implements government schemes for educated unemployed people, PMRY scheme, Jawahar Rojgar Yojana, etc.

(10) Helps entrepreneurs in obtaining licences from the Electricity Board, Water Supply Board, No objection certificate, etc.

(11) Helps the entrepreneur to procure imported machinery and raw materials.

(12) Organises marketing outlets in liaison with other government agencies.

Industrial Development Corporation (IDC)

Land is an important factor of production. The prices of land are very high and beyond the reach of a common man. People face innumerable difficulties and delays in obtaining power connection, water supply, telephone connection in remote places from the city. This inhibits the growth of industries. Particularly, the new entrepreneurs are frustratied while doing this exercise for all these facilities. In order to assist the entrepreneurs in acquiring land for their industrial units the government has initiated the Industrial Development Corporation (IDC).

The IDC is state level organisation which is established in every state. For example, in Maharashtra, it is known as MIDC, in Gujarat it is known as GIDC, etc. The IDCs have acquired land on the outskirts of the cities and at taluk places. The IDCs provide open plots of land, constructed galas and sheds as per the requirements of the entrepreneurs.

Objectives of IDC

- Initiating industrialisation in the economically backward regions of the state
- To create a network of industries all over the state by facilitating land and premises to the entrepreneurs
- To promote economic equality and decentralisation of economic growth in specific regions
- To facilitate infrastructure to entrepreneurs and to speed up the industrial growth of the state.

To achieve these objectives, IDC provides roads, power, water, street lighting, drainage and sewage disposal, post and communication, police station, security, fire brigade and other common facilities in the IDC zones.

If the industrial unit is located in IDC, it is easier for an entrepreneur to obtain loan from the financial institutions for the purchase of plot of land, shed or gala.

An entrepreneur can obtain plot of land or shed in IDC for following purposes:

(1) To establish small, medium or large-sca!e units

(2) Expansion of the existing unit

(3) To establish industrial units which are prohibited to be established elsewhere but are demarcated in a specific area. For example, chemical industries

(4) To change the place of the unit

(5) To start the supplementary service industries like banks, hotels, petrol pumps, weigh bridges, etc.

State Financial Corporations

State Financial Corporations (SFCs) came into being under the provision of the SFCs Act, 1951. At present, there are 18 SFCs, of which 17 were set up under SFCs Act and one, viz., Tamil Nadu Industrial and Investment Corporation (TIIC) Ltd. under the Companies Act. The main objectives of SFCs are to finance and promote small and medium enterprises in their respective States for achieving balanced regional growth, catalyse investment, generate employment and widen the ownership base of industry. Financial assistance to small and medium enterprises is provided by way of term loans, direct subscription to equity/debentures, guarantees, discounting of bills of exchange and seed capital assistance. They also provide financial assistance for small road transport operators, hotels, tourism-related activities, hospitals, nursing homes, etc.

SFCs provide financial assistance the- industrial units by way of term direct subscriptions, to equity/ debentures, guarantees, discounting of bills of exchange and seed/special capital. On behalf of IDBI/SIDBI, the SFCs operate a number of schemes of refinance and equity-type assistance. They have schemes for artisans, special target groups like SUST, women, ex-servicemen, physically handicapped, etc. SFCs also grant assistance for small road transport operators, setting up hotels, tourism related activities, hospitals and nurisng homes, etc. Over the years, the SFCs have expanded their activities and coverage of assistance.

With the expansion of the industrial sector SFCs are now providing assistance to units engaged in floriculture, tissue culture, poultry farming, setting up of commercial complex facilities, providing services relating to engineering, technical, financial management, marketing, etc.

Liberalisation in the financial sector has provided opportunities for the SFCs to diversify into newer areas. SFCs have now started offering equipment leasing facilities. They have also entered into areas such as consultancy, merchant banking, debenture trusteeship and capital market related services. Several SFCs have identified investment banking and equity participation as the thrust areas of their operations.

With the introduction of financial sector reforms, the business environment for all including the SFCs have become highly competitive. To enable the SFCs to adapt to the emerging environment, it would be necessary to restructure their organisation and management as also broaden their resource-base and carry out financial restructuring. A Committee under the Chairmanship of Chairman IDBI was constituted to under take a comprehensive review of the SFCs Act. The Committee has, after careful consideration and due deliberations, recommended amendments to the SFCs Act on aspects relating to capital restructuring, undertaking new activities and operational flexibility. The recommendations of the Committee are under the consideration of the Government of India.

State Industrial Development Corporations/State Industrial Investment Corporations

State Industrial Development Corporations/ State Industrial Investment Corporations (SIDCs/SIICs) were set up under the Companies Act, 1956 as wholly-owned undertakings of the State Governments to act as catalysts for industrial development in their respective States. At present, there are 28 SIDCs in the country, of which eleven also function as SFCs and are, therefore, termed as Twin-Function IDCs. SIDCs develop land and provide industrial infrastructure facilities in the form of factory sheds and/or developed plots together with facilities like roads, power, water supply, drainage and other amenities. Set up primarily for providing assistance to medium and large scale industries, SIDCs/SIICs also extend assistance to the small scale sector by way of term loans, subscription to equity and promotional services.

State Small Industrial Development Corporations

State Small Industries Development Corporations (SSIDCs) were established under the Companies Act 1956 as State Government undertakings to cater to the needs of the small, tiny and village industries in the respective States/Union Territories. Being operationally flexible, SSIDCs undertake a variety of activities for benefit of the SSI sector, the important ones are: Procurement and distribution of scarce raw materials; supply of machinery to SSI units on hire-purchase basis; providing assistance for marketing of products;

construction of industrial estates, provision of allied infrastructure facilities and their maintenance; extending seed capital assistance on behalf of State Government; providing management assistance to production units.

Functions of SSIDC

(1) Assists entrepreneurs in identifying products and preparing project reports
(2) Organises entrepreneurship training programmes
(3) Supplies scarce raw materials at reasonable rates by procuring these materials in bulk quantity from their main suppliers
(4) Arranges imported raw materials
(5) Provides credit facilities for raw material supplies
(6) Arranges for marketing assistance to products manufactured by small entrepreneurs
(7) Participates in the exhibitions to promote the products of the small entrepreneurs
(8) Arranges exhibitions of handicrafts to promote village and cottage industry
(9) Provides permanent display, exhibition and sale facilities for small entrepreneurs

Other Agencies

Other State-level agencies that extend facilities for promotion of SSIs are State Infrastructure Development Corporations, State Co-operative Banks, Regional Rural Banks, State Export Corporations, State Agro Industries Corporations and State Handloom & Handicrafts Corporations.

Technical Consultancy Organisations (TCOs)

TCOs were set up by the all India financial institution during the seventies and eighties in association with state-level financial development institution and commercial banks to cater to the consultancy needs of small and medium industries and new entrepreneurs.

TCOs provide a total package of consultancy services to small and medium scale enterprises, individual entrepreneurs, government departments and agencies, various state-level institutions, commercial banks and other institutions for activities relating to industrial development and financing. Though the initial thrust of TCOs was focused on pre-investment studies, over the years they have diversified their service to include:

- preparation of project profiles and feasilbility studies;
- undertaking industrial potential surveys;
- identification of potential entreneurs and provision of techaical and management assistance to them;
- undertaking market research and surveys for specific products;
- carrying out energy audit and energy conservation assignments;
- project supervision and wherever necessary, rendering technical and administrative assistance;
- taking up assignments on a turn-key basis;
- undertaking export consultancy for export-oriented projects based on modern technology;
- offering management consultancy services especially for diagnostic study of sick units or for improvement in the existing units and their rehabilitation programmes;
- conducting entrepreneurship development programmes; and skill upgradation programmes.

Financial Institutions

The Government of India and Reserve Bank of India (RBI) have been instrumental in devising a multi-agency approach/system to ensure credit dispensation to different sectors of the economy, including SSI. The distinctive feature of multi-agency set up is that each of the major institutions cater to the needs of a particular segment of the economy, e.g., agriculture, industry, export, housing, etc. Prior to setting up of Industrial Development Bank of India (IDBI) and Small Industries Development Bank of India (SIDBI), banks availed of refinance from RBI against their eligible loans to SSIs. IDBI and SIDBI have been the main providers of refinance to State Level Institutions such as SFCs and SIDCs.

For the purpose of credit dispensation to the SSI sector, the following major national and state level institutions are operating in the country:

Apex Level Financial Institution

Small Industries Development Bank of India

Banks

Commercial Banks

Regional Rural Banks

Co-operative Banks

State Level Institutions

State Financial Corporations

State Industrial Development Corporations

State Industrial Investment Corporations

State Small Industries Development Corporations

Other Financial Institutions and Agencies

National Bank for Agriculture and Rural Development

Khadi and Village Industries Commission

National Small Industries Corporation

North Eastern Development Finance Corporation Ltd.

Small Industries Development Bank of India (SIDBI) was set up in April 1990, as the principal financial institution for promotion, financing and development of industries in the small scale sector and to coordinate the functions of the institutions engaged in similar activities. SIDBI initially set up as a wholly owned subsidiary of IDBI, has since been de-linked from IDBI with effect from March 27, 2000 and is presently working as an independent autonomous body for financing of Small Scale Industries Sector. SIDBI's major operations cover three main areas: *(i)* Indirect Assistance, *(ii)* Direct Assistance, and *(iii)* Development and Support Services.

Chart Showing Financial Assistance to Entrepreneurs

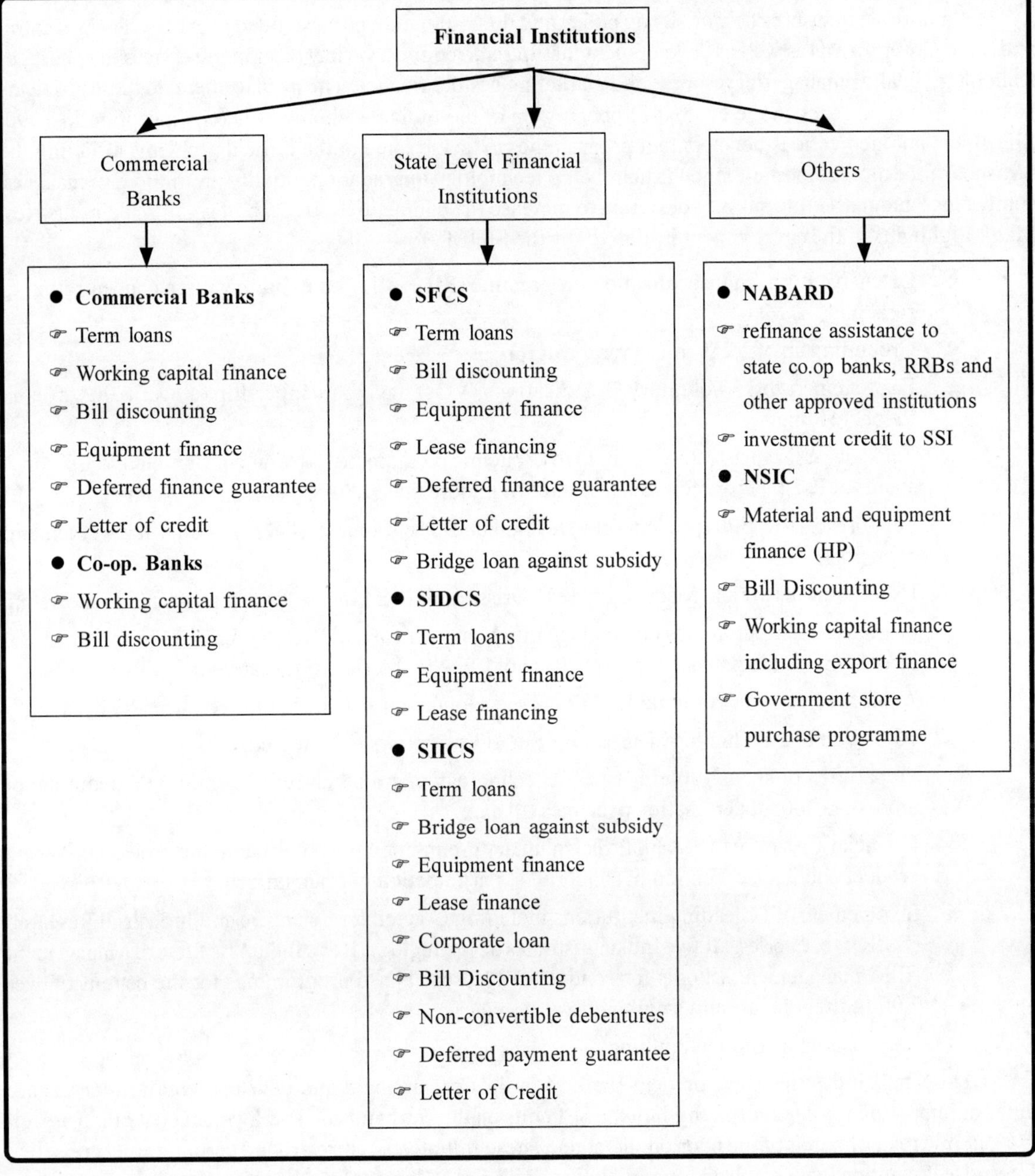

SIDBI Support to SSIs

Small scale industries despite strong policy and programme support extended over the years by Central and State,Governments as well as development institutions require a variety of support services in spheres of technology, quality, managerial resource and marketing besides finance. The need to attend to these problems has acquired an urgency in the context of opening up of the Indian economy. Since its inception in 1990. SIDBI has initiated various development programmes to tackle some of the critical problems afflicting the SSI sector; the more important among them being technology upgradation, quality promotion, managerial competence and marketing support designed to increase the competitive strength of small scale industries. Major highlights of the development initiatives by the SIDBI.

- Extensive Rural Industrialisation Programme (RIP) in 11 States having large concentration of rural poor.
- Grounding up of 2,250 micro rural enterprises.
- Fund support to 16 Voluntary Organisations (VOs) having membership of over 8,000 women for on. lending.
- Financial assistance to 22 VOs for their economic programmes for women. Cumulative assistance stands at Rs. 2.9 crore for 76 VOs benefiting more than 9,800 women.
- Support for 102 Entrepreneurship Development Programmes (EDPs) mainly for women and rural poor.
- Use of radio network in Madhya Pradesh, Orissa and Uttar Pradesh for spread of entrepreneurship.
- 60 awareness programmes on Total Quality Management and ISO-9000 and a special scheme of direct financial assistance for acquisition of ISO-9000 series certificate.
- A joint project with National Handloom Development Corporation for eco-friendly dyes.
- Setting up of a Technology Bureau for Small Enterprises at New Delhi.
- Preparation of about 400 unit-specific technology upgradation reports and implementation of more than 100 modernisation packages till date.
- Financial assistance to 8 small firms/voluntary groups for innovative marketing projects involving product publicity, execution of trial orders, participation in trade fairs, etc.
- Involvement of 71 leading institutions including Council for Scientific and Industrial Research (CSIR) laboratories, all five Indian Institutes of Technology (IITs), Indian Institute of Management (II M/management schools for conduct of 116 specialised programmes for the benefit of over 2,900 entrepreneurs and small industry managers.
- Emphasis on institution building.

The Small Industries Development Bank of India's promotional and developmental initiatives are aimed at improving the inherent strength of the SSI units on the one hand and employment generation as well as economic rehabilitation of the poor on the other. These initiatives centre around certain thrust areas like Enterprise Promotion (with emphasis on rural industrialisation), Human Resources Development, Technology Upgradation, Special Programmes on Environment and Quality Management and Infornation Dissemination. For the upliftment of the rural poor, the Bank operates a series of special schemes like Micro Credit, Mahila Vikas Nidhi, Entrepreneurship Development Programmes, Rural Industries Programme, etc. The Bank operates its schemes in collaboration with vast network of PLIs, reputed NGOs, Technology and Management Institutions and International Development Agencies.

Micro Credit has emerged as a powerful tool of empowering the poor people to alleviate their poverty. While there has been massive expansion of formal credit network in India, there still remains a perceptible gap in financing the genuine credit needs of the poor especially in rural areas. Under its Micro Credit Scheme, SIDBI provides assistance to well managed NGOs for onlending to the rural poor with an emphasis on women entrepreneurs. So as to provide undivided attention to this category of borrowers, the Bank has launched a separate outfit known as SIDBI Foundation for Micro Credit. With a thrust on institutional development, the SIDBI Foundation strives to create a coherent policy framework for accelerating the micro credit movement in the country.

Box – SIDBI Foundation for Micro Credit

Micro credit has emerged as a powerful tool of empowering poor people to alleviate their poverty. While the last three decades have witnessed a massive expansion of female credit network in India, there remains a perceptible gap in financing the genuine credit needs of poor, especially in remote rural areas. SIDBI, as part of its promotional and developmental activities, has been providing assistance to well managed NGOs for onlending to rural poor with an emphasis on women, under its Micro Credit Scheme. However, keeping in view the tremendous potential of reaching out to millions of rural entrepreneurs, a further impetus in development of micro credit in India is essential at this stage. With that objective, SIDBI, during November 1998 has launched a Rs. 1 billion SIDBI Foundation for Micro Credit. The SIDBI Foundation would make use of multi-channel credit dispensation routes to extend micro credit to poor people. The SIDBI Foundation would also focus on encouraging micro finance product innovations besides endeavouring to simplify the procedures in availment of assistance.

The renewed approach focusses on identifying major (nodal) micro finance institutions (MFIs) as long-term partners and providing credit support for their micro credit initiatives. These MFIs, which inter-alia include NGOs and community-based organisations (CBOs), would be selected on the basis of their credibility, track record, professional expertise, management practices and organisational capabilities/growth potential, ctc. Assistance to these MFIs would be based on a capacity assessment rating, business planning and resource forecasts exercise, appraisals and field visits, etc.

SIDBI Foundation would simultaneously help these MFIs by way of need-based loans and grants to strengthen their management capabilities (for achieving sustainability, economics of scale, desired outreach, etc.). It will endeavour to promote and develop these agencies into strong financial intermediaries who would act as major players in the informal credit segments, especially for reaching out to smaller NGOs and MFIs and for building their capabilities through management support inputs, training in credit delivery and usage. Focus will be on promoting best practices and the introduction of innovative features that would contribute to the financial viability of micro credit programmes which would, in turn, ensure appropriate financial services to the poor.

With a thrust on institutional development, SIDBI Foundation will also strive to create a coherent policy framework for accelerating the micro credit movement in the country. The Foundation would endeavour to function as the national financial institution for the micro finance sector and provide developmental and financial assistance for expansion of micro credit programmes for the poor. The SIDBI Foundation will, thus, endeavour to promote an entirely new channel conducive to the needs and psychology of the poor borrowers.

LENDING SCHEMES OF SIDBI

A. Schemes of Indirect Assistance

I. Schemes of Refinance Assistance

(1) General Scheme

(2) Schemes for Cottage, Village and Tiny Industries

- Composite Loan Schemes (CLS)
- Scheme for SC/ST and Physically Handicapped Persons

(3) Scheme for Small Road Transport Operators (SRTOs)

(4) Equity-type Assistance Scheme

- National Equity Fund Scheme (NEF)

(5) Scheme for Women Entrepreneurs

- Mahila Udyam Nidhi (MUN)

(6) Self Employment for Ex-servicemen (SEMFEX) Scheme

(7) Single Window Scheme (SWS)

(8) Refinance Scheme for Technology Development and Modernisation (RTDM)

(9) Refinance Scheme for Acquisition of ISO 9000 Series Certification by SSI unit (RISO 9000)

(10) Refinance Scheme for Rehabilitation of Sick Industrial units (RSR).

II. Bills Rediscounting Scheme (BRS)

(1) Bills Rediscounting Scheme (Equipment)

(2) Bills Rediscounting Scheme (Inland Supply Bills).

III. Resource Support to Institutions/Agencies Engaged in Financing SSI units

(1) To intermediaries, viz., SFCs/SIDCs/SSIDCs/Banks

(2) To Leasing/Hire Purchase companies

(3) To factoring companies

(4) To specialised institutions/corporations/corporate entities engaged in development of SSIs.

Schemes of Direct Assistance

(1) Project Finance Scheme

(2) Venture Capital Scheme

(3) Scheme for Financing Activities relating to Marketing of SSI Products

(4) Scheme for Direct Assistance for Development of Industrial Infrastructure for SSI Sector

(5) Equipment Finance Scheme

(6) Scheme of Integrated Infrastructural Development (IID) (Including technological back-up services) -

(7) ISO 9000 Scheme

(8) Scheme of Assistance for Saving-Cum-Credit Groups (Micro Credit Scheme)

(9) Scheme for Foreign Currency Term Loans to SSI units

(10) Pre-shipment/Post-shipment Credit to SSIs
(11) Scheme for Export Bills Financing
(12) Opening of Foreign Letters of Credits (FLCs)
(13) Technology Development and Modernisation Fund Scheme
(14) Vendor Development Scheme
(15) Working Capital Term Loan Scheme for SSIs
(16) Direct Discounting of Bills (Equipment) Scheme
(17) Direct Discounting of Bills Scheme
(18) Scheme for Domestic Factoring

PRODUCTS AND PROGRAMMES

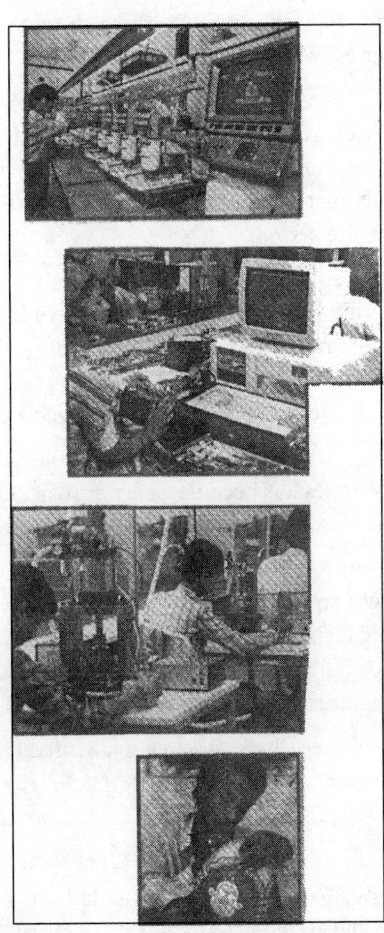

- Refinance
- Equity Finance
- Bills Finance
- Project Finance
- Venture Capital
- Marketing Assistance
- Infrastructure Development
- Assistance for equity certification
- Technology Development and Modernisation Fund
- Textile and Tannery Modernisation Funds
- International Finance and Cooperation
- Micro Credit and Rural Industrialisation
- Human Resource Development

... and many more

Credit Penetration in SMEs

Small and Medium Enterprises (SMEs) are not able to exploit their potential due to the low credit penetration into the segment. Almost 90 per cent of the units are not registered and close to 95 per cent of them do not have access to any kind of formal institutional credit. According to the Third All-India Census of Small Scale Industries, only 17.9 per cent had availed of credit of these 14.9 per cent could have had access to institutional credit. The report of the Committee on Financial Sector Assessment (CFSA) points to both a decline in the share of credit to SSIs and a widening of the credit gap to unreasonable levels. Further, the SME sector is underserved, especially in terms of working capital and trade finance.

The CFSA report goes a step further and points out that even in cases where credit is available for investment, the loan tenures are far too short to pay off any sizeable investment. Also, small scale units do not have access to competitive rates, which are usually reserved for blue-chip companies. The practice is that when banks lend to SSIs, banks charge a commission for the additional risks and apply tougher screening measures, which drive up costs.

The CFSA has made an attempt to gauge the extent of the credit gap by assuming the credit that would have been available, if the share of small scale credit in total bank credit remained at 13 per cent, its average share during 1998-2007. Figures show that credit gap expressed as a per cent of the actual lending to SSIs has steadily increased from 9 per cent in 2002 to nearly 100 per cent in 2007, the average gap being 69 per cent during the period.

The report cites three reasons for banks' increasing reluctance to lend to SSIs. One, banks consider them high-risk borrowers, as they have insufficient assets, high vulnerability to market fluctuations and high mortality rates. Second, there are issues related to high transaction costs, as the small amount of credit used by each unit raises administrative costs. Third, there are difficulties in assessing the creditworthiness of the units, due to the lack of accounting records or financial statements.

The third factor is especially relevant in the Indian context, where the growing sophistication of lending technologies has become a barrier to accessing, credit for small units, which are dependent on reelationship lending – where decisions are based on soft information gathered by the lender on the borrower.

In relationship lending, the banker has personal knowledge of a borrower's managerial skills and business strategy of the loanee firms over a period. This substituted for transparency of records. But as lending technologies of large banks become dependent on quantifiable transactions-based information, which is electronically stored and communicated across the institutions, the credit flows based on relationship lending are bound to fall, states the report.

Experts have stressed on the need to regenerate SME financing. According to *Finn Sizc and Business Environment* in *SME Financing,* a World Bank study, SMEs across the world face similar problems, due to inversely related factors, the problem areas being financing and regulatory policies.

Financing agencies are focussing on a cluster approach to achieve the twin objectives of their own business growth and development of the SME sector. The objective is to ensure that the fruits of development are spread across a vast majority of entrepreneurs and community and balanced regional development.

Regenerating SME financing in India is essential as the sector serves as a greenfield for nurturing entrepreneurial talent. An increased focus by Indian banks and financial institutions on providing micro finance, factoring assistance, etc, at reasonable costs will go a long way in making SMEs domestically and globally competitive, leading to economic growth.

Going forward, to ensure better accessibility of credit by SMEs, banks' ability to quickly evaluate the credit worthiness of small and medium enterprises will be critical. Due to limiting factors of financial statement lending and asset-based lending, credit scoring lending, long used in consumer lending, may be considered by banks in the case of SMEs. To make this a more effective option, it may be combined with relationship lending, universally the most popular lending technique for SMEs, where information and documentation are quite inadequate'. Under relationship lending, a lender's decision in substantial part is based on the proprietary information about the firm and its owner, acquired by the loan officer through a variety of sources.

Industry Associations

In addition to the Central and State Government agencies, industry associations also provide institutional support to the small-scale sector. Industry associations provide SSIs with a common platform to raise industry-related issues and to initiate cooperative efforts for promoting SSIs. Government's policies, in recent years, have stressed the increasing role of industry associations in setting up common facilities and other co-operative ventures in areas of technology, marketing and other support services. Some of the major industry associations providing services are:

- Federation of Tiny & Small Industries of India
- Indian Council of Small Industries
- Laghu Udyog Bharti
- Federation of Indian Export Organisations
- World Association for Small & Medium Enterprises
- Federation of Associations of Small Industries of India
- Consortium of Women Enterprises of India
- Manufacturers' Association for Information Technology
- Electronic Component Industries Association
- Federation of Indian Micro and Small & Medium Enterprises
- National Association of Software & Service Companies
- Hand Tool Manufacturers' Association
- Self-Employed Women's Association
- All-India Women's Association of Karnataka
- Tamil Nadu Small Industries Association
- Small Industries Association of Orissa
- Small Industries Association of Gujarat
- Confederation of Indian Industry*
- Federation of Indian Chambers of Commerce and Industry*
- PHD Chamber of Commerce and Industry*
- Associated Chambers of Commerce & Industry of India*

*(*These organisations are catering to large-scale industries and also have special cells for SSI units)*

Non-Governmental Organisations

Non-Government Organisations (NGOs) are an important link in the implementation of various developmental programmes of the Government. There is a team effort in the working of the NGOs and these organisations develop and apply new techniques and ways of working to achieve success. NGOs are registered under the Society's Registration Act and/or under Foreign Contribution Regulation Act and are generally non-profit organisations.

Table

Specialised Training Institutes

Name of Institute	*Place*	*Activities*
National Institute of Small Industry Extension and Training (NISIET)	Hyderabad	Training, Research and Consultancy activities
Indian Institute of Entrepreneurship	Guwahati	Training, Research and Consultaancy activities
National Institute for Entrepreneurship & Small Business Development (NIESBUD)	New Delhi	Co-ordinating & overseeing activities of various institutes/agencics engaged in entrepreneurship development
Integrated Training Centre (Industries)	Nilokher	Conducts EDP courses
Institute for Design of Electrical Measuring Instruments (IDEMI)	Mumbai	Render services to the Instrumentation Industry
Central Institute of Hand Tools	Jalandhar	Aims at rapid growth of the Hand Tool Sector
Hand Tool Design Development and Training Centre	Nagaur	Assistance for improvement in productivity, betterment in quality high value addition
Central Tool Room	Ludhiana	Provides services in the area of consultancy tool design & manufacture and technical training
Central Tool Room, &Training Centre	Kolkata	Training, design & manufacture of complicated precision tools for the telecom industry and other Common Facility Services.
Central Institute of Tool Design (CITD)	Hyderabad	Training, CAD/CAM Centre to train post graduate trainees, automatic process control unit etc.
Product-cum-Process Development Centre for Sports Goods	Meerut	Training, process & product development of sports goods, R&D.
Product-cum-Process Development Centre for Essential Oils	Kannauj	Modernise and upgrade technology status for the essential oils & perfumery industry
Product-cum-Process Development Centre	Agra	Provide better technology to small scale foundry & forging units, process & product development, provision of design for melting, equipment, testing facilities
Electronic Service & Training Centre	Ramnagar	Training, technical & consultancy services
Centre for the Improvement of Glass Industry	Firozabad	Development & adoption of new technologies & products
National Small Industries Corporation	New Delhi	Supply of machinery, marketing assistance, training

Export Promotion Councils

In order to overcome the problems in marketing of SSI products in foreign markets, it has been considered desirable to adopt a consortium approach. The export promotion councils for different industries make efforts to promote exports of their member units through direct marketing, developing vendor relations, opening respective sales outlets abroad as a collective export marketing strategy. The activities of different Councils are targeted to increase exports from the sector. The Export Promotion Councils (EPCs) are registered as non-profit organisations under the Companies Act /Societies Registration Act. SSI units get access to export related services from the Councils. Some of the Councils obtain bulk purchase orders from foreign buyers and distribute them among member units for supply to the Council for onward export. The EPCs also offer a package of other services to members and others by way of information dissemination, Export-Import policies and procedures, customs and excise duty rules etc. Besides, trade enquiries, tender notices are circulated among members in order to assist them to avail of business opportunities for augmenting overall exports.

Institutions to Assist Exporters

The following important agencies are available for assistance of exporters in their endeavour to increase exports from the country:

- Indian Institute of Foreign Trade
- Indian Institute of Packaging
- Export Houses, Trading Houses & Star Houses and Super Star Trading Houses
- Export Credit Guarantee Corporation of India Ltd.
- Export Inspection Council

Industry-related Research Institutes

There are a number of industry-related research institutes which undertake research in various aspects connected with growth of industry, including SSI sector. Important industry- related research institutes include:

World Asociation for Small & Medium Enterprises (WASME)

WASME is a non-governmental Organisation registered under the Societies Act, Delhi. It is managed by Governing Body comprising of representatives drawn from Chambers of'Commerce, Banks, Financial Institutions, Small Businclss Development Corporations, Department of Small Industries in various Governments. Among other activities, WASME's focus is on ensuring business cooperation amongst enterprises of the developing countries by facilitating technology transfer, training and marketing. The facilities provided by WASME include: (i) information on policies, strategies and support systems for SMEs in member conuntries, (ii) providing opportunities for marketing of products, (iii) facilitating contacts with sources offering latest technologies, equipment and services for SMEs and (iv) identification of facilities for training of entrepreneurs, managers and production personnel.

Some of the thrust areas of WASME activities include technology transfer, training, manintaining a roster of experts / consultants organising or sponsoring seminars/ workshops/ conferences, acting as a clearing house of information relating to SMEs, undertaking special studies and research on areas of relevance to SMEs and strengthening or assisting in the setting up of associations of SMEs and of women entrepreneurs.

Federation of Associations of Small Industries of India (FASII)

The Federation of Associations of Small Industries of India, set up in 1959 represents, associations of small industries and individual SSI units. The main objectives of FASII are: *(i)* to promote the development of small-scale, tiny and cottage industries, *(ii)* to cooperate with industrial, business, educational and research institutions in collecting and exchanging information pertaining to the small industries sector, *(iii)* to undertake professional, technical and management consultation services, *(iv)* to undertake studies, surveys and research assignments *(v)* to further the Cause of Small industries by interacting with Union and State Governments and other bodies, *(vi)* to establish and operate trade centres, display cantres, sub-contract exchanges and other promotional institutions for the benefit of the small-scale sector, and *(vii)* to establish test centres, laboratories and common facility centres for the SSI sector,

In this direction, the Federation offers scrvices such as organising meetings/conferences, liaisoning with such policy makers, analysis and interpretation of policies in taking the members' difficultics with the concerned departments/organisations for redressal.

Consortium of Women Entrepreneurs of India (CWEI)

In the context of the opening up of the economy and the need for upgradation of technology the consortium of Women Entrepreneurs of India is a common platform to help the women entrepreneurs in finding innovative techniques of production, marketing and finance. CWEI consists of NGOs, voluntary organisations, self-help groups, institutions and individual enterprises, both from rural and urban areas, which collectively support and benefit from the activities taken up by the Consortium. CWEI takcs up integrated activity linked with product development, manpower training and also acts as an intermediary between Indian entrepreneurs and overseas agencies for marketing and exports.

Laghu Udyog Bharati (LUB)

Laghu Udyog Bharati was established in 1995. The main objective of the organisation is to promote and safeguard the interest of small-scale industry. Entrepreneurial training, support for technology upgradation and marketing are within the extended scope of its activities. Laghu Udyog Bharati has its representation on the national and state level government bodies connected with SSIs.

Indian Council of Small Industries (ICSI)

Indian Council of Small Industries founded in 1979 represents around 1500 associations of the decentralised sector. The major objectives of the Council include extending help to small, tiny, small and cottage enterprises and artisans. In the process, the ICSI aims at enhancing the contribution of SSI sector in the overall growth of Indian economy. The major functions of ICSI are consultancy, information, dissemination, entrepreneurship development, training, research etc. ICSI represents the cause of is member enterprises by giving suggestions for appropriate policy making. The council follows consortium approach to provide market services and extends facilities relating to the testing centre and quality control outlets.

- Central Manufacturing Technology Institute
- Central Pulp & Paper Research Institute
- National Council for Cement & Building Materials
- Automotive Research Association of India
- Indian Rubber Manufaturers Research Association

- National Institute of Design
- Quality Council of India
- Centre of Leather Research Institute
- Council of Scientitic & Industrial Research

Conclusion

The entrepreneurship development movement, is primarily based on the belief that people can accept entrepreneurship as a career. In order to accelerate the speed of self-employment and entrepreneurship development various institutions and organisations were established by the government, particularly during the Third Five-Year Plan. These institutions and organisations cater to the business needs and requirements of the entrepreneurs. Particularly, the First generation entrepreneurs' is the focal point. Some of these institutions function at the State level to provide "single window" assistance and "on the spot" solutions to the problem of the entrepreneurs. The role of support institution in fostering entrepreneurs in general and small entrepreneurs in particular is qualit in the world. A coordinated effort to foster entrepreneurship will go a longway in speeding up economic development and economic growth.

ROLE OF ENTREPRENEUR AS AN INNOVATOR IN ECONOMIC GROWTH

Entrepreneurship development is getting a position of great importance for tackling evergrowing problem of unemployment due to rapid population growth. Though the last of 20th century experienced the growth of a large number of small entrepreneurs in our country, the number of innovating entrepreneurs is less than the imitating entrepreneurs; as a result of which, the country has been lagging behind in moving at a pace international communities demand. Therefore, to cope with the international order and dynamism of the society, an entrepreneur's role as an innovator is of prime importance. According to **J.A. Schumpeter,** an entrepreneur is basically an innovator who introduces new combinations of means of production. Development consists of carrying out new combinations. A new combination may be carried out by utilization of both used and unused means of production. According to **Schumpeter,** as an innovator entrepreneur forces the potentially profitable opportunities to exploit it. He is a risk bearer, problem shooter and gets satisfaction in confronting problems. As an innovator, entrepreneur performs the following activities:

(1) Bringing about the new combinations
(2) Emphasizing on purposeful and systematic innovation
(3) Implementation of mechanical skills
(4) Making use of potential technical knowledge for continuous technological progress.
(5) Giving rise to utilization of innovative talents which initiate and improve the economic growth.

***

10

Preliminary Project Report

Introduction

Soon after the identification of a project and its implementation, the project report is formulated after examining various relevant aspects. Usually, the entrepreneur gets a project report prepared before a project or investment is undertaken. That project report prepared before a project of investment is undertaken. That project report assesses the demand of the proposed product to be produced, works out the costs of investment as well as operational costs and thus estimates the expected profitability of the proposed investment. It is on this basis that not only the entrepreneur takes his decision on whether to proceed on the proposed project, but also financial backers, banks and state departments involved in the project base their decisions on the ways and the extent to which the help should be provided. If the entrepreneur has to go to the money market to raise some risk capital for his venture, the project report may serve as his main instrument in convincing the investors about the profitability of his venture.

In fact, the state financing and nationalised banks in India over the years have been insisting on first getting such a project report from the entrepreneur before taking any action on his application for financial and other support. This strategy has been in operation for several decades. However, the number of the closing down of comparatively new businesses, and the emergence of large number of 'sick' mills give a cause of concern about the strategies adopted at the time of project appraisal. These issues not only adversely affect the involved entrepreneurs, but also the financing institutions. Thus it is not only a serious setback to the budding entrepreneurs of a newly developing country; it wastes the scarce investable funds of the nation, and as the banks have to break-even, this situation hikes up the real interest rate in the economy, making development costly.

A Project Report

A project report incorporating relevant data in respect of a project serves as a guide to management and records merits and demerits in allocating resources to producion of specific goods or services. A project report is prepared for analysing the extent of opportunities in the contemplated project.

A project report is prepared by an expert after detailed study and analysis of the various aspects of a project. It gives a complete analysis of the inputs and outputs of the project. It enables the entrepreneur to understand, at the initial stage, whether the project is sound on technical, commercial, financial and economic parameters.

Parties Interested in Project Report

Financial institutions and commercial bankers are the interested parties in the. project report which is prepared for direct submission to financial corporations, banks for getting loans. It does not contribute substantially to future operations.

The entrepreneur gets the report prepared by a consultant. As such, these parties providing term loans go for the report because it spells out how production should be organised to yield maximum results.

Scope

Project report includes information on the following aspects:

1. Economic Aspects. The project report should be able to present economic justification for investment. It should present analysis of the market for the product to be manufactured. Market analysis basically pertains to the following issues: *(a)* How big is the present market? (b) How much is it likely to grow? (c) How much of the future market the proposed project can capture after allowing a margin for future entrants? It provides an analysis of the economics of production.

2. Technical Aspects. The appropriate report should give details about the technology needed, equipments and machinery required and the sources of availability.

3. Financial Aspects. The report should indicate the total investment required including sources of finance and the entrepreneur's contribution. It should present a comparison of cost of capital with the return on capital.

4. Production Aspects. It should contain a description of the product selected for manufacture and the reasons for such selection. The report should also bring out the fact whether the product is exportworthy. It should also give details of the design of the product.

5. Managerial Aspects. The report should contain qualifications and experience of the persons to be put on the management of the job. If the entrepreneur will look after management, the report must emphasise as to how he is qualified to manage the venture.

Feasibility Reports Setting

A feasibility report or a project report of a new enterprise or of an expansion provides, in general, primary economic information, financial data and technical details which serve a finite number of discrete economic processes or cost structures of the industry concerned. Here, the economic processes are defined as combinations of vectors of material inputs and fuels (distinguished by supplying sectors), labour (by types and skills), capital (by types of, function and capacities of categories), permitting different levels of output with varying costs of production but subject to the constraint of industrial capacities of the enterprise. The "industrial profile" is a similar document which also presents a brief history and technical descriptions of processes in terms of technical inputs coefficients for small-scale or medium or large-scale manufactures. Given these details, an entrepreneur is concerned with the local market prices and relative prices of substitutes and complements as to guide decision making for sales and purchases; and to enable to compute and check for profitability (social or private) of the enterprise expansion or of a new plant.

A researcher is, however, concerned with the computation of input, capital and labour vectors, based on the generally available contents of the project report. Further, he examines from the report three aspects: *(i)* Preparation of a number of possible alternative solutions to attain a production target; *(ii)* Comparison of the alternatives and final selection of them; *(iii)* Implementation of the project and scope for economies of scale.

A number of possible alternative solutions of attaining a production target is the result of studying available production techniques, of which choice for the best, singly or in combination can be made. For comparison of alternative solutions among a number of feasible alternatives to the project, a criterion has to be chosen to achieve substantial rate of return with a unique solution, sufficiently profitable to justify the decision to carry on the enterprise. However, the search for such a choice depends on a number of studies of the individual projects or of their combinations.

The feasibility report should contain the following details: *(a)* promoters(s) of the project, *(b)* product(s) of the project, *(c)* the level of output, *(d)* the raw materials used and the sources of supply, *(e)* the technical production method selected and the location of the plant, *(f)* the total cost of the project (in local currency and foreign currencies), *(g)* the proposed method of financing (proportions of the various sources of capital) and legal structure of the future enterprise, *(h)* the unit cost of the manufacture compared to those at FOB or CIF prices, *(i)* the size of the market (and the expected trading profits), *(j)* the effects of the projects on the economy, public finances and the labour market, *(k)* the existence of the market trend of demand, the structure of competing firms and the proposed methods of distribution, trends in imports, exports, income, prices, local producers etc. *(1)* possibility of producing at reasonable cost, alternative methods and brief reasons for selecting, *(m)* initial costs and costs of conversion: *(i)* investment costs and *(ii)* operating costs, *(n)* commercial profitability to ensure repayment of loans and a return on capital investment, *(o)* general information.

Contents of a Project Report

The following are the contents of a project report:

(1) Objective and scope of the report.

(2) Product characteristics (specifications, product uses and application, standards and quality).

(3) Market, position and trends (installed capacity, production and anticipated demand, export prospects and information on import and export, price structure and trends).

(4) Raw materials (requirement of raw materials, prices, sources and properties of raw materials).

(5) Manufacture (processes of manufacture, selection of process, production schedule and production technique).

(6) Plant and Machinery (equipments and machinery, instruments, laboratory equipments, electric load and water supply and the essential infrastructure).

(7) Land and building (requirement of land area, building, construction schedule).

(8) Financial implications (fixed and working capital investment, project cost and profitability).

(9) Marketing channels (trading practices and marketing strategy).

(10) Personnel (requirements of staff, labour and expenses on wage payment).

The project report is prepared for submission to the financial institutions for the grant of land and other financial concessions. An entrepreneur can himself prepare the report, otherwise assistance from experts can be sought. There are several organisations which help entrepreneurs in the preparation of reports. The Small Industries Service Institute (SISI) and Small Industries Development Organisation (SIDO) help the entrepreneur in this regard. State Government also help the entrepreneur in matters of financial assistance towards this end.

Importance of a Project Report

Project report is of great importance. It highlights the practicability of a project in terms of different factors like economy, finance, technology and social desirability. It is needed by the entrepreneur for carrying out expansion or starting a new production line. These may be carried on by individuals like engineers and scientists, bankers or institutions, consultancy services and development banks.

An important aspect of the report lies in determining the profitability of the project and minimising risks in the execution of the project.

Proforma of a Project Report

We give here a proforma of the Project report.

Proforma for a Project Scheme for the Manufacture of –

---

1. Introduction

Title/Name of the firm

(a) Scope
(b) Product (give specification, viz., ISS/BSS/ASS)
(c) Process
(d) Marketability
(e) Location
(f) Sources of finance/repayment schedule.

2. Scheme

(a) Land and Buildings: Rs.
(owned/rented or leased)
(b) Machinery and Equipment Rs.
(give detailed specification/capacity/imported or indigenous). For imported machine allowances (for duty on imported items, dock clearance charges, freight and insurance and local freight) Rs.
Total: Rs.
(c) Testing Equipment Rs.
(d) Other fixed investments:
(i) Packing and forwarding charges Rs.
(ii) Electrification and installation charges Rs.
(iii) Cost of tools/jigs/fixtures Rs.
(iv) Cost of office equipment Rs.

(e)	Total Non-recurring expenditure (a) + (b) + (c) + (d)	Rs.
(f)	Staff and Labour:	Rs.
	(i) Indirect labour nos. and wages/p.m.	Rs.
	(ii) Direct labour nos. and wages/p.m.	Rs.
	Total salaries p.m. [(i) + (ii)]	Rs.
(g)	Raw Materials and Consumables:	Rs.
	(Per month on single shift basis with specifications)	
	(i) Indigenous	Rs.
	(ii) Imported	Rs.
	Total:	Rs.
(h)	Other items of expenditure:	Rs.
	(Per month on a single shift basis)	
	(i) Power and water charges	Rs.
	(ii) Advertising and travelling	Rs.
	(iii) Transport	Rs.
	(iv) Commission to distributors/agents	Rs.
(i)	Total recurring expenditure: (f) + (g) + (h)	Rs.
(j)	Working capital for 3 months 3 x recurring expenditure	Rs.
(k)	Total Investment required:	
	(i) Non-recurring expenditure	Rs.
	(ii) Working capital for 3 months	Rs.
	Total:	Rs.
(1)	Total Cost of Production:	
	(i) Total recurring expenditure	Rs.
	(ii) Depreciation on machinery and equipment	Rs.
	(iii) Depreciation on building	Rs.
	(iv) Maintenance charges	Rs.
	(v) Interest on total investment	Rs.
	(vi) Welfare for staff	Rs
	(vii) Office stationery and postage, etc.	Rs.
	Total:	Rs.
(m)	Profit and Loss Account:	
	(i) By sale of... (qty.) of ... @ Rs. ex-factory *exclusive of* applicable taxes	Rs.
	(ii) Cost of production (1)	Rs.
	(iii) Profit *(i)* - *(ii)* Approx. percentage of the total capital employed`	Rs.
	Total:	Rs.

3. Profitability and Projections

(generally for about 5 to 10 years)

Phase of activity

Profitability of phases

4. Infrastructure

(i) Locational advantage

(ii) Availability of material/power/water/labour

(iii) Government policy Rs.

Break-even Point

(i) Fixed Costs:

(Executive salaries/depreciation / rent / interest on investment and administration costs) Rs.

(ii) Variable costs (direct labour/direct material/income tax/ commission and administration costs) Rs.

Item of Cost	*Fixed +*	*Variable*	*Total*
Materials	Rs.	Rs.	Rs.
Labour	Rs.	Rs.	Rs.
Other Expenditure	Rs.	Rs.	Rs.

$$Q = \frac{F}{P - V}$$

Where Q = Break-even Quantity

F = Fixed Cost

V = Variable Cost per unit

P = Sales Price per unit

5. Names and Addresses of Suppliers

(i) Raw Materials

(ii) Machinery and Equipment

6. Remarks

Seal and Date (Signature of the Consultant)

Project profile is a plan which enables a new entrepreneur to choose a suitable line of manufacture.

An entrepreneur usually finds it difficult to prepare this report due to heavy consultancy charges. In such circumstances, a project profile which is in the form of blueprints of different business ventures come to his rescue. It gives full information about the business opportunity of different projects.

Proforma of a Project Profile on a small printing press is given below: Product Introduction

A printing press can be started as a small business. The demand for printing jobs is increasing rapidly as the publicity through advertisements in papers, cartoons, pamphlets and booklets is needed in marketing of almost of every product.

The various educational institutions and other establishments also require printing facilities.

Process of Printing

The following is the process of printing:

(i) The material to be printed is first of all composed by the compositor.

(ii) The composed material is then fed into the printing machine and impression are got on the paper by mechanical operation of the printing press.

Accommodation Required

Floor Space	65 × 16 = 1040 square feet

Machinery and Equipment

The following machinery and equipments are required for a printing press:

(i)	Chandelier type printing press (17" x 22")	Rs.
(ii)	2 H.P. Motor 3 Phase = 1	Rs.
(iii)	Rubber Roller = 1	Rs.
(iv)	Paper Cutting machine (42") = 1	Rs.
(v)	Proof Press (Roller) = 1	Rs.
(vi)	Types, spacing materials, stars, monograms, etc.	Rs.
(vii)	Wooden type cases, racks, galleys, etc.	Rs.
(viii)	Type = 100 Kgs.	Rs.

Manpower Required

Supervisor 1	Rs.
Compositor 1	Rs.
Machinemen 1	Rs.
Helper 1	Rs.

Raw Materials

(i)	Papers	Rs.
(ii)	Cards	Rs.
(iii)	Inks	Rs.
(iv)	Gums, etc.	Rs.

Investment

(i)	Machinery and Equipment	Rs.
(ii)	Working Capital for 3 months	Rs.
(iii)	Total cost of production per year	Rs.

Total Production Per Year

(i)	Value	Rs.
(ii)	Profit	Rs.
(iii)	Rate of return	Rs.

A project profile specifies all the requirements such as raw materials, process of production, cost estimates, marketing facilities, expenditures which may be incurred if the industrial unit is to be established for operation. Project profiles can be prepared by different agencies. The Small Industries Development Organisation has been publishing model schemes on certain specific lines of production which provide immediate scope for development as small-scale industries as well as other enterprises.

Conclusion

The project report must contain the various detailed information which ultimately helps in the decision making process of whether or not to encourage the project conceived. The financial institutions insist upon such a project report in order to be sure about the feasibility of the project. Since the financial commitments would be huge in many cases, it is necessary that before they advance the money sufficient precaution should be taken or else it would result in a huge loss in case an unprofitable project is financed. Also they ascertain from the report the possibility of generation of funds by the project itself and whether or not it would be substantial enough to repay the amount advanced within the stipulated period also indicates the technical feasibility and on the proper verification of the information supplied, a conclusion can be drawn about the appropriateness of such feasibility. The report also indicates the economic and commercial viability of the project and whether or not adequate managerial competence required for successful running of the enterprise is available.

ANNEXURE 1

Insight into Objective Oriented Project Planning

The objective oriented project planning (oopp) designed by a German organisation for development cooperation can be easily adapted to the Indian context.

A project plan or a programme arises due to a desire to improve a situation which is found unsatisfactory. The idea may look realistic but the initial plan may not be appealing to the target groups or does not get the commitment from others. This is where objective oriented project planning proves beneficial.

The representatives of the relevant departments are brought together for discussions. Problems and possible solutions are discussed to come to an understanding of each others' viewpoints and a consensus is achieved. The problem elements are organised into a logical sequence, reformulated into objectives and focussed at the goal.

Subsequently while planning, a logical framework technique is used to prepare a project planning matrix (PPM) and management planning matrix (MPM). The matrix depicts the objectives of different levels.

Sequence of Adaption

Analysis phase:

Bring together the most relevant participants for discussion

— Determine the entity

— Discuss problems related to the entity

— Construct the "problem tree" with the "Cause-effect" relationship

— Reformulate problems to objectives, construct

"Objective tree" and check the 'means end' relationships

— Basing on predetermined criteria arrive at the project focus.

Planning phase:

— Use information from the anlysis phase to prepare PPM or MPM

— Schedule the activities

— Point out responsibility

Problem Formulation

Information is collected through surveys, log book entries, periodical reports and other sources. Perhaps the completeness and reliability of the data might be doubted. The participation of all parties will give an opportunity to make it precise.

During the planning session participants write their problems on cards. They are displayed on the wall and is anonymous. This gives an advantage to express unhesitatingly. The session moderator initiates a group discussion. In the process underlying difficulties are uncovered. All the participants have to identify problems in relation to a clearly described entity. Problems of those not represented also need consideration and thorough discussion. The data collected are useful in such situations.

A starter problem is then selected and cause/effect of this is identified. The causes can be identified from the cards. The effect is put above its causing. The problem tree thus emerges because of a problem which gets related to other problems. The logic has to be rechecked afterwards. Line will show the relationship between problems and arrows, the direction of effects.

The realistic objectives are reformulated by the participants. These objectives are then put on the wall. The sequence needs checking for reorganising. When the participants agree for the sequencing, the "means-ends" relationships are visualised. Related objectives are clustered and the topic required to address them is named. The last step in the anlysis phase is selection of clusters to be included in the project. The "project purpose" and "overall objective" then gets formulated.

Project Planning Matrix

Overall objective			
Project purpose	Indicators	Sources of verification	Assumptions
Results	Indicators	Sources of verification	Assumptions
Activities	Inputs	Costs	Assumptions
			Preconditions

This is used in the planning phase and is also known as the logical framework. The format is square in form with four vertical and four horizontal rows.

The first vertical column of the matrix has the project purpose and overall objective. Next, objectives leading to the project purpose on the objective tree are entered into the matrix as "results" or "outputs." Indicators of project purpose and each result are formulated in measurable terms: quantity, quality, place and time.

Objectives not to be addressed by the project are written on cards and can be considered as conditions. Other conditions are identified and then assessed as to whether they are important or likely to cause problems during implementation. If the project has no authority to address these crucial conditions, they are termed as "assumptions and are placed in the fourth vertical column at the respective levels in the matrix. "Assumptions" may become additional results if acted upon during the project implementation. Then they get shifted to the first column.

A brainstorming session brings ideas to light on activities leading to the various results. Participants discuss these ideas and put them in order of priority under respective results possibly a donor input can be estimated by marking the respective activities. A rough estimate of costs and inputs can be incorporated in the matrix.

The project planning matrix (PPM) shows the output of the project in relation to the outside world. However, internal problems of project organisation and management are often pressing. These problems, perhaps are best formulated in a management planning matrix by setting out as to how effectively the results could be achieved.

The bigger activities which require considerable resource, are identified with time duration. A bar chart can show the activities covering total project period. The resource availability can be taken into account. It is necessary that the responsibilities set out are clearly understood and agreed upon by the personnel involved.

Limitations of OOPP

Visualisation is the core of OOPP method. Therefore a session has to be conducted with a particular seating arrangement and in a special room. This makes the number of participants to be limited to optimal. Perhaps many sessions have to be conducted in a situation and findings integrated in a plenary session.

The OOPP tries to assure an anonymous presentation of viewpoints. But discussions become still a problem to the person of a low profile. In an organisation where a culture prevails for strong adherence to hierarchical order, open discussion gets inhibited.

Decision makers who do not participate in discussions are likely to disagree the plan developed. This perhaps may become a serious constraint. The possible solution will be a frank discussion in advance of the planning session to identify the project mandate.

The moderator is the key person to guide the participant of the planning session through each stage. It is a fact that open minded communication is a complex process needing a determined moderator. He has to be creative, flexible, objective and independent person too. If the moderator is not well trained, sessions will create conflicts and disappointments among participants. A well trained outsider can also make session effective.

Performance Management Systems

In an economy where nothing really seems broken, alignment still matters for two reasons. First, because it is possible to build performance management systems that are responsive to both business goals and to personal aspirations. Second, this nurturing of harmony opens up great possibility for individual and company potential to get realised. Currently, many companies feel forced to set limits on achievable, sustainable growth because they do not see any other way out. We suggest that neither companies nor employees need operate under such unnecessary and painful constraints.

Conserving Time: Performance Planning and Evaluation

Slack stealthily creeps into performance management system. Take for example the timing of performance related discussions. In India, there is a tendency to conduct performance planning – for the year ahead – and performance evaluation, for the year gone by, in the same meeting.

Though it may sound counterintuitive, companies need to have two separate sessions. This saves time because both processes – of setting strategic goals and of evaluating employees – then receive the attention they independently merit.

Organisations should synchronise their performance planning with their business planning and budgeting processes, usually held in March. This will ensure that goals are set and communicated before the start of the fiscal year. Performance evaluations should take place in the first quarter of the fiscal year, usually May-July, when all necessary date is available.

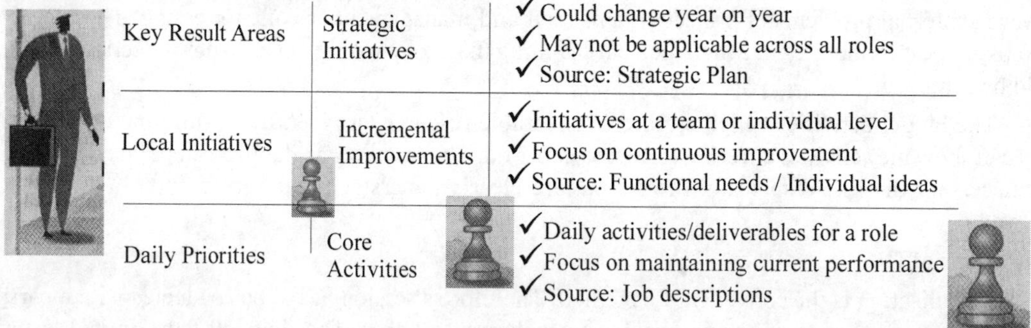

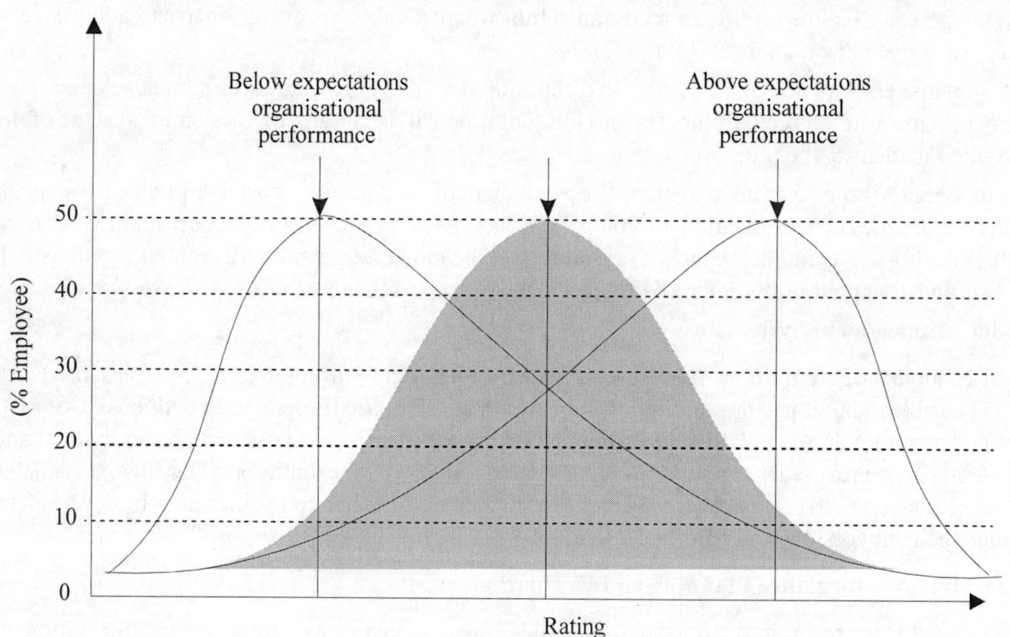

✸ ✸ ✸

GARNERING CUSTOMER LOYALITY

"Companies in all industries today are faced with double-barrelled problems of declining customer loyality and shrinking profit margins. One-to-one marketing strategies enable them to create long-term customer relationships that result in greater loyalty and improved margins." – ***Don Pappers, Guru of CRM***

UNIT – V

COST AND PRICING

11. Cost of Production

12. Pricing

13. Break-even Analysis

The mandate for change today is not merely for political leaders, but also for managers of businesses everywhere.

These volatile times have put the onus on businesses to focus on complex global systems now more than ever. And we have had an important learning from engaging in these systems: global integration impacts the way the world works.

We have also realized, as the world gets 'smaller' and 'flatter', merely being connected is not enough to survive, let alone thrive.

Fortunately something is happening right now: our planet is becoming 'smarter'.

Financial Information Network and Operations Ltd. a technology solutions provider focusing on micro customers, is helping many of the nation's disadvantaged gain access to simple financial products to improve their quality of life.

While it cannot eradicate natural disasters or even reduce them, technology can certainly help mitigate losses and alleviate human suffering. Based on analysis of affected regions, relief agencies can be guided to manage people, resources and logistics in a far more efficient manner.

Clearly, there is a pressing mandate for change today.

Breaking Boundaries

HERE, ALONG with changing the employee mindset, factors like IT systems and analytics also come into play. "In a company like Amazon or Google, analytics are essential as they enable the company to offer relevant options to each customer and make future recommendations on the basis of the data gathered," says Prahalad.

Setting up an innovation capability of this sort will not happen overnight, and Prahalad cautions companies from trying to do it instantly. "I don't believe in a revolution but fast evolution. Revolutions involve great risks and costs while evolutions give you time to adjust and make course corrections," he says. What's important is that the company have a clear point of view to work towards. Companies need to experiment and scale up rapidly and while not all experiments will succeed, the trick lies in the deployment of strategic intent, according to Prahalad.

The biggest breakthrough that needs to happen for all of this is for companies to realise that the relationship between the company and consumers is fast changing, says Prahalad.

Changing employee mindsets and thinking is another aspect which would need to be focused on. Employees need to be told that what they have done so far was correct in the given business environment, else they wouldn't have reached this stage.

While discussing the planning of production in small-scale industries in the previous chapters, we have laid stress on minimum cost. Cost control in small-scale industries is now a well recognised and most effective technique of managerial control. Cost, by and large, is the most important factor influencing sales in a competitive market. As a natural corollary, we shall now discuss three important features closely related to the cost of production, viz., product mix, full utilisation of production facilities and quality control.

Meaning: *Costing is not merely a tool of control but also a device of management planning, organisation and direction. The technique of cost control involves the determination of standard in respect of each item of cost, ascertainment of actual costs regarding those very items, detection of variations in actuals from the standard laid down, analysis of these variations so as to determine the responsibility and the cause, the cost of each variation, and then taking the necessary action to ensure that actual costs conform to standard costs in future.*

Usefulness: *Accurate costs of production estimates and records are of immense use in managerial decisions. Costing provides a scientific base for several other management decisions. Some important features are given below:*

(i) *Cost of production records provide ample informative material for planning material budget, labour budget, factory budget.*

(ii) *The cost of production aids the management to fix the competitive prices. It also enables small-scale industries to quote most competitive prices in their tenders without incurring losses.*

(iii) *The cost of production determines the level of production activity.*

(iv) *It determines the minimum acceptable quality and therefore enables the entrepreneur to avoid fixing quality levels which are higher than those desired by customers.*

(v) *Cost figures reveal the cost per unit of material consumed, labour, machine or process, and help in determining which materials prove comparatively costly or cheaper. This assists the small-scale entrepreneur to substitute other materials to minimise cost. Similarly, it is applicable to labour, machine and process. The cost of production can be maintained by a process of constant substitution.*

(vi) *A periodical review and analysis of the cost of production enables the entrepreneur to identify the causes of inefficiency, abnormal wastages, pilferages, over staffing and losses. It also suggests the possible reasons for variations in costs and enables the small entrepreneur to take timely corrective steps to overcome such deficiencies and distinguish between profitable products and non-profitable products; between profitable process and non profitable process; between profitable labour and non-profitable labour; between the profitable material and non-profitable material; and between profitable volume of production and the non-profitable volume of production.*

(vii) *The cost of production is dependent upon control over inventory receipts, issues, balance and flow of materials and on the maintenance of their records. The small entrepreneur has to give adequate attention to accounting systems.*

Prices play a pivotal role in the regulation of the entire spectrum of economic activities, particularly in small-scale industries. A pricing policy must act as a moving force for the accelerated growth of small-scale industries for production, distribution and consumption. It plays a central role in holding the various components of the price system in close inter-relationship and balance.

A competitive economic system is essentially based on price mechanism. Prices serve as guideposts in:

(i) Organising production;

(ii) Fixing standards (quality);

(iii) The distribution of the product;

(iv) Providing for economic maintenance and progress ; and

(v) Adjusting consumption over short periods.

Milton Friedman has aptly said: "They (prices) transmit information effectively ; they provide an incentive to users of resources to be guided by this information and provide an incentive to owners to follow this information."

Under competitive conditions, price is determined by the interaction of supply and demand. The demand is determined by the consumers desire and purchasing power, while the supply depends on the suppliers capacity, his costs and holding power. These four factors play a crucial role in price fixation.

Price Policy

In all business activities, whether in the public or private sector, large, medium or small-scale sector, the selling processes influence the management to fix the price of the product to be sold. The price is invariably fixed by the manufacturer. However, in the case of a controlled commodity, it is fixed by some statutory authority like the Tariff Commission.

Tips to Augment Your OPERATING MARGINS

- Avoid expensive lead database. Leverage newspapers, social sites, search engines and local directory sites instead.
- Get innovative in marketing. Use online tools for market surveys, promotions and capturing customer feedback.
- Leverage free communication medium. Use free, low-cost online SMS and chat services.
- Innovate your sales process. Identify steps that could be achieved remotely. Use field sales when unavoidable.
- Know your sales channel. Avoid unnecessary calls, centralise sales activities through cheaper online tools.
- Hire right. Invest more time in hiring right resource. Avoid hiring someone with short-term objectives.
- Eliminate some of your prospect or support calls by creating an online knowledge base and FAQ database.
- Avoid printing and paper cost by using online collaboration tools. Send electronic proposals, invoices and orders.
- Leverage students. Assign work like research, online marketing that can be executed independently to them.
- Know customers better. You don't have to spend much for your marketing, if they start speaking for you.

KANTANU KUNDU, CEO, A2ZAPPS.COM

11

COST OF PRODUCTION

While discussing the planning of production in small-scale industries in the previous chapters, we have laid stress on minimum cost. Cost control in small-scale industries is now a well recognised and most effective technique of managerial control. Cost, by and large, is the most important factor influencing sales in a competitive market. As a natural corollary, we shall now discuss three important features closely related to the cost of production, viz., product mix, full utilisation of production facilities and quality control.

Meaning: Costing is not merely a tool of control but also a device of management planning, organisation and direction. The technique of cost control involves the determination of standard in respect of each item of cost, ascertainment of actual costs regarding those very items, detection of variations in actuals from the standard laid down, analysis of these variations so as to determine the responsibility and the cause, the cost of each variation, and then taking the necessary action to ensure that actual costs conform to standard costs in future.

Usefulness: Accurate costs of production estimates and records are of immense use in managerial decisions. Costing provides a scientific base for several other management decisions. Some important features are given below:

(i) Cost of production records provide ample informative material for planning material budget, labour budget, factory budget.

(ii) The cost of production aids the management to fix the competitive prices. It also enables small-scale industries to quote most competitive prices in their tenders without incurring losses.

(iii) The cost of production determines the level of production activity.

(iv) It determines the minimum acceptable quality and therefore enables the entrepreneur to avoid fixing quality levels which are higher than those desired by customers.

(v) Cost figures reveal the cost per unit of material consumed, labour, machine or process, and help in determining which materials prove comparatively costly or cheaper. This assists the small-scale entrepreneur to substitute other materials to minimise cost. Similarly, it is applicable to

labour, machine and process. The cost of production can be maintained by a process of constant substitution.

(vi) A periodical review and analysis of the cost of production enables the entrepreneur to identify the causes of inefficiency, abnormal wastages, pilferages, over staffing and losses. It also suggests the possible reasons for variations in costs and enables the small entrepreneur to take timely corrective steps to overcome such deficiencies and distinguish between profitable products and non-profitable products; between profitable process and non-profitable process; between profitable labour and non-profitable labour; between the profitable material and non-profitable material; and between profitable volume of production and the non-profitable volume of production.

(vii) The cost of production is dependent upon control over inventory receipts, issues, balance and flow of materials and on the maintenance of their records. The small entrepreneur has to give adequate attention to accounting systems.

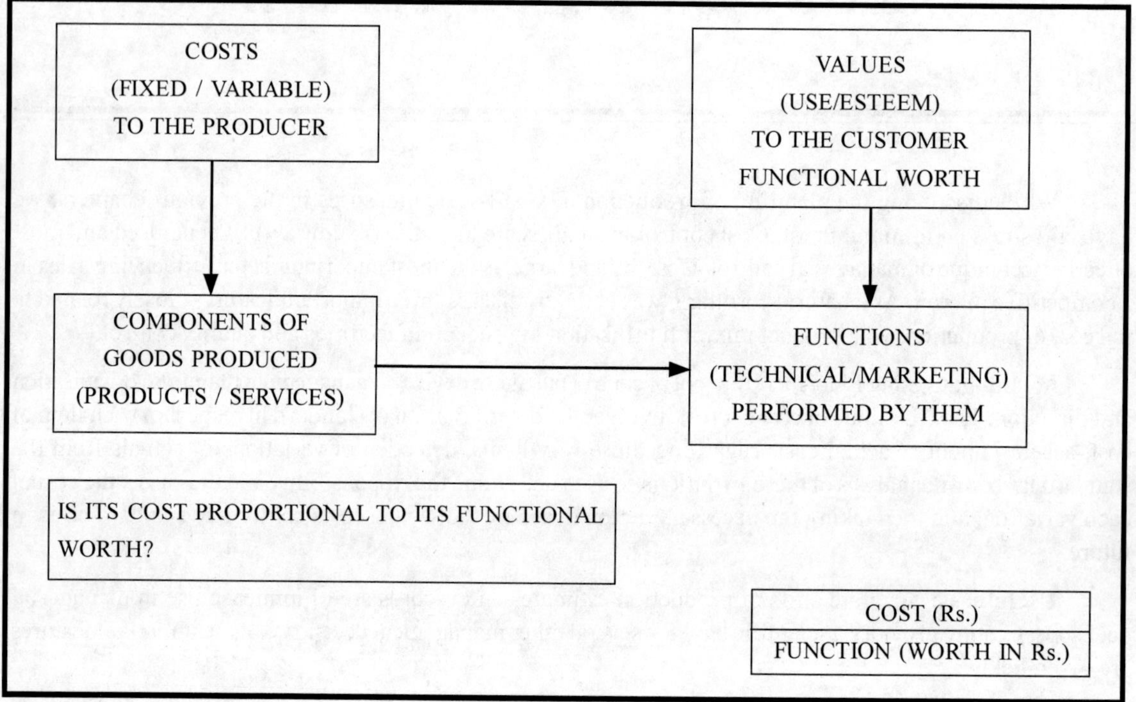

Elements of Cost

The cost of an industrial undertaking may be divided into three principal elements: *(i)* Materials; *(ii)* Labour; and *(iii)* Expenses.

The cost of materials may be divided into direct or indirect. If the material in question is used directly in the manufacture of product and becomes a part of the product, it is considered as a direct material charge. A material which does not become a part of the product but which is essential for the manufacture of that product is considered an indirect material. This category includes such supplies as cotton waste, lubricating oils, fuel, etc.

Labour costs, like material costs, may be classified into direct labour costs and indirect costs. Labour which is applied directly to the manufacture of a product and which changes the shape, form or the nature of the product is considered direct labour. Labour which has a more general and less direct application is considered indirect. Salaries of sweepers, carpenters, and electricians fall in this category.

Expenses or Overheads

Costs other than labour and material costs are classified as expenses are frequently referred to as overheads. They include such items as factory and office rent, local rates and taxes, insurance, depreciation, etc.

Overheads or expenses are usually divided into the following three categories: (i) Factory overheads, which include all expenses chargeable to the factory; (ii) Administrative expenses, which include such items as office rent, general office salaries and professional fees; and (iii) Selling expenses, which include salaries and commission for sales staff, advertising expenses, and other expenses connected with the distribution of the product.

Classification of Costs

The cost of production is also classified as under:

(i) Direct and Indirect Costs: Direct costs consist of those costs which are incurred exclusively on the production of a commodity, on the execution of a job work or on performing a service. Direct costs vary with the volume of production and the type of the product that is manufactured, and include expenses incurred on materials and stores and the labour charges incurred on the manufacture or servicing of a product.

Indirect costs are those costs which are incurred on carrying on the business as a whole. These costs are not incurred directly on a unit of production. Generally, these costs include factory costs, i.e., rent, insurance, lighting, fuel or power, depreciation, office costs, etc. These expenses are apportioned on some reasonable basis.

(ii) Fixed and Variable Costs : Fixed costs are those which are not influenced by the volume of production. Factory costs are generally annual charges and fall in this category. Fixed costs decrease per unit with the increase in the volume of production.

Variable costs vary in the same direction and in the same production in which the volume of production varies. For example, expenses incurred on direct materials, labour and other stores vary with the volume of production. However, variable costs per unit remain the same.

(iii) Standard Costs: The standard cost of production per units is estimated cost. It is a predetermined cost and is utilised in ascertaining the estimated cost of production. In order to estimate cost of production, standards have to be fixed in respect of each element of costs. For materials, standards have to be fixed in relation both to quantity and price. Similarly, standards are fixed in respect of time and wage rates of labour and overheads. Briefly, the standard cost is determined as follows:

The Totality of Total Cost Management

STRATEGY
Business Goals
OPERATIONS
Effectivity
PRODUCT DESIGN
SUPPLY-CHAIN
MANUFACTURING
MARKETING
SALES
SERVICE
DEPTH
Entire Hierarchy
HR
FINANCE
INFOTECH
ADMINISTRATION
WIDTH
Entire Value Chain
TIME
Continuous
SPACE
All Offices, Plants, Depots

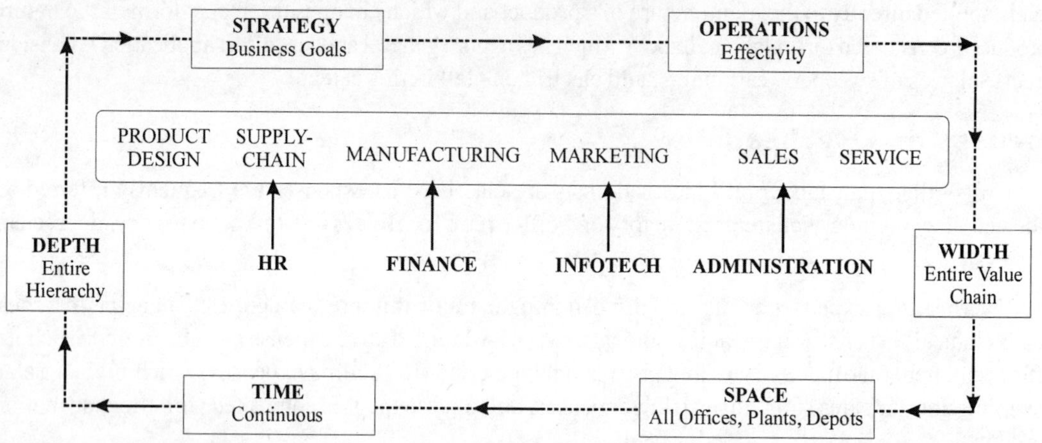

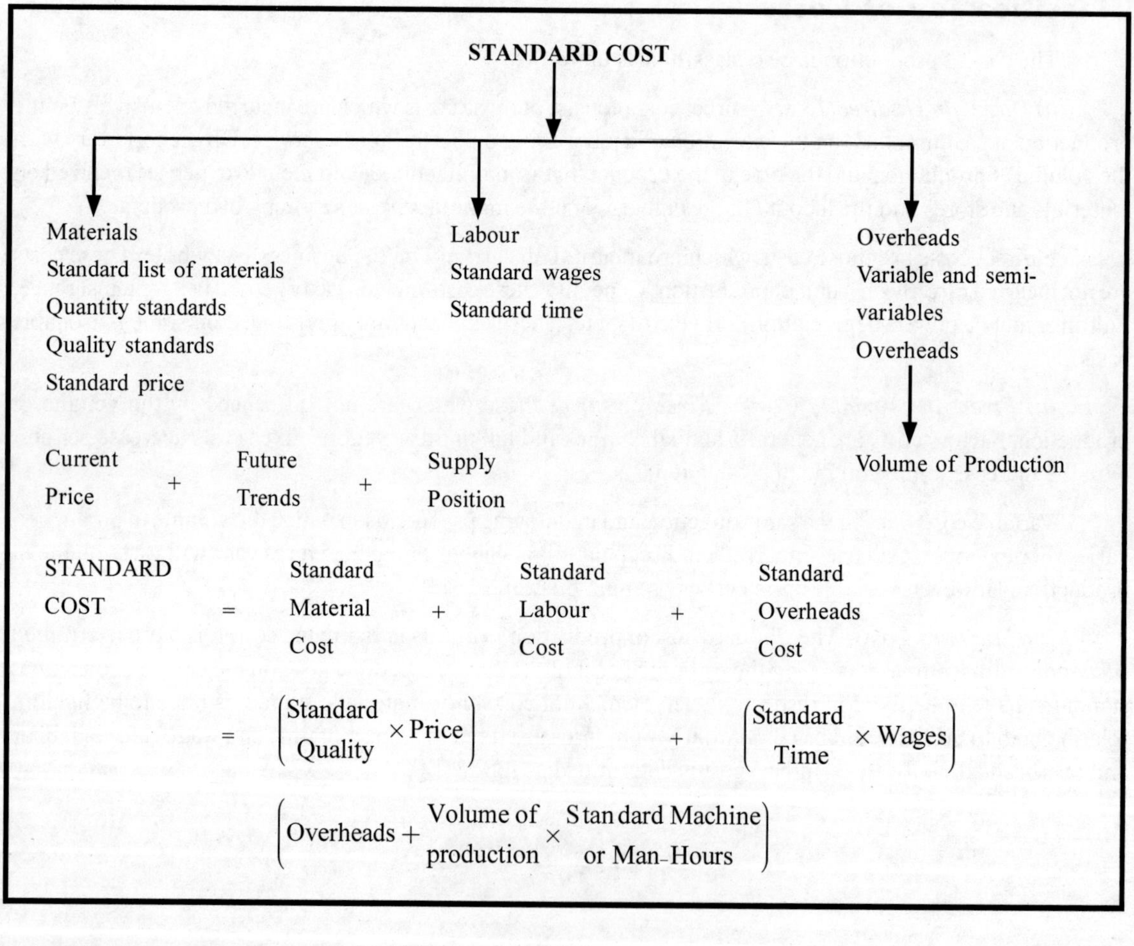

STANDARD COST
Materials
Standard list of materials
Quantity standards
Quality standards
Standard price
Labour
Standard wages
Standard time
Overheads
Variable and semi-variables
Overheads
Volume of Production
Current Price + Future Trends + Supply Position
STANDARD COST = Standard Material Cost + Standard Labour Cost + Standard Overheads Cost
= (Standard Quality × Price) + (Standard Time × Wages)
(Overheads + Volume of production × Standard Machine or Man-Hours)

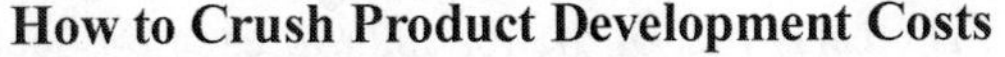

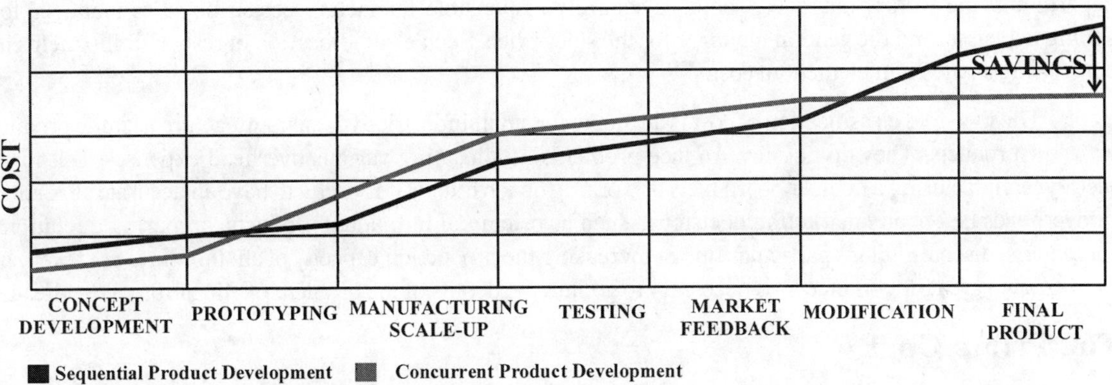

The advantages of the standard costs are:

(1) They are helpful in production and price policies.

(2) Serve as a barometer of the operating efficiency of a plant; and

(3) Work as incentive to workers.

The chart at the end of the chapter gives the application of the standard cost of progressive, average and weak small-scale industries.

(iv) Average Cost and Marginal Cost: The average cost is calculated by dividing the total cost of production by the number of units produced. The marginal cost is the cost of marginal unit produced over the lot of production.

Example : A small-scale industry produces 100 units at a cost of Rs. 2,000. The average cost is 2000 ÷ 100 = Rs. 20 per unit.

Now the cost of production of 99 units is Rs. 1,985 and the cost of the 100th (marginal) unit is Rs. 2,000 – 1,985 = Rs. 15, i.e., marginal cost.

An analysis of Average cost and Marginal cost helps the small entrepreneur to determine the volume of production and the overall production.

Costs may be classified further under the following five heads, each representing a distinct step in the breakdown of the total cost of the product:

(i) Direct Material + Direct Labour Prime Cost.

(ii) Prime Cost + Factory Expenses Factory Cost.

(iii) Factory Cost + Administrative Expenses = Manufacturing Cost.

(iv) Manufacturing Cost + Selling Expenses Selling Cost.

(v) Selling Cost + Desired Margin of Profit Sales Price.

This classification has the merit of locating clearly the responsibility for each of these categories of costs. For example, the responsibility for the prime cost is clearly that of the foreman in each production department; the factory manager would be squarely responsible for factory costs, the sales manager for selling expenses, and the general manager for the sales price. Such clear allocation of responsibility helps in controlling a particular element of cost.

The four-fold classification of cost is adequate for small industries which manufacture a single product or a few products. They do not have to face problems of allocating various overhead expenses. But for a factory manufacturing a number of products or working on job orders, it is useful to have an accurate allocation of overheads before any marketing decisions such as pricing of individual products, preparing quotations for tenders, discontinuing a particular line or increasing the production capacity of another line are taken. In view of such great importance, it is necessary to go into the details of the problem of allocation of overheads.

The Prime Cost

As has been stated earlier, the first stage in the determination of production costs is the prime cost. This includes the cost of direct material and direct labour which go into the making of a product. The determination of these charges for a product or for a specific order is relatively easy.

Direct Material Charges

May be easily ascertained from the stores controller who has supplied the material on the strength of a requisition note containing the name symbol, description, and the quantity of material requisitioned.

Direct Labour Charges

In order to ascertain the direct labour costs, it is necessary to get accurate reports of all the labour time that can be charged directly against a given product or order. A common means of obtaining this under a job order production is to give the workman a ticket when he starts on a new job. On this ticket are entered his name and number, the order number to which his time is charged, the kind and the quantity of the product, and any other information necessary for a proper control of production and costs. The tickets of all the workers working on a particular job order are collected and their wages calculated. To this sum must be added the amounts of dearness allowance and other allowances as well as payments made on their behalf towards the employee's state insurance. The total amount so arrived at constitutes the direct labour cost of a particular batch or order.

The Factory Cost

In order to arrive at an accurate figure of the factory cost for which the factory manager can be held responsible, it is necessary first to ascertain the indirect material charges, indirect labour charges and other expenses incurred and then allocate them to each product or order. The prime cost plus a share of the indirect expenses will constitute the factory cost.

Indirect expenses are made up of *(i)* Indirect material and indirect labour charges; *(ii)* Miscellaneous controllable expenses; and *(iii)* Fixed charges of rent, depreciation and interest.

Of these, the first two tend to fluctuate to some extent with changes in the volume of production, and so they can be controlled to that extent. It is, however, necessary to set up an adequate, comprehensive classification of these expenses if they are to be effectively controlled. Indirect materials include cotton waste, lubricating and other oils, sandpaper, etc. Indirect labour charges include wages and salaries of the foreman, shop clerks, set up men, inspectors, truckers, etc. Miscellaneous controllable expenses include departmental charges for power, light, machine repair, scrap, re work etc. Finally, the fixed charges include the ground rent, local rates and taxes, depreciation and interest.

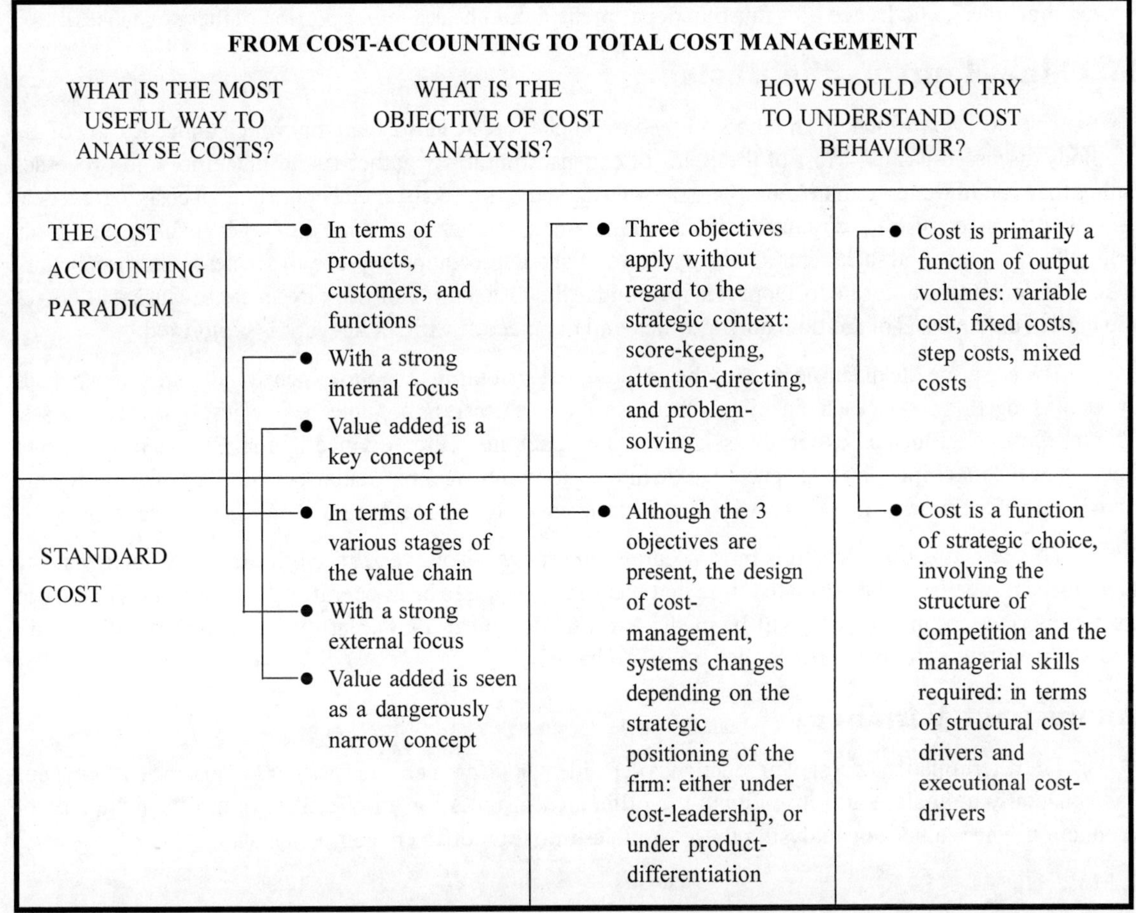

FROM COST-ACCOUNTING TO TOTAL COST MANAGEMENT

	WHAT IS THE MOST USEFUL WAY TO ANALYSE COSTS?	WHAT IS THE OBJECTIVE OF COST ANALYSIS?	HOW SHOULD YOU TRY TO UNDERSTAND COST BEHAVIOUR?
THE COST ACCOUNTING PARADIGM	• In terms of products, customers, and functions • With a strong internal focus • Value added is a key concept	• Three objectives apply without regard to the strategic context: score-keeping, attention-directing, and problem-solving	• Cost is primarily a function of output volumes: variable cost, fixed costs, step costs, mixed costs
STANDARD COST	• In terms of the various stages of the value chain • With a strong external focus • Value added is seen as a dangerously narrow concept	• Although the 3 objectives are present, the design of cost-management, systems changes depending on the strategic positioning of the firm: either under cost-leadership, or under product-differentiation	• Cost is a function of strategic choice, involving the structure of competition and the managerial skills required: in terms of structural cost-drivers and executional cost-drivers

Distribution on the Basis of Material Costs

In simple continuous processes, where the output consists of one uniform product as in a cement or salt works, the expenses incurred in a particular period may be evenly distributed over the output for the sample period. If two or more products are manufactured in a factory, the total work expenses for a period should be allocated to these products in that proportion which the total expenses bear to the total material costs.

Man Hours as the Basis

Under this method, work expenses are allocated on the basis of the number of hours put in by direct wage earners in different departments. The total number of direct man hours of each department is ascertained and that percentage of work expenses is apportioned to each department which its man hours bear to the total man hours.

This method removes the defect of the direct labour method and also gives more accurate results than that method does. The reason is that the longer the man hours work in a department, the greater is the use of power, machinery, etc. Hence, it is fair that department should bear a larger portion of these expenses.

Machine Hours as the Basis

The theory on which this method is based, is much more accurate than that which underlies any of the methods discussed earlier. Most of the items of expenses naturally gather round machines and processes rather than round wages or man hours. The rate of wages and time consumed being equal, it costs a great deal more to do a piece of work on a larger machine than on a smaller one, since the larger machine and tools originally cost more and such items as repairs, power, light, depreciation, etc. are all greater in like proportion. It is, therefore, more accurate to adopt this method for the distribution of work expenses because it allocates the burden on the basis of the time during which and the place at which, the work is performed.

To determine the machine rate for the purpose of distributing the total expenses, all items of expenses are pooled.together so that each machine or process would, as nearly as possible, bear its just share of expenses. The total of such allocated expenses assigned to any machine is then divided by the estimated number of hours that the machine may be expected to be in operation during a particular period. This *Would* give the hourly rate of thc machine; and every job that is performed on that machine will be charged accordingly.

Theoretically, this method is most accurate, in practice, however, difficulties crop up whenever any departure is made from the estimated time that the machines are to be in operation. If a machine fails to run for that period, an undercharge will be made; and this will mean that a part of the expenses will remain undistributed and will not appear in the cost of production.

Analysis of Variances

The determination of cost of production is dependent upon a number of variances. Thus, the entrepreneur has constantly to analyse and investigate the different variances for an effective control over the cost of production. The methods of analysing these variables into their different components are:

1. Material

(i) Material price Variance representing the excess Cost of saving resulting from purchases of direct materials at prices above or below the set standards

$$= \left\{ \begin{array}{cc} \text{Actual quantity} & \\ \text{Purchased X} & \\ \text{Actual price} & \\ (x) & (y) \end{array} \right\} \left\{ \begin{array}{ccc} \text{Actual} & & \text{Standard} \\ \text{Quantity} & \times & \text{Price} \\ (Q) & & (P) \end{array} \right\}$$

$$= XY - QP$$

(ii) Material usage variance indicating efficiency in the use of materials

$$\begin{Bmatrix}\text{Actual}\\\text{Quantity}\\(Q)\end{Bmatrix} \begin{Bmatrix}\text{Standard}\\\text{Price}\\(P)\end{Bmatrix} \begin{Bmatrix}\text{Actual}\\\text{Quantity}\\(Q)\end{Bmatrix} \times \begin{Bmatrix}\text{Standard}\\\text{Price}\\(P)\end{Bmatrix}$$

= QP– QP

II. Labour

(i) Labour wage variance showing higher or lower wage rates than contemplated

$$\begin{Bmatrix}\text{Actual direct rate}\\(R)\end{Bmatrix} - \begin{Bmatrix}\text{Standard wage rate}\\(W)\end{Bmatrix} \times \begin{Bmatrix}\text{Actual direct labour hours}\\(L)\end{Bmatrix}$$

= (R W) × L

(ii) Labour time variance. Revealing excess time taken or saving in time as compared to standard time

$$\begin{Bmatrix}\text{Actual labour direct hours}\\(L)\end{Bmatrix} - \begin{Bmatrix}\text{Standard direct labour}\\(S)\end{Bmatrix} \times \begin{Bmatrix}\text{Standard wage rate}\\(W)\end{Bmatrix}$$

= (L – S) XW

III. Overheads

(i) Overhead budget variance. Disclosing excess expenditure or saving in actual cost compared with the budget.

$$= \begin{Bmatrix}\text{Actual overhead for the budget period} & \text{Standard overhead for the same period}\end{Bmatrix}$$

(ii) Overhead capacity variance Highlighting the amount of overhead unabsorbed or over absorbed

$$= \begin{Bmatrix}\text{Standard direct labour hours as per the}\end{Bmatrix} - \begin{Bmatrix}\text{Actual direct labour hours as per}\end{Bmatrix}$$

$$- \begin{Bmatrix}\text{production budget Standard overhead rate}\end{Bmatrix} - \begin{Bmatrix}\text{payrolls for the above period}\end{Bmatrix}$$

(iii) Overhead efficiency variance showing the overhead cost of excess direct labour hours applied to the period's production or the saving resulting from the completion of the period's production in less than standard direct labour hours.

$$= \begin{Bmatrix}\text{Actual direct hours as per payrolls}\end{Bmatrix} - \begin{Bmatrix}\text{Standard direct labour hours}\end{Bmatrix}$$

$$- \begin{Bmatrix}\text{Standard overhead rate}\end{Bmatrix} \begin{Bmatrix}\text{for the period of production}\end{Bmatrix}$$

In each case, the plus balance shows a loss and a minus balance indicates a profit. Variances are very important indicators of the cost of production.

Product Mix

The product mix is generally adopted in case of multiple production. However, in a large number of cases, small-scale units manufacture a single product. With a view to maximising production, an entrepreneur has to produce ancillary by-products or components. In other words, the marginal cost of production of the by-product is lower, the profit of the entrepreneur therefore is higher. This apart, product mix can also be adopted in the production process without hampering the quality of the product. The entrepreneur should have analysed the strength and weaknesses of all materials, labour, etc. which can yield a higher production at a low cost.

Full Utilisation of Production Facilities

The small entrepreneur will increase his production by fully utilising his machinery and labour. Non-utilisation of these two important components, results in an increase in cost per unit. All the necessary raw materials are available, a fuller utilisation of machinery and labour therefore results in higher production. And every increase in production reduces the average cost per unit. This apart, the marginal cost is also considerably lower. Small entrepreneur has to plan in detail, so that no bottleneck crops up in between. In short, a full utilisation of production facilities will result in a lower cost per unit. The cost of overheads, too, will go down. Therefore, the aim of small-scale industries should always be to utilise the production facilities fully.

Inventory or Stores Control

Inventory control is a significant step in controlling the cost of production; one of the most complex and far reaching problems to the managements. A recent survey has shown that capital amounting to about Rs. 800 crores is locked up in inventories as against an annual sales turnover of about Rs. 2,500 crores, giving an inventory sales ratio of 1: 3.40 as compared to 1: 6 to 1: 8 in some of the developed countries. The figures indicate the tremendous scope for capital release through a control of inventories.

Inventories are stocks which are classified as:

(i) Raw materials (like oils, chemicals, cotton, steel, etc.);

(ii) Process stores;

(iii) Packing material, spare parts, ancillary goods, engineering stores, wrappers, bottles, bobbins; and

(iv) Finished goods.

The annual cost of carrying inventories adds to the cost of production. The objective of inventory control is to release the working capital for more productive uses and minimise the overhead costs. Generally speaking, an inventory, either of finished goods or of raw materials or of ancillary materials, should be adequate to achieve maximum production; at the same time, it should not be so excessive as to restrict the entrepreneur's ability to earn a high rate of return. As the inventory paradox has it, inventory control should "not be too much, not too little, and it should be practised at the lowest cost for the highest profit."

THE FOUR QUALITY COSTS

PREVENTION COSTS	APPRAISAL COSTS	EXTERNAL FAILURE COSTS	INTERNAL FAILURE COSTS
↳ Reciving inspection	↳ Quality engineering	↳ Warranty adjustments	↳ Scrap
↳ In-process inspection	↳ Quality planning	↳ Repair	↳ Rework
↳ Laboratory inspection	↳ Design of quality equipment	↳ Customer service	↳ Reinspection of rework
↳ Laboratory endorsement	↳ Design verification and review	↳ Returned goods	↳ Downgrading because of defects
↳ Testing set-up	↳ Quality training	↳ Returned repaired goods	↳ Losses caused by vendor scrap
↳ Test maintenance equipment	↳ Quality improvement projects	↳ Investigation of defects	↳ Downtime caused by defects
↳ Quality audits	↳ Quality data-gathering, analysis, and reporting	↳ Product recalls	↳ Failure analysis
↳ Quality equipment calibration	↳ Statistical process-control	↳ Product liability suits	
↳ Production equipment maintance	↳ Other process control activities used to prevent defects	↳ Last revenue from customer bad will (an opportunity cost)	
	↳ Cost-accounting for production variance		

Inventory control is not an isolated function, but a part of materials management. The main function of inventory control is to ensure a continuous flow of materials for production. This control will minimise the cost of production for a small-scale industry.

Life cycle phases and savings potential: The Life Cycle Phases of a product and savings potential are shown in Figure 11.2.

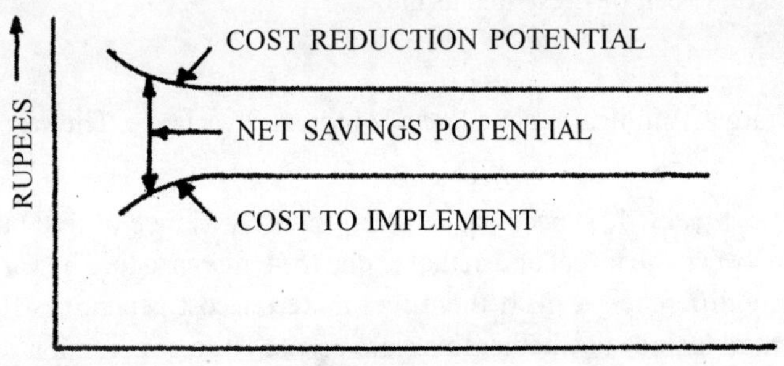

LIFE CYCLE PHASE

CONCEPT FORMULATION   INITIAL DESIGN   FINAL DESIGN   CONSTRUCTION   OPERATION

Fig. 11.2

Selection of items: The following can form the criteria for selection of items of Value Engineering study:

(1) Items of high annual consumption, say 'A' category items (of ABC analysis)
(2) Items complex in design
(3) Items made from scarce materials
(4) Items involving too many machine operations and difficult to make
(5) Items where chance of standardisation is bright
(6) Items with high scrap rate or wastage and of repetitive use
(7) Items with possibilities of modification or incorporation into a related product component
(8) Items purchased in large quantities
(9) Vital items where dependence on imports is too much
(10) Critical items of single source supply.

Steps in Cost Control

Cost control is an important executive function. Effective cost control can be attained successfully with the help of the following steps:

(1) To set up the target: The expense target should be set in advance for a specific period. This is properly known as budgets. Proper budgeting should be done for all important spending centres. They should be related to the production targets. Meticulous care should be taken while fixing the targets for the variable expenses.

(2) To measure the actuals: The detailed information about the actual performance should be collected on regular basis. As the actuals are to be compared with the targets, they should be measured on the same basis as the targets; e.g., if the targets are set on weekly basis, the actual data should also be made available on the weekly basis. Moreover, the actual data must be made available frequently otherwise, it is likely that the time lag might make it difficult to institute any prompt corrective action.

(3) *To compare the actuals with the target:* The actuals are compared with the targets with a view to ascertain any discrepancy between the two. Such discrepancies are known as deviations or variances. It is a simple arithmetical exercise and can be presented as under:

$$V = T - A$$

Where T indicates target, A indicates actual, and V indicates variance. The variances are expressed as favourable or (+) and averse or (–).

(4) To analyse the variances: It is necessary to analyse the variance to find out the facts behind the figures. The discrepancy between the target and actual is due to some reasons. The variances are analysed to find out the reasons for the difference; e.g., if the direct material cost per unit is Rs. 2.10 instead of the targeted Rs. 2.00, it is essential to find out whether this extra cost of 10 paise per unit is due to price fluctuation, inefficiency in purchasing, usage of wrong material, excessive usage of material with greater degree of wastage, incorrect setting up of machines producing more defectives etc. Unless the specific cause for the higher cost is identified, it will not be possible for the executive to institute any guiding or regulating action.

(5) To locate the responsibilities for unfavourable variances: The adverse variances arise due to either controllable or uncontrollable factors. The responsibilities for the controllable factors should be located properly and should be treated severely because they indicate lapses, omissions, negligence or carelessness; e.g. in the above example, high direct material cost resulting from the excessive usage of material is a serious matter to be attended to. Uncontrollable factors are beyond the control of management. However, the strategic decision may mitigate the severity of the uncontrollable factors.

(6) To take action for the correction of variances: The variances should be detected as early as possible and they should be corrected immediately. This is done through the preventive and corrective action.

Cost Accounting and Managerial Decision-Making

Cost accounting as a branch of accounting, has developed out of the need of management to have some precise and reliable data than can be used in shaping proper and effective decisions. Cost accounting data help in following types of managerial decisions:

(1) Cost ascertainment: It provides reliable cost data in respect of materials, wages and other expenses which help in ascertaining the cost of production precisely. Detailed cost data regarding materials, labour and overheads reveals actual and potential sources of cost savings and cost reduction.

(2) Cost control: Cost accounting provides the element wise cost for each product, process, department, job, contract etc. Thus the profitable and unprofitable areas are identified in the organization. These information serve as a good guide to the management for either shutting down the unprofitable activities or enhancing their profitability through changes in the technology, methods, machines or such other measures. The scarce resources are utilized efficiently with the minimum of costs and wastages.

(3) Pricing decisions: Cost accounting provides accurate cost data which serve as a good guide in the pricing decisions. Various types of pricing policies can be evolved on the basis of the cost data, e.g., "cost plus" pricing in contract business, wherein certain agreed profit margin is added in the cost of job; special offer of reduced pricing to tap unused capacity; incorporation of the escalation clause in the contractual business etc. The cost volume profit analysis serves as a basis in pricing decisions.

(4) Quotations and tenders: Historical cost data serve as a good guide for estimating the cost of future production. Such data as adjusted to the expected changes help in preparing quotations and submitting tenders. Due to the accurate cost ascertainment, the unprofitable commitment arising of the low tendering is eliminated. Conversely the chances of rejection of tenders resulting from higher-tendering are minimized.

(5) Planning and control: Cost accounting provides the valuable data for planing, budgeting and thus controlling the costs. It is highly essential to plan and control the activities so that the desired volume of production can be secured at minimum costs. Cost accounting attempts to ascertain actual historical cost as well as the estimated costs under the given situation and constraints. The pre-determined budgeted costs serve as the standards for judging whether the actual costs are what they should have been.

(6) Specific managerial decisions: The cost data provide invaluable information which help in sharpening some following types of important decisions: (i) to make or buy the component, (ii) to own or hire the fixed asset, (iii) to replace the existing plant before its useful life, (iv) to continue or shut down the whole or any part of the business.

Variances Analysis

Standard costing or variance analysis is much more than just a Cost accountancy method. It is a potent tool in the hands of management accountants. We shall axamine how standard costing procedures help the management function of a company.

First of all, it would be in the fitness of things to define certain terms commonly used in standard costing technique.

(a) A standard is a normal level which is established in advance of an activity, to be used as a yardstick for comparison when the activity takes place and the actual level is known, A standard hour is a predetermined unit of work measurement representing the amount of work which should be achieved in one hour under standard conditions.

A budget is a target or objective to be aimed for established in advance of an activity.

Variance analysis sets out to compare the predetermined standard for an activity with the actual level recorded when the activity takes place, i.e., what should happen compared with that did happen wrong quality of material, i.e., different from the standards specified.

(b) Material usage variance may arise through wrong methods of untrained employees, wrong quality of material or inefficient machinery, all of which may lead to waste if they they differ from the specified standards.

(c) Labour rate variance is another factor. Too many employees, or employees too highly skilled for the work, unsupervised overtime or work methods will lead to a higher wages cost than standard.

(d) Labour efficiency valiance may be the result of untrained or badly supervised workers, the lack of incentive schemes, outdated machinery, wrong-methods, labour turnover.

(e) Lahour idle time variance arises through the managements's inability to provide the conditions for continuity of work, e.g., shortages of material from stores, frequent breakdowns of badly mainained or outdated machinery or lack of sales orders for work.

(f) Variable overhead expenditure variance is the result of actual expenditure differing from the recovery derived from the actual hours worked. Actual spending on items such as heat, light, power, indirect wages etc. may be greater or less than planned, while actual hours worked could be different from planned hours due to changes in work conditions, customer orders, strikes etc.

(g) Variable overhead efficiency variance is caused by a productivity difference, i.e., standard hours of work produced being greater or less than the actual hours taken in performance of work. A favourable variance may be the result of an effective bonus system or good working conditions while an adverse variance usually, indicates badly trained indirect workers, inefficient machinery or poor supervision.

(h) Fixed overhead expenditure variance is the result of any over-or under-spending on items of a fixed nature such as rates, insurance etc.

(i) Fixed overhead capacity variance shows up the usage of the available or budgeted capacity of the factorv. If hours worked fall short of the available hours, an adverse variance will show how much this has cost, while overtime working could be reflected in a favourable variance.

(j) Fixed overhead efficiency variance is similar to variable overhead efficiency variance, i.e., a productivity difference, but the variance represents, the loss or gain brought about by absorbing overheads of a fixed nature over greater or lesser volume of output expressed in standard hours of work.

(k) Sales price variance change due to economic conditions, cost increases, competition in mark etc.

(l) Sales volume variance customer preference, competition, salesman's incentives, etc.

With a full set of predetermined standards the company is able to plan its profit target and exercise control over all operations towards the achievement of that target.

Variance analysis must be carried out regularly, usually. monthly, so that the management by exception technique can be applied. Trends disclosed in the early months of budget period may then be quick investigated and remedial action implemented to steer the operations along the planned path towards the company's objective. The fact that such a system is in operation will keep employee efficiency at a keen pitch with beneficial results for both management and workers.

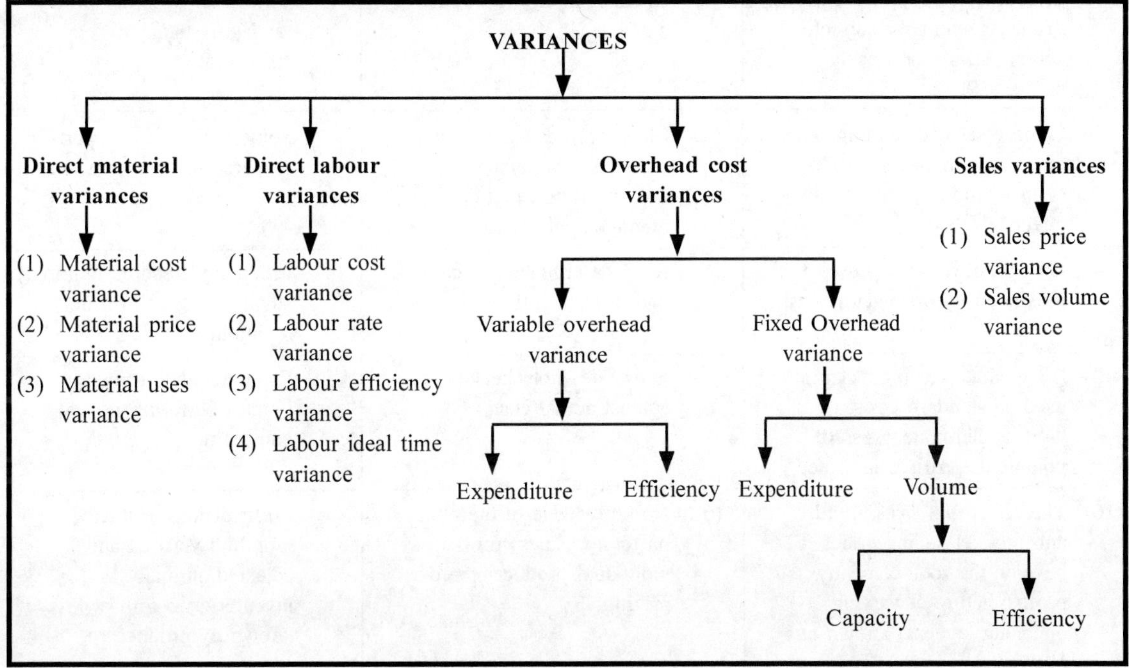

* As cost variances arise due to differences in price or quantity of cost element from specified standard so do sales variances. However, since these are concerned with revenue rather than cost, the adverse or favourable aspects are reversed.

Conclusion

The cost of production is an important determinant of the sale of goods produced by small-scale industries. It is, therefore, necessary for these industries to control costs through proper product mix, maximum utilisation of capacity, standardisation and quality control. The cost of production should always be related to the customer's needs and requirements. In a small-scale industry, it is generally dependent upon inventory management. The chart on the next page deals with production channels in three types of small-scale units, i.e., progressive, average and poor. The prime motive of every small scale entrepreneur is to earn maximum profit. The cost of production influences both his sales and his profit. The entrepreneur has to be progressive in his approach so that the small-scale unit contributes to the economic development of the country.

ANNEXURE – 1

Standard Costs in a Small-Scale Industry

Progressive Conditions	*Average Conditions*	*Work Conditions*
(1) Cost systems designed to reflect all variances between standard and actual costs.	(1) Cost accounting fairly accurate but not organized to provide standard cost information promptly.	(1) No standard costs. Job costs inaccurate and uncontrolled.
(2) Variances from standard performances supplied currently to management for corrective action– (Daily or weekly as needed).	(2) Records and reports not best suited to control cost and expenses.	(2) Cost information mostly estimated. Monthly profit and loss statements inaccurate.
(3) Unnecessary accounting records eliminated management control reports furnished as needed.	(3) Many records, reports and statistics maintained that are not useful as a tool of management.	(3) Some records and reports prepared have no practical advantage.
(4) All control records and costs integrated with standards costs.	(4) Records unrelated to control; therefore of little assistance.	(4) Production records required; suitable cost control not maintained.
(5) All estimate for product printing used on standard costs; guess work is eliminated; loss of volume or profit is indicated.	(5) Estirmates not checked against actual cost.	(5) Estimates determined by past performance and competition.
(6) The effect that sales mixture and product selling prices have on the total company profits picture at varying operating levels is known at all times.	(6) No knowledge of the effect on total business profits of individual product or order pricing.	(6) Profit or loss estimated monthly; verified and adjusted annually to inventory; no rofit or loss known by product break down.
(7) Effect of additional volume on cost and profit is easily determined. Break-even points determined.	(7) Effect of additional volume on cost and profit not easily determined. Break-even points not determined and their value underestimated.	(7) Additional volume usuallv authorized to keep plant busy without knowledge of effect on cost and profit. No knowledge of sales mixtures or break-even point.

❋ ❋ ❋

12

PRICING

Introduction

Prices play a pivotal role in the regulation of the entire spectrum of economic activities, particularly in small-scale industries — for production, distribution and consumption. It plays a central role in holding the various components of the price system in close inter-relationship and balance.

A competitive economic system is essentially based on price mechanism. Prices serve as guideposts in:

(i) Organising production;

(ii) Fixing standards (quality);

(iii) The distribution of the product;

(iv) Providing for economic maintenance and progress; and

(v) Adjusting consumption over short periods.

Milton Friedman has aptly said : "They (prices) transmit information effectively; they provide an incentive to owners to follow this information."

Under competitive conditions, price is determined by the interaction of supply and demand. The demand is determined by the consumer's desire and purchasing power, while the supply is based on the supplier's capacity, his costs and holding power. These four factors play a crucial role in price fixation.

Price is customarily referred to as one of the marketing-mix elements. Put in a different way, from the viewpoint of customers, price is one of the factors, which influence their buying decisions. The higher is the intensity of competition, the greater is the need to become competitive, including in terms of price. International markets are generally considered to be more competitive than domestic markets, because competition in export markets originates from three quarters, viz.,

PRICE = COST + PROFIT
Six years ago, corporate India was forced to bury that maxim, which dated back to the pre-liberalisation economy.

PRICE = RUPEE EQUIVALENT OF THE VALUE OF YOUR PRODUCT
For two years now, marketers have been confronted with the evidence that this is not a successful formula.

PRICE = WHAT THE CONSUMER WILL WILLINGLY PAY
Over the past six months, a small band of price-combatants have begun wielding this new equations.

(a) competing domestic producers in the export markets;

(b) producers in other competing supplying countries; and

(c) competing domestic producers in one's own country.

Since the larger is the number of sellers, the stiffer is the competition, there is no doubt that international business is highly competitive. There are, however, two points to be considered in this context. The first relates to the characteristics of exportable products and the second to the nature of competition.

(b) Minerals and metals, viz., iron, copper and mica.

(c) Manufactures — highly standardised, viz., steel and cement.

(d) Branded consumer products, both durable and non-durable.

(e) Branded industrial products.

(f) Ethnic products like handicrafts.

(g) Services.

The influence of price in the buying-decision process is the most for product categories listed in a, b & c. The influence of price for branded industrial products is not high, as specifications and performance characteristics happen to be a more important consideration. For branded consumer products, price is relatively more rtant but strong brand loyalty and other marketing-mix elements can make price relatively less influential in purchase decisions. Price is generally not a consideration for products like handicrafts, bulk of which are either tourists-purchases, impulse buying or for presentation. For many luxury items, price-demand relationship may, in fact, be positive, i.e., high price stimulates larger demand and *vice versa,* though it may not be universally true. But Still, as a generalization it can be said that price will not be a significant factor in the buying-decision process of luxury items. Buying of services, viz., consultancy jobs and management contracts will also depend more on the suppliers' credibility and image, rather than on the service fee quoted.

Many small manufacturers fix the prices of their products in a completely haphazard way. Often the procedure is to collect information on the prices at which competitors are selling and then either fix their prices at the same level or undercut their competitors' prices with the object of gaining a section of the market in the easiest possible manner. On the other hand, there is the manufacturer who has a new and original product and fixes his price at the highest level that the market will stand. Both policies are incorrect and commercially dangerous.

The first method, i.e., the method of fixing price by basing the price on competitors' prices without any comparison of quality or value and especially the method of undercutting competitors' prices is to be utterly condemned and might be likened to the man who tries to fly an aeroplane before he has learnt to take-off or land. Once price cutting had been started there is no end to it, and the small manufacturer with his limited resources is particularly unfit to engaging himself in a 'price-war.'

The manufacturer must not think that he can keep secret for very long the fact that he is selling at a lower price. Buyers are only too happy to take advantage of a price-war by revealing one manufacturer's prices to another manufacturer with the hope of getting even further reductions. Eventually prices go down all round, become completely uneconomical to any of the manufacturers and benefit only the buyer.

Not should the manufacturer think that by price cutting he can gift in on the market and then increase his prices later — this is a false assumption that never works in practice except may be for the large manufacturer who can make his products indispensable by force of nation-wide publicity.

Pricing is another important aspect to be taken into consideration while marketing a product. Pricing strategy followed by a unit influences its sales and profits. The strategies to be followed for an effective pricing policy depends on various factors like cost, competition, product/company image, stage of product life cycle, class of customers, price elasticity, legislation and governmental pressures, etc. These factors are briefly discussed below.

Cost: Costs and prices are inevitably linked. However, to what extent prices should be based on cost depends upon the situation. In any case, the price per unit should be so fixed that in the long run, all fixed expenses are fully covered for the proposed sales volume.

Competition: When competition is less, one can afford to keep his prices high. But when competition, is severe, prices automatically drop. A classic example is that of colour photograph prints. When there was no competition, postcard size colour print charges were six rupees per copy but today, when many competitors have entered the market, the charges have come down to as low as Rs. 2.25 per copy.

Company/product image: Pricing decisions also depend upon the image that the company wishes to project to its customers. The major effect of pricing with respect to product image is one of quality. A product from a reputed company or a highly priced product gives an image of good quality.

Stage of product life cycle: Every stage of a product life cycle calls for a different approach to pricing. At the introduction and growth stages there is considerable flexibility in fixing of the price, some entrepreneur using a low price to achieve market penetration and others using a high price to make maximum gain before competition increases. Prices stabilize as the market approaches saturation.

Customer: The type and standing of the customer and the quantities purchased by him also affect pricing decisions. Generally, permanent customers with large demand are offered a lower price.

Price elasticity of demand: Price elasticity refers to the sensitivity of sales volume to changes in the price. Whenever there is a change in price, customers react in one of the three ways — buy more, buy less, remain unaffected. Government legislations and pressures have a definite impact on prices. Under such conditions, the small manufacturers do not have much scope in price fixation.

Price Policy

In all business activities, whether in the public or private sector, large, medium or small-scale sector, the selling processes influence the management to fix the price of the product to be sold. The price is invariably fixed by the manufacturer. However, in the case of controlled commodity, it is fixed by some statutory authority like the Tariff Commission. The main issue facing the management is: at what price should the product be sold? In times of shortages, because of the failure of supply to meet the rising demand, at the same time, works as an incentive to the producer to produce more; and it is that which has been the central theme of the pricing policy, as summarised by the then Finance Minister, Shri Y. B. Chavan.

"The policy of price controls has also been reviewed in the interest of giving impetus to industrial growth. We sought in the past to maintain the stability of prices by controlling them, either by statutory notification or by some informal understandings with the industry. Such controls, when they work, are useful. But often they only tend either to restrict the growth of an enterprise or to create an unofficial market in which higher prices are realized without being shown in the books to the detriment, among other things, of the Government revenue.... In short, while we cannot rely exclusively on the market mechanism for the distribution of all essential and scarce materials, we have to be continually on the lookout for opportunities to minimise the reliance on controls by a judicious mixture of price incentives and disincentives."

The Planning Commission is of the view that a "price policy must seem to correct all the distortions in the structure of relative prices." The Commission has emphasized the need to:

(i) Provide an incentive to producer to adopt improved technology and maximize production;

(ii) Encourage optimum utilisation of land;

(iii) Work towards a better balance between demand and supply;

(iv) Export promptly: and

(v) Avoid adverse effects on the economy.

Objectives

The objectives of statutory price fixation in India are:

(i) To bring about a reasonable stability in factor and commodity prices with a view to protecting the standard of living of the people;

(ii) To ensure maximum production. Not only should the existing units be allowed to function more economically and efficiently, but a climate should be created to ensure that, when additional units are established and additional output produced, there is a possibility of reduction in prices;

(iii) Subserve the general objectives, of securing an increase in savings, investment and economic growth.

In implementing these policy objectives, the following points should be borne in mind:

(a) As far as possible, price fixation should be considered only as a short term device;

(b) Price fixation involves statutory intervention between the seller and the buyer and should be intro duced only in cases where there is sufficient justification for it;

(c) Prices must be fixed only when there is a reasonable chance that, if left free, they would adversely affect the interests of producers. The principle of equity, therefore, should necessarily determine the mechanism of price fixation and this principle should be extended to all the sectors of the economy — pubic or private, large or small.

While costs have a bearing on prices, the level of prices at a particular moment is a resultant of many factors.

Many a small-scale manufacturer fixes the prices of his products in two ways:

(i) By basing it on his competitor's prices without any regard to the quality or the value of the product. In this case, either the price is the same as competitor's price with the object of hailing a section of the market in the easiest possible manner;

(ii) By fixing the price at the highest level that the market will stand. This is done in the case of a new product.

Both these methods are wrong, unscientific, defective and commercially dangerous.

The small entrepreneur cannot indulge in price-cutting for a long time. By this method, he shortens the market. By fixing the prices at the highest level the markets can stand, one attracts imitators, and the process of price-cutting follows.

Prices, therefore, should be fixed on a properly scientific basis. They should be calculated from the bottom up, i.e., by finding out what the production of an item is going to cost. The cost of a product naturally includes direct and indirect costs and other overheads, plus a reasonable margin of profit.

A student of small-scale industry should understand that there are certain costs which are relevant only to small-scale operations. He should, therefore, be thoroughly familiar with the total composition of the various costs that make up the price of a small-scale product.

Pricing Strategy

In pricing steps have to be taken by the industries in the small-scale sector, including the tiny sector, to produce quality products for those market segments for which the marketing effort is made. Stanton organises the procedure for price determination into six steps:

(i) Estimate the demand for the product

(ii) Anticipate the competitive reaction

(iii) Establish the expected share of the market

(iv) Select the price strategy to be used to reach the market target

(v) Consider unit policies regarding products, channels and promotion

(vi) Select the specific price.

The aim of the pricing strategy is to win customer segments. Price also is influenced by operating methods, the quality of material required by the buyer and the quantity. In the circumstance, even when offering a single product, the small entrepreneur may have to charge different prices on the basis of the size, designs and features of his products.

When setting prices, it is important to take into consideration all of the following:

- Business and target market objectiveness
- The full cost of producing, delivering and promoting the product
- The willingness of the target market to pay for the product or service you provide
- Prices charged by competitors offering a similar product/ service to the same target market(s)
- The availability and price of substitute products /services
- The economic climate (local and national)
- The possibility of stimulating high profit products /services by offering related services at or below cost.

Cost Factor

7The cost of a product may broadly be classified into two groups:

(a) Ex-factory cost; and

(b) Sales and distribution overheads.

The ex-factory cost of a product includes all the costs incurred on it till it leaves the factory premises. This cost may be split into the following elements:

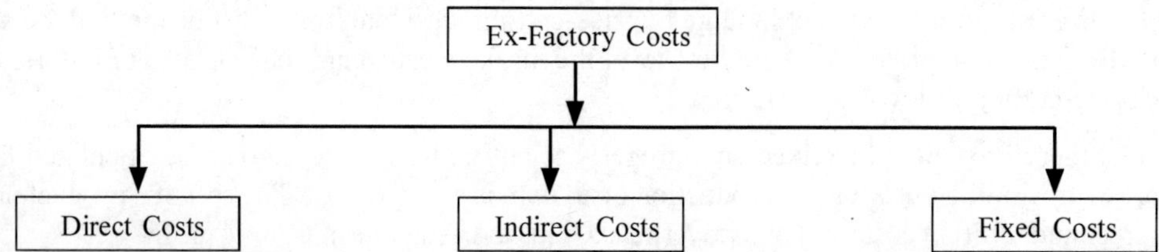

***(i)* Direct Costs:** These include the cost of raw materials, components, etc. which form part of the product; the cost of labour, which is directly related to the production of a product from the raw material to the finished stage; and any other expenses which have been incurred on the production of an item.

***(ii)* Indirect Costs:** These include the expenses incurred on supporting services such as plant maintenance, quality control, the cost of all the materials which do not form part of a product but which, at the same time, are essential for its production, and charges for lighting and heating.

***(iii)* Fixed Costs:** These include interest on capital depreciation, salaries for factory and office staff, rent, welfare expenses, etc.

The cost category matrix given in Fig. indicates the nature of the various cost elements which make up the ex-factory cost.

It may be noted here that the direct costs vary with production volume, and every additional unit produced adds a definite amount to the total cost. As against this, "Factory overheads" are more or less fixed and remain constant, regardless of the volume of production, or at least vary disproportionately with the volume of production.

A number of methods of costing are available to a cost accountant in collecting and categorising the various costs that are incurred on the manufacture of a product. It is obvious that, depending on the manufacturing process, costing methods would vary. Job or batch costing systems are used in the job-order type of work; the process costing system in industries using the continuous processing method, e.g., the chemical industry; and the standard costing system in a mass production industry.

Sales and Distribution Costs

Sales and distribution costs are necessarily to be included in the price. These cover all the costs incurred from the time the product leaves the factory premises — the cost of transportation to the warehouse, salaries in the sales departments, including those of sales personnel, advertising, sales promotional expenses and establishment expenses; this last cost is fixed, and changes little with the volume of sales.

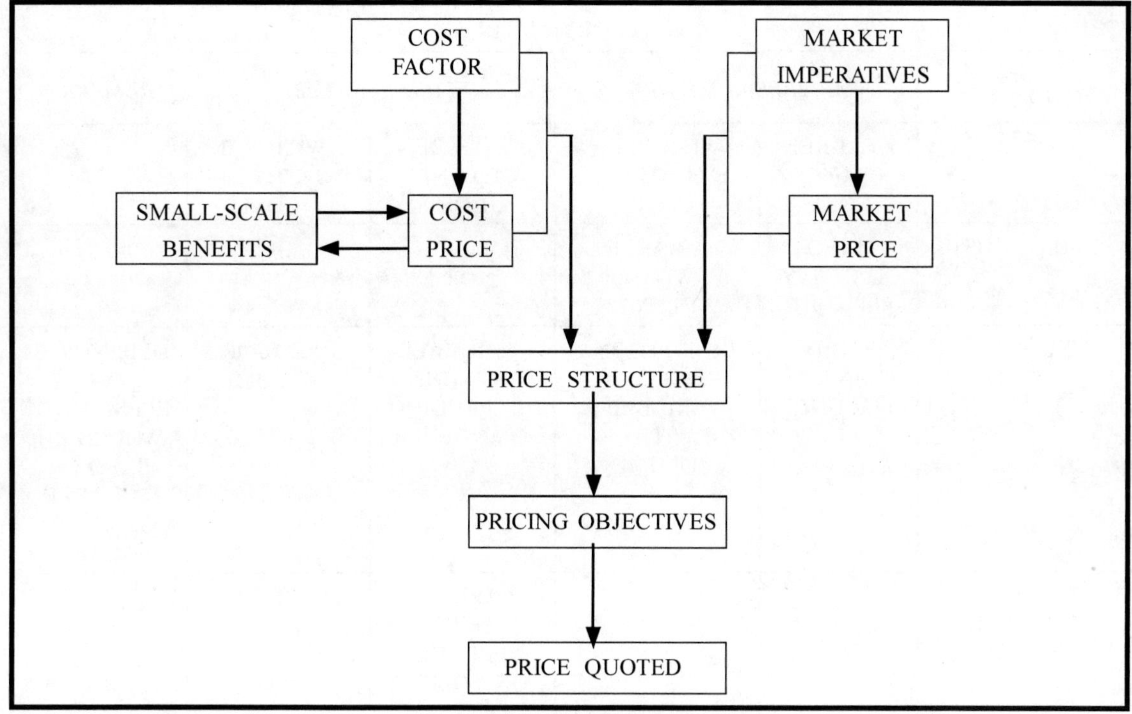

Fig. 12.1 Cash Pricing Decision

Credit Costs

The capital of a small-scale unit must be assessed and this should include fixed capital, working capital or loan capital, if any, and the cost of credit (borrowed money). All these should be included in the price.

Profit must be added to all the costs to arrive at the selling price. One of the guiding principles for fixing the margin of profit is that the small-scale entrepreneur should be able to earn more on his capital than he would if he merely invested it, say, in securities. The profit to be added is an amount which will be a reward for the investment risk. The return on capital should be reasonably sufficient to generate confidence in the financial soundness of the utility and should be adequate under an efficient and economical management, to maintain and support its credit and enable it to raise the money necessary for a proper discharge of its duties. The basic formula of return on capital is given below:

$$\text{Return on Capital Employed} \quad \frac{\text{Profit}}{\text{Sales}} \times \frac{\text{Sales}}{\text{Capital Employed}}$$

Thus, the return on elements employed depends on two factors: *(i)* the ratio of profit sales and *(ii)* the ratio of sales of capital employed. The former ratio measures the profit margin, while the latter shows the relationship of sales of the capital employed.

Ex-Factory Cost + Distribution Cost + Publicity Cost + Cost + Credit Cost + Profit and this may be termed as the Basic Price.

CATEGORY MATRIX					
CATEGORY OF COST	*VARIABLE IN NATURE*		*FIXED IN NATURE*		*REMARKS*
COST	WITH REF. TO UNIT COST	WITH REF. TO TOTAL COST	WITH REF. TO UNIT COST	WITH REF. TO TOTAL COST	
DIRECT COST	FIXED QUANTITY PER UNIT	VARIABLE WITH VOLUME	—	—	
INDIRECT COST	FIXED QUANTITY PER UNIT	PROPORTION-ATELY VARIABLE WITH VOLUME	VARIABLE PER UNIT DEPENDING ON VOLUME	FIXED FOR A VOLUME	DEPENDING ON COST ELEMENT IT WOULD BE FIXED OR VARIABLE MOSTLY IT IS VARIABLE
FACTORY OVERHEADS	—	—	VARIABLE PER UNIT DEPENDING ON VOLUME	FIXED FOR A VOLUME	—
SALES & ADMINISTRATIVE OVERHEADS	FIXED QUANTITY PER UNIT	PROPORTION-ATELY VARIABLE WITH VOLUME	VARIABLE PER UNIT DEPENDING ON VOLUME	FIXED FOR A VOLUME	DEPENDING ON COST ELEMENT IT WOULD BE FIXED OR VARIABLE BUT MOSTLY FIXED

Fig. 12.2: Cost Category Matrix

Indirect taxes in the form of duties and taxes levied by the Centre and the States and levied at the local level have increased the pressure on the prices of all commodities, essential or non-essential. Hence all indirect taxes — duties, octroi, sales tax, etc. — should be included in the sales price.

This method of pricing helps to prevent price cutting or fixing the price at the highest level — a fact which would promote the health of a small-scale unit.

Price Flexibility

Another important aspect of price fixation is the element of flexibility in price fixing. Flexibility is called for to ensure that prices are sensitive or responsive to changes in the factors that influence prices and should not fail to reflect changing conditions.

These are all the costs that are incurred inside and outside the factory before a product is ready for sale.

Fixation of Maximum Resale Prices

A suggestion for maximum resale prices by the manufacturer or supplier is permissible under the MRTP Act, provided that it has been made clear that the distributor is free to charge the prices which are lower than those which have been suggested. The logic behind this provision seems to be that, in a sellers' market, any suggestion made by a manufacturer to a distributor about the prices to be charged would be tantamount to a directive to adhere to those prices and to treat the maximum resale prices as the stipulated prices, unless it is conspicuously stated in the price circular or price list that prices which are lower the suggested prices may be charged on resale. In the absence of this statement, the practice of suggesting or prescribing the resale prices, even if they are qualified as "maximum", will attract provisions for registration under Section 33(1)(f) of the MRTP Act, which provides that any restrictive trade agreement to sell goods on the condition that the goods will be resold at stipulated prices will be subject to registration, unless it is clearly stated that lower prices than those which have been suggested may be charged.

The MRTP Commission may inquire into such cases, as in the case of another restrictive trade practice, and pass final orders under Section 37 of the Act.

Fixation of Minimum Resale Prices

The maintenance of minimum resale prices is prohibited under Sections 39 and 40 of the MRTP Act. As provided under Section 39, any term or condition of a contract for the sale of goods by a person to a wholesaler or retailer, or any agreement between a person and a wholesaler or retailer relating to such sale shall be void, in so far as it purports to establish or provides for the establishment of minimum prices to be charged on the resale of goods in India. This section forbids any supplier of goods from notifying to dealers, whether directly or through any person or association of persons acting on his behalf, or by publishing the price of goods stated or calculated to be understood as the minimum price, to charge such minimum price on the resale of goods. In other words, no persons may dictate the minimum resale price to a wholesaler or retailer.

Resale price maintenance is prohibited only in respect of the resale of goods in India. Sales abroad do not come under the purview of the MRTP Act.

As laid down under Section 40, no supplier shall withhold supplies of any goods from any wholesaler or retailer seeking to obtain them for resale in India on the ground that the latter has sold, or is likely to sell, the goods at a price below the resale price. A supplier shall be deemed to be withholding supplies of goods from a dealer if he:

(i) Refuses or fails to supply those goods to the order of the dealer;

(ii) Refuses to supply those goods to the dealer, except at prices or on terms or conditions as to credit, discount, or other matters, which are less favourable than the normal terms; or

(iii) Treats the dealer in a manner less favourable than that in which he normally treats other dealers in respect of the time or methods of delivery, etc.

However, a supplier is within his rights to withhold supplies of goods as "loss leader."

Any contravention of the provisions of Sections 30 and 40 is an offence punishable with imprisonment or fine or with both.

Exemption from Prohibition

The Commission is empowered to exempt particular classes of goods from prohibition of the maintenance of minimum resale prices, on a reference made to it either by the Registrar or any other interested person. An exemption can be granted if the Commission is satisfied that, in the absence of a system of maintained minimum resale prices:

(a) The quality or the varieties of goods would be substantially reduced to the detriment of the public;

(b) The retail prices of the goods would, in general and in the long run, be increased to the detriment of the public; or

(c) Services incidental to the sales (e.g., installation and repair services and the supply of spares) would either cease to be provided or be reduced substantially to the detriment of the public.

Generally speaking, it is difficult to make out a case for exemption from the prohibition of minimum resale prices.

Product Mix and Pricing

Small-scale industries generally have a tendency to price their products in the following way:

Cost — Raw material cost plus labour charges plus overheads added as a percentage of raw materials.

Price — Cost plus profit as a percentage of cost.

This method of pricing works reasonably well if the unit manufactures a single product. If there are more than one product, such a system of pricing can create great problems. For example, ABC Printing Press was doing well, having reached the break-even level of sales of Rs. 12 lakhs per annum. The accountant of the company was asked to suggest a method of pricing whereby sales and profits could be improved. He analysed sales and costs for the previous year. The analysis revealed that for every rupee-spent on raw materials, the company incurred one rupee by way of labour charges and Rs. 2 by way of overheads. Pricing accordingly was modified to hinge on raw material content of each other. For instance, if a particular order required Rs. 10 on raw materials, the price quoted was Rs. 44 (Rs. 10 on raw materials plus Rs. 10 as labour plus Rs. 20 on overheads plus Rs. 4 as profit). In the subsequent year the unit achieved a turnover of Rs. 14 lakhs (well above the anticipated break-even of Rs. 12 lakhs) but inexplicably incurred a loss. This was due to disproportional pricing of orders on art paper and kraft paper. Printing charges on kraft paper were extremely low. Printing charges on art paper were extremely high (due to kraft paper costing only Rs. 6 per kg. and art paper costing Rs. 15 per kg. and labour charges and overheads being charged proportionate to the cost of paper). This resulted in the unit getting all orders on kraft paper and no orders on art paper, and since the pricing was such that printing on kraft paper was unremunerative, the unit incurred losses. The pricing on percentage basis works if the product mix remains unchanged.

Price Discrimination

If different prices are charged to buyers, the attempt to do so may constitute a restrictive trade practice particularly if it has an adverse effect on competition in the relevant trade.

Price discrimination restricts competition because the dealers getting goods at higher prices cannot effectively compete with those buying goods at lower prices. Quantity discounts, or more favourable terms of delivery, credit, etc., in excess of what is justified by cost-saving effected in making bulk supplies, have the effect of charging lower prices from the large distributors who can resell the products at prices lower than those of the small distributors. Generally speaking, it is easier to justify discounts based on the size of the orders because of the obvious saving in the cost of the manufacture, sale, or delivery of large orders. But these quantity discounts must be same for buyers at the same stage of distribution. Aggregated rebates (discounts based on the amount purchased over a specified period), while not specifically prohibited, are harder to justify on the ground of cost savings. The costs would vary, depending upon whether the buyer has purchased small amount frequently, or large amounts infrequently.

As provided under Section 33(1)(e), an agreement which provides for granting or allowing, by a seller to a buyer, concessions or benefits, including allowance, discounts, rebates or credit, in connection with, or by reason of dealings, is subject to registration. This clause covers a wide array of quantity discounts, aggregated rebates, turnover bonus, over-riding commissions, and any other similar benefit granted by the seller to the buyer.

It is unlawful for a seller to discriminate in price if this leads to a substantially adverse effect on competition.

Not all price differentials are objectionable under the MRTP Act. Price differentials may be granted if they do not exceed the difference in the cost of production, sales or delivery resulting from differences in the quantity sold or from different methods of the sale or delivery of the product.

In sum, a manufacturer or supplier should not have a pricing policy which substantially limits competition among the distributors.

Predatory Pricing

Pricing discrimination can be used with a predatory intention by a dominant seller, by reducing prices below his costs in competitive markets with a view to driving out his smaller competitors or disciplining them against competitive pricing. This practice, referred to in the literature on economics as *predatory pricing* is covered Section 33(1) (0) of the MRTP Act.

An unreasonably severe price-cutting policy, with the object of lessening or trying to lessen competition, is against the spirit of the law. A.financially strong or a product-diversified company, which is making high profits in one area, is not permitted to reduce prices unreasonably in another area in order to eliminate local competition.

Collusive Price Fixing

In an ogliopolistic industry, the competing marketers are tempted to avoid price competition by fixing common prices and other terms of sale. Every collective arrangement among competitors ultimately turns out to be collusive pricing agreement. The coming together of two or more marketers in concert to fix, increase or quota the prices of their products or service harms the interests of consumers or buyers. The MRTP Commission has been of the view that a combination to fix prices is, *prima facie* anti-competitive in effect. In a number of inquiries relating to collusive price fixing, the commission has held that such a practice is prejudicial to the public interest and has accordingly passed “cease-and-desist” orders.

A collective agreement among marketers to fix price or any terms or conditions of sale falls under clause (d) of Section 33(1) of the MRTP Act. The clause also covers cases of collusive agreement among those submitting tenders to Government departments and other bulk buyers, and those concerned with the disposal of goods through auction or sealed tenders. The authorities concerned with tenders for the procurement of goods and services can lodge a complaint of collusive tendering with the MRPT Commission, which may inquire into such matters and take the necessary action provided under the Act.

In this context, it may be noted that any direction issued, or a recommendation made, by a trade or industry or association, to its members to adopt uniform prices or any other terms or conditions of sale or delivery, including the grant of credit, amounts to a collective agreement among the members of that trade, industry or association. It has been clarified under the MRTP Act made by or on behalf of a trade association to its members, or to any class of its members, as to the action to be taken or not to be taken by them in relation to any Matter affecting the trade conditions of those members, the Memorandum and Articles of Association of the association shall be deemed to be an agreement among all the members of the association and will accordingly attract the provisions of registration and inquiry under the MRTP Act.

Unreasonably High Prices

A marketer is generallv free to increase the prices of his products or services to any level. The MRTP Act forbids the practice of charging high prices only where it amounts to a monopolistic trade practice, i.e., where it has the effect of maintaining prices at an unreasonable level by limiting, reducing, or otherwise controlling the production, supply, or distribution of any goods or services, or in any other manner. Generally speaking, such a practice can be indulged in by a monopolistic undertaking, although any undertaking, or a group of undertakings acting in concert, can indulge in such a practice.

A monopolistic trade practice is deemed to be prejudicial to public interest if such a practice results, *inter alia*, in increasing unreasonably the cost of production, supply, or distribution of goods, or the performance of any service, or increasing unreasonably the prices at which goods are sold to derive profits from production or supply.

As pointed out earlier, the consequences of charging excessive or unreasonable price, if found to be prejudicial to public interest, can be serious. The Central Government can pass any order it considers appropriate in a particular case.

Any contravention of the orders of the MRTP Commission (in respect of a restrictive trade practice) and the Central Government (in respect of a monopolistic trade practice) is an offence, punishable with imprisonment, or with fine, or with both.

Pricing is also an interphase of different functions – marketing, sales, finance, accounts, legal and factory processes. All the interplay needs to converge to one number. It needs a well-coordinated organisational process to get to good strategy. The CEO could drive this or a price coordination committee (driven by marketing) could do so. But the crucial aspect is to explore alternatives. Can R & D and factory work at target costing? Can accounts think of innovative and strategic costing? Can marketing add value and increase price? The lazy option of "Equal to competition" may not always work.

A one per cent increase in price could increase price by three to four per cent or a few points decrease in price could lead to bigger share and hence greater contribution. The obvious fallout of not evaluating these is to pay a price.

The above analysis makes it evident that price as a marketing management instrument has an important role to play in business. Price is one element of the matrix of variables affecting the sales of small manufacturer. An integration of the variables is the key to marketing success. More importantly, proper and careful pricing and the adoption of a proper price policy are some of the most important steps towards the success of small-scale enterprises. Price policy should win over the confidence of the buyers.

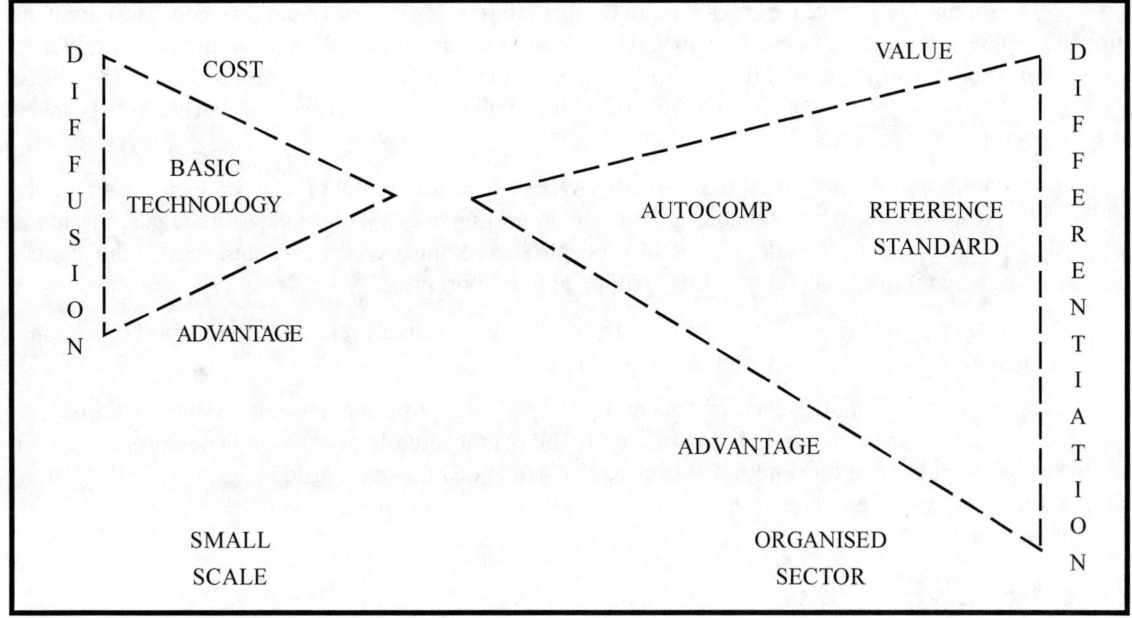

Fig. 12.3: The Price Squeeze

Export Pricing

In addition to these costs, however, there are certain other cost elements which are exclusively incurred in exporting a product. A few of these relevant costs are enumerated below:

***(a)* Export Packaging Costs:** Goods meant for export require special packaging to withstand rough handling in the process of loading and unloading at ports and during long sea voyages. When goods are loaded they need to be protected from the harmful effects of exposure to humidity and consequent deterioration. Special preventive treatments are carried out to avoid rusting owing to prolonged exposure to humidity.

***(b)* Export Handling Charges:** Export handling charges include the cost of transportation of a product from warehouse to port, all storage charges before it is loaded on to a ship, payment of port dues, charges for documentation for export, etc. Sometimes, owing to circumstances beyond the control of the exporter, goods may lie in the dock for quite sometime before they are loaded on to a ship. In such circumstances, port authorities, after an initial grace period of seven days, levy a charge called a "demurrage" charge on the storage and protection of these goods in the port premises.

***(c)* Sea Freight/Air Freight Charges:** Depending on the requirements of a customer, goods are shipped or despatched by sea or by air. The freight charges incurred by an export organisation in shipping or in airlifting involve a certain amount of incidental charges for the purpose of export pricing. Freight charges are usually recovered from the customer at actuals.

***(d)* Insurance:** Goods for export are usually insured against damage, deterioration and loss during transit. An exporter, at the request of the customer, insures the goods as soon as they are shipped and recovers the charges from him. Insurance charges on goods, until they are loaded, are a part of the "direct cost" for the exporters and have to be included in his costing for the purpose of pricing the product.

***(e)* Commission/Service Charges Paid to Export Houses/ Merchant Exporters:** Since an enormous effort is required to organise oneself for export, most small-scale and medium-scale industries prefer to export their products through established export houses. In such cases, the commission or service charge payable to an export house, through which the product is promoted in the international market, is to be taken as a direct cost for the exporter.

***(f)* Commission Payable to Agents Abroad:** Where the sales promotion of a product is sought to be achieved by the appointment of a suitable agent in the importing country, a pre-determined commission is required to be paid to him on the sale price of the product. This commission is a part of the cost of the product and should be taken into consideration while arriving at the export price.

It may be mentioned here that all these costs, which are exclusively relevant for transport operations, are direct in nature, i.e., they vary with the volume of sales.

A multi-product firm, however, will generally be in a better position than a uniproduct firm, so far as overhead allocations are concerned. It can distribute the overhead costs over a number of products, after taking into account the market conditions. If there is a strong demand for a product, proportionately more overhead charges can be recovered from it, while allocating little or no overheads on the products faced with a competitive market.

Export-Specific Costs

The amount of export-specific costs depends on a number of factors:

(a) Product characteristics : Some products need more promotional outlays than others. In general, primary products require such outlays less than finished manufactures.

(b) Mode of transport : Some products require to be airfreighted or require specialised transport services, e.g., refrigerated space.

(c) Method of distribution : For some products, the channel of distribution is longer than others. In general, the longer is the chain, the greater are the in-channel costs.

Export-specific costs in most cases will be greater than the domestic marketing costs. Therefore, exporting firms are in a disadvantageous position vis-a-vis domestic manufacturers in the importing country.

Price Discrimination

If there is a good domestic market, which is protected from overseas competition through import barriers, a company will have greater discretionary power to charge a lower price in an export market in order to become competitive. In the domestic market it will charge a higher price while in the export market, it will accept the going market price. This position is shown in the figure below:

DID is the domestic demand curve faced by the firm. The demand curve is downward sloping, as the firm is operating in an imperfectly competitive market. The corresponding marginal revenue curve in MR. XD is the export demand curve. The export market is perfectly competitive, i.e., the firm can export any quantity it wants, provided it accepts the going market price of OP. The firm, if it wants to maximize profit, will produce where the marginal cost curve interests the combined marginal revenue curve P'NXD, i.e., at Q. Out of the total production of OQ, OQ' will be sold in the domestic market at OP price, and the residual output, Q in the export market at price OPQ'.

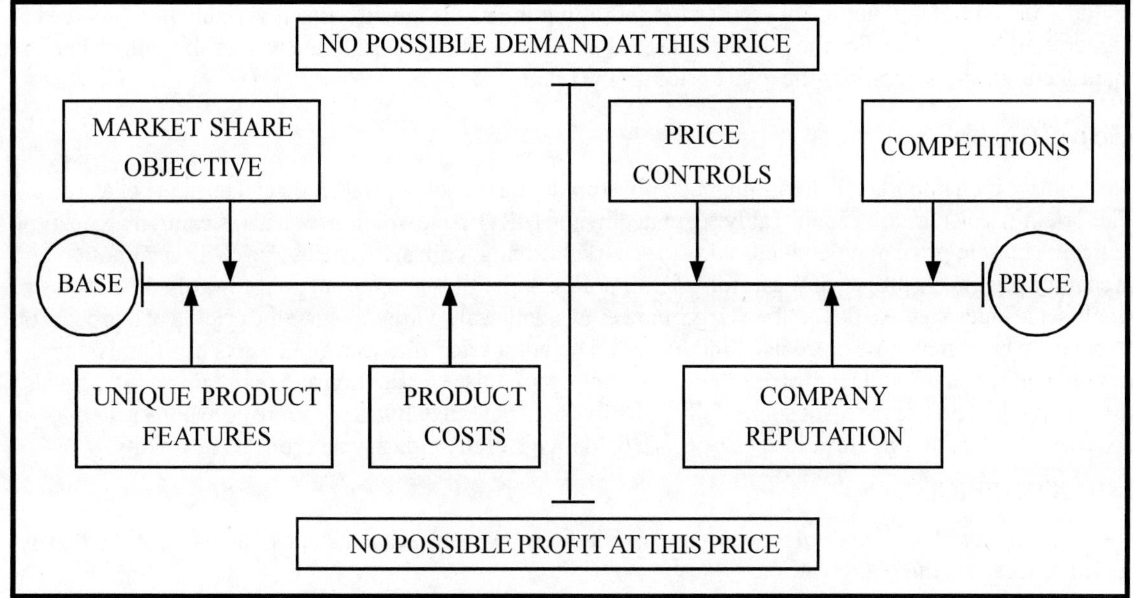

Fig. 12.4 Factors Determining the Base Price Level

The basic principle of price discrimination is that when there are two different geographical markets, for profit to be maximized, marginal revenues will have to be equalised, i.e.;

$MR_1 = MR_2$

If for example $MR_1 > MR_2$, it will be possible to increase total profit by shifting some output from market B to market A. The necessary condition to be fulfilled for practicing price discrimination is that *(a)* either re-import is banned, i.e., buyers in the export market cannot send these back in the domestic market to be sold at higher price or *(b)* even though it is not illegal, the transport and other charges are higher than the price difference, so that additional profit cannot be realised through resale.

If either of these conditions is satisfied and market conditions permit, the exporting firm can, if necessary, sell in the foreign markets at a price, which does not recover the fixed costs or allows a profit rate which is lower than what is otherwise expected, as the domestic market can be made use of to recover the rest of the fixed costs or to meet losses, if any.

It, however, need not be presumed that while following a differentiated pricing policy, it is always the export market which is to be charged a lower price. For many products, demand for which is basically a function of incomes or fashion, it would be possible to charge a higher price in export markets.

Resale Price

The resale price is the price fixed by the manufacturer for wholesalers and retailers. In other words, the small-scale manufacturer may fix the price at which the wholesaler must resell the product to the retailer and the retailer to the ultimate user, i.e., the consumer. This marketing mechanism ensures that the dealer gets a proper margin and that the consumer can buy products of a uniformly good quality at a fair price. In India, for example, the manufacturers of drugs, pharmaceuticals, detergents, etc., fix the retail price of a commodity, print it on the product packages. However, one of the common complaints is that, since the re-sale price includes the cost of the inefficient retailer for not selling the goods quickly, it is invariably fixed somewhat higher than it should be. For the products of small-scale units, it is generally the wholesaler rather than the manufacturer who determines the resale price for the retailer.

Conclusion

Price is an important determining factor in stimulating the sales, production and turnover of a product. The pricing decisions are considerably regulated by the MRTP Act, which necessitates caution against the policies of resale price maintenance, skim-the-market pricing, collusive pricing, price discrimination and predatory pricing. A proper and careful pricing policy is the most important step towards the success of small-scale industries. No doubt, for a large number of small-scale entrepreneurs, the pricing of a product on a scientific basis may pose a problem and a challenge; but a scientific price policy acts as a catalvst to the development of small-scale industries. It not only helps to regulate production and maintain quality, but also to step up sales and keep the Consumer fully, satisfied and contented. It has therefore been aptly said that the price of a product of a small-industry projects a bold image of the industry and reflects its quality.

INDEX OF PRICE CONTENT

(i) Cost of Production: (a) Raw materials; *(b)* Power; *(c)* Fuel; *(d)* Labour and establishment; *(e)* Repairs and maintenance; and *(f)* Overheads.

(ii) Depreciation: The depreciation at a rate varying between 4% and 6% is allowed on the gross block in estimating a fair ex-mill price.

(iii) Interest on Working Capital: As stipulated by the different commissions.

(iv) Return on Capital: (a) Managing Agency commission; *(b)* Taxation *(c)* Bonus (profit sharing); *(d)* Fair reasonable dividends; *(e)* Reserve; *(f)* Dividend to shareholders.

(v) Marketing Expenses: (a) Advertisement; *(b)* Packaging charges; *(c)* Sales campaign; *(d)* Sales promotion; *(e)* Wholesalers'/ Distributors' commission; *(f)* Retailers'commission.

(vi) F.O.B. Destination Selling Price: The following charges are added to the FOB Price: *(a)* Rebate on supplies against rate contract; *(b)* Excise duty; *(c)* Sales tax; *(d)* Average freight; *(e)* STC's remuneration; *(f)* Contingencies.

ANNEXURE – 1

GUIDELINES ON FIXING PRICES

The Union Government has prepared some guidelines for the fixation of prices of industrial commodities of mass consumption.

The guidelines assume significance in the context of the Government's proposal to enlarge the public distribution.system for essential commodities.

In the case of agricultural commodities, the Government fixes the prices on the basis of the recommendation of the Agricultural Prices Commission, and in consultation with State Chief Ministers. For industrial goods, the Bureau of Industrial Costs and Prices is an important agency for price fixation; and the guidelines are expected to help the Bureau in fixing fair prices.

The guidelines provide that the rate of return to manufacturers or producers should be calculated on the net worth of a company, rather than on the total capital employed.

The guidelines point out that the use of the concept of capital employed creates a bias in favour of borrowed capital against equity capital. The switch over to the concept of net worth would remove this bias and help to reduce the excessive demand for borrowed funds from public sector financial institutions.

Moreover, by focussing attention on the rate of return on the shareholders' equity, the new norm would encourage the flow of investible resources towards more essential commodities at the cost of relatively less essential commodities.

The other points made in the guidelines are:

(i) The minimum bonus payable under the law should not be considered as a part of the cost of production. However, the permissible net return to the firm should be calculated after allowing for the payment of bonus — up to the statutory minimum — from the likely gross profits of the firm.

(ii) Prices should initially be fixed on the basis of the average costs of the relatively more efficient firms which account for a large percentage of the output. For those among the remaining firms, which are likely to incur cash losses under such a pricing formula, the price fixing may be requested to suggest specific measures related to their particular problems.

(iii) Prices should be fixed according to an average debt-equity ratio calculated after a detailed examination of the financial structure of industry concerned.

(iv) Interest payments on borrowed funds should be considered as a part of costs.

(v) The rate of return should consist of two components — the basic minimum, which would be uniform as between industries, and an additional variable arising out of such factors as risk, priorities, growth prospects, need for internal generations of funds, and the extent of the obsolence of capital stock and capital structure, including reserves.

(vi) The basic minimum component of the rate of return may be equal to the going interest rate on bank deposits of five years' duration not of the rate of corporation tax.

(vii) The price fixing authority should suggest a suitable cost variation formula for major raw material inputs, accounting for a part of the costs of the firm: A thorough going review of price and costs in price controlled industries should take place every three years.

(viii) The problem of the excess profits of older units, wherever necessary, may be dealt with in two ways. In highly capital intensive industries, where the number of products is small, pooling may

be considered. In other industries, it may be stipulated that excess profits would be required in a statutory reserve, to be used with the permission or replacement and modernisation of the enterprise.

(ix) Price determining bodies should simultaneously be requested to suggest such cost reduction measures as may be considered necessary.

(x) Price determining bodies should be requested to suggest appropriate distribution arrangements in industries which are subjected to price control.

ANNEXURE – 2

FIXING THE PRICE

Price Cutting procedures are like a greasy pole where the climber slips back two feet for every one foot he climbs up. Frankly, the buyers who only consider price are of no permanent value to the manufacturer. No goodwill can be built up with such buyers because they move from one supplier to another. On the other hand, the buyer who is faithful to his suppliers and who considers quality, presentation and service above price is the buyer who is likely to have a more permanent business and whose customer is of real value. This type of buyer may even be antagonized by low prices and he may even be suspicious of the goods if the price is, in his estimation, too low. He will say to himself "it can't be any good if it is as cheap as that" and will refuse to buy unless the manufacturer has a ready and legitimate explanation as to why he can manage to offer good quality and low prices at the same time.

The second method of fixing the price at the highest the market can stand also has its defects. It is difficult, even impossible, to keep a new idea exclusive. Any new product which has reasonable sales potential will attract imitators. The higher the price the more imitators there will be. Other manufacturers will examine the preposition, and seeing that there is a good profit margin in it, will rush into its manufacture like bees flock around a honeycomb. To fix the price too high is to invite not only competition but also price cutting. Nor is it a legitimate argument for a manufacturer to say that he will start with a high price and reduce it later when competition appears. The customer can be permanently lost if he finds out that the manufacturer has been selling to him at a higher price than necessary and only brings down the price to a proper level when forced to do so.

Prices must be fixed on a properly scientific basis. Any manufacturer is in business to earn a profit and there is no point in his being in business unless he can claim a better profit on his investment than the return which he would get if he invested his money in securities. Therefore, he must price his products in a way which shows him the requisite profit on his investment. If he cannot sell his goods at such a price then he had better withdraw from business or at least take up the manufacture of a better line. It is all very nice to have a large sales turnover; but it must be remembered that it is true to say that the larger the sales the larger the loss when the price is uneconomical.

Prices must be calculated from the bottom up, i.e., by finding out first what the product is going to cost to produce. For the small manufacturer it may not be possible to have a precisely detailed cost system but there must be some form of costing which will give reliable results and which will give a reliable idea of what the cost of the product is. The manufacturers know how to account for raw materials, labour overheads, and other elements in arriving at a legitimate ex-works cost and now it must be decided how much has to be added to arrive at a sensible price and to show a proper proportion of net profit.

Example (1)

A factory producing 6 ft. lathes has a total capital of Rs. 2,00,000 and is producing and selling four lathes per month at an ex-works cost of Rs. 2,000 each. There is a certain amount of risk owing to competition and possible fluctuations of Government sponsored hire-purchase schemes and the proprietor considers that he is entitled to a net return of 12.5 per cent on his investment. Therefore, he will require to make an annual profit of Rs. 25,000. Because he estimates his continued sales at 48 lathes per year he must provide for the addition of Rs. 521 per lathe which is equivalent to a percentage of 26 per cent on ex-works cost. This appears a high percentage but is no more than is legitimate on the investment.

Example (2)

A factory producing assorted size and brands of hair oils has a total capital of Rs. 35,000 and it is estimated that the cost of annual sales will be Rs. 80,000. The risk is considered to be fairly high on this type of business and return of 17.5 per cent may be required on the capital investment, so that a total annual provision of Rs. 6,125 will be necessary. If this amount is divided by 80,000 the answer is 0.77 or in other words,. 7.75 per cent of the ex-factory cost of any item whatever its cost.

The addition for profit described above is calculated on the assumption that there will be no more than normal usage of working capital. The availability of capital is one of the prime factor in deciding whether or not the business can be expanded. If customers take longer credit than is normally provided for this is the same as if they were borrowing money to finance their enterprise. If the manufacturer is making or planning to make 12 per cent net profit then the giving of one month's extra credit will cost him I per cent and the customer should pay this. On the other hand, if the customer is prepared to pay at an earlier date the manufacturer should be prepared to pass to that customer a concession or reward for such payment.

Now all the elements of cost are accounted for and the price at which the manufacturer should sell his goods is said to be:

Ex-works cost + carriage or distribution cost + publicity cost + sales cost + profit + credit cost; and this may be termed the basic price.

These costs may well be calculated on the basis of production and distribution of the smallest economical quantity. For manufacturers of specialized equipment of reasonably sized machine tools, for instance, the smallest economical quantity may well one item but for manufacturers of consumer goods and repetition items the smallest economical quantity will be determined by the number of units which it is worth packing or the number of units which constitute a standard pack, or the number of items which make up the minimum value which is it worth a representative or salesman spending selling time upon.

If customers order larger quantities than the minimum economical quantity, certain savings will accrue to the manufacturer. For instance, the sales expenses (i.e., sales office costs, salesman's salary and travelling and daily allowances) may well be the same on a large order as they are on a small order although commission will increase proportionately. Carriage costs will reduce with larger orders and also raw material purchases may well be cheaper if larger quantities can be ordered to fulfil larger orders. Larger orders also mean longer production runs and, in consequence, lower works costs. It is only right, therefore, that there should be some inducement to customer to place orders in excess of the lowest economical quantity and this inducement is usually in the form of increasing discounts from the basic price of increasingly larger orders. Such quantity discounts may be arranged in relation to the total value of the order if the manufacturer is producing an assortment of goods with varying prices.

At this stage it is necessary for the manufacturer to decide as to what extent he is going to fix prices for his goods. Where the manufacturer is selling direct to the actual user there is no difficulty and he will price his goods in accordance with the considerations already studied. Where, however, the goods are to reach the user via wholesale and retail dealer channels the manufacturer will need to decide whether he will fix his price only to the customer who buys from him and leave that customer to mark up the prices to other buyers in the channel of sale or whether he will fix prices for each buyer in the channel irrespective of whether he has direct dealings or not.

If the manufacturer sell to wholesalers and only fixes his price to them he may well find that different wholesalers are fixing different mark ups on his prices with the result that there is unhealthy competition between the various wholesalers; because the less reputable wholesalers may work on a minimum mark-up in order to obtain the dealers' custom in the easiest way. In Western countries it is usual for the manufacturer to decide the price at which the product will be sold to the eventual user irrespective of the number of trade channels by way of distributors, wholesalers, and retail dealers who handle the product. This is done by adding on to the cost the amounts necessary to provide the margins required by the intermediate traders and to quote prices in terms of users' prices less trade and wholesale discounts. The price at which the product is to be sold to the public or actual user is most frequently marked on the item itself. For instance, a manufacturer of a certain consumer product will quote his price on the following lines:

Shino Hair Oil 4 11. oz. bottles — Rs. 2 each.

Trade (dealers) price Rs. 24 per dozen, less 25 per cent. Wholesale price Rs. 24 per dozen, less 25 per cent and less 20 per cent.

It is believed that this method of pricing helps to prevent price cutting. If the dealers are quoted Rs. 18 per dozen for SHINO HAIR OIL one dealer may sell at Rs. 1.75 per bottle and think he is doing well to make 25 paise on each whilst another dealer may think he is doing well if he makes 20 paise per bottle and accordingly sell at Rs. 1.80 paise. If the same two dealers are quoted Rs. 2 less 25 per cent there is a good chance that they will both sell at the same price and be less anxious to undercut as they will lose a profit they might have made if they do so.

Most buyers are suspicious that the manufacturer is trying to charge them more than is really necessary and this feeling is heightened by the absence of any regular form of price list. All manufacturers are well advised that when they have fixed their prices and have decided upon the discounts to be allowed for quantities and prompt payment to publish these prices and details in a proper manner. Handwritten and typewritten price lists often cause buyer suspicion and there is no substitute in helping schedule of prices, discounts and payment terms. Many small manufacturers are. reticent to publish their prices and accounts for fear of being copied by competitors but if competitors want to find out the manufacturer's prices they will do so any way and this should not deter the manufacturer from publishing an authentice price list.

Proper and careful pricing and the adoption of a proper price policy are some of the most important steps towards the success of small-scale industries.

✸ ✸ ✸

13

BREAK-EVEN ANALYSIS

Introduction

With the tremendous increase in the quantum of business activity, particularly in the small-scale sector, the quantitative approach (variedly known as ratio analysis) to management manifested. In recent years, these techniques proved beneficial in planning, controlling, co-ordinating and forecasting complex activities. Break-even analysis is one such technique which is a valuable key to the solution of complex problems in profit-planning, specially those relating to multi-product enterprises. Break-even analysis is not confined merely to the location of break-even point. It can be used to arrive at a point where a specified amount of profit/loss can be expected. Thus, break-even analysis, which forms the foundation of profit-planning, takes the garb of cost-volume-profit (CVP) analysis in its broader connotation.

Definition

Broadly defined, break-even analysis is concerned with the following questions:

- What is the relation between output and cost?
- At what level of output will revenues be expected to break-even with cost?
- What is the relation between profit and output?
- What is the relation between cost, volume (sales) and profit?

The break-even point is a level at which the organisation will be able to raise its output at a total cost which will be equal to the sales revenue of that output sold. In other words, a break-even point means a stage of production where total sales revenue is equal to total cost. Thus, at that point of production, the industry will neither make profit nor incur loss. If the sales revenue is above this point, the organisation earns profit and if it is below this point, the unit incurs losses.

The break-even analysis helps in revealing a clear projection of profit planning at different production stages vis-a-vis the financial needs. It also helps to gauge the rate of return on investment of capital at varying stages of production.

When once an organisation breaks even, from that period onwards repayment of debt may begin for the term loans granted by the banks. In the case of new projects, it indicates viability, i.e., when the organisation will start earning profits.

Break-even analysis is an important measure being used by the proponents and banks in deciding the viability of a new project, especially in respect of manufacturing activities. This technique is useful in dealing with a new project or a new activity of the existing unit.

The break-even analysis also determines the margin of safety, i.e., excess of budgeted or actual sales over the break-even sales so that the bankers would know how sensitive a project is to recession. This is an important factor in determining the strength of the project and its ability to absorb the ups and downs in the economy. The bankers, as lenders of funds, insist upon a reasonable margin of safety so that fixed costs are met at a fairly earlier stage.

From the banker's point of view, the project should achieve a break-even position within a reasonable time from the start of production. The project which reaches a break-even point earlier is considered as a viable project by the bankers. The bankers cannot only expect earlier repayment of their advances in the case of such projects but can also be assured that the project can fairly adapt itself to the day-to-day developing technology. The projects which are unlikely to reach the break-even point in the third or fourth year of its commencement of production will not be a viable proposal for the bankers.

The break-even point (BEP) establishes the level of output/ production which evenly breaks the costs and revenues. It is the level of production at which the turnover just covers the fixed overheads and the unit starts making profits.

Costs

The total cost can be divided into two categories, viz., fixed costs and variable costs. Fixed costs are those which are not directly related to the quantity or volume of production. Generally, these costs do not change over a particular period of time and/or upto a particular stage of capacity of the industrial unit. Variable costs are those which have a direct relationship with the volume of production, and almost proportionately vary with any change in the volume of production. As fixed costs cannot change percentage with the quantity of production, the cost per unit of output declines as output rises.

The operational strategy of a project is concerned with the interplay of profit operating cost and operating revenues. This interplay results either in loss or profit or break-even point. An analysis of cost-volume, profit relationship (operational leverage) is very useful to evaluate the operational strategy. The Cost-Volume profit analysis discuss the interrelationship of these variables; particularly its effect on Profit/Loss from a project with the changes in the level of project activity. In other words, the operation leverage also explains the manner in which project-fixed costs affect these changes. Normally, project operating costs are classified into two, i.e., fixed costs and variable costs. Fixed costs do not vary with the volume of production. Variable costs are, however, directly related to output. If production goes up, variable costs go up. When fixed costs and variable costs at a certain level of output are added, we get total cost. Now let us find out how total cost would behave if there is a change in output. We know the total costs include fixed costs and variable costs. If output increases, the latter would also increase and thus total cost would increase.

Yet another factor is income from the project. The total income which an organisation gets from producing its product is called revenue. Profit (or loss) as a variable is the reflection of a number of internal and external conditions which exert influence on sales revenue and costs. Outcome of these factors is interdependent and the volume is considered to be the dominant factor. This is probably because, changes in volume are more frequent, take place rapidly, and are subject to managerial control as changes due to outside factors which are outside the purview of management control.

Further, costs vary in direct proportion to the volume, and hence, a small change in the volume may have more than a proportionate effect on profits than the other factors mentioned above. It is thus the volume which is perhaps the largest single factor which influences costs. Hence, an intimate relationship exists among costs, volume and profit.

The relationship between cost-volume-profit variable can best be explained through the break-even analysis. Break-even analysis indicates at which level costs and revenue are in equilibrium. To speak broadly, break-even analysis is an analytical technique that can be used to determine the probable profit at any level of production.

Below is given a detailed break-even chart pointing out all the details of costs and profit.

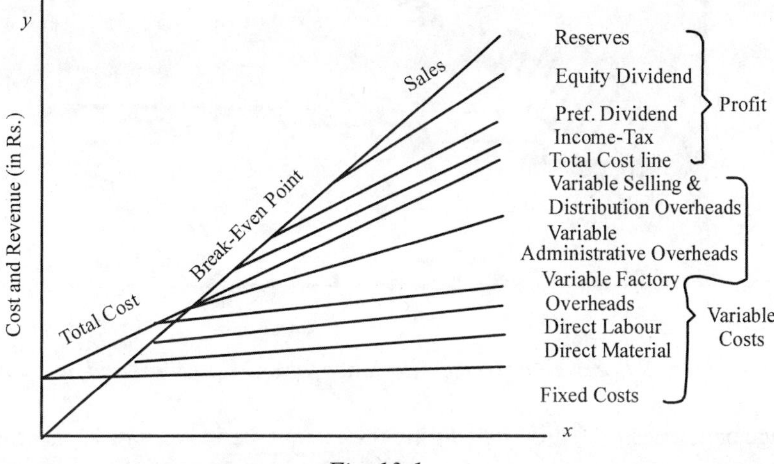

Fig. 13.1

Volume of production is shown on the X-axis and costs and revenue are shown on the Y-axis. Fixed cost line is parallel to the X-axis. Total cost line will start from the point of intersection of fixed cost line and the X-axis. Total cost line can be depicted by plotting the variable cost line above the fixed cost line. The sales line originates from the origin. The point of intersection of the total cost line and total sales line is the break-even point. A prependicular drawn from this point on the X-axis will determine the break-even sales. If the actual level of activity is less than break-even it will incur losses.

This break-even chart also shows each element of variable costs. Obviously, the area between fixed cost line and the total cost line is divided to show each element separately. In addition, to show the appropriation of profit, the area lying between sales line and total cost line is divided into different items of appropriations.

Basic Assumptions

The break-even analysis is based on certain assumptions which should be properly understood.

Some assumption is made regarding the expected volume of production in a period and this is described as 'activity', which should not he confused with 'efficiency.' The latter is related to the standards of performance. Activity is concerned only with the volume of production.

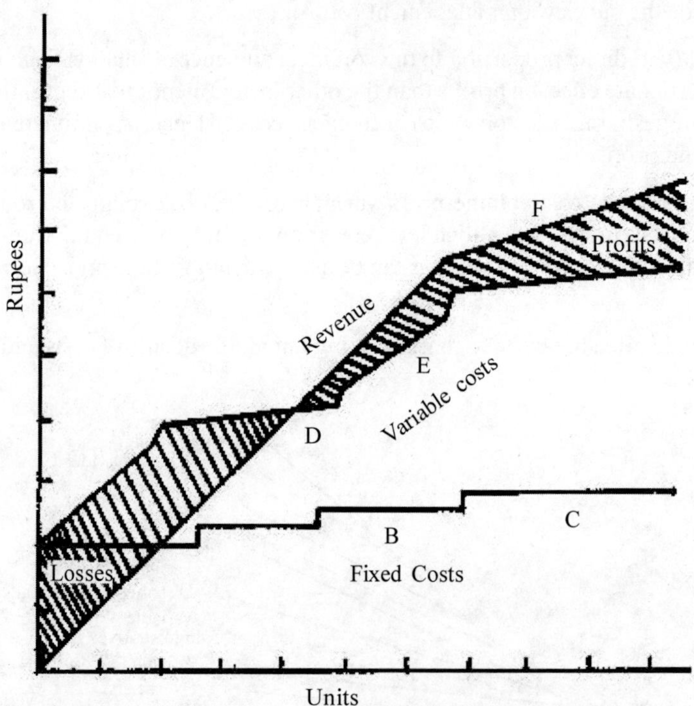

Fig. 13.2: Generalised Break-Even Chart Allowance for changing cost and revenue conditions.

An average output has to be projected during the ensuing period of, say, 12 months.

At the end of the period, actual production and projected volume of production would be reviewed and expected profits would be compared with the actual profit or loss, depending on over-activity or under-activity than anticipated.

(1) It assumes that the concept of cost variability is valid, i.e., the costs can be classified realistically as fixed and variable.

(2) There is a relevant range of validity for all facets of the analysis.

(3) The selling price does not change as the physical volume of sales changes.

(4) There is only one product, or in case of multiple products, their sales mix remains constant.

(5) The basic managerial policies relative to operations will not change materially.

(6) The general price level will remain essentially stable in the short run.

(7) There is synchronisation between sales and production, i.e., inventory remains constant or is zero.

(8) The efficiency and productivity per person and technology remain essentially unchanged.

Economic Characteristics

(1) Fixed costs, variable costs and total costs at varying levels of sales.

(2) Profit and loss potential, before and after income tax at varying levels.

(3) The margin of safety relationship of expected sales volume to break-even sales volume.

(4) Break-even point.

(5) The danger point the point below which preferred dividends are not earned.

(6) The dead point the point where management earns only the going rate on investment.

(7) The unhealthy point below which earnings are insufficient to pay the preferred dividends and the expected dividends on common stock.

It can be found out by application of this technique as to what extent physical capacity/ facility as represented by plant and equipment has been utilised and to what extent further potentials are available for profitable operations. Its use can be made to assess the feasibility of incurring capital expenditure on plant and machinery and effect of investment thereon on profitability.

Uses and Application of Break-Even Analysis

It has considerable value as a managerial tool. Essentially, it analyses the cost-volume-profit relationship. It is technique that provides greater insight into the economic characteristics of a unit and may be used to determine the approximate effect of various alternatives. It should be restaged that this analysis is based on estimates and the arithmetical manipulations generally involve averages. The results should never be viewed as precise. Rather the analysis may be characterised approximately as 'slide rule' approach that may be used to develop and test, with minimum effort, the approximate effect on costs and profits of several types of managerial decisions.

The Cost Volume Profit (CVP) analysis is a *device for* predicting the *effects of* various combinations of cost and volume upon the profit or net income of a business enterprise.

Uses of C-V-P Analysis

C-V-P analysis is useful in a variety of situations where the managers are required to take decisions. Some of the situations are as follows:

- Pricing decisions.
- *Make or Buy decisions:* Should we manufacture certain components which involves additional investment or buy them from outside?
- *Production Process Decisions:* If the same product can be produced by alternative processes, which one should be adopted?
- Acceptance of special orders at discounts.
- *Possible Ways of Sales Promotion:* Should we reduce the prices, or increase advertising, or incorporate additional features in the product?
- *Addition or Deletion of Product lines:* Which products can conveniently be added to the product line? Which can be discontinued?
- *Channels of Distribution:* Should we have our own distribution network or should we appoint distributors and stockists?
- *Sales Mix:* Given the present product line, which particular product should be manufactured in larger quantities and which product should not be emphasised?

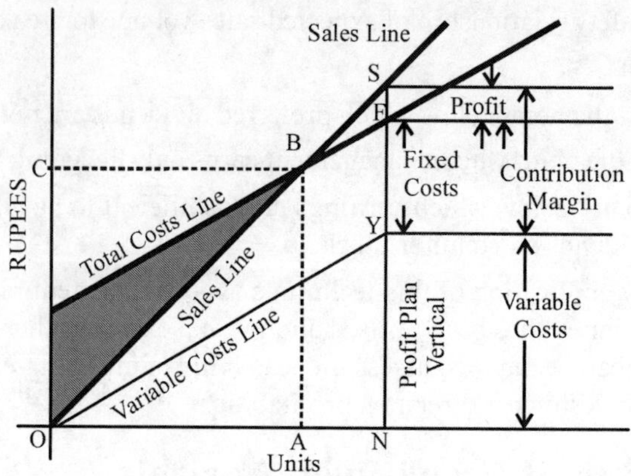

Fig. 13.3

Algebraic Formulate of Break-even Analysis

(A) Break-even point (BEP) in terms of sales:

$$\text{BEP} = \frac{\text{Fixed Cost}}{\text{Total contribution}} \times \text{Total amount of sales}$$

(Total Sales – Total variable costs – Total contribution)

Example:

Sales	1000	unit
Selling price per unit	Rs.	60
Variable cost per unit	Rs.	40
Fixed cost	Rs.	1,500

$$\frac{\text{BEP}}{\text{(Unit volume)}} = \frac{1{,}500}{60 \quad 40} = \frac{1{,}500}{20} = 75 \text{ units BEP in terms of units}$$

BEP in terms of sales = Rs. 75 × Rs. 60 = Rs. 4,500

(B) BEP (in terms of capacity utilisation)

$$\frac{\text{Total fixed costs}}{\text{Total contribution}} \times \frac{\text{Pr oduction in terms of per cent}}{\text{to installed capacity}}$$

In this method, BEP in terms of capacity utilisation is calculated with reference to the capacity utilisation in the normal year of production. For instance, if the unit is expected to achieve a capacity utilisation of 40 per cent, 45 per cent, 60 per cent, and 80 per cent of the installed capacity in the first five years, the BEP computation will be with reference to 80 per cent.

Calculation of BEP

The break-even point can be calculated in terms of physical units and in terms of sales turnover.

(i) In terms of physical Unit: The number of units required to be sold to achieve the break-even point can be calculated using the following formula:

$$BEP = \frac{FC}{SP - VC} \text{ or } \frac{FC}{C}$$

where,

FC = fixed cost

VC = variable cost

SP = selling price

C = contribution per unit (C = SP–VC)

Example, if:

FC = Rs. 1,00,000

VC = Rs. 2 per unit

SP = Rs. 4 per unit, and

Maximum productive capacity = 100,000 units per year.

$$BEP = \frac{100,00}{4-2} = 50,000 \text{ units (i.e., 50\% of the capacity)}$$

(ii) In terms of sales volume: BEP in terms of sales volume can be calculated using the following formula:

$$BEP = SP \frac{FC}{SP - VC}$$

where,

FC = fixed cost

SP = selling price per unit

VC = variable cost per unit

A different way of calculating BEP is

$$BEP = \frac{\text{Fixed Expenses} \times \text{Sales}}{\text{Total contribution}}$$

where total contribution is the total sales minus the total variable expenses.

In this case, the BEP will be in Rupees. Graphically, BEP is represented as below:

Shortcoming of the Break-Even Analysis

The BEP analysis is based on some assumptions, such as sales price, costs, production, sales, etc. The technique will be only of academic value unless all these assumptions are well-calculated. Besides, the technique is a preliminary and supplementary tool in the whole exercise of ratio analysis.

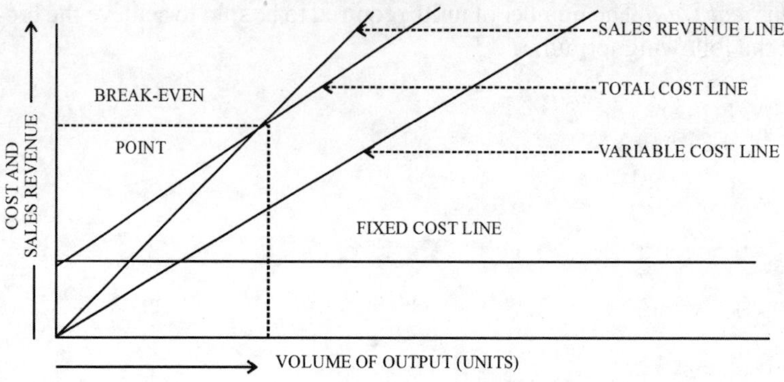

Fig. 13.4: Break-Even Analysis

Another important factor in using the technique is to provide for cost-escalation as a built-in safeguard against increase in prices.The most important factor while using the technique, however, is the proper analysis of various costs into fixed costs and variable costs, as there are some types of costs which do not fall into either of the categories. These are the expenses which are partly fixed and partly variable. In a break-even analysis, these semi-fixed costs cannot be treated independently but have to be isolated into the usual categories of fixed and variable elements.

Irrespective of these shortcomings inherent in the usage of this technique, it is an important tool for the profitability analysis of the new project.

Conclusion

Break-even analysis helps the entrepreneur to work out costs, revenues and profits at alternative levels of output. It also helps in profit forecasting and planning. Break-even point also indicates the level of production which will generate surplus. It helps the small-scale enterprise to determine product mix and alternative sales volume to maximise his profits.

From the banker's point of view, the break-even analysis determines the safety margin, repayment capacity of the enterprise and also useful to examine certain important points before taking credit decisions.

However, the break-even analysis is only one aspect of technique to take decisions relating to cost, production, prices and sales, its help to the entrepreneur are manifold. One can also measure the effect of cost changes on break-even point.

ANNEXURE - 1

ASSESSMENT OF BREAK-EVEN LEVELS IN SSI UNITS — A CASE STUDY

The high incidence of sickness in the small-scale sector is due to the fact that the margin for error available in assessment of the viability of the small-scale units is the correct assessment of break-even sales levels. This was most strikingly brought out in the diagnostic investigation of a small-scale unit engaged in the manufacture of bottles.

Brief Outline of the Facts of the Case

The initial project feasibility study indicated that the unit would break-even at a sales level of Rs. 11.9 lakhs (the costs indicated in this article relate to 1976-77) corresponding to 43% capacity utilisation. Full capacity production was estimated to be 1,460 tonnes (4.5 tonnes per day for 325 days) and sales realisation at full capacity working for the unit's contemplated product-mix Rs. 26.34 lakhs. The working capital required to maintain continuity of production, i.e., finance for the lock-up of funds in stocks, stocks-in-process, finished goods and bills receivables during the normal conversion cycle was envisaged to be Rs. 3 lakhs. A market survey also indicated a sales level of Rs. 13 lakhs to be well within the unit's capabilities and resources. Encouraged by the favourable viability investigation, the unit secured finance from the appropriate institutions at the levels envisaged in the feasibility study and commenced its operations. But it soon ran into rough weather. To start with, the unit purchased 20,000 litres of furnace oil for Rs. 20,000 and its furnace ran for 10 days (7 days preheating and 3 days furnace running) before shutting down on account of fuel run out. The unit, however, managed to obtain another tanker of 20,000 litres on credit and fired the furnace for another 10 days going through the same cycle leading to a second fuel run out and furnace shut down. Thereafter, the unit managed to obtain on further credit another tanker of 10,000 litres. This time the fuel was not adequate even to complete the pre-heating and the furnace was finally shut down on account of fuel run out as all sources of credit were fully drawn. In a period spanning two months (taking into account the gaps between arrival of fuel tankers), 50,000 litres fuel worth Rs. 50,000 was burnt for an effective production of 9 tonnes (4.5 tonnes per day for 2 days). Obviously, this was taking the unit nowhere.

Diagnosis of the Problem

Since the initial working suggested that the main requirement of working capital was for the purchase of fuel to ensure continuity of furnace firing, the investigation commenced with an examination of the fuel consumption pattern. The analysis revealed:

(a) Furnace oil was a compulsory high cost fixed item of expenditure for the unit.

(b) From the process point of view, availability of furnace oil on continuous basis without any let up appeared to be of paramount importance as otherwise fuel run outs would occur leading to furnace shut down, and every time a shut down occured there was the accompanying loss by way of pre-heating costs and loss of production time.

The unit's fuel requirement as it emerged, from the above pattern of consumption was as under:

(a) Pre-heating

2,000 litres per day for 7 days, 14,000 litres with three shut downs in a year. The annual pre-heating costs = Rs. 0.42 lakhs.

(*b*) For Normal Running

It was held by the unit that for its continuous tank furnace to maintain the required temperature, the daily requirement of furnace oil was 2,000 litres irrespective of the level of operations. In other words, according to the unit furnace oil was a fixed cost. But in the project report submitted by the entrepreneurs and in the appraisal exercise fuel was taken as a variable cost as is normally the case. The possibility that fuel was working to be a fixed cost on account of faulty furnace design and construction was also there. The fact that the furnace was designed by the entrepreneurs themselves seemed to reinforce this conclusion. Whatever the reason, the fact was that this shift in fuel costs from the variable (as originally envisaged) to the fixed category (as it turned out to be) changed to entire complexion of the project. This is evident from the following table:

Summary of Relevant Project Parameters

		As originally envisaged			*Actual (as it turned out to be)*		
Sr. No.	*Description*	*Value (Rs. in lakhs)*		*% Capacity utilisation to which the costs cerrespond*		*Value (Rs. in lakhs)*	*% Capacity utilisation to which the costs correspond*
1.	Fixed Costs						
	Fuel (pre-heating)	0.42			0.42		
	Fuel (running)	Nil			6.50		
	Other fixed costs	1.93	2.35		2.23*	9.15	
2.	Variable Costs						
	Fuel (running)	6.50			Nil		
	Other variable costs	14.20	20.70	100	14.20	14.20	100
3.	Total costs		23.05			23.35	
4.	Break-even sales		11.19	43		19.89	76
5.	Sales level at which unit must operate by yield nominal surplus		13-17	50		21.07	80
6.	Surplus at this level		0.47			0.56	
7.	Total working capital required to sustain sales level as at (5)		3.00			4.73	
8.	Sales realisation at full capacity working for unit's contemplated product-mix		26.34				

* The other fixed costs in actual working turned out to be Rs. 0.30 lakh higher than envisaged.

CALCULATIONS

(i) Originally envisaged break-even levels

$$\text{Break-Even Sales (BES)} = \frac{\text{Fixed Cost (FC)}}{1 - \dfrac{\text{Variable Costs (VC)}}{\text{Sales Realisation (SR)}}}$$

$$= \frac{2.35}{1 - \dfrac{20.70}{26.34}}$$

$$= \text{Rs. } 11.19 \text{ lakhs}$$

$$\text{Break-Even Capacity (BEC)} = \frac{11.19}{26.34} = 43\% \text{ capacity utilisation}$$

(ii) Originally envisaged sales levels at which unit was expected to operate and yield reasonable surpluses

Required Annual Sales = Rs. 13.17 lakhs

(Corresponding to 50% capacity utilisation)

Cost at this sales level

Total variable costs	=	10.35
Total fixed costs	=	2.35
Total costs		Rs. 12.70 lakhs
Surplus at this sales level	=	13.17
Less	=	12.70
		Rs. 0.47 lakh

(iii) Actual break-even sales levels

$$\text{BES} = \frac{\text{FC}}{1 - \dfrac{\text{VC}}{\text{SR}}}$$

$$= \frac{9.15}{1 - \dfrac{14.20}{26.34}}$$

$$= \text{Rs. } 19.89 \text{ lakhs}$$

$$\text{BEC} = \frac{19.89}{26.34} = 76\% \text{ capacity utilisation}$$

(iv) Sales levels at which unit was actually required to operate on a sustained basis to yield nominal surplus (considering the scale of working)

Required annual sales = Rs. 21.07 lakhs

(Corresponding to 80% capacity utilisation) Costs at this sales level

VC	=	11.36
FC	=	– 9.15
Total cost		20.51

∴ Annual surplus	=	21.07
Less		20.51
		Rs. 0.56 lakh

It is clear from the above that consequent to the shift of fuel from the variable to fixed category, the break-even sales level shot up from Rs. 11.19 lakhs (43% capacity utilisation) to Rs. 19.89 lakhs (76% capacity utilisation). It was envisaged that operating at a sales level of Rs. 13.17 lakhs (50% capacity utilisation) with working capital of Rs. 3 lakhs, the unit would earn an annual surplus of Rs. 0.47 lakh. The actual working revealed that operating at a sales level of Rs. 21.07 lakhs (80% capacity utilisation) with a working capital of Rs. 4.73 lakhs the unit would earn a surplus of Rs. 0.56 lakh.

Conclusion

The changed classification of fuel, from variable to fixed cost, completely altered the viability picture. The higher break-even sales meant higher capacity utilisation (80%) to yield even nominal surplus, larger volume of products to be marketed and what was equally important was the higher working capital requirements. Also it is to be noted that even if the market could absorb the production at 80% capacity utilisation, it was doubtful whether under Indian conditions the unit could on a sustained basis operate at this high capacity.

In the instant case, the fault may be either in the faulty furnace construction and design or in the failure to see the linkages between the various production costs and their classification into fixed and variable costs. If the furnace construction is at fault, its redesign and reconstruction may entail a huge cost immediately after the implementation of the project from which the unit may find it difficult to recover. If the technology (furnace construction) is without fault, it would mean that the project was marginally viable even at the conceptual stage. In the later case, the erroneously worked out break-even sales levels and the consequent lower capacity utilisation envisaged would have pushed the entrepreneur into the venture.

The above analysis clearly brings out the importance of correctly identifying the process parameters since a wrong identification may completely alter the viability of the project. Accurate estimation of the break-even levels will help in deciding whether a given project is within the manufacturing and marketing capabilities of the unit. At the project formulation stage, the entrepreneurs must not only understand clearly the technological processes involved but also be able to correctly categorise the different production costs into variable and fixed costs.

✱ ✱ ✱

READING CONSUMER BEHAVIOUR

"Cultural and consumer behaviour for every market needs micro understanding, and that requires a lot of focus. Hence, whether it's an expatriate in Japan or in India, the issues are the same." – ***Fumio Oshima, Head, International Operations, Dentsu***

UNIT – VI
MANAGEMENT

14. **Production Management**
15. **Marketing Management**
16. **Human Resource Management**
17. **Financial Management**
18. **Labour Legislations for SSI**

Asking 'What is right for the enterprise?' does not guarantee that the right decision will be made. Even the most brilliant executive is human and thus prone to mistakes and prejudices. But failure to ask the question virtually guarantees the wrong decision."

Management Functions

There are six basic functions of managemerit, viz., Planning, Organising, Staffing, Directing, Controlling and Communication.

(1) Planning: Planning is the function which determines in advance what should be done. It consists of selecting the sectorwise objectives, policies, programmes, procedures, etc. It is, looking ahead and preparing for the future. It bridges the gap between the present and the future. Planning is the codification and quantification of strategy, and the research and development of specific projects, e.g., strategic acquisitions. It also signifies the use of a rational approach to the solution of the problem. The banking system has imbibed this system for its operations, so that they always strive to achieve their objectives and discharge their responsibilities towards the various segments of society.

(2) Organising: Organisation is the means to an end. Organising involves determination and enumeration of the activities required to achieve the objectives of the enterprise, grouping of activities, assignment of such groups of activities to a manager. It requires a formal structure of authority and the direction and flow of such authority through subdivisions. It is a process of coordinating the physical resources, human resources, and monetary resources. Organisation is one of the cornerstones of the banking system, primarily because banks deal with money (deposits, advances, investments) and human resources (staff, customers, government, entrepreneurs). A co-ordinated effort will enable banks to mobilise resources and canalise them, into productive activities.

(3) Staffing: Staffing involves manning and keeping manned the positions provided for by the organisation structure. In other words, it is the management of human resources in the organisation. It is a continuous function; staffing function involves selection, training, remuneration and appraisal. The staffing function is concerned with the provision of right persons at the right time in the right place and in the right number. Indian banking problems reflect on the lack of staffing and more importantly, inadequacy of quality staff.

(4) Directing: Directing involves leading, motivating, guiding people to perform activities in the most efficient way possible in order to achieve the desired goals. This can be undertaken through teaching, counselling and issuing orders. Directing is concerned with instructing, guiding, counselling appraisal. In banking, directing plays a key role, in its day-to-day functioning.

(5) Controlling: Controlling involves those, activities that are essential and undertaken to ensure that people do not deviate from the plans formulated earlier. The activities include establishment of standards for work performance, measuring performance and comparing it with the established standards and take corrective actions as and when and where needed to correct deviations identified. Banking management is multi-directional and hence needs foolproof and effective controlling at all levels. Controllling also serves the purpose of making efficient use of scarce and valuable resources, for the rapid development of the economy. It improves customer, services, reduces frauds and scams raises efficiency and enhances the image of the banking system. Furthermore, it improves profitability and productivity of the banks.

(6) Communication: Communication is the base of understanding that integrates the members of an organisation from top to bottom and bottom to top. This apart, bankers (officers, clerks) have to be in communication with the customers, government and other developmental as welll as. financial agencies.

Chart

THE FUNCTIONS OF MANAGEMENT

Planning

1. *Forecasting*
2. *Objectives*
3. *Strategies*
4. *Policies*
5. *Procedures*
6. *Programmes*
7. *Schedules*
8. *Budgets*
9. *Rules*
10. *Methods*
11. *Projects*

***Note:** From 2 to 11 are types of plans — either standing plans or non-recurring plans.*

Organising

1. *Grouping tasks to form individual jobs.*
2. *Grouping jobs into sections, departments and divisions.*
3. *Delegating authority and fixing number of management levels.*
4. *Establishing relationships*
5. *Providing organisational climate for best results.*
6. *Communication systems for decision making, co-ordination and control.*
7. *Innovative, responsive and adaptive overall organisation to meet environmental changes.*

Directing and Motivating

1. *Selection, promotion, coaching, counselling, tranining and appraisal of employees*
2. *Direction and Supervision*
3. *Remuneration and Compensation.*
4. *Participation.*
5. *Communication.*
6. *Co-ordination.*
7. *Appropriate leadership style.*
8. *Non-finacial incentives.*
9. *Management development.*

Controlling

1. *Performance standards.*
2. *Measurement of actual performance.*
3. *Comparison of actual with desired standards of output.*
4. *Corrective action.*

***Note:** 2nd, 3rd and 4th together are referred as feedback. Positive feedback aggravates error. Negative feedback reduces error, i.e., the difference between actual and standards.*

14

PRODUCTION MANAGEMENT

Introduction

Production is the basic activity of all industrial units. All other activities revolve around this activity. The end-product of the production activity is the creation of goods and services for the satisfaction of human needs. The production activity is nothing but the step-by-step conversion of one form of materials into another either chemically or mechanically. This is done in factories which house manufacturing processes. The basic inputs of the production processes are men, machines, plant, services and methods. The products of the mine, farm, sea and forest are used as raw materials on which the processing is done to create or enhance the form of utility It should be noted that the finished product of one manufacturing unit does not always furnish a ready-made product for the ultimate consumption. In a chain of manufacturing activities, the finished product of the processor sometimes becomes the raw material (or component) for the other manufacturing firms falling next in the sequence.

Production Management

When principles of management are applied in the specific area of business such as production, we have production management involving planning, organising, directing and controlling the production function or production system — a subsystem of the business enterprise which itself is the subsystem of its environment. Production management is the process of effectively planning, programming, coordinating and controlling production, i.e., the operations of that part of an enterprise which is responsible for the actual transformation of materials into finished products. It deals with man-machine organisation to accomplish both productivity and satisfaction — the desirable end results.

The Meaning

The meaning of the term **"production management"** is clarified in the following definitions:

"Production management is the process of planning, organizing, directing and controlling the activities of the production function. Production function is the conversion of raw-materials into finished products."

According to H.A. Harding, "Production management is concerned with those processes which convert the inputs into outputs. The inputs are various resources like raw materials, men, machines, methods, etc. and the outputs are goods and services."

According to M.J.S. Harry, the word **production** is often used to mean the same as manufacture. In order to go through a process of manufacturing itself, we need basically three things: someone to do the job, his equipment and the necessary materials. To run production, we require service activities which make sure that the manufacturing activity can go on and control to make sure that it goes in the right direction.

According to E.S. Buffa, "Production management deals with decision making related to production processes so that the resulting goods or service is produced according to specifications, in the amounts and by the schedule demanded and at minimum cost."

The definition given by E.S. Buffa is simple, clear and exhaustive. It explains the following important aspects of production management:

(a) It is a decision making managerial function;

(b) The decisions are made regarding the production processes required for converting the raw materials into finished products, and

(c) The production or output should be according to specifications, in the specified quantities, as per the schedule and at minimum cost.

Scope of Production Management

Major activities included under the production management are (1) Product planning and development, *i.e.,* evolution of new product and designing of those products on the basis of specific demand received from marketing or sales department. (2) Production administration which deals with three specialised parts of production activity, namely, *(a)* production engineering, *(b)* production planning and *(c)* production control. (3) Execution of plans, policies and decisions, *i.e.,* implementation function. Here we have actual operation of manufacturing or processing of inputs into outputs. Please note that implementation of decisions is a continuous managerial function involving direction and motivation of people at work to get things done through them. (4) Dependent services and departments, *i.e.,* standardization, simplification, specialisation, inspection and quality control, inventory control, research and development, diversification employee amenities, etc.

The major thrust areas of production management are:

(1) Selection of the technique of production

(2) Selection, utilisation and maintenance of machinery

(3) Workplace layout

(4) Working conditions

(5) Production, planning and scheduling

(6) Easy flow of materials

(7) Inventory/stock control

(8) Cutting and controlling the material cost

(9) Skilled workers

(10) Materials handling

(11) Quality control.

Inputs are the factors of production. While output is the final finished product. Every entrepreneur aims at maximum output with minimum inputs. The main inputs are described as "Nine Ms" in production.

"Nine Ms" in production:

(1) Money	Capital resources
(2) Machine	Plant and machinery, equipment
(3) Men	Human resources
(4) Material	Raw material
(5) Motive Power	Fuel and Energy
(6) Metres	Space or premises
(7) Method	Technique of production
(8) Minutes	Time scheduling
(9) Management	Effective, innovative management

The capacity of the inputs to produce an output is known as its productivity. Production management is a systematic, scientific, planned approach to obtain maximum productivity from the given inputs. Higher productivity can be obtained by either higher production with same quantity of inputs, same production with less quantity of inputs. In other words, productivity is aptly described as the "War against Waste."

The Objectives of Production Management

Production is an organized activity in a manufacturing organization. Each organized activity must spell out its objectives so that its existence can be justified on the basis of the degree of the attainment of these objectives. Moreover, such identification of the consciousness of the objectives increases the personnel working in the respective organizations.

The objectives of the production function are broadly classified into; (1)Ultimate objectives, and (2) Intermediate objectives.

Ultimate Objectives

The ultimate objectives of production management is to produce a product or products at:

(1) Pre-established costs,

(2) At specified quality and

(3) Within the stipulated time schedule.

Every efforts have to be made by the entrepreneurs to (1) reduce variable costs (2) reduce fixed costs (3) Increase the volume of production, and (4) allocate fixed overheads on scientific basis.

Intermediate Objectives

The intermediate objectives strive to attain the optimum utilisation of varied inputs:

(1) Machinery and eqnipment

(2) Materials

(3) Manpower

(4) Manufacturing services

In a condensed form, it can be stated that the objectives of the manufacturing activities are — to manufacture a quality product, on schedule, at the lowest possible costs, with maximum asset turnover, to achieve consumer satisfaction. This statement is closely related to the ultimate and intermediate objectives of the production function.

To summarise, production has to

(i) Make sure. that it develops a product which can function as expected, i.e., product with the correct *Quality,*

(ii) Produce the product in correct *Quantity,*

(iii) Deliver the product in *Time* to the right *Place,*

(iv) And to perform these functions at the right *Price.*

New Product Idea

Excluding the continual search for new ideas, the time and costs involved in the activities relating to product planning and development process, from experience in the U.S.A., is as follows:

	Stage	*Time*	*Money cost*	*Ideas reduced from original 60 to*
1.	Screening	3 p.c.	2 p.c.	12
2.	Business Research	12 p.c.	7 p.c.	7
3.	Development	40 p.c.	31 p.c.	3
4.	Testing	20 p.c.	15 p.c.	2
5.	Commercialisation	25 p.c.	45 p.c.	1 (One successful new product)

Note: 1. Development, testing and launching are the most expensive stages.

2. They take more than 50 per cent of total time involved in the process.

3. About sixty new ideas are needed to find one good idea worth for commercialisation. About 48 of the new ideas fail to pass the screening stage. Only 12 ideas are compatible with the corporate resources and goals. Of these 12, five ideas are eliminated for lack of profit potential. Out of 7 ideas having profitability, only 3 ideas survive the product development stage. Finally, two more fail during test marketing and only one new product becomes eligible for market introduction and officially enters its life cycle.

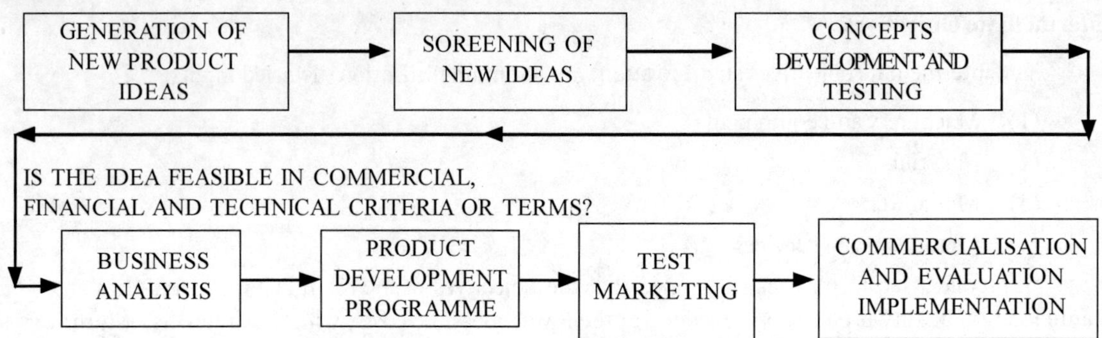

Fig. 14.1. New Product Development Process (Innovation Management)

Note:
1. Product life cycle requires the product development programme for new products and new profit opportunities.
2. New product development must be carefully planned and managed.
3. Special organisational wing is necessary to stimulate, collect, screen, evaluate, develop, test, and commercialise new product ideas.
4. Business analysis is the crucial stage. It concentrates on demand analysis, cost analysis and profitability analysis. It also considers social responsibilities of marketing the new product.

Product Planning and Development Process

There are seven steps in the planning and development of new product:

(1) New Product Ideas: We visualise the detailed features of a model product. Ideas may be contributed by scientists, professional designers, rivals, customers, sales force, top managment dealers, etc. We may need sixty new ideas to get one commercial viable product.

(2) Idea Screening : We have to evaluate all ideas and inventions. Poor or bad ideas are dropped and through the process of elimination, only the most promising and profitable ideas are picked up for further detailed investigation and research.

(3) Concept Development and Testing : All ideas that survive the process of screening (preliminary investigation) will be studied in detail. They will be developed into mature product concepts. We will have a precise description of the ideas and features of the proposed product. At this stage, we can incorporate consumer meaning into our product ideas. Concept testing helps the company to choose the best among the alternative product concepts. Consumers are called upon to offer their comments on the precise written description of the product concept, *viz.,* the attributes and expected benefits.

(4) Business Analysis: Once the best product concept is picked up, it will be subjected to rigorous scrutiny to evaluate its market potential, capital investment, rate of return on capital, etc. Business analysis is a combination of marketing research, cost-benefit analysis and assessment of competition. We have demand analysis, cost analysis and profitability analysis. Business analysis will prove the economic prospects of the new product concept. It will also prove the soundness and viability of the selected product concept from a business viewpoint. Now we can proceed to concentrate on product development programme. The proposed product must offer a realistic profit objective.

(5) Product Development Programme : We have three steps in this stage when a paper idea is duly converted into a physical product: *(a)* prototype development, giving a visual image of the product, *(b)* consumer testing of the model or prototype, and *(c)* branding, packaging and labelling. Consumer testing of the model product will provide the ground for the final selection of the most promising model for mass production and mass distribution.

(6) Test Marketing : The entire product marketing programme is tried out for the first time in a small number of well-selected test markets, i.e., test cities or areas. Test marketing is necessary to find out the viability of a full marketing programme for national distribution. Customer reactions can be tested under normal market conditions. It helps the company to learn through trial and error and to get additional valuable clues for product improvement and for modifications in our marketing mix. We can use test markets for testing the effectiveness of all ingredients of our marketing mix. Test marketing can answer such questions as: Is the new product labelled and packaged properly? Is the new product liked by the consumer? Is the firm justified in spending large sums on productive capacity? Has the communication (promotion) programme been right? Positive answers will reassure marketers.

(7) Commercialisation: Once the test marketing gives the green signal for the product with or without expected modifications, the company can proceed to finalise all features of the product. Now marketing management can launch a full-fledged advertising and promotion campaign for mass distribution. Mass production will start and all distribution channels will be only organised. The product is now born and will start its life cycle in due course.

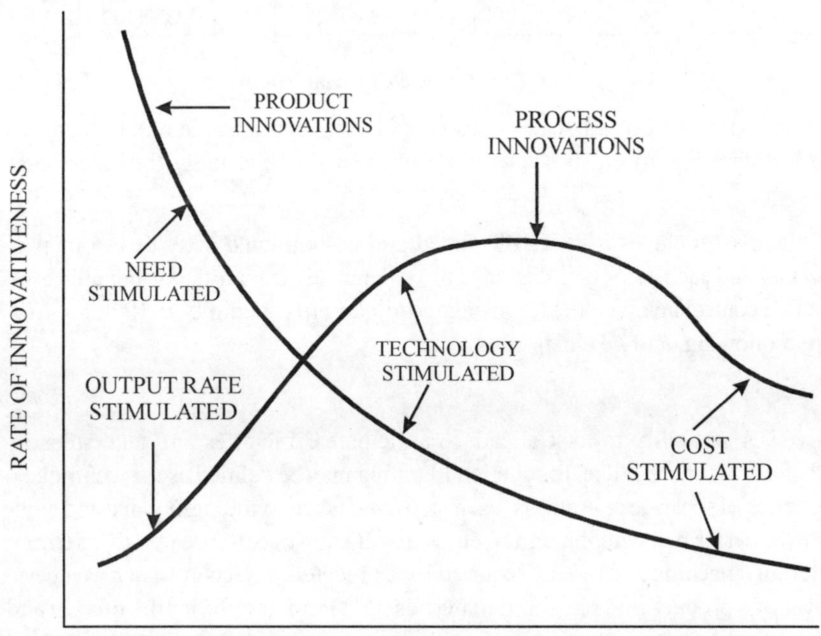

Fig. 14.2. Process Life Cycle Graph
(After Modern Production/Operations Management, Buffa, 1983)

No integration in process ———————— Full Integration in process

Maximisation of performance ———————— Minimisation of cost

In the third stage, the product reaches maturity. If there are innovations, they are all cost-based. The process of production becomes highly integrated. There are plants of large capacities and product-based operations. It helps achieve economies of scale.

Production management starts with sales forecasting, adjustment in production, control of production and motivating production. The channel of production follows the pattern of procurement, production control and scheduling, plant engineering, tool engineering, methods engineering, manufacturing and quality control, Fig. 14.3 indicates the channel of production in a small unit.

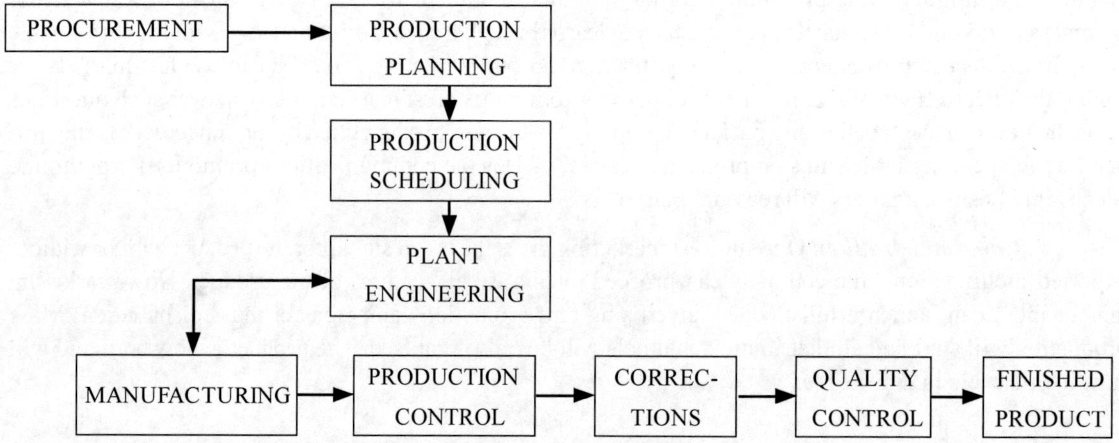

Fig. 14.3. Channels of Production

The production control in a small-scale industry is of a less complicated nature than in a large-scale unit in that the number of jobs at any one time is usually much smaller. Secondly, the processes are generally less complex.

Production planning includes a series of related and co-ordinated activities to be performed by a number of departments; and each activity is designed to systematise the manufacturing efforts in advance. In other words, production control involved the following techniques: *(i)* Planning, *(ii)* Routing, *(iii)* Scheduling, *(iv)* Dispatching, *(v)* Following, and *(vi)* Inspection.

***(i)* Planning**

Planning involves an ability to look ahead, to anticipate difficulties and take steps in advance to remove the causes before they materialise. Production Planning may be defined as the technique of foreseeing every step in a long series of separate operations, each step to be taken in the right place and at the right time, and each operation to be performed with maximum efficiency. It enables entrepreneur to determine in advance the manpower, materials, machine and money required for a predetermined output in given period of time. It calls for a breakdown of a product into parts and materials, and for determining the quality and quantity of products to be manufactured.

Objectives of Production Planning: The principal objectives of production planning are: (1) To determine the quantity of an item to be produced on the basis of the sales forecast; (2) To determine the quality of the product on the basis of a study of the products of the competitors (if any) or the needs of the market; (3) To determine the quantity and quality of men, materials and machines required to produce the product in the most economical manner; (4) To determine the time schedule and plan accordingly; (5) To make all the necessary preparations for the manufacture of the product as per the production budget; (6) To operate machinery and men at the pre-determined level of efficiency; (7) To utilise plant facilities to the maximum; (8) To aim at a determined level of profit; and (9) To ensure higher wages, bonus as other welfare facilities to employees.

(ii) Routing

Is the selection of the path or the route over which each piece is to travel while being transformed from raw material into a finished product. William Spriegel says: "Routing includes the planning of where and by whom work shall be done, the determinary sequence of operations; it performs a groundwork for most of the scheduling and despatching functions of a planning department." It establishes the operations, their path and sequence and the proper class of machines and personnel required for these operations. The object of routing to determine the best and the cheapest sequence of operations and to ensure that this sequence is strictly followed. Efficient routing is one which permits the best utilisation of physical and human resources employed in the manufacture of a product. In a small-scale industry, this is done by the entrepreneur himself, in a rather *ad hoc* manner. In fact, routing requires great ability and experience.

The Routing procedure consists of seven distinctive activities:

(a) An analysis of the article to determine what to make and what to purchase;

(b) To determine what materials are needed;

(c) A determination of the manufacturing operations and their sequence;

(d) A determination of the sizes;

(e) Determination of scrap factors;

(f) An analysis of the cost of an article;

(g) Organisation of production control forms.

(iii) Scheduling

Scheduling involves determining the order of priority, releasing the work to the plant at the proper time and in the correct sequence. Scheduling is the determination of the time that should be required to perform each operation and also the time necessary to perform the entire series as routed, making allowance, for all factors concerned. According to Alford and Beatty, scheduling is "fitting specific job into a general time table, so that orders may be manufactured in accordance with contracted liability, or in mass production, so that each component may arrive at and other into the assembly in order and at the time required." Scheduling is primarily concerned with the time element and priorities of a job. This becomes more important in these cases where several parts of components, with varying sizes, are to be produced for final assembly into a finished product. The pattern of scheduling varies from one job to another. it ensures increased production and a higher margin of profit. Different trends of scheduling are now briefly enumerated.

(a) Production Schedule: The aim in scheduling production is to schedule as great a volume of work as the plant and equipment can conveniently handle without interference. This depends upon the following facilities;

(1) Physical plant facilities of the type required to process the material being scheduled;

(2) Personnel who passes the desired skills and experience to operate the equipment and perform the type of work involved; and

(3) Necessary materials and purchased parts.

(b) Master Schedule: Scheduling usually starts with the preparation of a master schedule, which is simply a weekly or monthly breakdown of the production requirement for each product for a definite period of time. This provides not only a convenient means of keeping a running total of production requirements but also enables an entrepreneur to plan in advance for any shift from one product to another or for a possible overall increase or decrease in production requirements. Thus, it provides information which becomes the basis of all subsequent scheduling activities. A master schedule is followed by an operation schedule which fixes the total time required to do a piece of work with a given machine or which shows the time required to do each detailed operation of a given job with a given machine or process.

(c) Manufacturing Schedule: Next, depending upon the type of manufacturing process involved a manufacture schedule is prepared. It is primarily useful when a single product or a relatively few products are manufactured continuously or repeated at regular intervals. This shows the quantity that is required of each and the sequence in which each is desired.

(d) Scheduling of Job Order Manufacturing: Scheduling acquires greater importance in job-order manufacturing. This will enable the speedy execution of job at each focal point.

Scheduling plays an important role in a small-scale industry. This would certainly improve its working and reduce the cost price. In order to provide for a continuous scrutiny of all stages the small entrepreneur should maintain an enquiry schedule, a production schedule, a shop schedule, and an arrears schedule.

An enquiry schedule ensures a continuous scrutiny of all the stages of production, prior to its receipts by a firm. The production schedule records the progress of a manufacturing order through all the main stages until the delivery of goods by the factory. A shop schedule is maintained to provide the foreman with a list of jobs to be done by the shop in any period. This schedule is particularly suited to the small-scale industry because it enables the foreman to see at a glance.

(1) The total load on any section,

(2) The operational sequence, and

(3) The stage which any job has reached.

The jobs which are in arrears will usually become priorities in the succeeding shop schedule, provided that the work can proceed.

Progress Record: To ensure a scrutiny of the movement of work from one operation to another on a continuing basis, a progress record/chart is maintained. This record has to be utilised in conjunction with the production schedule and the shop schedule, for it provides detailed information which the production schedule does not give after the job has been entrusted to the shop and upto its completion.

***(iv)* Despatching**

The next logical step is the execution of the schedule plan as per the route chalked out. Despatching "consists essentially of the issue of orders in terms of their priority as determined by scheduling." It includes the assignment of work to the operators at their machines or work places. Thus, despatching in effect determines who will do the work, as routing determines where and scheduling determines when it shall be done. The production control, inspection and monitoring activities form an integral part of the despatching function.

Machine Loading: In most of the small industries Gantt charts are used as a planning technique to ascertain the existing load and to predict how soon a job can be completed. 'The greatest utility of these charts is that they compare what has been done and what ought to have been done. In these charts space is indicated to represent the amount of time and work to be done. Lines drawn horizontally through that space, as the work progresses, show the relation of work actually done in that period to the work scheduled. The chart is, therefore, an excellent diagnostic instrument for the supervisor.

In a small manufacturing plant, planning operations will probably first to be under the direction of the owner or manager. As the business grows, certain aspects will be handed over to someone else, either as a full-time or part-time job. Basically the sequence of planning will involve the following items in somewhat this order:

(i) Long-range planning for future production which includes product change, redesign or incorporation of substantial changes on a quantity scale.

(ii) Assignment of production facilities and such as plant, equipment and manpower with adequate training.

(iii) The purchase of equipment, materials and support facilities necessary to do the job.

(iv) The planning of production in such a way, that the maximum use is obtained from machines, manpower and facilities.

(v) Constant adjustment, reassignment and rescheduling based on the conditions that develop.

(vi) The constant improvement of jobs and processes including application of better methods, production knowledge and improvement of skills and machine operations.

Objectives of Production Planning

The main objectives of production planning are as follows:

(i) Production planning department studies the market demand for the products it manufactures. It takes into account sales forecast, programme for promotion of sales, expected orders, etc., and it plans production accordingly.

The production of overall quantity of product should be effected keeping in mind the potential market for the product.

(ii) A business enterprise conducts business with the aim of earning profits. In modern competitive business world, profit-making aspect of an enterprise is very important, if the enterprise intends to survive. Production planning department determines what is to be manufactured in what quantity and when keeping in mind the profit earning nature of the proposition. An enterprise earning good profits attracts capital for safe investment and labour by providing it with job security.

(iii) Production planning departments sees that the manufacturing unit is working at its optimum capacity of production. Optimum capacity refers to the rate of production achieved by best utilisation of men, equipment, space combined and by incurring the lowest cost of per unit product.

(iv) The production planning department does a good manpower planning. Jobs are created as per the pre-determined planning. No hiring and fixing of labour is resorted to position and it must see that there is no dissatisfaction among the employees.

(v) Optimum capacity of the plants in the manufacturing unit must be utilised for obtaining a fair margin of profit and reducing the cost of production. This matter is very important, because whether the plants are operating or not, certain fixed charges, like rent etc., and maintenance costs on the plants go on incurring for the management to bear. Hence, all plants must be kept busy.

Importance of Production Planning

The success of a small-scale industry often depends upon its ability to adhere to delivery schedule which *inter-alia* depends on production of quality goods in right time. In maintaining the production schedule at economic cost depends on production planning. Production planning, the entrepreneur should have to judge ahead of time what should. be done, how it should be done, where and when; and thus to leave nothing to chance once the work has begun. The small entrepreneur thus necessarily has to look into the following aspects of production programme carefully: Planning the use of manpower, materials (buildings and machines) and raw materials and supplies.

Production planning is an activity related to making available to the market a particular product in required quantity within given period of time. To achieve this goal, it organises in advance such aspect as men, materials, machines and money. Production planning starts with manufacturing and selling the product, in a competitive market. All these activities are done in cooperation between production and control department. Production department initiates the process of production by deciding: *(a)* What type of product is to be manufactured, *(b)* What materials are to be purchased, and *(c)* What facilities should be made available so that the product can be manufactured within the scheduled time.

Production planning is also concerned with personnel division, since to manufacture the required product, it is necessary to employ qualified and experienced people according to the skill and competence required in the performance of jobs. Production planning department, also handles getting materials, locates their supplies from outside sources and fixes time schedules and other aspects related to production. To perform these functions, it takes help of inventory control, purchasing and cost-departments.

Characteristics of Intermittent and Continuous Manufacturing

Intermittent and continuous manufacturing are the mutually exclusive activities. The following comparison will clarify their true nature of operations:

Particulars	*Intermittent Manufacturing*	*Continuous Manufacturing*
(1) Type of plant layout	Process layout is most suited	Product layout designed according to a separate line for each product is considered.
(2) Type of machines	As it necessitates frequent changes in the machine-setup required by the specifications of each order, the general purpose machines are more suitable.	As the production flow is permanently set in the form of product line, the special purpose machines are used.

(3) Types of labour	This type of production presupposes frequent changes in product design and machine set-up and thus, requires highly skilled workers.	The manufacturing activity becomes a routine function and so is carried on by the unskilled workers. The specialized team of plant maintenance looks after the repair and maintenance of the machines.
(4) No. of products and product designs	Wide range of products are manufactured in small quantities. The product design changes from lot to lot according to the product specifications.	Few standard products are manufactured in large quantities. Usually the product line is geared to only two or three products of standard design.
(5) Changes in the machines set up	As the specifications of each order changes, the machines are set according to the requirements of each order. Thus, frequent changes in the machines set up is a common phenomenon.	Under this type of manufacturing, the set up of the machines remains unchanged for a longer period. The standard products are manufactured in a continuous flow.
(6) Nature and size of the order	Generally the repeated small size of orders are received for unstandardized products. The order may involve the production of a single product of identical products in limited lot. Usually the production is carried on according to order. First the orders are received and then they are translated into actual production.	Generally the production is carried on for stock. The production is made of standardized products and so they are produced in anticipation of demand. Like intermittent production, there does not arise any problem about non-repeat orders or orders for unstandardized products.
(7) Investments in machines and equipment	As the machines are arranged according to process layout, less machines are required.	The machines are arranged according to the product layout. So it results in duplication of machines. Moreover, it is essential to maintain stand-by equipment to meet any breakdowns resulting in production stoppages. Thus, investments in machines are fairly high.

(8) Investment in inventories	It necessitates the reservoir of processed inventories and components in sub-stores. Moreover waiting and bottle-necks slow down the operating cycle. As a result, the investment in inventories increase.	Due to continuous flow of production, the need for the sub-storing of processed inventories is reduced to the minimum. Similarly the operating cycle is very fast reducing the necessity for the locking up of the in-process inventories.
(9) Material handling equipment	As the in-process materials are required to travel on varied routes, it is not feasible to employ mechanized material handling equipment.	Due to the movement of in-process materials between fixed points, it is possible to use mechanized material handling equipment. Mostly the materials are handled through conveyor belts, roller conveyors, pipelines overhead cranes etc. Under the automation, the materials are automatically handled from one machine to the next one.
(10) Material handling cost	The material handling cost tend to be high due to long-distance backtracking, movements of non-standard lots and lack of mechanization of material handling services.	The materials handling cost is less due to line balancing forward movement of materials and use of mechanized material handling equipment.
(11) Plant maintenance services	It is desirable to have the plaut maintenance services for repairs maintenance and replacements. However, like continuous production, there is no danger of the stoppage of whole line.	It is highly essential to have a sound plant maintenance services with a view to avoid any interruptions in the production flow.
(12) Balancing in the production capacity	The existence of imbalance in the production departments is likely to exist in such production resulting in the underloading or overloading of work on man and machines.	It is possible to ensure the perfect balance in the production line. The chance of overloading or underloading on men and machines are very little.
(13) The production planning and control	The function of routing, scheduling, dispatching and follow-up become relatively complicated to odd size of the order, non-repetitive nature of the order and awkward delivery dates resulting in imbalancing in the production capacity.	The routing, scheduling. despatching and follow-up functions are carried on smoothly due to the standard production underrated capacity carried on in anticipation of demand.

Regulation of the Production Process

Production management is related to a unique function where raw materials are converted into finished goods efficiently and economically. Efficiency in production is measured by the quantity and the quality of goods produced and economy in production is measured by the minimum cost at which the goods are produced.

The entire process of production has to be regulated, monitored and controlled. Control is, therefore, one of the important functions of production management. In fact, it is the other side of production planning. The managerial function of production control consists of a comparison of the actual production with production plan. Production control is an essential feature of all production/manufacturing activities. Effective control of men, materials, machines, and money is essential for the successful running of a small industry. Control is necessary to ascertain the deviations, adjusting to the changing environment channellising into the desired directions and guide the development of a small industry towards chosen goals/objectives. The important types of control in a small industry are: (1) Administrative control, (2) Financial control, (3) Production control, (4) Quality control, and (5) Quantity control. The types of control can better be understood with the help of the following diagram:

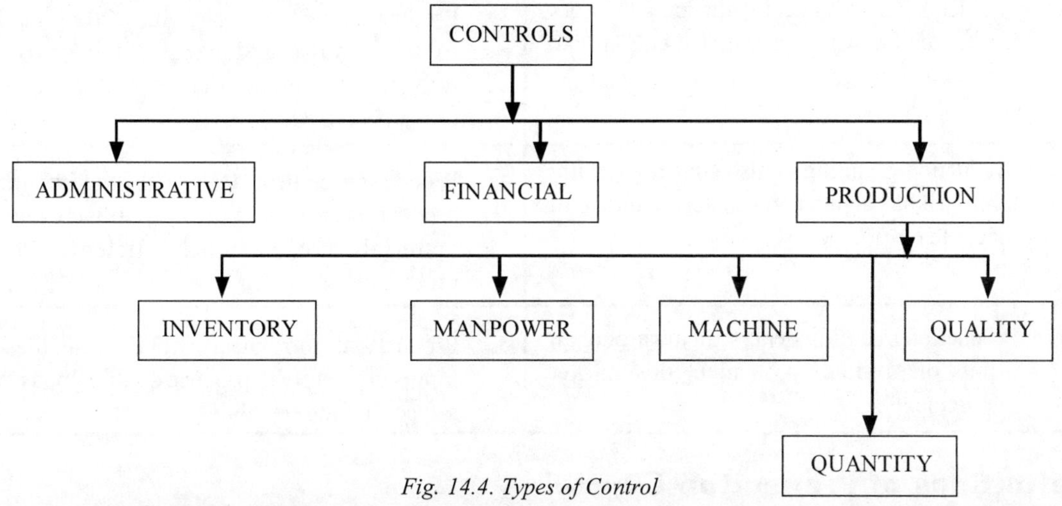

Fig. 14.4. Types of Control

Control is a management technique which aims to see that the activities are carried on in line with the predetermined standards. In case of production activities, production control tries to see that the actual manufacturing conforms to the predetermined standards and schedules of productions. Production control is considered to have a wider scope and thus, it includes production planning. In practice, a joint reference is made of production planning and control and it is popularly known as PPC.

Production Control

Production planning without production control is like a chariot without a character or a bank without a manager. Planning initiates action, while control in an adjusting process, providing corrective measure for planned development. Production control regulates and stimulates the orderly flow of materials in the manufacturing process from the beginning to the end.

In production control, all the operations are measured and evaluated from one stage to another and, if necessary, adjustments are made to maintain product quality and smooth flow of production. Production control coordinates the functioning of engineering, purchasing, production, selling and inventory management.

Production is an organised activity of converting raw materials into useful products and production control is the control of these organised activities. Production control in small-scale industry plays a key role in organising the most effective use of manpower, materials and machines.

Difference between production planning and production control:

Production Planning	*Production Control*
1. Production planning refers to the function which precedes physical action.	1. Production control refers to the feedback of information and the correction of the action.
2. Production planning takes place before the operation.	2. Production control takes place during the process of production.
3. Production planning deals with doing the work in accordance with the established plans to accomplish the goals.	3. Production control deals with feeding back to the planning department essential information in order to have correction made or plans revised.
4. Production planning is also concerned with, taking right people, right material and right machine for production.	4. Production control deals with maximising production at economic cost by utilising men, materials and machines efficiently and productively.
5. Production planning deals with arranging all inputs of production to meet the market requirements.	5. Production control deals with utilising these inputs efficiently to produce quality goods in a specific time schedule.

Definitions of Production Control

The production control in the small-scale industry is of a less complicated nature than other industries. However, the process is the same. According to Spriegel and Lansburg, "Production control is the process of planning production in advance of operations; establishing the exact route of each individual item or part and releasing the necessary orders as well as initiating the required follow-up to effect the smooth functioning of the enterprise."

Charles A. Korpke has defined production planning and control as, "the coordination of a series of functions according to a plan which will economically utilise the plant facilities and regulate the orderly movement or goods through their entire manufacturing cycle from the procurement of all materials to the shifting of finished goods at a predetermined schedule."

Kimball and Kimball observe that the fundamental object of production control is "that the product shall be produced by the best and the cheapest method, that it shall be of the required quality, and that it shall be produced at the right time." William R. Sprigel, in his *Industrial Management,* defines production control as "the process of planning production in advance of operations; establishing the exact route of each individual item, part or assembly; setting, starting and finishing date for each important item, assembly or the finishing products; and releasing the necessary orders as well as initiating the required follow-up to effectuate the smooth function of the enterprise." Production planning consists of breaking down a product into parts and materials, determining the quantity of products to be made and the materials to be purchased; determining physical facilities — buildings, machines, equipment tooling, layout and working conditions — required for planned manufacturing activities; determining qualitative and quantitative human resources, production material, labour and equipment; and budgeting and coordinating all these related activities. The Production Planning and Control Department can function at its best in a small-scale unit only when the Works Manager, the Purchase Manager, the Personnel Manager and the Financial Controller or Cost Accountant assist it in planning production activities.

According to Spriegel and Lansburgh, "Production control is the process of planning production in advance of operations; establishing the exact route of each individual item, part or assembly; setting, starting and finishing dates for each important item, assembly and the finished products; and releasing the necessary orders as well as initiating the required follow-up to effect the smooth functioning of the enterprise."

Thus production control involves the following stages:

(i) Planning setting targets of production.

(ii) Routing to decide the route or flow of production activity.

(iii) Dispatching — to issue materials and authorizations for the use of machines and plant services.

(iv) Follow-up — it compares the actual production with the targeted production. Deviations are found out and corrected and reasons are investigated.

Production Control Cycle

The production control cycle consists of operation, measurement of action in terms of quantity and quality of products, evolution of the operation in concurrence with production plans and adjusting the course of action, so that goods are produced as required. It is a continuous process. The production control cycle can be better explained with the help of the following diagram.

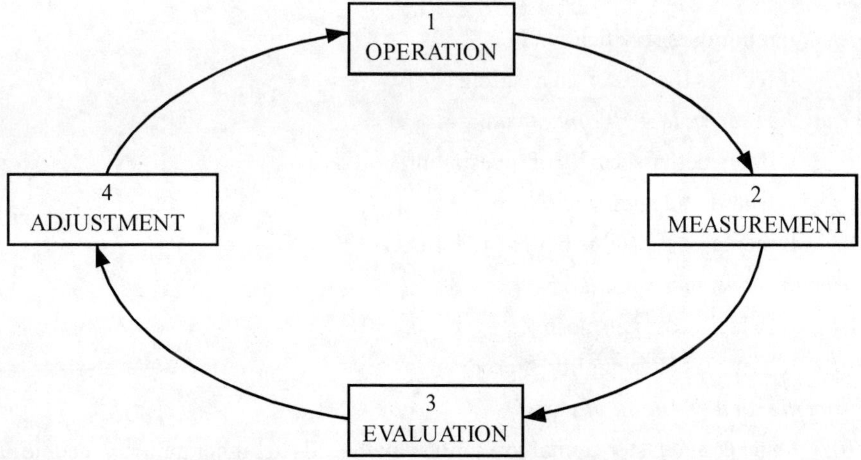

Fig. 14.5 : The Production Control Cycle

Objectives of Production Control

The aim of production control is to produce the right product, in the right quantity, at the right time, and by the best and least costly methods. In the words of James Lundy, "A successful production control programme minimises the idleness of men and machines, optimises the number of set-ups required, keeps in process inventories at a satisfactory level, reduces material handling and storage costs and consequently, permits quantity and quality production at low unit cost." In other words, good production means — less work-in-progress, decreased stock inventories, and more rapid turnover which in turn results in less capital tied up in idle material and greater earnings on the money invested. It enables on the one side production quality products at economic cost and on the other side maximises profits and improves productivity.

The objectives of production control are:

(i) To facilitate and co-ordinate activities;

(ii) To regulate the production of the desired quality product in right time;

(iii) To reduce the cost of production by an optimum combination of resources ;

(iv) To speed up turnover and improve productivity.

Advantages of Production Control

The advantages of production control can be viewed from various point of view such as *(a)* factory's point of view; *(b)* shareholder's point of view; *(c)* employee's point of view; and *(d)* society's point of view.

(a) Advantages from factory's point of view: Advantages of production control from the factory's point of view can be classified under the following captions:

(1) Production control:

(i) It increases the pace of production.

(ii) It reduces production cost.

(2) Quality control:

(i) It minimises waste, scraps, and rework.

(ii) It minimises rectification hours.

(iii) It reduces the cost of inspection.

(a) *From the shareholder's point of view:*

(i) It offers better security of investment.

(ii) It leads to adequacy of returns.

(iii) It increases the value of their holdings.

(b) *From the consumer's point of:*

(i) It reduces cost per piece.

(ii) It ensures better quality of products.

(c) *From the society's point of view:*

(i) Quicker and faster capital formation which leads to higher national income and per capita income which decides the standard of living of the people.

(ii) Better and efficient application of production control technique enables government to earn more revenue in the form of taxes on account of higher earnings.

(iii) National repute and self-dependence is boosted.

(iv) The nation progresses towards prosperity and progress.

(v) Security of the nation is achieved.

(3) Manufacturing cost:

(a) *(i)* It reduces maintenance cost.

(ii) It reduces raw material wastage.

(iii) It reduces material handling cost.

(iv) It exercises better control over manufacturing cost.

(b) *Advantages to management:*

(i) It helps in better planning of production.

(ii) Through feedback an effective control system can be installed in different spheres of activities.

(iii) It reduces conflicts with the trade union and management, and thus eliminates strikes and lockouts.

(iv) The management can efficiently and effectively instal the new techniques of production and automation if necessary.

(v) It helps in easing the burden of the supervisor.

(c) *Advantages to capital investment:*

(i) It helps in management of working capital, earnings and dividends.

(ii) It helps in reduced investment in machines and equipment by *(i)* Increased production per machine; and *(ii)* Utilising idle hours of machines.

(d) *Advantages to marketing management:*

(i) It increases the goodwill and reputation of the factory by *(i)* maintaining excellent quality of the product, and *(ii)* satisfying the customers by prompt delivery of the goods.

(ii) It helps introducing new products in the market.

(iii) It realises cost of advertising.

(iv) It reduces market research cost.

(e) *From the worker's point of view:*

(i) It reduces the efforts of workers.

(ii) It reduces the fatigue of workers.

(iii) It leads to specialisation.

(iv) It leads to efficient operations of workers.

(v) It leads to team spirit.

(vi) It reduces the number of accidents.

(vii) It leads to higher earnings.

(viii) It offers better working conditions.

(ix) It ensures job security.

Organisation of Production Control

Production control is a line function. The production controller directly reports to the works manager. The production control department has three sections:

(i) Material control

(ii) Planning; and

(iii) Control

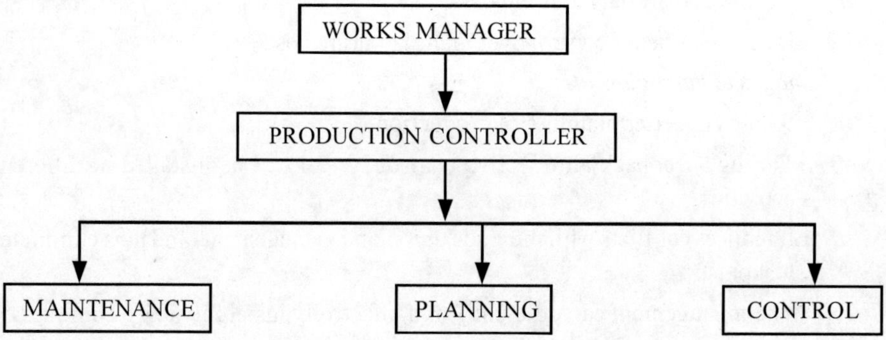

WORKS MANAGER → PRODUCTION CONTROLLER → MAINTENANCE | PLANNING | CONTROL

Fig. 14.6: Production Control Organisation

In a small-scale unit, all the three functions are often performed by the entrepreneur or works manager or foreman.

Functions of Production Control

The chief objective of production control is to co-ordinate and regulate all the production activities. The following are the important functions of production control — to achieve higher productivity, reduce the cost of production and improve the quality of goods in a specified period of time.

(i) To prepare production plan on the basis of sales forecastor demand forecast;

(ii) To prepare an inventory and arrange for production;

(iii) To procure resources and materials;

(iv) To organise inventory management;

(v) To prepare production programmes;

(vi) To assign work to workers and machines;

(vii) To motivate workers;

(viii) To regulate, control and direct the materials and men;

(ix) To receive reports of work done and evaluate performance;

(x) To adopt corrective measures;

(xi) To store the finished goods;

(xii) To re-plan, if need be and avoid breakdowns and ensure that workers do not resort to go-slow tactics.

(a) The procurement of necessary tools, dies, fixtures before they are actually required by the workers;

(b) The issue of the necessary work orders, diagrams, instructions to workers to initiate the job;

(c) Maintaining a record of the time of starting and completing each operation;

(d) Moving the work from one process to the next as per the route already determined; and

(e) Co-ordinating the plan of routing and scheduling.

Follow-up

Every production programme is to be preceded by a follow-up for the maintenance of a proper record of the work and expediting it by removing bottlenecks at appropriate times. "Follow-up, or expediting, is that branch of production control procedure which regulates the progress of materials and parts through the production process. Although it is the agency charged with the responsibility for the production orders after they are despatched, it is nevertheless closely interrelated with despatching." A follow-up serves as a catalytic agent to fuse the various separate and unrelated production activities into a unified whole. It primarily concerns itself with the reporting of production date and the investigation of variances from the predetermined time-schedules. As such, a follow-up action ensures that promise is backed by performance. This follows up action broadly covers (1) Materials ; (2) Work in process ; (3) Assembly and,erection ; (4) Production delays; (5) Excessive rejections; and (6) Errors in routing, scheduling and despatching,

Inspection

Inspection forms an important item in production control. This is introduced mainly to ensure the quality of goods. It can be regarded as an effective agency of production control.

Requirements of Production Control

The following are the requirements of a good production control system:

(1) Complete detailed drawings and other engineering information.

(2) Complete information regarding special tools, such as jigs and fixtures whether available or are to be provided.

(3) Complete information on time and cost of previous performances.

(4) Accurate uptodate information regarding the stores and finished stocks that are to be used.

(5) Exact knowledge of the progress of the work-in-process.

(6) Complete tabulated data on power, speeds and feeds of all machines.

(7) Records of the best performance on similar work with the. best combination of tools, feeds and speeds.

(8) Careful instructions to the workman by the speed boss or some similar person.

(9) Careful following up and correction of the department schedule.

(10) Careful inspection of all tools and appliances to make sure that they are up to the standard conditions.

(11) A financial incentive that will enlist the interest of the workman.

Recent Trends in Production Control

The following trends towards measures to increase production control are becoming evident:

(1) Manufacturing performance is improved by integrating controls at all levels of manufacturing endeavour from raw material inputs to the finished product output.

(2) A more responsible, accurate and flexible control is found in the use of mechanical office equipment. Examination of practices to shorten the clerical communication routines is also being initiated.

(3) Computers are frequently being used to solve the more complex manufacturing processes. Data generating and quick analytical abilities of the computers are being used to achieve efficient production control.

Inventory Control

Inventory control deals with the control over raw materials, work-in-progress, finished products, stores supplies, tools etc. The management of these items is closely related with the production function and so is included in production management.

The raw materials, supplies etc., should be purchased at right time, of right quality, in right quantity, from right source and at right price. Thes five 'R' consideration enables the scientific purchases.

Quality Control

The long-run success of the business largely depends on its amity standards as decided by the management and accepted bv ability to maintain customers. The quality standards arc prescribed in terms of specifications like size, colour, shape, tastes etc. The quality control is maintained by testing the actual production and by ascertaining whether they conform to the set standards. The raw materials, work-in-progress, finished products etc. are inspected at various stages of production. There may be 100% quality control where each unit produced is inspected or there may be a policy of testing the samples where the entire lot produced is either passed or rejected on the basis of the tested samples. Various statistical techniques are used for the effective quality control.

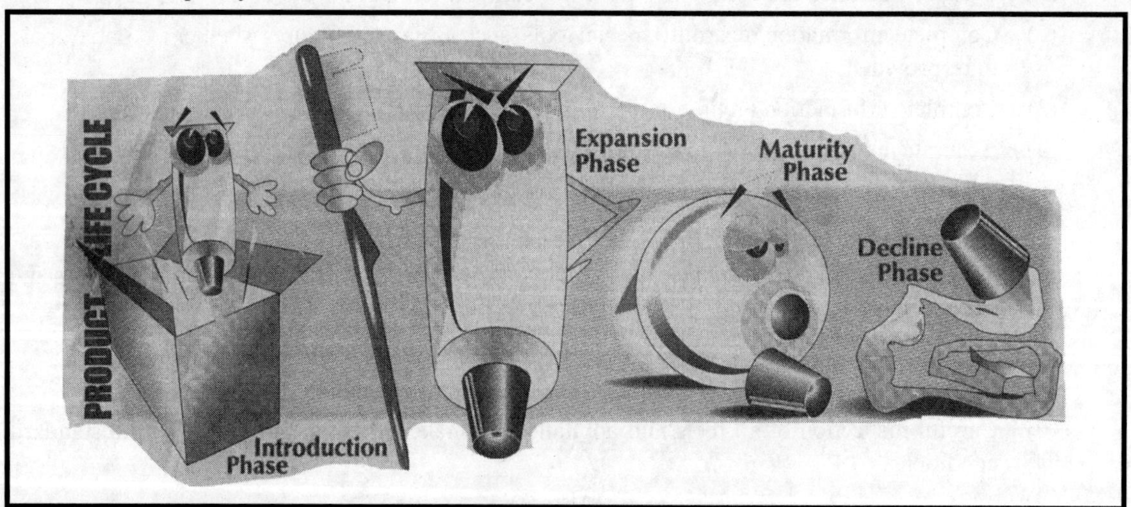

As a company moves to the expansion phase, the mandate is to increase volumes and expand the distribution network. During this phase, targets are established and actual performance is measured against the targets. In other words, we operate in an environment of operations and control. The managerial skill required in this phase is Quality Control. The accent is on conforming to specifications, delivering the product by the contracted time and keeping costs under check. Any deviation from the target is seen as non-conformance and needs to be corrected. Management through ISO 9000 Quality Systems is sufficient. With auto-crashing product life cycles, this phase should get reduced, operationally, it is adequate to have reactive managerial skills.

In the third phase, which is called the maturity phase of the life cycle, the accent is on retaining market shares. Within a product class, competition is rampant and customers seldom perceive differences between one brand and another. Nevertheless, market shares differ, based on the competitive advantage of prior franchise. And selling prices are established on the principles of demand and supply. So how does one retain one's customers without adding costs? How does one differentiate when the customer maps our products as having similar features as other brands? Simple. The managerial skills that comes to the forefront here is.that of Quality Improvement. Improve products incrementally and continuously at a rate faster than the competition. Apart from reducing chronic wastes in processes, improve what is important to the customers. Eliminate customer dissatisfaction and save costs associated with waste, warranty and cycle time. The objective of

THE DEMING CYCLE

Act
- Appraise, award, and appreciate
- Change process (Then go to 1)

Plan Approach
- Perspective
- Data to get
- Experiments to run

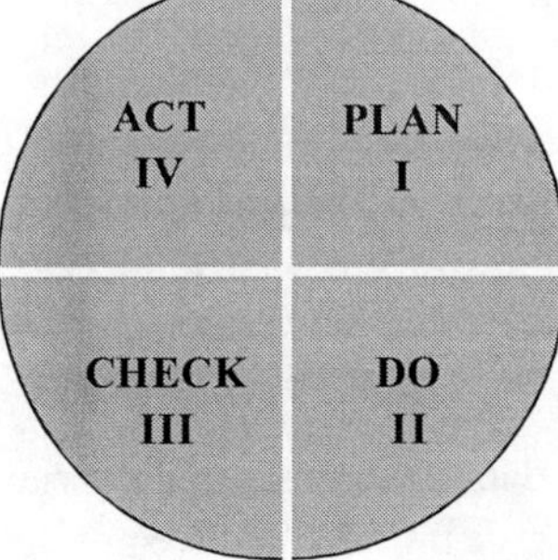

Check Results
- Analyse data
- Evaluate experiment
- Coaching and counselling

Do The Plan
- Gather data
- Run experiment
- Demonstrating
- Deploying

The Masters
The American Gurus
The Plan-Do-Check-Act-Cycle
Quality through constancy of purpose,
No Inspection,
Continuous Improvement,
Barrierless communication,
Pride of workmanship,
Constant training.
W. EDWARDS DEMING

"Many firms undertake to create quality. Few have actually reached quality leadership."
JOSEPH M. JURAN
Quality Guru

"My agenda would be quality leadership in government, business, and education."
PHILIP B. CROSBY
Quality Guru

competition is to nullify your strengths. Be pro-active in improving strengths because changing strengths is inevitable. If strengths are improved as a reaction to competition, a company will have lost its leadership. Hence, to retain leadership, continuously improvement of strengths is required.

Productivity and Production

The concept of productivity and that of production are totally different. Production refers to the absolute output, while productivity is a relative term wherein output is always expressed in terms of input. The production may rise without the corresponding rise in the productivity and vice versa. If inputs remain the same and the production of output increases, there is a rise in the level of productivity. If the output rises in greater proportion than the increase in the input, there is still a proportionate rise in the level of the productivity. But if the output rises at a slower rate than the input, there will be a fall in the productivity even though there is an increase in production on the whole.

Productivity, thus, refers to efficient utilization of resources. The improvement in the level of productivity refers to the efficient utilization of various types of inputs contributing to the output.

Importance of Productivity

The productivity consciousness has increased in all types of activities because it avails the following advantages:

(1) It emphasises the efficient utilization of all the factors of production scarce universally. It attempts to eliminate the wastage of every kind.

(2) It facilitates the comparison of the performance of the firm with that of its competitors or related firms, both in terms of aggregate results and in terms of major components of performance.

(3) It enables the management to control the performance of the firm by identifying the comparative benefits raising out of the use of different inputs, or varying proportions of the same inputs currently and over longer periods, as the basis for considering alternative adjustments over future periods.

(4) It also provides a reliable data for certain managerial decisions such as collective bargaining regarding wages with the trade union, effective presentation before the Government against the imposition of prospective restrictions etc.

(5) At national level also the concept of productivity is useful as under:

The statistical data about the productivity assist, the Government in framing certain economic policies regarding business community, trade unions, employment, hours of work, wages, price control, protection to industries, technological developments, taxation and fiscal policies, allocation of scarce natural resources, extension of labour welfare and social extension schemes etc.

Role of Scientific Methods in Operations Management

Scientific management techniques are much more relevant and widely used in operations management area than elsewhere. These techniques are an invaluable aid to decision making. They modify the purely subjective judgement of the manager.

Industrial Engineering (IE) which is an integrated system of men, materials and machines helps production systems tremendously.

Modelling where reality is approximated by studying the relationship of certain variables so as to understand, explain and predict the behaviour of the systems has done yeoman's service to production/ operations management. Of special interest are the optimisation techniques of OR like linear programming (LP), transportation, assignment, PERT/CPM ctc. We also fall back upon statistical techniques like central tendency, sampling, quality control by control charts etc. Some of these will be discussed in this book at appropriate places.

Computers have given us software packages for all these useful techniques. Computers also help us in MIS. Computer based production systems with cybernetic control have also come in vogue.

Behavioural sciences with emphasis on human element enlighten us about morale and motivation, group dynamics, supervising styles, merit rating and performance appraisals. Thus these also have a role to play in operations management.

Value engineering came forward as a cost reduction technique, trying to identify the unnecessary costs, not relevant to the functional utility of the product.

Computer applications in later years, especially for Industrial Engineering and OR problems, changed the very complexion of the Operations Management function.

Project Management techniques of PERT/CPM (1958) gave an effective tool of planning and control of large projects.

The fifties made production management as a science useful as a management function for diverse manufacturing organisations (like Petroleum, Chemical, Process Industries etc.). The sixties gave it a new status of Operations Management, embracing in its ambit the service sector of the economy also. The seventies gave us the Systems Approach, where the organisation is treated as a whole consisting of several sub-systems.

Computer simulation, computer aided design and manufacturing (CAD/CAM), group technology (GT), cellular manufacturing system (CMS) are some of the recent developments making us optimistic about operations management's role and utility in future.

Conclusion

Maximum production, highest quality and minimum cost is the guiding principle of production management. Production and productivity are two different concepts. Production implies the process of converting the raw material into a finished product. In other words, production implies the input output ratio. Productivity is the capacity of the inputs to produce a given output. Productivity is described as the "war against waste." Selection of proper techinique of production largely reflects in the efficiency of the production. The requirement of the plant and machinery, power supply, fuel, skilled workers, other infrastructure changes as per the choice of the technique of production. Entrepreneur has to choose from labour intensive and capital intensive technique of production.

The technique of production guides the entrepreneur in the choice of the machinery. Entrepreneur has to take vital decisions about the selection of machinery. Proper installation of the machines and equipment contributes to the higher productivity and quality of the product.

The essence of production management centres round a trio of forecasting, planning and control of production. Modern management of production uses scientific methods and disciplines. The results of good production management (production forecasting, planning and control) are reflected in the serving of many interested parties in production machine of a nation.

Product planning concerns itself with the creation of a product which is in demand in market. It includes:

(i) selection and development of a new product; *(ii)* product differentiation; *(iii)* packaging; *(iv)* branding; *(v)* value analysis; and *(vi)* product modification..

The proposed product can be a totally new product or an existing product with some modifications. It can also be a duplication of a competitor's product. The selection of product is an important process both for new and existing units. For an existing unit it is important because old products cannot survive indefinitely as every product has a 'life cycle.' Product life cycle consists of four stages, *viz.,* introduction, growth, maturity and decline. Depending upon the product, the cycle may vary from some months to even a few decades.

. Finally, we have to produce goods in required quantity, at the required times and with the required quality in the most economical manner. We must have low cost of production to make normal profit under keen competition. Hence, production management must look after method analysis, material handling, plant and office layouts, work management, and wage incentive plans. These measures will give maximum productivity and profits, without of course, sacrificing worker satisfaction and welfare, In short, production manager must evolve effective man-machine organisation to accomplish *both* productivity and satisfaction.

ANNEXURE – 1

Production Channel and Control

Progressive Condition	*Average Condition*	*Weak Condition*
	I. Procurement	
Purchase of all materials through competitive bids, in accordance with specifications, in quantities requisitioned by production control. Effective expediting procedure.	Purchasing function generally is well handled. Lacks complete co-ordination with Engineering and Production Control. Fair expediting procedures.	Purchasing not completely centralised. Poorly co-ordinated with Engineering. Production Control and other departments. Poor expediting procedures.
	II. Production Control & Scheduling	
Production completely planned and schedulel in accordance with sales requirements and manufacturing facilities.	Production planned, as to principal items. Scheduling of material and labour needs by department heads.	No central production control & scheduling, production often dictated by need to keep men busy — resulting in unbalanced, excess inventories.
	III. Plant Engineering	
Plant location determined by studies of material and labour supply, market location. Plant facilities arranged in accordance with production methods and processes, maintenance and replacement of plant, equipment and facilities well controlled.	Plant not located as a result of economic study. Machinery and equipment layout not well correlated to material flow. Maintenance and replacement of plant and equipment loosely controlled.	Plant location determined by available building space. Machinery location and plant layout arranged with little regard to economical material flow or handling. No facility for replacement programme and production control of maintenance.
	IV. Tool Engineering	
Tools developed, designed and tested to yield to lowest feasible manufacturing cost for each product. Tools efficiency maintained and controlled.	Tools well constructed, but not designed to produce lowest manufacturing cost. Fair tool maintenance and control.	Tool engineering not well correlated with manufacturing and processing to produce low production costs. Poor tool maintenance and inventory control.
	V. Methods Engineering	
Head of Methods and Process Engineering capable of developing, improving, standardising and simplifying manufacturing processes to reduce costs in co-operation with Factory and Engineering Departments.	Separate methods and standards department. Full co-ordination with Manufacturing, Tool and General Engineering Departments not maintained.	Methods worked out by various department heads — improvements low. Poor records and little control of manufacturing and processing. Manufacturing not well planned or supervised. Machinery old, material flow poor. Product quality fair. No incentive pay rates, supervision indifferent.

Progressive Condition	*Average Condition*	*Weak Conditionl Procurement*
	Vl. Manufacturing	
High quality, low-cost production for all products obtained by use of modern machinery, good plant layout and material flow, with high labour efficiency acquired by the offer of incentive pay and by able supervision.	Material flow needs improvement. Machinery up to date. Costs not low in field; loose incentive rates for labour. Improved supervision needed.	No separate quality control function except when complaints force extra precautionary measures.
	VII. Quality Control	
Quality control maintained as a separate function. Efficient inspection programme tailored to each product and used as aid to sales and manufacturing.	Quality control function not centralised. Inspection performed as a manufacturing necessity only, except when quality complaints are made by customers.	Inspection carried out independently by each department foreman.

Source : Nau Nihal Singh : *Scientific Management of Small-Scale Industries,* pp. 320-322.

ANNEXURE – 2

JIT (Just-In-Time) System of Inventory

It Is also called zero-inventory operation. It is atually a philosophy which can be installed after eliminating all unwanted operations and waste. It is a continuous process. It seeks to eliminate raw material stock and finished stock. It has to adhere to other norms of manufacturing excellence like right time delivery every time, perfect quality and right implementation of plan. It pre-supposes complete co-operation between management and workers.

JIT cannot be maintained if quality components are not continuously made available. Rejections of substandard components or faulty production operation leads to disrupted production. It consequently leads to non-delivery of finished product.

In India, it is difficult to get specified materials at the right time and at the right place. There is a factor of ancillarisation where ancillary industry feeds the parent industry. Due to absence of proper tooling and equipment, ancillaries face rejections at their level or at the buyer's level. The internal and external suppliers are the key to success in JIT system. Quality and timely supply schedule are necessary for it. JIT has been successfully employed in Taiwan, Korea and Japan. On installing JIT, they have reduced inventory level of only 2 days in place of 8-12 weeks inventory levels. Overseas supplies in a country Iike India also impede the installation of JIT. JIT reduces inventory carrying costs. There is scope to implement JIT in integrated companies where there is no reliance on external sources.

JIT in our situation, therefore, can be installed if suppliers carry stocks for us, which make them participators in our JIT programme. Perhaps, this is easier said than done in our situation. Even a slight trend towards JIT will be big step forward.

Just-In-Time Philosophy

The basic concept is not to make anything till it is needed. It further extends to producing anything needed to the highest level of quality. JIT is not restricted however to manufacturing but can be extended to distribution, sales, marketing and finance. It is applicable to both manufacturing and service industries. In JIT, we have to meet customer's requirements of quality, cost and delivery time. The factors which affect these requirement are wasteful, and so must be eliminated. For instance, factors like interest, unnecessary equipment and holding large inventories tend to increase costs, and so must be eliminated. JIT teaches us an effective method of manufacturing. We shall be able to appreciate JIT better if we compare it with traditional method of manufacturing.

Factor	*Traditional Method*	*JIT*
Quality	Quality has cost.	Quality is free. Do things right first time. It leads to good quality and also lowers cost. TQC and total employee involvement.
Workers-Managers-Engincers Relationship	Managers-engineers are experts. Workers execute their orders. Errors are to be eliminated by inspection.	Workers are experts. Managers-engineers are facilitators. Stepping stones to success. One must learn from them. They are not to be repeated, Closer to the concept of zero defects.
Inventories	Always in stock to keep production process continuous.	Inventories hide our inefficiencies. Low inventories (does not necessarily mean zero-inventory). Practise JIT selectively for big budget items and not for all items.

Lot Size	Mass production. Large-lot production.	Small lot sizes, preferably one. It means do a little bit of everything everyday. Study set-up times and reduce them. Modify some equipment.
Queue	Queues at work production stations lead to better machine utilisation.	Against queue formation small lot sizes and low inventories result in small or no queues.
Automation	Substitutes labour.	Preferred for consistency in quality.
Cost Reduction	*Tools:* High machine utilisation. High rate of production. Labour reduction.	*Tools:* Accelerated flow of product due to reduction in lead times.
Lead times	Increase in delivery lead time.	Decreases delivery lead time.
Flexibility	There is flexibility at the cost of excess capacity, general purpose equipment, accumulation of inventories and overheads.	Flexibility by reducing all lead times.
Line and staff functions	Separated.	Line workers perform the minimum staff functions like maintenance. Job-rotation.
Labour	Retrenchment when demand falls.	Relocation to other areas, e.g., sub-contracting.
Breakdowns	Accepted as routine.	Preventive maintenance.
Procurement	From multiple vendors.	Development of one vendor. Participation in vendor development process.
Purchasing	—	Purchase in small lots. Supplier evaluation is stringent. Makes inspection on arrival redundant. Over-specifications are avoided. Delivery-time insisted upon. Minimum paper work. Packaging in small standard containers with required quantity. Simple purchase agreement.
Implementation	Depends on attitude towards work.	Depends on attitude towards work.

Adapted from JIT write-up of Dr. Anshuman Khare, Research Scientist, UGC, TOI dt. May 1, 1995.

Productivity and Cost

The concept 'productivity' and 'cost' have gained great popularity, during and after the Second World War. Both are so closely related that they are sometimes treated as the Siamese twins. They are virtually inseparable and as a result if one of them is being referred to, the inference of the other, by implication is unavoidable. Productivity in its ultimate analysis, does not simply mean higher production divorced from cost. We always talk in terms of — How to increase productivity so as to reduce costs, or how to reduce costs so as to increase productivity.

There exists misconception about the productivity in the minds of the labour class. The workers mean that greater productivity means bigger work loads, greater efforts and increase in the profits of the owners. They also mean that it results into displacement of labour. However, these are not the correct observations. In fact, productivity integrates the objectives of the owners and workers. Greater productivity increases production through efficient utilization of inputs rather than the exploitation of workers. In principle, it emphasises that due share in the increased production and profits must go to the workers who are the key contributories to the productivity. Productivity strives to minimize the human hazards and human efforts with a view to utilizing them to those areas where they can contribute maximum to the output. At times, the techniques employed to increase the productivity may result into replacement of labour. However, the retrenchment of the workers can be minimized through effective manpower planning.

As productivity measures the output per unit of input, theoretically there are as many indices of productivity as there are inputs. However, for the purpose of simplicity, they can broadly be classified as under:

(i) Labour productivity;

(ii) Capital productivity;

(iii) Raw materials and fuel input productivity, and

(iv) Total factory productivity index.

***(i)* Labour productivity:** The labour productivity is obtained by dividing the gross value added by the average daily employment.

$$\text{Labour Productivity} = \frac{\text{Gross value added}}{\text{Average daily employment}}$$

The gross value added (i.e., numerator) is obtained by subtracting raw material inputs and fuel, electricity and lubricants consumed from the ex-factory value of the output. The depreciation is not deducted. The average daily employment (i.e., denominator) is obtained by the total attendance of the persons in all the shifts in all working days and dividing it by the number of days worked.

***(ii)* Capital productivity:** It is obtained by dividing the gross value added by the fixed capital.

$$\text{Capital Productivity} = \frac{\text{Gross value added}}{\text{Fixed Capital}}$$

In the denominator only the fixed capital investments are considered, such as land, buildings, plant, machinery etc. The working capital is excluded because under inflationary business conditions, the components of working capital, *viz.,* inventories, receivables, cash holdings etc., are more often determined by the supply and the market expectations rather than by the purely technological pipe-line requirements of the working capital.

Using HR for Cost Management

Design Organisational Structure	*Recruit People To Staff Positions*	*Appraise Performance*	*Institute Training Programmes*	*Manage Reward Systems*
Reduce Headcount	Prevent Over-Hiring	Institute Systems That can Highlight Skill-Gaps	Use Training to Prevent Expensive Hires	Ensure Competitive Pay to Reduce Replacement Costs
Flatten Layers	Pick/Promote to Avoid Expensive Mid-career Hiring	Zero In on Non-Performers & Reduce Headcounts	Try to Groom In-house Talent	Pay for Performance, Not for Position

***(iii)* Raw Materials and Fuel etc., input productivity:** It is obtained by dividing the gross ex-factory value of output by the combined value of inputs like raw materials, fuel, electricity, lubricants etc.

Raw materials and fuel input productivity

$$\frac{\text{Gross ex factory value of output}}{\text{Combined value of raw materials fuel etc., inputs}}$$

***(iv)* Total factory productivity index:** It is a ratio between output and the sum of combined inputs of labour and capital.

$$\text{Factory Productivity Index} = \frac{V_t}{W_o L_t + R_o C_t}$$

where V_t = Gross value added in year 't'

WO = Base year wage rate

RO = Base year return on capital

L_t & C_t = Labour and Capital inputs in year 't'

The indices of productivity focus on the measurement of output and various types of inputs and thus they help in determining which particular output-input comparisons are most relevant in evaluating the performance of various operations and units of concern to management and to interpret such findings with giving due regard to the influence of internally controllable and external imposed factors.

Tolls of Productivity

All progressive units strive to attain the higher level of productivity. The productivity a key factor which brings success to any establishment. The level of the productivity can be increased through the following means:

(i) Application of the scientific management techniques.

(ii) Devising better methods of operating the things with the help of time, motion and method studies.

(iii) Implementing simplification and standardization in operations.

(iv) Application of the principle of division of labour and specialization.

(v) Effectivating the control techniques, such as production control, quality control etc.

(vi) Improvement in the plant-layout and material handling facilities.

(vii) Provision of better working conditions, plant and personnel services.

(viii) Provision of the effective plant maintenance services.

(ix) Proper selection and training of workers.

(x) Amicable industrial relations.

(xi) Provision of fair wages and industrial relations.

(xii) Philosophy of management.

Factors affecting the Industrial Productivity

Productivity is a technique of extracting greater output from the inherent "input creativity" of various resources through the "conversion efficiency." The "conversion efficiency" which changes the level of productivity is largely affected by numerous factors. All these factors. affect the level of productivity either individually or jointly. Some important factors are classified as under:

(1) Technological, (2) Managerial, (3) Financial, (4) Natural, (5) Sociological and (6) Government.

The technique of economic ordering quantity (EOQ) strikes a balance between the ordering cost and the carrying cost. It devises such a quantity of each order at which the total ordering cost and carrying cost would be minimum. As both these costs are mutually exclusive the total of both costs will be minimum at a point where ordering cost equates carrying cost. This situation is explained by the graph as under:

The Technique of EOQ

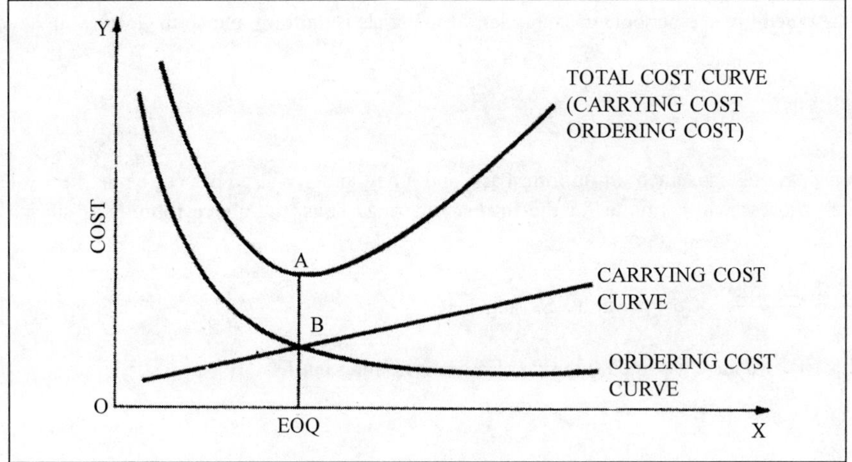

Fig. 14.6: Economic Ordering Quantity

It can be seen from the above figure that 'B' indicates the size of order where:

(i) The total ordering cost and carrying cost (i.e., AB) is at minimum. Any deviation from point B on left hand side will increase ordering cost and reduce carrying cost resulting into greater cost. If the deviation is made on right hand side from point B, it will result into increase in carrying cost and reduction in ordering cost with high total cost.

(ii) At point B, the ordering cost and carrying cost equates each other. Thus, B is the economic order quantity (EOQ) where the total ordering cost and carrying cost tend to be minimum.

Formula: The economic order quantity phenomenon can also be explained with the help of the formula. The formula is derived as under:

***(i)* Ordering cost:** Ordering cost (OC) is ascertained as under:

$$OC = \frac{\text{Annual Requirement (R)}}{\text{Size of order}} \times \text{Cost per order (D)}$$

Assume that the size of order is economic ordering quantity (EOQ)

$$\therefore OC = \frac{R}{EOQ} \times D \qquad ...(1)$$

It should be noted that $\frac{R}{EOQ}$ will give the number of orders placed during the year.

Thus, OC is nothing but numbers of orders, i.e., $\left(\frac{R}{EOQ}\right)$ multiplied by the cost per order (i.e., D).

***(ii)* Storing cost:** The storing cost (or the inventory carrying cost) is ascertained as under:

SC = Value of the units stored × Storing cost represented as certain percentage of the value of materials stored.

"The value of the units stored" is nothing but the average units stored × Cost per unit.

Now it is assumed that the periodic consumption of materials is uniform and so the average units stored will be equal to —

$$\frac{\text{Size of the order}}{2}$$

The materials will be consumed on uniform basis and a new order will be placed the moment the earlier lot is consumed and such process will continue for the further ordering. Thus, the above formula of storing cost can be reproduced as under:

$$SC = \frac{\text{Size of the order}}{2} \times \text{Cost per unit} \times \text{Storing cost}$$

Now in this case we have assumed that size of order is nothing but EOQ.

$$\therefore SC = \frac{EOQ}{2} \times C \times S$$

Where SC = Total storing – cost

EOQ = Economic ordering quantity

C = Cost per unit

S = Storing cost as a percentage of value of materials stored

Now principally we derived following two important characteristics of EOQ.

(i) EOQ is the ordering level at which the total ordering cost plus total storing cost is at the minimum.

(ii) EOQ is the ordering level at which total ordering cost will equate the total storing cost.

On the basis of the above (ii) characteristics, the aforesaid derivation (1) and (2) can be presented as under:

OC = SC

$$\text{or} = \frac{R}{EOQ} = \frac{EOQ}{2} \times C \times S$$

$$\therefore \frac{2RD}{CS} = EOQ^2$$

$$\therefore EOQ = \sqrt{\frac{2RD}{CS}}$$

where R = Annual requirement in units

D = Ordering cost per order

C = Cost per unit

S = Storing cost as percentage of value of materials stored.

❋ ❋ ❋

15

MARKETING MANAGEMENT

Introduction

Marketing is not merely a function of a business enterprise, but is one of the key business and is synonymous with the whole business. The primary function of marketing is to create and maintain a satisfied customer. Marketing management coordinates the various activities of its systems to achieve organisation goal. Although, the management concept of marketing is new, its utility to small enterprises is quite significant.

The Principal Marketing Functions

A marketing function may be defined as a major specialised activity or group of activities performed in the marketing of goods and services. Although the performance of a specific function may be inescapable, it is frequently transferable; in other words it has to be performed by someone regardless of his official title and responsibilities. Another characteristic of a function is that whereas its purpose may be unchanging, its content, in terms of the number and kinds of activities involved, may be subject to constant change. Newer and better ways of doing things and carrying out traditional functions are continually being developed.

Traditionally, some seven or eight so-called marketing functions have been listed and normally include *(a)* the exchange functions of buying and selling, *(b)* the physical distribution functions of transporting, warehousing and handling goods between producer and customer, *(c)* what are usually described as the 'facilitating' functions which take in product standardisation and simplification, commercial and market information, financing and risk-bearing. (It is questionable whether risk-bearing, in the true entrepreneurial sense of committing one's own resources to a speculative venture, really belongs in a fly list of marketing functions, risk-bearing is a responsibility jointly undertaken by the managers of a business or solely by the chief executive).

This kind of analysis is inadequate as a description of modern marketing activities since it fails to distinguish clearly between major functions and the specialised activities which comprise the different functions. Under the modern marketing concept there are four principal functions — marketing research and information, product planning, selling and distribution, and advertising and promotion. Chart sets out those major functions and the specialised activities involved in each.

Chart : 15.1

The Principal Marketing Functions

Specific Function	*Activities involved*
Marketing Information and Research	Economic, business, trade, industry, consumer, user, product, sales and advertising research and analysis. Information handling the data processing. Marketing operations research. Competitive intelligence.
Product Planning	Determining and developing the company's product mix. Matching the products' specifications, packaging, pricing, performance and servicing to customer needs through product and service improvements and new product development.
Sales and Distribution	Field selling/Selection of Distribution channels/Warehousing/Transport/ Sales Analysis/Sales Reporting/Sales Forecasting/Sales Budgets and Quotas Merchandising/Sales Communications.
Advertising and Promotion	Advertising to the customer or user in all media (press, television, cinema, radio, outdoor posters, etc.) Consumer promotion directed at the customer or user, e.g., reduced price offers, banded pack offers, premiums, competitions, couponing etc. Point-of-purchase display material. Trade promotion, e.g., incentive schemes, display competitions, sales contests.

Extracted from *Marketing* in *a Competitive Economy* by Lesile Rodger.

Responsibilities of Management

The major responsibilities of general management are to establish marketing objectives, to make policy decisions and communicate those decisions to the managers of the operating (or implementing) divisions of the company; to establish standards for measuring and guiding the overall performance of the company. The responsibilities of operational or line management are to plan programmes, methods and procedures and implement the decisions necessary to achieve the stated objective; to organise and co-ordinate the activities and resources necessary to carry out the programmes; and to see that operating results conform as nearly as possible to agreed plans and standards of performance.

The production division is responsible for the manufacturing aspect of marketing — organising men, materials, machines and time to. produce the requisite qualities and quantities at specified times and at a designated cost to meet market requirements, and sales forecasts. Quality control, production programining, raw materials procurement are included here.

The financial or accounting division of the company is concerned with the financial aspects of marketing — budgetary control, standard costing and profit planning. Business is based on the rigorous discipline of money and a major criterion of performance, but not necessarily the only one, must be profit earned. Nothing that a company produces makes money for the company until it is sold and paid for.

The marketing division is responsible for the sales, marketing research, product-planning and development, distribution and promotional aspects of marketing, for the detailed implementation of marketing and advertising plans and programmes and for achieving designated marketing goals. In some companies, the sales and distribution functions are separated from the research, product planning and promotion functions — the latter group sometimes being designated as 'marketing services.' This does not matter so long as both the sales division and the 'marketing services' division are co-ordinated by the same individual, irrespective of the latter's title, i.e., Marketing Director, Sales Director or Commercial Director.

Finally, the Personnel and Administration Division of the company, if this is separated from general management, is responsible for those aspects of marketing dealing with job evaluation, selection and recruitment, executive training and general administrative procedures laid down in company policy.

The line-up of top management and the four basic operating divisions of a company as described above is depicted in Fig. 15.1.

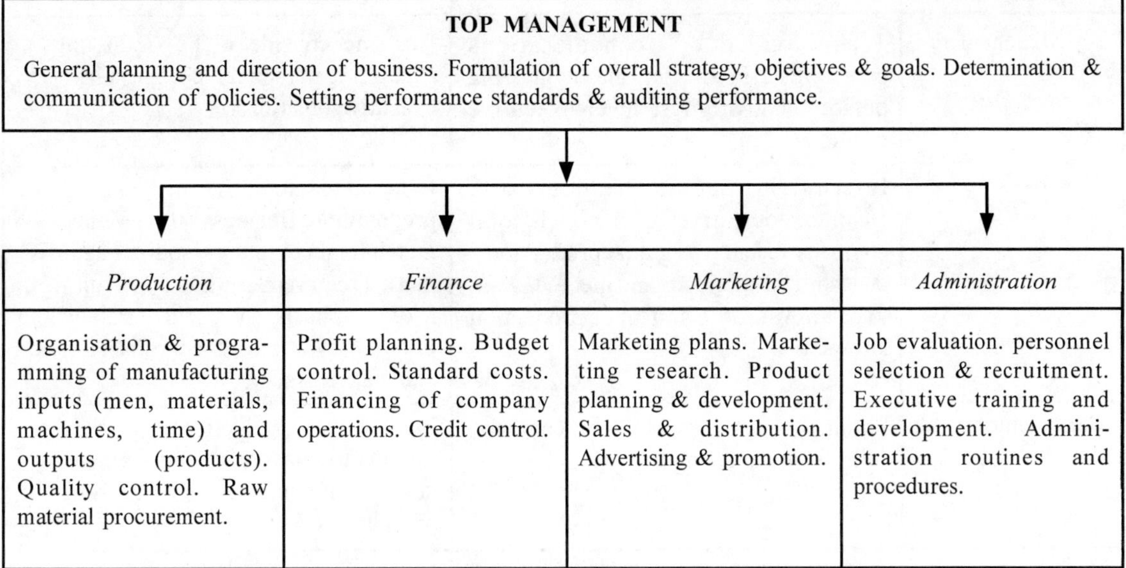

Fig. 15.1: The Responsibilities of Top Management and the Four Opening Divisions of a Company

Marketing is nothing more nor less than the profitable matching of total company resources against market requirements and opportunities. Production requirements are dependent upon the solution given to this commercial equation; in other words, a company should make what can be profitably sold. What is absolutely certain is that, if it remains unsold, it cannot yield a profit. In the parts, the business functions has been more concerned with matching total company resources against production, requirements that is the company has attempted to sell what it wanted to make. The task of marketing management is to identify, assess and realise market opportunities and potentials.

Marketing management is responsible for creating customers by persuading them through advertising and personal salesmanship that the company's products or services match their indicated needs and preferences more closely than competitors' offerings, by developing products and services through technical and market research which appear to offer profitable sales opportunities, and at a price, time and place the customers want.

The marketing process starts with knowledge of the customer and his needs and ends with a customer purchase and the satisfaction of those needs. Through technical product research and customer research, generalized needs are translated into specific product sales opportunities. Product planning identifies and specifies the particular product-price-package combinations to exploit these opportunities. Products are engineered or formulated (a number of variations of a single prototype may be made up), screened and tested with customers for overall acceptance and performance. Final decisions have to be taken on packaging design, pricing and trade terms. Assuming that one product stands out as eminently suitable in all major respects, the next step is to prepare a marketing plan, in writing, setting down all the relevant facts about the product, the market, and the competition the company's marketing objectives and sales goals and the means by which they are to be achieved.

The Basic Differences between Production-oriented and Marketing-oriented Organisation

Business Function or Activity	*Company Perspective*	
	Production	*Marketing*
Top Management	Technological considerations predominate. Production and engineering personnel in highest level executive positions.	Customer considerations paramount. Marketing personnel in highest level executive positions.
Objectives	Internal influences pre-dominate. Business objective is to match total company resources against production on technical efficiency and method. Want to be known for technical or production know-how.	External market influences predominate.Business objective is to match total company resources against market requirements and opportunities, More emphasis on market strategy and planning. Want to be regarded as style and market leader.
Manufacturing	Production less flexible. The company sells what can be made.	Flexibility in production so as to match product to sales opportunities. The company manufactures what can be profitably sold.
Marketing	Aims to fulfil existing needs and develop workable products to meet these needs. Company's future bound up with markets already supplied, and products already in existence. Marketing function not considered to be as valuable as, manufacturing, engineering or finance.	Seeks to create markets and develop saleable products. Company's future bond up with markets yet to be identified and developed, and with products not yet in. existence. Marketing to co-ordinate with manufacturing, finance and other major business functions.
Research	Leads in technical and scientific research. Marketing intelligence system relatively undeveloped.	Leads in analytical and marketing research. Market intelligence system well developed.
Product Planning	Based on technical research, suggestions for new or improved products system from functional performance and applications are prime considerations. Engineering consideration tend to predominate. Laboratory testing more prominent than sales or market. Packaging viewed as a shipping and protective engineering, materials handling and packaging machinery.	Based on market research. Suggestions for new or improved products stem from research into customer needs. Performance and applications are prime considerations regarded to be almost as important. Sales and market testing an integral part of planning. Packaging viewed as a sales tool in terms of its user convenience and advertising and promotional device. Chief concern is effectiveness.

Business Function or Activity	*Company Perspective*	
	Production	*Marketing*
Sales Organisation	Salesman regarded as an order-getter for the factory.	Salesman regarded as an order-maker who keeps the factory running and provides employment to production workers. Salesman accorded high status in the company and more likely to be promoted to top management positions.
	Salesman lacks the professional status of the engineer, chemist, lawyer or accountant. Less likely to be promoted to top management. Salesman lacks formal training. Tends to get left to his own devices as the man 'out there.' Motivation of the salesman minimal.	Salesman given formal and continuous internal and on-the-job training. Motivation of sales organisation given high priority. Chief sales executive regarded as part of the management team.
Advertising & promotion	Emphasis on cost rather than on the value of this contribution to the total selling effort.Advertising & promotion regarded as an extra cost, not a basic cost like machines, raw materials, research laboratories, etc. Not regarded as one of the skills required to run a modern business successfully.	Advertising & promotion is an integral part of the company's marketing effort and a basic cost. Outstanding advertising and promotion considered to be as equally important to the successful running of a business as outstanding manufacturing technique, technical research ability or financial and legal skills.
	Advertising & promotion not looked upon as an important source of competitive differential advantage.	Advertising and promotion regarded as a potential source of competitive differential advantage, particularly when the differences in own and competitive products become less & less distinguishable.

Problems of the Small Firm

It is sometimes asserted that "marketing is all very well if the firm is large, but a small firm has neither the men, the money nor the time at its disposal to be able to do very much about it" or words to that effect.

While conceding that the size of a firm largely determines the degree of management, division of labour or specialisation which is feasible, the facts remain that *(a)* marketing problems do not disappear simply because a business firm does not have personnel or resources to deal with, *(b)* the marketing functions must be carried out to a greater or lesser degree implicitly, if not explicitly, by someone either within or outside the firm and *(c)* the causes of small business failure seem to have a good deal less to do with size, availability of capital and product engineering skill than with basic management and planning weaknesses, in particular, poor product and marketing planning due to inadequate records and insufficient or inaccurate information, unbalanced management experience, and poor financial planning and control.

But accepting the fact that the problems remain and have to be dealt with as best the firm can, how can the smaller firm get over the limitations imposed by size, or its inability to employ the necessary marketing skills? Assuming that there is no one individual with the time, experience, and knowledge to co-ordinate the basic marketing functions, then there are two ways of meeting the difficulty. One way is to come to some point of association arrangement with another firm or group of other like-minded firms to finance and carry out certain centralised marketing services. Group market research projects, product testing facilities and information services, group advertising and promotion and reciprocal trading and purchasing arrangements these are just a. few areas in which greater co-operation should be possible.

The second method by which the small firm can partially overcome the size problem is the use of outside consultants. Numerous expert organisations in research and information, product planning, market testing, selling, advertising and public relations, are available to the individual firm or groups of firms on either an *ad hoc* or continuing basis.

Industrial versus Consumer Goods Marketing

Again, it has often been said that the techniques used with success in consumer goods marketing are not applicable to the marketing of industrial goods, that the marketing problems faced by industrial goods producers are quite different from those met within the consumer goods field.

The marketing difference between industrial and consumer goods are fairly clear, if not always appreciated.

(1) Industrial goods are destined for use by producers of other goods and services and include raw materials, buildings, equipment, supplies, fabricated materials and industrial services. The customers of industrial goods manufacturers and other service industries, institutions and government agencies. Consumer goods are normally for personal or household use without further processing. By way of illustration, the biscuit manufacturer makes a product for consumption by individuals and families in the home mainly. He must plan his marketing so as to make his products known and available in the areas where his consumers live and purchase their requirements. An assortment of industrial goods manufacturers will have supplied, among other things, the equipments with which the biscuit manufacturer makes, packages, and distributes his products to the ultimate consumer. By comparison with most consumer goods and services, the demand for industrial goods can be intermittent and change abruptly.

(2) Channels of distribution for industrial goods tend to be shorter than for consumer goods. Industrial goods suppliers and purchasers are very often in direct contact or use a few highly specialised middlemen. The discount manufacturer mentioned above may have to sell direct and/or through wholesalers to something like 1,50,000 retailers before his final consumers can buy his product. He has three tasks to persuade the trade to stock his product to persuade the consumer to try it and to keep on reminding people about it so that they will keep on buying it.

(3) There are relatively fewer customers for industrial goods than for consumer goods, although the former have far greater purchasing power at their command. For many industrial goods manufacturers, the total. number of buyers is determinable and a small proportion of major buyers may account for the bulk of a company's output.

(4) The criteria for purchasing industrial goods are primarily technical in nature, i.e., efficiency of performance, economy, durability. The customer is normally the user and an expert purchaser; the actual purchase is usually subject to multiple influences, both technical and commercial, within the customer organisation and to lengthy negotiation. Many industrial goods are supplied on a tendering basis, which raises special problems of estimating and pricing.

(5) The industrial goods salesmen is usually primarily concerned with finding the right people to influence — specifiers, contractors, technical experts, commercial buyers — with paying the way for his own technical experts. The consumer goods salesman, on the other hand, usually completes the sale to his wholesale and retail customers.

(6) The demand for industrial goods tends to fluctuate much more widely with ups and downs of the general economy. This is primarily due to the relative durability of such goods (hence it is easier to postpone purchase and extend the useful life of existing equipment) and to the fact of the demand for consumer goods and services and upon the state of business confidence about the present and future economic situation.

(7) Industrial purchasers buy products for their companies not for themselves. Having several different sources of supply is a sound buying policy. Consumers, on the other hand, may spread their purchases among a number of different brands or sources supply, but more from inquisitiveness and a desire to experiment than from the desire to protect their sources of supply.

Thus, in terms of the purposes for which they are bought, the markets to which they sell, and the methods by which they are marketed, industrial goods can involve more complex and widely differing marketing patterns than in the case of most consumer goods which tend to follow a common pattern. A British Institute of Management study group on industrial marketing, however, reported that "Within the field of industrial goods, the type of product and the nature of the market vary greatly. Despite this, it soon emerged from the discussion that there is a surprising amount of common ground. An initial reaction, that the problems of the various industries in the group were too different to allow useful comparison, quickly disappeared. The sugar manufacturer, for instance found that his problems were unexpectedly similar to those of the electrical engineer."

The differences between industrial and consumer goods in their respective markets in no way invalidates the applicability of the marketing concept to industrial goods. Indeed because of the high value of unit sales and unit purchases of many industrial goods and because of the longer manufacturing cycle and high cost of building and maintaining stocks associated with a wide range of such goods, the importance of the marketing concept may be even greater than for consumer goods to the extent that the consequences of being wrong through bad business and sales forecasting, faculty product planning, inadequate or inaccurate information, failure to identify, contact and follow up sales prospects with well-conceived sales promotional activity can be great deal more costly. This is not to say that the marketing techniques developed and refined by consumer goods manufacturers are immediately transferable to the industrial field. The use of such techniques adapted to the specific needs of industrial markets and without taking account of the real differences that exist between industrial and consumer goods marketing is deemed to failure.

Much of the disillusionment among any industrial goods manufacturers with the so-called marketing concept, stems from the undiscriminating use of methods ill-adapted to deal with peculiar problems met within industrial marketing or applied in completely wrong circumstances. But this is a matter of detailed application. The point at issue is not whether some of the techniques used in consumer goods marketing are adaptable to industrial goods marketing. New techniques are being developed in both fields and the cross fertilization of ideas and methods is by no means one-way. The argument put forward here is that manufacturers of industrial goods have something to gain by taking marketing perspective of their commercial operations, by looking at their business first and foremost in terms of customers and markets rather than in terms of production engineering and industrial processes.

The principles of competitive differential advantages and market segmentation apply with at least much force to the marketing of industrial goods as to the marketing of consumer goods. So far as differential advantages are concerned, technical patents are a much more common source in industrial goods than in consumer goods. This can be of critical importance because of the necessity to recover the high cost of research and development, tooling up and other investment costs associated with a large number of industrial marketing projects.

Again, the number and spread of markets or market segments supply or capable of being supplied by an industrial goods manufacturer. The more highly specialized the industrial product, of course, the less is this likely to be the case. A walking drag-line, for instance, has a highly specialist use and its markets are clearly predetermined, paint. On the other hand, is not only used in the home by 'do-it-yourself', professional builders and decorators, but also by a myriad of secondary users producing an infinite variety of consumer goods or other industrial goods. Thus, industrial goods manufacturers may have to tackle a much wider variety of markets with diverse requirements and different buying and selling conditions.

Accurate business and market forecasting is of major concern because (i) an industrial goods manufacturer's future is bound up to a much greater degree with that of the industries he supplies, (ii) the impact of technological innovation can be very much greater and more abrupt in industrial markets, (iii) it takes longer and, in general, requires a larger investment to undertake any major expansion or change of direction. Manufacturing, viewed as a single activity, makes use of a variety of technical skills, and facilities according to some central plan or objective. Likewise, marketing should be regarded as a single activity making use of a variety of research, selling and communication skills and facilities which is also based on central plan or objective. And yet, according to a recent survey carried out by Metal Working Production, 'A high proportion of industrial goods manufacturers must still be regarded as production-biased, managed by engineers and technologists (hardly ever by sales or marketing-oriented executives) and with little attempt being made to integrate all related marketing functions in an effective manner.'

The same survey of the buying and selling techniques used by machine tool builders, who can probably be taken as representative of a fairly wide section of the engineering industry, reports that fewer than one out of every two manufacturers approached properly integrate selling and promotional planning. Only one in ten had someone assigned to marketing, research. The report concluded: 'With few exceptions they (the manufacturers) undertake no market research. As a result, the majority are unable to draw up a really effective sales plan or apportion the necessary promotion expenditure in terms of reaching their market potential. It becomes quite clear that even the simplest of market research, designed to delineate their major prospects, which would enable companies to see it that all buying influences were covered by suitably planned promotion strategy, is not being carried out;

Selection and building a strong marketing team with able leadership
Selection of distributors and dealers
Negotiating terms and agreements
Coordination with Purchase and Production
Innovative and aggressive marketing plans
Product planning, Product demonstrations, Product development
Product promotion, Promotional tie-ups (short-term)
Formulation and Implementation of marketing strategies to achieve desired scheme of business and profit
Creating additional markets
Establishing the brand in the market
Market Research, market survey, marketing services of research
Introducing novel and innovative market ideas

Organizing advertisement campaigns
Effective utilization of media and other advertisement channels
Assessment of market potential
Brand management
Directing launch of new products
Monitoring product performance in a higher competitive environment
Monitoring Distribution Network
Arranging for shipments (in case of exports)
Train, develop and motivate a team of professionals
Product positioning, pricing, distribution and communication strategies
Transforming marketing strategies into sales
Strengthening the sale and distribution
Identification and analysis of customer segments
Competitor positions and market structures
Stock and credit control
Retailer network management
Sales promotion
Planning and Budgeting of all sales related activities
Achieving higher market shares at improved profitability
Proper study and analysis of project demand
Marketing communication
Dealer channel development
Dealer training and customer support
Market creation and development
Formulation of marketing-mix

Setting Business Objective

The first stage of this marketing process is setting up the business objective. The business objective may be to gain competitive advantage (a position which the company wants to occupy in the market place in relation to the competitors). It is quantitative in nature (for example, a 35 per cent market share or 18 per cent return on investment). It gives a sense of direction and purpose to all the functions of the company and channels all the efforts to achieve it.

The business objective by analysing the external environment of the company which gives the threats and opportunities and the internal environment which gives strengths and weaknesses. Thus the business objective is derived from the market opportunities balanced by the internal resources of the company.

Core Strategy

Once the business objective aimed at gaining competitive advantage is set, a core business strategy is derived to achieve it. Thus, strategies are really aimed at major competitors. The questions that the company has to answer here are:

— What sort of relationship to maintain with the competitor?

— Should the company improve its market position or just maintain it?

The core business strategy to attain the business objective can be based on: product differentiation and cost differentiation. In other words, the company has to decide how it is going to gain a competitive advantage. Does it want to pursue an improvement strategy based on enhanced performance advantage (product differentiation) or a strategy based on cost advantage (cost differentiation)? The core strategy is also determined by the available resources. Can the company invest or does it want to generate cash?

Thus the content of the marketing process is fundamentally affected by the direction taken here. A

SECOND P MARKETING: THE PRODUCT

Identify the Customer's Perception of Expected Price

Adjust Value Offering Accordingly

STRIP FEATURES

ADD FEATURES

ADD BRAND INTANGIBLES

IMPROVE PURCHASE EXPERIENCE

Compare Product Price with Costs To Check For Margins

SECOND P MARKETING: THE PLACE

Change Distribution For New Target Customer

Product Trade Margins And Profits

STEP OUT OF PREMIUM STORES

INCREASE GEOGRAPHICAL REACH

PENETRATE SMALLER MARKETS

ADJUST PURCHASE AMBIENCE

Change Retail Servicing Frequency

SECOND P MARKETING: THE PROMOTION

SECOND P MARKETING: THE PLACE

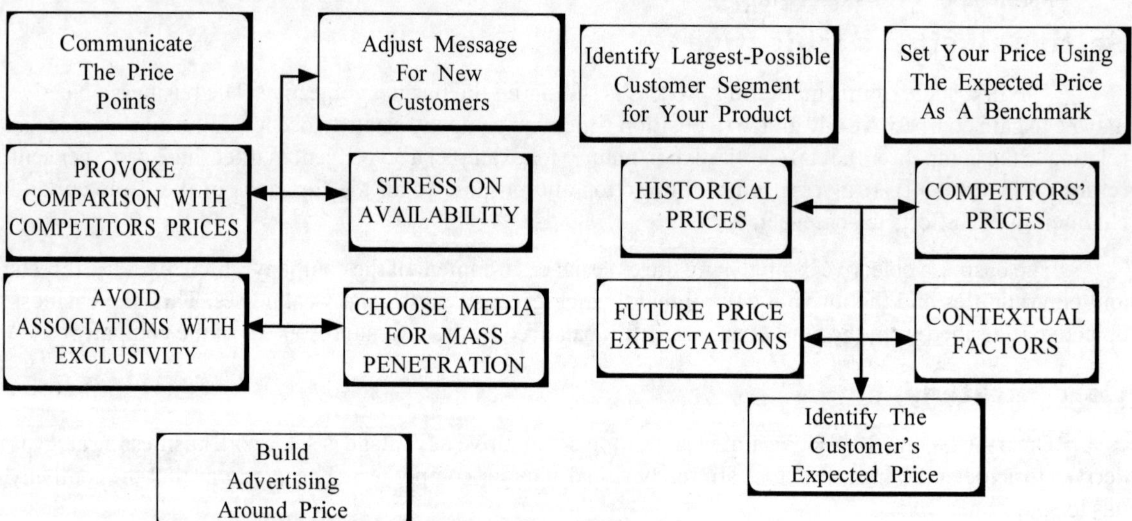

consistently derived core strategy focuses like a laser beam all the resources of the company in achieving the business objective. From the core strategy flow the various functional strategies. The direction of flow of these functional strategies will depend on which of the above paths is chosen to achieve the business objective.

Customer Segmentation

The second stage in the marketing process is customer segmentation, which is aimed at maximising customer advantage.

Here the heterogeneous market to which the business objective relates is divided into homogeneous sub-markets so that different marketing approaches can be adapted for different customer segments. This segments can be done based on customer profile and customer behaviour using factors such as

— Geographic
(regional, national, international)
— Size of order
(Small buyer or institutional buyer)
— Type of customer
(individual, private company, government)
— Customer industry
(bank, professional firm, manufacturing company)
— Customer buying criteria
(quality, price, service)

The important question to be asked at this stage is which target customers does the company want to reach?

The answer depends on the purchasing behaviour of the customer.
— Does he buy primarily according to price or according to performance?
— Does he want a standardised or a specialised product?

The company then puts itself in the shoes of the customers in each of these segments and evaluates its own strengths/weaknesses/capabilities in producing customer advantage. It selects that segment as the target segment where it can produce, as perceived by the customer, maximum advantage for the customers *vis-a-vis* the competitors.

Marketing Mix

The third stage in the marketing process is the marketing mix which focuses at providing appropriate marketing instruments (tools) to maximise the customer advantage for the target market segment. The marketing instruments to achieve this are the 4 'P's of marketing – product, price, promotion, place — giving the corresponding product strategies (product quality, product features, branding, packaging, service, warranty), pricing strategies (price level, trade discount, allowances, credit, payment terms), promotion strategies (advertising, sales promotion, mail order, telemarketing, personal selling) and distribution strategies (channels, locations, inventory, transport).

These instruments focus on the target customer and are tailored to form an appropriate marketing mix. For example, if the company wants to achieve a competitive advantage by way of enhanced performance, then the product policy is the focal point of the marketing mix. The marketing performance level and the performance features in the product are defined. Then the price-performance relationship is analysed. Next the, price or performance advantages are communicated to the target customers by appropriate methods. The

Fig. 15.2 : Elements of Marketing Mix

focal point of the communications policy is to establish a two-fold conviction in the minds of the customers.

— First, that the product capabilities are creditable.

— Second, that the product has a unique position against the competitor (USP: Unique Selling Proposition).

Finally, the high quality image established through the high profile advertising is reinforced by routing the product through select exclusive dealers.

The next stage should be the implementation of the marketing instrument. However, between marketing mix and implementation is the critical fourth stage, namely, the decision on functional programmes. This is the most important stage in terms of speeding up the marketing process since it helps conserve resources and valuable.

The marketing process should provide the link at each stage, from formulating the business objective via customer segmentation, the marketing mix, decision on functional programmes, to implementation. If this is done consistently and derived from the business objective then every function, every employee will be pulling on the same rope in the same direction — the one shown by the business objective.

The marketing process will then improve the way in which the business objective is put into practice, and transformed to the achievement of market success.

Market Segmentation

Market segmentation is the process of dividing the total, heterogeneous market for a product or service into several markets or segments, each of which tends to be homogenous in all significant aspects. Market segmentation is a customer-oriented philosophy.

Markets can be segmented on demographic bases like regional population distribution, urban-suburban-rural population, age, sex, family life cycle, miscellaneous such as race, religion, nationality, education, occupation, etc.

Market segmentation on the basis of income levels is:

(1) High Income Group *(Higher-higher, Higher-middle, Higher-lower).*

(2) Middle Income Group *(Higher-middle, Middle-middle, Middle-lower).*

(3) Lower Income Group *(Lower-higher, Lower-middle, Lower-lower).*

Market segmentation based on sociological factors such as: *(a)* Cultural groups; *(b)* Large social classes; *(c)* Small groups, including the family.

Market segmentation based on psychological factors. such as *(a)* Personality; *(b)* Attitudes; *(c)* Product benefit desired.

Bases for Marketing Segmentation

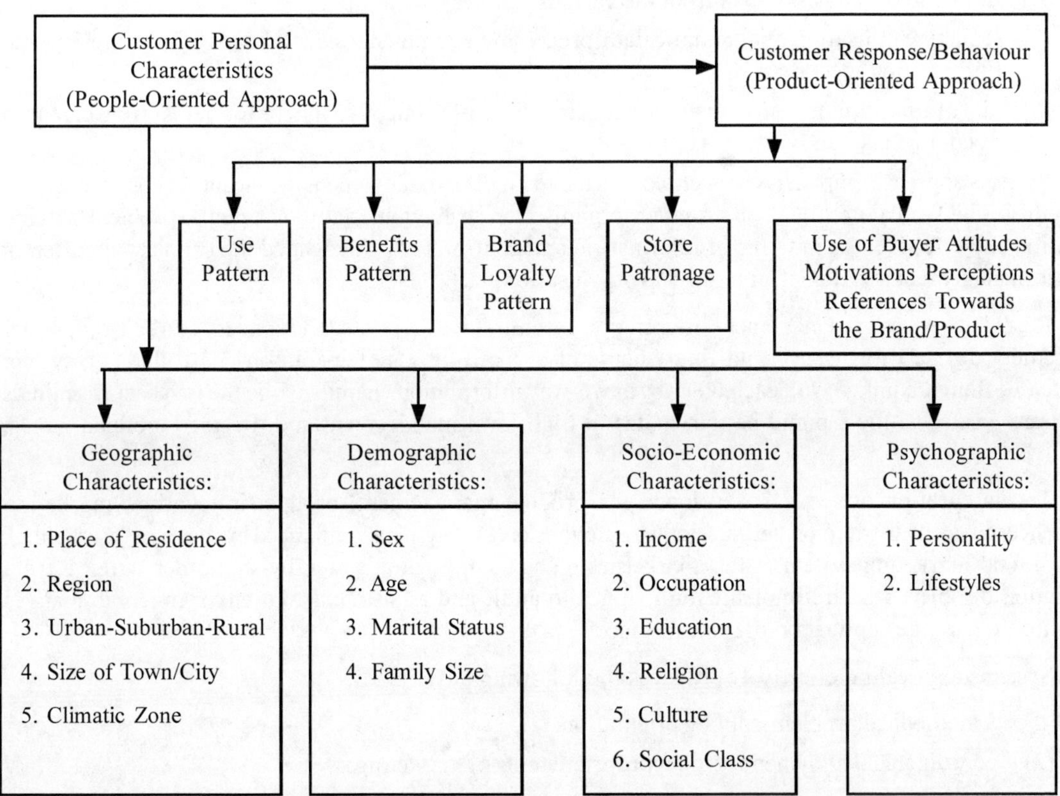

Fig. 15.3

Marketing Planning Systems Approach

The dynamics of market planning today basically aims at removing the mismatch that persisted over the decades till the advent of 90s. It was a dysfunction between management's product systems and the market place demand. In the initial stages, planning was constructed as a basic theoretical tool not related to actual strategic activity.

With the growing sophistication of product and market composition with the environment always shifting, the emerging problems ranged from a steadystate market demand to successive declining positions due to a large number of growing substitutes even though energetic reassimilation was applied in specific case. It was ultimately found that a dichotomy silently took its roots which became manifest later between the product/systems and the market place demand.

The role of the systems approach is to help evolve a marketing intelligence system tailored to the needs of each marketer, a system which would serve as an ever-vigilant nerve centre of the marketing syndrome. Briefly speaking, the following control areas are cited as the vital features of modern marketing operation system:

(1) surveillance of the market,

(2) a team of research techniques use in tandem,

(3) a network of data sources,

(4) integrated analysis of data from the various sources,

(5) effective utilisation of automatic data-processing equipment to distil heaps of raw unprocessed information speedily and,

(6) absolute emphasis not just on reported findings but also on practical action-oriented recommendations.

Systems approach emphasis or cybernetics is based on the two fundamental concepts of communication and control. The typical problems of structure, organisation, behaviour, activities, goals, problem-solving adaptation and effectiveness in terms of information and control have all engaged the primary attention of dynamic management division of an industrial organisation.

Recent advances in management information systems have facilitated the concept of a self-regulating management devise with its two vital ingredients of a controlling systems and a controlled sub-system respectively. Both are linked with each other by a two-way information channel while the two basic terminals of both are located at the top and bottom nodes of high-level management and diverse functional areas, respectively.

The integration of systems developed for product management, product innovation, marketing intelligence, physical distribution and such other functions or "sub-systems" embraced by the term "marketing" creates a total marketing system. Thus, marketing plans composed on a step-by-step order ranging from formulation of objectives and implementing stages to audit and adjustment to a environmental changes constitute a full-range application of systems theory.

Systems application effectively produces the following advantages:

(1) a methodical problem-solving orientation.

(2) coordinated deployment of all appropriate tools of marketing.

(3) greater efficiency and economy of marketing operations.

(4) an almost impulsive response to impending problems made possible by a better understanding of the complex interplay of diverse trends and forces.

(5) stimulates to innovation, and

(6) ensuring means of quantitatively varying results.

These advantages lead to the following functional gains:

(1) a deeper penetration of existing markets.

(2) a broadening of markets.

(3) an extension of product lines, and

(4) lessening competition and building up capacity to face increased competition.

The various consequential steps have to be followed to further ensure the quantitative approach to systems management:

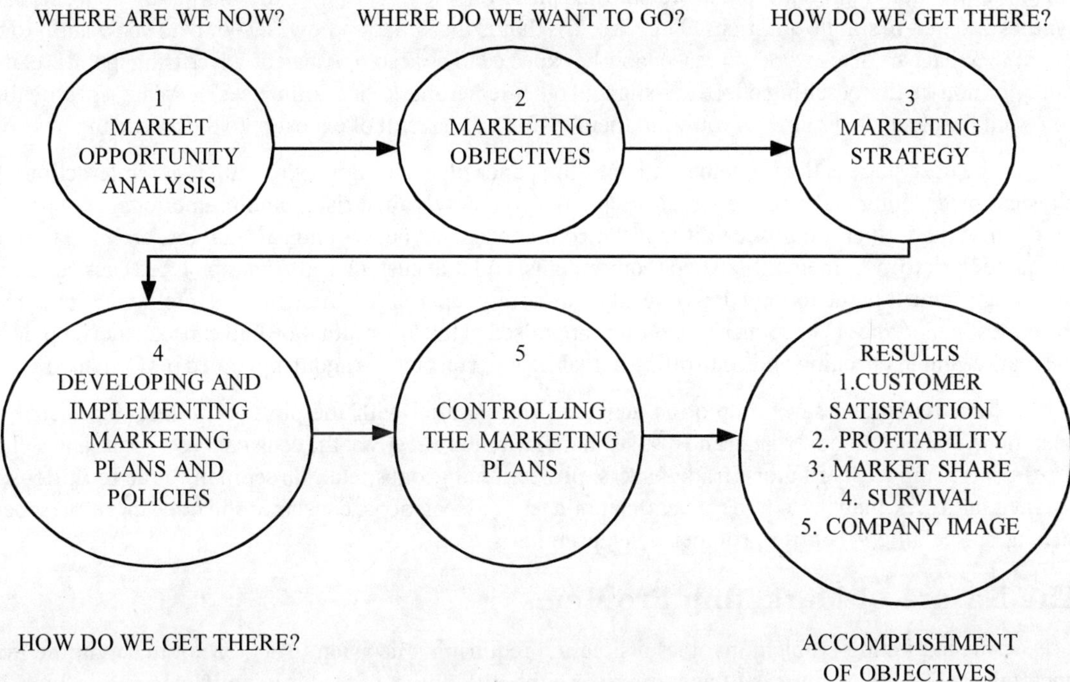

Fig. 15.4 : Marketing Planning Process

(1) a proper understanding of the problems and clarifying objectives.

(2) testing the definition of the problem *(expanding its parameters to the limit).*

(3) building a model.

(4) setting concrete objectives.

(5) developing alternative solution, and

(6) setting up objective.

Marketing Plan

The marketing plan is the key document which sets down preciously who is to do what, when, where and how. There must be liaison with production to determine product requirements and scheduling; ample stocks of the product must be available at the times required by the sales organisation. The advertising and promotional programme must be worked out in detail — the amount of money to be spent, the media to be used, the kind of advertising to be run. What is to be the basis of the advertising appeal, to reach what kind of audience with what degree of frequency and impact? Are there to be any introductory consumer efforts, coupons, premiums of competitions? On the sales side distribution and product sales targets must be set, by sales territory and by individual sales representatives. Physical distribution facilities have to be organised, delivery schedules worked out and so on. The financial people have to provide costing and profit estimates based on proposed expenditures and forecasted sales volume. Every part of the marketing plan has to be — costed out and budgets prepared.

A workable marketing plan, the starting place for the adoption of the marketing concept, can be synthesized in five simple questions. They are: 1. What is the situation now? 2. What do you want it to be in future? 3. What part of the work can reasonably be expected to be accomplished by advertising, public relations, sales promotion, direct selling effort, pricing and other lesser marketing influences? 4. What, specifically, do you want people to do, or how do you want them to think as a result of exposure to the marketing positively?

The next stage is the implementation of the paper plan through coordination and interaction of the physical field selling and distribution effort and the company's advertising and promotional activities. The function of the former are to see to it that the company's distribution and sales targets are met, that carry adequate stock to meet their anticipated requirements, and that customer information is fed back regularly to sales management in the form of daily, weekly or monthly reports. An efficient field intelligence system is of the utmost importance in keeping headquarters appraised of the latest situation and expected developments in the market and in checking and controlling actual field performances against planned performance.

Advertising and sales promotion activities run parallel with the physical selling and distribution operations, and include advertising and display material aimed directly at the consumer user; trade and technical press advertising to distributors, trade buyers, professional groups, etc., direct mail, trade receptions, and planned sales presentations to trade buyers, committees or associations; consumer and trade incentive schemes, such as special offers, bonuses, competitions, premiums, etc.

The Nature of Marketing Problems

Any marketing problem involves a situation requiring a decision to act, or not to act, in the face of uncertainty. The major sources of uncertainty are the difficulties of trying to anticipate and influence the future course of events, in determining the interactions of cause and effect, in allocating limited resources among competing ends, of choosing between different courses of action, and in obtaining accurate and a reliable information. The existence of uncertainty and therefore, the necessity of taking risks - and a decision not to take action can involve as great a risk, if not a greater degree of risk - is characteristic of all problems. Decisions to alter the prices of existing products or services, to introduce a new product, to increase the level of advertising for a product, all involve uncertainty and risk as to their probable outcomes in terms of achieving company objectives.

Seen in this light, problemsolving means finding ways of progressively reducing uncertainty and risk in business judgements, assumptions, decisions and actions, at least to more tolerable limits.

The Scientific approach to problem-solving involves the basic steps shown in the Chart.

Chart 4.1

The Six Basic Steps in Problem-Solving

Step 1. *The Identification of the Problem*

Isolation of the key determining factors and areas of decision

Prior to

Step 2. *The Evaluation of Relevant Information*

Gathering, processing and analysing all relevant information and drawing conclusions

Relevant to

Step 3. *The Setting of Objectives and Goals*

Distinguishing between generalised aims (objectives) & specific qualified targets (goals)

which will determine

Step 4. *The Selection of a Particular Course of Action*

Representing the most favourable balance of risk, effort, timing and expected results

necessitating

Step 5. *The Planning and Control of Action*

Specifying who does what to whom, when and how

leading to

Step 6. *The Evaluation of the Action Taken*

Measuring the effectiveness of the action taken in terms of the complete or partial solution of the original problem or total failure to solve the problem. Compering actual operating results against planned performance.

The ability to identify and assess a particular problem is related to the quantity, accuracy, relevancy and timeliness of the information available, and to how well the information is analysed and interpreted.

The setting of objectives and goals and the selection of the particular course of action to follow are related, on the one hand, to management's ability to forecast or anticipate events over which it either can or cannot exercise some degree of control and the probable customer of its own and other's actions; on the other hand, it is also related to management's capacity for perceiving the possibilities and potentialities in a given or expected situation not apparent at first sight, and what can be made to happen by purposeful action.

Planning and control relate to the organisation and allocation of limited resources to a particular course of action, chosen from a number of possible alternatives, and to the evaluation of the results achieved by such action against planned performance. If at the end of this sequence of steps the original problem remains then the cycle must start again 'in the hope of coming closer to the final solution through successive approximations and corrections. The original as well as new information, including the results yielded by the previous plan must be reappraised; assumptions, conclusions, objectives and goals must be critically re-examined and either reaffirmed or changed in the light of newer or more accurate knowledge; a fresh course of action must be embarked upon and its results evaluated.

Linear Programming

It is mathematical technique for selecting the most favourable or desirable course of action in terms of least cost, highest profit, least time or least effort from among a number of alternative courses of action, using limited resources. Programming means planning activity to achieve a given objective through the optimum use of allocation of available resources. Programming is linear when there is a straight-line relationship between the variables as when a change in the number of calls a salesman brings a proportional change in the number of value of orders he collects. A non-linear relationship would exist where change in the former produces a less than or more than proportional change in the latter. The very large number of computations usually called for in all but a limited range and this represents a major limitation on the extension of the use of the technique at this time. The cost of marketing problems that linear (and non-linear) programming should help to solve include determining the most profitable combination of products to be made from limited resources, determining the optimum location of warehouses and depots to minimise transport and delivery costs, determining the optimum stock levels to meet sales requirements.

Communication Theory

As its name implies, this theory originated in the electrical communications field and is concerned to evaluate the effectiveness of the flow of information and communication within a given system. Consequently, many problems in communication theory can be translated into models. One branch of the theory, cybernetics, deals with self-regulating and control mechanisms and. has provided greater insight into the workings of human behaviour systems. The study of the mechanism of 'feedback' has been of particular importance to communication and., a control theory, for control of an operation involves reporting back 'whenever it goes outside certain specified limits so that corrections can be made. When a human being, sensing that he may fall, corrects his balance, he is making use of a built-in, self-regulating, information feedback control process. Industrial automation is one practical commercial result of the theory of cybernetics.

The two best known applications of the network principle are PERT (Programme Evaluation and Review Technique) and CPM (Critical Path Method). The PERT technique was developed as a method of planning and controlling the co-ordination of the Polaris, Fleet Ballistic Missile Programme for the Special Projects Office of the U. S. Navy's Bureau of Ordnance. Several thousands of contractors and agencies involved in the programme had to be integrated and as a result of the use of PERT the completion date is reported to have been advanced by more than two years. Both PERT and CPM have found their wide application to-date outside of military uses, that is, in the programming of constructional and installation work.

J. S. Pickup and D. A. Thwaites have summarised the main advantages of these network techniques as follows: *(i)* they record all the activities necessary for the completion of a project; *(ii)* they display the reasoning behind the forecasting of completion dates; *(iii)* they enable potential trouble areas to be foreseen; *(iv)* they pin-point responsibility; *(v)* they save time and money by simulating changes in cost variables; *(vi)* they define objectives; *(vii)* they provide a good communication medium; *(viii)* they permit management by exception whereby only significant deviations from planned or standard performance, abnormal situations and trouble spots are brought to the attention . of management. The authors conclude — 'One of the greatest benefits of drawing horizontally and vertically. The necessity to analyse in detail the activities and events of a project not only. bring out the relative "time" importance of interrelated activities, but for people to think and discuss with others the sequence in which operations are done and the associated problems which emerge.

Management by exception is a natural outcome of using networks, for by concentrating control on the critical path activities, time is not wasted by progressing other activities which could not shorten the overall length of the project.

The application of network analysis to marketing operations is still in the experimental stage. Its use in planning new product development, test marketing, planning and the co-ordination and scheduling of selling and advertising plans and programmes can be expected to become much more widespread during the next few years. Networks can give the marketing executive a better planning perspective in which the relative importance of time, costs and profits can be taken into account. Operating management is concerned with two basic problems. On the one hand, activities must be organised, scheduled, and co-ordinated. On the other hand, limited resources must be assembled and allocated to various tasks at the time and place and in the quantity necessary so as to maximise or minimise some magnitude of importance to management. It is not enough to merely allocate resources to ensure a successful and efficient plan. Although the simultaneous optimisation of all phases of a project may be desirable, in some cases it is usually necessary for the different parts of the programme to be optimised in a particular sequence. But there is always a danger that the whole programme is actually weakened rather than strengthened by making one part more efficient in isolation from or at the expense of others. For example, spending a sum of money on advertising too far in advance or the sales force's capacity to obtain the minimum level of distribution necessary is a common error of marketing management policy.

Segmentation of the Market

India has many diversities with regard to consumption patterns. Thus, in reality, it is a conglomeration of several markets in which people tend to differ. People can be regrouped demographically, economically and socially, but even within these groups, each set of consumers can be differentiated further. For instance, individuals sharing a common demographic profile may show variations in terms of a cultural and demographic mosaic. The marketer has to recognise all these differences since each individual represents a unique opportunity.

Segmentation is dynamic and extends beyond the traditional two-dimensional classification. We need to treat it as three-four or five-dimensional segmenting. Many intelligent companies have been able to do beyond two-dimension. However, it is only the gut feeling of the marketer that will help him into the fourth and fifth dimensions of segmenting. Thus, segmentation itself becomes a multi-dimensional issue, and a marketer has to face a complex matrix in terms of positioning products.

Segmentation or subdivision of the market is based upon the modern marketing concept, i.e., market-oriented strategy and philosophy. Segmentation places special emphasis on the demand side of the market. It is a more rational and more precise adjustment of the product and marketing effort is tuned to the consumer or user's needs and requirements. Segmentation implies that there are 'several demand schedules and not necessarily a single demand schedule or curve. For each demand schedule representing of group of buyers with similar needs and characteristics, we can prepare a separate and precise market offering or marketing mix.

Market segmentation is a method for achieving maximum market response from limited marketing resources by recognising differences in the characteristics of the various parts of the market. In a sense, market segmentation is the strategy of divide and conquer, i.e., dividing markets in order to conquer them. Its philosophy is something for everybody, within practicable limits. Marketing strategy is adjusted to inherent differences in buyer behaviour. For different groups of customers, i.e., market segments, we have different sets of marketing strategies. Segmentation strategy is an answer to the question: "To whom should we sell our products, and what should we sell them. It is a strategic choice concerned with "doing the right things as opposed to the tactical choice, 'doing things right."

Market segmentation enables the marketers to give better attention to the selection of customers and offer an appropriate marketing mix for each chosen segment, or a group of buyers having homogenous demand. Each subdivision or segment can be selected as a market target to be reached with a distinct marketing mix.

Marketers must go beyond the age-old classifications based on consumer locations, age-profiles, gender, and economic strata, among others, and take into account several other factors that differentiate the markets.

Market Assessment

Successful innovation is a necessary condition for effective marketing. 'Innovate or perish' is a current slogan which has a rich meaning for business operating in an economy with customer-oriented marketing. An innovation is considered as a successful invention. An innovation is the act of develo ping a novel ideal into a process or product. For an innovation to be successful, the new product or new process must be feasible and must have commercial acceptability. The successful innovation passes through three stages: (i) idea or invention, (ii) implementation of the idea and (iii) market acceptance. Implementation refers to the development of the idea or invention from its conceptual stage to an output — a developed product or service. Market acceptance is the third stage and it is the most critical to any successful innovation. A firm can control partially the first two stages. However, the acceptance decision is an external factor and it depends upon consumers and their reactions Markets rely on all modes of promotion or marketing communication to exert influence on consumer behaviour and induce the potential customers to adopt the innovation.

In this changing world, attitudes, habits, preferences, values and trends change. A change in income, or instance, alters the demand pattern to unrecognisable dimensions. There are a number of variables which have a direct bearing on the demand pattern of a product. It is therefore, necessary to gather data and information on these variables to the extent possible with a view to making sound decisions. A sound decision based on sound facts should certainly reduce risk. This is the role of marketing research.

Marketing research is needed to determine the kind of product you should manufacture on the basis of the needs, uses and preferences of the consumers; what size, package and presentation will be most effective in persuading the consumer to choose your products; the number of units that may be sold; the time and season for peak sales, optimum price, sales promotion methods and so on.

In other words, marketing research involves and study of consumer preferences, habits and attitudes; it helps to decide how immediate market operation should be directed. It also involves an examination of trends so that the subsequent findings indicate the future pattern of the market and assist in planning future programmes.

In a free economy, the consumer has the right to choose and the prerequisites of his choice are free competition and enough production to meet the demand — that is the demand does not exceed the supply. His second right is to be informed of the products, its characteristics and its capacity to satisfy his needs. His third right is that the product. Finally, he has the right to benefit from technological progress in terms of the satisfaction of his needs at reasonable cost. Therefore, any marketing research programme must begin with ascertaining the need, habits and preferences of consumers.

How to Grow A Stagnant Market
Promote the product, rather than specific brands, to convey the generic benefits
Break down usage barriers by eliminating the misconceptions that consumers have about it
Break the limitations of existing offerings to present new reasons to use the product
Offer added benefits that require increased usage of the product for better effect
Attach unique attributes to each brand to build customer involvement and increase usage
Offer entry to new customers at a price-per-unit that makes purchasing the product possible
Identify the key benefits, and make the USP of new brands in order to win over customers
Use countrywide sampling activity to acquaint potential customers and back up with advertising to convert intent to purchase
Multiply both brands and segments to add value

A System

Marketing is a system of integrated activities defined to develop strategies and plans including marketing mixes to the satisfaction of customer wants to selected market segments or targets. It is an ongoing process involving a set of multi-directional as well as multi-dimensional activities. Marketing is a matching process by which a producer provides marketing mix (product, price, promotion and physical distribution) that meets consumer demand of a target market within the limits of society.

Promotion is the process of marketing communication involving information, persuasion and influence. It is a systematic attempt to move forward from a stage of awareness to purchase action.

Of late, marketing management has been given much importance, especially by the SSI sector. This could be attributed to the vastly different market situations existing now. The demand for most products then exceeded the supply and anybody having the resources could normally do well. In a competitive environment, small-scale industries face marketing problems from stage to stage.

Some of the factors which contribute to marketing problems of the small-scale industry could be identified as under:

(i) Increasing competition from within the small-scale sector as well from large industries with established brand names and marketing set up;

(ii) Consumer awareness, even in rural and semi-urban areas, for quality goods;

(iii) The need to set up distribution networks for reaching out widely dispersed markets and

(iv) Inability of the SSI units to exploit the export markets.

Considerable difficulty is being experienced by small-scale industrial units in marketing their products due to their size, limited scale of operations and inability to set up an adequate network of retail outlets. With a view to facilitating the marketing efforts of small-scale units, it is considered desirable to encourage the operations of marketing organisations specially engaged in promotion of sales of products cottage, tiny and small-scale industrial units. Any requests from such marketing organisations for financial assistance to meet their working capital needs should, therefore, be favourably considered by banks with due regard to the performance of such organisations in respect of recycling of bank credit.

Table 15.3 Promotion Strategy

Push Strategy	*Pull Strategy*	*Push-Pull Strategy*
It is called a pressure strategy. Emphasis is on personal selling at all stages in distribution. We have aggressive and high pressure salesmanship. Conditions favouring push strategy: (1) Quality product with unique product features and talking points for salesmen (2) High-priced product and (3) Higher profit margins to resellers. Advertising plays a minor role in the push strategy.	It is called a suction strategy. Emphasis is on extensive advertising to generate consumer demand. Product is literally pulled through the marketing channel by the consumer. Salesmen are mere order takers and distributing agents. Less emphasis on personal selling at all stages in distribution. Lower trade margins are offered to resellers. Lower retail prices but higher turnover rates. Heavy emphasis on consumer advertising and large investments required.	In the consumer goods market very large companies generally adopt a push-pull or a combination strategy to sell their products. Salesmen are employed to push products through the marketing channels. Extensive advertising is also employed to accelerate sales and to increase the market share. We need extensive promotion expenditures and only very big national companies can resort to combination strategy. All tools of promotion work together as a total communication process.

Note:

(1) Strategy lays down plan of action to secure an advantage over competitors, demonstrate attractiveness to buyers and try to achieve fuller exploitation of company resources.

(2) Pull strategy gives emphasis on mass promotion. Push strategy gives emphasis on personal selling.

(3) Conditions indicating a favourable opportunity to promote are: (1) A favourable trend in demand, (2) Major product differences, (3) Hidden qualities (purity in drugs, cleaning power in detergents, flavour in foods), (4) Emotional buying motives to change the psychological climate or buyer's predisposition. Promotion strategy is expected to exploit such opportunities partly through information, partly through motivation and partly using promotion as a form of non-price competition.

(4) In the push strategy, the middlemen have an active role for creating demand. In the pull strategy, he is responsible for serving demand.

Table 15.4 Promotion Plans

Advertising Plan	*Publicity Plan*	*Personal Selling Plan*	*Sales Promotion Plan*
An advertising plan covers advertising: 1. Targets. 2. Objectives. 3. Strategy. 4. Appeal. 5. Copy theme. 6. Media schedule. 7. Budget. 8. Methods for measuring advertising results.	A publicity plan covers: 1. Targets and objectives. 2. Schedule of company products and events with news value. 3. Media possibilities. 4. Budget. 5. Means of measuring the results of publicity.	A personal selling plan covers: 1. Sales targets. 2. Objectives. 3. Strategies. 4. Major appeals. 5. Budget. 6. Methods of measuring personal selling results.	A sales promotion plan covers: 1. Sales promotion targets. 2. Objectives. 3. Strategies. 4. Schedules of events. 5. Budget. 6. Methods of measuring the results of sales promotion.

Note:

(1) Objectives indicate where a firm wants to go: strategy shows the way or means of going there and achieving objectives.

(2) Promotion plans should be: (1) relevant, (2) practical, (3) complete and detailed. They should include specific costs and schedules of activities. They should be coordinated. They should allocate responsibilities and give necessary authority to those who are required to carry out each part of the plan.

(3) Typical promotion objectives are: (1) increase sales, (2) improve market share, (3) create or improve brand recognition, acceptance, insistence etc., (4) inform and educate the market, (5) create a competitive difference and (6) create a favourable climate for future sale. Please note that promotion is only one tool to achieve these objectives.

(4) A strategy is a plan for achieving objectives through the use of scarce resources in the face of intelligent competition.

The requirement, therefore, of systematic marketing efforts for survival and growth of small-scale industries, cannot be overemphasized. Basically, marketing involves:

- Finding out what consumers want;
- Planning and developing a product or service to satisfy these wants and
- Determining the best way to price, promote and distribute that product or service.

The various activities required to be looked into in detail for arriving at a sound marketing strategy comprise product planning, market segmentation, market research, sales promotion, advertising, pricing and distribution. However, depending upon the product, the market and the environmental conditions, the intensity of usage of these activities will differ.

Marketing begins with the choice of a product and its planned production.

Product planning concerns itself with the creation of a product which is in demand in the market. It includes:

(i) Selection and development of a new product;

(ii) Product differentiation;

(iii) Packaging;

(iv) Branding;

(v) Value analysis; and

(vi) Product modification.

The proposed product can be a totally new product or an existing product with some modifications. It can also be a duplication of a competitor's product. The selection of product is an important process both for few and existing units. For an existing unit, it is important because old products cannot survive indefinitely as every product has a life cycle. Product life cycle consists of four stages: introduction, growth, maturity and decline. Depending upon the product, the cycle may vary from some months to even a few decades. Graphically, the product life cycle can be shown as under:

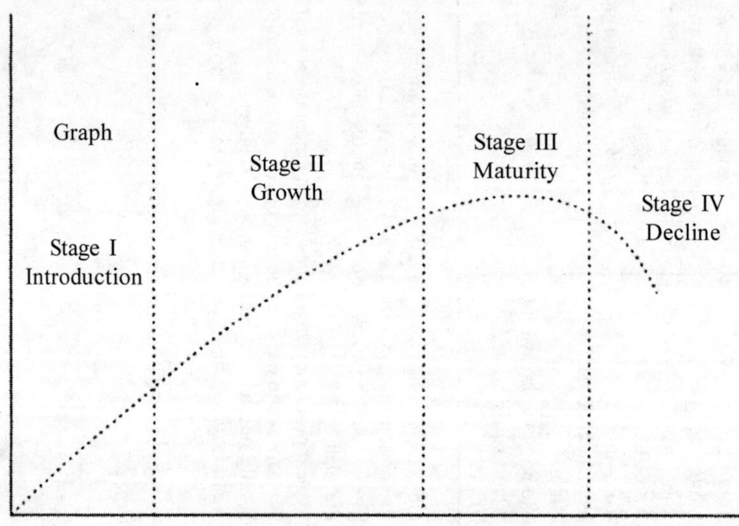

Fig. 15.5: Product Life Cycle

A segmentation of the market may be done on the basis of consumer goods, both durable and non-durable. It may even be done in terms of producer goods in some cases. Let us take the example of durable goods. One proposes to manufacture builder's hardware. The different segments of the market in this case are house-builders aristocratic middle class, lower middle class, lower class; houses in hilly areas and so on. Officers, shops and other similar buildings are other examples. The railways require this hardware for their wagons. Shipbuilders constitute another segment of the market.

The advantages of segmentation of the market are:

(i) Narrowing the range of products;

(ii) Ease in preparing the design of the product, its colour scheme, shape, size and the type of package it may require;

(iii) Ease in determining the trade channels and avenues for direct selling;

(iv) Ease in preparing sales forecasts;

(v) Ease in planning marketing programmers; and

(vi) Ease in selecting the media for appeals that will be most effective for promotion, e.g., displays etc.

Marketing Management

Marketing management represents marketing concept in action, i.e., preplanned demand management under customer-oriented marketing philosophy. Marketing management may be defined as the 'process of management of marketing programmes for accomplishing organizational goals and objectives. The process of management is the set or managerial functions known as planning, implementation and control of programmes to achieve predetermined objectives. Marketing management involves planning, or implementation and control of marketing programmes or campaigns. Marketing management is directly in charge of: 1. the setting of marketing goals and objectives. 2. developing the marketing plan. 3. organises the marketing function, 4. putting the marketing plan into action and 5. controlling the marketing programme. We have the management cycle of planning action-control-replanning. Marketing management would be influenced by: 1. the forces operating in the marketing system, and 2. the philosophy and objective of the organisation. At present the philosophy and objective of the organisation are reflected in the broadened marketing concept, i.e., societal marketing concept, wherein we have socially responsible marketing. As an agency of demand management, marketing management is in charge of regulating the level, timing and character of market demand in such a manner that the enterprise will be enabled to achieve its objectives, viz., productivity, customer and social satisfaction.

Marketing management represents an important functional area of business management efforts for the flow of goods and services from the producers to the customers. It looks after the marketing system of the enterprise. Marketing management perfonns all managerial functions in the field of marketing. It has to plan and develop the product on the basis of known consumer demand. It has to build up appropriate marketing plan or marketing mix to fulfil the set goals of the business. It has to formulate sound marketing policies and programmes. It looks after their implementation and control.

Marketing management is responsible for organising, directing and controlling all marketing activities included in the process of marketing. It has to implement the marketing programme and conduct the marketing campaign. Finally, it must evaluate continuously the effectiveness of each part of the marketing-mix and introduce necessary alterations or modifications to remove discrepancies and deficiencies discovered in the actual execution of all marketing plans, policies and procedures.

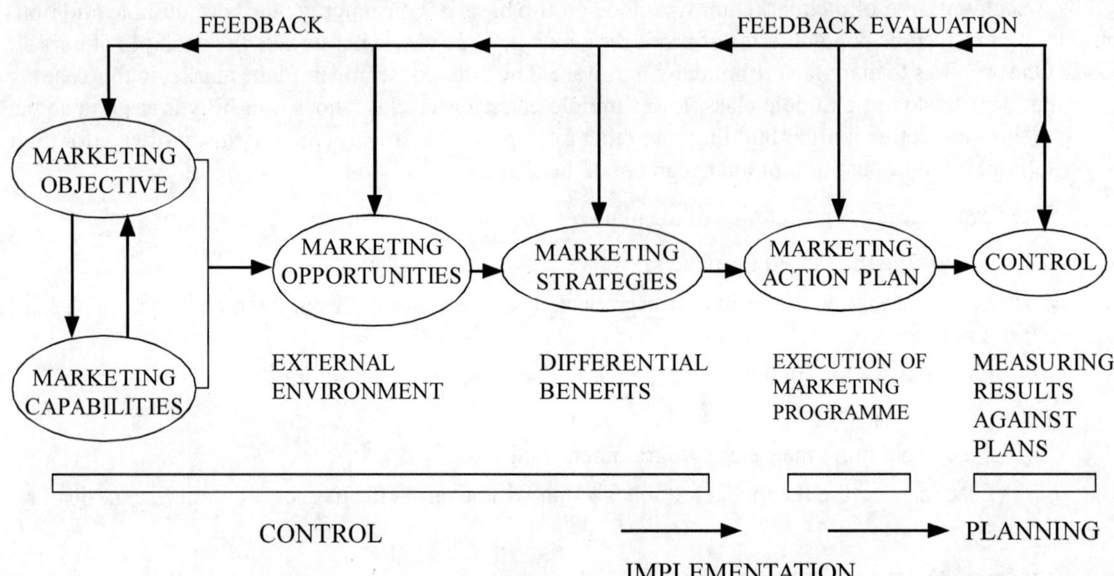

Fig. 15.6: Marketing Management Process

Marketing Organisation

There will usually be a number of transitional stages through which a business enterprise will pass from being a production-oriented organisation to being a marketing-centred organisation. The following three-stages: transition-pre-marketing organisation, sales-oriented organisation and marketing-centred organisation illustrates the process.

The main point to note in this chart, which is not untypical of many organisations as they were or as they exist today, is the absence of coordination between an integrated control of sales, information and research order processing, sales forecasting, product planning, advertising and public relations. While it is true that each of these activities is the responsibility of one or other or the management team, they are not grouped on a functional basis, and are not under the control of one coordinating executive. How competent is financial management to make market and sales forecasts and budgets? Since when was personnel management a repository of advertising expertise? How accurate and objective are the findings of sales and market research carried out by interested parties with as take in the Outcome?

Chart shows what the line-up might be after certain changes have been made to give greater emphasis to the selling function.

There has been a noticeable increase in the responsibilities of Sales management and in the number of supporting staff needed to carry out the duties now assigned. The transition reflects the development on a salesdirected appraoch to the firm's problems. Certain activities previously carried out by some other individuals or departments have been regrouped and are now overseen and co-ordinated by one responsible sales management executive. However, not all of the key marketing activities have been brought together under a single management executive. The responsibility if services remains with Personnel and product *planning responsibility* with Production. At outset Sales Management is still held responsible for researching ties and auditing its own performance.

Chart I
Pre-Marketing Organisation

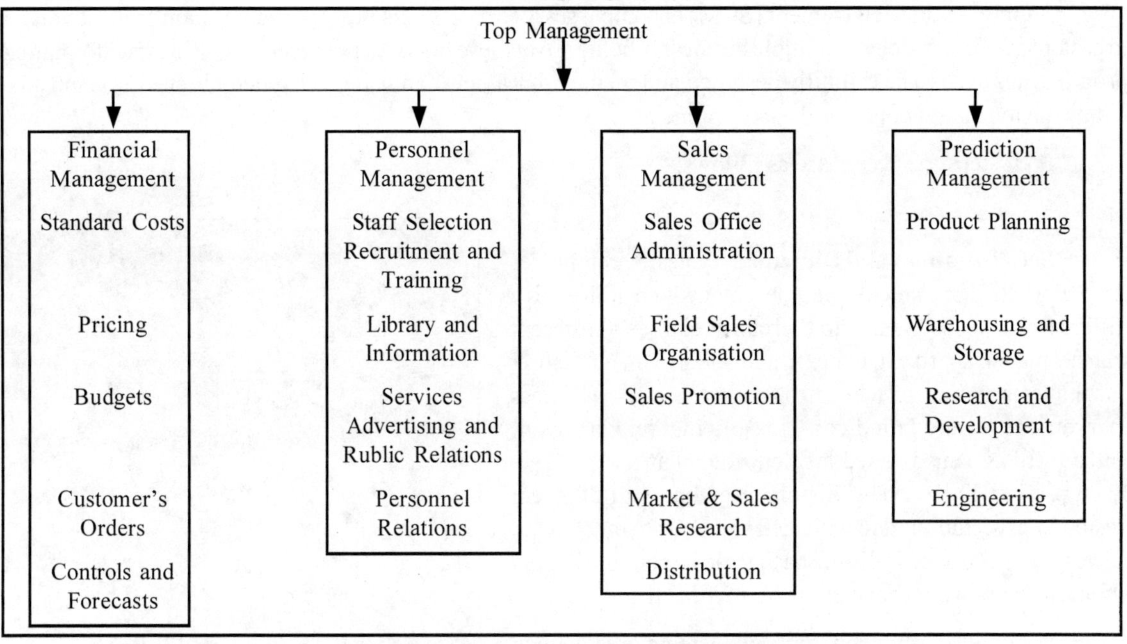

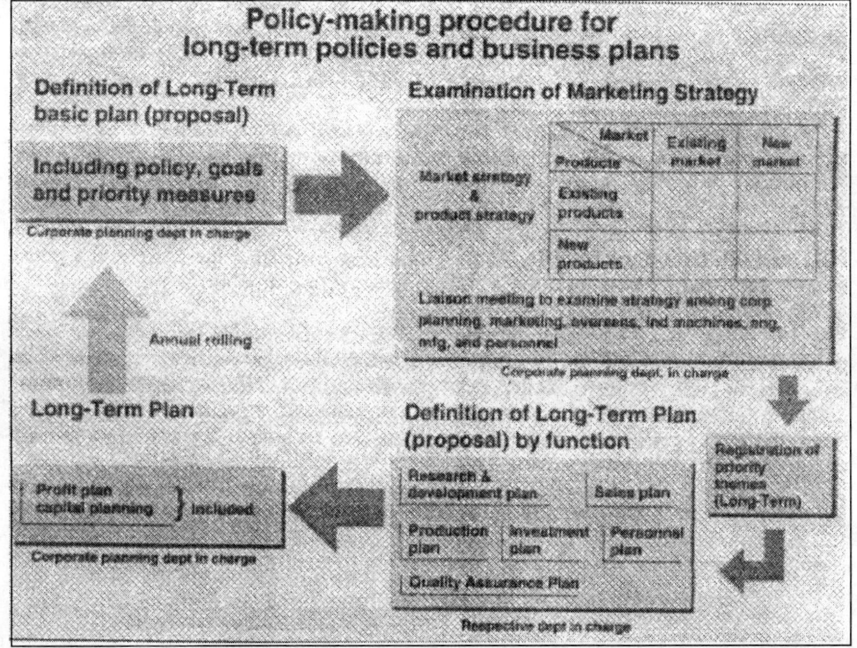

(1) Buying and selling Technique, used in the British Engineering Industry Special Report prepared by the Research Department of Metal-Working, McGraw-Hill Publication, May 1963.

(2) *Ibid.*, p. 20.

SUPPLY CHAIN MANAGEMENT — FOUR STEPS TO SUCCESS

Supply Chain Management (SCM) encompasses all aspects of company's value chain from suppliers to customers and can deliver multiple business benefits. To achieve best-practice levels, the SCM transformation programmes need to be carefully designed and managed. Rather than being delegated, these efforts must be led by the top management or the entrepreneur.

Four steps to success are as follows:

Step 1

Set Aspirations and Direction: Typically, companies have more than one supply chain, each of which addresses a different market segment and therefore requires a different transformation approach. For example, a watch manufacturer can have three product lines: one for the low-cost mass market, one for the brand-conscious, upmarket consumer, and a third as a customised fashion statement for the elite. Each product-line serves a distinct segment with different customer expectations and with different costs to meet them. Clearly, a one-size-fits-all approach to designing the supply chains will not work for such distinct segments.

For each supply chain, top management must launch the transformation effort by defining stretch aspirations along multiple dimensions; extent of inventory, response time to customers, level of stockouts at the front-line, extent of distribution costs, etc.

Step 2

Priorities, Levers and Design Solution: Having identified multiple supply chains within a company and set improvement aspirations for each of them, companies should design various components of each supply chain (i.e., define how the physical, information and financial flows would work from supplier to customer).

Rather than design the supply chain for the entire market (e.g., all plants, suppliers and distributors that constitute a supply chain for a given segment), companies should develop and test the solution on a supply chain microcosm. A microcosm is a supplier-to-consumer slice of the entire supply chain, which contains all processes and participants, and yet is small enough to ensure manageability. For example, it could include all stock-keeping units within one family of products, a plant, a warehouse, all retailers supplied by that warehouse, and the suppliers that provide raw materials to that family of products. Once the new solutions have been designed and pressure tested in the microcosom, they can be expanded to over all other products, plants, warehouses and markets that constitute the entire supply chain.

While designing solutions within a microcosm, companies should pick the right sub-set of 3-5 improvement levers (not 15-20), such as good forecasting processes for the fashion industry, efficient and effective logistics infrastructure management for basic materials supply chains, production management for engineered goods, etc. Clearly, these 3-5 levers vary according to the type of supply chain, level of aspiration relative impact of each improvement lever and the starting position of the company, and must be thoughtfully chosen. Our experience suggests that a detail fact-based diagnostic of underlying root causes helps companies identify the right subset of levers.

Stop 3

Provide Appropriate IT and Organisation Support: While it is a key enabler of the supply chain solution, it is not the silver bullet. It is therefore prudent to define the IT architecture only after the basic supply chain blueprint for a company is ready, and the prototype IT tools have been tested within a microcosm using simple applications such as spread-sheets.

On the organisation front, most Indian companies operate their supply chains sub-optimallyas fragmented pieces controlled by multiple functional departments (e.g., sales, distribution, manufacturing, purchasing, etc.). Given the critical need for cross-functional integration in successful SCM, the transformation effort must be managed by a cross-functional team of star line managers, and in some cases, by a full-time supply chain manager. Equally importantly, the top management across areas (CEO, CFO and relevant functional heads) must actively drive the supply chain transformation process and stay involved in ongoing management of the supply chain.

Stop 4

Monitor Performance: While a new supply chain design may be state-of-the-art, it may not provide the desired results if the metrics for the stake-holders are not appropriately defined. A balanced set of metrics, encompassing 'outputs' (e.g., inventories, service levels and lead times) and'inputs' (e.g., forecasting, productiong sourcing and dispatch accuracies) is crucial towards ensuring large, sustainable benefits. Here again, our experience suggests that a comprehensive set of metrics does not exist in several companies, or is incorrectly defined and monitored only intermittently.

Overall, supply chain transformation programmes are complex and need significant CEO attention and organisational energy. However, the pay-offs from doing it right are immense: not just to reduce costs and to improve customer service levels, but also to potentially redefine competitive position.

A Change Agent

Industrial liberalisation, globalisation, marketing economy and heightened competition is changing all this permanently. While labour laws have become antiquated and virtually ineffective, government policies which encourage dispersal of industries into backward area locations have helped improve matters. Market forces are now compelling modernisation, productivity improvement and value of additional efficiency like never before. Some parts of the country where industry had been severely affected by obscurantist trade unionism, are today showing heightened pragmatism to generate and safeguard employment as well as to attract new investments. Industrially better endowed states do not seem to appreciate that in order to stay ahead in the game of economic and industrial development, only one thing counts — efficiency of value addition and an enabling climate along with a degree of reassurance about the future.

With market forces changing rapidly, marketing has been seen as a change agent — a means of continuous adjustment and adaptation. This refers to significant orientation in marketing management and priorities. The imperatives of market exploitation demand understanding meaningful marketing facts, observations and opinions. The dynamics of successful marketing calls for selecting the right question, getting answers, organise, evaluate and form strategies to deal with competition and technological changes. Marketing perspective focuses on what we want to find, how and where we find and what we believe it means to the business. It is an integrated approach to generate market power by critical analysis of the market logistically, segment proportion of the customers, understanding profile of customers and the competitors, finding new products and services, customer preferences, customer records as to retention and defection etc.

Since the market place in the decade has been registering rapid transformation, we are witnessing that the business events reflect a distinct pace and capacity for expansion. The moments signal continuous shift in the way of performing — both in style and behaviour. Market is now being defined and perceived as a group of competitors. Hence there is an entrepreneurship surge in the market — the triumph of the entrepreneur. It suggests great opportunities in the fast growing market where there are many under served market niches. Marketers are always competing to locate the markets that will value the products and would pay for them. It calls for concentrating on market efforts of targeting and positioning the product. 'ME TO' profile of a market man is the formidable force enabling him to acquire distinct competence and chalk out specific strategies for business emphasis. The competing dynamics is resulting in reinventing the marketer. It is the only stimulus today in the development of 'new' market concepts. Today 'operating salesman' is reborn as a marketer because he is to take strategic decisions in the new market requirements.

Market focus therefore demands:

- Perceiving market as market intelligence;
- Targeting customers;
- Managing for profitability and not sales volume alone;
- Building customer relationship and loyalty; and
- Growing with the market.

So, 'Compete' is the buzzword. It is forcing market operators to develop innovative strategies to sway over the market.

Today's salesman, nay the marketing man, must always edge closer to the market call to transcend the adventurous customers and excel by solving daunting problems continuously to be different in the market.

Marketing information will become a highly valued asset in today's information age. Monitoring and scanning scenario building and continuous planning would be the marketing privately. As the future will occupy a prominent position in marketing research concerns, marketing research is expected to change both in technique and orientation. Marketing intelligence, therefore will be a critical factor to be given greater attention to. While assessing the strategic situation, executives will be focussing on marketing factors and strategies, corporate affairs and public relations activities. Marketing environment is expected to be paradoxical — keenly competitive, but exhibiting more cooperation, making marketing more important in the management hierarchy.

Marketing intelligence is supposed to explore real demand of the customers and the steps the competitions are taking to fulfill the same. Marketing intelligence is a way to understand the customers's perception of values and purchase preference. It shall be imperative for the organisations to be alert about competition's approach towards marketing determinants like dependability and reliability, consumer-friendly features, technical specification, high quality and service uniqueness.

In the year ahead, industrial location will be guided primarily by commercial considerations and sustainability rather than by regulatory of social demands alone. An investment which does not maximise the generation of surpluses cannot contribute to the country's social goals. Thus, location in backward regions where there is a great deal of willingness and native skill amongest the first generation workers proves very attractive to the decaying environment of cities where industry has been traditionally located.

In the current rising wave of economic growth and liberalisation and in the absence of systematic market research, capacities far in excess of demand have been set up in many industries. Thus, in addition to some of the old and obsolete industries, many relatively new investments have either turned sick or have shut down. The Government has taken several imaginative measures to revive many of these. The Board for Industrial Finance and Reconstruction (BIFR) was created to expedite revival schemes.

The Indian economy and the business environment, currently undergoing important structural changes, will grow faster than ever and will encounter myriad complexities of a free enterprise system. The private sector, which had always clamoured for freedom to conduct its affairs, is now face to face with the realities of standing more or less on its own. We had not realised that change would be upon us as fast as it has.

Business now has an opportunity to transform individuals and organisations into vibrant and competitive entities. Industries which cannot generate surplus can neither have any place in our country nor can they achieve the goal of a more egalitarian society. It is through productive endeavours and mutual cooperation of those engaged in the industry and agriculture, that the larger issues of population control, unemployment and poverty alleviation can be effectively tackled.

The era of mutual distrust, government controls and disruptive trade union movements must, under these changing circumstances, *recede into* the background. Our economy, to get progressively drawn into the sphere of a new international trade and export, will have to grow faster.

Conclusion

Marketing are aware of the paradigm shift that is ushering in a new economic era for business. The prime mover of this shift is the emergence of the information society. In the information society, unlike the industrial and capitalist societies, the fundamental drivers of wealth creation are intangibles, that is, the development, exploitation and communication of ideas, knowledge and information. This changes the perception of marketing in the information society.

Marketing today embraces total value propositions, a departure from the erstwhile emphasis on unique selling propositions. This implies that when a customer finds the solution to his problem, he not only takes into account the money spent, but also the total transaction cost which includes the time spent and his experience chain. Brand strategy therefore now involves delivering the best possible total brand experience at the lowest possible total cost.

Successful brands involve customers as partners in the process of wealth creation. Consequently, brands are really treated as gateways to ongoing relationships between the customers and the organisation. There is no doubt that customers who are 'involved' tend to be more loyal than customers who are merely 'satisfied.'

An organisation's share of customer trust and share of market goes up proportionately with its ability to balance the live product with the sensory perception of the user (touchy-freely experience). For example, the Bofors gun may be branded and be important for a country like India, but it can't offer any touchy-freely experience to attract premium for its service. But, when an aircraft is combined with the brand experience of, say, British Airways, the brand experience involving the whole value chain that differentiates one airline company from the other. The same holds true to hotels and all other branded service organisations.

Today, the concept of brand experience permeates every conceivable product category. The better an organisation manages this experience process, the better its chance of survival. It also improves its ability to attract a premium for its offerings. On the heap of brands from the lowest to the highest level in a product category — the differentiations are increasingly based on non-price factors. The higher the hierarchy of a brand, the higher the intangible, sensiry perception engendered through the customer experience process. Over a period of time, the intangibles need to get embedded as part of the total brand offering.

Industrial liberalisation, globalisation, marketing economy and heightened competition is changing all this permanently. While labour laws have become antiquated and virtually ineffective, Government policies which encourage dispersal of industries into backward area locations have helped improve matters. Market forces are now compelling modernisation, productivity improvement and value of additional efficiency like never before. Some parts of the country where industry had been severally affected by obscurantist trade unionism, are today showing heightened pragmatism to generate and endowed states do not seem to appreciate that in order to stay ahead in the game of economic and industrial development, only good thing counts — efficiency of value addition and an enabling climate along with a degree of reassurance about the future.

Marketing management is responsible for creating customers by persuading them through advertising and personal salasmanship and prefers more closely their competitiors' offerings, by developing products and services through technical and market research which appear to offer profitable sales opportunities and at a price, time and place the customers want.

As with societies *so with markets change with the passage of time. Only those* companies that can adapt to these changes and innovate to serve the evolving needs of customers can hope to survive. To do this *Marketers will have* to *continuously go back to 'the basics. Niches or segments are not made by* product managers — the changing needs and perceptions of consumers create them. As man produces, to fill them up. The future, therefore, belongs to the pro-active challenger.

Social behavioural insights have a huge role to play in the art of Neuro-marketing. Studies have proven that humans like to get associated with popular people because of the positive triggers rated that are generated in the brain because of that association. This is one of the main reasons why celebrity endorsements work. in the case of celebrity endorsements, the association of the celebrity with a given product aids the stimuli when the product is seen at retail shelves. The more popular the celebrity the better the chance of success. Naturally when unknown faces endorse a brand, the consumer and his brain take more time to get closer and know your brand better.

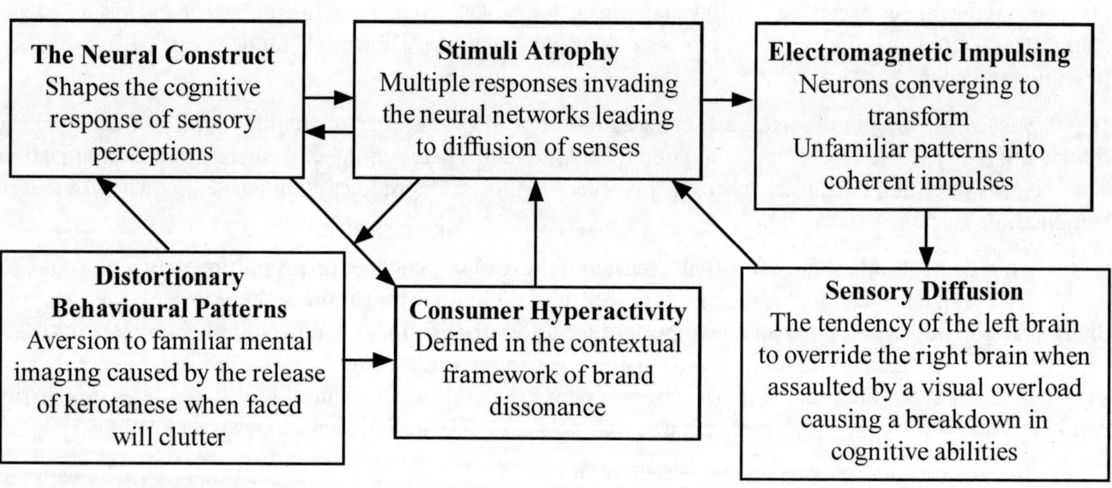

Chart II
Stages of Development in Marketing Management

Production Orientation	*Sales Orientation*	*Customer/Market Orientation*
Market is viewed as dependent variable and production capacity as the independent variable. Production Dept. → Market	Market as dependent variable and sales department capacity as the independent variable. Sales Dept. → Market	Market and the firm are mutually interdependent; firm is highly dependent on market; it is an extension of the market. Market → Firm.
Emphasis is on the production process – on technical unit. Focus is on problems of manufacturing/ finance.	Emphasis is on own products of the firm – *on sales.*	Emphasis is on the customer needs and wants – on demand. Focus is on problems of marketing.
Marketing means: 'Sell what is produced.'	Marketing means: 'A good product does not sell by itself. It has to be pushed. Customers have to be manipulated.'	Marketing means: 'Targeting on customer needs/present or future purchasing patterns of demand.'
Prevalent in a situation of absolute scarcity, or during seller's market.	Prevalent in a situation of surplus production, surplus capacity, or when the market has not been surveyed properly.	Prevalent in a situation of relative affluence or during buyer's market. Prevalent in the developed and affluent countries since 1955.
Prevalent in the West Prior to 1930. Prevalent in areas, e.g., development nations at a production economy stage.	Prevalent in the West during 1930-1950 and when demand declined in certain industries.	Customer satisfaction is the focus of marketing universe.
Production was the centre of the universe.	Salesmanship and promotion acted as the focus of marketing universe.	It is assumed that goods are bought and not sold and profit is through customer satisfaction only.
It was assumed that best product could attract buyers automatically. Consumer choice could be based on quality in relation to price.	It is assumed that goods are not bought. They have to be sold at any cost, and profit is through sales volume.	
No need of aggressive salesmanship and publicity. Company sells what it can make.	Special selling efforts and promotion to capture and maintain demand.	If demand clicks with supply, no special selling efforts are necessary, problem is only of distribution, i.e., serving of demand. Company makes what it can sell.

Note: Since 1965 under environmental approach, marketing concept has been widened in the West. Government, market and pressure groups influence the firm and its marketing strategy. The firm has to adopt socially responsible marketing strategies. It has to cater to the needs of consumers as well as society – market needs in a social framework. It has to ensure quality of life, e.g., absence of food, air and water pollution. Consumerism and Government should achieve consumer protection and environmental protection. The firm now aims at benefits for both sides, i.e., customer satisfaction and profitability. Societal or social marketing concept appeared in many affluent countries from 1965. It is slowly spreading over also in other developing countries. It is now said that the so-called affluent countries have become really effluent countries. Developing countries should not be effluent countries.

Chart III

Types of Communication (Promotion) Influencing Various Stages in Buyer Behaviour

Components or Dimensions of Attitude	*Movement toward Purchase (Six-stage Sequence)*	*Types of Communication Relevant at each Stage*
(1) The Conative (Behavioural) Dimension It is the region of drives or motives, i.e., activated unsatisfied wants. Advertisements and sales promotion must stimulate and direct desires so as to motivate the consumer to buy a product. The buyer should be made ready to respond and he should have the conviction that the purchase would be wise. Purchase is the last step converting this attitude into actual purchase.	↑ 6 Purchase 5 Conviction	Point-of-purchase Material, Retail Store Advertising, Special Deals, 'Last Chance Offer', Price Appeals. Testimonials, Source Credibility, i.e., expertness and trustworthiness of the source, personal selling, interpersonal communication, word of mouth communication are essential in evaluation and adoption stages. Believability of company as a communicator is called source credibility.
(2) The Affective (Feelings and Emotions) Dimension It is the region of feelings and emotions. Consumer moves from knowledge to liking and preference, he develops a favourable attitude toward the product (liking) and then develops the point of preference. Promotion tools must stress the affective aspect of behaviour, i.e, the area of feelings and emotions must be tapped. Advertisments and sales promotion will change emotions and feelings.	↑ 4 Preference 3 Linking	Competitive Advertising, Argumentative Advertising Copy, Image Advertising, Status, Glamour Appeals stress on changing emotions and feelings of buyers. Opinion leaders are used as a good source of information and opinion – to change attitude of buyers through interpersonal communication.
(3) The Cognitive Dimension It is the region of awareness and knowledge. Promotion tools must emphasize the cognitive aspects of buyer behaviour in order to create awareness and knowledge. Advertising provides adequate information and facts.	↑ 2 Knowledge 1 Awareness	Announcements Advertising, Descriptive Avertising Copy, Classified Advertisements, Slogans, Jingles, Sky Writing, Television, Radio Advertisements. Mass media must be adopted to create awareness, provide knowledge and information.

Note: (1) Buying process involves six-stage sequence related to three basic psychological states: (1) The cognitive dimension (Awareness and Knowledge), (2) The affective dimension (Liking and Preference), and (3) The conative dimension (Conviction and Purchase).

(2) A firm does not have separate strategies of advertising, selling and sales promotion. It has one promotional mix, and this mix is an integral part of the overall marketing plan. The elements of promotion mix are not independent strategies. Each one supports the other. They are complementary tools of promotion. Taken together advertising, personal selling and sales promotion are the "Three Musketeers" of marketing programmes. Their motto is: "All for one and one for all." An integrated marketing mix means this, and nothing short of this can be thought by a marketer.

(3) Promotional plan should be in harmony with overall corporate objectives, policies, organisation and its competence. Promotional plan should be evaluated against specific promotional objectives as well as against the rest of the marketing mix.

(4) The proper coordination and integration of selling, advertising and promotion produces a far more efficient programme than an attempt to carry out thew activities without regard to their effects upon each other.

(5) Movement towards purchase is upwards. It starts from awareness and ends at purchase action or decision.

(6) The company reputation, created through advertising and other forms of mass communication, can enhance the effectiveness of the salesman. Company image is the personality or reputation of the company as perceived by customers, prospects, supplied shareholders, and the general public company image is created by communications, particularly through public relations.

❋ ❋ ❋

16

HUMAN RESOURCE MANAGEMENT

Introduction

Human resources are one of the key factors in economic development. Empirical studies in the past three decades have shown that the most efficient and effective means for the development of any society lies in an improvement in the quality of its human resources. Human resources are both a supplier of basic inputs like skills and a beneficiary of development. Basically, human resources are thought of as "the total knowledge, skills, creative abilities, talents, attitudes and aptitudes of an organisation's workforce, as well as the values, systems, ethics and benefits of an individual involved .... It is the sum total of inherent abilities, acquired knowledge and skills represented by the talents and aptitudes of the employed (work) persons."

It is now well-recognised that people are the key to success in any organisation.

Constituents of Human Resources

Human resources constitute the principal asset of an organisation. They consist of the total knowledge, skills, creative abilities, talents and aptitudes of an organisation's workforce as well as the values, attitudes and beliefs of the individuals involved in them. They are the sum total of the inherent abilities, acquired knowledge, skills represented by the talents and aptitudes of the employees. The quantity and quality of human resources of an organisation thus, become their edifice. An organisation such as a bank, industry or government can only be as strong as the people manning it are at various levels. It is, therefore, obvious that any organisation interested in real and rapid progress should exercise particular care about the personnel manning the posts at the various levels. One of the important and dynamic activities is the management of people, of the human resources. Management of human resources is the heart and soul of a manager. It is a challenging task because of the dynamic and unpredictable nature of the people. The employees should be equipped to handle their jobs effectively. They should also be given opportunities to expand their knowledge and thus, extend its utility to other jobs so that they may develop themselves and get equipped to handle higher responsibilities efficiently.

Quality and Utilisation of Human Resources

The success of any organisation depends on the quality of its human resources. Studies in the growth pattern of advanced countries have shown that improvements in the quality and utilisation of personnel have been a major factor in accelerating the pace of economic growth. It is the effectiveness of the human system, therefore, that differentiates successful, dynamic and progressive organisations from the others. As noted by Thomas J. Peters and Robert H. Waterman in their management classic, *In Search of Excellence:*

"Treat people as adults. Treat them as partners; treat them with dignity; treat them with respect. Treat them — not capital spending and automation — as the primary source of productivity gains. These are the fundamental lessons from the excellent companies' research. In other words, if you want productivity and the financial reward that goes with it, you must treat your workers as your most important asset."

"There was hardly a more pervasive theme in the excellent companies than respect for the individual. That basic belief and assumption were omnipresent. But like so much else we have talked about, it's not any one thing — one assumption, belief, statement, goal, value, system, or program — that makes the theme come to life. What makes it live at these companies is a plethora of structural devices, systems, styles and values, all reinforcing one another so that the companies are truly unusual in their ability to achieve extraordinary results through ordinary people."

The functional requirement of effective utilisation of human resources, be it in a macro social system or in a micro commercial organisation, for achieving the desired goals cannot be gainsaid. While in the traditional mould the human resources constitute only one of the factors of production, the very human nature has provided this factor with pre-eminence, as a vibrant, motivated and conscious human element imbued with the "quality of work life" which alone can make any enterprise work in today's complex and highly demanding environment. Human resources are a potential highyield investment and effective and optimum utilisation alone will yield — capacity, coupled with quality.

'HUMAN RELATIONS': CONCEPT AND FEATURES:

In simple terms, 'Human Relations' refer to the interaction of people in all walks of life. In the context of business organizations, the term 'Human Relations' refers to the interaction of people employed within the organizations and also the interaction between the organization and persons and groups outside it.

In its broader sense, the term 'Human Relations' refers to an area of management practice in integrating the people into work situation in a way that motivates them to work together productively, cooperatively and with economic, psychological and social satisfaction. It is a process of providing effective motivation to individuals in a given situation inorder to achieve balanced objectives which yield greater human satisfaction thereby help accomplishing corporate goals. It is a medium through which both employees and the organization mutually co-operate for the maximum satisfaction of the economic, social and psychological needs of the people having relations with the organization for increasing productivity. The above conceptual understanding unveils the following features of 'Human Relations':

- It is a strategic process whereby the work and attitudes of the individuals are integrated;
- It is an art of getting along with people either as individuals or as a group;
- It is the study of how people can work effectively in groups in order to satisfy both organizational as well as personal goals for greater productivity at work and greater human satisfaction;
- The objective of this process is to achieve a willing co-operation from the employees for meeting corporate objectives;

HUMAN GROWTH PROCESS

1
IDENTIFYING
THE HUMAN POTENTIAL
2
BASIC EDUCATION &
DEVELOPMENT OF THE
HUMAN POTENTIAL
3
EMPLOYMENT
TRAINING DEVELOPMENT
7 STAGES OF DEVELOPMENT
OF HUMAN POTENTIAL
4
ON THE JOB DEVELOPMENT AND
EXPERIENCE & MOTIVATION
5
REALISATION OF
INDIVIDUAL POTENTIAL

SCHEMATIC APPROACH TO HUMAN GROWTH

1
IDENTIFYING THE HUMAN POTENTIAL OF INDIVIDUAL
2
1ST STAGE OF DEVELOPMENT OF HUMAN
POTENTIAL THROUGH BASIC EDUCATION
3
EMPLOYMENT
2ND STAGE OF DEVELOPMENT OF HUMAN POTENTIAL
THROUGH TRAINING AND DEVELOPMENT
4
3RD STAGE OF DEVELOPMENT OF HUMAN POTENTIAL
THROUGH THE RIGHT OPPORTUNITY AT THE
RIGHT TIME IN THE CAREER PROGRESSION
5
4TH STAGE OF DEVELOPMENT OF HUMAN POTENTIAL
THROUGH THE RIGHT MOTIVATION, CHALLENGE, ACHIEVEMENT,
RESPONSIBILITY, WORK, POWER, STATUS,
LEADERSHIP, LEARNING & RELEARNING
6
5TH STAGE OF DEVELOPMENT OF SELF ACTUALISATION &
MAXIMUM HUMAN GROWTH

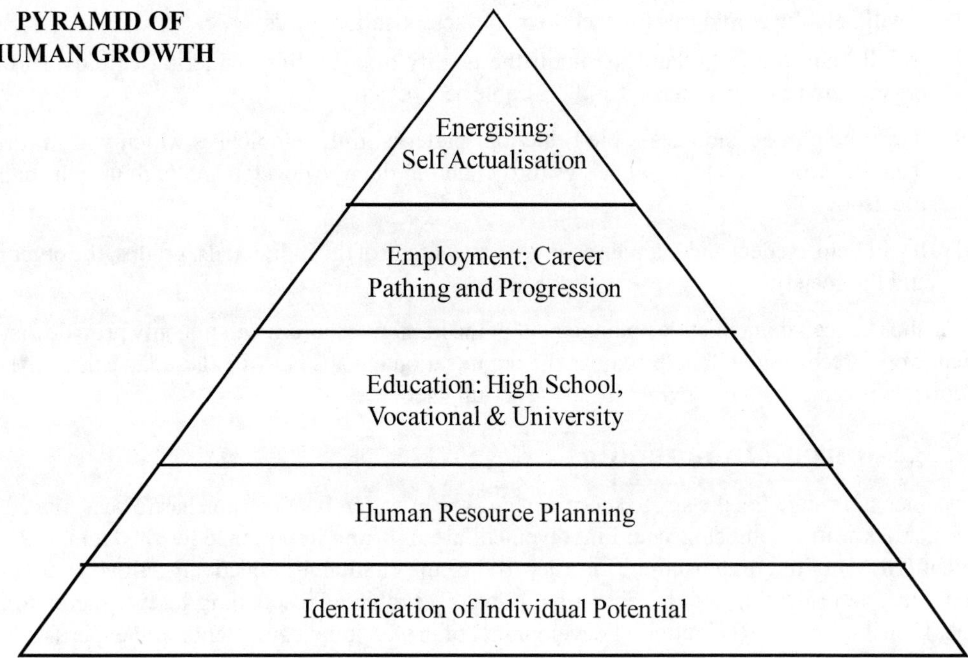

- Its purpose is neither to discover techniques strategies for winning friends and influencing people through personality development nor to enable the management to manipulate people as though they were puppets, but to assist the management in working more effectively.

Any human relations effort should aim at to achieve organizational goals and human goals. While the organizational goals consist of growth, productivity, profit maximization etc. which can be augmented to some extent by non-human factors like organizational complexity and structure, level of technology etc., the human goals encompass social and psychological factors like job satisfaction, recognition, career growth of employees which are possible to achieve only through providing motivation, Quality of Work Life (QWL) and congenial work environment etc.

Driven by the growing class-conflicts created by status and positions in the organizations, the industrial progress of future may largely depend upon the willingness and ability of the concerned industry in establishing mutual responsibility between the highest paid executive and the lowest paid worker in the organizational hierarchy. Obviously enough, one of the principal objectives of the human relations movement must be to attain a much needed congruence and integration between these structural elements, both in terms of psychological and social framework.

The Advantages

The advantages of managing the human resources are many. In fact, a careful examination would reveal the following advantages:

(a) It will help the organisation. to reach the set goals.

(b) It will help to effectively utilise the skills and abilities of the workforce.

(c) It will help to provide the banks with motivated and developed employee potential.

(d) It will help to develop employee job satisfaction.

(e) It will help the employees to meet their self-actualisation needs.

(f) It will help to develop and maintain the quality of work life, rendering employment in the organisation a highly merited and desirable occupation.

(g) It will help to develop desirable behaviour patterns in the employees which will in turn help them to become better social beings thus enabling them to develop and maintain the quality of life itself.

(h) It will help to effect and manage change to advantage of the individuals, groups, the organisation and the society.

It can thus be seen that effective management of the human resources will not only provide motivated and efficient workforce which will help achieve the organisational goals but will also enable them to become more functional citizens, thus improving the social set-up itself.

Human Resource Management

Customer satisfaction is the key to success of any organisation but the same has to be achieved by the internal customers whose competence and involvement are of prime importance for the Human Resource Management (HRM) of the organisation. In order to face the challenges effectively, HRM has to develop strong and effective leadership for the operational levels, capable of responding to every situation, be it Production, Distribution or FRD including development of professional competence and expertise.

Leadership at operational level is the most critical position where a company cannot afford to place people with less experience and less exposure to interact with customers who demand immediate and satisfactory solution to their problem. But the common phenomenon in control based organisations is that people with higher maturity and exposure drawn to the control layers and operational units are deprived of benefit of their expertise. Their responses to the customer are needed on the shop floor, across the table and not where the customer is asked to wait for the reply from the traditional 'Head Office.' One has to remember that today's customer has no time to wait. Deployment of people with maximum exposure and expertise to lead the operational units will enable the organisation to achieve the much talked about and much needed customer satisfaction.

Management system and managerial style are highly significant as to what extent, people would identify themselves with the organisation and its goals by taking initiative and remaining creative. In order to achieve the identification and involvement of people in a natural and spontaneous manner, the organisation has to ensure that the culture of management system and managerial style consists of 'sharing and caring' elements instead of threats and authority under which people work out of fear of losing the favour of the quantity managers who reduce people into virtual robots with pre-set programmes and whose concern is output for today and not survival for tomorrow. Hence, the organisation has to moderate its management system and style to maintain proactive and positive environment for building a pragmatic work culture. The same can be generated by the shop floor managers by supporting people to develop internal stimulations rather than developing through external stimulation. What is really required is more freedom and less interference for boosting up the creativity and initiative among the people for their developing a stake in the Organisation.

Advantages of Human Resources Management

The advantages of managing human resources are many. In fact, a careful examination would reveal the following advantages:

(a) It will help the banks to achieve the set goals.

(b) It will help to effectively utilise the skills and abilities of the workforce.

(c) It will help to provide the banks with motivated and developed employee potential.

(d) It will help develop employee job satisfaction.

(e) It will help the employees to meet their self-actualisation needs.

(f) It will help develop and maintain the quality of work life, rendering employment in the organisation a highly merited and desirable occupation.

(g) It will help develop desirable behaviour patterns in the employees which will in turn help them to become better social beings, thus enabling them to develop and maintain the quality of life itself.

(h) It will help effect and manage change to the advantage of the individuals, groups, the organisation and the society.

It can thus be seen that effective management of the human resources will not only provide a motivated and efficient workforce which will help achieve the organisational goals but will also enable them to become more functional citizens, thus improving the societal set-up itself.

SCOPE OF HUMAN RELATIONS IN ORGANISATIONS

The necessity for pursuing a good human relations approach can be better understood from the constraints that are associated with managing people at work. As discussed, managing human element in organizations is quite difficult but equally challenging. Every employee possess a unique set of educational standards, intellectual capabilities, talents, skills, attitudes, needs, drives, ambitions and work experience towards the job.

As the human being is mostly conditioned by his formative experiences, he often tries to change the course of his personal attributes according to his responses to such past experiences. Meaning thereby, if his experience towards an incident is positive, he may be motivated to improve his behaviour and attitude. This apart, it is rightly said that the man is identified with the company (group) he belongs. This statement emphasises that the collective behaviours of the group or team to which they belong are the potential influencers of his individual behaviour. Hence, his personal attributes also vary from time to time according to the friend circle or formal and informal group in which he is a member. While the technology is of late making massive inroads into the Indian organizations, integrating the varied sets of such personal attributes with the highly standardized technology as a responsive tool, is a potential challenge and this can be possible only through maintaining cordial human relations.

In the organizational framework, the scope of work and activity of each functional unit is determined largely having regard to the organizational structure, size, location, reporting relations, decision making pattern, geographical spread, financial status, level of technology etc. The organizational effectiveness can be achieved if and when the management succeeds in getting all these factors properly assimilated in an orderly manner, which cannot be possible without maintaining human relations within and outside the organizations.

Technology perforce the organizations to continuously innovate and change in its content and strategies. The winds of 'change' are of late blowing hard in all walks of life and the organizations, being the products of society, have no exception to this global phenomenon. Given the fact that the Indian organizations are mostly multi-union entities co-existing with intense political interference and inter & intra union rivalries,

Functions	Activities	Profiles	Educational background	Careers
Creators	Invention and innovation Very high technology content		Third level Emphasis on research and development	Scientists and engineers
Teachers	Communication and transformation High technology content		Third level Emphasis on science and technology	Educators and trainers
Managers	Activation and cordination Medium technology content		Third level Emphasis on business and commerce	Entrepreneurs, executives and supervisors
Operators	Operation and correction Low technology content		Second level Emphasis on vocations and crafts	Technicians and craftsmen
Workers	Production and construction Very low technology content		First level Emphasis on literacy and vocation	Skilled and unskilled labourers

Education Know-why Knowledge

Experience Do-how Practice

Training Know-how Technique

attempting such a change initiative in any form including innovation in technology, production methods, organizational structure etc., may invite strong resistance from workforce and its representative unions on the premise that such changes may be detrimental to their interests and infringement of their rights. Such individual and collective resistance although cannot be eliminated altogether, but can be reduced to a greater extent by maintaining cordial relations among workforce and their representative unions.

What is Human Resources Development?

HRD is defined as "activities and processes undertaken by an organisation to promote the intellectual, moral, psychological, cultural, social and economic development of the individuals in an organisation, in order to help them to achieve the highest human potential as a resource for the community." It means to bring about a total all-round development of the people so that they can contribute their best to the organisation, community, society and the nation. HRD does not cover only a set of mechanisms or techniques but it is a process by which employees in an organisation are helped in a planned way to:

(a) *acquire or sharpen capabilities* required to perform the various functions associated with their present or expected future roles;

(b) *develop their general capabilities* as individuals and discover and exploit their own inner potentials for their own and/or organisational development purposes; and

(c) *develop an organisation culture* in which superior-subordinate relationships, teamwork and collaboration among sub-units are strong and contribute to the professional well-being, motivation and pride of employees.

The human resources development (HRD) concept is much wider and embraces almost all areas of an organisation. In the context of banking, HRD would mean not only the acquisition of knowledge and skills but also acquiring capabilities to anticipate and manage both internal and external environment and attaining self-confidence and motivation for public service. Further, HRD is not a piecemeal or a one-time exercise; it is a continuous process requiring to keep pace with the changes and developments taking place.

Manpower is utilised to the maximum possible extent to achieve individual and organisational goals. Manpower planning is, therefore, an important segment of the business plan. In a service-oriented industry like banking, manpower planning is quite significant. It is a means to human resources development.

What is Manpower Planning?

Manpower planning is a useful guide. It gives both balance and direction, i.e., manpower input and its multi-faceted uses. It is the identification of various action steps committing human resources towards achieving results beneficial to the organisation. It involves clarity of objectives. In the words of Peter F. Drucker, "Objectives must be derived from *our need both in quantitative as well as qualitative* (italics author's) terms. They are the fundamental strategy of a business." Manpower planning is the process of examination and re-examination, of continual consideration of the future, of constant searching for more effective methods of accomplishment and improved results.

Definitions of Manpower Planning

Coleman has defined "manpower planning" as "the process of determining human resources requirements and the means for meeting those requirements in order to carry out the integrated plan of the organisation."

Edwin B. Flippo states: "An executive manpower planning programme can be defined as an appraisal of an organisation's ability to perpetuate itself with respect to its management as a determination of measures necessary to provide the essential executive talent."

Edwin Geisler defines it thus: "Manpower-planning is the process (including forecasting, implementing and controling by which a firm ensures that it has the right number of people and the right kind of people at the right place, at the right time, doing things for which they are economically most useful."

Welter has defined manpower planning as "the process by which a management determines how an organisation should move from its current manpower position to its desired manpower position. Through planning, a management strives to have the right number and the right kinds of people at the right place, at the right time, to do things which result in both the organisation and the individual receiving the maximum long-range benefits."

According to Wickstrom, manpower planning consists of a series of activities, viz.:

(a) Forecasting future manpower requirements, either in terms of mathematical projections of trends in the economic environment and developments in industry, or in terms of judgemental estimates based upon the specific future plans of a company;

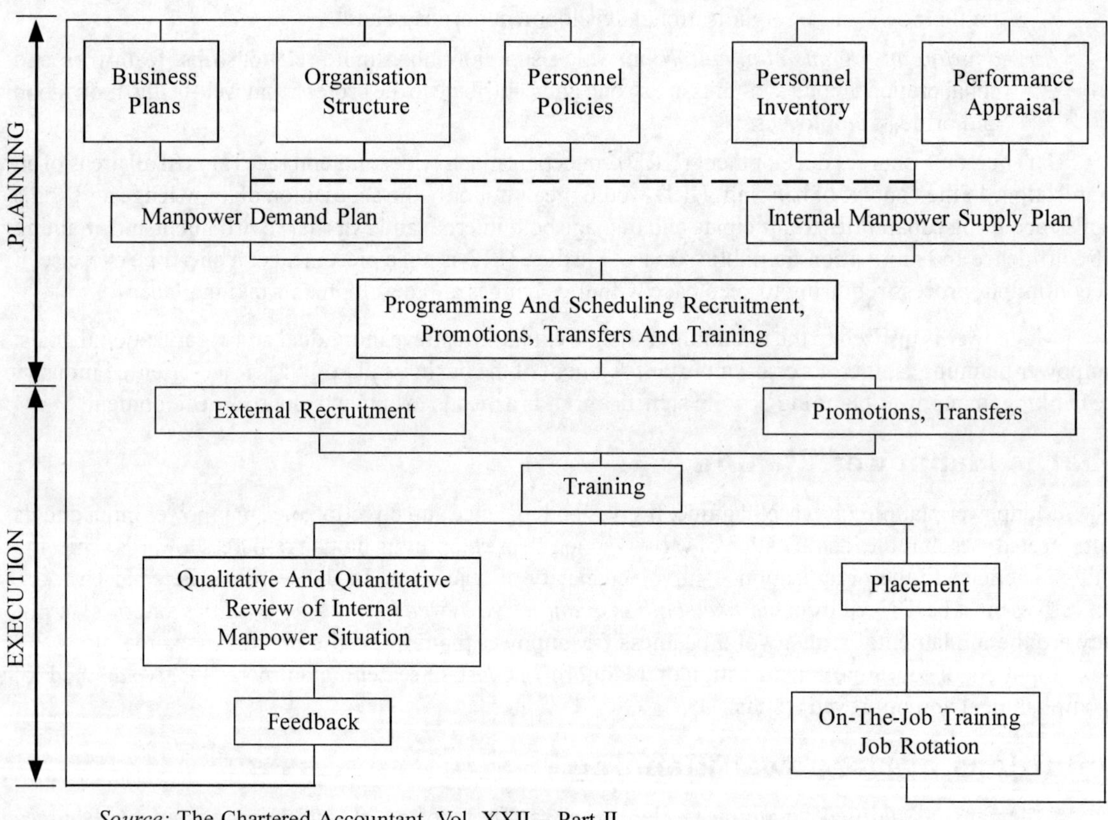

Source: The Chartered Accountant, Vol. XXII – Part II

Fig. 16.1: Diagrammatic Representation of Manpower Functions in a Bank

(b) Making an inventory of present manpower resources and assessing the extent to which these resources are employed optimally;

(c) Anticipating manpower problems by projecting present resources, the future and comparing them with the forecast of requirements to determine their adequacy, both quantitatively and qualitatively; and

(d) Planning the necessary programmes of recruitment, selection, training, development, utilisation, transfer, promotion, motivation and compensation to ensure that future manpower requirements are properly met.

Thus, it will be noted that *manpower planning consists in projecting future manpower requirements and developing manpower plans for the implementation of the projections.* This planning cannot be rigid or static; it is amenable to modification, review and adjustments in accordance with the needs of an organisation or the changing circumstances.

Human resources planning is a double-edged weapon. If used properly, it leads to the maximum utilisation of human resources, reduces excessive labour turnover and high absenteeism; improves productivity and aids in achieving the objectives of an organisation. Faultily used, it leads to disruption in the flow of work, lower production, lower job satisfaction, high cost of production and constant headaches for the management. Therefore, for the success of an enterprise, human resources planning is a very important function, which can be neglected only at its own peril. It is as necessary as planning for production, marketing, or capital investment.

For an individual, it is important because it helps him to improve his skills and utilise his capabilities and potential to the utmost. For an organisation, it is important because it improves its efficiency and productivity. It is only through initial human manpower planning that capable hands are available for promotion in the future.

The definitions of manpower planning stated above possess the following features:

(1) It includes all activities in regard to human resources.

(2) It is concerned with finding out the manpower requirements of the organisation in the right number and at the right time.

(3) It determines in advance the manpower requirements so that there will be enough time for training and development of manpower.

(4) It includes inventory of present manpower of the organisation. An analysis of the existing inventory helps in determining the status of available personnel and to discover the untapped talent presently within the organisation.

(5) With the knowledge of total needs of manpower and the present supply of available personnel, it takes decisions to meet the difference between demand and supply of manpower. If future needs are more than the available talent, it initiates programmes for recruitment and development of manpower. On the other hand, if future needs are less than the available talent, it takes measures such as retiring personnel, etc.

(6) To be effective, manpower planning must include not only recruitment, development of workers, etc., but also their working conditions.

Objectives of Manpower Planning

Manpower planning fulfils individual organisational and national goals. The principal objective of manpower planning is to match the power or integrate it with the organisational plan to achieve the goals or objectives.

The objectives of manpower planning are:

(1) Identify and assess future human resource needs.
(2) Analyse and improve upon utilisation of existing resources.
(3) Relate future human resources to future organisational needs so as to maximise the future return on investment in human resources.
(4) Match employee abilities to organisational requirements, with an emphasis on future instead of present arrangement.
(5) Plan for the required human resources in terms of skills, knowledge, aptitude, attitude of the existing and newly-recruited human resources.
(6) Ensure optimum use of human resources currently employed.
(7) To assess or forecast future skills requirements of the organisational overall objectives are to be achieved; and
(8) Provide control measures to ensure that the necessary resources are available as and when required.
(9) Integrate and coordinate human resource policies so that the present and future human resources are met easily.

A few more specific reasons for attaching importance to manpower planning and forecasting exercises are:

(1) To determine recruitment level;
(2) To anticipate redundancies and avoid unnecessary dismissals;
(3) To determine optimum training levels;
(4) To provide a basis for management development programmes;
(5) To cast the manpower in new projects;
(6) To assist productivity bargaining; and
(7) To assess future accommodation requirements.

Need for Human Resources Planning

Human resources planning is deemed necessary for all banks for the following reasons:

(1) To carry on its work, each organisation needs personnel with the necessary qualifications, skills, knowledge, work experience and aptitudes. These are provided through effective planning.
(2) Since a large number of persons have to be replaced who have grown old, or who retire, die or become incapacitated because of physical or mental ailments, there is a constant need for replacing such personnel.
(3) Human resources planning is essential because of frequent labour turnover which is unavoidable and even beneficial because it arises from factors which are socially and economically sound such as voluntary quits, discharges, marriage, promotions; or factors such as seasonal and cyclical fluctuations in business which cause a constant ebb and flow in the workforce in many organisations.
(4) In order to meet the needs of expansion programmes which become necessary because of increase in the demand for goods and services by a growing population, a rising standard of living, which calls for larger quantities of the same goods and services as also for new goods; the competitive

position of a firm which brings it more business arising from improvements effected in the slump period; and the rate of growth of the organisation, human resources planning is unavoidable.

(5) The nature of the present workforce in relation to its changing needs also necessitates the recruitment of new labour. To meet the challenge of a new and changing technology and new techniques of production, existing employees need to be trained or new blood injected into an organisation.

(6) Manpower planning is also needed in order to identify areas of surplus personnel or areas in which there is a shortage of personnel. If there is a surplus, it can be redeployed; and if there is a shortage, it may be made good.

Steps in Manpower Planning

Manpower planning is a process. The important steps in manpower planning in banks are:

(1) Formulation of long-range, short-range objectives, plans, programmes, and budgets of banks regarding their key activities like branch expansion, deposits and other sources of mobilisation, loans and advances, organisation and other key services.

(2) Estimation of overall manpower requirements — occupational, category and skill-wise analyses at different levels of the bank's hierarchy.

(3) Find out the current inventory or manpower, principal dimensions of manpower inventory being:

(a) Head counts — total, department, sex, designation, skill-wise.

(b) Job family inventory — clerks, typists, officers — General, Technical, and at different levels like grade A, B, C and D.

(c) Age Inventory.

(d) Inventory of experience, skill, talent, ablilty, aptitude, knowledge and the like.

(e) Inventorv of qualifications, training and executive development.

(f) Inventory of salary grades.

(i) Inventory of performance.

(h) Inventory of potential.

(4) Forecast the changes in human resources inventory due to employee turnover, transfers, promotions, demotions, training and career plan and development.

The plan factors and forecasts will help the banker to determine the quantity and quality of work to be turned out and thereby to estimate the total number and kind of personnel (branch-wise, department-wise, category-wise, job-wise etc.) required to meet the future demand in terms of knowledge, skill, creative abilities, talents, aptitudes, attitudes, and the like. In this connection, the banker also takes into consideration short-term goals, plans, programmes and budgets, etc.

(5) Find out the difference between the current inventory and future total human resources requirements.

(6) Correcting the imbalances between demand and supply.

(7) Action programmes for recruiting and selecting for the needed human resources or adjusting the employees through transfers, promotions or adjusting human resources through moulding and developing.

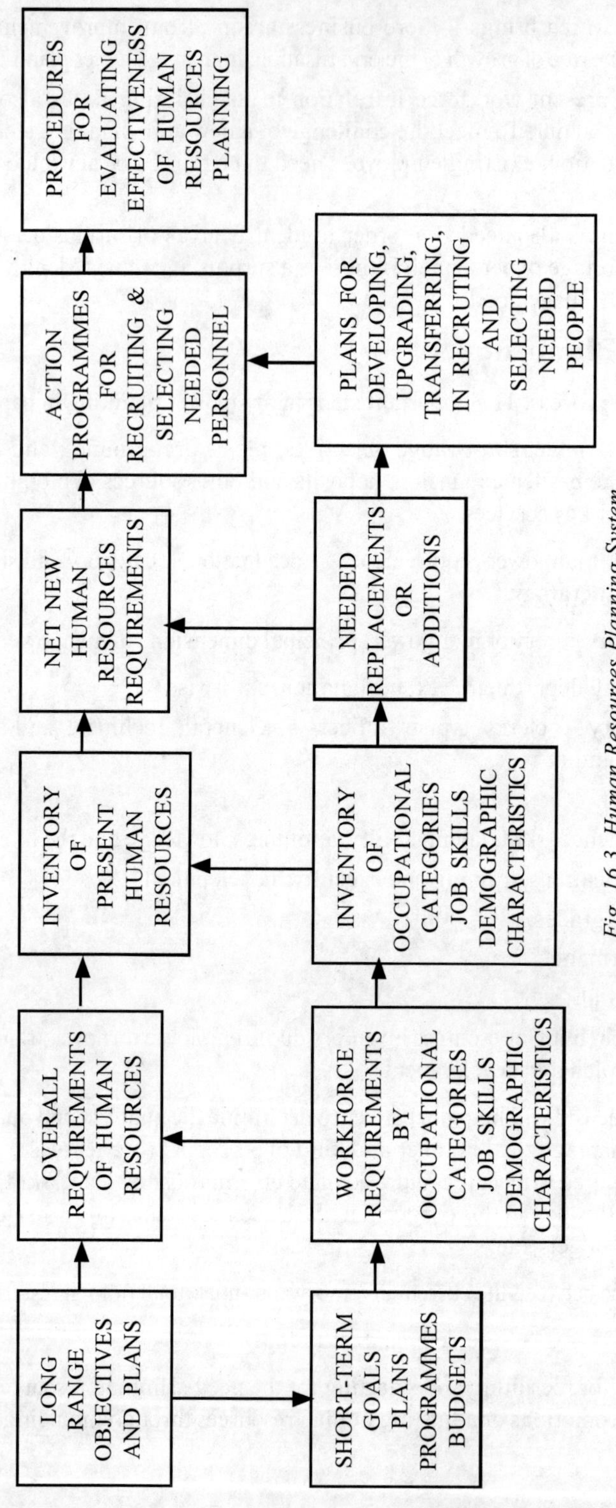

Fig. 16.3. Human Resources Planning System.

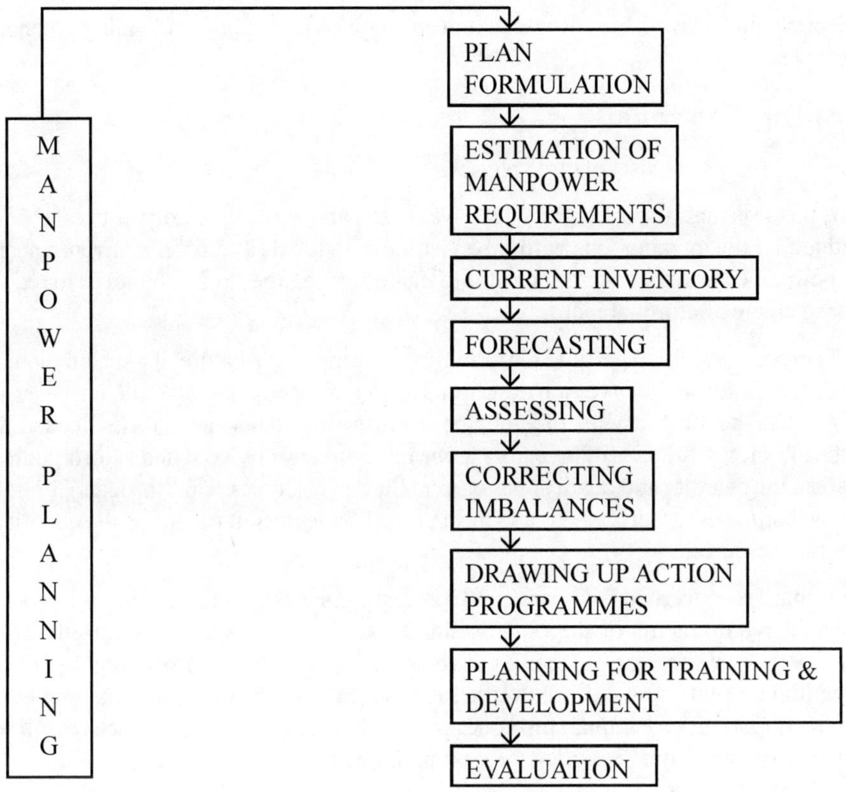

Fig. 16.4. Steps in Manpower Planning.

(8) Prepare the plans for training, development, promotions, transfers, demotions, etc.

(9) Evaluating the performance.

Factors affecting human resources supply are:

(1) Internal Factors: (a) Present inventory; *(b)* Possible changes in the present inventory.

(2) External Factors: (a) Local population density in the area, local unemployment level, availability of employees on part-time/temporary basis, current competition for similar categories, outcome from local educational institutions, pattern of immigration, residential facilities available, local transport and communication facilities.

(b) National: Trends in the growth of the working population, training institutes, schemes, technical, professional, vocational and general educational institutes, social security measures, unemployment benefits, lay off, retrenchment, cultural factors, customs, social values and the like.

Time Period for Manpower Planning

Manpower planning can be classified on the basis of time span. On this basis, manpower planning can be made short-term, medium-term or long-term. Generally, short-term planning is made for a period of up to two years, medium-term planning up to 5 years and long-term planning for more than 5 years. While short-term manpower planning is essentially concerned with matching the existing jobs with the existing individuals and filling current vacancies with the available talent, medium and long-term manpower planning is concerned mainly with future vacancies.

Manpower Planning Process

Manpower planning process consists of three phases:

Phase One: This phase is mainly concerned with job analysis and skills inventory. It tries to find out its current position and match the existing jobs with the existing individuals and filling current vacancies with the available manpower, because the time is too short to make any changes in personnel or to recruit or to develop personnel or to create or eliminate jobs.

Job analysis is the process by which pertinent information relating to the nature of a specific job in the organisation is obtained. Jobs analysis involves job description and job specification. While job description describes the job and specifies the requirements of a job, job specification states the qualities needed for an individual to perform the job successfully. Skill inventory as we have already observed helps the organisation in getting infonnation about the quantity and quality of its current human resources. Thus through job analysis, an organisation can know its current resource needs and through skill inventory, it can know the quantity and quality of its current human resources.

Phase Two: This phase is concerned with personnel forecasting. Personnel forecasting is a process by which the future personnel requirements of the organisation to achieve the organisational objectives is determined. For making personnel forecasting, many variables such as composition of present workforce, skill required in the potential new business venture, future sales projections, technological changes etc., are considered. Because of the important role human resources play in attaining enterprise objectives, all levels of management should be involved in the personnel forecasting process.

Phase Three: This phase is concerned with the taking of measures to obtain the quantity and quality of human resources to achieve the enterprise objectives. In the second phase, human resource requirements have been estimated to achieve enterprise objectives. These human resource needs indicate gross personnel requirements. The skills inventory which has been done in the first phase of the manpower planning process indicates the current quantity and quality of human resources with the enterprise. The difference between the gross personnel requirements and the organisation's current level of human resources is referred to as the net 'personnel requirements'. It may be positive or negative. The organisation takes measures to bring the current level of quantity and quality of its human resources in tune with the requirements as forecast. To achieve this, the methods adopted are recruitment, selection, training, promotion, transfer, lay offs and retirement of employees.

Career Planning

Career planning is choosing an occupation keeping in view one's resources and environmental conditions. Career planning is not an event or an end but a process which requires continuous examination of the goal, the strategies to be chosen, the resources and limitations on the part of the individual, the organisation and the environment. Career planning is of less importance in a stable society but has greater importance in an adaptive society. Career planning requires that individual employees, particularly those in the supervisory and managerial role, develop early in their careers, insights into their suitability for creative vs. ordinary or routine work. Those who do not possess or cannot develop the ability required for top level managerial positions might look towards routine jobs in large organisations.

From the above, it clearly follows that career planning is an essential aspect of managing people to obtain the maximum performance. It is aimed at:

(a) improving the performance of subordinates on their present job in terms of results to be accomplished;

(b) to prepare employees to accept increasing responsibility in their present jobs; and

(c) to help subordinates grow and develop for higher level jobs.

Career planning is thus an important and an integral part of the manpower planning and development system.

The overall aim of career planning is to give individuals the guidance and encouragement they need to bring out their potential and have a successful career in the organisation matching their talents and aspirations.

Myths of Career Planning

There are many myths related to career planning which have surfaced over the years. These myths are often misleading and can inhibit career growth. One such myth is that there is always room for one more person at the top. The major lesson to be learned is to choose career paths that are realistic and attainable. The second myth is that career planning is the sole responsibility of the organisation. But career planning and development is a two-way process and both the organisation and the individual must play their part. The ultimate responsibility for career planning, however, rests with the individual. Successful career planning results from the joint efforts of the individual and the organisation. The individual does the planning and the organisation provides the necessary guidance and resources.

A person is more likely to experience satisfaction as progress is made along the career path. A good career plan identifies certain milestones and when these are consciously recognised and reached, the person is likely to experience a sense of achievement. The feeling of accomplishment increases the individual's personal satisfaction and motivation.

Responsibility for Career Planning

A fundamental question regarding career planning arises as to who is responsible for career planning: is it the employee or the management? Career planning is basically an individual's responsibility. However, in the organisational context, it is the organisation's responsibility to guide and direct the employees to develop and utilise their knowledge, abilities and resources toward organisational development and effectiveness. Employee goals have to be integrated with organisational goals. The organisation must provide career counselling services. Such a programme has the following objectives:

(a) Provide a normal, mature person with guidelines to help him understand himself more clearly and develop his thinking and outlook.

(b) Enable the individual to study the immediate and personal world in which he lives, a world different from all others and possibly more exciting.

(c) To bring about a closer relationship between people as well as increase one's awareness of human needs.

(d) To understand the forces and dynamics operating in a system.

(e) To achieve and enjoy greater personal satisfaction, pleasure and happiness.

The individual and the organisation will have to operate in close coordination in the 'career exercise' and the organisation has to provide timely intervention at various stages of the career programmes to make it a fruitful and satisfying experience, both for the employee and the institution. Any attitudinal slackness on the part of the organisation can result in demoralisation leading to frustration and ultimate collapse of the Career Planning System. The phasewise close monitoring remains the prime responsibility of the organisation.

At the start of the career, new skills are acquired, knowledge increases rapidly, and aspirations and inclinations are clarified. Job rotation programme opens up 'career paths' that were previously blocked to a person because he lacked the necessary experience.

The first step towards attaining the skills for a higher position in the hierarchy is identifying and defining those skills. This can be done either by the organisation or by the individual aspiring for promotion. The relative importance of the various skills at different levels can be highlighted diagrammatically. As one moves higher, the importance of technical skills is reduced, and that of conceptual skill gains prominence. Broadly speaking, the skills at different level areas shown in Fig. 16.2. The organisation plays a prominent role at this stage in providing opportunity for all-round experience and enables the employee to identify skills and qualities needed for the current and future jobs.

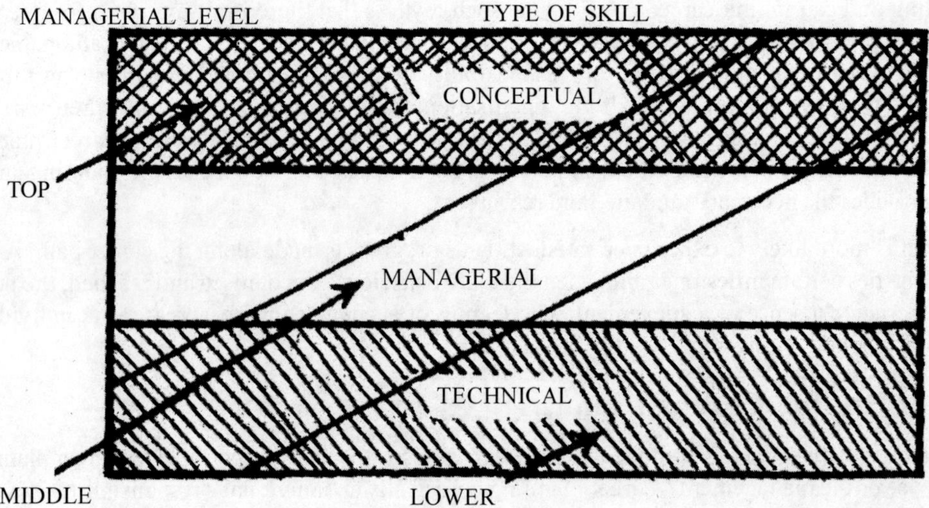

Fig. 16.2: Types of Skills

The all-round multifarious experience gained in the initial years brings the employee to a critical point, where he has to choose his career path. The skill and knowledge gained in the formative years is applied, tested identified and consolidated, and aspirations are confirmed and amended accordingly. The organisation's role in the career development of the employee at this juncture is to help him align and integrate personal, aspirations with organisational objectives. The organisation also, keeping in view the future needs, should make available career paths not just for upward mobility but lateral too.

Persistent people know they can succeed where cleverer and more talented people fail. It involves making choices, which is risky. Successful people understand that no one makes it to the top in a single bound. What truly sets them apart is their willingness to keep putting one step in front of the other — no matter how rough the terrain.

Career Planning Process

On the basis of manpower planning, the organisation will have the following information:

(a) An inventory of manpower resources.

(b) Manpower needs, in terms of numbers, types, skills, levels and time dimensions.

(c) Changes in functions and activities expected in the next two or five or ten years hence, if not for a longer period.

(d) Nature and extent of behavioural changes required to meet the manpower needs.

(e) Availability of human resources within and without the organisation, training opportunities, training resources and training time, etc.

On, the basis of the above information, an effective organisational career planning process should include the following:

(A) Assessment of occupational and career choice.

(B) Personnel assessment.

(C) Annual appraisal and development programme.

Career Growth of Employees

Employees can feel the organisational interest in their growth, if they are provided with constant information on banking, its schemes, ways of improving business, etc., as this would give them confidence and motivation to achieve better and give them a taste of success. A newsletter providing this relevant information which also encourages their participation and suggestion would facilitate "information explosion". Open communication should be encouraged through various ways and employees should talk about bank schemes. Without proper dissemination of work-aiding information, the employees are conspicuously oblivious of the progress of their own bank and its services and do not get a visible feel of the organisation. By professionalising in any fashion, they would feel that the organisation means business. For if newly inducted employees are straightaway put in the field to collect deposits, it would help in developing them as field people and also help the organisation by adding to its deposits.

Successful Career Planning Programme

(1) An organisation must have clear corporate goals for the next five, ten and fifteen years.

(2) On the basis of corporate plans, an organisational analysis should be conducted periodically to determine the types of changes, its functions, activities, procedures, technology, materials.

(3) Unless the above two are completed, an organisation cannot develop the manpower planning system, thus reducing the need for career planning.

(4) Career planning requires selecting the right man for the right job. Job design systems require understanding employee resources and clarity of organisational, divisional and unit goals. In an employment-oriented organisation, there is hardly any place for career planning except at the top level. In most government organisations in India, employees stagnate at the very level they join. In most cases, getting a job and holding on to it is a blessing and an achievement.

(5) Career planning is a top management philosophy and commitment. The success of career planning programme will depend upon the sincerity of the top management and the interest it takes in the development

and utilisation of the employee to achieve organisational effectiveness, development, innovation, health and vitality.

(6) Career planning is a continuous process. This process may be followed yearly, two-yearly or five-yearly. In organisations such as space research, electronics and other adaptive organisations, the process should be carried out more frequently and consistently.

(7) An effective career planning programme requires interested, goal directed, motivated and hard-working employees. An organisation can create an environment and show genuine concern for the development of the employee but the employee must be willing to make use of the resources and opportunities available.

Career planning is an integral part of manpower planning. It contributes towards individual development and utilisation as well as organisational development.

Human resource planning is a continuous process. HRP is a futuristic planning. Considering the growth areas of the organisation in the next five years, the HRP department analyses and identifies the requirements of human resource of each department and each functional area of the organisation.

The human resource is classified mainly into four categories: (1) Skilled, (2) Semi-skilled, (3) Unskilled and (4) Administrative staff. A thorough assessment is made about the posts vacant, job requirements, future demand for and supply of various categories of people in both management and non-management cadres. Depending upon the product or the service scale of operation and technique of production, different organisations will have different requirements of human resource. Accordingly year wise requirement of various categories of employees is assessed. Further details about the desired qualifications, and experienced expertise are also scrutinised and a master plan of human resource requirement is prepared.

Human resources is an asset of an organisation. It is responsible for either the success or the failure of the organisation. It has been seen that many organisations have survived in adverse situations only because of their dedicated, committed human resource in spite of a conducive environment. Some are wiped off from the industrial scene only because of unproductive, uncommitted, indisciplined human resource. Thus, human resource employed in the organisation plays a vital role in the "making or breaking" of the organisation.

From the organisational point of view, human resource has an economic contribution. Organisations compare the contribution to the productivity by a worker and the cost incurred on that worker. Human resource constitutes a major cost component as in most of the organisations, nearly 50 per cent of the total cost is spent on the wage bills and other benefits to the human resource. Therefore, while planning the human resource, it becomes obligatory for the organisations to assess the productivity of the employees and to plan for the optimum utilisation of human resource. The following specific issues are considered for the efficient and effective utilisation of human resource.

- Whether right people are appointed for right jobs?
- Are they doing the job in the right manner?
- Do they need further training?
- Is there a surplus workforce?
- Is there a deficiency in workforce?
- How to resolve the surplus/deficient workforce situation?

A solution. to the above issues cannot be given in isolation. Its impact on production, finance and general administration has to be considered in minute details. Therefore, HRP is a part of the strategic, integrated planning process.

The Art of Managing People

Supervision of your employees is an art that varies from country to country, and situation to situation. What follows is for consideration only, and should be supplemented with the appropriate art of supervision for our country, our culture and our situations. However, while you are working through this section, look for a few working clues for your initial thinking.

What do Employees Expect From Their Employers?

***(i)* Fairness:** The first answer to this is probably fairness. They want to be treated fairly and equitably.

***(ii)* Training:** The first step in being fair suggests developing confidence that the employee can do the job. It is your responsibility to train him, and he expects to be trained. Assume the stance that if the employee has not learned, you have not taught.

***(iii)* Clear understanding of role and responsibilities:** It is necessary that your employee knows what exactly is expected of him. This should be covered both in job description and in written statements of policies, procedures, rules and regulations. If things are written down and periodically discussed informally with the employee you will eliminate a major source of friction in a small business. Be clear about what you want and expect, and measure the performance based on that.

***(iv)* Fairness in Handling Problems:** It does no one any good to handle a problem in a combative role, as this will activate defence mechanism of the others' mind, and the need for the preservation of both egos can often lead to something harsh, such as terminating employment. Most problems should be treated in such a manner that they do not occur again. Discussing it with the employees should be to make them understand when the problem was created, learning how to do it differently next time.

Many societies are adopting the stance that if an employee commits an error:

(1) For the first time, make sure that there were no extenuating circumstances. If not, assume that the employee did not really know and then inform the employee what is expected. This may be done verbally or as a written notice to the general attention of all employees.

(2) If it happens the second time and is within a reasonable period of time after step 1, it is fair to discuss the situation with the employee. If you determine that the employee did not have extenuating circumstances and should be forgiven, advise that it must stop, or else disciplinary action will be necessary. This may be put in writing, a copy must be given to the employee and a copy must be kept in his personal file.

(3) If within a reasonable time, the problem persists, take disciplinary action and ensure that the employee knows and accepts why action was taken.

In this process you should demonstrate fairness even if a situation turns bad. Of course, there are some standard situations where quicker action is needed and expected, such as fighting on the job, etc. In handling any situation, remember that you are to be seen to be fair in the eyes of all employees.

***(v)* Pleasant and safe working conditions:** The work environment should be a pleasant place in which one can work. This has less to do with the physical facilities (with some comfort and health exceptions) than with the development of a friendly and helpful atmosphere among fellow workers and management. If people enjoy working for you (this does not infer they do not work hard), they will enjoy coming to work and doing a good job. There is a great advantage in sharing your goals and aspirations with your workers so that their level of motivation may be along the same lines.

***(vi)* Sense of growth:** Many employees want to feel that they are growing in their employment with you. People grow in maturity over a period of time, and may wish to assume new responsibilities in their work.

***(vii)* Sense of belonging:** Most employees want to feel that they play an important part in operation of the business. They want to be seen as contributing to the overall well-being of the business.

SELECTING EMPLOYEES

When recruiting employees, there are some basic points to consider. Such points are as below:

(1) Hire a person who can grow into the job, when suitable opportunities are developed. Recruiting/hiring an overqualified person will usually lead to that person becoming bored unless there are other considerations that will contribute to the employee being content to work with you, such as part-time work close to home, wanting a change, etc.

(2) Recruit/hire and train personnel in order to be prepared if someone leaves or gets sick. There is a merit in cross training people to do the jobs of others, although it may threaten the feeling of being uniquely valuable to a firm.

(3) Avoid hiring persons with a history of possessing bad habits such as addiction to drugs, drinking or with social problems. Do not try to salvage people until you are well established and have the time and energy available to do so.

(4) Avoid someone begging for a job as there may be a good reason why they did not get any other job.

(5) Avoid hiring the first applicant on the first interview. It is a motivator to let employees know that they had to compete for a job and that they were the successful applicants.

(6) Be extremely cautious of glowing references and recommendations. Follow them up and find out. Always probe further the validity of recommendations.

(7) Do not hire for good looks and a suave manner unless you just want to decorate your office. Select on the basis of the ability to do a job well, first and foremost.

(8) Do not assume that a high salary will assure productivity. High salaries are often paid because the employer is too lazy to train and wants to purchase the qualifications. High pay can be a temporary motivator but there are other major motivators that also have to be at play, i.e., can the person really do the job to your time standards, contribute in accomplishing the aims of business/organisation, etc.

(9) Do not change a job description just because a higher qualified candidate comes along. Who will handle the lesser work chores ? Hence once the job description is decided, keep that as focus for selection.

(10) Have a probationary period. It will help both employer and employee.

(11) Have standards of performance that are easily quantifiable and to which you should measure the performance of the person during the probationary period. Do make it clear to the employee, what the standards of performance are, and how they will be measured.

(12) Be fair on measurement of the standards of performance by allowing a reasonable time for the person to learn the job and get up to speed before you assess them. But do not alter the standards of a job just because the new employee cannot accomplish them. It may be better to dismiss an employee during the probationary period and find someone who can do the job to suit your standards (assuming that others have been able to do so).

(13) Be careful in hiring friends and/or relatives because your emotional bias may interfere with your judgement to the point where you upset other employees who may feel that you are not treating all fairly and equally or prevent you from recognising that they are not up to standard. Too many relatives in a business will discourage other employees as they will not consider they have room to grow.

FORMULATING WORK POLICIES

As soon as you decide to recruit/hire your first employee, you must make decisions relating to personnel policies, The selection and management of your employees is critical to the success of your business. You must anticipate how you will deal with the situations that you expect to arise in the daily operations of your business. Most of all, you must treat everyone fairly.

Formulating your personnel policies in writing will put them on record and will make it easier to enforce them. Each employee will thus have the same information. These policies are also very useful for the orientation of new employees.

Personnel policies should include all matters that would affect employees. You might want to consider written policy decisions for the following areas:

- Hours of work — number of hours per week, number of days per week, overtime, evening and week-end work.
- Safety — accident prevention.
- Compensation — hourly wages.
- Fringe benefits — group life insurance, pension plan, extended health benefits, group disability plan.
- Vacations — length, time of the year, with or without pay.
- Time off — for personal needs, emergencies in the family, holidays, special days such as election days.
- Education and Training — on the job training, costs of training.
- Personnel Welfare — profit sharing, social get-together, housing, transport.
- Retirement — pension plan.
- Discipline — improvement, disciplinary action, penalties.
- Grievances — procedure for handling grievances, employees' right to demand review, provision for third party arbitration.
- Promotions, Transfers — normal increase of wages, change of job titles.
- Disputes — settlement of disputes, arbitration, adjudication.
- Personnel review — frequency of review, factors to be considered, effect on salary adjustments, training recommendations.
- Termination — lay offs, seniority rights, severance pay, conditions warranting summary discharge.

When you have developed your personnel policies for all matters which affect your employees, give each employee a copy. For a small company, this statement may only consist of one or two typed pages. Matters such as the following should be standardised and not left to one's whims.

- Hours of work
- Time record keeping
- Paid holidays
- Promotions and transfers
- Deportment and safety practices
- Wage payment system
- Separation procedure
- Discharge or dismissal
- Pension and retirement plan
- Health and medical care benefits
- Grievance procedure.

PREPARING A JOB DESCRIPTION

The trick to getting the right person for a specific job is in deciding what kinds of skills are needed to perform that job. Once you know what it takes to do the job, you can match the applicant's skills and experience to suit the job requirements. A job description for the position to be filled will guide you in this task.

The first step in writing a good job description is to identify the tasks that must be performed in a job. If you are already performing the work that you want to delegate, prepare a detailed list of all the tasks you will assign to your future employee. Begin the task statement with an action verb, that is the action to be performed such as "record all cash transactions on a daily basis" or "install the wiring in single-family dwelling." If there are special tools or equipments that must be used on the job, mention them.

Once you have described the job on paper, decide what skills or experience the person must have to fill the job and what type of training you will expect the person to have received. A good example of format job description is given on the following pages.

Once you have a good job description, the hardest part of your work is finding and hiring the right employee. You need some method of screening the applicants and selecting the best one for the position.

The application form is a tool which you can use to make your tasks of interviewing and selection easier. The form should have blank spaces for all the facts you need as a basis for judging the applicants. A sample form is provided on the following pages.

Have the applicants fill out the application form before you talk to them. This form makes an excellent starting point for the interview. It is also a written record of experience and provides information about the former employers' names and addresses.

Job Specification

Job specification is a declaration of the minimum qualifications necessary to perform a specific job competently.

In contrast to a job description, this is a standard of personnel and designates the qualities required for acceptable performance of the job duties.

Once you have listed the basic requirements, it is helpful to classify each requirement as "essential" or "desirable." If essential, specify:

(1) If the attribute is basic or advanced in nature, and

(2) If it should be possessed on job entry or if it can be developed soon after on the job.

If you classify the requirement as desirable, indicate its level of importance to job performance.

For example, Job Title: Computer System Supervisor

Job specification qualification 1: Having a basic understanding of the computer software system in use.

Basic knowledge, essential knowledge possessed at entry of job.

Job specification qualification 2: Having advanced understanding of software systems.

Name of the company, job description and title of the job are important.

General Statement of Duties

Write a general description of the job in a sentence or two such as "record the book keeping and the payroll on a regular basis" or "perform commercial remodelling (plumbing)."

(1) ***Example of work performed:*** Use the list of task statements you have already prepared.

(2) ***Materials, tools, equipment used list:*** Any particular tools, equipment or materials that the employee must be familiar with.

(3) ***Supervision received:*** Indicate whether the employee will work independently or be supervised. If the employee is to be supervised, mention the supervisor.

(4) ***Supervision exercised:*** Indicate if the employee will supervise subordinates.

(5) ***Required training and experience:*** Mention the educational and/or work experience necessary to perform the job.

(6) ***Other requirements:*** Mention any special requirement like physical fitness certificate, a driver's licence, whether agreeable to accept transfers, undertake tours, furnish sureties (in case of employment dealing with cash transactions), furnish a bond, etc.

TIPS FOR SUCCESSFUL INTERVIEWING

- Preparation before the interview is critical. The interviewer must get the job in his own head (job description, job specification) and should note the things he wants to cover.
- The primary purpose of the interview is to gather further information about the candidate. Therefore the candidate should do approximately 80% of the talking and the interviewer 20%.
- Past performance record, not present aspirations, is the important determinant for how well a person will do in a job. Look for past achievements, as those who have succeeded in the past are the most likely to succeed in the future.
- The interviewer must deliberately set out to relax and establish rapport with the candidate and to win the candidate's confidence in him. Unless he does this, his search for the necessary information will not be successful. Interview in a private and relaxed environment. The furniture set up should be informal, removing any barrier (e.g., desk) between the interviewer and the candidate.
- Ideally, the interviewer should meet the candidate in the reception area to avoid the candidate's being ushered into his office by a third party. From the moment of contact, the candidate should have the undivided attention of the interviewer. No telephone interruptions.

- Start with some brief weather talk then lead into the questioning gently, in order to build the trust.
- The interviewer should acknowledge the candidate's answers briefly and simply. A nod or smile in the right place is usually enough. It is the interviewer's challenge to be objective during the interview and to keep personal opinions to himself. The occasional comments should be encouraging but never critical. However, when the interviewer comes across a topic the candidate would rather avoid, this is a signal not to back off politely but to probe further.
- Use closed questions which require only one word answers sparingly. Aim to use an appropriate mixture of open probing, what would be self-appraisal questions. There are, however, times when a closed question is highly appropriate, for example, when the candidate gives an ambiguous answer. 'Were you fired from your last job ?' leaves little room for avoidance because it calls for a simple yes or no.
- The interviewer must keep control of the interview and indicate its pace. Sometimes this may mean interrupting a verbose candidate.
- Use silence creatively to encourage thinking time, further reflection and complete answers.
- Ask about problems and solutions to them, not just past successes. How a person has coped with difficulties and how he has overcome and avoided them can indicate likely future behaviour. Motivation to address challenges and overcome adversity can be revealed by asking such questions.
- During the interview, only brief notes should be taken. They should be completed immediately after the interview; facts, suppositions and subjective feelings should all be documented.

Training is an integral input of managerial development. The lack of adequate and skilled personnel is one of the bottlenecks in a developing economy. Staff training is essential for entrepreneurs and workers employed in small enterprises.

Training is the systematic instruction of staff at all levels in new attitudes or new skills; random bits of continuing education or mere learning on-the-job cannot be called training: the term implies a scheme of instruction which is more-or-less formal and ongoing, which is planned, systematic, consistent, pervasive and monitored to measure its effectiveness. Although it may be usually reactive to a response to a perceived demand or pressure, it should be developed to become proactive — an advance response, instigating new services, skills and methods, identifying unsuspected problems and leading the way towards an improved standard of service. As a term, it implies a trainer and a trainee; it suggests an institutional context, but it is in fact open to anybody to be a trainee and we should not mislead ourselves into assuming that an institution is essential.

The word 'training' consists of eight letters, to each of which could be attributed some significant meanings in the following manner:

(i) T : Talent and Tenacity (strong determination)

(ii) R : Reinforcement (something positive to be reinforced into memory and system again and again, until it becomes a spontaneous affair)

(iii) A : Awareness (with which one can easily take long strides of progress)

(iv) I : Interest (which is invariably accompanied by excitement and enthusiasm)

(v) N : Novelties (the new things, the like of which would sustain our interest and fill our hearts with thrills and sensations)

(vi) I : Intensity (the training instilled into the trainees' mind must acquire experience-oriented intensity)

(vii) N : Nurturing (it does refer to incessant nurturing of talent, which otherwise would remain latent and dormant)

(viii) G : Grip (a fine grip over the situation solves multiple problems and enables one to acquire a practical and pragmatic approach along with all tricks and tactics to achieve success after success in one's endeavours)

The following points of warning must be given to the person *who* undergoes the process of *any one* training programme:

(i) One has no right, to be complacent and stagnant about one's own progress.

(ii) One need not be unethical and crooked while being on the track to achieve one's goals.

(iii) One doesn't have to disturb others, or obstruct others' progress while sustaining one's own profitability.

(iv) One need not resort to deception, fake and fraudulent, means to achieve success or triumph in marketing, customer satisfaction and such other activities.

All said and done, training does become an essential and inevitable factor for any one who still finds himself in the process of achieving excellence in his own sphere of work.

Why should we Train Staff?

Very few individuals indeed do their jobs in an 'ideal' way, many jobs are done for the wrong reasons or in the wrong place, or by the wrong staff and many jobs that should be done are overlooked. Currently the pressures on the public sector make any of these 'mistakes' unsupportable. The costs of staff are so great and their role in a service profession so crucial that their work must be demonstrably effective. Effective staff do not happen; they must be created through training.

A service profession must enjoy a careful relationship with its public; attitudes of the staff towards their clientele is the most vital area of training. Banks are becoming more market-oriented; there is change in emphasis and to cope with this, the staff need training to understand the need to change and to become familiar with the needs of their clientele.

All individuals have a need for training; new recruits need induction into the rationale and objectives of their jobs, and need to be trained in specific skills and routines. New professional staff may need additionally a programme of training to enable them to obtain their professional qualifications. Certain individuals may need training for a specific purpose, the development of a new service, taking on a new role in the organisation, preparing for retirement.

But, in a world where development and promotion happen more rarely, everyone still needs training, or rather needs it even more; if a job at any level becomes drudgery, then it cannot be effectively performed. The role of training is to develop the critical awareness of staff and prevent ingrowth. An employee who can make some appraisal of her or his role, can. compare the situation of colleagues elsewhere, and can feel that management promotes this process, is likely to experience satisfaction in the job, however great the constraints on achievement, And job satisfaction is a clear way towards effectiveness; if individuals at all levels can contribute towards the formulation of goals, then those goals are more likely to be the most appropriate in this context.

Importance of Training

The importance of training employees results in the following advantages:

(i) It makes sure the availability of skilled workers at all levels of management.

(ii) It increases the potential abilities of workers and thus to improve their performance to the maximum attainable level through the training process.

(iii) It enables the workers to perform the work more efficiently and precisely so as to maintain the quality of products.

(iv) It minimises excessive scraps, defects and wastage in the production process.

(v) It minimises the number of accidents, as unskilled and semi-skilled workers are more prone to industrial accidents.

(vi) Training reduces fatigue.

(vii) Training enables the workers to work speedily and thus increases the earning of employees.

(viii) When the speed of production increases, overtime work can be avoided and therefore, the payment of overtime does not arise.

(ix) A trained worker does not feel the need to join other factories and thus reduces the labour turnover.

(x) Training improves the good relations between employees and the management.

(xi) New techniques can be easily adopted through trained employees.

(xii) Standardization can be adopted in a factory where trained employees are available.

(xiii) Team spirit and teamwork can be promoted when employees are fully trained.

(xiv) Training enable employees to occupy higher position of authority.

(xv) As trained workers do not require any consolation and because of less spoilage resulting from their performance, the supervision cost can be minimised.

Objective of Training

The training programme is designed to subserve the following objectives:

(i) To impart basic knowledge about the industry, product and production methods;

(ii) To build the necessary skills of new entrepreneurs and workers;

(iii) To assist the entrepreneur/worker to function more effectively in his present position by exposing him to the latest concept, techniques and information;

(iv) To build up a second line of workers and prepare them to shoulder additional responsibility and/ or watch on the production of a new product, if there is any diversification;

(v) To expose the entrepreneur to the latest developments which directly or indirectly affect him;

(vi) To broaden the vision of entrepreneurs by providing them suitable opportunities for an interchange of experiences within and outside an industry;

(vii) To impart customer education and

(viii) To impart knowledge of the marketing goods.

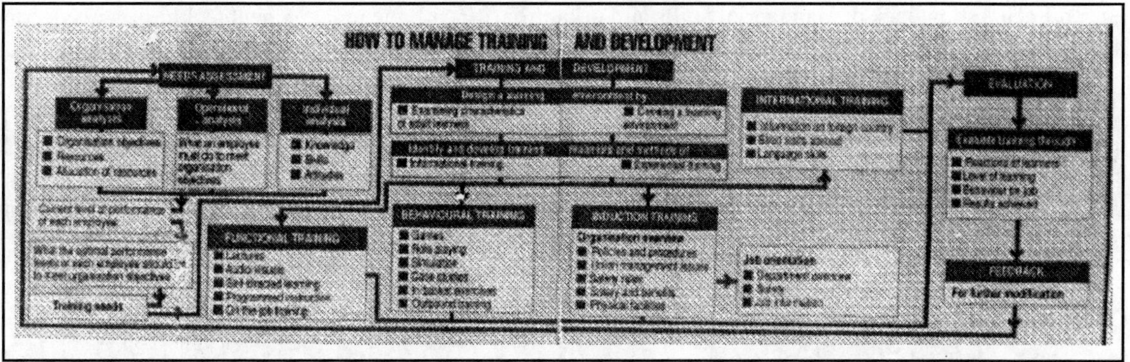

Fig. 16.3: How to Manage Training and Development

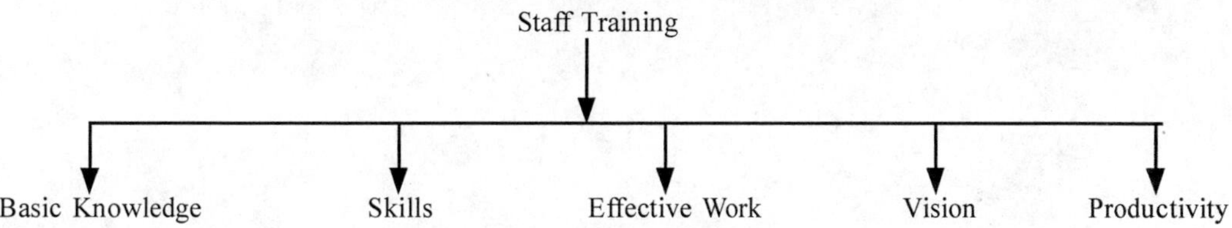

Fig. 16.4: Objectives of Training

The principles of training may be enumerated as under:

(i) Training should be given in a proper atmosphere and that too systematically through duly qualified and trained instructors.

(ii) Training should be of reasonably long duration so as to enable the workers understand the theory and develop skills for managing the job accurately.

(iii) Training should be given at all levels. This means training programme of a factory should include induction training, job training, training for promotion and refresher training.

(iv) The level of training should be high. It must be comprehensive and the participant should be made familiar with the latest trends in production technology and

(v) Training should consist not only of theory; it should be supplemented by practical training and made interesting to all participants.

Achievement motivation training is designed to increase the achievement orientation of the trainees with the idea that positive behaviour, such as striving for excellence, learning from feedback and moderate risk taking is required. Likewise, it strengthens the ability of an individual to generate alternatives as well as to solve problems creatively. It also develops the ability to define and set goals in life. As such, entrepreneurship development is viewed as behaviour oriented. One of the factors contributing to the success of this training intervention in entrepreneurship development is that it is based on experience. In entrepreneurship training, learning by discovery is usually preferred. Here, one is able to learn from one's actions and behaviour in training. The learning process becomes a *positive reinforcement.*

Although there are some variations of and/or models for this intervention, the overall objective of any achievement motivation training is the transformation of the entrepreneur into a new person as a result of the training. The training intervention may also take the form of management skills development. Most entrepreneurs show lack of managerial skills and unfamiliarity with the management techniques needed to deal with the management problems of the enterprise. Therefore, for any entrepreneurship development programme to succeed, it is important not only to motivate the trainees but also to provide them with all the skills necessary to run their business successfully. In Malaysia, where this training intervention is utilized in entrepreneurship development programmes, Majlis Amanah Rakyat (MARA) maintains a pool of small enterprises to act as host to the trainees. For two weeks trainees work in the factories where they obtain practical know-how and guidance on how to manage and operate an enterprise. In turn, MARA hosts the cost of training.

Nurturing Leaders: Mentor-in-chief N.R. Narayana Murthy addressing Infoscions

Inputs for Entrepreneurship Development Training

The objective of the programme of training in entrepreneurship development is to develop motivation of potential entrepreneurs, help them in taking up suitable enterprises and activities, enable them to prepare economically viable and technically feasible project reports and enhance their enterprise building skills. The motivational inputs include psychological games, tests, goal setting exercises and role play. The objective of these inputs is to enable the participants to understand their own entrepreneurial personality and behaviour and bring about thorough self-study changes in self-concept, values and skills leading to positive entrepreneurial behaviour.

The training programme further enables entrepreneurs to develop skills in identifying suitable items for manufacture or other self-employment ventures. The technique of conducting studies, market survey and research should further be covered in-the programme of training based on which project reports have to be prepared. For organizing an industry, information on government policies and programmes is helpful to the entrepreneurs. A number of institutional agencies offer finance, raw materials, readymade sheds, power, machinery and equipment and water etc. Some countries have also introduced schemes of incentives and concessions available to entrepreneurs.

A programme for training for entrepreneurship development should also cover information on programmes of assistance and support systems.

Any programme of training should not only develop proper entrepreneurial motivation and skills for project preparation but should also ensure that entrepreneurs are able to develop their enterprises well by application of scientific managerial techniques in various fields of management. The managerial contents of programme of training should be considered as vital for developing enterprise building skills and as such various aspects of management such as financial management, marketing management, production management, inventory control, labour laws and taxation should be covered in the programme. There is also the need for visits to the industrial units, consistent with the items identified by the entrepreneurs, to gain more knowledge on production processes and machines required for the purpose. Facilities for inplant training will futher heighten the usefulness of the programme, particularly when the enterprises are very small or in areas where there is paucity of skilled personnel.

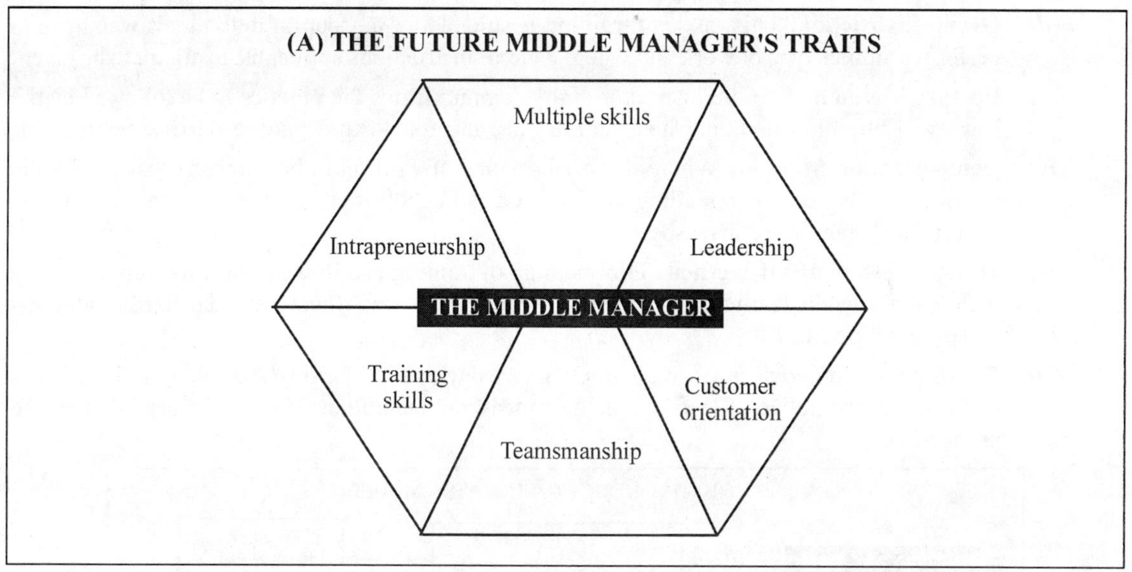

Fig. 16.5

Training is expected to be more close to *learning by doing, learning by practice* rather than by just listening to theories and principles. Obviously, there are limitations but if the following things are taken care of, training can become effective:

(1) **Trainee's approach towards training:** Trainee's perceptions about training, how serious he or she is, the openness with which they receive inputs.

(2) **Discussion on the objectives of the training program with trainees:** Agreeing to a common agenda, both trainers as well as trainees taking responsibility for making it mutually beneficial and satisfying.

(3) **Continued involvement of trainees:** More and more of case studies, management games, exercises rather than one-sided lectures.

(4) More and more examples, anecdotes, illustrations, practical tips, daily review and follow up exercises.

(5) An action plan to put learning into practice, to be prepared by trainees.

(6) **Reinforcement mechanism back at the work place:** The learning acquired needs to be nurtured, reinforced and opportunities given for translating learning into performance by the superior, and by Refresher Courses.

An effective training program is characterised by activity, variety and direction.

"Experience is the worst teacher. It gives the 'Test' before presenting 'lessons' – Wisdom need not be a comb given to a man only after he is bald."

Methods of Training

The following are the important methods by which training may be imparted:

(i) **Individual Instruction:** Under this method, a single individual is selected for training. This mode of training is undertaken where a complicated skill is to be taught to an individual.

(ii) **Group Instruction:** This mode of training is suitable for a group of individuals who have to perform a similar type of work and where general instructions applicable to all are to be given.

(iii) **Lecture Method:** Here the instructor orally communicates the practice to be followed by the learners. Under this method, whenever there are any doubts, they may be clarified on the spot.

(iv) **Demonstration Method:** Where the performance of work is to be shown physically by the instructor for better understanding, this method can be followed. This is more concerned with the practical than theoretical aspect.

(v) **Written Instructional Method:** This medium of training is followed where a future reference is to be made by the learners. This method is mostly followed where a standardized production system is followed.

(vi) **Conference:** Conferences are frequently organised wherein experts in the field share their ideas and bring to the notice of learners the new ideas and techniques that can be used to increase production.

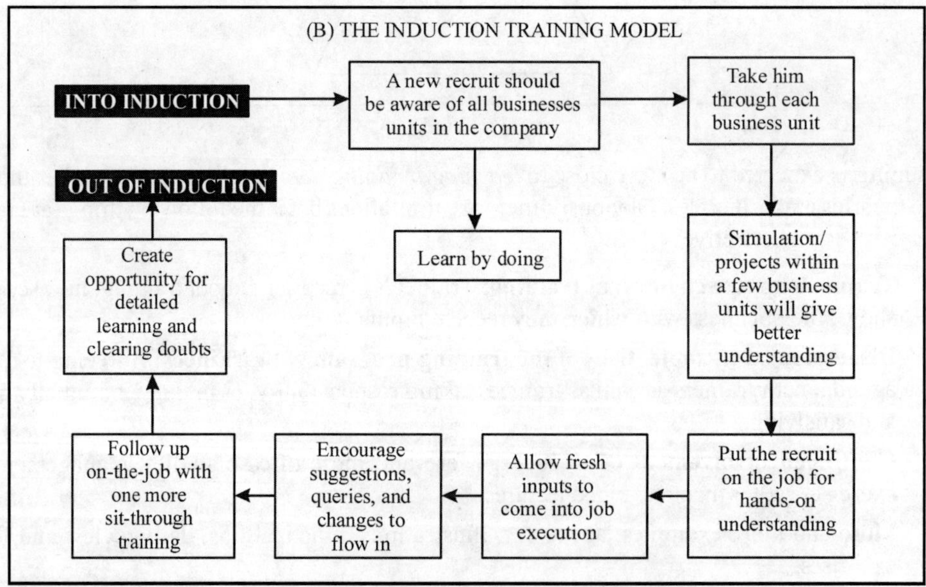

Fig. 16.6

(vii) **Meetings:** Meetings are a mode of training involving a group of people who discuss the various problems confronting them. They involve exchanging ideas and views and later on, coming to a firm conclusion based on the various proposals and alternatives.

Small-scale industries in India suffer from various handicaps compared to large-scale industries; one of the most important among these is the non-availability of technical and managerial personnel of the required calibre. Large industries can employ qualified staff who are specialized in different areas of production and management. Further, they can afford to retain from time to time their own supervisory personnel and workers. As against this, the small industrialist cannot afford to employ workers and supervisors having a sound educational background and the requisite experience in production and in trade. Besides, they do not have the equipment and resources to train their own staff. To meet this lacuna, the training of small industrialists and their workers has been taken up as an important part of the Industrial Extension Service rendered by the Development Commissioner and Small-scale Industries Organisations (DCSSIO). The courses provided are designed to familiarise small industrialists and their workers with the latest tool and techniques in their respective fields. The object of the training of personnel for and from small-scale industries is to equip them with improved management/technical know-how and to appraise them the kinds of assistance available from various government organisations. The training programme of such personnel is suitably geared to the needs of individuals with different background and performing different functions.

The training of instructors at various levels was *sine qua non* of the programme. Besides training officers of the DCSSIO, it became imperative that state government officers, entrusted with the development of small-scale industries, should be given similar training, since the development of small industries is a State subject under the Constitution. Indeed, the training programmes of this organisation commenced with orientation training for its own officers in charge of the Pilot (Industrial) Projects under the Community Development Programme. The small-scale industries organisation has extended the benefit of its training resources and programmes to other developing countries, which being interested in the development programmes of small-scale industries, have been deputing their officers for participation in training programmes, study visits etc., specially arranged by it for them.

In the post-independence period, the nation laid stress and put its faith in science and technology. The country has made tremendous investments in scientific institutions and scientific and technical manpower. These investments need to be harvested. We have learnt that the managerial skills necessary to harvest business are different from the skills required to create businesses. Similarly, to create technology enterprises, we may also require different kinds of managers in our science and technology institutions. Development of technical entrepreneurship and the management of science and technology cannot be dealt with in mutual exclusion.

Training in Technical Trades

Regular and *ad hoc* training courses in various technical trades are conducted by Small Industries Service Institutes, SISI's Extension Centres and Production Centres for Artisans, both skilled and semi-skilled, sponsored by small-scale industries for upgrading their existing skills and broadening their areas of competence to meet the specific requirements of small-scale industries.

TRAINING PROGRAMME: COURSE CONTENT AND CURRICULUM

The EDP training will be set up according to the training needs of participants, who are both existing and potential entrepreneurs, and industrial prospects of the area. The training programme lasts for four weeks, and consists of six modules.

(a) *Introduction of Entrepreneurship:* This module covers general knowledge on the role, of entrepreneurs in economic factors affecting small-scale industries, the role of entrepreneurs in economic development, entrepreneurial behaviour and the facilities available.

(b) *Motivation training:* Motivation training is a three-day live-in-module aimed at increasing the participant's level of achievement and confidence and developing the right attitude and behaviour toward business. Successful entrepreneurs are invited to speak about their experience in setting up and running a business.

(c) *Essentials of management:* This module is aimed at providing participants with basic management and technical know-how required to enable them to operate their business enterprise effectively and efficiently. It consists of the following subjects:

(i) General management.

(ii) Marketing management.

(iii) Production management.

(iv) Financial management.

(d) *Fundamentals of project feasibility study:* This ratio provides guidelines on the effective analysis of feasibility of the project in view of marketing, organisation, technical, financial and social aspects.

(e) *Organising the business:* The purpose of this module is to enable participants to know the environment in which they will operate their business. This covers such aspects as government incentives, industrial opportunities, policies, business laws and regulations, etc.

(f) *Plant visit:* Plant visits are necessary to familiarise the participants with real life situations in small business. Such trips also provide participants with opportunities, to learn more about an entrepreneur's behaviour, personality, thoughts and aspirations, including his plans and projects.

The training method is a combination of group dynamics, lecture discussions, case studies, actual preparation of project assignment, and workshop exercise.

German Experience

The worldwide acclaim achieved by the German companies has been due to the rapid adaptation to change and restructuring the training accordingly. The common features of restructuring are:

(1) Broadbased training to start with, followed by specialisation. This has led to a reduction in the number of trades.

(2) Development of multi-craft skills.

(3) Development of unique training modules and units.

(4) Industry's lead and initiative in restructuring the training.

(5) Change in complexion of the workforce leading to more skilled workers.

(6) Retraining programmes for skill upgradation of the existing workforce, and

(7) The overall personality development of the workforce through emphasis on 'key qualifications' which will equip the workforce with the ability to cope with change. This is illustrated in the diagram.

Two important recommendations emerged when there was an interchange of German and Indian experiences, through a workshop organised by the Confederation of Engineering Industry.

Multi-skill Concept

(1) The pattern of Indian training system needs to be overhauled. This is needed particularly in respect of offering broad training with limited number of trades and offering specialised modules in tune with the hitech requirements. Also, the multi-skilled concept which is fast emerging as a response to hitech needs would necessitate this approach.

(2) At the operational level, the modification of the existing training programmes to include the allied elements. In particular, the maintenance aspect has been much stressed, whether it be mechanical, electrical, electronics or the processing sector.

To make training successful, the German experiences point to the absolute necessity for developing good training materials and updating the instructors on their use.,

SPECIAL DISCIPLINARY PROBLEMS

Behaviour of employees at the place of work represents the work culture of the organisation's recent years, it is observed that employees come under heavy influence of various social evils — drug abuse, alcoholism, emotional distress, depression, criminal mentality, theft, violence, etc. These are the products of the deterioration of the social and cultural values and materials. This results in delays, absenteeism, industrial accidents, frequent quarrels with co-workers inefficiency, low quality output and damage to the machinery and equipments. When these elements, affect the work life, employers are directly concerned and are supposed to take disciplinary action. The mere dismissal of an employee is not the solution to such a problem. But employers should. arrange for help, support, guidance and counselling in these areas. It benefits the employees. Establishment of welfare centres and appointment of a welfare officer has become common, particularly, in the large-scale industrial sector. Code of conduct of the organisation is introduced, and employees are made aware of it at the time of recruitment and induction itself. Disciplinary Actions Policy is prepared and communicated to the employees.

The important assumption of the entire discussion on Human Resource Management is the fact, that in the initial stages of business, most of the small-scale units are "one man show." The entrepreneur himself looks after all the functions and takes the decisions. Due to the resource-constraint and the limited scope of the business, initially, it may not be possible and necessary for him to delegate the responsibility to other people. The discussion will bring clarity about the many facets of the Human Resource Management and the role he has to play in this regard. For implementation of the Human Resource policy, Appendix II provides all the formats and proforma outline of the letters and applications useful for him for the recruitment and appointment of the employees. Appendix-II provides the details about performance appraisal, counselling, etc. Chapter on "Labour Legislation for SSI" will be helpful to know the various Acts and their provisions to be complied by him wherever necessary and applicable.

IMPROVING HUMAN RELATION IN ORGANISATIONS: MODUS-OPERANDI:

As discussed above, in view of the innumerable advantages of human relations in organizations, there is a dire need to give required attention to this approach by, not only strengthening the relations but also by practicing the same as a corporate objective thereby making this movement as a way of corporate philosophy. Organizations may adopt the following, measures to maintain good relations with their employees :

Table 16.1 : Comparison of Six Training Strategies

Strategy	*Emphasis*	*Characteristic Methods*	*Assumptions*	*Action Steps*
1. Academic	Transmitting content and increasing conceptual understanding	Lecture Seminar Individual reading	1. Content and understanding can be passed on from those who know to those who are ignorant. 2. Such knowledge and understanding can be translated into practice.	Devising a syllabus to be covered in the programme Examination to test retained knowledge and understanding
2. Laboratory	Process of function and change Process of learning	Isolation Free exploration and discussion Experimentation	1. It is useful and possible to pay attention to psychological factors for separate attention. 2. Understanding of own and others' behaviour help in the performance of the jobs.	Unfreezing participants from their usual expectations and norms Helping participants see and help others see their own behaviour and develop new habits.
3. Activity	Practice of specific skill	Work on the job under supervision Detailed job analysis and practice with aids	1. Improvement in particular skill leads to better performance on the job. 2. Production and training can be combined rather simply.	Analysing skill and dividing it into parts. Preparing practice tasks, standards, and aids.
4. Action	Sufficient skills to get organisational action	Field work, setting and achieving targets	1. Working in the field develops people. 2. Individual skills and organisational needs will fit together.	Preparation of field programmes. Participation according to schedule.
5. Personal development	Improved individual competence in a wide variety of tasks and situations	Field training, simulation methods, incident and case sessions, and syndicate discussion	1. Training in job requirements with emphasis on process will help a participant develop general skills and understanding 2. Organisation will support the individual in using understanding and skills acquired	Identifying training needs, preparing simulated data.
6. Organisational development	Organisational improvement	Study of organisational needs Work with small groups from the organisation	1. Attention to organisational needs as process develops understanding 2. Organisational change will result in individual's change	Survey of organisational needs Determining strategic grouping for training Working on organisational requirements

- Create a congenial work atmosphere, pleasing surroundings and better job facilities;
- Don't be conservative in praise and appreciate the individual when due to him and practice to reprimand in private and praise in public;
- Treat the employees with dignity and respect, so as to foster. organizational loyalty and job interest;
- Provide abundant opportunities for career advancement and job satisfaction;
- Delegate authority commensurate with responsibility and to allow complete and active independence to employee;
- Promote a healthy competitive, spirit among the employees while simultaneously ensuring that such an endeavour should not create avoidable ego-based tendencies like jealousy, contempt, bias and fight etc. among the workforce;
- Provide reasonable security and safe working conditions. Be strategic in dealing with the general demands of unions by not easily giving away the concessions and let the unions/employees feel that they have earned them fairly;
- Empower the employees, not with an intention to punish for their faults, but with a genuine intent to develop them;
- Give heed to the problems of the employees and give them sympathetic consideration if deserve or else to explain as to why their grievances cannot be considered;
- Put in place a robust and 'well established grievance resolving machinery and to ensure speedy settlements of employee grievances;
- Reduce response time in decision making and improve quality, fairness and objectivity in decisions;
- Develop a well-planned communication system to communicate and get speedy feedback on changes they may be contemplated in the work processes etc.;
- Encourage active employee participation in goal setting and decision making ;
- Develop a positive attitude towards life and the organization and encourage the employees to improve their creative abilities;
- Provide an enlightened leadership and set examples by your own actions being a role model to be emulated by the subordinates;
- The organizational policies and procedures should be followed faithfully and uniformly, both in letter and spirit.

Apart from the above, as a prelude to set out to remedy the human relations problems, one should have open mind and learn to control his temper and be friendly with the people. Further, it should be ensured to separate the facts from the opinions, sentiments, imaginations and one should not be conditioned by the extraneous factors about the people.

Conclusion

As discussed in the foregoing, in the world of organizations, the employees are not to be viewed as mere 'economic tools' but they have to be recognized as 'complex human beings' endowed with varied personal attributes whose normal human interactions are bound to affect the organizational effectiveness, no matter as upto what level the organization has attained the technological sophistication in its work processes.

Further, normal interactions of employees at work always create a social network which is popularly called as'informal groups'and such informal interactions would greatly influence the behavioural patterns of the group members. It is therefore, essential to understand the needs of both management and employees and of the social and psychological aspects of work performance. Here comes the importance of fostering human relations which yield interpersonal relationships for the proper realization of the potential of individuals and their formal and informal groups.

Organisations, being social systems, are governed by the social and psychological laws which are heavily guided by the theory of interdependence and, mutuality of interest. Such a mutuality of interest enables the people to act cooperatively in meeting the organisational conflicts and problems. The extensive studies carried out on 'human behaviour in organizations' suggest that the employees work better not in obedience to compulsion but on the basis of co-operation, not by force but by persuasion and not by rule of fear but by affection. In order to secure such a caused behaviour from the employees, there is a dire need on the part of organizations to lay greater attention to sharpen the human relation skills among the managerial flock. Hence, skill in human relations has since become an essential ingredient of effective management.

In a quest to maintain the 'people systems' in the center stage of organisation's prime activities despite large-scale technological advancement being attained by the organizations, there appears a felt need to carry the funnel of 'people administration' further to transform the existing role of 'HRM' into 'Human Response Management' function through the strategic approach of 'Human Relations.' The response time within which the organizations achieve better understanding and congruence on the dynamics of human relations, may perhaps differentiate them from each other on the degree of genuine intent to stay committed to the human element and its group efforts, in their respective domains.

ANNEXURE – 1

CHECKLIST FOR EMPLOYEE MANAGEMENT

Have you made any decisions concerning the following aspects of employee management ?

Areas of Responsibility	*Yes*	*No*
Recruiting/Hiring Workers		
Number of full/part-time employees	________	________
Where to look for workers	________	________
Previous training and experience required	________	________
What to look for during an interview:		
Motivation	________	________
Interest in the job	________	________
Attitudes	________	________
Salary expectations	________	________
Trades'skills	________	________
Expectations about new employees	________	________
Job description	________	________
Trial period.	________	________
Training and Supervision		
Training apprentices and journeymen	________	________
Giving responsibility for the job	________	________
Degree of autonomy	________	________
Checking the employee's work	________	________
Safety standards on the job	________	________
Dress code	________	________
Sales goals.	________	________
Compensation and Benefits		
Working hours	________	________
Wage	________	________
Pay period	________	________
Rest periods	________	________
Travel time to and from jobs	________	________
Statutory holidays	________	________
Overtime pay	________	________
Absence from work	________	________
Sick leave	________	________
Jury duty	________	________
Fringe benefits	________	________
Promotion of employees.	________	________
Motivating Employees		
Handling of problems carefully and quickly	________	________
Rewarding employees	________	________
Attention to worker's needs and grievances	________	________
Two-way communication with employees	________	________
Building Relationships		
Group activities:		
Social and business		

ANNEXURE – 2

THE MOTIVATION AUDIT

Do you cultivate a positive environment for your team and bolster everyone's spirits? Take this audit to find out:

(1)	Do you rally your workers by treating them to special food, prizes, and cook-outs?	Yes	No
(2)	Do you prod people to express their appreciation for others through spoken praise or notices?	Yes	No
(3)	Do you look for ways to make jobs rewarding, such as training and friendly competitions?	Yes	No
(4)	Do you help your people laugh and bear adversity by giving them something to smile about?	Yes	No
(5)	Do you take advantage of scheduling flexibility by giving deserving workers extra time off?	Yes	No
(6)	Do you describe your group's achievements whenever you have a chance?	Yes	No
(7)	Do you support other groups within your company, and let them know about it?	Yes	No
(8)	Do you invest your group's time in being helpful to your customers, both internal and external?	Yes	No
(9)	Do you tell your team that you are committed to help it get the recognition it deserves?	Yes	No
(10)	Do you ask your team members what they need from you to get through the crunch?	Yes	No

THE SCORING

Give yourself 10 points for every YES and 0 for every NO

TOTAL

THE RATING

0-30 You are a miserable motivator. Learn to utilise your greatest asset: your people.

40-70 You are a mediocre motivator. Strive to improve your communication sklills.

80-100 You are a master motivator. You know how to get the best of your people.

THE NEW CREDO AT LEVI STRAUSS

BEHAVIOURAL CHANGE

Management must expemplify "directness, openness to influence, commitment to the success of others, and willingness to acknowledge our own contributions to problems."

DIVERSITY

Levi's "values a diverse workforce (age, sex, ethnic group, etc.) at all levels of the organisation .... Differing points of view will be sought; diversity will be valued and honestly rewarded, not suppressed."

RECOGNITION

Levi's will "provide greater recognition — both financial and psychic — for individuals and teams that contribute to our success ... those who create and innovate and those who continually support day-to-day business requirements."

ETHICAL MANAGEMENT PRACTICES

Management should epitomise "the stated standards of ethical behaviour. We must provide clarity about our expectations and must enforce these standards throughout the corporation."

COMMUNICATIONS

Management must be "clear about company, unit and individual goals and performance. People must know what is expected of them and receive timely, honest feedback ......"

EMPOWERMENT

Management must "increase the authority and responsibility of those closest to our products and customers. By actively pushing the responsibility, trust, and recognition into the organisation, we can harness and release the capabilities of all our people."

INTERVIEW QUESTIONNAIRE

(1) What are your weaknesses?

This is a trick question. Minimise your weaknesses as much as possible and also talk about the steps you're taking to overcome your hurdles. It would be better for you to focus on your professional aspects rather than your personal qualities. While you're at it, emphasise on your strengths.

(2) Why should we hire you?

The answer lies in emphasising your strengths and telling them what you can do for the company and how having you will add value to the company Recollect your experiences and tell the interviewers about how your contribution has proven valuable for your previous employer.

(3) Why do you want to work here?

The key is to come up with an answer that is well throughout. The interviewer should not get the impression that you sent across your resume just because there is an opening. You could give an answer that says the long-term goals of the company match your own and that you're confident of the contribution you can make in the company.

(4) What are your goals?

Instead of elaborating on long-term goals, it would be better if you concentrated on your short-term goals and link your goals with that of the company.

(5) Why did you leave (or why are you leaving) your job?

Whether you're employed or unemployed, state the reason of your state in a positive context. If you're unemployed you can talk about the useful things that you did on your break from employment. If you're currently employed then you can talk about why you want to leave your present job. Make sure you do not come across as a job hopper.

(6) What can you do for us that other candidates can't?

What makes you unique? This will take an assessment of your experiences, skills and traits. Summarise concisely: "I have a unique combination of strong technical skills, and the ability to build strong customer relationships. This allows me to use my knowledge and break down information to be more user-friendly."

(7) "What do you know about this industry?"

This question assesses the depth of your knowledge about the industry in question. If you are new to the area, you may have to research this question before you attend the interview. You should not spend a long time answering the question. After all, the interviewer already knows the answer. Give a brief synopsis of the industry and where you believe the firm sits within the industry.

(8) "What kind of salary are you seeking?"

When preparing for the interview you should try to discover the salary range for the job from the recruitment consultant or human resources department. This information can put you in a strong position when the time comes to negotiate a salary.

Unless pressed, you should not give a specific number here. Instead you should specify your value relative to a 'salary band.' Most firms have salary bands for each position. You should aim to negotiate a salary towards the peak of the range for the position in which you are interviewing.

If you are pushed for a specific salary, respond with a target range. This will help lay the groundwork for future negotiations. You should qualify yourself by specifying that your answer is based on the information that you have in hand about the job. Do not give the actual range that would satisfy you, as your prospective employer may try to bargain you down at a later point. For example, if your target salary range is 26,000 - 30,000, you should specify a higher range such as 28,000-32,000.

(9) "Tell me about yourself."

This is a deceptively difficult question to answer. The key to answer this question is staying focused on your primary objective here selling yourself as an employee. With this in mind, answer this question in light of your overall interview strategy. Don't describe your record collection, your favourite movies or you pets' names. Do, for example, describe what motivates your career and drives your passions.

(10) "Do you expect to work regular hours?
Would working irregular hours cause a problem?"

In today's modern working environment most jobs require flexibility with respect to your working hours. By expressing your willingness to work irregular hours or do overtime you will impress upon the interviewer your eagerness to succeed and contribute to the firm.

Set Your Soft Skills Right

In today's competitive world, it is not only difficult getting a job, but it is equally if not more challenging to maintain the job. What can give you an edge over others are your interpersonal skills or 'soft' skills in popular parlance. As the corporate world gears up to take up the challenges of the never ending competition, more and more of the companies realise that apart from having a great business strategy, good products and services they also need to ensure that the team that constitutes the organisation that knows how to handle themselves at work and how to relate to customers!

Soft skills are intangible — cannot be taught. So the next time you see a job ad that says, "Should be able to work under pressure", or "should be flexible", understand that the employer is looking at a person who is equipped with all the right soft skills. They are basically non-technical skills and include a cluster of personality traits, social graces, and facility with language, personal habits, friendliness and optimism that mark each of us to varying degrees. Persons who rank high in this cluster, with good soft skills, are generally the people that most employers want to hire. Soft skills complement hard skills, which are the technical requirements of a job. If two candidates have the same technical skill set, be assured that the company will end up hiring the outgoing, friendly, well-adjusted candidate.

There is no easy way to train for soft skills; the basics stem from early childhood and the family environment. A few of the illustrative soft skills include:

Have a "winner" attitude – For example, instead of complaining about a stressful workload, think about it as an opportunity to show off your abilities by getting through it productively and efficiently.

Be a team player – The next time a conflict arises within your team, take the initiative to mediate. When you find your team getting stuck in a project, take the lead to move things forward.

Communicate effectively – Good communication skills are essential to someone's job performance. Communication is what allows you to build bridges with co-workers, persuade others to adopt your ideas and express your needs.

Exude confidence – While it's important to accept your limitations and act humble when you receive praise, it's also important to acknowledge your strengths and embrace them.

Accept and learn from criticism – Be aware of how defensive you get in reaction to negative feedback. Never reject a piece of constructive criticism completely without acknowledging that at least part of it is helpful. And when you dish out criticism, make sure it's done diplomatically.

Soft skills are the underlying principles that trademark a company for professionalism and excellent customer service. They provide differentiation between all the cookiecutter look-alikes and play a vital role in customer loyalty. In today's working environment, where customers and employees are demanding more, instilling the use of soft skills in your team members is important.

Value-added Attitude

Nurturing a value-added attitude and action will benefit you personally, those for whom and with whom you work, and those who are your customers. You ought to have generated several specific actions you can take to add value to your life and those about you.

Work groups and organisations that are trained to understand value-added attitudes and action enhance both customer and employee satisfaction.

Adding value begins with working on self-improvement. Those who layoff self-improvement become susceptible to corruption. Those who increase their skills, enhance their knowledge, and develop their emotional intelligence and in the process become more valued by others.

Adding value is linked to loving what you do and the person for whom you work. Loving what you do, hinges upon believing your efforts are meaningful. Finding purpose in what you do generates task commitment and that extra effort. Working for a boss crushes motivation, working for one's beloved and for those who love you energizes you to give of yourself. Working for making the production numbers does not create lasting motivation. Consumers and customers have different meanings. Consumers are statistics and working for statistics is not intrinsically motivating. Customers are people and people are what we can care about. People are intrinsically worthy objectives of value-added action.

Adding value flows from "owning" what you do and "wanting" to do what you do. A sense of ownership does not come from following orders or from being bossed, but from a feeling of pride in inserting yourself into a service, a mission.

Adding value means doing what lasts. Wisdom dictates that we weigh evils that come from short-term acts. Adding value flows from writing negative scenarios for tomorrow and planning for positive outcomes today.

To add value, make believe you do not know who you will be or where you will live tomorrow. Not knowing who you or I will be tomorrow prompts us to make rules that are fair to everyone. It prompts us to treat others as they want to be treated, because you or I could be those others. It prompts us to sell good products and deliver good service because in our imagination we see ourselves as buying those goods and services.

True value is robust. There is no such thing as too much value-added attitude and action. Not knowing where we will live tomorrow prompts us to protect the land, water and air everywhere today.

Adding value results from making good connections. We are not self-made individuals, but interdependent people. This time is not his, hers or their story, but it is our story that we as a people are living out.

Making good connections means living less fragmented and isolated lives. Our interactions are safer and we as a people are happier when we know each other, when we build the parks to play in, when we support the schools, and when we promote the arts.

Willingness to Change

Adding value requires willingness to change. Adding something innovative springs from nurturing attitudes. And as research and development build a critical mass, new products and services increasingly happen.

The journey of change is not without its obstacles. But it is also a journey that is full of rewards. The key to reaping the rewards and minimising the breakdowns is to lead with your heart, not your head. Your heart is where you will find your willingness. Your head is where you will find resistance and fear.

When we begin to feel resistance and fear that it can be easy to lose touch with the willingness that we had at the beginning of the process. When this happens, we need to focus on reconnecting with the part of us that originally wanted make the change – the part that is excited about learning new things, facing new challenges, and bringing more joy and fulfillment to our life.

Adding value is not simply a matter of doing good rather it is a synergistic process. It is a collaborative process of problem solving and of designing robust systems that produce goods and services that meet customer needs and specifications. It is a process of making thousands of moments of truth happy experiences for those involved.

Adding value is easier when we use the right tool for the job. Adding something new can come from the tool of stretch goals. Cutting waste, reducing failure costs, and delivery problems comes from tools of subtraction, from employing the tool of simplicity.

Intensification of effort can come from incentive tools, and from the tool of division — from focus of effort upon specific tasks. Adding value can come from teaming up to do a job, from enlisting others in a pyramid of effort.

Adding value goes beyond customer satisfaction to customer confidence. Trust is generated from honest relationships that are built into goods and services. It means being able to depend upon those who have earned that trust.

Add value to your life by self-improvement. The Japanese have a term for the kind of attitude and action they want their employees to nurture; it is kaizen. Kaizen means to continuously find small ways of improving yourself in whatever you do. It is an attitude that manifests itself in action. How does one do that? It is a matter of improving one's character, one's personality, one's relationships, and by increasing one's skill level.

At the company level, less rather than more, means finding ways to cut waste, cut costs, and to make one's product and service better fit for one's customers: more durable, easier to use, more beautiful, and more accessible. Some gurus of quality refer to this as cutting failure costs — the aggregate cost of failure to do things right. Not doing it right costs in inspection, complaints, loss of customers and rework. Less waste is more profit.

Every drop of water contains all the elements of the entire ocean and each drop sustains the other drops. Together they make the ocean into a critical mass whose tides can swell and carry forward great ships. It is an environment that resists autocracy and encourages employees to defy bosses who seek to kill their pet projects.

❋ ❋ ❋

17

FINANCIAL MANAGEMENT

Introduction

Financing is the most important activity for running smoothly a small-scale enterprise. Its influence permeates throughout the organisation and encompasses every facet of the enterprise. It is closely linked with all the activities of the enterprise. It is both a service input and an effective controlling instrument.

Finance is one of the basic requirements of a project. The entrepreneur needs capital to start with and he needs financial assistance at every stage of the project. Project finance is needed both for short-term and long-term. The sources from which the entrepreneurs can meet their financial needs for their enterprises are broadly grouped as: *(a)* internal source and *(b)* external source. Besides, the entrepreneur raises his finance by availing of available subsidies, state aid to industries, etc., finance, therefore, is very crucial to the success of a project. In this chapter, the various facets of project financing are discussed.

"One of the key problems of planning, therefore, is where to strike this balance between enough credit for the small man to develop and not giving him so much that there have to be large write-offs every year."

Finance is one of the constant problems, and if small-scale industries are to develop in the way the Government policy wants, they must have adequate credit. Credit is available on the basis of the credit worthiness of the entrepreneur. In regard to capital structure and working capital management, there are many differences between large, medium and small-scale industries.

Finance is the life-blood of any business enterprise. Its management is an art and merits special attention. The financial function of management is to:

(a) Ensure a fair return on investment;

(b) Generate and build up surpluses and reserves for growth and expansion;

(c) Plan, direct, and control the utilisation of finances so as to ensure the maximum efficiency of operations and build a proper relationship with suppliers, financiers, workers and members; and

(d) Co-ordinate the operation of the various departments through appropriate measures to ensure discipline in the use of financial resources.

Wheeler defines business finance as "that business activity which is concerned with the acquisition and conservation of capital funds in meeting the financial needs and overall objectives of a business enterprise." Capital funds refer to the money available to business from the money and credit markets. Top management of a company views its financial problems in terms of: (1) use of circulating and fixed capital; (2) sources of capital; (3) protection of capital; and (4) distribution of earnings.

Primarily these problems are concerned with cash flow — what the cash will be used for, and where it will come from.

Financial Management

It is an applied branch of general management. It looks after the financial function of the enterprise. In itself it constitutes a sub-system of the business enterprises, inter-related very closely with production, marketing and personnel functions or sub-systems. Financial management is concerned with planning, organising, directing, controlling and co-ordinating the financial activities of an enterprise. A successful small entrepreneur is in fact a shrewd and intelligent financial manager. The success of a small enterprise is the reflection of sound and effective financial management.

Financial management is the custodian of corporate funds. It has to .plan, organise and control the finances of the enterprise. The chief duties of financial management are, however, planning of corporate finances. Planning is the key to sound financing and control will ensure the realisation of the above-mentioned major objectives of the finance function.

Financial management is called upon to take three major decisions: (1) investment decision, e.g., capital budgeting or financial plan; (2) financing decision or formulation of the best financing mix or capital structure of the enterprise; and (3) dividend decision or dividend policy. Financial management involves the implementation of these three major decisions. The decisions are inter-related and should be implemented jointly. Together, these vital decisions determine the value of the enterprise to its shareholders and investors. Financial management makes use of analytical tools in the analysis planning and control of the activities of the enterprise involving funds.

Financial management is not merely concerned with raising resources in the most economical and suitable manner, using these resources both productively and profitably to achieve a preferable economic growth but also with all these aspects which relate to financing, viz., proper assessment of financial needs, raising sufficient funds, capital gearing, cost of financing, financial budgeting, maintaining liquidity, determining financial objectives and policies and financing organisation and control. More so with planning future operations; and controlling current performances and future developments through financial accounting, budgeting and other means. In short, financial management implies the designing and implementation of plans. It is interwoven intimately into the fabric of the management itself.

Financial management, unlike the other functional areas of a business, relates both to the enterprise as an operating entity and to the interests of the owners. It should, therefore, look in two directions. On the one hand, its responsibility is to ensure that financing contributes to efficient day-to-day operations; on the other, the long-range objectives of the owners should be achieved. Financial management is thus, an integrated and composite subject. It welds together much of the material that is found in accounting, economics, mathematics, systems analysis and behavioural sciences, and uses other disciplines as its tools.

Although financial management is mainly concemed with the problems of planning and financing the recurring, long-term and short-term needs of the enterprises, the less frequent but equally important problems — such as those associated with mergers, financial reorganisations and the like – require careful attention.

Guthmann Dougall says, "It is in the handling of these more complex problems that the skill and effectiveness of the financial management are most rigorously tested."

Objectives of Financial Management

Financial management evaluates how funds are used and procured. In all cases, it involves a sound judgment, combined with a logical approach to decision making. The core of a financial policy is to maximise earnings in the long-run and optimise them in the short-run. This calls for an evaluation of the conditions of the alternative uses of funds and of the allocation of resources after a consideration of production and marketing inter-relationships. Financial management is concemed with the efficient use of an improved resource, mainly capital funds. Profit maximisation should serve as the basic criterion for the decisions arrived at by the financial managers of privately-owned and controlled firms.

The availability of funds depends upon the kind of commercial strategies adopted by a firm during a particular period of time. The theory of financial management provides an analytical framework for an evaluation of the courses of action that have already passed a higher level of policy screen and have been judged to be consistent with the firm's commercial strategy.

The maximisation of profits is often considered to be a goal or an alternative goal of a firm. However, this is somewhat more narrow in concept than the goal of maximising the value of the firm because of the following reasons:

(1) The maximisation of profits, as reflected in the earnings per share, is not an adequate goal in the first place because it does not take into consideration the time value of money.

(2) The concept of the maximisation of earnings per share does not include the risk of the streams of alternative earnings. A project may have an earning stream and will attain the goal of maximum earnings per share; but when compared to the risk involved in it, it may be totally unacceptable to a stockholder, who is generally hostile to risk-bearing activities.

(3) This concept of the maximisation of earnings per share does not take into account the impact of the dividend policy upon the market price or value of the firm. Theoretically a firm would never pay a dividend if the objective is to maximize earnings per share. Rather, it would reinvest all its earnings so as to generate greater earnings in the future.

The criterion for financial management decisions on long-range profit maximization requires careful consideration. Benefits are often difficult to classify; sometimes, it is impossible to classify them. Where the benefits and the costs of a course of action can be quantified, value maximisation is an appropriate criterion. Where only costs can be quantified, a cost benefit approach is useful, with cost estimates compared to benefits in qualitative terms. Where mutually exclusive alternatives are under consideration, cost minimisation is an appropriate criterion. Financial management techniques, therefore, are applicable to decisions of individuals, non-profit organisations and of business firms. These techniques are useful in proprietary as well as non-proprietary organisations, for business firms as well as for organisations, which are motivated by objectives other than profit-making. They are applicable to different situations in different organisations. funds must be provided so that the economic functions of a business organisation may be carried out. This may be achieved, in part, by the preservation of property and rights are preserved, the confidence of profits. Unless property and rights are preserved, the confidence of the owners and creditors is not likely to be won; and unless sufficient profits are retained for the organisation, it is not likely to gain its financial health which, again, would be detrimental to the interests of the owners as well as of the creditors of the organisation. Profitability must be preserved and growth must be sustained in order to serve the interests of all those who are interested in the survival of the corporation.

The objective of a firm is to maintain its integrity and ensure its future prospects. In this way, it will create confidence among creditors and investors. Though profit-making is not the sole objective of financial management, it is nevertheless an important determinant and a major expectation of the investors. Financial management has a leading part to play in the decision making processes which ensure the profitability and growth of a firm.

Briefly, the objectives of the financial management are:

(1) Sufficiency of funds;
(2) Flexibility in financial planning;
(3) Reduced cost of capital;
(4) Liquidity;
(5) Creditworthiness;
(6) Safety of funds;
(7) Profitability;
(8) Fair return on investment;
(9) Bring efficiency in the enterprise; and
(10) Maximisation of profit and wealth.

Aspects of Financial Management

Financial management can be divided into the following main aspects:

(i) *Size of capital:* Proper assessment of financial needs and determining the size of capital is the first important decision on the part of the small entrepreneur.

(ii) *Structure of capital:* Next, the entrepreneur has to decide the form of capital, that is, to decide the ratio of ownership capital, etc.

(iii) *Source of finance:* To choose the available finance in terms of adequacy, cost and liquidity.

(iv) *Utilisation of funds:* To utilise the funds productively to assure a fair return to the entrepreneur and also that the objectives of safety, liquidity, solvency are simultaneously served.

(v) *Profit disposition:* To utilise the profits of the enterprise for paying dividends, taxes, bonus and ploughing back for sustained expansion.

(vi) *Financial organisation :* To organise the financial activities in accordance with the nature and size of enterprise.

(vii) *Financial controls :* To utilise several financial techniques to derive the maximum rate of return;

(viii) *Other financial aspects: (a)* Liquidity of funds, *(b)* Borrowing policies; and *(c)* Lending policies.

Goals of Financial Management

The goals of financial management may be such that they should be beneficial to the owners, the management, the employees and the customers. These goals may be achieved only by maximising the value of the firm. The elements involved in the maximisation of the value of a firm are:

(1) Increase in Profits: A firm should increase its revenues in order to maximise its value. For this purpose, the volume of sales or any other activities should be stepped up. It is a normal practice for a firm to formulate and implement all possible plans of expansion and every opportunity to maximise its profits. In theory, profits are maximised when a firm is in equilibrium. At this stage, the average are equal. A word of caution, however, should be sounded here. An increase in sales will not necessarily result in a rise in profits unless there is a market for the increased supply of goods and the overhead costs are properly controlled.

(2) Reduction in Cost: Capital and equity funds are factor inputs in production. A firm has to make every effort to reduce the cost of capital and to launch an economy drive in all its operations.

(3) Sources of Funds: A firm has to make a judicious choice of funds so that they may maximise its value. The sources of funds are not risk-free. A firm will have to assess the risks involved in each source of funds. While issuing equity stock, it will have to increase ownership into the corporation. While issuing debentures and preferred stock, it will have to accept fixed and recurring obligations. The advantages of leverage, too, will have to be weighted properly.

(4) Minimise Risks: Different types of risks confront a firm. "No risk, no gain" — this is a common enough adage. However, in the world of business uncertainties, a corporate management will have to calculate business risks, financial risks or any other risks that may work to the disadvantage of the firm before embarking on any particular course of action. While keeping the goal of maximisation of the value of firm, the management will have to consider the interest of pure or equity stockholders as the central focus of financial policies.

(5) Long-run Value: The goal of financial management should be to maximise the long-run value of the firm. It may be worthwhile for a firm to maximise profits by pricing its products high, or by pushing an inferior quality into the market, or by ignoring the interests of *employees,* or, to be *precise,* by resorting to cheap and "get-rich-quick" methods. Such tactics, however, are bound to affect the prospects of a firm rather *adversely over a period of time*. For a permanent progress and sound reputation, it will have to adopt an approach which is consistent with the goals of financial management in the long-run. "More haste, less speed" — this is the principle it may profitably follow.

Financial management should not only maintain the business in financial health, but should help to produce a rate of earnings which will reward the owners adequately for the use of capital they provide. To the creditors, the managenient owes it to have an administration which will keep the business liquid and solvent. Moreover, financial management will have to ensure that the expectations raised by the corporation are fulfilled with a proper use of the several tools at its disposal. In other words, it should ensure an effective management of finance so that it may bear the desired fruits for the organisation. If it is properly supported and nurtured by efficient activities at all stages. It will positively ensure the desired results.

Financial management should take into account the enterprise's legal obligations to its employees. It should try to have a healthy, going concern which can maintain regular employment under favourable working conditions. However, a good financial management alone cannot guarantee that a business will succeed. But it is a necessary condition for business success, though not the only one. It may, however, be described as a prerequisite of a successful business. In other words, there are various other factors which may support or frustrate the financial management by supportive or non-supportive policies.

Wealth maximisation is as important an objective as profit maximisation. The operating objective of financial management is to maximise wealth or the net worth of the enterprise.

Financial management is a key input of overall management of small-scale enterprises.

Importance of Financial Management

Prof. Solomon says that financial management is an integral part of overall management rather than *merely a* staff activity concerned with fund raising operations. At *present,* a financial manager occupies a central position in any business firm and financial management involves the application of all managerial functions such as planning, organising, directing, and controlling in the finance function — as *sine qua non* of industrialisation.

Managerial personnel connected with financial planning and policies will have the specific responsibility for the following: (1) Fair return on capital invested in business. (2) Plough back of profits for growth and expansion. (3) Planning, directing and controlling the use of financial resources in order to ensure optimum efficiency of operations and establish cordial relations with financiers, suppliers, workers and members. (4) Co-ordination of operations of different departments of the business. (5) Control through appropriate measures to secure financial discipline in the use of available financial resources.

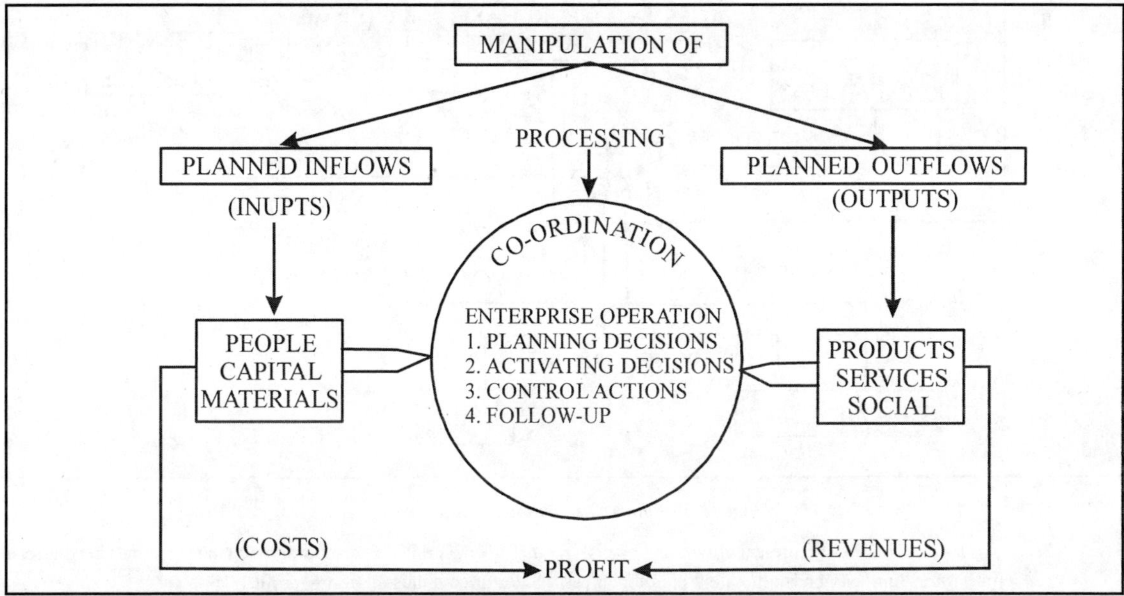

Fig. 17.1. Process of Financial Management

Note: Financial Management can manipulate controllable variables and plan for the non-controllable variables to achieve the long-range objective, viz., Return on Investment.

Role of Financial Management

A business enterprise as a system has a dynamic flow of funds represented by the funds-flow cycle. Financial management is in charge of efficient planning and control of the cycle of flow of funds — inflow and outflow of funds. There are three responsibilities of the financial manager in connection with the direction of the flow of funds as per plan: (1) The appropriate magnitude or volume of funds needed for efficient operations (capitalisation). (2) The wise allocation of financial resources to particular assets - fixed and current. (3) The fund raising activities — short-term and long-term liabilities and their composition.

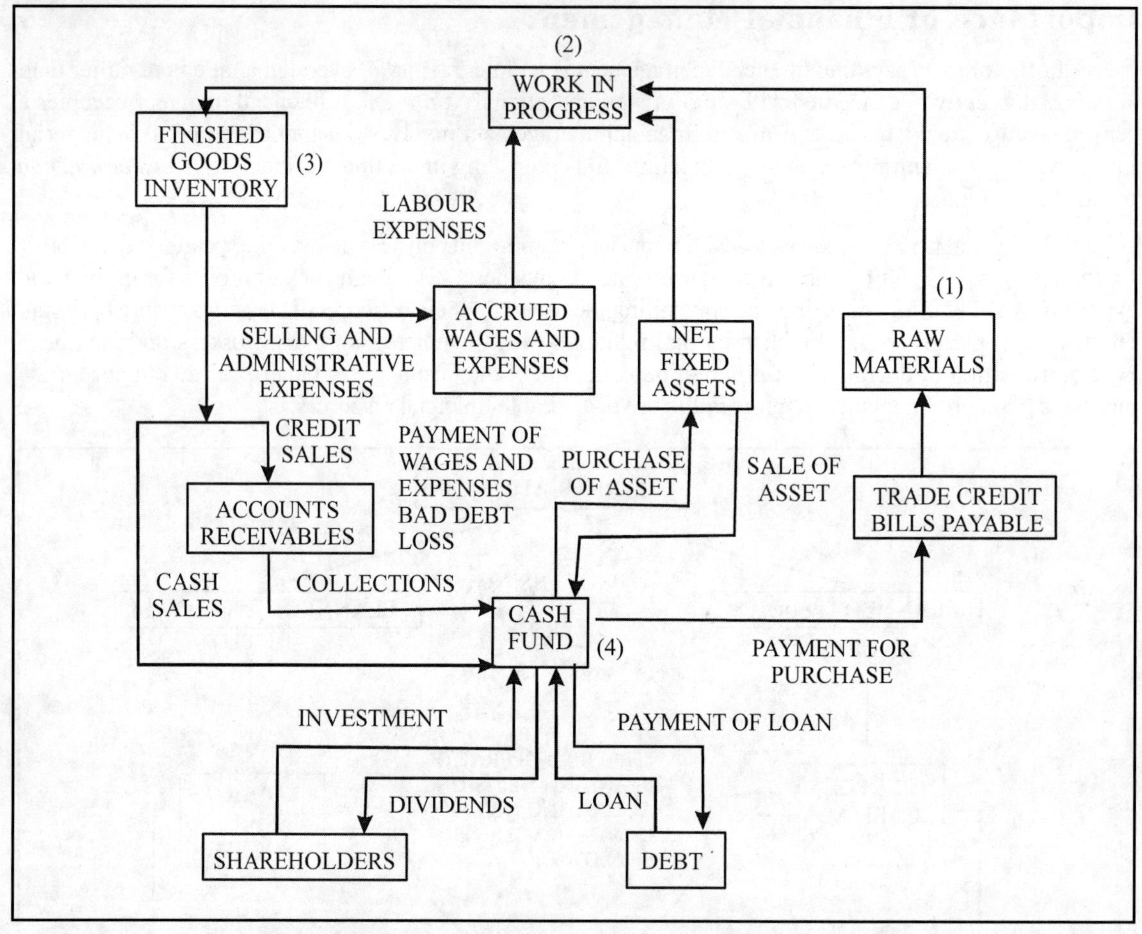

Fig. 17.2. Funds Flow within the Enterprise

Note: *(1), (2), (3)* and (4) represent circulating assets. *Input:* Raw materials, work-in-progress, labour and net fixed assets. *Output:* Finished goods ultimately paid for in cash. Sales price minus all cost = profit.

Managing Capital

Capital for any size of business is what oxygen is for any size of a living being – it's an absolute necessity. However, the relative importance of capital, amongst others factors that are essential for any business to survive and grow, has changed over time. A decade ago, capital was the primary bottleneck to start or grow the business but during current times that's not true to a very large extent. Today, bankers line up in front of entrepreneurs with their best possible offers. Secondly, Indian stock markets have evolved and the retail investor base has grown with a larger share of their savings now being diverted towards equity products. But a recent and probably the most prominent factor is the entry of a new source of capital in the form of venture capital, private equity, hedge funds, which can collectively be termed as 'private capital'. Therefore, the above mentioned trends along with increasing domestic wealth have actually put today's entrepreneurs in a commanding position.

India has plenty of aspiring entrepreneurs and some of them are already testing their mettle in real market conditions. Going by the success achieved by entrepreneurs over the last 4-5 years, be it through IPOs, PE or strategic deals, the entrepreneurial drive has only gone up and it is great for the nation in the long run. However, when you add 'easy capital' to the entrepreneurial fire of creating and growing existing business to unrealistically large size or expanding into other businesses, things could take an ugly turn and sometimes destroy what's been built over the years. The primary culprits for such a condition could be that entrepreneurs get swayed by what others are doing without regard to their core strengths and weaknesses or simply the lack of meticulous execution skills.

If a SME promoter were to view PE capital as just another source of funds, then he/she would not see much value in that proposition. We need to understand that there are different levels of value addition that PE firms do in a small business. They can play a, role in the simplest of tasks such as reporting an organisational structure, management remuneration, and business lead generation, to more significant areas such as guiding the company to thin through a long-term vision, formulation of business strategy, connecting with the right people to gain technological or process tie-ups, helping sell-off parts of the business or finding acquisition targets and helping in the decision process.

When PE firms tell promoters that we both are on same side of the table it is true to a very large extent. PE firms are the closest partners promoters can get who are genuinely concerned about growing the value of the company at a sustainable level without taking undue risks. Their interests are clearly interwoven with the interests of the promoters.

PE capital should never be compared to bank lending because fundamentally the risk-reward profile of these two forms of capital are divergent ends of a pole. Each has its own purpose and importance in helping the company do business and grow.

Box 17.1: Transaction costs and the supply of credit

The impact of financial intermediation and interest rate ceilings on credit can be demonstrated geometrically. In the diagrams in Box figure 17.1 the horizontal axis measures the quantity of borrowing or lending per unit of time (x), and the vertical axis measures the cost of borrowing (r) and the return for lending (i). The economy's demand for credit is depicted in the first diagram by the downward sloping curve labeled D. Its negative slope reflects, in part, the increasing quantity (per unit of profitable investment as the cost of borrowing declines. The upward-sloping curve labeled S depicts intermediaries such as banks. Its positive slope reflects, in part, the increasing share of total saving provided for financial assets as their return rises relative to the return on real assets or investment abroad. If there were no transaction costs or interest rate regulations, the market-determined rate of interest would be r = 1, and the amount of credit per period would be X.

It is costly, however, for lenders to locate creditworthy borrowers directly. In the center diagram, the amount lenders must charge borrowers to cover that cost is reflected in the curve S_d. The wedge between the cost to borrowers and the return to lenders is now the banks' spread. Assuming that bank spreads are less than the costs of direct lending, the amount lent increases from X_d to X_b the return to lenders increases from l_d to l_b, and the cost to borrowers falls from r_d to r_b. The better banks are at reducing transaction costs, the greater these effects. Reducing taxes on banking (such as unremunerated reserve requirements, which are a part of these costs) has the same effect.

The third diagram shows the effect of an interest rate ceiling (the horizontal orange line at i_c. If the ceiling is applied to deposit rates, it will reduce the amount lent (to X_c) and raise the cost to borrowers (to rc). If the amount deposited and, when abstracting from reserve requirements will be X'_c. The excess demand for credit ($x_0 - X'_c$) cannot be satisfied, and lenders will ration the available supply.

The supply of and demand for credit

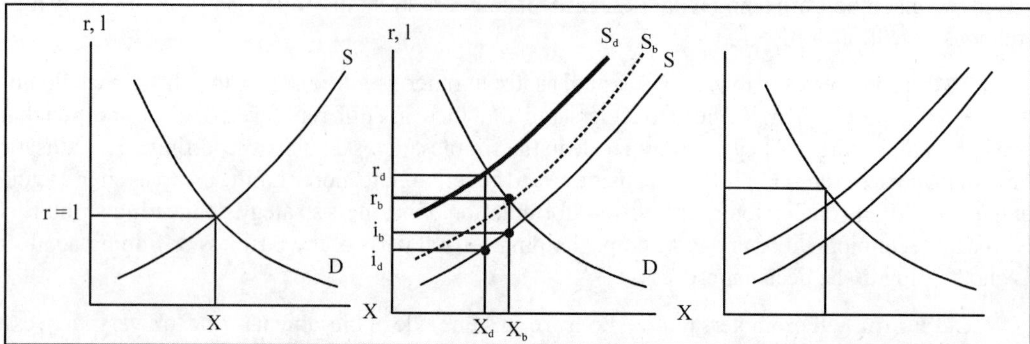

From the banker's point of view, credit appraisal involves a detailed financial analysis of the past and projected viability of a firm's operations, determination of the need, purpose and quantum of short-term credit, and what follow-up and control measures require stipulation to ensure that the firm's operations continue to be viable and short - term funds are utilised by it for approved purposes.

Conclusion

Financial management is a unique technique that shapes the small enterprises. So the experts do not consider routine managerial problems relating to the functioning of a firm. Problems of a firm — problems of profit planning and control, budgeting, finance and cost control, and working capital management which constitute the crux of the financial problems of modern financial management. The central issue of financial policies is a wise use of funds and the central process involved is a rational matching of advantages of potential sources so as to achieve the broad financial goals which an enterprise sets for itself. The new or modern approach is an analytical way of looking at the financial problems of a firm. Financial problems are a vital and an integral part of overall management.

In this connection, Ezra Solomon observes: "If the scope of financial management is re-defined to cover decisions about both the use and the acquisition of funds, it is clear that the principal content of the subject should be concerned with how financial management should make judgments about whether an enterprise should hold, reduce, or increase its investments in all forms of assets that require unit funds.

A judicious application of financial management techniques in setting up a new venture in the small-scale sector and running it, will yield good results in bringing economies of scale, effective operation, and maximisation of profit and wealth. A well-informed and competent financial management is, therefore, an absolute necessity for the development of small-scale enterprises, ancillaries and accelerate the process of industrial development.

ANNEXURE – 1

Comparative Study: Preference vs. Equity Shares

Points of Difference	*Preference Shares*	*Equity Shares*
(1) Right of receiving dividend	They enjoy first preference to get dividend.	Second claim to receive dividends, if there is balance or surplus profit.
(2) Right of reciving back their capital	They enjoy first right of priority even in this respect.	They rank next to preference share in the return of capital.
(3) Rate and Magnitude of dividend	Dividend fixed by Articles, e.g., 8 per cent per annum, It is usually subject to income tax. No rise in the dividend when company is prosperous, except when shares are participating perference shares. Unpaid dividends can accumulae if they are cumulative preference shares.	Dividend fluctuating according to asset value, earning power and stability of the company. Rising dividends when the company is prosperous. Equity Shares have non sub-divisions. They are always non-cumulative.
(4) Voting Rights	They are entitled to enfoy voting rights only under exceptional circumstances, e.g., dividends unpaid for 2 years or resoulution affecting their rights is to be passed.	They enjoy normal voting rights. They are the real risk bearers. Voting rights shall be in proportion to the paid up amount in shares.
(5) Face Value	Relatively higher. Usually Rs. 100.	Neither too high nor too low. Usually Rs. 50.
(6) Redeemability during lifetime of the company.	They can be redeemed at the end of a certain period (e.g., 10 years). They are very useful for raising temporary additional finance for further expansion.	Equity shares are always irredeemable and they constitute a permanent share capital of the company, not subject to redemption during the lifetime of the company.
(7) Appeal to Investors	They involve a small risk. Their rights are secured and stable. The cumulative type has practically no risk. Hence, they appeal to cautious investors who prefer stable and regular dividend.	The equity shate capital, in the absence of deferred shares, is called the risk capital of the company. They have ordinary investors, who perfer rising though unstable income.
(8) Capital.	No capital appreciation as no chance to share in Co.'s prosperity.	Capital appreciation possible due to prospects of rising dividends.

Comparative Study: Shareholders vs. Debentureholders

Points ot Difference	*Shareholders*	*Debentureholders*
(1) Nature of Capital	Share capital is the owned capital, an external source of getting capital, generally non - repayable during the lifetime of the company. It is a permanent capital.	Debenture capital is loan capital, an external source for raising capital usually repayable during the lifetime of the company, having a fixed period of maturity say 20 or 30 years.
(2) Status	A shareholder is the proprietor or owner of the company, a registered member.	Debentureholder is the creditor of the company either secured or unsecured.
(3) Income	A shareholder may get a dividend fixed or variable depending on the distributable annual net profits. Dividends shall be payable only out of annual or undistributed profits.	Income on the debenture is a fixed rate of interest lower than the normal rate of dividend. Interest must be paid irrespective of annual profit, even out of capital when the company makes no profits.
(4) Repayment	No repayment possible except (1) under winding up, (2) when reduction of capital is approved by special resolution and confirmed by Court when shares are redeemable preference shares.	Can be paid off as per agreement or at the option of the company. They can become payable automatically at the time of winding up or when the company makes a default.
(5) Position at winding up	They stand last as claimants for the return of capital. All creditors must be satisfied first and if there is a surplus or residue, it may be shared by them as per Article.	Debentureholders have a prior claim to the return of capital. If they are secured creditors, they can realise their security and prove for the balance at the time of company's liquidation.
(6) Rights and Privileges	They are governed by the Articles of Association. Members are entitled to receive notices, annual accounts and report, attend general meetings, exercise their right of vote. In case of partly-paid shares, they are able to pay calls.	Debentureholders have no such rights and privileges enfoyed by shareholders. As per trust deed they may be entitled to get copies of annual accounts and appoint one or two directors as their are representatives on the Board.
(7) Taxation	Dividend not deducted from profits for taxation on Co. income.	Interest deducted from profits of the Co. to arrive at the taxation base.
(8) Issued	Shares cannot be issued at a discount without fulfilling cretain legal conditions.	Debentures can be issued at a premium or even at a discount without any restrictions.

ANNEXURE - 2

VARIOUS SCHEMES FOR FINANCING SMALL-SCALE INDUSTRIES

Banks have various schemes for financing Small-scale Industries. The general facilities offered by banks are detailed below:

TERM LOAN FOR FIXED ASSETS

Banks grant term loans for acquiring fixed assets like land, buildings, plant and machinery. Such loans are repayable in stipulated instalments ranging between three and seven years linked to profit accruals. A suitable moratorium period is granted for the commencement of repayment depending upon the lead period necessary for the first batch of products to reach the market.

CASH CREDIT

Working capital loans are granted in the form of cash credit, i.e., running accounts in which drawings are allowed within the limits sanctioned in proportion to the value of goods pledged/hypothecated.

BILLS PURCHASED OR DISCOUNTED

Banks purchase demand bills accompanied by invoices and documents like railway receipts or lorry receipts evidencing the despatch of goods, and discount bills maturing after a specified period mentioned thereon. Banks also grant advances against book debts arising out of trade transactions.

EXPORT FINANCE

Banks grant pre-shipment and post-shipment finance to units engaged in exports

(i) **Pre-shipment credit** which is also known as packing credit, is granted to a unit where an irrevocable letter of credit in its favour has been received or a firm order has been secured by the unit from an overseas buyer/export house. This credit helps the unit to purchase raw material, pack/manufacture the goods ordered and export the goods.

(ii) **Post-shipment credit** is granted to an exporter after the shipment of goods against export bills.

LETTERS OF CREDIT

Banks establish letters of credit in favour of an exporter in another country when their clients have to import machinery, equipment or raw materials.

Some banks have Consultancy Cells and Technical Officers whose services can be utilised by those desirous of setting up small-scale units for drawing up their projects or for ascertaining whether any areas in the projects already drawn up by them require any toning up.

EQUITY FUND SCHEME

Some banks have schemes under which those who are unable to meet the usual margins from their resources are offered interest-free assistance to supplement the capital they can introduce, provided they do not have any other unit and do not borrow from any other bank. The amount of assistance is repayable on a longterm basis.

Many State Development Corporations have capital subsidy schemes.

ASSESSMENT

The working capital management is an integral part of overall management of small-scale industries. There is a need for greater coordination between small- scale industries and financial institutions. Towards this direction, the Small Industries Development Bank of India (SIDBI) is shaped to provide a strong support to small-scale industries.

It is essential that financial institutions should safeguard their interests with adequate security. At the same time, small industrial concerns should not, as far as possible, be denied the assistance they deserve or need. Lack of finance is often not the cause but the result of difficulties in other financial assistance fruitful. It is common knowledge that the small-scale sector needs non-financial assistance–marketing assistance, technical gudance and training in management, etc. In order to assist it, the Government has already established special institutions like the small Industries Service Institutes, the National Small Industries Corporation, and industrial estates with necessary facilities. It has also arranged training programmes for small enterpreneurs; but the scope of operations of these need to be expanded. Above all, there is need for greater coordination at all levels between the financial and non-financial institutions and agencies engaged in the promotion of small-scale industries.

In the present Indian context, the socio-economic obligations of a banker include identification of project ideas, formulation of projects, location of managerial talent and provision of technical assistance, assisting in the creation of more employment opportunites in the country. The banker who controls credit is a "supply leader" as opposed to his erstwhile role of a "demand follower." He is no longer a "wholesale" banker sitting in an ivory tower. His new role as an agent of economic development is to assist in the development and growth of economic activities.

Planning and control of working capital centres, around sound cash planning which includes setting of cash policies and procedures and the control over cash and credit. The working capital has, therefore, to be managed properly, especially by the small-scale industries, because over or under circulation may create volatile problems.

✱ ✱ ✱

18

Labour Legislation for Small-scale Industries

Introduction

Regulations are the basis of steady growth. In a society, regulations are the governing factors, ensuring that everything occurs in conformity with the Plan and Policy adopted, the instructions issued, the principles established. They pinpoint the weaknesses and errors so that they may be rectified and their recurrence may be prevented. They operate on everything — people, objects and actions. Thus, a regulation is a process by which we may check whether or not plans are being adhered to, whether or not a proper progress is being made towards the objectives, whether the environment is saved from pollution whether law and order is maintained or not, whether the interests of the workers are safeguarded or not, whether the small entrepreneurs are getting the raw materials or not, and whether there are any deviations for which a corrective action needs to be taken.

Objective

The basic objective behind the whole process of regulations is to ensure that the results of operations conform as closely as possible to established standards of goods, specified procedures or instructions. The small-scale industry has to develop as an important segment of society; as such it has to adhere to the rules of the land, i.e., it has to be subject to the various regulations. Regulations governing the small-scale industry are of two types: *(i)* Protective and *(ii)* Promotional. Protective regulations are in the nature of various safeguards, while promotional regulations are in the nature of giving a push to the small-scale industry, i.e., they are growth-oriented.

Labour Legislation

Labour legislation is intended to regulate the employment of labour to avoid its exploitation, ensure proper and adequate working conditions in the form of hours of work, leave and holidays, and also of employment of children, adolescents, and women and payment of minimum wages. Labour legislation also seeks to promote harmonious relations between labour and management so as to avoid disputes and to encourage settlement thereof by mutual negotiations. Measures of social security provide medical aid and financial assistance during sickness and disability, maternity benefits, provident fund and gratuity. Important enactments are included in this chapter in an alphabetical order. Under each enactment, the purpose of the Act, the factories or establishments to which it applies and its important provisions are spelt out. As this publication is meant for industrial enterprises in private sector, applicability of these Acts to the said sector has been kept in view. It is thus likely that application of a particular Act or its provisions to a public sector enterprise or mines, or plantations etc., may not have been dealt adequately. Important forms in which applications are required to be submitted for seeking registration /licence etc., are also added wherever considered necessary for purposes of reference.

The aim of labour legislation is to regulate and provide safety to labour, so that the labour productivity in small-scale industries improves considerably.

LABOUR LEGAL	
	Regulate the employment of labour
	Avoid exploitation
	Ensure proper working conditions
	Ensure minimum wages
	Seek to promote harmonious relations
	Provide social security
	Enhance productivity.

Fig. 18.1 Role of Labour Legislation

Labour Legislations

(1) The Apprenticeship Act, 1961
(2) The Contract Labour Act, 1970
(3) The Employees' Provident Funds and Family Pension 1952
(4) The Employees' State Insurance Act, 1948
(5) The Employment Exchange (Compulsory Notification) 1959
(6) The Employment of Children Act,. 1938
(7) The Equal Remuneration Act, 1976
(8) The Factories Act, 1948
(9) The Industrial Disputes Act, 1947
(10) The Industrial Disputes (Amendment) Act, 1956
(11) The Industrial Employment Act, 1946
(12) The Industrial Relations Act, 1946
(13) The Maternity Benefit Act, 1961
(14) The Minimum Wages Act, 1948

(15) The Payment of Bonus Act, 1978
(16) The Payment of Gratuity Act, 1972
(17) The Payment of Wages, 1936
(18) The Sales Promotion Employees Act, 1976
(19) The Shops and Establishment Act & Rules, 1948
(20) The Trade Unions Act, 1926
(21) The Workmen's Compensation Act, 1923

The salient features of the labour regulations governing the small- scale industries are summarised in this chapter.

(1) Industrial Development (Regulation) Act

The IDR Act is an instrument in the hands of the Government for the control and direction of private sector industrial investment through the mechanism of the industrial licensing system, which enables it to exert pressure on the applicants in a variety of ways. Conceptually, the Government ought to direct further industrial investment in such product lines as would better serve the overall national interest and in such geographical areas as needed, the most.

It is a complicated, time-consuming and costly exercise to acquire an industrial licence. Sometimes, it takes years before it can be obtained. Obviously, it cannot be the intention of the Government to extend this procedure to the small-scale sector because it would be impossible of implementation. A small unit cannot even prepare an application for an industrial licence; and there is nobody to help it in preparing it. There is no agency which is capable of checking the veracity of what the applicant says in his application, much less comment thereon.

In recent years, there has been quite a clamour from various associations of small-scale industries for their legislative protection. A little more than ten years ago in August 1971, the Small-Scale Industries Board, at its 29th meeting, had recommended to the Government to set up a committee to examine the feasibility of enacting suitable legislation for the development of small-scale industries. Always eager to form committees, the Government speedily acceded to the recommendation of the Board and constituted a committee in January 1972, under the chairmanship of Mr. A. R. Bhat to draft legislation for the small-scale sector. It was, moreover, required to identify specific areas where legislation was considered necessary and to submit drafts for the purpose.

In its report submitted in August 1972, the Bhat Committee prepared a total of five draft legislations for the Government's approval. They were: The Small Industries Development Act, which included a definition of the small-scale industry; the Restricted Partnership Act; the Small Industries Reservation Act; the Small-Scale Ancillary Industries Act and the Public Stores Purchase and Disposal Act for Small Industries.

The committee has quoted extensively from similar legislative enactments in the USA and Japan. However, though well over nine years have passed since the recommendations were submitted to it, the Government has not been able to take any decision on them, perhaps because it has reservations on the desirability of enacting such legislation. If this is so, it should come out in the open and share its viewpoint with others.

The small-scale sector in this country is an important sector, for it is capable of meeting the consumer goods needs of the community. It is, therefore, only fair that the Government should keep the interests of the community uppermost in mind while extending legislative protection to the small-scale sector. At the same time, the small-scale sector must fulfil social and moral obligations if it desires protection against large houses, it should, on its part, safeguard the interests of millions of those who depend on it for their livelihood.

(2) Factories Act, 1948

***(i)* Definition of a Factory:** Section 2 (m) defines a factory as any place wherein ten or more persons are working and in which a manufacturing process is carried on with the aid of motive power supplied by steam, oil or electricity. Premises in which power is not used come under the term of a factory if twenty or more persons are working in them. This definition brings a greater number of places under the purview of this Act than was the case under the Act of 1934.

***(ii)* Employment of Children:** The Act fixes the minimum age of persons who can enter a factory for work at 14 years. It prohibits the employment of children up to the age of 13.

The Act further lays down that a qualified surgeon must certify that a person has completed the age of 14. Such certificates must be obtained by a factory manager and must be available for inspection by a factory inspector.

***(iii)* Hours of Work for Children:** The Act reduces the hours of work for children between the ages of 14-17 from 5 hours a day to 4½ hours a day. It also prohibits work at night for such persons.

***(iv)* Hours of Work for Adult Female and Male Worker:** The Act prohibits employment of women in between 6 P.M. to 7 A.M. It reduces the hours of work for adult men and women workers from 54 to 48 per week and from 9 hours to 8 hours a day.

The Act also lays down that the eight hours of work will be spread over a period of not more than 10½ hours. Further it provides that no worker shall work for more than 5 hours before he has had an interval or rest of at least half an hour. Lastly, the Act lays down that those workers who are made to work for more than 8 hours a day or 48 hours a week shall be paid for the extra hours at the rate of twice their ordinary rates of wages.

***(v)* Cleanliness:** The Act lays down that every factory shall be kept clean and free from effluvia arising from any drain, privy or other nuisance. Accumulation of dirt and refuse shall be removed daily from the floor and the benches of workrooms, from staircases and passages and disposed off in a suitable manner.

The floor of every workroom in a factory shall be cleaned once a week.

All inside walls, ceilings and partitions shall be white-washed at least once in fourteen months; if they are painted or varnished, they shall be re-painted or revarnished once in five years.

Effective arrangements shall be made in every factory for the disposal of wastes arising out of the manufacturing processes carried on therein.

***(vi)* Ventilation and Temperature:** Effective and suitable provision shall be made in every factory for securing and maintaining in every work-room adequate ventilation by the circulation of fresh air and the maintenance of such temperature as will secure therein reasonable conditions of comfort for those working there. Where excessively high temperatures are necessary for technical reasons, adequate measures shall be taken by the management to protect the workers from such temperatures.

The State Government may prescribe a standard of adequate ventilation and reasonable temperature for any factory or class of factories and can suggest ways and means for reducing excessively high temperatures.

In any factory, where dust or fumes injurious to the health of workers arise in any manufacturing process, effective measures shall be taken to prevent their inhalation or accumulation in any workroom.

***(vii)* Artificial Humidification:** In factories where humidity is artificially increased, the State Government may make rules:

(a) Prescribing standards of humidification;

(b) Regulating methods used for humidification;

(c) Directing prescribed tests for determining humidity, and directing that such tests are carried out — their results recorded: and

(d) Prescribing methods to be adopted for securing adequate and cooling of the air in those rooms where artificial humidity is introduced.

Water used for the purpose of humidification shall be such as has been certified by the municipal authorities as fit for drinking.

***(viii)* Overcrowding:** To prevent overcrowding in a factory, the Act lays down that, in factories built before the passing of this Act, there shall be a space of at least 350 cubic feet per worker and in factories built after the Act came into force, it shall be at least 500 cubic feet. To arrive at these figures, a height above 14 feet shall not be taken into consideration. In accordance with this rule, the Chief Inspector of Factories will communicate each factory manager the maximum number of workers that may be employed on any premises. He has, however, the power to exempt any factory or workroom from this rule, if he is satisfied that its observance of this rule is not necessary in the interest of the workers employed therein.

***(ix)* Lighting:** It is the duty of the management of a factory to maintain sufficient and suitable lighting, natural or artificial or both, in a factory and in all the workrooms.

All glazed windows and skylights shall be kept clean on both the inner and outer surfaces, and effective measures shall be taken for the prevention of glare and formation of any shadows which may cause eye-strain or create a risk of accidents.

The State Government may make rules as to what is sufficient and suitable lighting, for a factory or a class of factories.

***(x)* Drinking Water:** In every factory, effective arrangements shall be made to provide, at suitable points conveniently situated for all workers employed therein, a sufficient supply of wholesome drinking water.

In every factory, where more than 253 workers are ordinarily employed, provision shall be made for cool drinking water during the hot weather.

***(xi)* Latrines and Urinals:** In every factory, sufficient latrine and urinal facilities of the prescribed types, shall be provided at places which are conveniently situated and are easily accessible to workers at all times while they are at the factory.

The State Government may prescribe the number of latrines and urinals to be provided in any factory in proportion to the number of male and female workers ordinarily employed therein.

***(xii)* Provision of Spittoons:** In every factory, there shall be a sufficient number of spittoons in convenient places and they shall be maintained in a clean and hygienic condition.

***(xiii)* Safety Provisions:** According to the Act of 1934, a factory manager could afford to wait till an Inspector of Factories gave instructions as to what ought to be done to ensure the safety of workers. The Act of 1948, has placed the responsibility for safety matters on the shoulders of the occupier or the manager of a factory. He must comply with all the safety provisions without waiting for the inspector's instructions.

Secondly, the Act places legal responsibility on the management for the maintenance and use of safety guards. It is its duty to supervise the use of these guards by the workers.

The specific provisions for safety are as follows : In every factory, all dangerous parts of all machines, such as the moving parts of prime movers, flywheels, electric generators, motors, rotary converters, etc., shall be securely fenced by safety guards of substantial construction which shall be kept in position while the parts of machines are in motion.

***(xiv)* Dangerous Fumes:** Adequate provision shall be made in a factory where dangerous fumes are present in any chamber, tank, pipe, etc., for egress of such fumes.

***(xv)* Explosive Gases, Dust, Fume:** If, in any factory, the manufacturing process raises dust, gas, fume or vapour which is likely to explode on ignition, all measures shall be taken to prevent any such explosion by —

(a) Providing an effective enclosure of the plant or machinery used in the process, or

(b) The removal or prevention of accumulation of such dust, gas or fumes.

***(xvi)* Safety of Factory Buildings and Machinery:** If it appears to the Inspector that any building or part of factory is in such a condition that it is dangerous to human life or safety, he may serve on the manager of the factory an order in writing specifying the measures that should be adopted and the specific date by which they should be carried out to ensure the safety of the building or factory. He may also serve an order on the manager, prohibiting its use until proper repairs or alterations have been carried out.

***(xvii)* Welfare Provisions: *(a)* Facilities for Washing:** In every factory, adequate and suitable facilities for washing shall be provided and maintained for the workers. Adequately screened facilities for washing shall be provided for male and female workers separately. Such facilities shall be conveniently accessible and shall be kept clean.

***(b)* Storing and Drying Clothes:** The State Government may require any factory or class of factories to make provision therein of suitable places for keeping clothes not worn during working hours and for drying wet clothing.

***(c)* Facilities for Sitting:** In every factory, suitable arrangements for sitting shall be provided and maintained for all workers obliged to work in a standing position in order that they may take advantage of any opportunity for rest which may occur in the course of their work.

***(d)* First-Aid Appliances:** First-aid boxes, equipped with the prescribed contents, which will be readily accessible during all working hours, shall be provided and maintained in every factory. The number of such boxes shall not be less than one for every one hundred and fifty workers.

***(xviii)* Penalties for Breach of Provisions of the Act:** For any contravention of the provisions of the Act, the occupier and the manager of a factory shall each be guilty of an offence and be punishable with imprisonment for a term not exceeding three months or with a fine up to Rs. 500 or with both.

If any person, who has been convicted of any offence punishable under the provisions of this Act, is again found to be guilty of an offence involving contravention of the same provision within a period of two years from the date of conviction with imprisonment up to six months or with a fine up to Rs. 1,000 or with both. This Act, for the time, provides that if any worker contravenes any provision of this Act or any rules or orders, such as the use of safety guards, spitting only in spittoons provided for the purpose, he shall be punishable with fine up to Rs. 20.

India's ratification of International Labour Convention No. 90 prohibiting the employment of young persons in factories at night necessitated an amendment of the relevant sections of the Factories Act, 1948. This was achieved by passing an Amendment Act in April 1954. This Act added a new chapter on "Annual Leave with Wages" to the Factories Act, 1948. It lays down a period of 240 days as the minimum attendance necessary during a calendar year to qualify for leave with wages. It also prohibits employment of young persons in cleaning, lubricating or adjusting any prime mover or transmission machinery while it is in motion, if such work exposes them to a risk of injury.

(3) Income-Tax Act

The tax concessions provided in the Income-Tax Act for small-scale industries are of minor significance. Under section 80 HHA, which came into effect from the assessment year 1978-79, an assessee is entitled to a deduction in respect of profits and gains derived from a new small-scale industrial undertaking set up in any rural area at the rate of 20 per cent for the first ten assessment years. One of the conditions is that the unit should have commenced its manufacturing activity after September 30, 1977. This concession is discriminatory, for there is no justification for denying the benefit to those units which commenced manufacturing activity before September 30, 1977. Moreover, the units in urban areas have been neglected. Unless we have correct statistics of the proportion of small-scale units in rural areas to those in urban areas and the proportion of the tax collected from rural units to the tax collected from urban ones, the significance of such a discriminatory tax concession cannot be evaluated.

Another incentive is the investment allowance under section 32A of the Act, under which a small-scale unit is entitled to a deduction at the rate of 25 per cent of the cost of plant and machinery installed after March 31,1976. This allowance is capital-oriented whereas most of the small-scale units are capital-saving and labour-oriented.

At present, these is no Central Government definition of the term *small-scale industrial undertaking* — a fact which indicates how unimportant these undertakings are in the eyes of the tax department. According to the definitions given under Sections 32A & 80HHA, the term is used to mean an industrial undertaking whose aggregate value of machinery and plant — other than tools, jigs, dies and moulds — installed on the last day of the previous year for the purpose of the business of the undertaking, does not exceed Rs. 10 lakhs. In Section 58A of the Companies Act, however, the term is defined as any industrial undertaking registered with the Directorate of Industries or the Directorate of Small-Scale Industries.

(4) The Industrial Employment (Standing Orders) Act, 1946

The absence of standing orders clearly defining the rights and obligations of the employer and the workers in respect of recruitment, discharge, disciplinary action, holidays, leave, etc,. was one of the most frequent causes of friction between management and workers. On the recommendations of the Tripartite Labour Conferences held in 1943, 1944,1945, the Government of India passed the Industrial Employment (Standing Orders) Act in 1946. This Act provides for the framing of standing orders in all establishments employing 100 or more persons. It requires employers to submit within six months of the enactment of the law standing orders covering the classification of workmen (permanent, temporary, etc.), the manner of intimating to them their hours of work, holidays, pay days and wage rates, the procedure to be followed while applying for leave and holidays, the termination of employment or notice of discharge and for disciplinary action. In pursuance of this Act, the Central Government published the Central rules in 1946, which were applicable to Commissioner's provinces and to the undertakings under the Central Government. Its lead was promptly followed by all State Governments. In Maharashtra State, it has been made applicable to establishments in which fifty or more persons are employed.

(5) The Indian Trade Unions Act, 1926

The experience of the working of the system of free enterprise in the industrial field revealed that though theoretically both the employers and workers were free to enter into a contract and to agree upon the wages to be paid and received, in point of fact, for various reasons, this freedom did not benefit the workers in any way. Firstly the commodity that a worker has to sell is highly perishable in the sense that if he refuses to work on a particular day because the wages offered are low, he cannot store up his labour of that day to be used the next day. This compels him to accept work even if the wages offered are unsatisfactory. Secondly, as his income is very low, he is noable to accumulate any savings on which he can fall back if and when he refuses to work. The only alternative to refusal to work because of low wages is, therefore, starvation. These two factors compel a worker to accept low wages and so the theoretical freedom of contract is not of much use to him. Lastly, the fact that a worker is a small-scale seller and the employer is a large-scale buyer reduces his bargaining power to a very great extent. It is possible for the employer to refuse the wage which a worker demands because it is possible for him to engage somebody else who is willing to work on a lower wage. It is, however, relatively difficult for a worker to find an alternative employer who would pay him the wage he demands. His weak bargaining position thus compels him to accept whatever wages are offered to him.

Rules of a Trade Union: The rules of a union must contain the following provisions: *(a)* The name, *(b)* the objects for which it has been established, *(c)* the purpose for which its general funds will be applicable, *(d)* maintenance of the list of members for inspection by officers and members of the Union, *(e)* the admission of ordinary members who shall be persons engaged in the industry with which the Union is connected and also the admission of honorary members to form the executive of the union, *(f)* the conditions under which members are entitled to the benefits ensured by the rules and under which fines or forfeiture may be imposed on them, *(g)* the manner in which any rule shall be amended, altered or rescinded, *(h)* the manner in which the members of the executive and other officers of the Union shall be appointed and removed, *(i)* the safe custody of the funds of the union, the audit of accounts and inspection of the account books by the officers and members, and lastly, *(j)* the manner in which the Union will be dissolved.

Rights of Registered Trade Unions: A registered trade union has a right:

(a) To collect membership fees on the premises of the factory without interference from the management;

(b) To put up notices of the meetings of the union and of other activities of the union on the premises of the factory;

(c) To use the general funds for specific purposes;

(d) To raise funds for political purposes at the option of the members;

(e) To conduct a strike by peaceful methods;

(f) To be exempted from the provisions of Section 120B, subsection (2) of the Indian Penal Code if the members conduct a peaceful strike;

(g) To appoint outsiders in a number which is not more than one-half of the total number of office bearers to the executive of the union; and

(h) To send to the Registrar, every year, an audited statement of receipts and expenditure.

(6) The Payment of Wages Act, 1936

The payment of wages to factory workers in a particular form and at regular intervals without any unauthorised deductions is the objective of this Act.

Scope of the Act: The provisions of the Act are applicable to workers engaged in factories as defined by the Factories Act of 1948, and to persons employed on any railway by contractor or sub-contractor. The State Government may, after giving three months notice of its intention of doing so by a notification in the official Gazette, extend the provisions of this Act to any class of persons employed in any industrial establishment. The provisions of this Act are applicable to those persons whose wages do not exceed Rs. 400 per month.

The date of payment of wages: The wages of every person employed in a factory, industrial establishment, or a railway, where less than 1,000 persons are employed, shall be paid before the expiry of the seventh day after the completion of wage period, generally a month; the wages for a month, for example, shall be paid before the seventh day of the next month. In the factories which more than a thousand persons are employed, the wages shall be paid before the expiry of the tenth day of the next month. The wages of a person whose services have been terminated shall be paid on the next working day after such termination.

The payment of wages shall be made on a working day.

Authorised deductions: The Act authorises an employer to make deductions from wages for the following purposes only: *(a)* fines, *(b)* absence from duty, *(c)* damage to or loss of goods or money, where such damage or loss is due to the negligence or default on the part of the employee, *(d)* housing accommodation supplied by the employer, and *(e)* such amenities and services supplied by the employer as the State Government may authorise.

(i) Fines shall be imposed for those acts of commission and omission which the employer, with the approval of the State Government, may have specified by notice to his employees.

(ii) Fines shall not be imposed on any employee unless he has been given an opportunity to show cause why the fine should not be imposed.

(iii) No fine shall be imposed on persons below the age of fifteen.

(iv) A fine imposed on any employee in any wage period shall not exceed an amount of half an anna or three naye paise in the rupee of the wages payable to him for the period.

(v) The fine so imposed shall be recovered in instalments or after the expiry of sixty days from the day on which it was imposed.

(vi) The fine and the actual amount recovered shall be recorded in a separate register in the prescribed form and all amounts of fines realised shall be utilised only for such purposes as are beneficial to the employees and as are approved by the prescribed authority. Applications for the recovery of fines, or of deductions not authorised under the Act, for delay in payment of wages shall be presented within six months of the date on which such fines were imposed or deductions were made or wages were due.

(7) The Workmen's Compensation Act, 1923

Within the installation of machinery operated by motive power, the number of accidents in factories have increased considerably. Many times, workers lost their fingers, sometimes their hands and feet and in some cases even their lives while working on machines in factories. This meant the loss of earnings for those who were involved in accidents and, in cases where a worker died, his dependants were left to starve. From a purely humanitarian point of view, it would be natural to expect that employers should give some compensation to such workers or their dependants. Further, even on economic grounds, it could be argued that the amount of compensation is a legitimate element of the cost of production under the factory system and, therefore, neither society nor employers should grudge to pay it whenever workers were involved in accidents. Some enlightened employers did pay compensation to their employees when they suffered accidents; but a large majority was not willing to accept this responsibility. The workers, however, could not claim compensation as a matter of right; and even when compensation was paid, there was bound to be an honest difference of opinion between an employer and an employee as regards the fairness of the amount paid. In order to provide some bases for a statutory claim for compensation to be paid to the disabled factory worker, Workmen's Compensation Acts have been passed in almost all the countries.

The following are the provisions of the Indian Workmen's Compensation Act:

Employer's Liability for Compensation: If a personal injury is caused to a worker by an accident arising out of and in the course of his employment, his employer shall be liable to pay compensation in accordance with the provisions of this Act.

When Employer is not Liable: The employer, however, shall not be liable if (a) the injury results in a partial or total disablement of the worker for less than three days; (b) if the injury can be directly attributed to the worker having been under the influence of drink or drugs; or (c) if the injury can be directly attributed to the wilful disobedience by the worker of an order expressly given; or (d) to the wilful removal or disregard by the worker of any safety guard or other device which he knew to have been provided for these of securing his safety.

Occupational Diseases: If a worker engaged in any employment which involves the handling of wool, hair bristles or animal carcasses or loading or unloading of such merchandise, or in processes carried on in compressed air, or in processes which involve the use of lead or tetraethyl or in processes involving exposure to nitrous fumes, contracts diseases like anthrax, compressed-air illness, lead poisoning, or poisoning by nitrous fumes respectively; or when engaged continuously for not less than six months in any employment specified in Part B of Schedule III, contracts any disease specified in this schedule as an occupational disease, the contacting of such a disease shall be regarded as an injury by accident and shall be deemed to have arisen out of and in the employment. The State Governments in the case of employments specified in Part C of the schedule may make additions to the list of employments in Schedule III and specify the corresponding diseases after giving three months' notice in the Gazette.

Types of Injuries: Injuries for the purposes of this Act have been classified into the following categories: (1) death, (2) permanent total disablement, (3) permanent partial disablement, and (4) temporary disablement, partial or total.

Amount of Compensation: The Act provides for compensation for these categories of injuries in Schedules I to IV.

Medical Examination: A worker who has given notice of an accident shall submit himself to a medical examination, if the employer insists on it by a qualified medical practitioner and free of charge. Similarly, a worker who is in receipt of half-monthly payments under this Act shall submit himself to such medical examination from time to time.

If a worker refuses to submit himself to such a medical examination without sufficient cause, his right to compensation shall be suspended.

(8) The Employees State Insurance Act, 1948

Experience in the working of the Workmen's Compensation Act of 1923, revealed that the benefits conferred by it upon factory workers in many cases, did not reach them. This was due to various reasons. Firstly, a claim for compensation for injury had to be filed in an ordinary court of law and the lack of finance often made impossible for a worker to file such a suit and fight it out. Secondly, armed with expert legal advice, it was often possible for an employer to prove that the accident either did not arise out of and in the course of employment or that it was due to the worker concerned being under the influence of drink or drug at the time of the accident, or that it was due to his negligence or his disobedience of safety rules. In such conditions, workers were generally unwilling to go to court of law, and preferred to accept whatever compensation employers chose to pay out of a sense of pity or charity. The Employees' State Insurance Act of 1948, was framed to prevent such victimisation of the worker by the employer.

Contributions: Every person, who is employed for wages in or in connection with the work of a factory or establishment to which this Act applies, shall be insured. All the insured workers, except those who earn wages of less than one rupee per day, shall pay their contributions to the Employees' State Insurance Corporation at the rates specified in the First Schedule to the Act. The employers shall pay their contributions at the rates specified in the above schedule.

Distribution of Benefits under the Act: The insured persons or as the case may be, their dependants shall be entitled to the following benefits, namely :

***(a)* Sickness Benefits:** Periodical payments, to any insured person in case of his sickness certified by a duly appointed medical practitioner;

***(b)* Maternity Benefits:** Periodical payments, in case of confinement, to an insured woman certified to be eligible for such payments, by an authority specified in this behalf by the regulations;

***(c)* Disablement Benefits:** Periodical payment to an insured person suffering from disablement as a result of an injury sustained in the course of his employment;

***(d)* Dependants' Benefits:** Periodical payments to such dependants of an insured person who dies as a result of an injury sustained in the course of his employment; and

***(e)* Medical Benefits:** Medical treatment for and attendance on an insured person.

The Corporation may at the request of Government of India extend medical benefits to the family of the insured person. Accordingly, these benefits have been so extended from 1st January 1962.

A person who is in receipt of sickness or disablement benefit, must observe the following conditions:

(a) He shall remain under medical treatment at dispensary, hospital, clinic or other institution provided under this Act and shall carry out the instructions of the medical officer or medical attendant in charge thereof;

(b) He shall not, while under treatment, do anything which might retard or prejudice his chances of recovery;

(c) He shall not leave the area in which medical treatment provided under this Act is being given without the permission of the medical officer or such other authority as may be specified in this behalf under the rules framed for this purposes; and

(d) He shall allow himself to be examined by any duly appointed medical officer or any other person authorised by Corporation in this behalf.

Penalties: If a person makes a false statement for the purpose of causing any increase in payment or benefit or for the purpose of causing any payment or benefit to be made where no payment or benefit is authorised, or for the purpose of avoiding any payment to be made by himself, he shall be punishable with imprisonment for a term up to three months or with fine up to Rs. 500 or with both.

If any person fails to pay any contribution which he is liable to pay, or deducts from the wages of an employee the whole or any part of the employee's contribution, or reduce the wages or any privileges or benefits admissible to an employee, dismisses, discharges, reduces or otherwise punishes an employee in contravention of Section 73, or fails or refuses to submit any return required by the regulations or makes a false return, or obstructs any Inspector or other official of the Corporation in the discharge of his duties, or is guilty of contravention of, and non-compliance with, any of the requirements of this Act, he shall be punishable with imprisonment up to a period of three months or with fine up to Rs. 500 or with both.

(9) The Industrial Disputes Act 1947

Industrial disputes, strikes and lock-outs were not very common occurrences in India till 1914. It was, however, during the Great War of 1914-18, that the strike came to be regarded as an ordinary weapon of industrial warfare. During the War while the cost of living went on rising, the wages did not keep pace with it. This gave rise to serious discontent among industrial workers and led to a series of strikes, notably in the textile industry in Bombay, in the post-war period. In addition to low wages, there were many other causes which were partly responsible for the outbreak of strikes during this period. The more important of these were long hours of work, bad conditions, insanitary housing conditions, absence of any provision till 1922, for compensation for injuries sustained in the course of employment, absence till 1925, of the right to form a trade union, illtreatment of workmen by foremen or other mill officials etc.

The important provisions of the Industrial Disputes Act of 1947, are:

(i) If any industrial dispute exists or is apprehended, the appropriate Government may, by order in writing, *(a)* refer the dispute to a Board for promoting a settlement thereof or *(b)* refer any matter appearing to be connected with or relevant to the dispute to a Court of Inquiry; or *(c)* refer the dispute to a Tribunal for arbitration.

(ii) If either of the parties to a dispute or both of them apply to the Government to refer a dispute to a Board, Court or Tribunal, the appropriate Government, if satisfied that the person applying represents majority of each party, shall make the reference accordingly.

(iii) If a dispute has been referred to a Board or a Tribunal, the Government may prohibit the continuance of any strike or lock-out in connection with such a dispute.

(iv) A settlement arrived at in the course of conciliation proceedings under the Act, or an award which is declared by the Government as binding on all the parties to the dispute for at least six months.

(v) An award declared by a Government shall come into operation on such date as may be specified by the Government and shall remain in operation for a period of one year, or a shorter period, if so fixed by the Government.

(vi) Workers employed in public utility industries shall not go on a strike and the employers in such industries shall not resort to lock-outs

  (a) without giving a fourteen days' notice and before the period of notice expires; or

  (b) during the pendency of conciliation proceedings.

(vii) Workers employed in any industrial establishment shall not go on strike –

(a) during the pendency of conciliation proceeding; or

(b) during the pendency of proceeding before a Labour Court, Tribunal or National Tribunal; or

(c) During a period in which a settlement or award is in operation.

A strike or a lock-out, in contravention of any of these provisions, shall be illegal.

No person shall knowingly expend or apply any money in direct furtherance or support of any illegal strike or lock-out.

Penalties: Any worker who commences, continues or acts in furtherance of an illegal strike shall be punishable with imprisonment up to one month or with fine up to Rs. 50 or both.

(10) The Employees Provident Fund Act, 1952

The Act provides for the institution of a contributory provident fund in estabishmcnt in which 20 or more persons are employed. The contribution, which shall be paid by the employer to the fund, shall be $8^1/_3$ per cent of the basic wage and the dearness allowance payable to each employee, while the employee's contribution shall be equal to the contribution payable by the employer.

DEATH RELIEF

A Death Relief Fund was set up under Employees' Provident Fund Scheme in January 1964, for affording financial assistance to the nominees or heirs of deceased members of unexempted establishments.

EMPLOYEES DEPOSIT LINKED INSURANCE SCHEME

Another important social security measure, the Employees' Deposit Linked Insurance Scheme, 1976, was introduced for the members of the Employees' Provident Fund and the exempted Provident Funds with effect from Ist August, 1976. On the death of the member, the person entitled to receive the provident fund accumulation would be paid an additional amount equal to the average balance in the provident fund account of the deceased during the preceding three years.

FAMILY PENSION

To provide long-term financial security to the families of industrial employees in the event of their premature death, the Employees' Family Pension Scheme was introduced from Ist March, 1971 by diverting a portion of the employers' and employees' contribution to the Employees' Provident Funds with an additional contribution by the government.

GRATUITY SCHEME

The Payment of Gratuity Act, 1972, is applicable to factories, mines, oil-fields, plantations, ports, railways, motor transport undertakings, companies, shops and other establishments. The coverage under the Act is restricted to employees drawing wages not exceeding Rs 1,600 per month. The Act provides for payment of gratuity at the rate 15 days' wages for each completed year of service, subject to a maximum of 20 months' wages. In the case of seasonal establishment, the gratuity is payable at the rate of seven days' wages for each season. The Act does not affect the right of an employee to receive better terms of gratuity under any award or a agreement or contract with the employer.

(11) The Indian Boilers Act, 1923

An owner of a boiler shall not use it or permit to be used,

(a) unless it has been registered in accordance with the provisions of this act;

(b) in the case of a boiler transferred from one State to another, until the transfer has been reported in the prescribed manner;

(c) unless a certificate or provisional order authorising the use of the boiler is obtained under this Act;

(d) at a pressure higher than the maximum pressure recorded in such certificate or provisional order;

(e) unless the boiler is in charge of a person holding a certificate of competency.

Procedure: The owner of a boiler may apply to the Inspector to have the boiler registered. Every such application shall be accompanied by the prescribed fee. The Inspector shall examine the boiler and submit a report to the Chief Inspector in the prescribed form.

The permit is a "must" for boilers.

Summary

Industrial relations have always been a burning issue in all industries all over the world. Capitalist and labour, even though two sides of the same coin, have always treated each other as the enemies in a battle. Yet, it is not the conflict but the compatibility between the owners of the industry and the labour that is the key to the success of any enterprise. The unions also changed their agendas during the last couple of decades. Initially. these started with organising collective bargaining power against exploitation of labour, trade unions brought on their agenda subjects like maximum profit sharing by workers, industrial safety, betterment of working conditions, skill upgradation programmes, workers' participation in management and human rights. But more important is their recent realisation that unless and until they work with devotion and high work values, they will not succeed in meeting the challenges of competition.

Labour legislation should not be looked at as a device to restrict and restrain entrepreneurial growth in the country. It acts as a safeguard to protect the interests of the workers, entrepreneurs and the society.

Contract Labour (Regulation and Abolition) Act, 1970, ensures the welfare and interests of the contract labour.

Employees' Provident Funds and Miscellaneous Provisions Act, 1965, describes how the provident fund benefits should be calculated, the beneficiaries of the provident fund scheme and the method of payment.

Employees' State Insurance Act, 1948, overcomes the drawbacks of the Workmen's Compensasation Act, 1923, and prevents the victimization of the employees by the employers. Employees covered under this Act are entitled to get benefits in cash for sickness, maternity, disablement, dependant benefits and medical benefits.

The Factories Act, 1948, aims at protecting the workers in the factory against the industrial and occupational hazards.

The Industrial Disputes Act, 1947, introduces provisions for investigation and settlement of the industrial disputes.

Minimum Wages Act, 1948, ensures that the entrepreneur pays a minimum wage notified by the Central and State Governments to his employees.

Payment of Bonus Act, 1965, makes a provision of rules and regulations for the calculation and payment of the bonus to the entitled employees.

Payment of Wages Act, 1936, has provisions for making prompt and regular payment of wages to the employees. The employer should not make any arbitrary fines and deductions from their wages.

Workmen's Compensation Act, 1923, describes the compensations to be paid to the workers in case of partial or total disablement due to the accidents caused at the place of work.

Other important Acts are *Trade Unions Act, 1926, Indian Boiler's Act, 1923,* and the *Indian Electricity Act,* 1910.

Conclusion

Rules and regulations governing small-scale industries act as a governor ensuring steady growth of the industry as well as the environment (ecosystem) and the labour force. It not only ensured healthy growth but also ensures rapid growth. The basic objective of rules and regulations governing small-scale industries is to ensure that the results of operations confirm as closely as possible to established standards of goods, specified procedures or instructions. The need for rules and regulations are meant to develop small-scale industries on the successful track.

They are the directions, for excellence, growth and development. And, regulations is a monitoring mechanism of rules. Since, small-scale enterprise is concerned with land, environment, goods, people and consumer, rules and regulations have been formulated to safeguard these varied interests. If there is greater awareness among the entrepreneurs, these rules and regulations have minimum effect and disturbance. Thus, rules and regulations ensure steady and rapid growth of small-scale industries, develop new products and markets, produce quality goods, promote healthy development of human resources. More importantly, small industries are located nearer to the natural resources and human resources. And, do not pollute or degrade the eco-system, intimidate and exploit labour and cheat the consumer on all counts. Rules and regulations are, therefore, the basic component of small-scale indutries. They are like the lamp post and direct the growth of this sector on a firm ground.

The Indian MSME faces major challenges when it comes to legal issues. The Micro, Small and Medium Enterprises Development (MSMED) Act, 2006, requires certain legislative reforms. There are several glaring discrepancies between the provisions of the Act and its implementation.

ANNEXURE – 1

Applicability of Various Labour Acts

204. A table indicating the factories or establishments to which various Labour Acts are applicable is given below to enable the entrepreneur to know the Acts applicable to his enterprise:

Name of the Act	*Factories or establishments to which applicable*	*Remarks*
Apprenticeship Act, 1961	——	Apprenticeship Adviser shall give a notice in writing to the employer.
Contract Labour (Regulation and Abolition) Act, 1970	Where contract labour is permitted.	It is permitted if work is intermittent or of sporadic nature.
	Esablishment or contractors who employ or had employed 20 or more workers on any day in preceding 12 months.	Principal employer/contractor is required to seek registration/licence.
Employees' Provident Fund and Family Pension Fund Act, 1952	Factories employing 20 or more persons and those industries which are specified in the Schedule.	Employer required to furnish particulars to Regional Commissioner within 15 days of the application of the Act to his establishment. Those employees are eligible to become members whose wages do not exceed Rs. 1,000 per month.
Employees State Insurance Act, 1948	Factories employing 20 or more persons, except specified seasonal factories.	
Employment Exchanges (Compulsory Notification of Vacancies) Act, 1959	Establishments where ordinarily 25 or more persons are employed.	Vacancies are to be notified to local Employment Exchange one week before the date on which interviews/tests are to take place.
Employment of Children Act, 1938	Workshops engaged in specified processes; these processes are 10 in number.	Employment of children in these processes is prohibited. Child is defined as one who has not completed his 14th year.
Equal Remuneration Act, 1976	——	Act enjoins every employer to pay equal remuneration to men and women workers.
Factories Act, 1948	Factories where 10 or more workers with the aid of power or 20 or more workers without aid of power are working or were working on any day in preceding twelve months and where manufacturing process is carried on.	Occupier is expected to obtain prior permission for construction of factory premises and seek licence for the factory.

Name of the Act	*Factories or establishments to which applicable*	*Remarks*
		Act is applicable to other places where manufacturing process is carried on, even though number of workers is less than 10 or 20, if so notified bv the State Government.
Industrial Disputes Act, 1947	Any business, trade, undertaking, manufacture or calling of employer and includes any handicraft, or industrial occupation.	It deals with procedures for settlement of disputes and stipulates compensation for lay off, retrenchment and closure of establishments.
Industrial Employment (Standing Order) Act, 1961	Industrial establishments employing one hundred or more workmen.	Standing Orders relating to classification of workmen, terms and conditions of service, etc., are to be got approved from certifying officers.
Maternity Benefit Act, 1961	Factories where 10 or more workers with aid of power or 20 or more workers without aid of power are/were workng; mines and plantations or other establishments notified by the State Government.	Act is not applicable to any factory or establishment to which Employees' State Insurance Act applies. A woman is entitled to maternity benefit at the rate of average daily wages for 12 weeks (6 weeks before and 6 weeks after delivery) if she has worked for 160 days in 12 proceding months.
Minimum Wages Act, 1948	Certain specified employments or processes.	State Governments have fixed minimum wages for skilled, unskilled, manual and clerical workers, and have specified other conditions of service. Payment of Wages Act, 1936 is also applicable to these specified employments and processes.
Payment of Bonus Act, 1965	Factories where 10 or more workers with aid of power or 20 or more workers without aid of power are/ were working; and establishments employing 20 or more persons.	A minimum bonus 8.33% of the salary or wages earned or Rs. 10, whichever is higher, is payable even if the establishment has made no profits. Maximum amount of bonus payable is 20 per cent of the salary or wage earned. Newly set up establishments are exempted from payment of bonus till they start deriving profit or for 5 years from their establishment, whichever is earlier.

Name of the Act	*Factories or establishments to which applicable*	*Remarks*
Payment of Gratuity Act, 1972	Factories where 10 or more workers with aid of power or 20 or more workers without aid of power are/were working; and mines or plantations, and shops or establishments employing 10 or more persons	An employer is required to furnish particulars to the controlling authority when Act becomes applicable, notify any change or closure of establishment. Gratuity is payable, after an employee has rendered five years of continuous service, at the rate of 15 days of wages for a year's service, subject to a maximum of 20 months' wages.
Payment of Wages Act, 1936	Factories where 10 or more workers with aid of power or 20 or more workers without aid of power are/were working; other industrial estabishments as are specified; specified employments included in the Schedule to Minimum Wages Act.	This Act seeks to *regulate timely* payment of wages in respect of persons, whose wages average less than Rs. 1,000 a month.
Sales Promotion (Conditions of Service) Act 1976	Establishments engaged in Pharmaceutical industry.	—
Shops and Establishments Act of State Governments	Shops, commercial establishments, residential hotels, restaurant, eating houses, etc.	Act is not applicable to such undertakings which are covered under Factories Act, 1948.
Workmen Compensation Act, 1923	Certain specified employments.	Compensation is payable to workmen, whose monthly wages do not exceed Rs. 1,000, for injury by accident or occupational disease.

✱ ✱ ✱

OPENING UP THE WORLD WIDE WEB TO THEM

"Just translating the Web into multiple languages is not enough. It still assumes that people who are using it are very literate. How do you get people who cannot read to participate? People think beyond just keywords, yet databases, websites and search engines are structured only that way. We need to go from just the ability to search for information to the creation of knowledge and insight that people can act on." – ***CK Prahalad, Management Guru***

UNIT – VII

TAXATION AND EXPORT MARKETING

19. Taxation
20. Export Marketing
21. E-Commerce

Taxation and Export Marketing

Every entrepreneur has to fulfil tax obligations. It facilitates the smooth functioning of the enterprise. It helps the entrepreneurs to avail various government facilities, schemes and incentives. Entrepreneur has to concentrate mainly on the following three taxes:

***Income tax:** It is a direct tax imposed by the Central Government on the earnings of the unit in the period of one year. Every year, the government announces the tax rates, standard deductions, tax saving facilities etc., in its taxation policy.*

***Sales tax:** The State Government imposes. Entrepreneur needs to register for state sales tax on the sales and also for the central sales tax. While acquiring sales tax registration, Entrepreneur must know whether he needs such a registration, the rate applicable for the commodity sold by him, whether he is supposed to pay the state sales tax or central sales tax, whether he has to submit 'C' form, incentives given by the government etc.*

***Excise duty:** Excise tax or duty is imposed by Central Government. It is applied on the goods cleared from the factory. Different rates are applied for different products.Entrepreneur must know the rates charged for his goods, set-off and other concessions given by the government and other necessary provisions.*

With market forces changing rapidly, marketing has been seen as a change agent — a means of continuous adjustment and adaptation. This refers to significant orientation in marketing management and priorities. The imperatives of market exploitation demand understanding meaningful marketing facts, observations and opinions. The dynamics of successful marketing calls for selecting the right questions, getting answers, organise, evaluate and form strategies to deal with competition and technological changes. Marketing perspective focuses on what we want to find, how and where we find and what we believe it means to the business. It is an integrated approach to generate market power by critical analysis of the market logistically, segment proportion of the customers, understanding profile of customers and the competitors, finding new products and services, customer preferences, customer records as to rentention and defection etc.

Since the market place in the last decade has been registering rapid transformation, we are witnessing the business events reflect a distinct pace and capacity for expansion. The moments signal continuous shift in the way of performing — both in style and behaviour. Market is now being defined and perceived as a group of competitors. Hence there is an entrepreneurship surge in the market — the triumph of the entrepreneur. It suggests great opportunities in the fast growing market where there are many under served market niches. Marketers are always competing to locate the markets that will value the products and would flay for them. It calls for concentrating on market efforts of targeting and positioning the product. "ME TOO" profile of a market man is the formidable force enabling him acquire distinct competence and chalk out specific strategies for business emphasis. The competing dynamics resulting in reinventing the marketer. It is the only stimulus today in the development of "new" market concepts. Today 'operating salesman' is reborn as a marketer because he has to take strategic decisions in the new market requirements.

Market focus therefore demands —

Perceiving market as market intelligence.

Targeting customers.

Managing for profitability and not sales volume alone.

Building customer relationship and loyalty.

Growing with the market.

So, 'Compete' is the buzz word. It is forcing market operators to develop innovative strategies to sway over the market.

Today's salesman, nay the marketing man must always edge closer to the market call to transcend the adventurous customers. And excel by solving daunting problems continuously to be different in the market.

Marketing information will become a highly valued asset in today's information age. Monitoring and scanning scenario building and continuous planning would be the marketing priority. As the future will occupy a prominent position in marketing research concerns, marketing research is expected to change both in technique and orientation. Marketing intelligence, therefore will be a critical factor to be given greater attention to. While assessing strategic situation, executives will be focussing on marketing factors and strategies, corporate affairs and public relations activities. Marketing environment is expected to be paradoxical — keenly competitive, but exhibiting more cooperation, making marketing more important in the management hierarchy.

Marketing intelligence is supposed to explore real demands of the customers and the steps the competitors are taking to fulfil the same. Marketing intelligence is a way to understand the customer's perception of values and purchase preference. It shall be imperative for the organisations to be alert about competitor's approach towards marketing determinants like dependability and reliability, consumer-friendly features, technical specification, high quality and service uniqueness.

Marketing intelligence has a greater value today in view of market complexities consumer preferences vis-a-vis the product availability. Consumer, therefore goes wholeheartedly for the quality product and the excellence in services. Based on these premises, the success of marketing organisation should be measured — how far the organisation is adapting itself to the customer's aspirations. It is in this context that marketing intelligence has its importance. It enables the organisation to be pro-active in terms of futurology.

Marketing intelligence addresses to the constant research and a deeper insight of the market changes and consumer preference and the organisation's response in terms of products and services. The recent phenomenon in consumer market suggests a continuous adapting to the changes in technology and products. Today, when there is a shift from micro to macro business environment, it is high time we thought of an organised market intelligence for regular communication and integration for market exploitation at all operational levels.

It is therefore, imperative:

- *To go deeper into the mechanism of the sales and profit element of business,*
- *Assess the market potential,*
- *Monitor and measure the market place,*
- *Locate and attract new customers,*
- *Identify the customer's preferences, review the customer's defection percentage and the reasons thereof,*
- *Fight competition with competitive edge,*
- *Adopt competitive technology to enhance performance and profitability.*

Market has been aspiring lately for more products and a faster pace. The market operators therefore must rush to move markets using abundant marketing intelligence.

19

TAXATION

Introduction

In most developing countries, the taxation policy aims at the promotion of agriculture and industry. Industrial development may, however, be stimulated by means of a reduction in the normally applicable tax liability in the form of either an exemption from income-tax on the amount invested or a concession in the tax rate. In the early stages of the developmental programmes for small-scale industries, the Government had provided a number of taxation benefits with adequate incentives. In fact, special tax concessions to small-scale industries are desirable for the accumulation of capital and for directing it into the right channels. In the present context of rapid economic development, particularly in the rural hinterland, taxation benefits must be viewed in relation to the need for increasing investment in small-scale and ancillary industries and discouraging speculative investments in unproductive activities. At the same time, there is need for increasing the productivity of the various factors of production utilised in the industrial advancement of the country.

Taxation benefits relate to:

(i) Income-tax;

(ii) Excise duty;

(iii) Sales tax;

(iv) Electricity duty; and

(v) Octroi.

Apart from these, small-scale industries are entitled to Central capital and transport subsidies.

Taxation Support for Small-Scale Sector

Concessions in matters of taxation for industries have three supportive roles, viz., marketing support, investment support and raw materials support. Concessions in excise duties and sales-tax primarily aim at marketing support; concessions in profit tax/dividend tax etc., offer investment support, whereas concessions in custom duty offer raw-materials support.

Chart Showing Tax Concession to SSIs

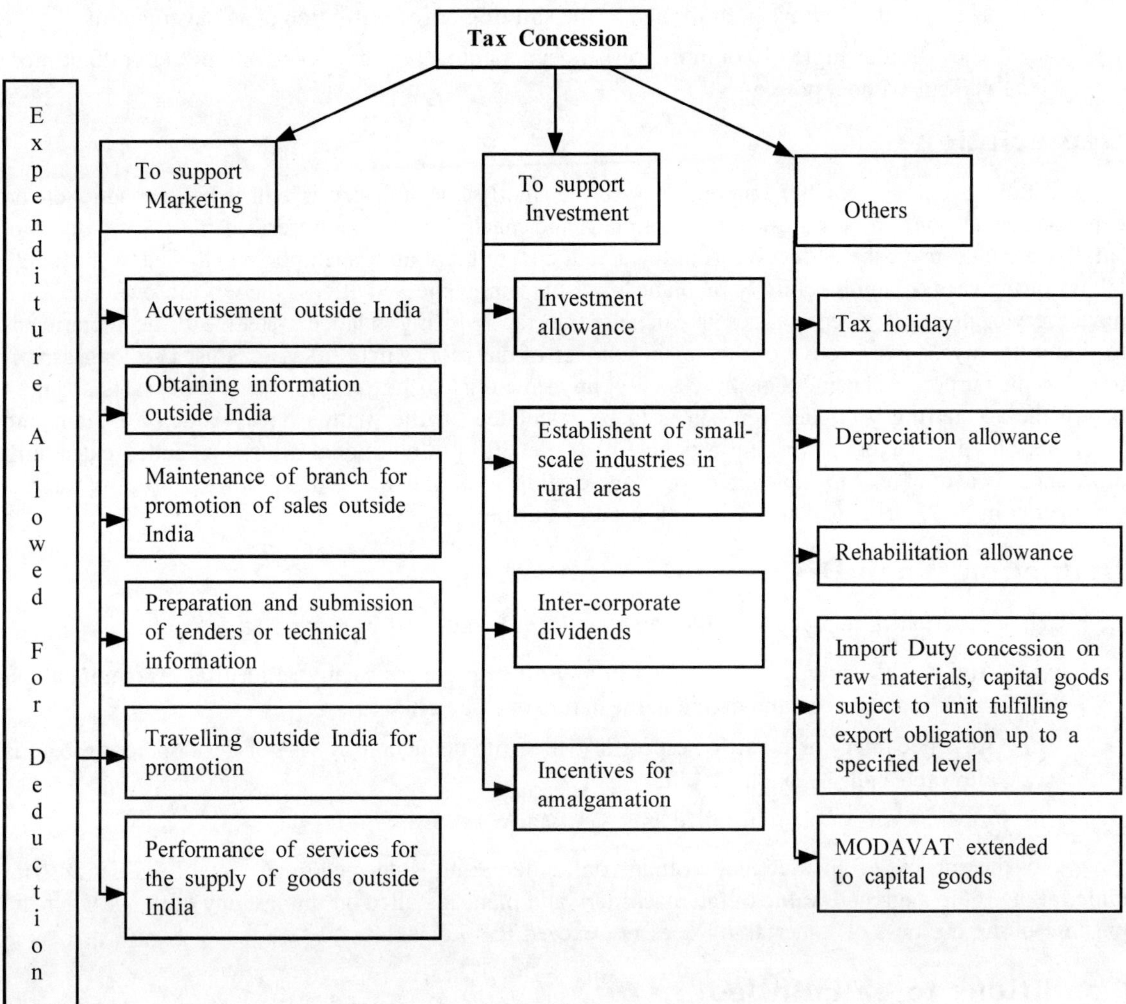

Every year this office formulates pre-budget proposals in consultation with the Technical Divisions of this office and appropriate suggestions/modifications in respect of direct and indirect taxes are sent to the Ministry of Finance for their consideration.

The taxation benefits available to small-scale industries, are enumerated below:

Tax Holiday

New industrial undertakings, including small-scale industries, are exempted from the payment of income-tax under Section 90J of the Act on their profits up to 6 per cent per annum of the capital employed. The deduction at the rate of 6 per cent (7.5 per cent for companies) from the total income is allowed in the assessment year in *which* the unit begins to manufacture, provided that the conditions specified in Section 80J are fulfilled by small-scale industries. This concession is for five years from the commencement of production. Small-scale units should satisfy the following conditions before they become eligible for tax benefits:

(i) They should not have been formed by the splitting or reconstitution of an existing unit;

(ii) They should employ 10 or more workers in a manufacturing process with power or 20 or more persons without power.

Depreciation

Under Section 32 of the Income-Tax Act, a small-scale industry is entitled to a deduction on depreciation account on buildings, furniture, plant and machinery at the prescribed rates. In the case of small-scale industries, the deduction from the actual cost of plant and machinery is allowed up to Rs. 20 lakhs; in the case of any machinery or plant hired by a unit, the actual cost thereof the owner of such machinery or plant. The depreciation is calculated on the reducing balance system. Full depreciation is available for a year irrespective of the actual number of days for which the asset is used so long as it is used for the purpose of business or profession at any time during the year. In the case of assets acquired before the accounting year, depreciation is to be calculated on the written down value. For plant and machinery used in factories working a double or triple shift, an additional allowance called extra shift allowance, is available. Any machinery or plant costing less than Rs. 750 is allowed to be written off completely in the year in which it was first used in business.

Deduction When Disallowed

The deduction of depreciation allowance will not be allowed in respect of:

(i) Any machinery or plant installed in any office premises to any residential accommodation, including any accommodation in the nature of a guest house;

(ii) Any machinery or plant in respect of which the deduction by way of development rebate is allowable under Section 33; and

(iii) Any machine or plant installed after 31st March 1976.

For the purpose of this Section, an industrial undertaking is deemed to be a small-scale industrial undertaking if the aggregate value of the machinery and plant installed on the last day of the year for the purpose of the business of undertaking does not exceed Rs. 7.5 lakhs.

Conditions to be Fulfilled

The following conditions have to be fulfilled for eligibility:

(i) The assets should be owned by an assessee;

(ii) The assets should actually be used for the purpose of the assessee's business or profession;

(iii) The prescribed particulars should be furnished as required under Section 34 (1) of the Act. If they are not furnished the Income-tax Officer would be justified in refusing to grant such allowance;

(iv) The aggregate of the initial depreciation and normal depreciation over the year should not exceed the actual cost to the assessee of the building, machinery, plant or furniture;

(v) Depreciation allowance is granted only for buildings, machinery, plant and furniture and not for any other capital asset.

The word "plant" is defined by Section 43(3) to include ships, vehicles, books, scientific apparatus and surgical instruments and rebate as specified below, is allowed under Section 33, in addition to normal depreciation.

In the case of machinery or plant:

(i) Thirty-five per cent of the actual cost, if it was installed before Ist April 1970 and 25 per cent of such cost if it was installed after 31st March 1970.

(ii) Where the machinery or plant was installed after 31st March 1967, being an asset representing expenditure of a capital nature on scientific research related to the business carried on by a unit, development rebate is given at the specified rates.

Rehabilitation Allowance

Under Section 33B, a rehabilitation allowance is granted to any small-scale industrial undertaken in India, whose business is discontinued on account of:

(i) Flood, typhoon, hurricane, cyclone, earthquake, or other natural upheaval;

(ii) Riots or civil disturbances;

(iii) Accidental fire or explosion;

(iv) Action by an enemy or action taken in combating an enemy—

Provided that this rehabilitation allowance is used for business purposes within three years. The re-established, reconstructed or revived unit is allowed a deduction of a sum, by way of rehabilitation allowance, equivalent to 60 per cent of the amount of the deduction allowance to the unit.

Expenditure on Scientific Research

Under Section 35, the following deductions in respect of scientific research are allowed:

(i) Any expenditure (not being in the nature of capital expenditure) incurred on scientific research related to the business;

(ii) Any sum paid to a scientific research association which has as its object, the undertaking of a scientific research, or to a university, college or other institution to be used for scientific research.

Patent Right and Copyright

Under Section 35A, any expenditure of a capital nature, incurred after 28th February 1966 on the business, shall be allowed, subject to and in accordance with the provisions of this Section.

Export Markets Development Allowance

If a domestic company, whether directly or in association with any other person has after 28th February, 1969, incurred any expenditure on this account (not being in the nature of capital expenditure or personal expenses), a deduction of a sum equal to one and one-third times the amount of such expenditure incurred during the previous year shall be allowed under Section 35B.

The expenditure incurred, wholly and exclusively, on the following items is eligible for deduction:

(i) Advertisement or publicity outside India;
(ii) Obtaining information regarding markets outside India;
(iii) Maintenance of a branch office or agency for the promotion of sales abroad;
(iv) Preparation and submission of tenders, samples or technical information;
(v) Travelling outside India for the promotion of sales;
(vi) Performance of services outside India in connection with, or incidental to the execution of any contract for the supply of such goods, services or facilities outside India;
(vii) Such other activities as may be necessary for the promotion of sales outside India.

Amortisation of Certain Preliminary Expenses

Under Section 35D, Indian companies and resident persons are allowed deduction for the specified expenditure:

(i) Before the commencement of business;
(ii) After the commencement of the business in connection with the extension of an individual undertaking or in connection with the setting up of a new industrial unit;
(iii) Expenditure in connection with the preparation of a feasibility report necessary for the business;
(iv) Engineering services relating to the business; and
(v) Legal charges for drafting any agreements.

The aggregate amount of expenditure allowed to be deducted is limited to 2.5 per cent of the total cost of the project.

Under Section 80HH, a newly-established small-scale industrial unit located in a backward area, is allowed a deduction of 20 per cent on its profits and gains, provided that:

(i) It has begun, or begins, to manufacture or produce articles after 31st December, 1970, in any backward area;
(ii) It has not been formed by the splitting up or reconstitution of a business already in existence in any backward area;
(iii) It has not been formed by the transfer to a new business machinery or plant previously used for any purpose in backward area;
(iv) It employs ten or more workers in the manufacturing process carried on with the aid of power, or employs twenty or more workers in the manufacturing process carried on without the aid of power.

The deduction shall be allowed for ten years, beginning with the commencement of production.

Investment Allowance

Rate of Deduction: It was in 1976. that the investment allowance was introduced, replacing the initial depreciation allowance. One of most valuable tax concessions offered to small-scale industrial undertakings under the Income-tax Act is the deduction, by way of investment allowance, granted under Section 31A. The investment allowance is allowed at the rate of 25 per cent of the cost of acquisition of new plant or machinery installed, unlike the development rebate, which was allowed at different rates, ranging from 10 per cent to 40 per cent.

Items of Low Priority — Eleventh Schedule: Although the benefit of investment allowance has been made available for the articles or things except certain articles and things of low priority specified in the Eleventh Schedule, a special dispensation has been provided for the plant and machinery installed in small-scale industrial undertakings. Such machinery and plant are eligible for investment allowance irrespective of whether they are used for the purpose of the business of construction, manufacture or production of low priority items listed in the Eleventh Schedule. Small-scale industrial undertakings are, in comparison with other industries, at an advantage in claiming a deduction of investment allowance.

When Forfeited: In order to avail itself of the benefit of investment allowance, a small-scale industrial unit must put to use machinery or plant either in the year of installation or in the immediate following year; otherwise the benefit will be forfeited.

Conditions to be Fulfilled: An investment Allowance Reserve must be created during the relevant financial year. This reserve is required to be utilised for the acquisition of machinery or plant for the purpose of the business of the small-scale industrial undertaking. Its utilisation for distribution by way of dividends or profits or for remittance outside India is prohibited.

When Withdrawable: The investment allowance will be withdrawn:

(i) If machinery or plant is sold or otherwise transferred by the assessee to any person (other than the Government, a local authority, a corporation or a Government company) at any time before the expiry of eight years from the end of the financial year in which it was acquired or installed. It is not withdrawn if the sale or transfer is made in connection with the amalgamation of a partnership firm into a company or where a firm is succeeded by a company in the business carried on by it.

(ii) If a small-scale industrial undertaking ceases to be a small-scale industrial unit by virtue of the total value of the machinery or plant installed exceeding Rs. 10 lakhs.

Small-scale Industries in Rural Areas

The Finance (No. 2) Act of 1977 has inserted a new Section 80HHA in the Income-tax Act, 1961, under which the tax-payers are entitled to claim a deduction from the gross total income to the extent of 20 per cent of the profits and gains derived by them from small-scale industrial undertakings newly set up in any rural area, and which begin manufacturing activity after 30th September 1977. The expression rural area means any area as defined — under the Explanation to Section 35CC(I) of the Act. The small-scale industrial units engaged in mining are not allowed this tax concession. The deduction of profits and gains derived by an assessee from small-scale industrial undertakings will be allowed in computing the total income in each of the ten assessment years in which the small-scale industrial undertaking begins to manufacture or produce articles. For the purpose of this section the term *small-scale industrial undertaking* will have the same meaning as assigned to it under Section 32(2) of the Act.

Conditions to be Fulfilled

The conditions for eligibility are:

(i) The small-scale industrial undertaking should not be formed by splitting up or by reconstructing a business already in existence in a rural area or any other area. In other words, machinery and

plant must be newly acquired and put to use in its business for the first time, and the business should not have been in existence prior to the establishment thereof in the rural area.

(ii) It should not be formed by the transfer to a new business of machinery or plant previously used for any purpose. This condition will not apply in cases in which the total value of machinery or plant or a part so transferred does not exceed 20 per cent of total value of machinery or plant used in the business.

(iii) It should employ ten or more workers in manufacturing process carried on with the aid of power or twenty or more workers in a manufacturing process carried on without the aid of power. When an industrial undertaking is located in a rural area which is also a backward area. The assessee has the choice of claiming the deduction to the extent of 20 per cent of the profits from the new business in the small-scale sector for the first 10 years either under Section 80HH or under Section 80HHA, but not under both the Sections.

Small-scale Industries in Backward Areas

The small-scale industries, which have been newly established in the backward areas specified in the English Schedule to the Income-tax Act and which produce or manufacture any article or thing in backward areas, are entitled to the benefit of deduction from gross total income to the extent of 20 per cent of their profits and gains. This deduction is allowed for ten assessment years beginning with the assessment year in which the small-scale industrial unit begins to manufacture or produce goods. The small-scale industrial unit must also fulfil the other conditions prescribed in Section 80HH of the Act before it can avail itself of this tax concession. If it has already been established in a non-backward and shifts to backward area, the profits derived from the industrial undertaking in the backward area after the shifting would qualify for this tax concession for a period of 10 years. The small-scale industry engaged in the business of mining is not entitled to claim the benefit of this concession, even though it may have been established in a backward area.

Other Concessions

Publication of Books: A small-scale industry engaged in the business of publication of books is entitled to claim a deduction of a sum equal to 20 per cent of the profits and gains derived from such business under Section 80QQ of the Act. “Books” for the purpose of this Section do not include newspapers, journals, magazines, diaries, brochures, pamphlets and other publications of similar nature.

Small-scale industrial undertakings are also entitled to claim the various tax benefit granted to other tax-payers, such as rehabilitation allowance, expenditure on specific research, a mobilisation of the cost of patents and copyrights, agricultural development allowance, rural development allowance, amortisation of preliminary expenses, allowance of expenses by way of contribution for rural development and other deductions allowed in computing the taxable income from business, in addition to the tax concessions admissible in respect of capital gains.

Small-scale industrial undertakings should plan in such a way that it should be possible for them to avail themselves of the tax concessions to the maximum extent so that the aim of the Government to encourage more and more small-scale industries to establish in rural and backward parts of the country may be fulfilled.

In addition, deductions are available in respect of:

(i) Inter-corporate dividends (Sec. 80M);

(ii) Royalties from any company in India (Sec. 80M);

(iii) Dividend from certain foreign companies (Sec. 80N);

(iv) Royalties etc., from certain foreign companies (Sec. 800);

(v) Income of co-operative societies (Sec. 80P);

(vi) Profits and gains of the business from the publication of books (Sec 80QQ); and

(vii) Carry forward and set off of business losses (Sec. 72).

Tax Benefits for Amalgamation of Sick Units: Sickness in an industry, whether large or small, is quite widespread in the country and has become a national problem which has caused a great deal of concern. It is estimated that the aggregate amount involved in the sick units is more than Rs. 2,000 crores.* The policy of the Government has been to encourage the amalgamation of sick units with profit-making larger units. For this purpose, some tax concessions have been announced to include healthy units to take over sick concerns in the public interest. Tax concessions for the amalgamation of sick units are discussed below.

What is Amalgamation? The Income-tax Act defines the amalgamation of companies as a merger of one or more companies with another company or a merger of two or more companies to form another concern, in such a manner that all the property and liabilities of the amalgamating company become the property and liabilities of the amalgamated company, and the shareholders holding not less than nine-tenths of the shares in the amalgamating company, become the shareholders of the amalgamated company, by the virtue of amalgamation. However, the shares which are already held immediately before the amalgamation by, or by a nominee of the amalgamated company or its subsidiary are not to be taken into account for arriving at 90 per centof the shares held. An "amalgamating company" is a company which merges and the company with which it merges or which is formed as a result of the merger is the "amalgamated company." There can be no amalgamation when a company is wound up and another company purchases the assets of that company or receives its assets as a result of the distribution made by the company in liquidation. It is essential that all these conditions are satisfied before an amalgamation is said to have been effected.

Business Losses and Tax: The assessees are permitted to carry forward and set off business losses against income under the provision of Section 72 of the Income-tax Act. Under the existing provisions of this Act, the business loss of a year, which cannot be set off against the other income of the assessee for the relevant year, is allowed to be carried and set off against the profits of the following assessment year from any business in which he is engaged. If the loss cannot be wholly set off against the profits, the amount of loss not so set off is allowed to be carried forward to the following assessment year, and so on up to a maximum of eight assessment years immediately succeeding the assessment year for which the loss was first computed. This concessions is allowed only when the assessee continues to carry on business in which the loss was originally computed. Further, the assessee who has incurred the loss has the right to carry forward the same; a successor in business, if any, cannot claim the right to carry forward the loss incurred by his predecessor. Again, if the business of an assessee is taken over by another, the unabsorbed depreciation allowance due to the predecessor in business is not allowed to be carried forward by successor in business and set off against his profits in subsequent years. In view of these provisions,

* Of this amount, small-scale units account for about Rs. 800 crores, or 40 per cent of the total.

no unit was prepared to take over a sick unit because the accumulated loss and unabsorbed depreciation allowance of the amalgamating company could not be carried forward and set off by the amalgamated company against its profit.

Incentives for Amalgamation: The Finance (No. 2) Act of 1977 has inserted Section 72A in the Income-tax Act, relaxing the aforesaid provisions relating to carry forward and set off accumulated business loss and unabsorbed depreciation allowance in certain cases of amalgamation. Section 72A provides that when there has been in amalgamation of a company owing an industrial undertaking or a ship with another company, and when the Central Government, on the recommendation of the specified authority, has made a declaration to that effect and that, thereupon notwithstanding anything contained in any other provision of the Income-tax Act, the accumulated loss and unabsorbed. depreciation of the amalgamating company will be the loss or the allowance for depreciation of the amalgamated company for the previous year in which the amalgamation was effected. It, therefore, follows that, as the unabsorbed loss of the amalgamating company is considered to be the loss for the previous year in which the amalgamation was effected, the amalgamated company will have the right to carry forward the loss for a period of eight assessment years immediately succeeding the assessment year in which the amalgamation was effected. The Government will make this declaration in respect of amalgamation provided:

(i) That, immediately preceding the amalgamation the amalgamating company was not financially viable by reason of its liabilities, losses and other relevant factors;

(ii) That the amalgamation was in the public interest; and

(iii) That such other conditions as the Central Government may by notification in the Official Gazette specify to ensure that the benefit under this Section (72A) is restricted to an amalgamation which would facilitate the rehabilitation or revival of the business of the amalgamating company.

Even after the said declaration by the Central Government, the concessions in respect of the accumulated loss and the unabsorbed depreciation allowance will not be granted to the amalgamated company unless the following further conditions are fulfilled:

(i) During the assesment year, for which such set off are allowance is claimed the business of the amalgamating company is carried on by the amalgamated company without any modification, or with such modification or reorganisations as may be approved by the Central Government to enable the amaigamated company to carry on such business more eonomically or more efficiently.

(ii) The amalgamated company furnishes, along with its return of income for the assessment year for which such set off or allowance is claimed, a certificate from the specified authority to the effect that amalgamation were not in a position to know in advance whether, after amalgamation, they would be entitled to the tax benefits offered under Section 72A. This lacuna has now been removed by the Finance Act of 1978, which has amended Section 72A. By virtue of this amendment, a unit seeking amalgamation with another unit will now be informed in advance whether, after the amalgamation, it will be entitled to benefits under Section 72A.

Guidelines for the Merger of Sick Units

In February 1978, the Central Government announced certain guidelines for merger of sick industrial units with healthy ones. The specified authority has to scrutinise the proposals for amalgamation and recommend the grant of the tax concessions offered by the Government. The guidelines are for the purpose of determining whether a scheme of amalgamation can be considered to be in the public interest or not.

According to the guidelines, the amalgamating company should have employed at least 100 workers during the accounting year in which the amalgamation is effected as well as in the two preceding years. Alternatively, the fair market value of the fixed assets (excluding land), as on the date of amalgamation, should not be less than Rs. 50 lakhs. However, these general criteria may be relaxed if the sick unit is engaged in the manufacture of mass consumption goods or goods which have a high priority, or a unit which has an industrial capacity which is required for the manufacture of such goods. Special consideration will also be given to those sick units which are located in any rural or backward area, or in any city or town with a population of less than one million.

The amalgamated company should have formulated a satisfactory programme for the rehabilitation or revival of the sick units, after taking into account the interests of the workers employed by the amalgamating unit. It should also have the necessary managerial and financial resources to execute the programme. If either the amalgamating or the amalgamated company owns an industrial undertaking governed by the Monopolies and Restricted Trade Practices Act, amalgamation will be recommended by the specified authority only after the requirements of this Act have satisfied and certain other conditions have been fulfilled. If the amalgamated company is a foreign majority company, the amalgamation will be recommended only if it conforms to the provisions of the Foreign Exchange Regulation Act and fulfil certain other conditions. Although a formal recommendation to the Central Government under Section 72(A)(1) of the Act will be made by the specified authority only after the amalgamation has been effected, an application for the approval of the scheme may be made to the specified authority even before such amalgamation actually takes place.

Other Provisions

The other provisions of the Income-tax Act containing tax concessions for companies in the course of amalgamation are summarised in what follows:

(i) There will be no computation of any profit under Section 41(2) of the Income-tax Act in the case amalgamating company with reference to the consideration receivable by it in respect of any building, machinery or plant or furniture transferred by it to amalgamated company. The profit under Section 41(2) of the Income-tax Act is the excess of sale proceeds or money receivable by the assessee in respect of any building, machinery or plant or furniture over the written down value thereof, to the extent of the depreciation allowance actually grated on such assets. As a corollary to this, there will also be no computation of any "terminal allowance" (i.e., the allowance for the net capital loss, if any, suffered on the transfer of an asset eligible for depreciation) in respect of such assets.

(ii) As a corollary to the above provision, the actual cost as also the written down value of the building, machinery, plant or furniture transferred by the amalgamating company of the amalgamated company, will be taken in the assessment of the amalgamated company to be the same as in the case of the amalgamating company. Further, for the purpose of the provision in the Income Tax Act that the aggregate amount of the depreciation allowed from year to year in respect of any asset will be limited to its actual cost, the depreciation actually allowed to the amalgamating company in respect of such assets is equal to the actual cost of the asset in the hands of the amalgamating company, the amalgamated company will not be entitled to any further depreciation on such assets.

(iii) When the amalgamating company transfers to the amalgamated company special capital assets used by it for scientific research in connection with its business, or for promoting family planning amongst its employees, or any capital assets of the nature of patent rights or copyrights, the amalgamated company will be entitled to amortise the capital costs of such assets against its profits under the existing provisions

of the law in this behalf, as if the amalgamation had not taken place.

(iv) No capital gain or loss will be computed in the case of the amalgamating company in respect of any capital assets transferred by it to the amalgamated company.

(v) For the purpose of computing, in the case of amalgamated company any capital gains or loss in respect of assets which were transferred to it by the amalgamating company and are subsequently sold or otherwise transferred by the amalgamated company to any other person, "the cost of acquisition" of such assets will be taken to be the same as in the hands of the amalgamating company.

Such capital gains will be computed by taking the cost of acquisition thereof to be the cost of acquisition of the shares in the amalgamating company.

(vi) An amalgamating company, which is a closely held company will not be liable to any gift tax in respect of the assets transferred by it to the amalgamated company. (Widely held companies have already been exempt from gift-tax under the Gift-tax Act.)

(vii) Where, in a scheme of amalgamation, the amalgamating company sells or otherwise transfers to the amalgamated company any ship, aircraft, machinery or plant in respect of which an investment allowance has been allowed to the amalgamating company under sub-section (1) of Section 32A:

(a) The amalgamated company shall continue to fulfil the conditions mentioned in sub-section (4) Section 32A in respect of the reserve created by the amalgamating company and in respect of the period within which such ship, aircraft, machinery or plant shall not be sold or otherwise transferred; and in default of any of these conditions, the provisions of sub-section (4A) of Section 155 will apply to the amalgamated company as they would have applied to the amalgamating company had it committed the default; and

(b) The balance of investment allowance, if any, still outstanding to the amalgamating company in respect of such ship, aircraft, machinery or plant will be allowed to the amalgamating company in accordance with provisions of sub-section (3), subject to the provisions that the total period for which the balance of investment allowance shall be carried forward in the assessment of the amalgamating company and the amalgamated company shall not exceed the period of 8 years specified in sub-section (3), and provided that the amalgamated company shall be treated as the assessee in respect of such ship, aircraft, machinery or plant for the purpose of this section.

(viii) Where the amalgamating company sells or otherwise transfers to the amalgamated company any ship, machinery or plant in respect of which a development rebate has been allowed to the amalgamating company, the amalgamated company would continue to enjoy the benefits of the development rebate provided that it satisfies the conditions specified in sub-sections 34(3) *(a)* and *(b)*. The amalgamated company is allowed to carry forward the unabsorbed development rebate; but the total period for which the amount of this rebate is carried forward in the assessment of the amalgamating company and the amalgamated company should not exceed eight years.

The objectives of Section 72A in the Income-tax Act of 1977, are in keeping with the approach adopted by the Government to help accelerate rehabilitation type of sick units. It remains to be seen, however, how far the concerned industries take advantage of the scheme of amalgamation and tax incentives offered to them. The Section has empowered the Central Government to lay down any other conditions that may be necessary by a notification in the Official Gazette. It is hoped, however, that such further conditions will not hamper but will speed up, the process of amalgamation. As stressed by the Chokshi Committee on Direct Tax Laws, such further notifications, which may be issued by the Central Government, should apply only prospectively to the schemes of amalgamation which may be submitted for approval after the date of the issue of the notification.

In the guidelines recently issued by the Government, it has been indicated that an application for the approval of a scheme for amalgamation may be made to the specified authority even before such amalgamation has actually taken place, and if the specified authority is satisfied, it may make a formal recommendation to the Government to make a declaration under sub-section (1) of Section 72 A. The Chokshi Committee has recommended that the substances of the assurance should be incorporated by a specific provision in the law to permit an application for amalgamation to the Central Government. After the application has been approved, the concerned companies may go ahead with the scheme, obtain the court's approval for it and implement it accordingly. It is, however, felt that, with the right spirit of flexibility in the administration of the scheme, a codification of the substance of the assurance may not be necessary. The Chokshi Committee has suggested that the two proceedings, one before the specified. authority and the other before the Central Government, should be coalesced. The Section should provide for a declaration to be issued by the Central Government or, alteratively, by the specified authority that an application by an amalgamated company be treated as a single proceeding. A consideration of this recommendation may, perhaps, be necessary in the interest of expediting the process of amalgamation. The Committee has also suggested that the Section should spell out the conditions relating to the employment of workers, the use of productive capacity and the finance to be raised. A certification in regard to these matters would help in the simplification of the amalgamation process.

The amalgamated company has, with its return of income, to furnish a certificate from the specified authority to the effect that adequate steps have been taken by it for the rehabilitation or revival of the business of the amalgamating company. Here, again, the issue of such a certificate by the specified authority is subject to its satisfaction as to the method and manner in which the business operations are carried on by the unit. These checks are considered essential by the Government; otherwise the objects for which the scheme of amalgamation has been formulated may not be achieved, and the tax benefits may be misused.

MODVAT and Small Industries

The Long-term Fiscal Policy has envisaged that the best solution to the vexatious question of the taxation of inputs and the cascading effect of this on the value of the final product would be to extend the present system of proforma credit to all excisable commodities with the exception of a few sectors. This scheme has been referred as Modified Value Added Tax (MODVAT) Scheme. It is a good beginning.

It is intended to greatly expand the scope of the provisions for set-offs for excise and countervailing duties and paid on inputs, with a view to coming as close to a generalized set-off for excise (and countervailing duty) taxation of inputs as is administratively feasible. The basic approach will be to move towards an extension of the present system of proforma credit to all excisable commodities with the exception of a few like petroleum, tobacoo and textile product. This programme will be implemented in a phased manner over a period of years, taking due account of the revenue implications, the need to revise administrative procedures and the lessons from experience gained in the early stages of the reform.

It must be emphasized that the MODVAT programme is intended to be broadly revenue neutral. It is not the purpose to use MODVAT to give substantial net reliefs on excise. The loss of duty on inputs will be recouped through higher excise taxation of final products. Indeed, shifting the effective burden of excise taxation away from inputs and on to final products is at the heart of the proposed reform. Aside from reducing distortionary effect on production and thus increasing the competitiveness of Indian industry, the shifting of excise to final products will help in tailoring excise duties in such a manner that the well off bear a higher proportionate burden than the poor.

For the progrcss towards a generalised system of reliefs on input taxation, it will be necessary to co-ordinate this move with the fiscal concession to Small Scale Industries (SSI). At present, input purchases from SSI do not qualify for set-off for the good reason that excise is not, generally, paid on them. Introduction of MODVAT will require further ration alisation of excise concession to SSI units and other excise exemptions. This will be done in a phased way.

Reform of Excise Concession of Small-scale Producers

An established feature of the excise duty structure is the concession schemes for small-scale producers. These have been granted in recognition of the employment potential of the small-scale sector and also the vital role of this sector in the industrial development. The eligibility criteria for exemptions and concessions to small-scale units have varied over time. However, the multiplicity of the criteria has been reduced considerably in recent years and there are at present two major schemes of concessions for the small-scale sector, namely, *(i)* a general scheme applicable to specified groups of commodities, and *(ii)* for commodities coming under Tariff Item 68 of the Excise Tariff. There are also a few special schemes applicable to particular commodities.

Government attaches high priority to growth of small-scale industries in view of their employment intensity, particularly in traditional sectors. Fiscal policy will continue to encourage growth of this sector through excise concessions. An important objective will be to provide an environment for growth of these industries, while at the same time, ensuring that tax concessions are not used as loopholes by large-scale units for abuse. The modifications made in the last Budget were designed to remove the disincentives for growth and promote efficient expansion of the small-scale sector.

The recently submitted report of the Technical Study Group on Central Excise Tariff has identified certain areas for further reform. For example, it has been noticed that a large number of small-scale units had been set up by large companies, solely to avail of concessions for small-scale units without adding significantly to employment or output. It has also been noted that the vast majority of small-scale units (over 90 per cent) have investment in plant and machinery of less than one lakh rupees. In respect of such units, it is particularly desirable to ensure that the fiscal environment is conducive to their growth. The report of the Technical Study Group is under consideration of the Government and changes in respect of the small-scale sector as well as other areas of excise will be announced as necessary. As a step towards simplification of the existing concessions, the Government also intends to move towards a uniform system of excise concessions for all commodities irrespective of the tariff classification.

Manufacturing Budget 2006-07

- In manufacturing sector, textiles, food processing, petroleum, chemicals and petro-chemicals, leather and automobiles and in services sector, tourism and software, have been identified as the industries having the potential to create a large number of jobs.
- Allocation for Technology Upgradation Fund (TUF) enhanced from Rs. 435 crore to Rs. 535 crore.
- Jute Technology Mission to be launched; a National Jute Board to be established.
- Food processing to be a priority sector for bank credit; NABARD to create a refinancing window with a corpus of Rs. 1,000 crore, especially for agroprocessing infrastructure and market development; National Institute of Food Technology Entrepreneurship and Management to be set up; Paddy Processing Research Centre, Thanjavur to be developed into a national-level institute.

Small & Medium Enterprises

- 180 items identified for dereservation; to give impetus to lending by SIDBI, SMEs to be recognized in the services sector and small-scale enterprises in services sector to be treated on par with small-scale enterprises in manufacturing sector.
- Corpus of Credit Guarantee Fund to be raised from Rs. 1,132 crore to Rs.2,500 crore in five years; Credit Guarantee Trust for Small Industries to be advised to reduce guarantee fee from 2.5 per cent to 1.5 per cent for all loans; insurance cover to be extended to 30,000 borrowers; ten schemes drawn up under a five-year National Manufacturing Competitiveness Programme, including promotion of ICT, mini tool rooms, design clinics and marketing support for SMEs; implementation to be in the PPP model.

Conclusion

Tax concessions have two important objectives, *viz.,* to promote investment in small-scale industries and to provide relief to them. Tax concessions are used to stimulate the establishment or expansion of small-scale industries in a desirable manner. They are granted on the basis of product line, and the concessions refer to excise duties, sales taxes on specific input such as capital equipment, intermediate goods etc. Of all the privileges that small-scale industrial firms enjoy, excise duty concessions are probably the most important, which give small enterprises an important competitive edge. In addition, tax concessions are also provided for new investments in particular industries or specific localities. The idea is to stimulate investments in specific directions which in the eyes of the government are particularly helpful from a macroeconomic development standpoint. Lowering of tariffs and sales tax concession enables the small-scale industry to push up their share in the domestic and international markets. Thus, taxation concessions not only stimulate growth of small-scale industries but also stimulate entrepreneurship production and marketing of quality goods. There is increase in employment, industrial production, national income and in return increased revenue to the exchequer, which will offset the loss on account of tax concessions.

During the last one year, the Centre has initiated a number of changes in the policies and programmes. In view of these, the next few years are of crucial importance to the small-scale industries. To achieve sustained economic growth, it is necessary to develop the infrastructure, particularly essential facilities like railway, communication, power, road transport etc. In addition, the policies and programmes for this sector should emphasise rationalisation of the fiscal and taxation regime, provision of appropriate infrastructure, the introduction of modern management techniques, upgradation of skills of artisans and propagation of appropriate technology and the adoption of a coherent marketing strategy both for internal and export marketing. The policies should not, on the other hand, be such as would discourage the natual growth in size of tiny and small industries. The organisational set-up will have to be revamped to meet the changing higher technological needs in terms of a well-programmed human resources development. Adequate and well organised programmes of extension, training and entrepreneurial motivation will have to be undertaken. R&D efforts will have to be stepped up and commercial production and distribution of improved tools and equipment undertaken. Special programmes and taxation incentives should be provided to the tiny sector having investment below Rs. 5 lakhs.

The future of the small-scale industries by and large depends upon the industrial policy pursued by the Government during the nineties. The small-scalc sector requires the active support of the government. *It is, therefore, necessary to adopt a policy conducive to the growth of this sector, so as to enable it to face the 21st century with confidence and bright prospects.

---

* Taxation benefits should be adequate, meaningful and free from undue harassment. It should aim at motivating an enterpreneur to go to set-up a SSI.

ANNEXURE – 1

Comprehensive Policy Package for SSI Sector and Tiny Sector

SSI SECTOR

Policy Support

- The investment limit for the SSI sector will continue to be Rs. 10 million.
- The Ministry of SSI and ARI will bring out a specific list of hi-tech and export-oriented items which would require the investment limit to be raised to Rs. 50 million to admit suitable technology upgradation and to enable them to maintain their competitive edge.

Fiscal Support

- To improve the competitiveness of the Small-scale Sector, the exemption limit for excise duty has been raised from Rs. 5 million to Rs. 10 million.

Credit Support

- The composite loans limit has been raised from Rs. 1 million to Rs. 2.5 million.
- The Small-scale Service and Business (Industry Related) Enterprises (SSSBEs) with a maximum investment of Rs. 1 million will qualify for priority lending.
- The eligibility limit for coverage under the recently launched (August 2000) Credit Guarantee Scheme has been revised to Rs. 2.5 million from the present limit of Re. 1 million.
- Under the National Equity Fund (NEF) Scheme, the project cost limit will be raised from Rs. 2.5 million to Rs. 5 million. The soft loan limit will be retained at 25 per cent of the project subject to a maximum of Rs. 1 million, per project. Assistance under the NEF will be provided at a service charge of 5 per cent per annum.
- The Department of Economic Affairs will appoint a Task Force to suggest the revitalisation/ restructuring of the State Financial Corporations.
- The Nayak Committee's recommendations with regard to the provision of 20 per cent of the projected turnover as working capital is being recommended to the financial institutions and banks.

Infrastructural Support

- The Integrated Infrastructure Development Scheme will progressively cover all areas in the country with a 50 per cent reservation for rural areas.
- Regarding the upgradation of the industrial estates, that are languishing, the SSI Ministry will draw up a detailed scheme for consideration of the Planning Commission.
- A plan scheme for cluster development will be drawn up.
- The funds available under the non-lapsable pool for the North East will be made use of for Industrial Infrastructure Development in the North East region including Sikkim, for the setting up of incubation centres and for cluster development.

Technological Support and Quality Improvement

- Capital subsidy of 12 per cent of investment in technology in select sectors. An interministerial committee of experts will be set up to define the scope of technology upgradation and sectoral priorities.
- The setting up of incubation centres in sunrise industries will be supported.
- The TBSE set up by SIDBI will be strengthened so that it functions effectively as a Technology Bank. It will be properly networked with NSIC, SIDO (SENET Programme) and APCTT.
- SIDO, SIDBI and NSIC will jointly prepare a compendium of available technologies for the R&D institutions in India and abroad and circulate this among the industry associations for the dissemination of the latest technology-related information.

- Commercial banks are being requested to develop schemes to encourage investment in technology upgradation and harmonise the same with SIDBI.
- A one time capital grant of 50% will be given to Small-scale Industries Associations which wish to develop and operate Testing laboratories, provided they are of international standards.

Marketing Support

- SIDO will have a Market Development Assistance Programme, similar to the one operating in the Ministry of Commerce. It will be a plan scheme.
- The Vendor Development Programme, Buyer-Seller Meets and Exhibitions will take place more often and at dispersed locations.

Streamlining Inspections/Rules and Regulations

- To minimise harassment to the SSI sector a group will be set up to recommend within 3 months, the means for streamlining inspection. This will include a repeal of laws and regulations applicable to the sector that have since become redundant.
- Self-certification will be progressively encouraged in lieu of inspections, which should be prescribed under the following three conditions:

  — On receipt of specific complaint;

  — Selection of unit for sample check (Say 10 per cent of total units); and

  — For audit and safety purposes.

Entrepreneurship Development

- Capacity building in the SSI sector, both for entrepreneurs as well as workers will be given top priority. The Ministry of SSI and Labour Ministry will jointly work out the strategy.

Facilitating Prompt Payment

- The Reserve Bank of India is being requested to appoint a Task Force to go into the question of strengthening and popularising factoring services, without recourse to the SSI suppliers. The Task Force shall give its report within six months of its constitution.
- RBI is being requested to take up with the banks the question of sub-allocating the overall limits to the large borrowers specifically for meeting the payment obligations in respect of purchases from the SSIs, either on a cash basis or on bills basis.

Rehabilitation of Sick Units

- RBI is being requested to draw up revised guidelines for the rehabilitation of currently sick but potentially viable SSI units. Such guidelines should be detailed, transparent and non-discretionary.

Promoting Rural Industries

- To support the Handloom Sector the 'Deendayal Hathkarga Protsahan Yojna' has been announced. The scheme has a total financial impliction of Rs. 4.47 billion and will provide comprehensive financial and infrastructural support to weavers.
- The Government is working out new comprehensive package to strengthen Khadi and Village Industries that will further upgrade the skills of khadi workers.

Improving Data Base

- A fresh Census of Small-Scale Industries will be conducted covering inter-alia, the incident of sickness.

TINY SECTOR

Policy Support

- The investment limit for the tiny sector will continue to be Rs. 2.5 million.
- Under the Prime Minister's Rozgar Yojna, which facilitates the setting up of micro enterprises and generates employment for the educated unemployed, the family income eligibility limit of Rs. 24,000 per annum being revised to Rs. 40,000 per annum.

Credit Support

- The Nayak Committee's recommendations regarding the provision of 20 per cent of the projected turnover as working capital is being recommended to the financial institutions and banks. In respect of tiny units also 20 per cent of the projected annual turnover would qualify for working capital loan.
- The National Small Industries Corporation will continue to give composite loans upto Rs. 2.5 million to the tiny sector and continue to charge one per cent concessional interest rate.
- SIDBI will continue to give concessional rate of refinance to the tiny sector which is now at 10.5 per cent as compared to 12 per cent for the SSI sector. This policy will continue.
- In the National Equity Fund Scheme, the project cost limit will be raised from Rs. 2.5 million to Rs. 5.0 million. The soft loan limit will be retained at 25 per cent of the project cost subject to a maximum of Re. 1.0 million per project. Assistance under the NEF will be provided at a service charge of 5 per cent per annum. Under the National Equity Fund Scheme, 30 per cent of the investment will be earmarked for the Tiny Sector.

Infrastructure Support

- The Integrated Infrastructure Development (IID) Scheme will progressively cover all areas in the country with 50 per cent reservation for rural areas. Under this scheme, 50 per cent of the plots will be earmarked for the tiny sector (as against the 40 per cent done earlier).
- Under the National Programme for Rural industrialisation, cluster development is being taken up by KVIC, SIDO, SIDBI and NABARD. The major beneficiaries of the cluster development programme will be tiny sector units. The sponsoring organisation for each cluster will provide for design development, capacity building, technology intervention and consortium marketing. A cluster development fund will be created under the Plan.

Technological Support

- Under the Capital subsidy of scheme of 12 per cent for investment in technology upgradation in select sectors preference will be given to the tiny sector.

Marketing Support

- Preference will be given to the tiny sector while organizing buyer-seller meets, vendor development programmes and exhibitions.

Source: *Office of the DC (SSI)*

New Package for Khadi and Village Industries

Options of Rebate and MDA

Market Development Assistance (MDA) at the rate of 20 per cent of the annual turnover has been introduced as an option in place of rebate to the institutions for producing innovative designs and marketable products.

Additional Working Capital

The term loan of Rs. 3 billion given to Khadi Institutions is being converted into working capital. Further, a fresh line of credit of Rs. 2.5 billion as working capital would be provided to those institutions that are willing to switch from Rebate Scheme to MDA Scheme.

Insurance Cover to Khadi Artisans

Insurance cover for khadi artisans against death, disability and disease will be provided.

Quality

The quality of products of this sector will be certified through labs accredited by NABI.

Marketing

- To create Packaging and Design Facilities, Brand Building Exercise, in the form of Heritage Khadi, standard logo and standard design of sales outlets.
- To undertake Marketing Blitz and Campaigns through the use of multimedia and sustained publicity.

Cluster Development Programme

To create common facilities for innovation, technology upgradation, packaging, processing, testing and e-commerce.

Focus on Core Areas

An amount of Rs. 2.75 billion has been earmarked for a few selected areas where there exists a competitive advantage, namely, herbal cosmetic and medicines, honey, organic foods, edible oils and essential oils to begin with.

Source : *Office of the DC (SSI)*

Measures taken for Development of North Eastern Region

- Small Industry Service Institutes (SISIs) have been setup in all the North Eastern States to provide assistance/ consultancy services to prospective and existing entrepreneurs, conduct entrepreneurship development, management development and skill development programmes for SSI entrepreneurs and also to provide common facilities through workshops/laboratories attached to SSIs.
- The Prime Minister's Rozgar Yojana (PMRY) has been liberalised for the North Eastern Region. The family income limit for each beneficiary and his/her spouse has been enhanced from Rs. 24,000 to Rs. 40,000 per annum and the age limit for eligibility has also been enhanced from 35 years to 40 years. Activities like horticulture, piggery, poultry, fishing and small tea gardens have also been included as economically viable activities, which are distinctive for the North Eastern Region.
- Under the Integrated Infrastructure Development (IID) Scheme meant for improvement of infrastructure in rural and backward areas for SSIs, one IID Centre has been sanctioned for Assam in district Darang (Village Dalgon) and another for Manipur in district Chandel (Village Moreh).
- Indian Institute of Entrepreneurship (IIE), Guwahati was set up in 1994 as a full fledged Institute to act as a catalyst to encourage entrepreneurial development in the North East. The Institute organises training programmes and undertakes research and consultancy services in the field of small industry and entrepreneurship.
- Transport Subsidy Scheme was introduced in 1971, with a view to promoting industrialisation in hilly, remote and inaccessible areas. Under the scheme, transport subsidy ranging from 50 per cent to 90 per cent is admissible on the transport cost incurred on movement of raw materials and finished goods from the designated rail heads/ ports upto the location of industrial units and vice versa. The scheme has been extended upto March 31, 2007 for North Eastern Region.
- Industrial undertakings set up in Integrated Infrastructural Development Centres and Industrial Growth Centres to be notified by the Central Government are exempt from income tax for ten consecutive assessment years. A similar benefit is given to such other industries in the North Eastern Region as are notified by the Central Government. The above are effective from April 1, 2000.
- A Tool Room and Training Centre at Guwahati to create facilities for manufacture of quality tools and dies and for training in tool making is under implementation.
- On June 1, 1998 the Government of India has notified the Central Capital Investment Subsidy Scheme for industrial units in the North Eastern Region. A scheme of interest subsidy on the working capital loans for industrial units in the North Eastern Region called the Central Interest Subsidy Scheme, 1977 has also been notified on February 18, 1999 with a view to accelerating the industrial development in the region.

Source : *Office of the DC (SSI)*

* * *

20

Export Marketing

Introduction

In the achievement of the strategic objectives of a self-reliant and dynamic economy, the Government considers a substantial expansion in export earnings to be of great importance. Exports enable the country to pay for critical imports — machinery, metals, petroleum, fertilisers and new technological inputs and step up the pace of economic development, put the resources of those goods in which India has a long-term comparative advantage. This apart, exports are an important instrument for the creation of employment opportunities in small-scale industries, cottage industries and in the agricultural sector as well as in the medium and large industrial sector.

Although the quickening pace of industrialisation in the nineteenth century has opened up vast markets for the commodities produced by developing countries, the volume of their exports began to decline with the changes in the economic climate in the middle of the twentieth century.

In order to achieve national objectives, the Government adopted a new and scientific approach to its export policy, which has been made an integral part of the country's overall strategy for economic development. The new export policy aims at consciously and systematically developing the export of items in which India has a comparative advantage and which promises long-term growth prospects. More practically, stress has been laid on greater participation by the small-scale sector and the labour-intensive sector in the export trade with a view to providing wider employment opportunities to the people.

Export promotion of products manufactured in the small-scale sector has been given considerable importance, and efforts are being made to increase its share in total exports.

GLOBALISATION OF MARKETS

Globalisation is the trend toward a more integrated global economic system. Figure 20.1 shows the components of globalisation. The components of globalisation are: *globalisation of markets, globalisation of production, globalisation of investment and globalisation of technology. First,* we discuss the globalisation of markets.

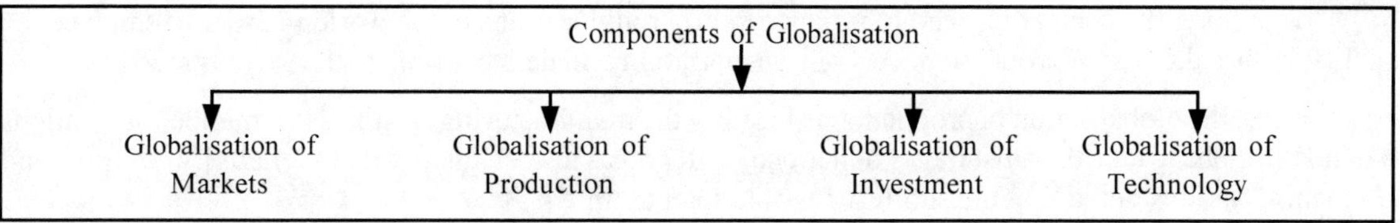

Fig. 20.1. Components of Globalisation

Globalisation of markets refers to the process of integrating and merging of the distinct world markets into a single market. This process involves the identification of some common norm, taste, preference and convenience and slowly enables the cultural shift towards the use of a common product or service.

A number of consumer products have global acceptance. *For example,* Coca Cola, Pepsi, McDonalds' burgers, Music of Madonna, MTV, Sony Walkmans, Levis jeans, Indian masala dosa, Indian Hyderabadi biryani, Citicorp credit cards etc.

Features of Globalisation of Markets

Features of globalisation of markets include:

- The size of the company need not be too large to create a global market. Even small companies can also create a global market. *For example,* Harry Ramsden — a small British company with an annual sales of US $ 16 million is trying to sell its product of fish 'n' chips in Japan based on the Japanese culture. *(See Box 20.2).*
- The distinctions of national markets are still prevailing even after the globalisation of markets. These distinctions require the companies to formulate different strategies for each market. *For example,* Coca Cola, Levis jeans and McDonalds' employ separate strategies for each country.
- Most of the foreign markets are the markets for non-consumer goods like industrial products, machinery, equipment, raw materials, computers, software, financial products etc.
- The global business firms compete with each other frequently in different national markets including their home markets. *For example,* Coca Cola is the global rival of Pepsi. Similarly Ford and Toyota, Boeing and Airbus, Caterpillar and Komatsu. Though these companies compete with each other they create a global market.

Reasons for Globalisation of Production

Companies globalise the production facilities due to the following reasons:

- Imposition of restrictions on imports by the foreign countries forces the MNCs to establish the manufacturing facilities in other countries. For example, Toyota of Japan established its plants in USA and UK due to the import restrictions.
- Availability of high quality raw materials and components in other countries.
- Availability of inputs at low cost in foreign countries.
- Availability of skilled human resources at low cost.
- Liberal labour laws in foreign countries.
- To reduce the cost of transportation and easy logistics management.
- Facility of exporting to other neighbouring foreign countries.
- To design and produce the products as per the varying tastes of customers in foreign countries.

Therefore, the companies tend to produce in different locations of the world in order to enhance the quality, reduce the cost of production, cost of transportation and delivery time to the various markets.

Thus, the globalisation of production is locating the manufacturing facilities in a number of locations around the globe to take the advantages of national differences in cost, quality and availability of inputs and of reaching various markets at the shortest possible span of time.

The process of globalisation of production helps the companies to design the following strategies:

- Low cost leadership
- Superior quality and
- Superior speed.

For example, Jet airlines – Boeing 777 has 132,500 major components. These components are produced in 545 different locations of the globe. A small optical company in USA, *i.e.,* Swan Optical, manufactures its eyewear in low cost factories in Hongkong, China, Japan, France and Italy.

In addition to the globalisation of markets and production, a number of factors enable the process of globalisation at a fast rate. Now, we shall discuss the investment factor.

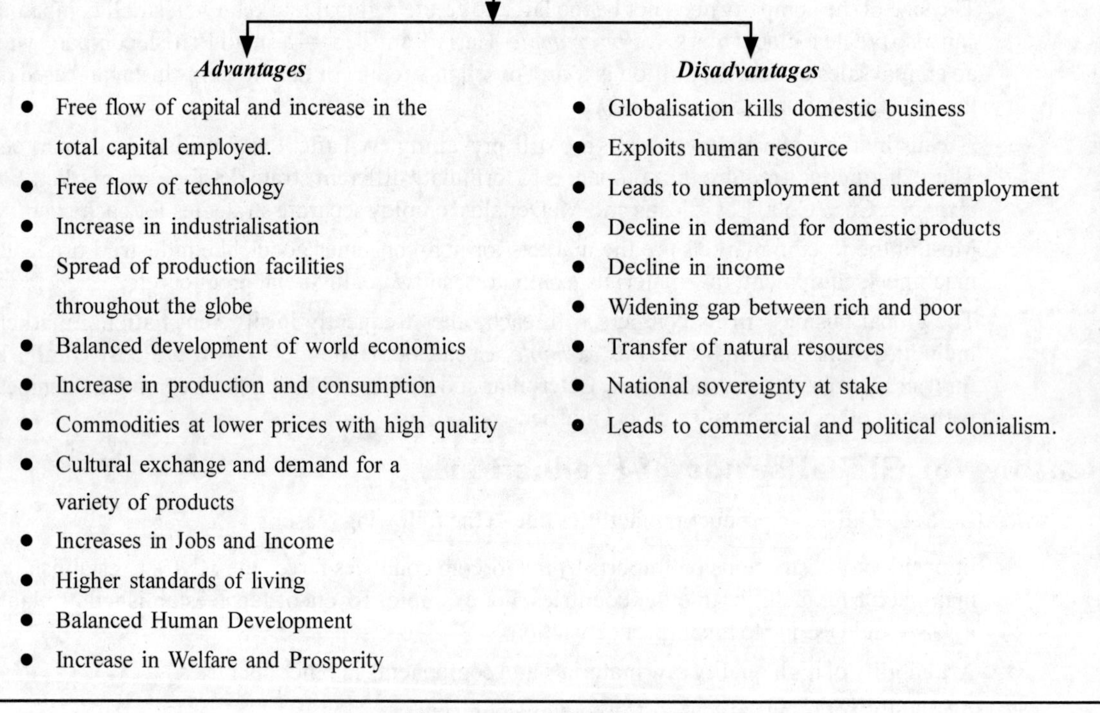

Fig. 20.2. Advantages and Disadvantages of Globalisation

Export Marketing

Marketing is "the process of planning and executing the conception, pricing, promotion and distribution of ideas, goods and services to create exchange that satisfy individual and organisational objectives" and extension of these activities across the globe is referred to as International Marketing. Companies entering into international markets must deal with varying economic, social, cultural, political and legal environments and advertising media and distribution channels.

One of the Nikes' advertisement features a coach telling his players "visualize your opponent as your worst enemy." This advertisement was banned by New Zealand's regulators for being too violent. Similarly, they banned the Coca Cola's advertisement featuring aboriginal dances for being culturally insensitive.

In addition export marketing managers capture synergies by efficient co-ordination of the markets. Environmental factors in different countries make the marketing different from one country to another country. Hence, we have to study International marketing although we have studied a course on marketing.

Domestic marketing managers mostly go for standard products. But a standard product may not be acceptable to the customers of a foreign country. Hence, export marketing managers have a dilemma whether to standardise the product or customise it.

Export marketing is based on standardised and quality goods. The branding of goods takes a precedence.

Brands play a key role in export marketing. The future of branding lies in telling a story. Successful marketers are those that would have moved beyond to the 31st second, they are the ones who are not just telling the story but weaving it. It's about crafting a story that is relevant to the consumer and telling it to them at a time when they want to listen. It's about telling them a story in a way they would like to remember it and in a place they won't mind you sharing with them.

The consumer has the power. The consumer will absorb only when she wants. It's not the right of the brand owner, nor the right of the retailer. It's the right of the consumers. Marketer's who fail to engage with her, fail to create a brand.

The future of branding is when consumers give in to the seduction happily and willingly. That's the magic that will create the lasting consumer devotion to a brand.

Competitive Advantage

The competitive advantage of export (international) maketing are as follows:

High Living Standards: Comparative cost theory indicates that the countries which have the advantage of raw materials, human resources, natural resources and climatic conditions in producing particular goods can produce the products at low cost and also of high quality. Customers in various countries can buy more products with the same money. In turn, it can also enhance the living standards of the people through enhanced purchasing power and by consuming high quality products.

Increased Socio-economic Welfare: International business enhances consumption level, and economic welfare of the people of the trading countries. *For example,* the people of China are now enjoying a variety of products of various countries than before as China has been actively involved in international business like Coca Cola, McDonalds' range of products, electronic products of Japan and coffee from Brazil. Thus, the Chinese consumption levels and socio-economic welfare are enhanced.

Wider Market: International business widens the market and increases the market size. Therefore, the companies need not depend on the demand for the product in a single country or customer's tastes and preferences of a single country. Due to the enhanced market the Air France, now, mostly depends on the demand for air travel of the customers from countries other than France. This is true in case of most of the MNCs like Toyota, Honda, Xerox and Coca Cola.

Reduced Effects of Business Cycles: The stages of business cycles vary from country to country. Therefore, MNCs shift from the country, experiencing a recession to the country experiencing 'boom' conditions. Thus international business firms can escape from the recessionary conditions.

Reduced Risks: Both commercial and political risks are reduced for the companies engaged in international business due to spread in different countries. Multinationals which were operating in erstwhile USSR were affected only partly due to their safer operations in other countries. But the domestic companies of then USSR collapsed completely.

Large-Scale Economies: Multinational companies due to the wider and larger markets produce larger quantities. Invariably, it provides the benefit of large-scale economies like reduced cost of production, availability of expertise, quality etc.

Potential Untapped Markets: International business provides the chance of exploring and exploiting the potential markets which are untapped so far. These markets provide the opportunity of selling the product at higher price than in domestic markets. *For example,* Bata sells shoes in UK at £ 100 (Rs. 7,000) whose price is around Rs. 700 in India.

Provides the Opportunity for and Challenge to Domestic Business: International business firms provide the opportunities to the domestic companies. These opportunities include technology, management expertise, market intelligence, product developments etc. *For example,* Japanese firms operating in US provide these opportunities to US companies. This is more evident in the case of developing countries like India, African countries and Asian countries.

Similarly, the MNCs pose challenges to the domestic business initially. Domestic firms develop themselves to meet these challenges. Thus, the opportunities and challenges help the domestic companies to develop. Maruti helped Telco to come up with Tata Indica, Foreign Universities helped IIMs, IITs and Indian Universities to enhance their curricula.

Division of Labour and Specialisation: As mentioned earlier, international business leads to division of labour and specialisation. Brazil specialises in coffee, Kenya in tea, Japan in automobiles and electronics, India in textile garments etc.

Economic Growth of the World: Specialisation, division of labour, enhancement of productivity, posing challenges, development to meet them, innovations and creations to meet the competition lead to overall economic growth of the world nations. International business particularly helped the Asian countries like Japan, Taiwan, Korea, Philippines, Singapore, Malaysia, and the United Arab Emirates.

Optimum and Proper Utilisation of World Resources: International business provides for the flow of raw materials, natural resources and human resources from the countries where they are at excess supply to those countries which are in short supply or need most. *For example,* flow of human resources from India, consumer goods from UK, France, Italy and Germany to developing countries. This, in turn, helps for the optimum and proper utilisation of world resources.

Cultural Transformation: International business benefits are not purely economical or commercial, they are even social and cultural. These days, we observe that the West is slowly tending towards the East and *vice versa.* It does mean that the good cultural factors and values of the East are acquired by the West and *vice versa.* Thus, there is a close cultural transformation and integration.

Knitting the World into a Closely Interactive Traditional Village : International business, ultimately knits the global economies, societies and countries into a closely interactive and traditional village where one is for all and all are for one.

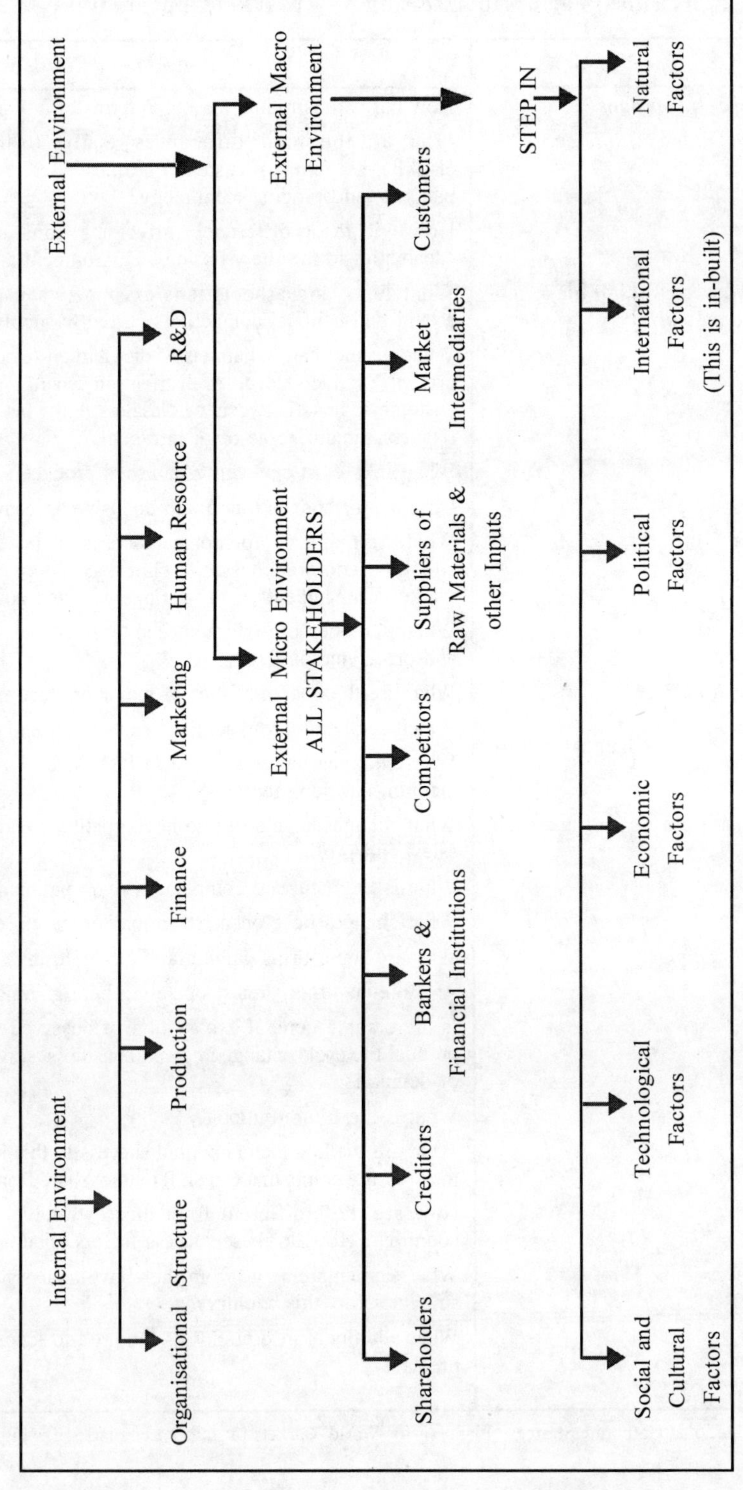
EXPORT MARKET ENVIRONMENT
Internal Environment
External Environment
Organisational Structure
Production
Finance
Marketing
Human Resource
R&D
External Micro Environment
ALL STAKEHOLDERS
External Macro Environment
Shareholders
Creditors
Bankers & Financial Institutions
Competitors
Suppliers of Raw Materials & other Inputs
Market Intermediaries
Customers
STEP IN
Social and Cultural Factors
Technological Factors
Economic Factors
Political Factors
International Factors
(This is in-built)
Natural Factors

Exhibit 20.1 Critical Factors in Assessing New Market Opportunities

Topic of Appraisal	*Items to be Considered*
Product-market dimensions	How big is the product market in terms of unit size and sales volume?
Major product-market "differences"	What are the major differences relative to the firm's experience elsewhere in terms of customer profiles, price levels, national purchase patterns, and product technology?
	How will these differences affect the transferability of the firm's capabilities to the new business environment and their effectiveness?
Structural characteristics of the national product market	What links and associations exist between potential customers, established national competitors currently supplying these customers?
	What are the major channels of distribution (discount structure, ties to present products, levels of distribution separating producers from final customers, links between wholesalers, links between wholesalers and retailers, finance, role of government)?
	What links exist between established producers and their suppliers?
	Do industry concentration and collusive agreements exist?
Competitor analysis	What are major competitor characteristics (size, capacity utilization, strengths and weaknesses, technology, supply sources, preferential market arrangements, and relations with the government)?
	What is competitor performance in terms of market share, sales growth, and profit margins?
Potential target markets	What are the characteristics of major product-market segments?
	Which segments are potential targets upon entry?
	What changes have occurred in total size of product market short, medium and long-term?
Relevant trends (historic and projected)	What changes have occurred in competitor performance market share, sales, and profits?
	What is the nature of competition *(e.g.,* national or international)?
	What changes have occurred in market structure?
Explanation of change	Why are some firms gaining and others losing?
	Are foreign firms already operating here gaining or losing?
	Is there some general explanation of observed change, for example, product life cycle, change in overall business activity, and shift in nature of demand?
	What is the future outlook?
Success factors	What are the key factors behind success in this business environment, the pressure points that can shift market share from one firm to another?
	How are these different from those we have experienced in other countries? How do these success factors relate to our firm?
Strategic options	What elements emerge from the above analysis that point to possible strategies for this country?
	What additional information is required to identify our options more precisely?

Source : Multinational Corporate Strategy: Planning for World Markets by James Leoutiades, Lexington Books, 1985.

Components of Exports

The main components of exports of products manufactured in the small-scale sector are: khadi and handloom, processed foods, engineering goods, computers, handicrafts including gems and jewellery, garments (all types), project exports, consultancy exports, ancillary exports outsourcive, export services, outsourcive and so on.

Exports from the SSI Sector

The value of exports from the small-scale industries (SSI) sector has been rising from year to year. The value increased from Rs. 1,643 crore in 1980-81 to Rs. 97,644 crore in 2003-04. The share of exports from the small-scale sector as percentage of India's total exports also rose from 24.5 per cent in 1980-81 to 33.2 per cent in 2003-04. This increase in SSI exports is mainly due to the powerlooms, measures undertaken by the government as well as entrepreneurial push.

Major sectors contributing to SSI "Exports include readymade garments (27%), engineering goods (14.5%), chemicals and pharmaceuticals, electronics and computers and processed foods (11% each). In terms of export orientation, sports goods have 100% exports from SSI sector, followed by readymade garments (90%), leather (70%), marine products (47%) and chemicals and pharmaceuticals (44%). More and more exporting units from the SSI sector have been increasing their capital investment to come out of the SSI net and emerge as global players. Such a trend is happening in: basic chemicals, pharmaceuticals, engineering goods, leather goods and textiles.

If exports of powerlooms, handicrafts, handlooms and khadi are included, the share of the SSI sector is likely to be nearly half of the total. Even in the global market, the SSI units have been successful in enlarging their share every year. This goes to prove that the SSI sector is quite significant in the ever-changing economic scenario.

An analysis of the data on product group wise exports shows that the entire exports of sports goods are from the SSI sector. The substantial shares of the SSI sector in the total exports of other commodity groups are: woollen garments (95 per cent), readymade garments (90 per cent), processed tobacco, snuff and bidi (70 per cent), processed food (65 per cent), finished leather and leather products (52 per cent), basic chemicals, pharmaceuticals and cosmetics (44 per cent) and marine products (44 per cent).

Factors Affecting SSI Exports

(i) *Technological Constraints:* The technology used by small-scale units in India is of low to medium quality. The products of the SSI sector in terms of quality are not comparable to products from foreign countries. Research and Development which are crucial for producing high technology products has not been the focus of the Indian SSI sector. A large number of SSIs in India manufacture products for the domestic market only and exports from the larger ones among the SSI units have a low skill and technology content. In order to step up its exports, it is, therefore, important for the SSI sector to undertake research and development and focus on technology based product lines.

(ii) Size *Constraints:* The small size of the SSI units limits their activities mainly to production for the domestic market, as the resources required for venturing into exports, is beyond the capacity of the lower end units.

(iii) *Inability to Undertake Promotional Activities:* Enterprises undertaking advertising and promotional activities perform better than others in the international markets because of their conscious building of brand images and trade names and to maintain quality as well as satisfactory after sales services. Due to lack of resources for competing with multinationals in the international market, many of the SSIs sell their products to trading agencies or merchant exporters to avoid international competition. Similarly, it is difficult for SSIs to establish their own marketing channels in foreign countries or to establish formal links with marketing companies to promote exports.

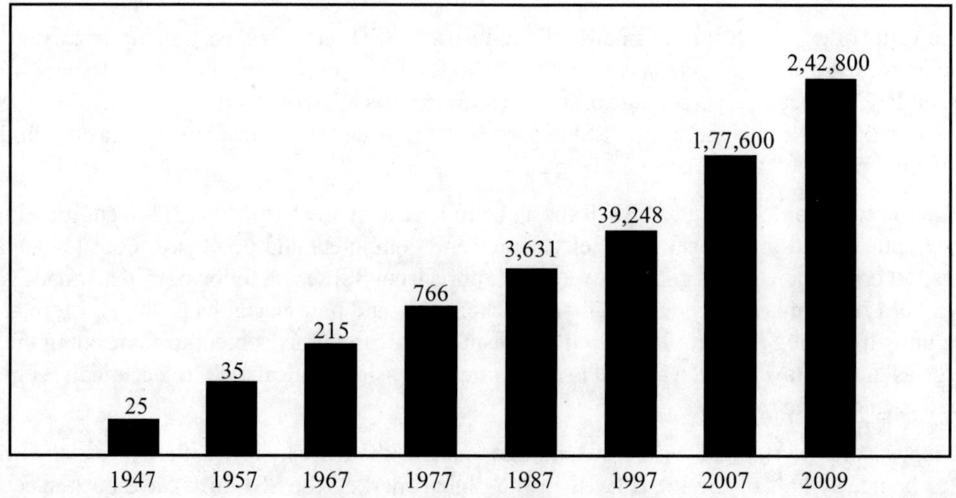

Fig. 20.3. SSI Exports (Rs. Crore)

Export Prospects

The small-scale sector in India now produces a wide range of products, from simple consumer goods to such sophisticated products as scientific and precision instruments, hearing aids, electronic components, tape recorders, television sets etc. With a lower level of labour costs than in the western countries, India enjoys an advantage in exporting both traditional and non-traditional labour-intensive products. This apart, there is favourable climate for SSI exports in foreign markets because frequent wage hikes and pollution hazards in industrialised countries tend to favour imports from developing countries, particularly the import of SSI products.

Tech Mart India'96, Pragati Maidan, New Delhi

Container handling at one of the ports

In order to promote exports, the Government has drawn up a number of schemes for promotion of exports from the SSI sector, which includes organisation of specialized training programmes on packaging for exports in collaboration with the Indian Institute of Packaging, Mumbai, assistance to SSI units for participation in the international and internal exhibitions, dissemination of export information at the doorstep of SSI units through Technological Information Promotions Systems (TIPS) and incentives for quality production in the SSI sectors.

In order to strengthen the export production base, manufacturers of items reserved for SSI sectors are permitted to increase their capacity by way of investment in plant and equipment beyond Rs. 100 lakhs provided they undertake a minimum export of 76 per cent of their annual production.

The new revised export and import policy extends equal opportunity to small and medium exports. Bulk of the country's exports, in terms of value, are taking place through export/trading/ star trading/super star trading houses and such status is granted on the basis of prescribed export performance level and all exporters, including small and medium exporters, are extended equal treatment.

If the status is claimed in terms of FOB value of exports, double weightage is given to the export of products manufactured by the Small Scale Industry (SSI), handloom and handicrafts including sports goods, hand-knotted carpets and silk products.

If the status is claimed in terms of Net Foreign Exchange (NFE) earned, double weightage is given to the export products manufactured by SSI and triple weightage is given to the NFE earned on the exports of hand-knotted carpets and silk products manufactured by the handloom and handicrafts sectors.

Such status holders are extended equal treatment for getting transferable special import licence valid for the import of specified items of the negative list of import. Under the duty exemption scheme, SSI units have been extended the facility to give the bank guarantee wherever applicable, at 50 per cent of the normal requirement.

Table 20.1 SSI Export

(Rs. Crores)

Year (1)	*Total Exports (2)*	*SSI Exports (3)*	*3 as % of 2*
1980-81	6,711	1,643	24.5
1981-82	7,806	2,071	26.5
1982-83	8,803	2,071	23.2
1983-84	9,771	2,164	22.1
1984-85	11,744	2,553	21.7
1985-86	10,895	2,773	25.5
1986-87	12,452	3,631	29.2
1987-88	15,674	4,535	28.9
1988-89	20,232	5,681	28.1
1989-90	27,658	7,990	28.9
1990-91	32,553	9,763	30.0
1991-92	44,042	13,883	31.5
1992-93	53,350	17,785	33.3
1993-94	69,546	25,307	36.4
1994-95	82,674	29,068	35.2
1995-96	1,06,353	36,470	34.3

Year (1)	*Total Exports (2)*	*SSI Exports (3)*	*3 as % of 2*
1996-97	1,18,817	33,248	33.4
1997-98	1,30,100	44,442	34.1
1998-99	1,39,752	48,979	35.0
1999-2000	1,59,561	54,200	33.4
2000-01	2,03,571	69,197	34.3
2001-02	2,09,018	71,244	34.6
2002-03	.2,55037	86,013	33.7
2003-04	2,93,367	97,644	33.2
2004-05	3,75,340	1,24,417	33.1
2005-06	4,56,418	1,50,242	32.9
2006-07	5,71,779	1,77,600	31.0
2007-08	6,55,864	2,13,500	32.5
2008-09	7,66,935	2,42,800	31.6

Export Thrust Areas

City	*State*	*Commodity*
Tirupur	Tamil Nadu	Knitwear & hosiery
Moradabad	Uttar Pradesh	Brassware
Ludhiana	Punjab	Heavy machinery, Hosiery
Surat	Gujarat	Handloom
Alleppey	Kerala	Cori
Jallandhar	Punjab	Sports goods
Ranipet/Ambur	Tamil Nadu	Leather
Nagpur	Maharashtra	Handtools
Vishakapatnam	Andhra Pradesh	Marine products
Meerut	Uttar Pradesh	Sport goods
Aligarh	Uttar Pradesh	Brass locks
Agra	Uttar Pradesh	Leather footwear
Khurja	Uttar Pradesh	Pottery
Kanchipuram	Tamil Nadu	Silk
Sivakasi	Tamil Nadu	Safety matches
Salem	Tamil Nadu	Handtools
Ambala	Haryana	Scientific instruments
Jamnagar	Gujarat	Brass parts
Rajkot	Gujarat	Engine pumps
Vapi-Ankleshwar	Gujarat	Chemicals
Batala	Punjab	Machine tools
Bhagalpur	Bihar	Weaving

Box 20.1: Our Heritage

India's handicrafts have been renowned from time immemorial for *their* intricate workmanship and exclusive designs. The sector has got a significant boost over the last decade from the efforts of the Export Promotion, Council for Handicrafts (EPCH), which has been actively working to promote India's arts and crafts in overseas markets. The EPCH. has been organising the IHGF since 1994 under the aegis of the Development Commissioner (Handiicrafts), Ministry of Textiles. The institutionalisation of IHGF over the past 10 years and its role as a "one-stop sourcing centre" for buyers has made it the largest gifts and handicrafts exhibition of South-East Asia. The basic objective of IHGF is to display under one roof the range of handicrafts available in India, The fair presents a huge business opportunity to exhibitors and offers overseas buyers the opportunity to directly interact with the manufacturers.

For several centuries, almost every region of India has had its own distinct form of art and craft. Handicrafts production predominantly happens in the small-scale and medium secdtor. It plays a vital. role in the economic development of India by providing employment at the village and town level. The office of the Development Commissioner (Handicrafts) in the Textiles Ministry has played a key role in the rise of this sector by providing regular jssis[ame to the industry for further growth Today, it is estimated that over 60 lakh artisans arc involved in producing and creating Indian handicrafts.

The strength of the Indian handicrafts industry lies, in its low capital investment, abundant skilled manpower, negligible import content and high export potential, The other strength of the industry is the rich -hidden' treasures" that are to be found across India.

The marketing approach adopted by EPCH lays considerable emphasis on development, presentation, packaging, production and finishing techniques for the products. The National Centre for Design and Product Development is equipped with the latest methods of design computing, Assisted by a team of Indian and foreign designers, the centre is expected to be fully operational during the loth Plan. The integrated design and technology project in the cane and bamboo sector implemented in the Northeast by the Office of the Development Commissioner (Handicrafts), rafts), under a UNDP-assisted programme, had tremendous impact and opened up immense export opportunities in the Northeast. EPCH has taken this mission forward with the support of the Ministry of Commerce for promoting exports from the Northeast.

An analysis of the export trend of handicrafts shows 48 per cent of the total exports of the country emanating from four centres of production, Moradabad, Saharanpur, Jodhpur and Narsapur, Moradabad is the centre for art metalware production, which accounted for exports worth Rs. 2,165,21 crore (23.12 per cent of total handicraft exports) in 2002. Saharanpur is K, known for its wooden wares,, The export *of* woodware in 2002 was Rs. 5 1135 crore, or 18.47 per cent of exports. Jodhpur is famous for textiles, embroidered goods, art metalware and woodware while Narsapur is known for lace and crochet. This category la st year accounted for 20 per cent of total exports, amounting to Rs. 2,477.75 crore.

The handicrafts sector will receive a major boost with the opening in 2605 of the India Exposition Mart 1, in Greater Noida, on Delhi's outskirts. The mart will provide marketing support to cottage and small-scale handicrafts exporters and serve as a centralised facility and a permanent contact point (open throughout the. year) for foreign buyers.

To boost India's handicraft industry, EPCH has also finalised plans for the opening of permanent showrooms and warehouses in the US and the Netherlands. It intends to double the export of handicrafts from India in the next five years with integrated tie-ups with international Marketers. The proactive approach of EPCH, strongly supported by the Development Commissioner (Handicrafts), Ministry of Textiles, in association with industry, the Government and overseas buyers, will project India as the preferred handicrafts destination, It will also increase employment generation, earning of foreign exchange and safeguard India's cultural heritage.

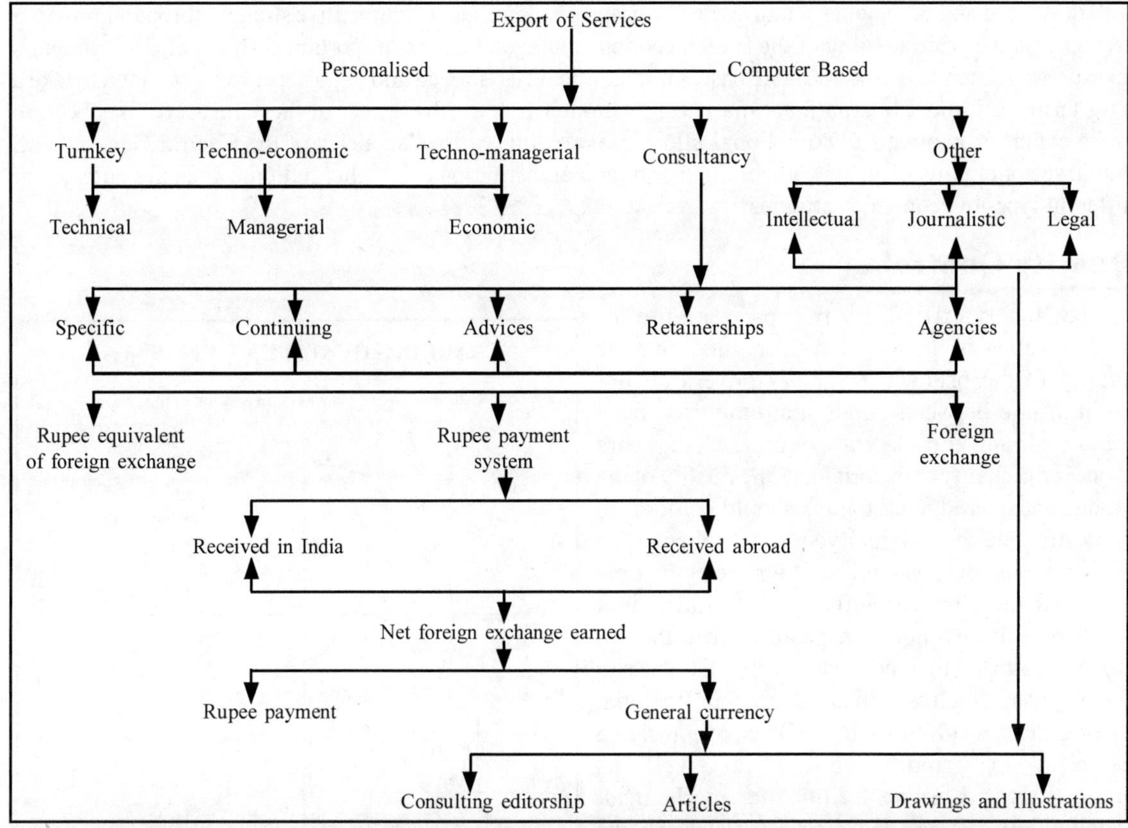

Box 20.2: Planning to Export?

With renewed emphasis on the country export efforts, a number of policies concerning special economic zones (SEZs) are being fine-tuned. It was the 2000-1 Exim Policy which for the first time talked about setting up of SEZs; with a view to provide an internationally competitive and hassle-free environment for exports. This and other extensive information is now available on www, sezindia.nic.in, a website set up and managed by the department of commerce, under the Ministry of' Commerce and Industry. The website has separate sections on setting up of SEZs, criteria for approval, application criteria, facility for developers, policy related to an SEZ developer, and a list of operational and approved SEZs. The Website informs visitors that all the import/export operation, of SEZ units would be on a self-certification basis, and though these have to be a net foreign exchange carrier, they shall not be subject to any pre-determined value addition or minimum export performance requirements. The high-point of the website is the FAQs section, which lists almost every bit of information a visitor needs to know about SEZs, and the low-point is the section on 'Articles', which lists just three clippings from newspapers and that too, of 2001 vintage! But this in no way undermines the basic information dissemination objective of the website.

Export Promotion Measures

To ensure a secure base for India's export, the Government initiated various measures that would *(i)* strengthen export production, *(ii)* encourage capacity expansion in export-oriented industries, *(iii)* augment bargaining power of our exporting community, *(iv)* encourage entry of our products in the new markets of both developed and developing countries and *(v)* improve our inherent competitive strength through imparting greater relative price stability of the Indian economy. One of the most important features of Government's measures has been to provide a stable base, uncertainties are removed and exporters are encouraged to take a long-term view about international marketing. Another noteworthy aspect of these measures has been to make export promotion truly a national effort by involving various agencies of the Central Government, public sector organisation, state governments, financial institutions and other national agencies engaged in different types of economic activities.

Quality Control

Closely allied to the programme of modernisation is the question of maintaining the quality of the product. Overseas buyers do not differentiate between goods manufactured by a small-scale unit and a large-scale unit. All they care about is the quality of the product. The quality of the products delivered to customers should conform to the sample design originally shown to them. The products, moreover, should be fit for use at the time specified therein. Recognising that, individual entrepreneurs are not in a position to establish laboratories to test their products, the Small Industries Development Organisation has set up four Regional Testing Centres at New Delhi, Kolkata, Mumbai and Chennai to provide general as well as product-oriented testing facilities for mechanical, metallurgical, chemical and electrical products. In the course of time these Regional Testing Centres plan to open sub-centres in other parts of the country to cover small units in the remotest parts.

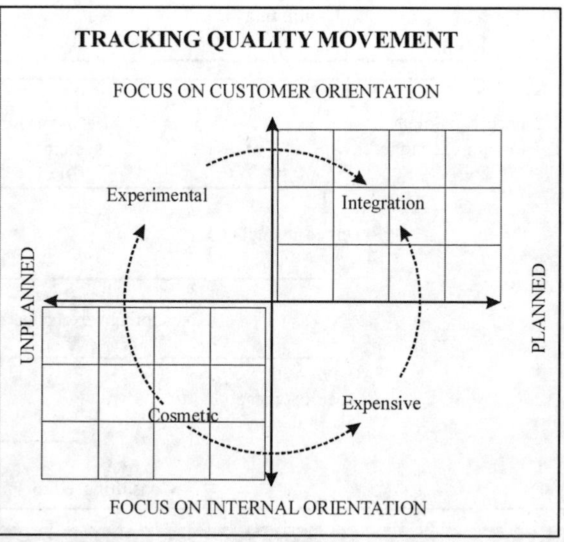

Marketing

Attempts have been made to obtain raw materials for small entrepreneurs, help them to update their products and ensure their quality. But not enough has been done to provide marketing facilities for them, particularly for the export of their products. The problems which small entrepreneurs face when they market their products within the country become acute, varied and complex when they enter international markets. These problems range from lack of export consciousness to the absence of infrastructural facilities in marketing abroad. Here, steps have to be taken, on an urgent basis, to assist the small entrepreneurs.

Export Consortia

One way of overcoming the problems of marketing is through the increasing participation of small entrepreneurs. They can adopt a group approach by forming themselves into export houses or export groups to maximise the opportunities available in the marketing of their products. Their combined efforts may lead to, among other things, better packaging methods and overseas publicity campaigns. It is essentially with a view to encouraging small-scale industrialists to join together for this purpose that the Union Government has announced liberal concession for small-scale export consortia.

Chart 2

Export Promotion — Export or Perish

I. Institutional Organisations	*II. Export Policy*	*III. Facilities for Exports*	*IV. Quality Control and Pre-shiptnent Inspection*	*V. Reorganisation & Reorientation of Trading Practices*
1. Export Promotion Councils 2. C;ommodity Boards 3. Board of Trade 4. Advisory Councils of Trade 5. Trade Development Authority 6. Zonal Export Advisory Committee 7. Chambers of Commerce 8. Associations of Trade and Industry 9. Federation of Indian Export Organisations 10. Export Processing Zone 11. Indian Institute of Foreign Trade 12. Export Inspection Council 13. S.T.C. 14. Indian Council of Arbitration 15. Trade Representatives and Commissioners 16. Commercial Intelligence Services 17. Indian Standards Institution	1. Export Control Relaxation 2. Export Duty Reduction 3. Excise Duty Reduction 4. Import Duty Reduction 5. Tax Relief to Exporters 6. Cash Compensatory Allowance 7. Import Licence for Raw Materials and Equipment Import 8. Devaluation	1. Bilateral Trade Agreements 2. General Agreement of Tariffs and Trade 3. Trade Delegations 4. Trade Fairs and Ex-hibitions 5. Transport Concession 6. Liberal Export Credit 7. Export Credit Insurance 8. Show Rooms Abroad	We must have compulsory Quality Control Marketing and Quality Control and Issue of Certificate of Quality after Pre-shipment Inspection	1. Standardisation 2. Simplification of Procedure 3. Mediation and Settlement of Disputes

INFRASTRUCTURAL SET-UP

The Government has established adequate and appropriate institutions, mainly to assist export promotion in particular. They are:

(1) 18 Export Promotion Councils, for the promotion of specific commodities of groups;
(2) Commodity Boards for coffee, tea, cardamom, rubber, coir, silk, handicrafts and handloom;
(3) The Board of Trade; Advisory Council of Trade; Zonal Committees;
(4) Chamber of Commerce and Industry and Associations of Trade and industry;
(5) The Trade Development Authority (TDA);
(6) The Federation of Indian Export Organisations (FIEO);
(7) Export Processing Zone;
(8) Indian Institute of Trade;
(9) Export Inspection Council;
(10) Indian Council of Arbitration;
(11) State Trading Corporation of India;
(12) The Minerals and Metals Trading Corporation;
(13) Export Houses and Trading Houses;
(14) Free Trade Zones;
(15) 100% Export-oriented Units and
(16) Trade Fair Authority of India (TFAI), to concentrate exclusively on fairs and exhibitions in furtherance of exports directly and derive immense benefits to the sector.
(17) Marine Products Export Development Authority, Cochin;
(18) Agricultural and Processed Food Products Export Development Authority, New Delhi;
(19) Export Credit Guarantee Corporation of India Limited;
(20) Projects and Equipment Corporation of India Ltd.;
(21) Spices Trading Corporation of India Ltd.;
(22) Tea Trading Corporation of India Ltd.;
(23) Export-Import Bank of India.

Export Promotion and Marketing

Small Industries Development Organisation (SIDO) is functioning as a Nodal Agency for promotion of exports of the SSI Sector. Besides providing export consultancy and export market intelligence, SIDO is also organising specialised training programmes for promoting exports in various parts of the country. With a view to augmenting the exports from the small-scale sector and to assist them in internal marketing, SIDO has been implementing the following schemes:

Export Oriented Units

The scheme of 100 per cent Export Oriented Units (EOUs) was introduced in 1980 with the objective of generating additional production capacity for exports by providing appropriate policy framework and incentives. The predominance of small-scale enterprises in EOUs and their key role in generating additional production capacity, producing quality goods and enlarging. The scope for export is well recognised. The scheme needs to be reviewed and streamlined, so that it plays a pivotal role in enhancing exports.

The growth of EOUs is imbalanced.

Five states Andhra Pradesh, Tamil Nadu, Maharashtra, Gujarat and Karnataka account for more than half the number of EOUs in the country. Between August 1991 to April 1997, these five states received investment of Rs. 28,177 crores spread over 18,91,000 units. The level of export performance for the purpose of export house recognition shall be as per the following table:

Table 20.2
Level of Export Performance

Category	*FOB Criterion*		*NFE Criterion*	
	Average FOB value of exports made during the preceding three licensing years	*FOB value of exports made during the preceding licensing year*	*Average net foreign exchange value of exports made during the preceding three licensing years*	*Net foreign exchange value of export made during the preceding licensing year*
Export Houses	20 crores	30 crores	16 crores	24 crores
Trading Houses	100 crores	150 crores	80 crores	120 crores
Star Trading Houses	500 crores	750 crores	400 crores	600 crores
Super Star Trading Houses	1500 crores	2250 crores	1200 crores	1800 crores

Problems

The small-scale sector is beset with a number of problems. Basically, the three aspects that affect the SSI exports relate to:

(a) Availability of raw materials;
(b) Quality control; and
(c) Marketing facilities.

A major difficulty facing the small-scale industry is the procurement of raw materials, both imported and indigenous. Big industries have resources to maintain special staff for liaison with the various government agencies and are able to use their influence to expedite their applications and obtain raw materials on a priority basis. In this respect, though small-scale industries get some government help, the small-medium scale industries with no special staff to liaise with the government agencies are left with inadequate supplies and often they have to resort to open market purchases at very high prices.

Another major problem facing the small-scale sector is that at least 40 per cent of them are connected with the company organisation. Only few companies have detailed sales plans, and only 50 per cent of the units allocate and control department costs. Application of modern methods of management would enable small-scale industries to lower production costs, standardise and improve the quality of their products and achieve sustained growth, thus consequently making the products more competitive overseas.

The procedures for claiming export assistance have been considerably streamlined. However, the dynamism and sense of dedication should percolate to the working levels of the ITC office and sustained dialogue maintained with the industry not excluding the smaller units to evaluate and assess what has been done and what remains to be done.

Export Processing Zones

Special incentives for companies to undertake manufacturing of export items have been provided by the Government of India through the establishment of Export Processing Zones or through 100 percent Exportoriented Units set up outside the EPZs, EPZs and EOUs fall under the purview of the Ministry of Commerce, Government of India.

EPZs are special areas designated for providing export production or the processing of manufactured products at a low cost. Each EPZ provided basic infrastructural facilities at reduced rates and included other incentives like developed land sites, standard designed factory buildings, roads, power, water and drainage. Other provisions included banking, post offices and custom clearing agents. Units located in EPZs/EOUs are permitted to sell upto 25 per cent of the value of production in the Domestic Tariff Area.

The Government of India has established 7 EPZs across the country. The Kandla Free Trade Zone, the Santacruz Electronics Export Porcessing Zone and the Falta EPZ were set up in 1965, 1974 and 1984 respectively. The EPZs set up at Chennai, Cochin, Vishakapatnam and NOIDA are of more recent origin.

Special Economic Zones

The Government of India declared a new liberalised customs framework for the Special Economic Zones (SEZs) with a view to boosting exports by making necessary changes in the EXIM policy with effect from November 1, 2000. The SEZ scheme envisaged a simple and transparent policy and procedures for the promotion of exports with minimum paper work. This will make the customs process in the SEZs free of controls to a great extent and will provide for green channel clearances. The important features of the scheme are as follows:

- The SEZ area shall be deemed to be a foreign territory for the purpose of duties and taxes.
- Goods supplied to SEZ from Domestic Tariff Area (DTA) will be treated as deemed export and goods brought from SEZ will be treated as deemed import.
- Goods may be imported procured from DTA duty free for the purpose of manufacture of goods and services, production, assembling, trading, repair, reconditioning, re-engineering, packaging or in connection therewith and export thereof.

Prospects

With the functioning of District Industries Centre and by reserving 827 items for production in the small-scale sector, there will be greater industrial production in the small-scale sector as a result of which there will be more avenues of employment. It is further necessary to find more outlets for this increased production as there are limitations to absorb all the production in India.

In harnessing the growing international market, the small-scale units should maintain high quality of the goods and channelise their products through the Export Promotional Agencies. Exports of Small-Scale Industries are going to play a crucial role in the export performance during the Sixth Five Year Plan.

Export Management: In the seventies, the small-scale sector emerged as a principal contributor to the country's exports. The pattern and direction of trade have been diversified, and an increasing number o small-scale units have switched over to non-traditional exports and export-oriented industries to cater to the specific needs of the export market. These industries have played a very significant role in pushing up exports through large-scale undertakings. These developments have called for the organisation of exports on sound lines. Export management in the small sector calls for professionalisation and sound organisation. The basic principles of export management are:

(i) Planning;
(ii) Organisation;
(iii) Building a team;
(iv) Executive action; and
(v) Management control.

Planning

Planning for export, even though extremely difficult, is the most important function. It involves forecasting, programming, procedures and budgeting. While forecasting leads to objectives and potential, programming spells out the ways of accomplishing them. A properly prepared programme spells out the ways of accomplishing them. A properly prepared programme becomes an administrative tool of much significance. Procedures help in the performance of work in a uniform manner. Budgeting in export marketing is a vital element in planning.

Organisation

A sound export organisation determines the economy and effectiveness with which the export business is managed and operated. The three basic activities of an export organisation are:

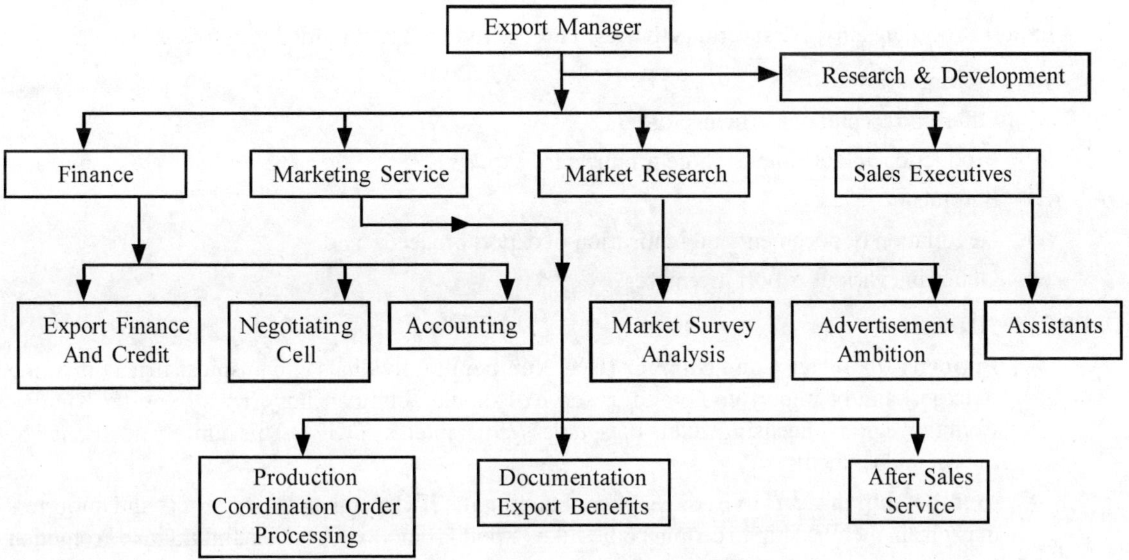

Fig. 20.3 Organisation Chart for a Small-scale Unit

(a) Designing organisation components, that is, identifying the work that has to be performed to reach the objective and grouping this work in well-balanced jobs, territories, divisions and other operational segments.

(b) Defining and delegating responsibility and authority and

(c) Establishing relationships.

The organisation chart indicates all the important functions of an export activity. Since many a small unit may not be in a position to have a specialised organisation of this type, efforts should be made by a group of small-scale industries to form a consortium to promote their exports on a larger scale.

The future of exports of the small-scale sector hinges on their concentrating as sub-contractors and vendors. For growth of exports during the Tenth Plan, the Study Group has made the following recommendations:

- Strengthening the international linkages;
- Encouraging brand building to create a distinct identity;
- Buyer-seller meets to be organised in target markets;
- Upgrading technology with the help of international experts wherever it is needed;
- Encouraging consortia approach in selected clusters to meet bulk orders;
- Focus on product design. Avail of updated market information;
- Indian Trade Missions abroad to play an active role in popularising Indian products;
- Timely availability of finance; and
- Laws and rules to be simplified.

EXPORT PROCEDURES

Export Procedures involve several activities. These activities are classified into five-stages, *viz.*,

(i) Preliminaries

(ii) Offer and receipt of confirmed orders

(iii) Production and clearance of the products for exports

(iv) Shipment

(v) Negotiation of document and realisation of export proceeds and

(vi) Obtaining various export incentives.

(i) PRELIMINARIES

- **Importer-Exporter Code Number (IEC Number):** Individuals and business firms intending to export and/or import goods and/or services should obtain an importer's Exporter Number from the regional licensing authorities, unless expempted by DGFT- This number mentioned be shown in documents.

- **Membership in Certain Bodies:** After obtaining the JEC member, the exporters and importers may obtain membership in certain bodies like Export Promotion Councils, India Trade Promotion Organisation etc. Membership in these organisations, help the exporter and importer regarding information and documentation.

- **Registration:** The exporter/importer have to register themselves with the Export Promotion Councils (EPC), Sales tax authorities etc.

(ii) INQUIRY, OFFER AND RECEIPT OF CONFIRMED ORDER

Inquiry is the request made by a prospective importer regarding his wish to import certain goods. *Offer* is a proposal submitted by an exporter expressing his intention to export specific goods at specific price with specific terms and conditions. Exporters usually makes an offer in the form of a *'Proforma Invoice.' (See Annexure 15.4 for format of proforma invoice).*

The proforma invoice includes the following items:

- **Name of the Buyer:** The complete name and address of the buyer/importer.
- **Description of Goods:** A brief description of goods indicating technical, physical and chemical features. If necessary, a detailed description is provided.
- **Price:** Unit wise and total price of the goods in internationally accepted currencies or mutually agreed currencies. It should also cover the quantity discounts and cash discounts both in unit wise and total. The price indicated in the invoice should be f.o.b., c and f, c.i.f. or in other internationally accepted form.
- **Conditions of Sale:** Conditions of sale should be incorporated in detail. Important among them are:
  - *(i)* *Validity : The* period for which the invoice is valid. The importer can accept the invoice any time before the validity period. Buyer can stipulate the validity period in case of tenders.
  - *(ii)* *Escalation Clause:* The prices of the products may increase before the delivery-period due to increase in the cost of inputs and thus, cost of production. Therefore, the exporter may include an escalation clause for escalation of price.
  - *(iii)* *Delivery Schedule:* A realistic delivery schedule should be indicated. Based on the pricing mode, the exporter has to indicate the delivery schedule. In case of c.i.f. quotations, the goods have to be delivered to the port of destination.
  - *(iv)* *Inspection:* The authority who will conduct inspection of goods, (if necessary) should also be indicated.
  - *(v)* *Force Majeure Clause:* The exporter may sometimes fail to deliver the goods in case of uncontrollable situations like war, riots, natural calamities etc. Therefore, the exporter indicates the force majeure clause in order to get rescue in such conditions.
- **Payment Terms:** Payment terms like letter of credit, bill of exchange etc. should be included.
- **Other Obligations:** Other obligations of the following nature should also be included: Post sales service to be provided by the exporter; Providing spare parts; Warranty/guarantee for the equipment/technology.
- **Confirmed Order:** The buyer sends the confirmed order to the exporter by signing the duplicate copy of the invoice. The signed invoice by the importer becomes the *confirmed order.*
- **Export License:** The exporter has to obtain the export licence from the authorities concerned, if the items to be exported require licence.
- **Procuring Finance:** If the exporter does not have required finance to undertake the exports, he/she should obtain finance from different sources.

(iii) PRODUCTION/PROCUREMENT OF GOODS

The exporting house after obtaining confirmed order should produce the goods exactly as specified in the invoice. If the exporting house does not have production facilities, it has to procure the products from others.

- **Packing and Marking:** After the goods are procured, the exporter should arrange for packing and Standards has prescribed packing standards for certain items. Similarly, the British Standard Packing Code and the Exporters' Encyclopedia published in the USA provides detailed packing instructions. Shipping companies also provide packing instructions. The International Carao-Handlina Coordination Association has also prescribed packing instructions.

  The exporter has to follow these instructions while packing the goods.
- **Quality Control and Preshipment Inspection:** The exporter has to arrange for quality control and preshipment inspection in order to ensure the quality of products as indicated in the invoice. Export Inspection Council or other appropriate body conducts the quality control inspection, if the goods to be exported are included under the Compulsory Quality Control and Preshipment Inspection Scheme in accordance with the provisions of the Export (Quality Control and Inspection) Act, 1963.
- **Excise Duty Rebates:** Government has exempted the goods meant for exports from the imposition of excise duty. Exporters can export the excisable goods either under claim for rebate of excise duty or in bond without payment of duty. The rebate is provided under Rule 12 of the Central Excise Rules of 1944. Exporter has to submit the following forms for rebate after the excise duty is paid.
  - Gate Pass,
  - GP-1, AR-4 form

  The next stage is the shipment stage. Now, we shall discuss the shipment stage.

(iv) SHIPMENT

Transporting the goods by ship is cheaper compared to that by air. In addition, physical size of the products create hurdles for transporting by air.

Regarding shipment, the exporter has to contact shipping companies for space, after getting the confirmed order. Sometimes getting the space in ships is easy through agents as they have information of all shipping companies throughout the world.

The shipping company may issue shipping advice or shipping order, depending upon the requirement of the exporter. In case of shipping advice, the shipping company has no obligation to accept the cargo as the shipping advice is only providing information of availability of space at the time of issue of the acceptance. But in case of shipping order, the shipping company has the obligation to accept the cargo.

- **Customer Clearance:** The exporter has to get custom clearance of the goods before, they are loaded in the ship. Custom authorities accord their formal approval after scrutinizing, complete set of shipping documents, copies of shipping bill etc. These documents include:
  - Proforma Invoice in original and duplicate
  - GR-I Form (in duplicate)
  - AR-A Form (in original and duplicate)
  - Export Licence (if required)

- Letter of credit covering the export order, export contract or order in original
- Certificate of inspection (where necessary)
- Form of declaration (in duplicate)
- Shipping bill (five copies)
- Quality Control Inspection Certificate (if required)
- Original contract wherever available
- Packing list
- Letter of Registration Certificate (if applicable).

- **GR-I Form:** This form is an exchange control document required by the Reserve Bank of India. The exporter has to realise the proceeds of the goods exported within 180 days from the date of the shipment from India. This form is not necessary in case of export to Nepal and Bhutan. *(See* Annexure 15.5 *for format of GR form).*
- **Shipping Bill:** This is an exchange document needed by the customs officials for granting permission for shipment. This bill contains the following information:
  - Name of the Exporter/shipper including his address and IEC number
  - Description and quantity of goods to be shipped
  - Value of goods
  - Number of packages and marking on them
  - Amount of drawback claimed (drawback duty is allowed when the goods are produced in India)
  - Port of destination
  - Names of the ship and agent.

  Five copies of the shipping bill are to be provided to the custom officials.
- **Export Licence:** Export licence is necessary for certain categories of goods. Export licence can be obtained from the Joint Director General of Foreign Trade (JDGFT).
- **Carting Order:** Once the goods are ready for export and the shipping order is available, the exporter has to approach the Superintendent of the concerned Port Trust for the latter's permission to move the goods physically inside the port area. The Superintendent of the Port Trust issues the order for moving the goods in to the port area after verifying the shipping bill and shipping order. This order given by the superintendent is called the *Carting Order.* After getting the carting order, the exporter physically moves the goods into the port area.
- **Customs Examination of Cargo at Docks:** The custom authorities after checking the documents, check the products to be exported at the docks. The exporter can arrange for the physical check of the products in his factory or warehouse. Applications for this facility can be made to the Assistance Collector of Customs. The Customs Appraiser after checking the consignment, will seal the packages, after his satisfaction. Such packages are normally not checked when at the port, unless otherwise bonafides of the exporter is doubtful.

The custom authorities accord form, approval for export, once they are satisfied with the products and documents. After obtaining the approval from the customs authorities, the exporter can make the arrangements for loading the cargo on a ship.

- **Let Ship Order:** After getting the approval from the custom officials, the exporter arranges for loading the products in the ship. Before loading takes place, the exporter's forwarding agent has to get the permission from the Preventive Officer of the customs department. This permission is called the *Let Ship Order.* Let ship order authorises the shipping company to accept the cargo on board the vessel. The goods are to be loaded in the ship after obtaining let ship order in the presence of custom officials.
- **Mate Receipt:** After the goods are loaded in the ship, the captain of the ship furnishes a document to the Port Superintendent. This document is called *'Mate Receipt',* which certifies the loading of the cargo. This document provides the details of the products, condition of the products at the time of loading etc.
- **Port Trust Dues:** The Port Trust Authorities after receiving the 'Mate Receipt', from the captain of the ship, issues the 'bill of lading' to the exporter.
- **Bill of Lading:** The Exporter's forwarding agent collects the 'Mate Receipt' and submits the same to the authorities and in turn collects the bill of lading from the port authorities.

The exporter's forwarding agent provides the following docurnents to the exporter at this final stage. They are:

- A copy of the invoice duly attested by the customs
- Drawback copy of the shipping bill
- Export promotion copy of the shipping bill
- Full set of 'clean on board' bill of lading together with the non-negotiable copies
- The original letter of the credit
- Customer's order or contract
- Duplicate copy of the AR-4 form.

- **Shipping by Other Modes of Transport**

All the goods are not transported through ship. Other modes of transport like air and land are also used for exporting the goods.

Shipping by Air: Mostly perishable goods, goods of less weight and goods those are needed by the importer urgently are transported by air.

Shipping by Post: Certain goods of less weight are exported by post. The emergence of *'e-comimerce'* increased the export trade by post. *Postal Notice No. 13 dated 3rd December 1973 regulates the export trade by post.*

Shipping by Land: Export of the excisable goods to the nearby countries is similar to the one laid down for export by sea. AR-4 form is different for export by land. The excisable goods are presented to the Frontier Customs Officer/Board Examiner along with form 4A.

After the Goods are exported, the exporter is interested in getting payment for the exports made. We shall discuss the payment procedure.

(v) NEGOTIATION OF DOCUMENT AND REALISATION OF EXPORT PROCEEDS

The exporter submits the relevant documents to his banker for getting the payment for the goods exported. Submission of relevant documents to the bank and the process of getting the payment from the bank is called *"Negotiating the Documents"*, through the bank. These documents are called *Negotiable Set of Documents.* This set normally includes:

- Bill of lading
- Commercial Invoice together with the packing slip and bill of exchange
- Certificate of origin
- GR-I form (in duplicate)
- Marine Insurance Policy (in duplicate)
- Letter of credit (in original). *(Annexure 15.2 provides model of confirmed and irrevocable letter of credit).*

The letter of credit is opened by the importer through his bank authorities drawing a bill of exchange. Payment will be made against this bill of exchange by the importer bank. The exporter's bank realises the export proceeds and pays to the exporter. *(See Annexure 15.3 for Bank Certificate of Export and Realisation)*

- **Aligned Documentation System:** Government of India appointed a committee to suggest on the documentation regarding export trade. Government of India accepted the recommendations of the committee and introduced standardised docurnents with effect from last October 1981, which is known as *'the Aligned Documentation System.'* This system is based on the UN layout key. Standardised documents for Indian exporters based on the Aligned Documentation System include :
  - Invoice
  - Exchange Control Declaration (GR) form
  - Shipping Bill (Dock Challan/Duty Draw back and Port Trust Copy)
  - Bill of Lading.

***(vi)* EXPORT INCENTIVES**

- Export incentives include
- Duty Drawback and Excise
- Duty Refund.

- **Duty Drawback:** Exporter is eligible to get back the excise duty and central excise paid on all raw materials, components and consumables used in the production of goods exported, under this scheme.
- **Excise Duty Refund:** Exporter is eligible for refund of the excise duty. He/she can recover if after export, if he paid at the beginning. He/she also can execute a bond with the Excise authorities without making the payment.

Having discussed the export procedure, we now discuss the import procedure.

IMPORT PROCEDURE

Importing refers to the purchase of foreign products for the consumption or sale in the home country. Import process consists of five stages, *viz.*,

- Determining the market demand and purchase motivation
- Locating and negotiating with sources of supply
- Securing physical distribution

- Preparing documentation and custom processing to facilitate movement among countries and organisations
- Developing a plan for resale or consumption.

Different kinds of institutions import goods and services from the foreign countries. Different kinds of importers include:

- Private industrialists
- Government agencies
- Facilitating Agencies and
- End users.

Stages in Import Procedures

Stages in import procedure include:

(i) Preliminaries
(ii) Enquiring and Placing the Indent
(iii) Obtaining the Foreign Exchange
(iv) Arranging for Payment
(v) Payment of Customs Duties and taking the Delivery of Goods.

Now, we discuss these stages of import procedure in detail.

***(i)* Preliminaries**

The importing firm or an individual has to obtain a licence and Importer-Exporter Code Number *(See Annexure 15.1)* from the Controller of Exports and Imports. The firm can become an established importer by importing the goods it intends to import during the prescribed period. The import licences are usually issued for a period of one year at a time.

***(ii)* Enquiring and Placing the Indent**

After obtaining the import licence, the importer has to enquire with various exporters of exporting countries regarding the goods, he would like to import. Importer at this stage asks the exporter to send the invoice. The importers may accept the invoice and send the indent directly to the exporter. Otherwise, they may send the indent through specialised intermediaries called *indent houses.*

Indent may be open or closed. Open indent does not specify the price and other details of the goods and leaves them to the discretion of the exporter. On the other hand, the closed indent specifies the brand, price, number, packing, shipping mode, insurance etc. The indents incorporation the exact price is called *'Confirmatory indent.'* Indent Houses help the Importers in negotiating for price, discounts etc. as they maintain close links with the foreign firms. As such, some importers use the services of indent houses. Thus, the importers order for the goods either directly or through indent houses.

***(iii)* Obtaining Foreign Exchange**

The importer, after sending the indent, has to procure the required foreign exchange from the Exchange Control Department of the Reserve Bank of India. He/she has to produce the import license and the prescribed forms for securing foreign exchange which is needed to pay for the import of goods.

Reserve Bank releases the foreign exchange based on the strength of the application, availability of foreign exchange and foreign exchange policy of the government.

(iv) Arrangement for Payment

The importer has to make arrangements for paying for imports after obtaining the foreign exchange. He may do it by obtaining letter of credit from his banker. Alternatively, he may request the exporter to forward the documentary bill through his banker which would be delivered to him either against acceptance of the bill of exchange or against its payment.

Thus, the documents may be received by the importer either through D/A (documents against acceptance of bill of exchange) or D/P (documents against payment). The importer's bank after receiving the documents from the exporter bank, hands over the documents to the importer if it is D/A bill. The banker delivers the documents to the importer only when the latter pays the amount of the bill on maturity. Normally, indent houses help the importer if he fails to pay the amount on maturity date of the bill.

After obtaining the documents the importer awaits the information of the ship carrying the goods. He gets the information from the newspapers and the custom authorities. The importer obtains the *'Endorsement for Delivery'* on the back of *'Bill of Lading'* from the shipping company by paying for the freight, if it is not paid by the exporter. Then the importer presents 'Port Trust Dues Receipts' (two copies) and Bill of Entry to the Port Trust Office to obtain clearance regarding dock dues.

Bill of entry certifies the fact that goods of specified quantity, value and description are entering the country.

(v) Payment of Custom Duties and Taking Delivery of Goods

The importer has to pay for the custom duties, if necessary. The custom duty may be based on the weight and size of the goods or based on the value of goods. The custom duty may also be paid under the *'Permanent Deposit System.'* Under this system, the importer maintains a running account with custom office and deposits money from time to time which is adjusted to the duty payable.

The importer then gets the delivery of goods.

Special Economic Zones (SEZs)

The Special Economic Zones Policy was announced in April 2000 with the objective of making the Special Economic Zones an engine for economic growth, supported by quality infrastructure and an attractive fiscal package both at the Central and State level with a single window clearance. The experience in last 55 years with the Industrial areas and Industrial clusters has been that large slums come up in the neighbourhood of these areas. Besides, the additional population creates pressure on the Municipal System. The SEZ concept recognizes the issues related to economic development and provides for developing selfsustaining Industrial Townships so that the increased economic activity does not create pressure on the existing infrastructure.

The main objectives of the SEZ Act are:

- generation of additional economic activity;
- promotion of exports of goods and services;
- promotion of investment from domestic and foreign sources;
- creation of employment opportunities; and
- development of infrastructure facilities.

Box 20.3: Smart Tips for doing Business Overseas

- A good website must be developed and maintained with detailed catalogues for product and service offerings.
- ISO or other certifications must be obtained. Govt offers subsidy to MSMEs seeking ISO certification.
- Business should be operated through secure credit-mechanisms.
- Ensure that product samples are clearly approved or service delivery SLAs are signed off.
- Strictly adhere to timelines for product/ service delivery.
- Have a portfolio of standardised or modular products and services, which establish confidence.
- To understand the complete procedures, be a member of your industry association or FIEO.
- Effectively utilise pre- or post-export incentives offered by the Government. Ministry of MSME offers incentives to participate in exhibitions and conferences abroad.
- Price your services properly and work back from the endprice at which a product will sell in the market.
- Identify and focus on limited markets and geographical locations for better results.

Rajeev Karwal, Founder, Milagrow

Need for Improvements

While the Govt Policies has resulted in the simplification of procedures and formalities for the exporters, there are still many areas which needs to be addressed. High transaction cost is a huge burden on our exporters which has been eroding their export competitiveness. The new scheme as proposed in the FTP should, therefore, be introduced as early as possible to neutralize the transaction costs. Other issues like the inadequate facilities at our ports which are not upto the desired level resulting in longer turnaround time for export and import goods needs immediate attention. Besides, port congestions takes place very frequently. The roads needs upgradation to reduce the transportation time from the place of production to the ports. Towards this end, the involvement of the State Govts in export facilitation also needs to be increased with greater fund allocation under the ASIDE scheme in the The foreign (Trade policy) FTP. Another constraint is that Bank interest rates continues to be higher especially as compared to our neighbouring countries like Pakistan, Bangladesh etc.

New Initiatives

While it is necessary to comply with the World Trade Organisation Rules, it is to be noted that most of the countries in the world including the advanced countries extend various schemes to promote exports from their countries and we should not ignore this fact while deciding on the level and extent of export assistance measures. We should ideally continue with the existing schemes besides introducing new instruments for export promotion to enable Indian Synthetic Textile Industry to increase its share in World markets.

With the impact of globalization and technological advancements world wide, business development in the international markets has become more challenging. Nevertheless, there are opportunities as well with rise in consumer demand and purchasing power besides the opening up of the markets across the world. However, the rapidly changing scenario with competition intensifying steadily demands new approach, attitudes and strategies to sustain and succeed in the export markets.

Finance for Exports

Export marketing reguires the financial support at various stages of the process.

The key institutions catering to the export trade are:

(1) Export-Import Bank of India (EXIM BANK)

(2) Export Credit Guarantee Corporation of India

(3) Small Industries Development Bank of India (SIDBI)

(4) Reserve Bank of India (RBI)

(5) Commercial Banks

These financial institntions play a vital role in promoting exports.

Export-Import Bank of India (EXIM BANK)

The Exim Bank was established in 1982 with the main objective of providing long-term finance as well as medium-term finance to exporters.

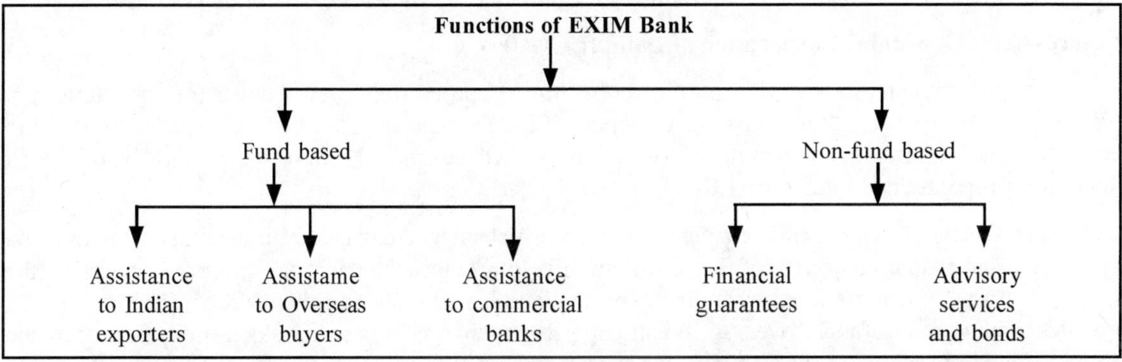

Fig. 20.4. Functions of EXIM Bank

Assistance is given to Indian exporters with respect to the following:

(1) Exports on deferred payment terms

(2) Export and import of machinery and equipment on lease basis

(3) 100 per cent financial assistance to EOUs and units set as in FTZs and EPZs

(4) Preshipment finance to eligible exporters for procuring raw materials and other inputs required to produce machinery and equipments for purposes of exports

(5) Credit facilities to deemed exports

(6. Foreign exchange loan to computer software exporters (subject to RBI clearance)

(7) Finance facility against deferred credit to exporters of consultancy, services and technology

(8) Export marketing activities in India and in foreign countries through Export Marketing Fund

(9) Export development fund to finance techno-economic survey, research or any other study for the development of exports

(10) Indian joint ventures in foreign countries

Assistance to Overseas parties is given with respect to the following:

(1) Overseas buyer's credit facility to foreign importers for imports of Indian capital goods and related services with repayment spread over a period of years

(2) Long-term finance underlines of Credit to finance government and financial institutions abroad which extend finance to importers of their respective countrics to buy Indian capital goods

(3) Relending facility to overseas banks

Assistance to Indian commercial banks with respect to the following:

(1) Refinance facility to commercial banks to enable them to provide credit to Indian exporters who extend term credit to importers

(2) Export bills rediscounting facility to commercial banks in India to enable them to provide financial assistance for post-shipment credit extended to Indian exporters

Non-fund based activities of the EXIM Bank cover the guarantees and bonds, executing contracts abroad, global exchange control practices, advisory services to Indian construction projects abroad, access to Euro financing sources and global credit sources and guidance to small-scale entrepreneurs.

Export Credit Guarantee Corporation of India (ECGC)

The government established Export Risks Insurance Corporation in 1957 under the companies Act, 1956 to provide export credit and insurance support of Indian exporters. In 1964, it was transformed and restructured as Export Credit Guarantee Corporation Limited and since 1983, it is known as Export Credit Guarantee Corporation of India Ltd. (ECGC)

ECGC is the premier organization in the country, which offers credit risk insurance covers to exporters, banks, etc. The primary objective of the Corporation is to promote the country's exports by covering the nonpayment risk of exports faced by Indian exporters and banks financing the exports. The Corporation provides a range of insurance covers to Indian exporters against commercial risks of nonpayment by the overseas importers as well as the country risks caused due to political developments. It also provides credit insurance covers to banks against the nonpayment risks of exporters availing preshipment, post-shipment as well as other non funded export credit facilities. These covers to banks enable the latter to extend the credit facilities on a more liberal basis The paid up capital at the end of 2008-09 is Rs. 900.00 crore. ECGC has registered itself with the IRDA on 27th September, 2002.

ECGC also provides guarantees to banks to protect them from the risk of loss inherent in granting various types of finance facilities to exporters. The covers issued by ECGC are:

- Standard policies
- Specific policies: export on deferred terms of payments, services rendered to foreign parties, construction work and turnkey projects undertaken abroad
- Financial guarantees: Packing Credit guarantee, Export Production Finance Guarantee, Export Finance Guarantee, Post-shipment Export Credit Guarantee, Export Performance Guarantee, Export Finance (Overseas Lending) Guarantee
- Special schemes: Transfer guarantee, Insurance cover for Buyer's credit and Lines of Credit, Overseas Investment Insurance

Small Industries Development Bank of India (SIDBI)

SIDBI is a wholly owned subsidiary of IDBI. It was set up in 1990 as an apex institution for the promotion, development and finance for the small-scale industries. It also coordinates the activities of the other institutions set for this purpose.

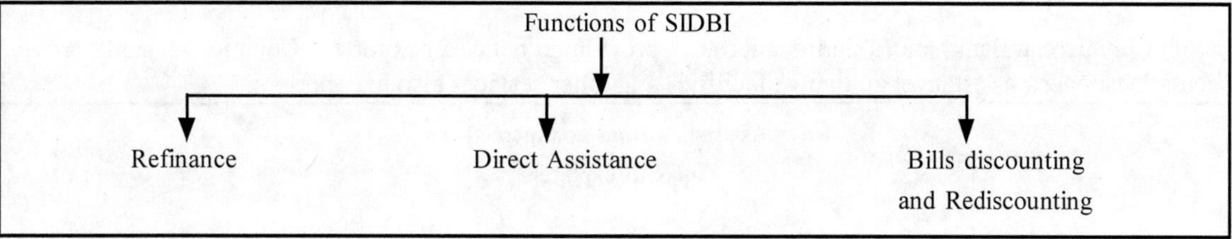

Fig. 20.5: Functions of SIDBI

The details of these functions are as follows:

Refinance

- Provision of term finance
- Schemes for tourism related activities
- Seed capital scheme
- Single window scheme
- Equipment refinance scheme
- Line of credit against PCFC of commercial banks
- Other refinance schemes for hospitals, hotels, small road transport operators, women entrepreneurs, ex-servicemen, etc.

Direct Assistance

- Special markeling agencies
- Equipment finance
- Project finance
- ISO 9000 Scheme
- Foreign currency loans for SSI Units
- Preshipment credit foreign currency loans

Bills discounting and Rediscounting

- Direct Discounting Schemes (DDS)
- Bills Rediscounting Schemes (BRS)

Reserve Bank of India (RBI)

RBI plays a pivotal role in providing finance to the exporters. Even though RBI does not finance the exporters directly, it guides, initiates and frames the measures to be taken by the other specialised financial institutions and the commercial banks. To enable the commercial banks to provide finance to the exporters liberally, the following schemes are implemented by RBI:

- Preshipment Credit Scheme
- Export Credit Interest Subsidy Scheme
- Duty Drawback Credit Scheme

Commercial Banks

Commercial Banks play a significant role in providing finance for exporters. Commercial banks provide necessary support, assistance, guidance, facilities and other services also to exporters.

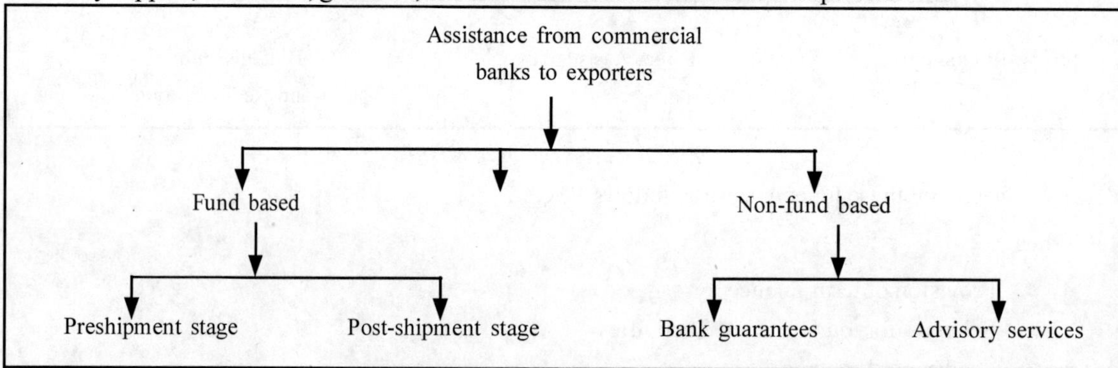

Fig. 20.6: Assistance from Commercial Banks

Fund based assistance are as follows:

Pre-shipment stage

- Cash packing credit loan
- Advance against hypothecation
- Advance against pledge
- Other services

Post-shipment stage

- Negotiations of bills drawn
- Purchase/discounting of bills
- Overdraft against bills under collection
- Other services

Non-fund based assistance are as follows:

Bank guarantees

- Performance guarantee
- Guarantee for foreign currency loans
- Guarantee for payment of retention money
- Advance payment guarantee
- Bid bonds

Other services

- Collection of export proceeds
- Information about foreign buyers particularly their creditworthiness

- Issue of certificate in form XC and CBX in case of blanket permits
- Issue of bank drafts in case of payment of freight charges
- Information about exchange rates
- Issue of certificate in respect of export sales value which is required for claiming the incentives

EXPORT PROMOTION ORGANISATIONS

State Trading Corporation of India (STC)

STC was set up on 18th May 1956 primarily with a view to undertake trade with East European countries and to supplement the efforts of private trade and industry in developing exports from the country. STC has played an important role in the country's economy by arranging imports of essential items of mass consumption (such as wheat, pulses, sugar, edible oils, etc.) into India and developing exports of a large number of items from India. The core strength of STC lies in handling exports/imports of bulk agro commodities. However, during the past few years, STC has diversified into exports of steel raw materials, gold jewellery, iron ore, chemicals & pharmaceutical items and imports of bullion, hydrocarbons, minerals, metals, fertilizers, petrochemicals, etc. This has helped STC achieve record breaking performances in the recent years. STC is today able to structure and execute trade deals of any magnitude, as per the specific requirement of its customers.

The main functions of the STC are:

(1) To implement the government policies regarding foreign trade

(2) To explore potential markets for Indian products

(3) To strengthen the structure of India's foreign trade and increase the share in the international market

(4) To provide complete package service of raw materials supply, warehousing facility, exports market development, shipping, etc.

(5) To provide off-the-shelf deliveries of imported raw material with the help of its Industrial Raw Materials Assistance Division

To strengthen its operations, STC has set up subsidiaries:

(i) Handicrafts and Handloom Experts Corporation of India (HHEC)

(ii) Cashew Corporation of India (CCI)

(iii) Projects and Equipment Corporation of India (PEC)

(iv) State Chemicals and Pharmaceuticals Corporation Ltd. (SCPCL)

(v) The Tea Trading Corporation of India (TTCI)

(vi) Central Cottage Industries Corporation (CCIC), a subsidiary of HHEC

(vii) Minerals and Metals Trading Corporation of India (MMTC)

(viii) Mica Trading Corporation (MITCO), a wholly owned subsidiary of MMTC

(ix) Spices Trading Corporation

MMTC Limited

MMTC is widely recognized as India's largest international trading company and the first Public Sector Undertaking to be awarded Premier Trading House status in the country. It is actively involved in exploring overseas markets for exports and sourcing material for domestic needs. With focus on 'bulk' operations, MMTC primarily has seven core commodity groups viz. Minerals, Precious Metals, Coal & Hydrocarbons, Fertilizers & Chemicals, Agro, Metals and General Trading.

The company achieved a milestone turnover of Rs. 36,905 crore during the year (Exports – Rs. 4,579.84 crore and Imports – Rs. 30,767.20 crore, Domestic – Rs. 1,557.58 crore) as against Rs. 26,423 crore in 2007-08.

Export Promotion Council (EPC)

Export Promotion Councils are non-profit organisations registered under the Companies Act or The Societies Registration Act. The EPCs are established to promote and develop the exports for the specific product for which the EPC is established. At present, there are 20 EPCs in India. They are as follows:

(1) Apparels
(2) Basic chemicals, pharmaceuticals and cosmetics
(3) Chemicals and allied Products
(4) Cotton textiles
(5) Carpets
(6) Cashew
(7) Engineering
(8) Gems and jewellery
(9) Handloom
(10) Indian silk
(11) Council for leather export

Conclusion

The exports of small-scale sector have been continuously expanding. As such, the share of the small-scale sector in the total exports showed a perceptible increase over the years. However, the increase was generally larger among the small-scale industries. The share of exports of the smaller sector among the small-scale industries — with less than Rs. 2 lakhs fixed capital — declined sharply. Those industries which showed improvement in exports had relatively lesser dependence on exports in their total output. Hence the export performance of these industries was only a subsidiary function, while catering to the domestic market constituted their major activity. At the same time, the smaller among the small-scale industries had a high degree of dependence on export.

Small-scale units are flexible in product adaptation because of their small size. That is why the items which are frequently modified according to the customer's demand can be produced by them and should be undertaken for export production.

The export market is a highly competitive market. It would, therefore, not be worthwhile to try to export the products of all the SSI units. It is desirable to identify some and to select a few export-worthy SSI units. This should be done on a continuing-basis. Once the products and units have been identified, every effort should be made to develop the exports of the products of these units.

The small-scale sector, which is rightly called the unorganised sector, require organisational assistance, particularly in the marketing of its products abroad. Some of the State Export Corporations have rendered useful services in an organised way to market the products of the SSI units situated in their respective states.

But most of the states either do not have any State Export Corporation or, when they have one, the desired services are not available. Merchant exporters and some of the export houses have no doubt played an important role in exporting the products of small-scale units; but this is insignificant in view of the large export potential of this sector. Small-scale units producing identical products should form a consortium of their own to market their products. But no satisfactory progress has so far been achieved in this system which is developed in marketing the exportable products of the SSI units abroad in a bigger way, the small-scale units should organise and mount their own export marketing effort. For this purposes, arrangements should be made by public institutions to render package assistance in respect of:

(i) Locating markets and buyers abroad;

(ii) Getting price indications and samples;

(iii) Arranging exhibitions of their products abroad; and

(iv) Advising identified export-worthy SSI units on the trade practices and formalities in the buying countries.

The study also brings into focus that export performance of industries with high capital intensity was remarkable during the period, while the share of labour-intensive industries in the total export showed a declining tendency throughout the period. The share of highly labour-intensive industries in the total export also showed a sharp fall. Though it may be admitted that the export performance of capital intensive industries has enlarged the scope for employment generation both directly and indirectly through employment linkages, additional employment creation would have been much higher had the labour-intensive industries showed better export performance.

The expansion of export of semi-processed and manufactured goods during the period under study had benefitted mostly the large-scale capital intensive industries and larger among the small-scale industries. It is true that small-scale and labour-intensive industries could expand their exports to an extent and thereby contribute towards the avowed objective of reduction in inequality of wealth and economic power, but the inequality would have been reduced by a large extent, had these industries strived to secure a larger share in the total exports of semi-processed and manufactured goods.

Small-scale industries are not in a position to achieve the necessary thrust in marketing their products in competitive international markets. Since the small units' resources are quite meagre, they cannot go in for an aggressive drive in marketing their products in competition with large-scale and/or multinational units. The small-scale units do not only require professional managerial supports, they also need the active support of financial institutions. In particular, the commercial banks and the newly constituted Export-Import Bank of India can play a very crucial role in promoting export of the small-scale units.

Small-scale industries are poised for a leap under the Eighth Five Year Plan, and the SSI sector offers immense scope. It is, therefore, necessary for the small-scale units to increasingly exploit export demand for their products as a supplementary demand outlet. Given the inherent potential of India, Government's new thrust of export promotion, stability of policies, simplified procedures and the national commitment to rapid economic growth, the Government is confident that it shall be possible for India to overcome the present situation and to attain a sustained growth in export to meet not only important requirements but also the needs for development. in harnessing the growing international market, the small-scale units should maintain the high quality of the goods and channelise their products through the Export Promotional Agencies. Exports of small-scale industries are going to play a crucial role in the export performance.

ANNEXURE – 1

Key Objectives of the Foreign Trade Policy -2009-14

- The short-term objective is to arrest and reverse the declining trend of exports and to provide additional support to sectors hit badly by recession in the developed world;
- The policy aims to achieve an annual export growth of 15% with an annual export target of US$ 200 billion (Rs. 9.8 trillion) by March 2011;
- In the remaining 3 years of the Policy, i.e. upto 2014, the country should be able to come back on the high export growth path of around 25% per annum. By 2014, India's exports of goods and services is expected to double;
- The long term policy objective for the government is to double India's share in global trade by 2020.

In order to meet these objectives, the Govt. would follow a mix of policy measures including fiscal incentives, institutional changes, procedural rationalization, enhanced market access across the world and diversification of export markets. Improvement in infrastructure related to exports; bringing down transaction costs and providing full refund of all indirect taxes and levies would be the three pillars, which will support to achieve this target.

Stability of the Foreign Trade Policy

- To impart stability to the policy regime, the Duty Entitlement Passbook (DEPB) Scheme is being extended by a year till December 31, 2010. The interest subvention of 2% for pre-shipment credit for 7 sectors was extended till March 31, 2010 in Budget 2009;
- Duty Entitlement Passbook (DEPB) rate shall also include factoring of custom duty component on fuel where fuel is allowed as a consumable in Standard Input-Output Norms. DEPB will continue upto December 2010;
- Income Tax exemption to 100% Exports Oriented Units and to Software Technology Park units under Section 10B and 10A of IT Act has been extended for the financial year 2010-11 in Budget 2009-10;
- The adjustment assistance scheme initiated in December, 2008 to provide enhanced ECGC cover at 95% to the adversely affected sectors is continued till March 2010.

A. Promotional Measures:

- **Assistance to States for Developing Export Infrastructure and Allied Activities (ASIDE):** The objective of the scheme is to establish a mechanism for involving the state Govts to participate in funding of infrastructure critical for growth of exports by providing export performance linked financial assistance to them.
- **Town of Export Excellence:** Selected towns producing goods of Rs. 750 crore or more will be notified as Town of Excellence based on potential for growth in exports. However, for Handloom, Handicraft, Agricultural and Fisheries sector, the limit would be Rs. 150 crore.
- **Brand Promotion and Quality:** IBEF (originally called India Brand Equity Fund and later renamed as India Brand Equity Foundation) aims to promote India as a business opportunity by creating positive economic perceptions of India globally as well as effectively present the India business perspective and leverage business partnerships in a globalised market place.
- **Test House:** Central Govt. will assist in modernization and upgradation of test houses and laboratories to bring them at par with international standards.
- **Focus Market Scheme ('FMS')**
  - The objective is to offset high freight cost and other externatilities to select international markets with a view to enhance India's export competitiveness in these countries.

- Percentage of credit entitlement increased from 2.5% to 3% and benefit of credit entitlement extended for exports made to 26 more countries (including 16 from Latin American Block and 10 from Asia-Oceania block).
- The following categories of exports products/sectors shall be ineligible for Duty Credit Scrip, under FMS scheme:
  - Supplies made to Special Economic Zone (SEZ)
  - Service Exports
  - Diamonds and other precious, semi precious stones
  - Gold, Silver, Platinum and other Precious metals in any form, including plain and stubbed jewellery
  - Ores and concentrates, of all types and in all forms
  - Cereals, of all types
  - Sugar, of all types and in all forms
  - Crude/Petroleum based products covered under ITC HS codes 2709 to 2715, of all types and in all forms
  - Exports of Milk and Milk Products covered under ITC HS codes 0401 to 0406, 19011001, 19011010, 2105 & 3501

Focus Product Scheme ('FPS'):

- The objective is to incentivize export of such products which have high export intensify/employment potential, so as to offset infrastructure inefficiencies and other associated costs involved in marketing of these products,
- Percentage of credit entitlement increased from 1.25 % to 2 % and scope expanded to specified products including engineering products, electronic products, plastic products, textile products, green technology products (like wind mill, wind powered generating sets, electrically operated vehicles etc), etc.

Market Linked Focus Product ('MLFP') Scheme:

- The Export of Product/Sectors of high export intensify/ employment potential (which are not covered under present Focus Product Scheme list) would be incentivized at 2% of Free On Board value of exports (in free foreign exchange) under Focus Product Scheme when exported to the Linked Markets (countries), which are not covered in the present Focus Market Scheme list as notified, for exports made from 27.08.2009 onwards.
- Percentage of credit entitlement increased from 1.25 percent to 2 percent and benefit of credit entitlement extended to products including pharmaceuticals, articles of iron and steel, articles of aluminium, dyes, paints, soaps etc exported to countries like Brazil, South Africa, Australia etc.

Directorate of Trade Remedy Measures:

- To enable support to Indian Industry and Exporters, especially the Micro, Small and Medium Enterprises (MSMEs), in availing their rights through trade remedy instruments under the WTO framework, a directorate of Trade Remedy Measures is proposed to be set up.

Advance Authorization Scheme (AAS):

- This policy is expected to encourage value addition in manufactured exports and towards this the Govt. has stipulated a minimum 15% value addition norm on imported.

* * *

21

E-Commerce

Introduction

Electronic commerce or e-commerce is not just a jargon, but a ground reality at the dawn of the third millennium in India. E-commerce has emerged as a search-engine for success in the territory of free enterprise. India's entrepreneurs are storming the digital frontier with new business ventures. They are trying to capture a piece of the action in cyberspace. Businesses are realising the importance of being a part of the wired world and its change or perish rule. The objective of this chapter is to give a synoptic view of the relevance of e-commerce to small-scale industries and the entrepreneurs including then entrepreneurs.

New Technology

Every new technology introduced in this world has transformed the way business is conducted and now, it is the turn of e-commerce. Alvin Toffler, the famous futurologist, predicted few decades ago that the new networked digital economy would drive and change the 21st century and today e-commerce is making it true. The proliferation of the new 'infonomics' is forcing the traditional assumptions of economic theory to be rewritten. The customer interaction with business is being transformed. The 'Amazon effect' is driving well-established 'skyscraper' corporations to build attractive online shopping malls.

The corporate world is feeling the pressure — from customers, partners and even the shareholders — to rapidly develop e-commerce capability. The strong positive factors such as growing web usage, well evolved standards, rapid application development tools, single market place, global reach and Euro make the organizations feel confident of e-commerce. The IT industry is responding favourably by throwing up effective application development tools every other day. The whole world is witnessing an e-commerce explosion, which is likely to intensify in the third millenium.

Businesses cannot succeed in their e-commerce venture unless careful steps are taken towards redefining the business flow, populating corporate data from legacy systems integrating with the existing ERP system, efficiently modifying the SCM and CRM and implementing stringent security measures. By introducing a wide range of WYSIWYG development tools, the IT industry makes e-commerce development look much simpler. But e-commerce is not just about creating attractive web stores.

E-Commerce

E-commerce is the use of computer applications communicating over networks to allow buyers and sellers to complete a transaction or part of a transaction. Due to differences in the markets involved, two categories of e-commerce have emerged — Business-to-Business (B2B) and Consumer-to-Business (C2B) — with different business models and different business drivers.

In simple words, E-commerce is an electronic business. It is the capability of exchanging value electronically. E-commerce relates to the electronic exchange of all trading relationships external to the enterprise. E-commerce involves exchange of money, goods, services as well as information. E-commerce, according to the World Trade Organisation (WTO)

".... production, distribution, marketing, sale or delivery of goods and services by electronic means. A commercial transaction can be divided into three main stages; advertising and searching stage; ordering and payment stage; and delivery stage. Any or all these may be carried out electronically and may, therefore, be covered, by the concept of electronic commerce."

The use of Net technologies for consumer sales has dominated the media and has led to the rise of high profile business. Not only retail business, but corporate attention is focussed on the use of net and web technologies to streamline the procurement process and raise the volume of automated B2B transactions. Advocates of e-commerce envision zero-latency enterprises, in which buyers and suppliers are integrated into an electronic supply-chain so tightly that the transaction buyers initiate results in immediate triggering of all the processes necessary to fulfil the order.

Historically, 13213 transactions occurred across value-added networks supporting Electronic Data Interchange (EDI), but the high cost and technical complexity of that process has limited its use to large enterprises and their trading partners. On the other hand, Net 13213 transactions are becoming more affordable. But key issues remain. Of primary importance is the need for companies to agree on standards for automated transactions. Some standards such as the Open Buying on the Net standard already have emerged. Standards for web-based e-commerce have been not available for their slow adoption by corporations.

In C2B e-commerce, security for consumers and fraud-detection for merchants have merged as key issues. The Secure-Electronic Transactions specification, championed by Master Card and Visa, appears to solve these issues simultaneously, with a complicated network of software for banks, merchants and consumer desktops. However, slow adoption on all three levels has led to the rise of service companies that provide the security for fraud detection.

The Net, as a medium for shopping and buying, opens new alternatives for consumers, offering them a different set of trade-offs between cost, selection, convenience and experience than any other channel. Retail merchants are rushing to exploit characteristics in their competition for getting more consumers.

The consumer has a much wider choice on the Net. They can compare product's features, prices and even look up reviews before they select what they want. They also have the convenience of having their orders delivered right at their doorstep. Consumers are driven to e-shopping in hordes as even branded goods cost lesser on the Net. E-commerce ventures need not maintain huge inventories or expensive retail showrooms. Their marketing and sales force is a fraction of that traditional mortar-based business. And as the volumes are large, the economies of scale come into play. Businesses are also realising the advantages of direct interaction with consumers in today's evolving economy.

Types of Application

The application spawning out of the e-commerce initiative can be broadly grouped into seven categories. While not being all inclusive, these seven categories cover most of the common business transactions:

- B-to-B procurement (e-procurement).
- B-to-B and B-to-C sales (e-sales).
- B-to-B virtual market places and enterprise portals (e-portals).
- One-to-one marketing and e-promotion (e-promotion).
- Customer service (e-CS).
- Electronic payments (e-pay), and
- Employee self-service (e-ESS).

In additional to these, e-commerce can be implemented between government organisations and between the government and the public. However, these applications can also be broadly classified B-to-B or B-to-C.

E-ventures: Portfolio

Company	*Domain*	*eVI's Role/State of Investments*
GLOBAL INTERNET SERVICES		
3Genesis	Wireless Internet application development services serving European wireless software and consulting companies.	Funded to the extent of $2 million by Connect Capital Holdings and e-Ventures in October 2000.
Customer Asset	Customer Asset is a global e-CRM company providing customer interaction and database management services to e-businesses in the US, UK and India.	Second round of $9 million funding in July 2001; e-Ventures, which had put in $3.3 million in the first round of funding in April 2000, also participated in the second round.
Intigua	e-Solutions provider, which helps companies digitise, conceptualise and build successful businesses.	In April 2001, e-Ventures had consolidated two companies in its portfolio-exchange, one of Singapore's largest e-Consulting firms and Net Across OLS, one of India's leading Web integration companies – to from Intigua.
Netpilgrim	e-recruiting portal, targeting the best technology professionals.	Sold its 96 per cent stake for Re. 1 to Ashok Advani of Business India.
Turbograd	Offers customissed, adaptable and highly scalable hosted solutions to e-learning companies, global corporations and educational institutions.	Aptech, e-Ventures India and a Silicon Valley company — Turbograd launch Mentorix Technologies. e-Ventures invested $5 million in January 2001.
Vergil Technologies	Creates an intellectual Property (IP) driven Services network-based applications. Vergil's initial focus on the Network Service Provider (NSP) market.	Last of the entrepreneurs in residence with e-Ventures at its Worli office and now based in Cochin. The venture was launched in April 2001.

Company	Domain	eVI's Role/State of Investments
B2C CONTENT AND COMMERCE		
Chaitime.com	Online community and affinity marketing site for South Asians living at home and abroad.	Shut down India operations.
Clubgreetings.com	Electronic greetings, messaging and gaming.	e-Ventures invested $2.2 million in March 2000. The portal is refining its revenue model and organisational structure.
Contests2win.com	Internet-based brand promotion site using contesting and gaming.	One of the winners in e-Ventures portfolio Cash break-even achieved.
Makemytrip.com	An India-centric travel and leisure focused site that facilitates online transactions backed by offline fulfillment.	e-Ventures invested $2 million in March 2000. Helped in business plan refinement, assistance in management team recruitment, introduction to global partners.
B2B AND LOCAL INFRASTRUCTURE		
Intigma	Intigma provides e-catalogue content management services to B2B exchanges worldwide.	In March this year entered into a strategic alliance with exchange 21 (an e-Ventures backed venture) to increase the efficiency of B2B marketplace.
Mediaturf	Online advertising venture that aims to provide end-to-end internet advertising services.	N.A.
Netmagic Solutions	Provider of internet hosting solutions for enterprises with mission-critical internet operations.	e-Ventures invested $4 million in March 2000 and helped in definition of corporate structure, assisted in recruitment and initial business development.
Junction96	A national retail chain of internet parlours.	e-Ventures invested $2 million and helped in consolidation of the business model.

An Integrated Business Solution

According to Mr. Richard Campbell, President of Bright Star Systems, e - commerce is a dynamic set of technologies, applications and business practices that link enterprises, customers and suppliers through electronic transactions. E-commerce implementation should be an integrated solution of the existing business practices, namely:

- The customers, suppliers, vendors and set-service providers.
- The organisation's business processes and the technology.

The adoption of e-business standards also means drastic changes in the ways of conducting business. The important points to consider here are:

- The business is on for 24 hours a day and 365 days a year (no holidays)
- The organisation displays its products/services in the virtual market place (complete transparency).

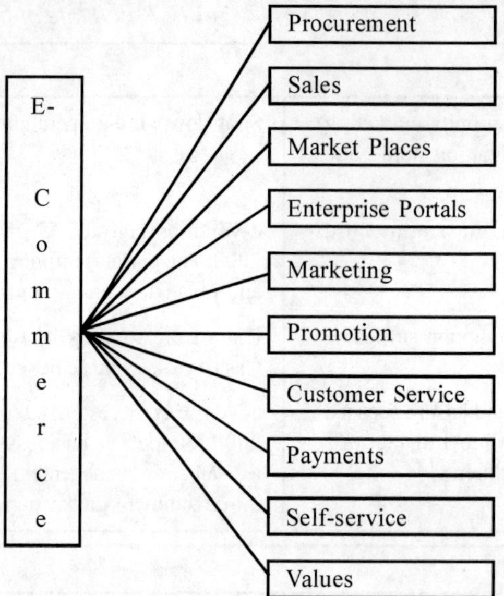

Fig. 21.1: Application of E-Commerce

- The orders are going to pour from almost every part of the globe (global market place) and
- The customer wants a product according to his specifications by yesterday (high-customer expectations).

An executive might order a book at Amazon.com on the way to airport at 11 p.m. and might need it to be delivered for inflight reading.

A customer might want to send a camera to his college going grandson in a remote village in India for his tour programme that might start the very next day.

A doctor might order for a medicine at Medicines.Com through his mobile phone in the middle of a heart surgery to save the patient.

Business at the speed of light may be a little exaggerated but e-consumers worldwide will force the organisations to be extremely fast. In order to keep up the pace, the organisation should carefully handle complex issues such as pricing, multiple tax, government policies, shipping modes, effectiveness in supply chain management, procurement, resource availability, just-in-time delivery systems, efficient customer relations management, competition and much more. The following section discusses the architecture of e-commerce and the investment of different units in creating e-commerce applications.

Benefits of E-Commerce Brand

E-commerce brands have the following distinctive benefits vis-a-vis the conventional retail brand. The benefits are:

- Transaction cost economising,
- Efficient channel alternative,
- Reduces inventory costs
- Provides better buying options

- Mass media,
- Interactivity, and
- Adaptation to the external market.
- Widens market coverage
- Reduces dependance on middlemen
- Improves customer service

Other than this some more advantages/benefits of e-commerce can be Iisted as follows:

(i) Provides better exports prospects;

(ii) Better awareness of business;

(iii) Increased profitability;

(iv) Increased productivity;

(v) Effective information gathering;

(vi) Increased market share; etc.

It is worth noting that e-commerce is a significant competitor to the traditional retail channel. Though its potential is immense and benefits increasing by the day with advancing technologies, traditional retail channels are here to stay as significant players. It is difficult to visualise a scenario of either/or with the e-commerce medium supplanting the conventional retail channel or for the retail channel to completely overcome the e-commerce emergence, the scenario of parallel offerings of the e-commerce brand and supermarket brands more likely.

Architecture of E-Commerce

A simple web application can be designed as a three-tier (browser, web server and database) architecture constituting three modules, namely, presentation logic, which deals with the HTML pages that help the user to navigate through the organisational information, Data logic, which deals with databases related to the application and Business logic the interface between presentation logic and data logic.

But e-commerce applications should be based on a multi-tier architecture. Compared to other web applications, e-commerce applications should be highly secure and depend more on third party service providers such as security service providers, merchant bankers and financial institutions.

Application layer	
Security layer	
User interface layer	Transaction layer
Data management layer	
(Legacy) Systems interface layer	

System interface layer

Marketing	Procurement	Logistics
Inventories	Order management	Customer service

Fig. 21.2: Cobra. COM/DCCOM. RMI. Apls ERP etc.

E-commerce cannot be an independent system that would take care of the business on the Internet on its own. It should be viewed as a giant integrated information warehouse extended from the existing resources that would cater to the information needs of the employees, customers and suppliers. Organisations should leverage their back-end systems at the point of every transaction, providing relevant and timely information to customers, today, an organisation's data is not in a single source.

It is distributed on Oracle, MFG; PRO, Ingress, DB2 and so on. The system interface layer should be designed to integrate these legacy systems and make them more transparent on the Web. For instance, when a customer orders an item online, the order should immediately get into the order management system that might be residing in an Oracle database and the supply chain management (SCM) that might be residing in an Ingress database.

Money transaction is the essential feature of e-commerce. It is important to implant secure, cost-effective and reliable ways to collect payments and process transactions over the Internet. There are plenty of software products that will take care of the actual transaction.

The transaction system of e-commerce should take care of the 24 x 7 (24 hours a day, 7 days a week) uptime of the application, transaction integrity, concurrent system interface, ability to handle the increase in volume of transaction, risk management and recovery system. While building the transaction layer, the organisation should aim at achieving faster response time and transaction closure.

User interface layer

Membership directory	Foot-print analysis	Dynamic pricing
Application guidelines	Content catalogue	Client-side verification

HTML. DHMTL. ASP. Java. JSP Java Script, VB Script. Etc.

User interface involves building attractive online storefronts. The e-commerce site should provide well-organised HTML/ASP/JSP pages that display the required information. They should be able to navigate through the pages and get the relevant information with a few mouse clicks. The user interface module should also take care of personalising customer relations, sending periodic product catalogues, client-sideverification systems, efficient search engines, foot-print analysis, online help and frequently asked questions and answers. The core consideration here is in providing a look and feel that would make using the site a pleasure.

Application layer

e-portals	e-customer service	e-procurement
e-shopping	e-payments	e-auction

B-to-B, B-to-C. etc.

E-commerce implementation should be in a phased manner. Before actually getting into the development stage, the organisation should plan the type of e-commerce application that has to be built first. A sample approach for a phased e-commerce introduction is provided herein:

- Start with e-employee self-service (e-ESS) and test it with the employees.
- After evaluating success and performing a SWOT analysis, an extranet can be implemented for e-procurement with select vendors in select regions.
- Next target could be implementing e-procurement for all procurement activities from all regions.

- After a couple of B-to-B implementations, the organisation can be ahead with B-to-C implementation.

Opportunities in India

During 1998-99, e-commerce transactions were estimated to be worth Rs. 131 crore and only Rs. 12 crore of this was from retail business while the rest constituted business-to-business transactions. However, this scenario will definitely undergo a change with the various corporates focussing on activities related to e-commerce. Moreover, the potential of 13213 (business-to-business) transactions in India is huge, and estimated by industry experts to reach Rs. 43,500 crore by 2008. Even consumer-to-consumer (C2C) transactions, comprising sale of second-hand goods, classifieds, etc. is expected to touch Rs. 783 crore by 2008.

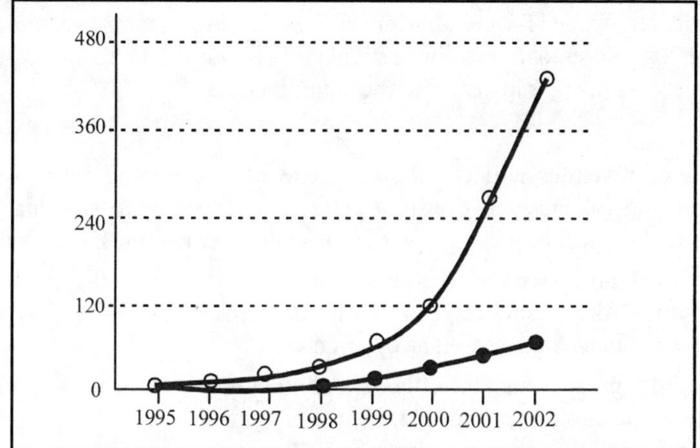

***(Sources:** IDC's Global market Forecasts or internet usage and commerce)*

Fig. 21.3: The E-Commerce Explosion

Apart form software, the products that can sell through e-commerce (Net) include books, clothing, apparel, recorded music, handicrafts, handlooms, carpets, gift items, consumer electronics, tour and travel and other types of entertainment. Internet also plays a unique role in the multidimensional service sector. It offers immense opportunity to the small-scale industry and entrepreneurs to provide customised products and services.

But these figures need to be considered in light of the fact that internet reaches 100 towns and cities, having less than 12,00,000 internet accounts and the largest private ISP reaches only 25 cities. Given, this, how can the critical mass levels estimated at 50 million e-com.net browsers per annum be achieved? The answer lies in creating a facility where those individuals who do not have internet access (either due to not owning a PC or living in a town where internet connectivity is not present) are networked to the world or e-commerce.

The other side of the coin is that India has a vast and vibrant middle class segment that can logically stand to gain substantially from the e-commerce revolution. The price and convenience advantages are clear indicators that this form of business is sustainable. The challenge lies in overcoming the obstacles of lack of connectivity and shortage of PPC penetration.

There is an installed base of 3.5 million home PCs in India. Now compare this with the population of 950 million spread over 500 towns and 6,00,000 villages and growing by 22 million each year. Now compare this with a PC growth rate of 25% p.a. The gap will get wider and wider with each day.

The industry has also identified action points giving a thrust to e-commerce which includes earliest passage of a comprehensive cyber-law, setting up national digital certification authority, providing global level telecom infrastructure with competitive tariffs and allowing private ISPs to set up gateways.

The trade aspect of the network is a two-tier system with the Strategic Business Associates (SBA) overseeing the operations of a minimum of forty franchises. These franchises will operate public kiosks at strategic locations in their cities/ towns with commuters linked via the VSATs.

Integral for any new concept or service to achieve penetration in the market is communication. With the boom being experienced by the IT sector, players are sending big budgets to communicate to the masses on the benefits of the Net and e-commerce in particular. Through the large spends on this segment, the excitement of e-commerce is being transferred to the common man.

The Forecast

- E-commerce revenues will continue to grow at exponential rates, with 13213 revenues overshadowing Business To Consumer (B2C) revenues by a wide margin. However, 132C transaction volus will be much greater because the average transaction value is lower.
- The number of businesses of sizes involved in e-commerce will grow substantially, aided by hosting and other services that can take care of network, system, security and transactions-management as well as other tasks.
- To appeal to a broader audience, the use of e-commerce will need to offer some compelling advantage to the buyer over traditional purchasing methods.
- Web-advertising revenues will continue to grow rapidly and will continue to subsidise a growing number of websites.
- The adoption of B2B e-commerce will be driven most frequently by large corporate purchasers that make the use of e-commerce, requirement for selling to them, thus paralleling the adoption path EDI pioneered.

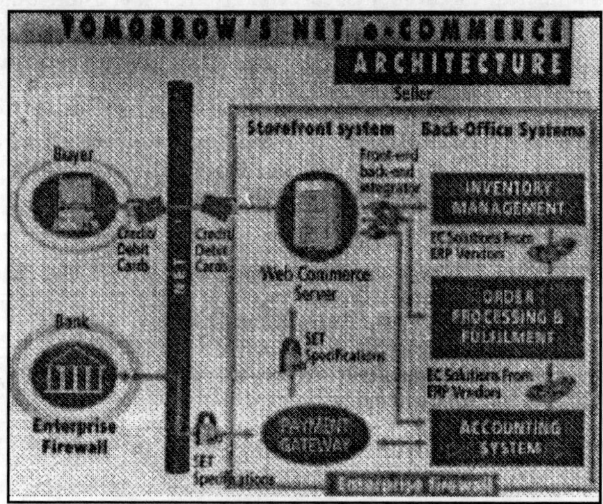

Fig. 21.4: Tomorrow's E-Commerce

- The growth of B2C e-commerce will be limited by net-access problems that prevent high seed access to e-commerce websites.
- Most B2C e-commerce transactions will use credit or debt-cards for payment throughout the forecast period. By the end of the forecast period, it should become clear whether alternative payment systems such as stored value (smart) cards or other forms of digital cash have prospects for widespread adoption as part of e-commerce.

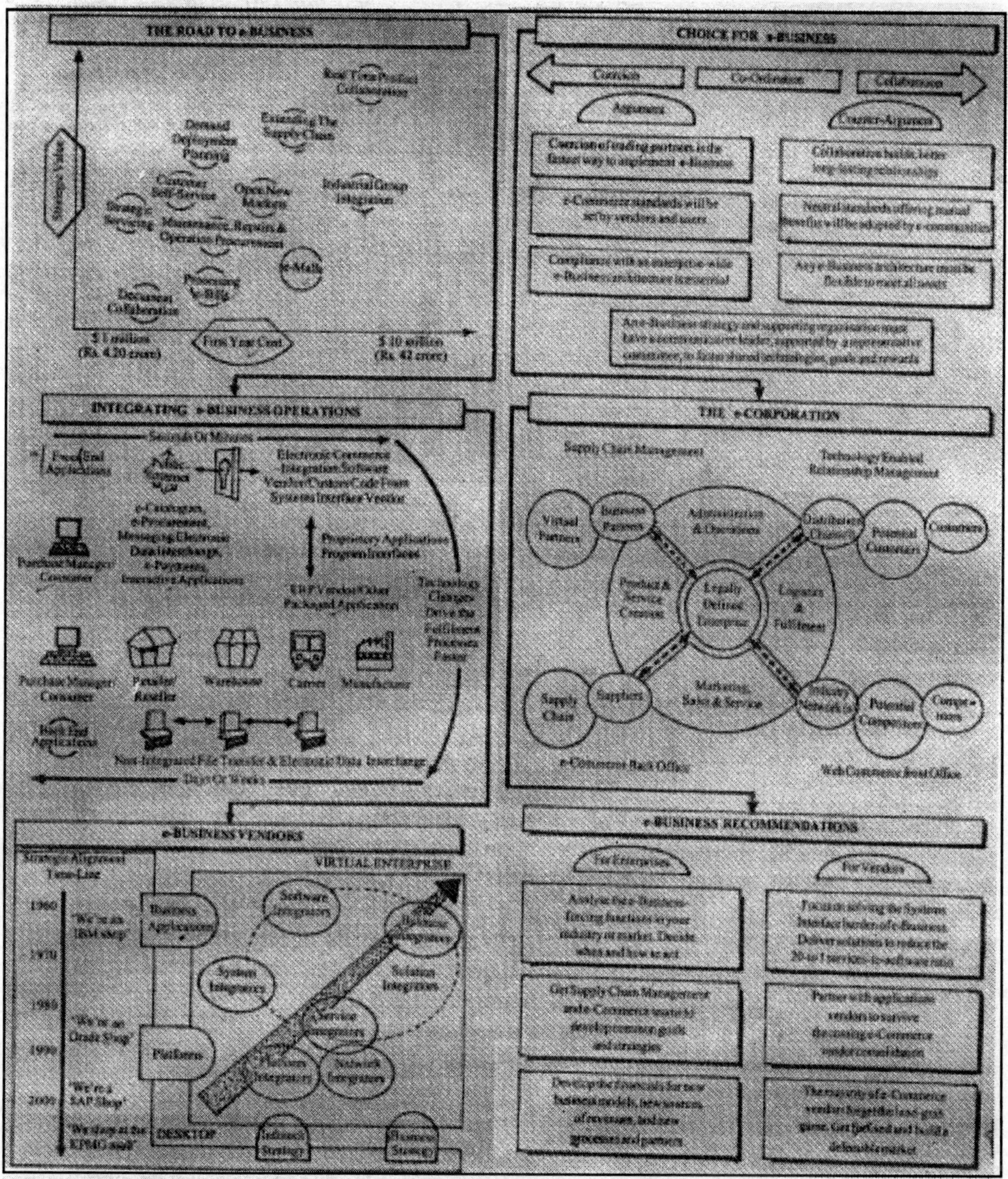

Fig. 21.5: Business Process

- Credit-card payment will continue to be made predominantly via Secure Sockets Layer SSL encrypted transmission of credit-card information to the merchant throughout the forecast period.
- Development of Secure Electronic Transactions (SET) by merchants and banks in North America will continue to lag with somewhat greater acceptance in Europe.
- In the short-term, B2B payments for e-commerce and supply-chain processes will primarily use existing processes. By the end of the forecast period, additional solutions will evolve from the Bank Internet Payment System's (BIPS) focus on inter-enterprise and inter-bank transactions.
- E-commerce software products will continue to be characterized by vendor specific APIS. The one major expectation is in payment processing, where plug-in modules that inclement various payment mechanisms will be available for use with most major e-commerce products.
- ERP vendors will evolve e-commerce strategies, initially for procurement and subsequently, for other supply chain integration along with supporting processes.
- Integrating web-based e-commerce systems with existing corporate applications will be a major challenge for companies implementing e-commerce.
- A variety of companies, including financial services firms, banks, securities firms and non-bank providers, will compete to provide enhanced services such as bill presentiment and electronic payments to consumers.
- Issues involving cross-border e-commerce will occupy the attention of the European Union, The Organisation for Economic Co-operation and Development and the World Trade Organisation.
- Debate will continue over whether state regulation or industry self-regulation is better to ensure consumer-protection and data-privacy on the Net.

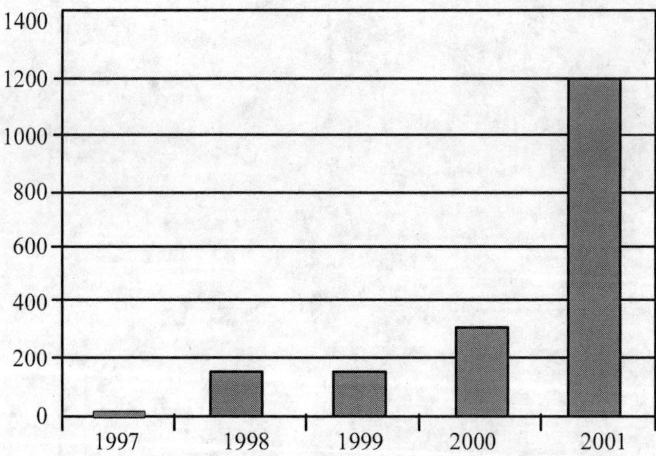

How quickly the government formulates cyber-commerce laws and allows international financial transactions on the Net will determine the pace of growth.

Fig. 21.6: Internet Commerce

The Future E-commerce

WWW and other forums for electronic commerce hold tremendous potential to change the way we work, shop, bank and communicate. Experts opine that, despite the fact that hundreds of thousands of people are already functioning in this virtual world, still it is only the beginning. Electronic commerce will continue to revolutionise entire industries and radically alter the way people live. There is no doubt that the potential rewards of electronic commerce are worth the initial risks. E-business will take off in a big way. And this will open new vistas in customer relations management where e-commerce will be the buzzword. Here too, wireless systems will probably take over the anytime-anywhere-concept which will fructify.

Further business will be founded upon the ability to be direct, flat, close and quick. Organisations must understand the changing scenario and its implications and should take necessary steps. For companies willing to make bold moves, the opportunities to succeed in the emerging e-commerce are boundless. In e-commerce, there will be a shift from producing for a mass market and front marketing through mass communications to customising products for individuals with whom the companies must build one-to-one relationships. Goods are no longer made to stock, they are made to order.

The future of e-commerce in India depends to a large extent on government involvement to providing the basic infrastructure necessary for this emerging business.

Whatever maybe the type, development should start only after implementing the legacy system interface layer and the data management layer. Chuck Shih, Research Director, Gartner Group, feels that organisations should make a checklist of the best business practices, infrastructure and the customers/partners, before and after implementing the e-commerce applications.

The e-commerce development team should by default include professionals drawn from various divisions, namely, MIS, ERP, procurement, inventory, marketing, quality, and software development. The accompanying diagram (Fig. 21.7) tries to provide a planned approach towards e-commerce implementation.

E-commerce and Small-Scale Industry

Alvin Toffler in his book *'Power Shift'* described the landscape of tomorrow (next millenium) as terra incognito, which implies an unknown terrain where accelerating pace of change will create immense opportunities as well as challenges. It will be a world where small enterprises can outsmart giant corporations. It is the mindset of small enterprises that will set in excellence.

The trend of the aforesaid scenario is already visible in the varied segments of the economy. In these circumstances, e-commerce opens up immense opportunities to expand the horizon of their activities and excel. E-commerce is a boon to small-scale enterprises, entrepreneurs and the customers. The critical task is to achieve a unique position and offer the highest perceived value product at the lowest delivered cost.

E-commerce is empowering the small industry at a great speed and is becoming a widely spread opportunity for them to avail. Globally, it has already been adopted to a large extent but Indian SSIs are yet to make a strong grip. E-commerce is spreading its wings in rural areas also. E-commerce sites are emerging everywhere, selling everything from groceries, bakery items, gifts, books, audio, video cassettes to computers and machines. But various bottlenecks are obstructing the SSIs as compared to large ones because the amount of investment and technology solutions can't be very large in SSIs. SSIs usually lack the right technical and advertising methods to get themselves known in the Net. EC, if used effectively by SSIs can serve as a shopping window for their product range.

Barriers to E-commerce Growth in India

For the growth of e-commerce in India, there are some external and internal barriers. External barriers include:

- Tele-density and band width
- Lack of Transport infrastructure
- Cyber Laws
- Financial transaction facilities

***(i)* Tele-Density and Bank Width:** The telecommunications infrastructure in India is unreliable, weak and expensive. The penetration of telephones and PCs is still very low in India. In US, people can make unlimited local calls for a fixed monthly rental, whereas the telephone rents are .very high in India. Unless this situation is changed, internet and e-commerce will still be a luxury for the masses. It is imperative to increase tele-density in India, and to give internet access to more people in rural areas.

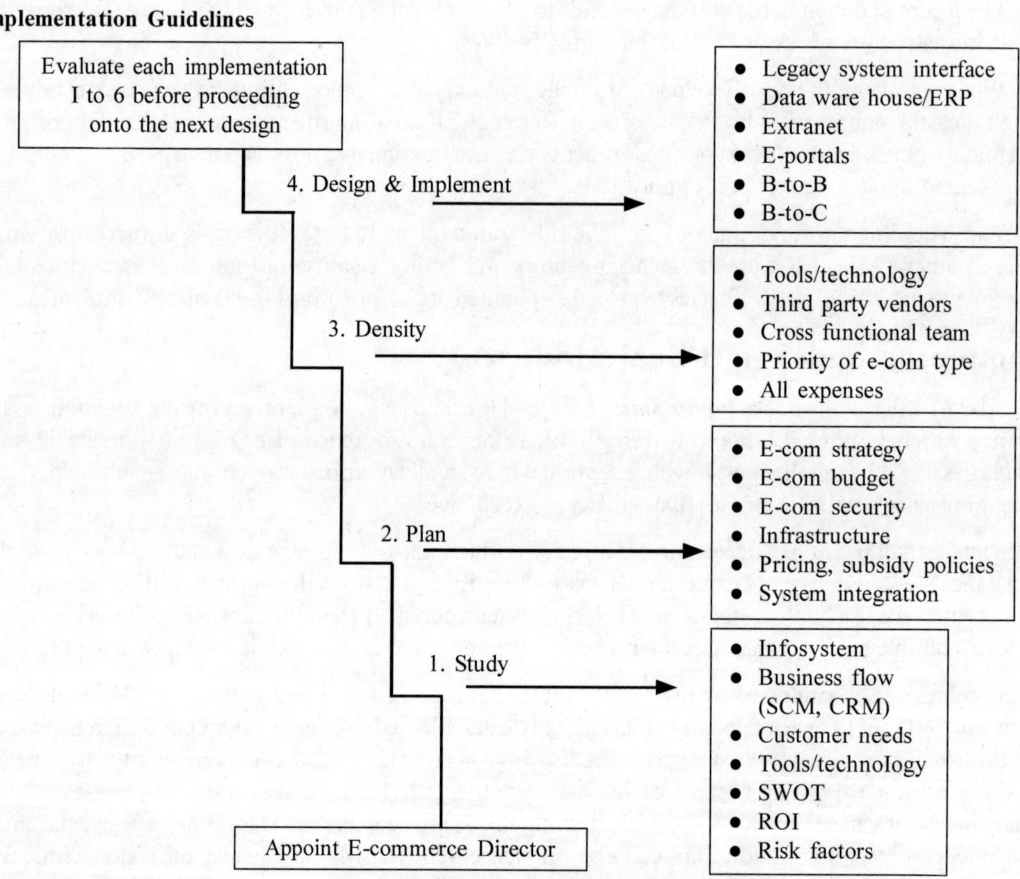

Fig. 21.7: Implementation Guidelines

In urban areas, there is better telecom infrastructure but long ordering times and failed transactions due to lack of fast internet access continue to frastrate online buyers. However, privatisation may come up as a hope to the users.

(ii) **Lack of Transport Infrastructure:** Internet will be able to make its place in the Indian market if it increases the speed of transaction, eliminates steps in the distribution chain and delivers products faster and more reliably. Even if high-speed telecommunication were in place, much of the transactional advantages of the Internet in commercial practice would be lost due to poor roads and inefficient railway facilities. Unless transport facilities are fast and reliable, the growth of e-commerce may be restricted.

(iii) **Cyber Laws:** Indian laws are insufficient for growth of e-commerce, e.g., Indian contract law is not covered under IT Act. The Act is not clear on the issues of taxation of electronic transactions. It is also silent on protection of intellectual property rights like patents and copy rights in the Net space. No consumer protection exists if people are dissatisfied while transacting online.

(iv) **Financial Transaction Facilities:** These facilities are not yet established in India for e-commerce. People are reluctant to use their options like smart cards or debit cards or credit cards. Firstly, because the number of such cardholders is very low in India. Secondly, the holders of such cards don't trust the quality and delivery system of the internet for making purchases.

E-commerce may prove out to be a boon in information technology after a few years but at present, it is facing a number of challenges. These impediments are flowing from all the directions. As per a survey conducted by a researcher on 463 industries covering large, medium-sized and small-scale industries, the following barriers were concluded being faced in the adoption and implementation of e-commerce by industries.

Conclusion

The forces extended by rapid change in technology and customer expectations are unstoppable. So, the need to constantly re-evaluate and reinvent the existing business processes becomes inevitable. The key in ensuring success in any major exercise or initiative will be a focus on fundamental guidelines. They are : do not rush, lay the foundation strong and plan carefully and implement these guidelines.

For starters, e-commerce offers enormous opportunities in every sphere of business. It allows trade at low costs worldwide and offers enterprises a chance to enter the global market at the right time.

With e-commerce solutions being available from several infotech majors providing the technical infrastructure for online ordering credit verification, payment acceptance, and seamlessly linking orders to the delivery system is not a major problem anymore.

Most importantly for entrepreneurs in the small sector, it is a boom of opening up of abundant opportunity for their quality and artistic products. E-commerce in fact, will change the working conditions in this sector, and small-scale sector activities will be more focussed in their activities in a global competitive environment.

E-commerce or internet commerce has come to stay in India and play a unique role in exploring new avenues of business opportunities within the country as well as globally. Its role in the new millennium is quite unique.

To one and all, young and N-Entrepreneurs, here's a golden opportunity to seize. The excitement of e-commerce is building up away from the metros, moving towards rural India. Catch it young today, tomorrow will be too late.

Finally, the Net is becoming the market place. Quick to recognise this, smart enterprises all over the world are now trying to transform their purely information-oriented home pages into commercial sites. In the process, they are beginning to realise that they need to address two critical issues — e-security and financial e-relationships. After all, any e-commerce site should delight customers by providing a means of information. Dissemination leads to a sale, enable users to place orders online, facilitate a payment mechanism (usually, credit cards) and offer customers a window that allows them check the status of their orders. The Net offers tremendous opportunities to understand customer needs one at a time and offer customised products and services.

Inventing the future and competing in it is a dynamic activity. In this, speed and quality are given assumptions. It is the attitude, the learning ability and quality of leadership that will differentiate one small industry from another. As the future has already arrived, the small-scale industries better see the writing on the wall and assume the role of wealth to face a disequilibrium future is to embrace it. Do it now.

✸ ✸ ✸

BENCHMARK FOR SURVIVAL

"Total customer satisfcation has been a battle cry taken up by organisations in all sectors of the economy. But this paradigm that provided a competitive quality advantage 15 years ago is today fundamental to survival." – ***Stephen R. Covey, Management Expert***

UNIT – VIII

ENTREPRENEURSHIP SOLUTIONS

22. Activity Based Costing

23. Business Process Re-engineering

24. ERP Solutions

25. Logistics

26. Networking

27. Success Strategy

28. Technology — The Competitive Weapon

29. Enterprise Mobility

30. The SWOT Analysis

31. The Enterprise Risk Management

APPENDIX

Innovate in Business Process

Entreprenueurship Solutions

Emerging Practices, Innovative Approaches, Changing Mantras

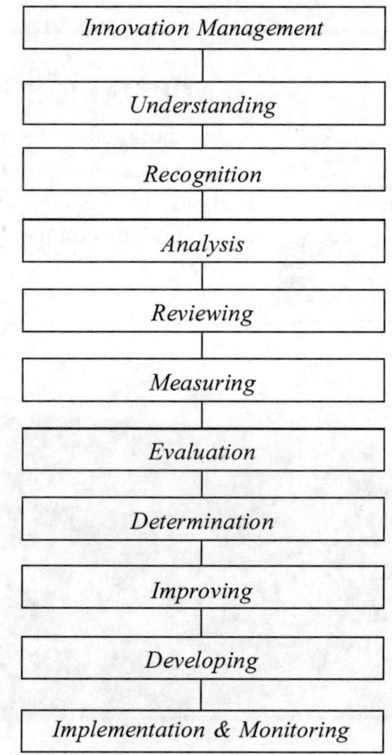

Ten Commandments of Improved Innovation Management

Seven Steps to Success

A major part of the process of achieving success and living the kind of life that you dream of is to give. Many people think that to get what you want you have to take it. There is a universal truth though that the true path to get what you want is to give. When you give, you get. What you sow, you shall reap. If this is true, then what is it we must give? I'll show you the way..

Give Others Your Honesty: *The world we live in has a simple rule that most follow: Lie when you have to. Unfortunately, this may make some people wealthy but it make us humans poor. To achieve success is to become wealthy not only in money, but in character. To be successful, truly successful, is to be able to attain your goals and keep your character at the same time!*

"Honesty is the most single most important factor having a direct bearing on the final success of an individual, corporation, or product." Ed McMahon

Mister McMahon is right, though others will tell you otherwise. Some people will say, You have to bend the truth to get ahead. Not true. Some of the most successful people who have ever lived were honest people.

How about you? Are you honest in all things? The problem with little lies is they become big ones. Lies spin out of control. You get caught in one lie and you lie to get out of it.

Give Others Your Respect: *Most of the time we give people respect based on what they have done or what they have accomplished. We gauge whether or not they are worthy of it based on what we know of what they have achieved or who they know or are related to.*

But I believe we should have a higher standard We respect people not for what they have done or for who they are related to or for what they can do for us. Instead, we respect people for simply being.

What would happen in our world, in our company, and yes, even in our families if we started with respect for everyone else rather than making them earn it? I think we would see that most people would live up to the respect that we give them!

Give Others Your Vulnerability: *We are taught to be strong. And yes, we should be strong. But we have also embraced something that I think keeps us from having the kind of life that we long for. It is an idea that keeps us from experiencing the kind of relationships that would bring deep meaning to us. It is the idea of vulnerability.*

But Chris, make yourself vulnerable and people will step all over you! It is true that this will happen. But I have also seen that most people will be drawn to you. They will help you. They will open up to you. You see, we are all broken people inside. We all have secrets. Yet everyone plays the poser. When one lets down their veil, others soon follow and we all win.

Give Others Your Care: *Too many people are running around this old earth not caring about others. Take the time to show people you care. Listen to them. Empathise with them. Love them. Now, I don't mean that you have to go around hugging everyone that probably wouldn't fly in corporate America anyway but we can take some time to step back from business and be human! And I have found that when we do so, our business succeeds as well!*

Give Others Your Passion: *There is nothing this world needs more than passionate people. And people need passionate people. Living in this day and age can be tiring. The hustle and bustle of it all can wear you down and tire you out. Give your passion to others and fire them up.*

Don't just be humdrum be excited. Give people all the energy you can muster up. And you will find that energy reciprocal. They will get energised and passionate. This in turn will fire you up more when you are already charged and get you going altogether when you don't feel like moving at all!

Give Others Your Experience: *We all have areas that we excel in and they are usually areas that we have experience in. One of the things we can do to make our lives more meaningful and be of utmost help to others is to show them the way through the experiences we have.*

Sometimes it will be what they should do: Shortcuts to take, people to meet etc. Sometimes it will be what they should not do: Shortcuts not to take and people to stay away from! Whatever it is, we can be of service to others by giving them our experience and ultimately it will make us all better!

Give Others Your Help: *All in all, what we want to do is to help others. Zig Ziglar says that if we will help others get what they want, we will in turn get what we want. If we want to be successful, we should consider ourselves servants of other people. What can we do to help them and make them better? This is the true path to greatness and success, not only in business but in life!*

Benefits of Integration Solutions

After implementation of the solution there was a considerable efficiency enhancement in the company's business operations. Some of the benefits Sunrise Kitchens experienced are:

Integrated business operations: *The new solution integrates the business operations, thereby enabling employee access and allowing the company to track information across varibus departments with ease.*

Fast Order-to-Production Cycle : *The new solution enabled multiple designers to transfer their designing details to the NAV sales order menu simultaneously. It helped the production planners to plan in a better way thereby reducing the overall cycle time from sales order to production.*

Inventory Management: *With a new solutiion in place, the company is now able to keep a proper track of the ongoing and incoming inventory items. It helped the company to manage the inventory and enabled a considerable optimsiation of the inventory items in hand.*

Multi-user Environment: *Its multi-user mode nature enabled multiple people to enter sales orders, simultaneously resulting in better resource utilisation.*

Streamlined Business Operations: *The new solution centralised all inventory, financial, sales, and purchasing data in a single database which can be accessed by any authorised user from any location. It improved data visibility and decision making across the entire, organisation.*

22

Activity Based Costing

Introduction

In the modern business world, profitability, growth and survival are considered as the basic economic goals of any business organization. Among these, profitability is the key goal because growth and survival are incidental to the profitability. No enterprise can survive if it does not prove profitable in the long-run. Similarly, there is a case for growth only when the existing and the proposed projects seem profitable. Without undergoing into certain technical controversies about the terms "cost" and "profit", it can plainly be put that profit determinations is dependent on cost. From the revenue and cost data expressed in monetary value, the profit is determined as under:

Revenue – Cost = Profit

Thus, profit is the positive difference of revenue and cost. Profit is a derived rather than a direct figure. The margin of profit can be increased by the maximization of revenue or reduction of cost or maximization of revenue along with the reduction of the cost.

The reduction in the cost presupposes the ascertainment of cost per unit.

Activity Based Costing (ABC) offers a way to calculate the real costs of products. The new tool of costing is designed to wipe off the inadequacies of conventional cost accounting practice for strategic and management decision making. ABC will transform costing exercise into enterprise-wide process management activity aimed at reducing costs in every activity.

The Concept

Activity based costing or ABC is an accounting system that tries to remove distortions of overhead costs between products.

THE ABC OF ABC

- **Advances:** Partial or entire processes or procedures that meet a particular work need of the organisation.
- **Activity Costs:** All conversion costs that are not material costs. These costs are assigned to specific activities.
- **Cost-driver:** A measurable factor that is used to assign costs between activities and from one activity to other.
- **Cost Objective:** An end item, in the form of a product, a job, or a product line, for which the accumulation of costs is desired.
- **Material Costs:** All non-payroll costs that are obviously related, and specifically traceable to a particular product or service.
- **Multiple-stage Approach:** The approach to ABC that attempts to mirror the actual flow of costs through the organisation.
- **Two-stage Approach:** The approach that attributes costs to activities using cost-drivers, and distributes the accumulated costs among the activities.

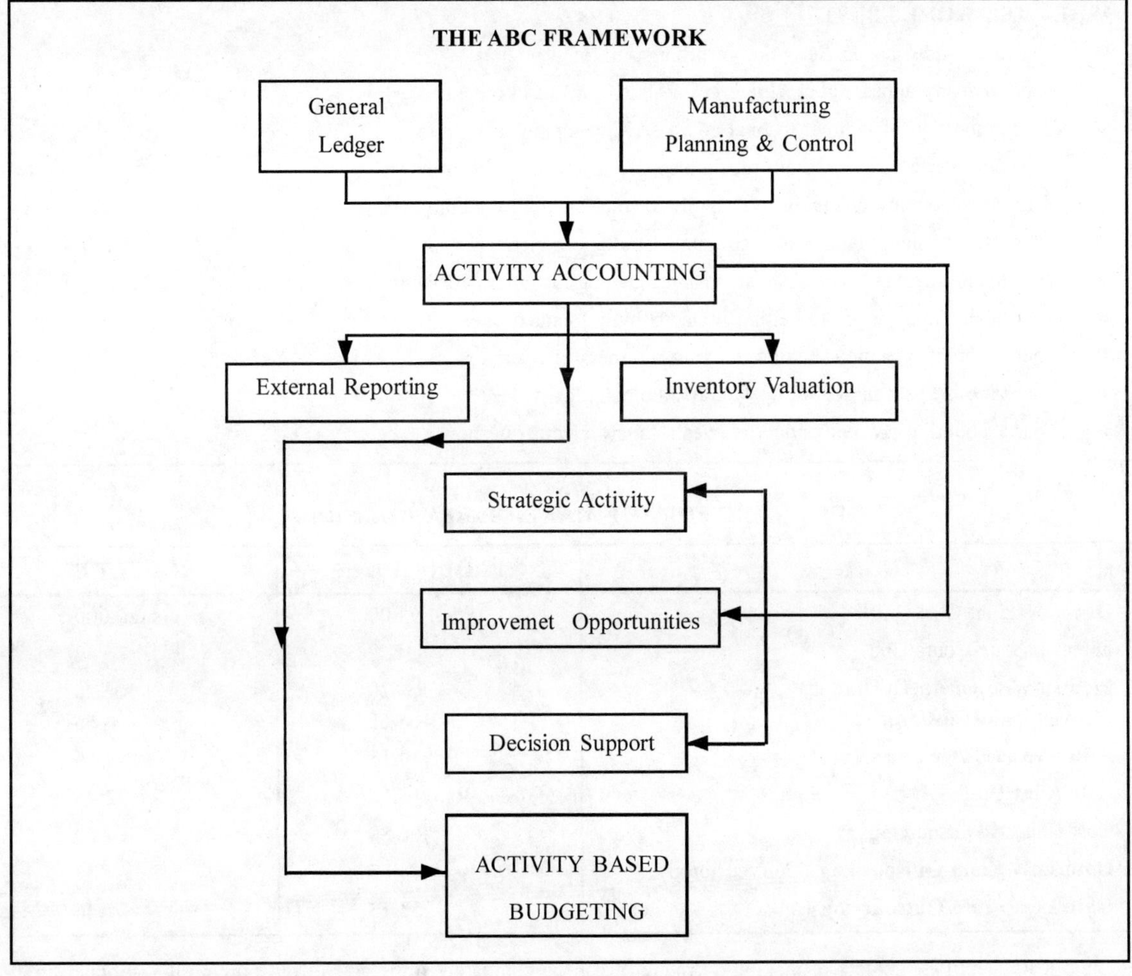

Benefits of ABC

The benefits of ABC are :

- Provides necessary inputs for cost management
- Helps you to discover which of your products or branches, or costumers are profit-makers
- Provides enterprise-wide cost process management opportunities
- Leads into reengineering a quality drive
- Provides insights for strategic decision-making, budgeting and accurate production planning
- Translates strategic intent into performence measures
- Creates cost awareness
- Enables in reducing costs.

WHEN ABC WORKS BEST

- You're confused about the optimum product-mix and pricing.
- Your company appears competitive in one line, but not in others.
- Your proportion of indirect to total costs is rising rapidly.
- Your turnover is rising without profits keeping low with sales growth
- Your customers are changing too rapidly to track their profitability
- Your entering new markets is becoming a strategic imperative
- Your quality management costs are rising, but not customer satisfaction
- Your labour operations are getting replaced by automated ones
- Your different operations require varying numbers of operators
- Your time is spent in setting up largely automated activities
- Your accounting people conduct studies to answer your questions

USING ABC FOR THE MAKE-OR-BUY DECISION

	PRODUCT A	**PRODUCT B**
Direct Material Cost/Unit	Rs. 5,000	Rs. 20,000
Direct Labour Hours/Unit	2	2
Product-Wise Overhead/Unit	Rs. 20	Rs. 20
Conventional Cost/unit	**Rs. 65**	**Rs. 55**
ABC ovetheads/Unit	Rs. 70.15	7.46
ABC Cost/Unit	**Rs. 115.15**	**Rs. 42.46**
Cost/Unit Of Outsourcing	Rs. 80	Rs. 20
Gain/Loss From Outsourcing (Conventional)	**–15**	**35**
Gain/Loss From Outsourcing (ABC)	**35.15**	**22.46**

Once ABC identifies the cost of making a product it can be compared to the cost of outsourcing that product, to check whether making is cheaper than buying. The conventional system offer details between making and buying.

USING ABC TO CHANGE PRODUCT-MIX

	PRODUCT A	PRODUCT B
Conventional Cost/Unit	Rs. 65	Rs. 55
ABC Cost/Unit	Rs. 115.15	Rs. 42.46
Margin (Conventional System) [%]	35	45
Margin (ABC) [%]	–15.15	37.54
Original No. Of Units	5,000	20,000
Profits (Conventional System)	Rs. 175,000	Rs. 500,000
Profits (ABC)	Rs. –75,750	Rs. –750,750
Optimum No. Of Units (ABC)	0	33,560
Optimised Profits (ABC)	**0**	**Rs. 1,259,758**
With ABC providing an accurate picture of costs and profits, a company can switch its resources, without making additional investments, from loss-making or low-profit products to the more profitable ones. The results will boost the bottomline.		

The powerful results it delivers is making ABC the epicentre of several different approaches to management accounting. For instance, Kaplan and David P. Norton president of Nolan, Norton & Co. of the US have integrated it into their concept of the balanced scorecard, which measures strategic objectives and operational performance across four perspectives — financial, customer, process, and learning balancing short-term financial performance with the drivers of growth opportunities for the future. Just how does ABC fit in? In two ways. First, it can generate the metrics for gauging the efficiency of different activities under the balanced scorecard system. And second, the cost information it provides can guide the strategic and operational decisions that are taken in response to the balanced scorecard. Thus, a pure costing exercise cascades into an enterprise change management system.

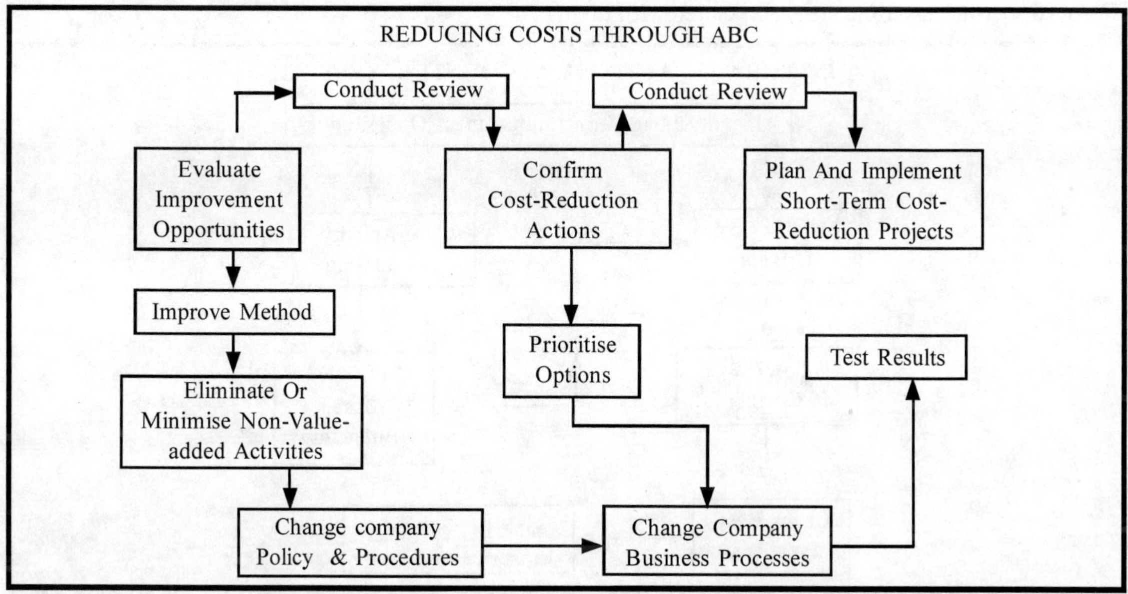

CONVENTIONAL COSTINGS VS ABC

	PRODUCT A	PRODUCT B	TOTAL
No. Of Units	5,000	20,000	25,000
Direct Labour Hours/Unit	2	2	*
Total Labour Hours	10,000	40,000	50,000
Direct Material Cost/Unit	Rs. 25	Rs. 15	*
Direct Labour Cost/Unit	Rs. 20	Rs. 20	*
Total Overheads Cost	*	*	Rs. 599,000
Overheads/Direct Labour Hrs.	*	*	10
Product-Wise Overheads/Unit	Rs. 20	Rs. 20	*
Conventional Cost/Unit	**Rs. 65**	**Rs. 55**	*
ABC Overheads/Unit	Rs. 70.15	Rs. 7.46	*
ABC Cost/Unit	**Rs. 115.15**	**Rs. 42.46**	*

Under conventional costing, overheads are distributed between products in the same proportion as the total labour hours that each product needs. But because ABC allocates differently, costs per unit are found to be vastly different.

THE ABC OF ACTIVITIES

THE STARTING POINT — THE A OF ABC – is, of course, to identify activities correctly. Distinct from transactions or processes, an activity in this context refers to a repeatable, adaptable action, or a series of such actions, that make a meaningful, complete contribution to the completion of the process or product in question. Most important, it acts as a causal factor in incurring a cost. Thus, a quality check, or inventory movements, or the power consumed, all qualify as activities whose costs can be measured. For the purposes of ABC, that would be enough. But when it comes to ABM, the activities must also be of the kind that can be improved so as to lower the costs associated with them.

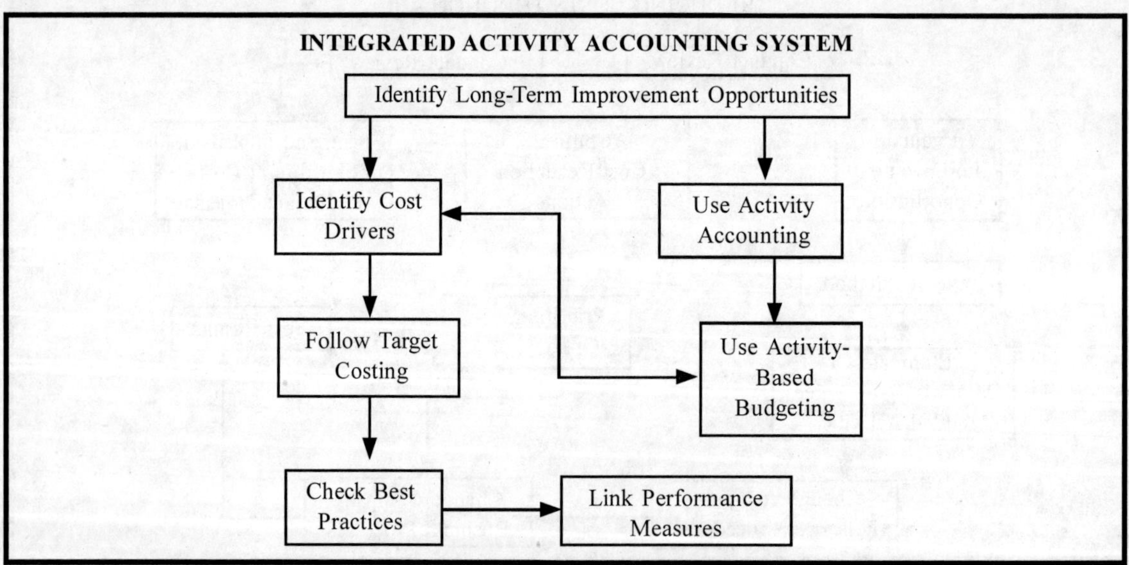

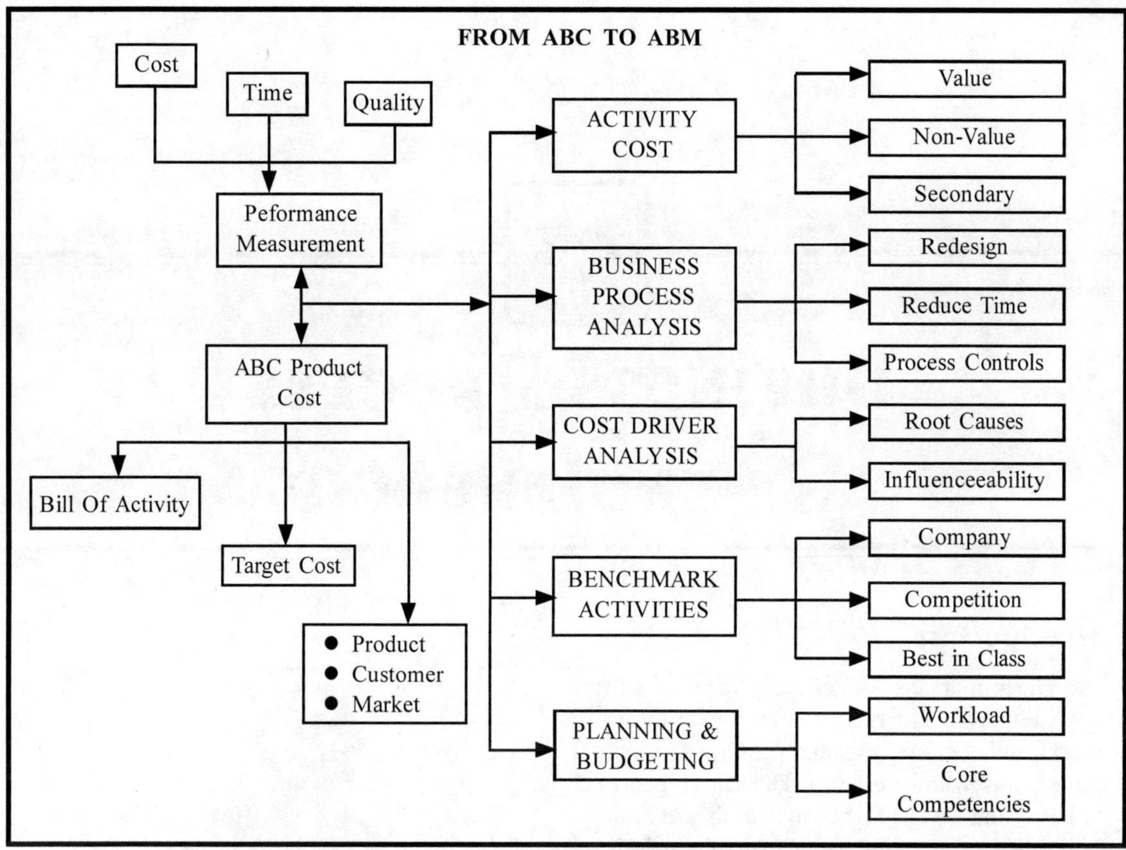

The next step: attributing as accurate a cost to the activity as Possible. And while that's relatively simple for activities like power consumption or use of a specific and quantifiable resource, other activities like making quality checks or addressing customer complaints are far tougher to address. That's why involving the actual performers of those activities is vital for ABM. The most effective way to sustain ABM is to create user-driven cost systems. Prepare for prolonged exchanges between your ABM consultant, the ABC champion within the company, and the activity performers.

THE ABC OF EVALUATION

TO GET THE BEST OUT OF ANY MEASUREMENT system — whether it's economic value added or productivity per employee smart CEOs inevitably link the findings to departmental, functional, team, and individual performance evaluation. The alternative can be disastrous in case of ABM in particular. A prominent foreign bank, for instance, had introduced ABC in a few chosen branches. Using the results from the new applications, these informed branches immediately reshuffled their product portfolios and focused on the most profitable ones.

The benefits of ABC are unquestionable, the jury is still out on whether the system can entirely replace conventional costing models. But even for those benefits to flow, you must ensure that the model is applied — and the findings acted on — by every employee. For, the objective of ABM is — not just to understand the activities, but also to ensure that the employee realises the costs of his or her activity, and tries to control them. Ultimately, the real benefits of ABC only accrue when the actual line employees proactively manage their activity costs. Only then will ABC be as easy as well, A-B-C.

* * *

23

BUSINESS PROCESS RE-ENGINEERING

Introduction

The primary concern of every business is to achieve, retain and enlarge customer loyalty for its products and services and maintaining onward march for growth and prosperity. The focus is hence on efficient management wherein both the external and internal customers are happy to maintain their wedlock with the company. Customer loyalty can be achieved by the Company when it is able to make goods and services available at competitive cost and quality, and so the question of managing the business more effectively and economically than the competitors, becomes important. Under an open sky, various technologies relating to manufacturing, distribution including information technology, are available to all. But the real differences stem out of the various ways the business processes are managed by various companies. Due to varied ways with which the organisations are managed, there is a striking difference between a business organisation and a non-business one for as much as a business organisation has to generate growth and profit whereas it is not so stringent in the other case.

Michacl Hammer

Re-engineering

- Business process re-engineering (BPR), enshrined in the management caffiedral as re-engineering, is simultaneously the most powerful and most maligned management tool today. Used casually to describe many a half-hearted attempt at catalysing change in corporates, re-engineering is actually a sharply focused practice that has delivered extraordinary benefits, but only to those who have adhered to its four fundamentals.

- It's process-centric. If you're searching for a product with which to invade a hot new market to fend off an attack from a challenger re-engineering will leave you none the wiser. The tool comes in on processes: the activities that convert inputs from suppliers into outputs for the customer; the steps that go into your manufacturing, your marketing, your accounting, and even your presentations, When you re-engineer, it is these processes that you must change.
- It's redesign-ruled. Modification is the one word that re-engineers abhor. Making small improvements to your, processes in the hope that they will add up to a major gain is not the route on which re-engineering travels. To re-engineer. start with a clean sheet of paper and lay out the steps of your from scratch, the way you would like them to be.
- It's dramatic. Don't even consider re-engineering if you're trying to scrape five per cent off your costs; conventional methods like supply chain management will work better. The tool aims to burn away large chunks of expenses — a third, a half, or even more. If you're trying to achieve incremental improvement, you're not re-engineering.

Ingredients

BPR, as expounded by its gurus, Michael Hemmer and James Champy, has the following ingredients:

(a) Assumptions: "it is a jungle out there" and only the fittest will survive in today's and tomorrow's business environment. Change is a permanent fact of life and will continue to come thick and fast. Customers are getting finnickier and finnickier and niche marketing is inescapable. Technology is, and will be, changing fast. Globalised competition is a fact of life.

(b) Goal: In the context of the foregoing assumptions, an organisation has to do whatever, repeat whatever, is necessary to survive and grow. There will be no more sacred cows in any organisation (except, of course, the customer).

(c) The tool: Irrespective of the product or service offered, an organisation has to re-engineer its business processes, so as to attract, fully satisfy and retain its customers. A business process, in this context, is defined as a sequence or set of activities delivering value to the ultimate customer. Re-engineering a process means making it fully and competitively effective in satisfying customers. In the words of its originators, Hammer and Champy, it is a "radical re-invention of how corporations do their work."

(d) Aspects covered: Improve productivity aspects like cost, efficiency, cycle time etc. Break through conventional functional barriers and encourage cross-functional team-working. Inform and empower employees, especially those closest to customers. Remain focussed on customers — let every employee serve either a customer or another employee who does. All employees must be involved so as to result in what Matsushita total wisdom management.'.

Re-invent your industry if You must, runs the argument, but only in the last of a sequence of seven steps:

(1) Sell more to current customers by inducing increased usage.

(2) Find new customers and markets by adding value to existing products.

(3) Innovate on products, targeting either existing or new customers.

(4) improvise on the delivery system, offering more value to win customers from competitors.

(5) Change the industry structure through alliances and acquisitions.

(6) Step out into new geographical market, home or globally.

(7) Expand into new business areas, vertically or diversifying.

The Process

The best of methods fail if the application is flawed. There are certain key precepts that have to be kept in mind:

Process view of business

The traditional view that companies are driven by vertical functions needs to be changed. No single function, such as manufacturing, can re-engineer itself. The re-engineered outlook involves a process that includes sourcing, production, human resource rnanagement and distribution.

Break the mould

Re-engineering works only if it is allowed to dissipate and cross the traditional borders. The sequential processing and isolated islands of information suddenly become accountable, forging cross-functional teams. It is important to provide the teams with catalysts who are eager, open-minded and focussed on driving the broad process; not concentrating on the traditional functions.

Exploit technologies

KISS - Keep It Simple Stupid , i.e., simplifying a complex process can yield good results. Re-engineering means that expanding technologies and inventing an old process to yield better results.

The potential of powerful client/server distributed processing, using powerful workstations dedicated to share information across the organisations is phenomenal. At Honeywell, sales staff access the plant production and inventory status that result in accurate delivery schedules, correlating customer needs to the organisation's production flows.

Trans-organisational outlook

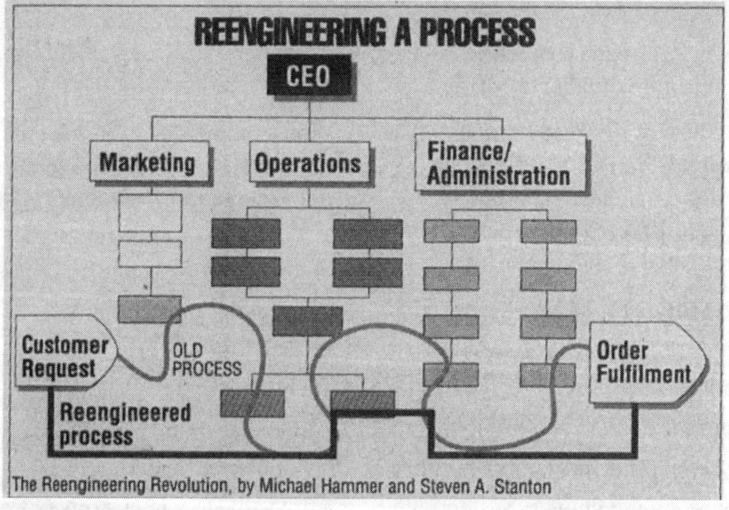

The Reengineering Revolution, by Michael Hammer and Steven A. Stanton

The span of an organisation is to be measured; this means that not only the organisation's clients but also the client's clients need to be addressed. Conversely, the suppliers' supplier must be informed about the common objective — serving the customer better.

Champion re-engineering

The efforts of re-engineering should start from the top and be supported down the line. The CEO should have a clear vision of the process and the time involved in the whole exercise, and encourage participation.

Re-engineering should never be viewed as cost cutting. It is a procedure involving the entire organisation and not just a strategic step taken by the top management.

Assess readiness for a change

For a company to change, it has to demonstrate need, good opportunities to effect the change and a strong will to make it happen. If any of these conditions is missing, the results of re-engineering would be disappointing.

CREATE A VISION: Before corporations re-engineer, they dream up a vision of what they want to achieve. Precision is critical since it is the vision that will energise everyone for the anaesthetised surgery that re-engineering often involves. A vision strategy will also doubles as a fundamental dicision maker.

PICK THE PROCESS: Choose the processes to be re-engineered. The first step for the choice: mapping your company's business not in terms of its organisational structure, but as an outcome of its processes. Only then will the processes where the most value is added and where dramatic improvement will deliver the greatest benefits to the bottomline be identified. Picking processes is doubly critical because re-engineering every one of the company's operations simultaneously can be fatal.

FIND THE FACILITATOR: Who, besides you, should lead re-engineering at your company? Successful re-engineers recommend picking people who are not only proven leaders, but are also wellliked and accepted by employees. For, BPR involves many a hard decision — for instance, breaking the news to a manager that his functions no longer exist — which your employees will not greet with joy. It is essential that their trust not be demolished by foisting weak, unlikeable change agents on them.

MANAGE CHANGE: Smart corporations ensure that their processes re-engineered or not — are owned by the people manning them.

THE DO IT–TRY IT–FIX IT METHOD

The Do It-Try it-Fix it approach is quick; it produces results in months — not years; links process reforms to competitive strategy; tests whether the organisation is ready for the early implementation of this unique approach; and, eventually, delivers the changes likely to benefit the company as a whole. This approach is based on four simple steps:

- Do It: diagnose the most critical problems facing the company and work out solutions.
- Try It: quickly convert the solution into new work processes and systems, and begin using them to manage only a few products at plants and warehouses.
- Fix It: determine whether, or how, these new processes and systems succeed, or fail, and fix the process failures or organisational barriers that impede implementation.
- Roll out the new processes and systems across the whole organisation. To build momentum for change, the success of the trials should be communicated across the organisation.

This approach is successful because it ensures learning from doing. The speed with which it is carried out has several advantages. While change is always relevant, trade-offs are essential, ensuring that limited resources are devoted to pursuing truly valuable goals. Top people can participate in the change process and ensure its momentum. Further, by trying out the new ideas in the real world, their shortcomings are exposed through real experience, and their successes are indisputably established. And, finally, by emphasising speed, and using the real world as a laboratory, this approach makes change and improvement a fact of corporate life.

The Benefits

Done correctly, BPR cle livers the results. The benefits accruing out of re-engineering are:

- Best way to dismantle the creaking systems of the past
- Reduces cycle times
- Improves productivity and profit
- Brings radical improvements in cost, quality, service and speed.

THE STAGES AND TASKS OF RE-ENGINEERING

PREPARATION
- Recognise Need
- Develop Executive consensus
- Train Team
- Plan Change

IDENTIFICATION
- Model Customers
- Define Measure Performance
- Define Entities
- Model Processes
- Identify Activities
- Extend Process Model
- Map Organisation
- Map Resources
- Prioritise Processes

SOLUTION: TECHNICAL DESIGN
- Model Entry Relationships
- Process Linkages
- Instrument and Informate
- Consolidate Interfaces and Information
- Redefine Alternatives
- Redefine and Retime Controls
- Modularise
- Specify Deployment
- Apply Technology
- Plan Implementation

VISION
- Understand Process Structure
- Understand Process Flow
- Identify Value-Adding Activities
- Benchmark Performance
- Determine Performance Drivers
- Estimate Opportunity
- Envision the Ideal
- Integrate Visions
- Define Sub-visions

SOLUTION: SOCIAL DESIGN
- Empower Customer Contact Personnel
- Identify Job Characteristic Clusters
- Define Jobs/Teams
- Define Skills and Staffing Needs
- Specify Management Structure
- Redraw Organisational Boundaries

TRANSFORMATION
- Complete Business System Design
- Perform Technical Design
- Develop Test and Roll-Out Plans
- Evaluate Personnel
- Construct System
- Train Staff
- Pilot New Process
- Refine and Transition
- Continuous Improvement
- Specify Job Changes
- Design Career Paths
- Define Transitional Organisation
- Design Change Management Programme
- Design Incentives
- Plan Implementation

Source: The Re-engineering Handbook, by Raymond L. Manganelli and Mark M. Klein.

Objectives of BPR

- Concerned with reducing cost, waste and cycle time
- Aim at eliminating non-value-adding activities
- Emphasise on working smarter
- Reducing paper work
- Envisage multi-skilling or combining of jobs
- Enables saving on labour
- Aim at radical improvements
- Improve end to end process
- Customer-focussed
- Emphasise on benchmarking
- Bridge the gap between the organisation and the market
- Re-invent the business.

GOAL

The object of efficient management is ultimately linked to the survival of the business in the long run to uphold the trust of the owners, i.e., shareholder and customers, whose loyalty is dependent on the company satisfying their basic demands, i.e., lower costs and better quality. Thus, continuous vigil, research and development have assumed central stage in the management of modern organisations. The objective is to find out superior ways and means to match the growing expectations of the shareholders and customers who are continuously chased by the competitors to change their loyalties.

STRUCTURE

Organisational structure plays a pivotal role in deciding its effectiveness so far as its grcwth and profitability is concerned. Structural features directly influence the functional efficacy of any Organisation. Basically, there are two types of structures: One is multilayered pyramidic structure and the other is flat structure. The pyramidic structure is the oldest one linked with the origin of organisation right from the feudal days and adopted by bureaucracy whose prime objective is exercising control, power and authority on the masses. However, business organisations gradually started shedding the intermeiary layers and adopted flat structure by reducing the gap between the apex and the bottom line making the organisation more direct and economic. The state bureaucracy in sharp contrast, continued its pyramidic organisational structure as it could afford the luxury since cost is no major consideration for it.

In a market economy, no organisation can afford to run its business profitably with a lavish multi-layered structure with a set of people engaged in merely exercising control. i.e.. laying down, reinforcing 'Lakshman Rekha'(boundary lines) for the bottom line operators and thereby interfering with their freedom of thought, action and creativity.

It is interesting to observe that the organisations like the state and even monopoly business, who operate in a captive market, find it convenient to follow the pyramidic structure as the same play host to their enjoying authority and power. But in a fast changing environment, where the world is converging into a global village, no organisation can remain an island and has to maintain its structural advantages with the passage of time and the solution is a lean, flat and vibrant organisation.

Multi-layered pyramidic structures are more formal and act as Safety Nets for diffusing and diluting the element of accountability which ultimately results in misdirection and wastage. Successful companies, therefore, promptly identified the same and flattened their organisations, making them lean and strong at the bottom-line, combining competence with expertise. But the question was 'Could the state-run companies and monopolies do it and if so, how promptly?'

Once the organisation is restructured, the monitoring centres can coordinate between the apex and operating units. This should enable the company to reinforce its operating capabilities and reduce the overheads eliminating the unproductive expenses on hypothetical and imaginary control elements which do not have natural bearing on business output.

Bottomline Operations

The vitality of an organisation is the inherent strength of its bottomline operations which play pivotal role of producing goods and services at a competitive cost and quality and making them available to customers. They earn the much needed market friendliness for the organisation. Utmost care and consideration are essential for achieving the optimum utilisation of the potentialities of men and material engaged in operations. Sharpening the skills and competencies of people and updating the infrastructure at the bottom-line of the operations are basic concerns, because there lies the success of the organisation in achieving a competitive edge for its survival and onward march. This calls for redefining the role and responsibilities of the bottomline operations as a profit centre with uninterrupted freedom for taking decision within the framework of the organisational objectives and guidelines. This, should enable the people manning the profit centres, to understand and accept their individual and collective responsibilities in specific and realistic manner.

While redesigning the management system, a close scrutiny of the traditional element of control adopted by some organisations purported to reinforce the operational effectiveness, should be reexamined to assess their efficacy on the basis of their net contribution (not notional). However, it has been found that controls, besides imposing additional burden on cost of management, proved counter productive and an interference instead of support to operations. Promoting performance through control is like 'Cooking on treetop while fueling from bottom.' The objection is not against control as such but the manner in which it turns futile in the process. 'What is therefore, practised by most successful business houses is the combination of operations and its control, i.e., self-control.' The process will provide the unique combination of professional competence and expertise under the same roof to cater to the needs of the customers. The interesting aspect of the change under the redesigned system is the development of stake 'in the organisational goals and objectives by all concerned. Because the principle is'perform or perish.'

Human Resource Management

Customer satisfaction is the key to success of any organisation but the same has to be achieved by the internal customers whose competence and involvement are of prime importance for the Human Resource Management (HRM) of the organisation. In order to face the challenges effectively, HRM has to develop strong and effective leadership for the operational levels, capable of responding to every situation, be it Production, Distribution or HRD including development of professional competence and expertise.

Leadership at operational level is the most critical position where a company cannot afford to place people with less experience and less exposure to interact with customers who demand immediate and satisfactory solution to their problem. But the common phenomenon in control based organisations is that people with higher maturity and exposure drawn to the control layers and operational units are deprived of benefit of their expertise. Their responses to the customer are needed on the shop floor, across the table and not where the customer is asked to wait for the reply from the traditional 'Head Office.' One has to remember that Luuay's customer has no timeto wait. Deployment of people with maximum exposure and expertise to lead the operational units will enable the organisation to achieve the much talked about and much needed customer satisfaction.

Management system and managerial style are highly significant as to what extent, people Would identify themselves with the organisation and its goals by taking initiative and remaining creative. In order to achieve the identification and involvement of people in a natural and spontaneous manner, the organisation has to ensure that the culture of management system and managerial style consists of 'sharing and caring' elements instead of threats and authority under which people work out of fear of losing the favour of the quantity managers who reduce people into virtual robots with pre-set programmes and whose concern is output for today and not survival for tomorrow. Hence, the organisation has to moderate its management system and style to maintain proactive and positive environment for building a pragmatic work culture. The same can be generated by the shop floor managers bv supporting people to develop internal stimulations rather than developing through external stimulation. What is really required is more freedom and less interference for boosting up the creativity and initiative among the people for their developing a stake in the Organisation.

THE TOP TEN WAYS TO FAIL AT RE-ENGINEERING
1. Don t re-engineer but say that you are.
2. Don't focus on processes.
3. Spend a lot of time analysing the current situation.
4. Proceed without strong executive leadership.
5. Be timid in redesign.
6. Go directly from conceptual design to implementation.
7. Re-engineer slowly.
8. Place some aspects of the business off-limits.
9. Adopt a conventional Implementation style.
10. Ignore the concerns of your people.
Source: *The Re-engineering Revolution,* by Michael Hammer and Steven A. Stanton

Re-engineering in India

India has taken its first step towards amalgamating its business with the outside world and is slowly gearing up to free market economy. Indian companies would need to turn to re-engineering to face the competition from multinationals. The winning attitude would be to tailor to one's own need. A host of Indian companies have adopted the process and a few are already in the process of implementing it.

More importantly, new technology-based players, such as on-line retailers, Internet banks, electronic purchasing agents, and remote logistic managers, will leverage technology to create more efficient processes and businesses. And there is no running away from the fact that companies will have to embrace new technologies and re-engineering. Therefore, to serve them well, companies will have to ensure that re-engineering efforts are truly strategy driven and appropriately piloted. For, only then can they re-engineer a healthy future for themselves.

THE PROFILE OF A RE-ENGINEER

Process-orientation	Optimism
Holistic perspective	Persistence
Creativity	Tact
Restlessness	Team player
Enthusiasm	Communication skills

Re-engineering is a time and human intensive procedure, it is also a process fraught with challenges and is not a very comfortable one. The key to successful re-engineering is linking people, process, strategy and technology, It is not a fad buzzword any more — it is here to stay. It is better to re-engineer by choice than by chance.

World class companies have benefited by BPR efforts. Many Indian companies are complacent with their ISO 9000 accredetion. It is high time the Chief Executives of these companies realise that to compete with World class companies is like competing with an Olympic Champion. Often these companies, both public and private have inherited feudal systems and archaic attitudes. Often they are plagued by bloated bureaucracy, several layers of management and outmoded systems and procedures which are killing the enterprising mentality of Indian managers and workers. Management attitudes and practices are not questioned. They are rooted in the past.While re-engineering questions everything from the top to bottom, the Xerox corporation uses benchmarking as a corporate strategy. For example, when Xerox discovered that Fuji Xerox was selling copy machines for less than it costs Xerox to manufacture them, it believed it could do the same, so it did. Indian managers are going to deal headlong with this type of competition. Are we prepared, in short Re-engineering efforts start from the desired future state and work backwards not constrained by today's way but considering lessons learnt — do not repeat the past.

Structure strategic change around core business processes and customer outcomes. Flatten the organisational hierarchy and use teams to manage work processes. Create "one-stop" work cells rather than sequential processes. Link parallel activities instead of integrating their results. At this point a student of information technology who is working with me in a re-engineering project pointed out that it is very similar to concurrent engineering which information technology people are familiar with. Not only information technology, re-engineering currently has elements resembling total quality rnanagement, world class manufacturing, industrial engineering, team building, organisational learning, organisational re-structuring, systems thinking, etc.

EVALUATING YOUR SCORES

The following list indicates the minimum numbers we believe an organisation should score tackling re-engineering; that is, prior to launching the effort. Some issues are more vital than others, and hence, have a higher minimum score. If your score on a statement is lower than the indicated minimum you should take steps to raise it. While there is no precise mathematical formula for success, a higher score obviously means you are better positioned to achieve it. Scoring above the minimum does not absolve you of further effort. You may be ready to begin, but you should strive to raise each number as high as possible to further improve your position.

Grab a pencil before you start this chapter. You will be quizzed on your knowledge of your own organisation and tested on your ability to assess its capabilities. The only right answer is the truth.

This diagnostic, designed to help you determine your company's strengths and weaknesses at re-engineering, consists of 20 statements that characterise an organisation that is well positioned for successful re-engineering. These statements are organised around three major themes.

You should ask yourself how true each statement is of your organisation. The answer scale runs from I to 5, with representing strong disagreement, i.e., the statement is not at all true of your organisation and 5 representing strong agreement, i.e., the statement is very true of your organisation.

After you complete the diagnostic, use the next section, Evaluating Your Scores, to do precisely that. Minimum scores are given for each statement, for each section, and for the diagnostic as a whole. While there are obviously no passing or failing grades, these base scores are intended to help you identify problem areas.

Are You Readv To Re-engineer ?

RE-ENGINEERING LEADER

(1) The leader of re-engineering is a senior executive who is strongly re-engineering and who possesses the title and authority necessary to institute fundamental change. ☐

(2) The re-engineering Ieader truly understands the nature o re-enngineering and the magnitude of the organisational change in particular that it entails. ☐

(3) The re-engineering leader has a vision of the kind of organisation the or she wishes to create and is able to express that vision clearly and simply in operational terms. ☐

(4) The re-engineering leader is ready and able to exercise leader through communications, personal behaviour, and systems of measurement and reward in order to make re-engineering succeed. ☐

(5) The re-engineering leader is prepared to commit both, the organisational resources and personal attention that re-engineering requires. ☐

(6) The entire senior management team shares the leader's enthusiasm for re-engineering. ☐

ORGANISATIONAL READINESS

(7) The organisation as a whole recognises the need for Re-engineering and fundamental change. ☐

(8) The organisation understands the nature of re-engineering, including the fact that it results in multidimensional change that impact processcs, jobs, organisational structure, management responsibilities, and so on. ☐

(9) The organisation believes that the re-engineering leader and the senior management team are truly committed to re-engineering and that this commitment will be long lasting. ☐

(10) The organisation has none of the complacency and often follow a sustained period of success. ☐

(11) The organisation is free of the scepticism, mistrust, and umbivalence that often follow a programme of downsizing or restructuring. ☐

(12) The organisation has the financial and human resource needed to implement re-engineering. ☐

(13) Key staff organisations, human resources, finance, and information systems are positive about the prospect of re-engineering and capable of innovative responses to its demands. ☐

(14) The organisation's experience with total quality management (TMQ) has created an environment that is receptive to re-engineering. ☐

(15) The organisation places a high value on serving customer and has a solid understanding of customer needs. ☐

STYLE OF IMPLEMENTATION

(16) The organisation is comfortable with the way in which re-engineering proceeds through risk taking, learning, and ambiguity ☐

(17) The members of re-engineering teams will feel empowered to break the rules and to challenge long standing assumptions. ☐

(18) The re-engineering effort is direct at key business proceses rather than organisational units. ☐

(19) Managers have been given end to end responsibility for the processes to be re-engineered and are motivated to assure that the proceses are successfully re-engineered. ☐

(20) Measurement systems and performance goals have been established to chart the progress of re-engineering. ☐

MINIMUM SCORES

RE-ENGINEERING LEADERSHIP

Statement 1: 3
Statement 2: 3
Statement 3: 4
Statement 4: 4
Statement 5: 4
Statement 6: 3

Minimum score for section: 24

ORGANISATIONAL READINESS

Statement 7: 3
Statement 8: 2
Statement 9: 4
Statement 10: 2
Statement 11: 2
Statement 12: 3
Statement 13: 2
Statement 14: 3
Statement 15: 3

Minimum score for section: 28

STYLE OF IMPLEMENTATION

Statement 16: 3
Statement 17: 4
Statement I8: 4
Statement 19: 3
Statement 20: 3

Minimum score for section 18

Minimum score for diagnostic as a whole 75

These minimum scores, as we said, are what you need before you start. Once implementation is under way, however, required minimum scores go up; sometimes, way up. In particular, scores for statements 1, 5, 9, 12, 18, and 19 must be 5. The rest should consistently grade out at 4 or 5. As implementation progresses, intensity increases meaning that leadership, resources, and focus, already strong, must get stronger. So, don't just take this test once and then forget it; use it again and again. During implementation, the diagnostic can help you monitor your progress and identify areas requiring attention and improvement. If you think these minimum scores are somewhat high and even intimidating, you are right. We never said it would be easy. The entrance requirements for re-engineering are stiff.

Extracted with permission from The Re-engineering Revolution: A Handbook by Michael Hammer and Steven A. Stanton. Published by Harper Business and distributed by Rupa.

* * *

24

ERP Solutions

Introduction

The infusion of technology in business has changed how the modern enterprise functions. With growing pressure to deliver in the high-stakes, high-risk marketplace, most organisations use some or the other form of enterprise software that helps them work faster, reduce costs and be more competitve. Good 'technology architecture' is also essential for any organisation that wants to limber up and streamline processes, according to experts. "Nobody today says 'I don't want an ERP.' The real question they're asking is 'Can I handle one?"

In this age of competition for survival it is essential for any industrial organisation or business enterprise to evolve ways and means to keep its operational efficiency at the peak. With the advent of information technology there have been efficiency to utilise its gifts for the purpose of improving all kinds of industrial and commercial activities. But the latest trends involve the total integration of information technology with operational domains. Enterprise Resource Planning (ERP) is an excellent exercise which achieves such an integration with remarkable results in terms of productivity.

The Enterprise Resource Planning (ERP) which is essentially a software application package has emerged as a new concept for providing a total information system solution to a business enterprise in an integrated manner. Most of the business organisations in India are in the process of either evaluating or implementing an ERP system in their organisations. Selection and implemention of an appropriate ERP package among various options such as SAP R/3, BAAN IV, ORACLE Applications, People Soft, MFGIPRO, MARSHAL is a difficult and challenging job. However, the ERP system, if implemented successfully, will enable companies to improve upon their contemporary measures of performance such as cost, quality, speed and service which can ultimately provide a competitive business advantage. The chapter discusses in depth the dynamics of ERP solutions to business.

The Need for ERP

The business environment has changed more in the last five years than in the previous five decades. The pace or changc continues to accelerate and corporations around the world seek to revitalize, renovate and resize its efforts to position themselves for success in the 21st ccnttury.

The ability to respond to new customer needs and seize market opportunities as they arise is crucial. Successful companies today, recognize that a high level of interaction and coordination along the supply chain will be a key ingredient to their continued success. Enterprises are continuously striving to improve themselves in the area of quality, time to market, customer satisfaction, performance and profitability.

Tomorrow's winner will be those business that can most effectively gather vital information and quickly act upon it. Making informed business decisions in this manner would enable organisations to accomplish their business growth while also enabling them to utilize information for competitive advantage.

To enable the companies to execute this vision there is a need for infrastructure that will provide information across all functions and locations within the organisation. The enterprise resource planning software provides this infrastructure to the organisation.

The Concept

ERP, or enterprise resource planning, is a software that helps to integrate nearly all the functions of an organisation, enabling it to plan, track and see its resources (material, people and money) in the best possible way to service its customers. For example, ERP has allowed companies like computer firm Dell and communication equipment company Cisco in the US, to take orders and service customers through the Internet.

ERP System

Enterprise Resource Planning (ERP) systems which are coming into vogue are built with the vision to provide businesses with an integrated information system. These systems implement business processes within the organisation to achieve synergy in operation across various business units. The challenge for ERP systems is to set up and integrate information resources across geographically spread business units to enable optimization across the organisation. Even though a multitude of technologies is involved in building ERP systems, the business fitment, implementation and post-implementation maintenance should be made simple. Towards this objective, it is imperative that the ERP systems satisfy some basic requirements of the customer.

Objectives of ERP Systems

- Provides support for all variations of best business practices.
- Enable implementation of these practices with a view towards enhancing productivity.
- Empowers the customer to modify the implemented business processes to suit their needs.
- Enables to create a sustainable competitive business advantage.
- Ensures the implementation of the supply chain management effectively.
- Networks the operations of the organisation.
- Improves productivity and enhances competive edge by optimising use of resources.

The Evolution

The evolution of the Enterprise Resource Planning (ERP) solutions has a long history. Earlier packages used to come in different forms and in a non-integrated fashion. But slowly the need to integrate various segments of an enterprise and go beyond back office and front office, growth of business to business requirements and large databases, and rise of concepts like supply chain management, just-in-time and order-to-manufacture, ERP has become a compulsory addition. In short new dynamics of business have forced the corporates to employ ERP solutions.

Shrinking geographical borders integration of currencies, ever decreasing product life cycles, reduced profit margins and the need to raise productivity — each of these problems is addressed by ERP solutions. The physical, inventory, financial, market and human resources are to be properly pooled and maintained and ERP solutions do just that.

Earlier, only global organisations, MNCs and large corporations with multi country operations thought that the ERP solutions were necessary for them. But even a small company, if it is looking at the global market, has to implement ERP solutions. And now, with liberalisation and international market integration, any company can target the global market and expand beyond borders.

In fact, some companies are developing ERP solutions at a lower cost aiming at smaller companies. Some companies have also brought out ready-made templates to be used by smaller corporations.

The experience in other countries shows that the productivity levels have gone up three times with the implementation of ERP solutions. However, in India, we arc still in the early stages of implementation and we do not have information on the rise in productivity. But certainly it would help more in Indian scenario and I am sure the results will start coming in shortly.

Aims of ERP

ERP aims at definite competitive advantage in manufacturing, marketing, accounting, human resources and other areas in industrial organisations. It cuts across the interdepartmental boundaries in an enterprise. It is said that ERP links information islands. We often find that in several organisations there is a tendency for the various departments to function as if they were independent empires maintaining unhealthy rivalries.

Functions

The fact that the functions carried out by them are complementary may be forgotten. ERP however effectively integrates islands of information within the organisation ensuring total transparency, information sharing, healthy dialogue, a uniform system, elimination of wastage caused by misunderstandings and improvement in overall productivity. ERP is sometimes defined as an integrated suite of application software modules which will provide adequate information for the enhancement of productivity and competitiveness. This is achieved by optimising the use of 4M resources: Men, Machines, Materials and money.

ERP integrates the entire enterprise starting from supplier / vendor to the customer covering Financials, Logistics and Human Resources.

The various areas covered are:

Financials: Financial Accounting, Treasury Management, Entcrprise Controlling, Asset Management.

Logistics: Production Planning, Materials Management, Plant Maintenance, Quality Management, Project Systems, Sales and Distribution.

Human Resources: Personnel Management, Training and Development, Skills Inventory.

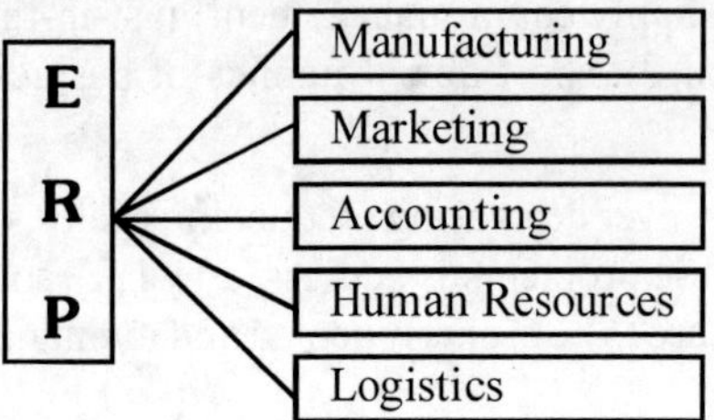

Implementation

An effective ERP system should necessarily fulfil various requirements. We have to realise that the system implementation involves substantial financial inputs and the end results should invariably justify the investment. The system should not be rigid; it should permit easy customisation, adaptation to new environments and periodical upgradation. It has to be tailor made to suit to the requirements of the organisation. Its client/server capabilities and security are significant concerns. Initial investment as well as maintenance cost should be within affordable limits. Most importantly it should give early results.

In-house development of ERP solutions may be ideal from the point of view of the best fit. But it has to be borne in mind that individual organisations may neither able to develop them quickly, nor would their documentation be exhaustive. It would be much more practicable to go in for packages marketed by reputed software product developers. They can be customised to meet specific requirements. They would be in general cheaper, more flexible, and easier to maintain. Customisation may sometimes be rather expensive. Trained personnel well-versed in such packages will be available in the employment market. The names of some of the well-known EPP packages are: SAP R/3, BaaN, Oracle Financials, Peoplesoft, Control and BPCS.

Whatever might be the package used, total commitment of the top management is essential for success. There should be a single-mindedness of purpose moving steadily from the basic to the sophisticated in incremental steps during implementation. Probably temporary setbacks may torment, but confidence and unflinching should steady the continued activities.

The entire enterprise will have a pool of information making processes of operational cascading easy and effective. Lead time delays will be reduced and workflow systematically automated. Tools for decision making will be at the fingertips of top management, rendering even crisis management relatively smooth and easy. Performance evaluation and the prompt supply of feedback will become routine, and corrections for improvement quick. ERP solutions such as SAP and Oracle Financials contain diverse functional modules to meet almost all business requirements. Modules like Order Entry, Inventory, Purchasing, Bill of Materials, Work in Progress, General Ledger, Accounts Payable, Accounts Receivables, Fixed Assets, MRP/MPS and Client/Server Technology are sufficiently comprehensive to meet general needs of most organisations.

Training

Training is sensitive area. Since certain ERP trained personnel are very well-placed in lucrative job positions, there is a virtual scramble for admission to the training programmes, the objective of the candidates being nothing other than minting easy money. Training institutions with inadequate infrastructure are also in the scene admitting candidates without the knowledge and skills essential for appreciating the contents of the course and developing competency for ERP implementation. As a general rule, we should remember that no high position can be reached through shortcuts; perhaps we may have to go by winding stairs.

Who can take the training usefully? There are indeed two options. In either option, you should have some knowledge/experience in one professional field and in software development.

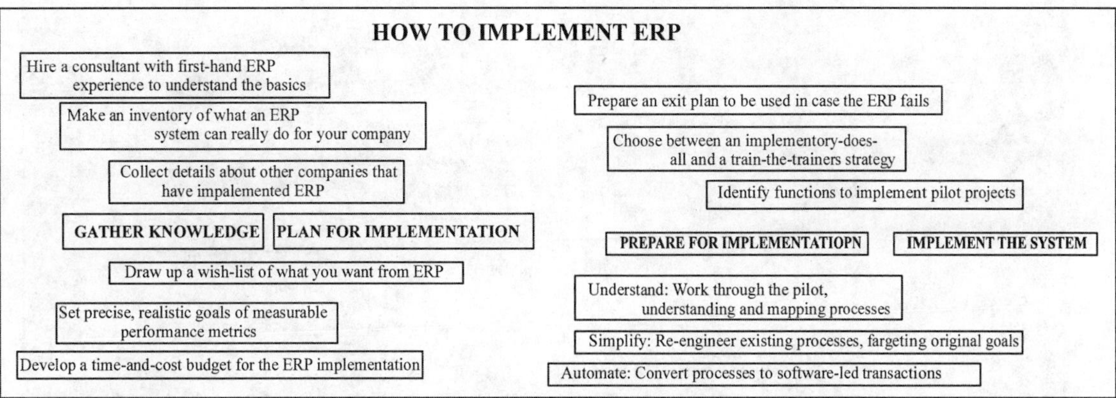

Objectives

- To provide the participants an indepth understanding about the ERP systems and its business and managerial implications in the organization.
- To provide a structured framework for selection and implementation of an ERP package.
- To provide an overview of features of major ERP packages.

Contents

- Cost-benefit analysis of ERP systems in a business organisation.
- Feature analysis of various ERP packages.
- Selection and implementation strategy for an ERP systems.
- Business Process Reengineering (BPR) through ERP.

Force Multipliers Software that helps extract more out of an ERP suite

	SCM	**Data Warehousing**	**Business Intelligence**	**CRM**
Definition	Art/science of managing the entire process from sourcing of components to delivering product	Repository of information that can be queried, extracted from heterogeneous ssources	Makes sense of disparate data from top management's point of view	Helps learn more about consumer behaviour to help build strong bond with them
Goal	Helps plan, source, make, and deliver	Source for decision-making tools such as BI and CRM	Helps analyze trends and performance by products, brands etc.	Gives better insights about consumers
Benefit	Improves efficiency cuts inventory	Improves quality of decision-makings.	Improves quality of decision-making	Improves customer service
Implementation	Challenging. Involves interfacing with disparate systems	Needs customisation to incorporate unique business concerns	Requires some customization.	Same as BI

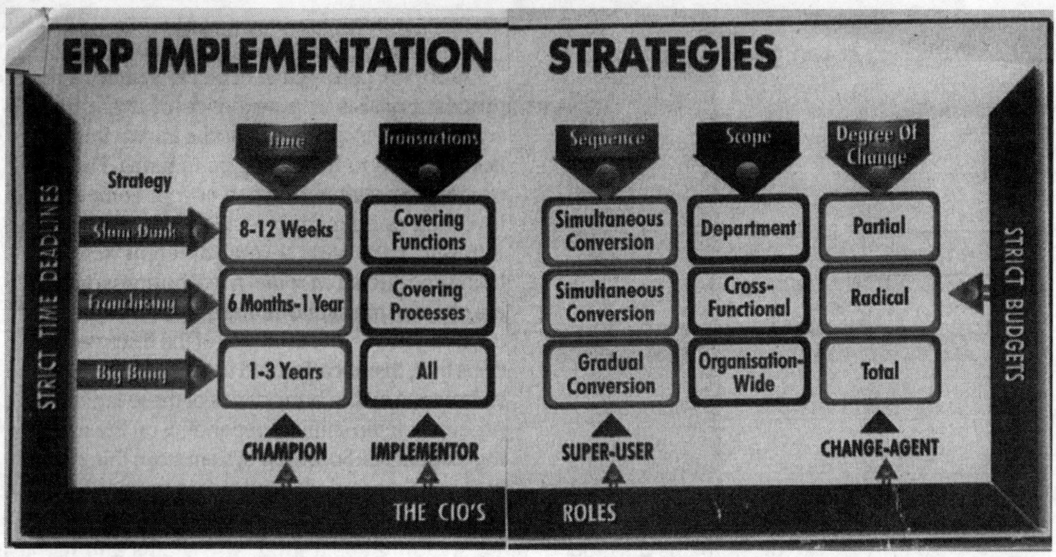

Benefits of ERP?

ERP helps:

- bring together people who work on shared tasks; within the same enterprise or in their dealings with suppliers and customers;
- organisations ensure a smoother flow of information at all levels and between all parts of the organisations;
- to access up-to-date information;
- enterprise replace legacy systems that are expensive to support and maintain;
- workflow integrates business processes.

Who has implemented ERP?

Traditionally it has been manufacturing enterprises that are looking to improve efficiency, lower costs and increase profitability. The manufacturing industries that have successfully implemented are in Automotive, Discrete, Consumer goods, and Chemical and Pharmaceutical industries. But this has not prevented other diverse enterprises such as Banking and Insurance, Health care, Telecom and Utilities to realise that ERP is the way to go in the right direction. These diverse enterprises have found that the basic core business processes in the area of Financials, logistics and human resources are no different than in the manufacturing segment. This has to some extent dispelled the myth that ERP solutions can be implemented only in manufacturing or processed industries.

With the Indian economy opening up to liberalisation and competition enterprises in India have realised the need for adopting ERP solutions. Though infrastructure bottlenecks like telecom and power exists, a number of Indian enterprises have found innovative methods to overcome these problems and implement ERP successfully. The fact that technological advancements have been happening simultaneously world wide and in India has helped the advancement of ERP. India customers in areas like Automotive, FMCG, Steel, Pharmaceutical etc. have already shown that integrated systems have provided tangibly to their organisations.

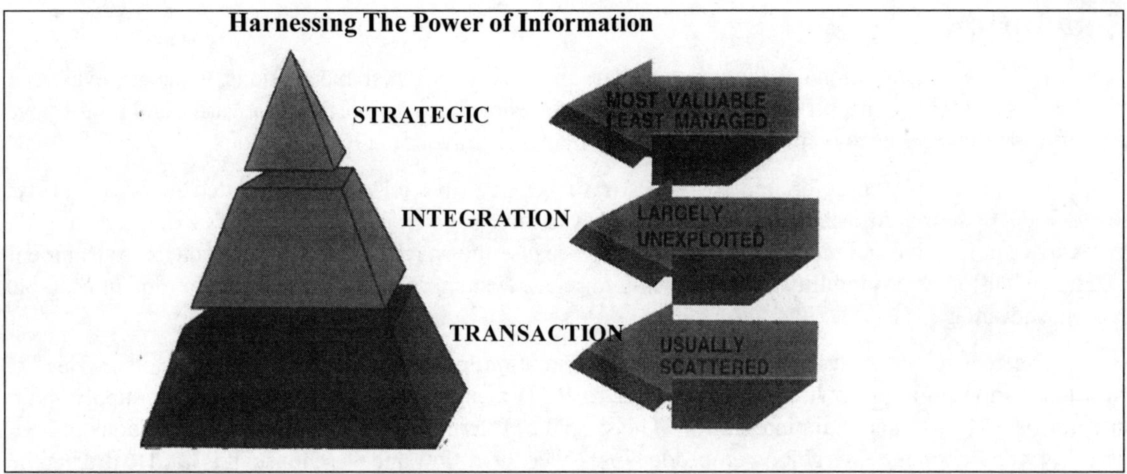

ISME Needs of small Enterprises

There is a greater need for information integration in small and medium sized organisations which lack the money power and business resilience of large enterprises. The need of the hour is to provide micro ERPs i.e., near ERP capabilities build into a product and sold at an affordable price, including implementation.

Ctitcria for selection

Small and medium enterprises should look for and demand that they get a software package which meets the following criteria:

Affordable

Attractive prices, including implementation support.

Domain knowledge of suppliers

It is important that the software developer or supplier knows your industry and is willing to implement the softwarc for you. If you are a Manufacturing enterprise, buy the software from people who have the experience in manufacturing industries.

What Next?

ERP systems are platform architecture, RDBMS technology and GUI capabilities. Due to the evolution background, initially ERP had its place only in manufacuring organisations. Today it has universal application, irrespective of nature and scope of the business.

Today, the thrust is towards achieving business objectives through optimum utilisation of resources backed by BPR and new IT technologies as emblem. The system which offers managerial capabilities to correlate appropriate technologies to business processes according to changing demands is the key for enterprise success. In this context, it may be appropriate to refer such system as Enterprise-wide Resource Management System or ERMS.

Today's market basically offers enterprise application systems following two different approaches. One is the software solutions covering core common business processes which is easily customisable by building additional features according to customer requirements. The other is application package, which requires extensive parameterisation for customisation.

Conclusion

The smart organisation's today can anticipate and exceed customer expectations, which are evaluated on the basis of quality, time, service, availability and efficiency. The one tool that innovative and progressive organisations have come to increasingly depend on in this endeavour is : ERP solutions.

The waves of change brought by ERPs have begun to be. felt and appreciated by organisations world-wide. Customer focused applications and analysis have begun moving from theory to implementation by creative, innovative and motivated organisations because they have realised that in today's environment measuring customer profitability and organising to retain customers provide a tremendous and unbeatable strategic advantage.

The tremendous strides in technology make the solutions progressively cheaper and customer-friendly. New innovations have given rise to terms such as EERP (Extended ERP), and operations like supply chain integration and customer chain integration. The spread of Internet has made its own contributions to ERP whereby we speak of the 3Ws getting embedded in its web, workflow and warehouse. It is hard to predict the possibilities; but one could easily say that they are immense.

Key Capabilities from my SAP ERP Suite

Self-service *Provides two types of self-services* • Enable employees manage tasks like travel management, purchasing, training etc. • Manager self-services for budgeting (planning, monitoring), and personnel responsibility (recruitment, reviews, compensation planning.) **Analytics** *Provides comprehensive analytic capabilities combined with forecasting and reporting tools* • Strategic enterprise management (performance measurement, business planning for each unit) • Financial analytics (define financial targets, monitor costs and revenue during execution) • Operational analytics (compilation of detailed operations reports) • Workforce analytics (design, implement and monitor workforce optimization activities) **Human Capital Management** *Spans four areas to maximize workforce profitability* • Employee lifecycle management (applicant tracking process, worldwide recruiting, e-learning) • Employee transaction management (complex payroll processes, tracking, monitoring, record-keeping, and time-data evaluation) • Service delivery (self-service capabilities, collaborative relationships via portals, help desk etc.) • Workforce deployment (create, monitor and analyze project-based teams.)	**Financial Management** *Provides control corporate finance functions* • Financial and management accounting (financial reporting by user groups, transactions for country-specific statutory purposes) • Financial supply chain management (credit management, invoicing, cash management) **Operations** *Spans value generation and support activities* • Procurement • Inventory and warehouse management • Manufacturing • Transportation • Sales order management • Customer service • Support activities (project management, quality management and enterprise asset management) **Corporate Services** *Optimizes centralized and decentralized services* • Travel management (expense statements, new reports and expense entry) • Incentive and commissions management (sales and brokerage commissions, profit sharing and bonuses) • Real-estate management (contract management, service charge settlement, contract renewal) • Environment, health & safety (compliance with government regulations)

Case Study : Asian Paints

Asian Paints operates manufacturing facilities in 22 countries around the world, and is one of the largest paint companies in nine overseas markets. The subsidiaries that were started by Asian Paints — and also acquired — used different systems and solutions, leading to issues such as high IT administrative costs and duplicated efforts in reporting. The company's executives saw a critical need to standardise operations in its international markets. With this objective in mind, the company chose the Microsoft® Business Solutions Navision® software, now called Microsoft Dynamics NAV.

Employees spent too much time in populating Microsoft Excel sheets and updating numbers instead of focusing on the business. This led to frustrations, long hours and wasted time. This is where Aashish Kshetry, Chief Information Officer, Asian Paints stepped in..... He realised the key to successfully plugging the gaps would have to come from the IT division of the company.

Solution

The key objectives in deploying the business solution were to:

- Create a stable transaction system across all subsidiaries that would last at least seven to 10 years.
- Implement a solution that had built-in international modules on taxation and multilingual capabilities to support its offices in 22 countries.

Additionally, Microsoft Dynamics NAV offered a hub-and-spoke model which was ideal for Asian Paints. The hub-and-spoke concept refers to a parent or holding company that uses one business software system (the hub), which is integrated with the systems used by its individual subsidiaries or divisions (the spokes).

Benefits

"Our key objective was to standardise technology platforms and business processes across subsidiaries and regions. Microsoft Dynamics NAV has helped us achieve this objective quickly, efficiently, and cost effectively " comments Aashish Kshetry, Systems Development Manager at Asian Paints.

- Standardised technology platform reduces IT administration.
- Faster, quicker, improved data flow to parent company and regional teams.
- Removes the need for double reporting.
- Multilingual software integrates companies around the above.

Pooja Forge Limited

Business Situation

Pooja Forge Limited manufactures a wide array of precision cold-forged high tensile fasteners and components of various grades of carbon, alloy, and stainless steel for automobile, electronics, and construction industries. The key issue across the company was the lack of control because of the lack of available information, be it on the shop floor or in the financial group.

Solution

Trident Information Systems, a Microsoft® Certified Partner implemented Microsoft@ Business Solutions Navision® software, now called Microsoft Dynamics NAVTM, to deliver greater visibility into business activities through improved access to information.

Benefits

Though the new system has been in use since July 2005, Pooja Forge has already seen some significant benefits. Better access to necessary data has led to better control over production and finances. And most importantly, it can track production through the supply chain which helps maintain high product quality and reduces inventory carrying costs.

- Better product quality achieved
- Financial control improves cash flow
- Easy to track inventory
- Control and visibility over shop floor
- Data backup made easy
- Easily generated reports

✹ ✹ ✹

Your competitiveness is driven by those mega-tonne monsters on the highways. And by the science of logistics, which gets those trucks on the road — and your products to the shops, your components to the plants, and your services to your customer.

25

LOGISTICS OF ENTREPRENEURSHIP

Changes encompass technology, government policy, product life cycles, and manufacturer retailer relationships. It is vital that the survival of an organisation depends largely on its capability to anticipate and prepare for change rather then just react to it.

Global trade is growing more streamlined, even as the networks become more and more complex. Today global sourcing, shared technology and changing distribution processes are more a norm than an exception, and this has led to a more holistic approach to logistics management with outsourcing of logistics requirements that further leads to substantial cost reductions.

As the volume of cargo grows, so does the demand for integrated logistics solutions and efficient, costeffective options. These requirements have thrown open countless opportunities for companies that are engaged in the business of providing logistic services.

Competition and a rapidly changing environment have brought at number of new factors into play. Changes encompass technology, govemment policy, product life cycles, and manufacturer-retailer relationships. It is vital that the survival of an organisation depends largely on its capability to anticipate and prepare for change rather than just react to it. Reactive organisations and proactive organisations are distinguished as tactics and strategy are. Many organisations consider logistics as merely the management of activities related to finished goods distribution. This view however does not take into account the materials management role of logistics which deals with the inward flow of raw materials, manufactured parts, packaging material etc. It is the combination of materials management at one end, and the distribution of finished goods at the other, which comprise logistics and logistics management. And complementing this physical flow is the two-way flow of information.

Organisations have now realised that logistics is more than just another operational variable. It manages the interrelationship of all the factors which affect the flow of information and goods which begins when the customer decides to place an order and ends when the order is delivered and the payment made. This means that priorities have to be decided and trade-offs made.

The logistics manager plays a crucial role in today's organisation, and ought to be involved in strategy formulation. He is the person who is involved in every stage of the flow of information and materials from conception to consumption. He is therefore best equipped to determine the organisation's capacity to respond to expectations.

Strategic planning calls upon management to strike a balance between long-term goals and short-term customer requirements. Three vital components of strategic planning are vision statements (what the organisation stands for), aims (directions it wants to go in), and objectives (specific quantified targets). While aims are a qualitative aspect, objectives are quantitative. Therefore it will not suffice to merely state that a company wants to increase its sales. This is an aim and has to be quantified in order to be considered an objective. So specifying that sales have to be increased by 5 per cent within six months makes it an objective.

After aims and objectives are established, operational plans can be formulated. These plans include procedures for implementation, control and evaluation. Whether plans are a success or a failure depends on the logistics manager.

A strategic plan is not an end in itself. It enables an organisation to respond to changes in the surrounding environment, whether these changes are expected or not. What are the environments that affect an organisation? Organisations are directly affected by five environments: the market, government, suppliers of materials and services, the labour market and the finance market. Four other environments that indirectly or directly affect the organisation are the economy, the community, the nation's resource base, and the world environment.

In order to make the adoption of strategic thinking and acting a way of functioning throughout the organisation, there are certain guidelines that can be adopted.

– Establishing a disciplined framework for undertakings, the planning process.

– Tying up this framework with a clearcut marketing intelligence function.

– Converting plans into strategic behaviour.

When an organisation decides to launch into a strategic framework it has to first analyse the underlying social forces and trends in the external environment. With changes in the external environment taking place at an increasing rate, organisations must necessarily take stock of these changes because of their growing interaction with the external environments.

Strategic planning is an approach that tries to answer four questions: Where are we now?

Where do we want to be?

How do we get there?

How do we know when we have arrived?

Having a plan does not mean the organisation will face no problems in the future. Since the environment is constantly changing, how does the organisation cope?

A strategic plan is not watertight. It is adaptable to the incessant changes in the environment. It is this ability which is termed 'issue management.'

An issue is a condition or a pressure which affects an organisation's performance, aims or future. Whatever the perceived nature or gravity of the issue, a strategic response is required. Issue management is a focused way of defining those issues to be addressed through the strategic planning process. Thus it is the trigger for actions and responses rather than hasty reactions.

It is important to get every level of the organisation sensitive to the changes in the internal and external environments. If different areas of the organisation are entrusted with monitoring the environment, it will enhance the overall commitment to the strategic process.

An issue usually arises with litter or no warning. Dealing with then must be in keeping with the corporal plan. Senior management is best suited to deal with issues and must be kept informed. A task force senior management should be responsible for analysing issues. Senior management is chosen because it is in the best position to gauge the significance and potential impact of an issue, and senior management can actually implement action rather than just recommend it.

Depending on the potential impact of an issue and the immediacy of it, issues can be prioritised and resource allocated accordingly. In this way resources are not wasted, particulary if they are scarce.

Successful issue management comprises an in-house system which can respond to the strength and complexity of emerging issues, and action that is appropriate to the resources available to the organisation.

Issue management has a two-fold benefit in that orients the organisation to respond to changes in the environment, and it makes the response a team effort.

Within the framework of strategic planning, scanning and issue management are very vital. The role of logistics is growing to be recognised as crucial for survival in an environment that is constantly changing, and logistics managers must rely on strategy if they are to cope with the challenges that emerge.

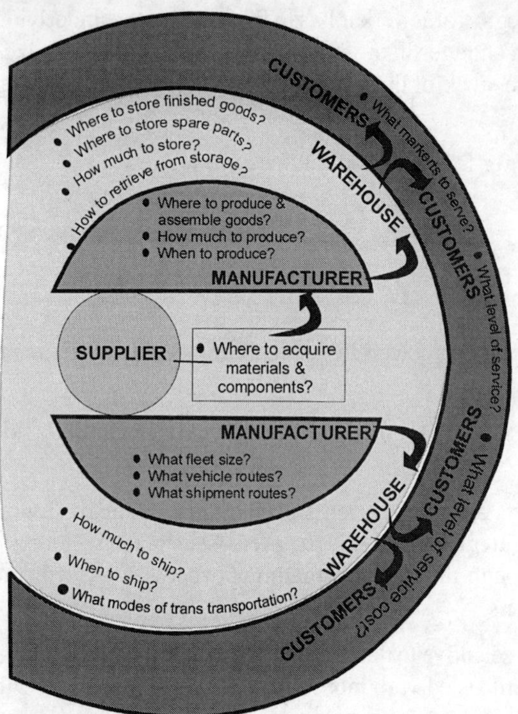

Fig. 25.1: Logistics as Strategy

Logistics will not operate on operational efficiency, but will also demand a strategy aligned to once's business objectives.

Strategic logistics will look beyond its own parish to check for optimisation at the other nodes on your value chain. After all, with linkages to most of the other activities in your company, logistics is more likely to deliver better results if it can operate in those areas as well. The involvements, usually, tactical, being the result of on-the-spot innovations rather than of established principles. The only rule: do what it takes.

Laws of Logistics:

(1) Hone your operations
(2) Channel your resources
(3) Serve the end user
(4) Attack the inventories
(5) Apply tactical solutions

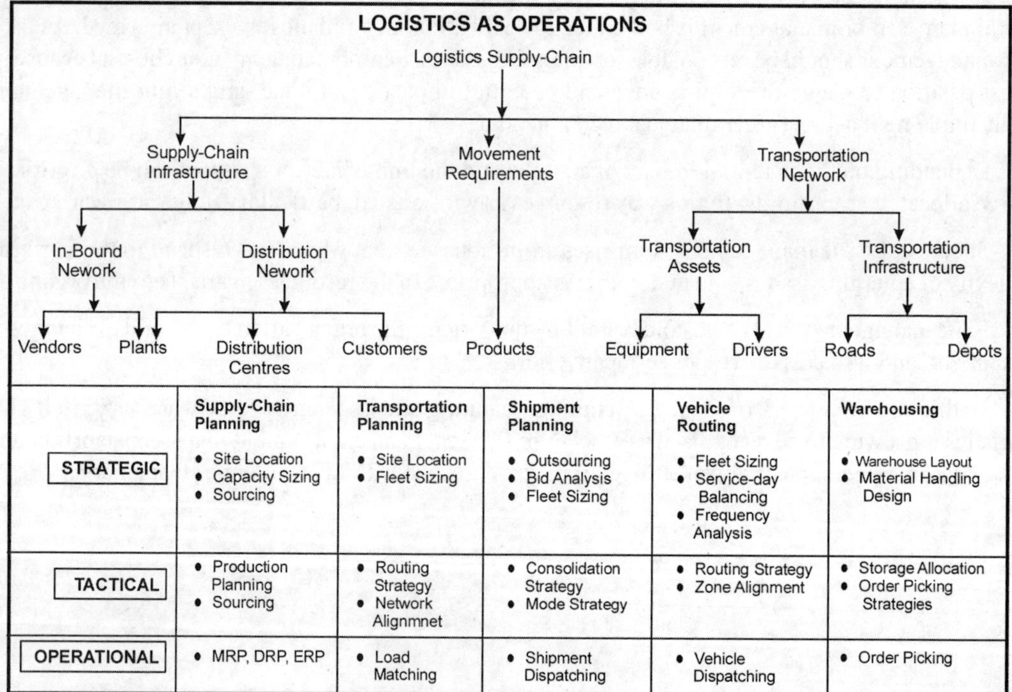

	Supply-Chain Planning	Transportation Planning	Shipment Planning	Vehicle Routing	Warehousing
STRATEGIC	• Site Location • Capacity Sizing • Sourcing	• Site Location • Fleet Sizing	• Outsourcing • Bid Analysis • Fleet Sizing	• Fleet Sizing • Service-day Balancing • Frequency Analysis	• Warehouse Layout • Material Handling Design
TACTICAL	• Production Planning • Sourcing	• Routing Strategy • Network Alignmnet	• Consolidation Strategy • Mode Strategy	• Routing Strategy • Zone Alignment	• Storage Allocation • Order Picking Strategies
OPERATIONAL	• MRP, DRP, ERP	• Load Matching	• Shipment Dispatching	• Vehicle Dispatching	• Order Picking

Fig. 25.2: Logistics as Operations

❋ ❋ ❋

26

NETWORKING

Networking — A Giant Leap towards Global Competitiveness

One of the top-of-mind concerns in the small and medium enterprises is the lack of in-house expertise and hence the need to have a dedicated IT(MIS) department once the computers are networked which adds significantly to the cost of running the small business organisation.

More than 2/3rd of world-wide Small and Medium Business offices today have islands of automation with productivity applications such as Finance/Acounting/lnventory management running on these computers. Given that there are no IT department/personnel manning these computers, we need to examine how networking of these computers help organisations become more productive keeping the simplicity intact at the same time. Let us examine the benefits of networking computers in today's small and medium business office and the steps involved in achieving the same.

First of all, why network? How does getting connected benefit me as a small office? These arc the questions, which need answer from business perspective. Some important reasons are improving co-ordination and communication between departments which help in improving overall productivity. Charles River

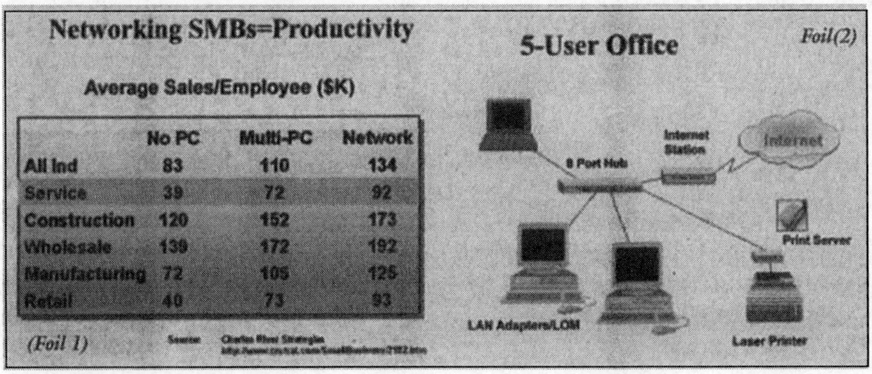

Networking SMBs=Productivity

Average Sales/Employee ($K)

	No PC	Multi-PC	Network
All Ind	83	110	134
Service	39	72	92
Construction	120	152	173
Wholesale	139	172	192
Manufacturing	72	105	125
Retail	40	73	93

(Foil 1)

5-User Office *Foil(2)*

Internet Station
Internet
8 Port Hub
Print Server
LAN Adapters/LOM
Laser Printer

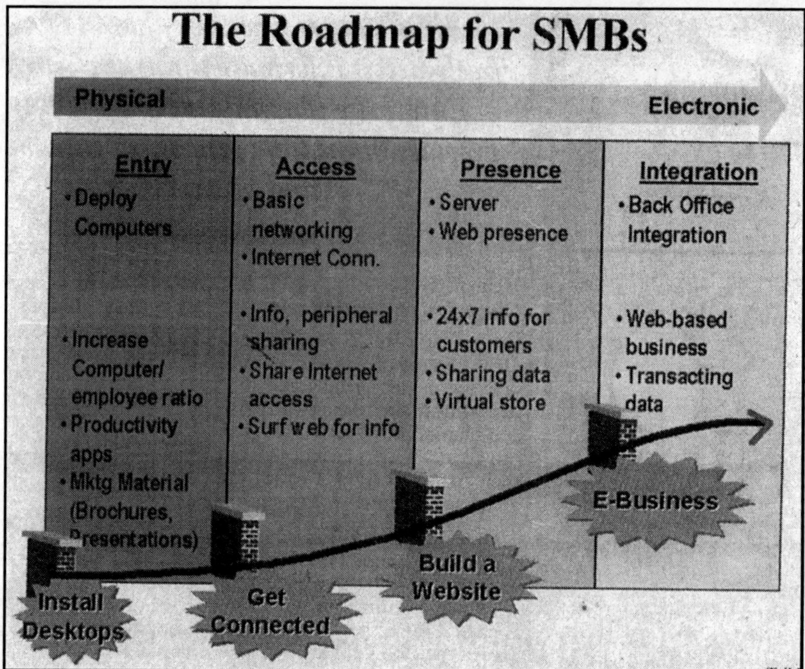

Strategies, a renowned research firm in US conducted a study on the productivity per employee of segments of organisations with stand-alone computers versus computers, which are networked. The interesting outcome is that the organisations which are networked have 21% more average productivity per employee when compared with small and medium organisations with stand-alone PCs. This is a significant business advantage to go for. (Foil 1)

One of the top-of-mind concerns in the small and medium enterprises is the lack of in-house expertise and hence the need to have a dedicated IT(MIS) department once the computers are networked which adds significantly to the cost of running the small business organisation. This brings about the need for simple, easy-to install and use networking products for small and medium business. With breathtaking advancements in silicon technology, companies are now offering networking building blocks which are true plug-and-play devices and very costffective. Features such as 10/100 MbPS LAN on Motherboard (LOM) and 10/100 MbPS ethernet cards are standard in computers today.

What to look for in network building blocks?

- *True plug-and-play features for easy . installation and maintenance*
- *Ability to start from networking connections for as low as five-eight nodes*
- *Ability to grow with the organisation and number of networked users by stacking and cascading*
- *Compactness and ruggedness*
- *Fewer controls for the user to operate*
- *10/100 MbPS fast-ethernet connectivity for visual computing*
- *Sharing of networking resources such as printers, peripherals using sharing devices.*
- *Connectivity to Internet for multiple users using Internet stations*

Let us take a look at how a five user computer net-work would look like

With the hubs and internet stations from companies spccifically meant for small and medium business, it is comparatively easy and very cost effective to build networks and grow the network with the organisation. Internet connections to all users in the network with dialup connection on ordinary telephone line are easy using Internet station and one ISP connection. Current Desktop Operating Systems such as Windows 95 support such networks. This helps the staff surf the net for more info on products and use e-mail as means of business communication between organisations. Expensive device such as Laser Printer can be shared as a resource by the networked users using print server, which is again a highly cost-effective solution than deploying expensive, network-ready printers.

Starting from scratch, the entire network with five Pentium® II based systems, 100 MbPS network, Laser printer with print server, E-mail, Internet access and basic Finance and accounting applications, MS Access Database, DTP software, would cost in the range of Rs. 6.0 Lakhs.

Let us now take a look at how the network would look like with scaling to 20-nodes. *(Foil 3)*

As you can see, the number of users are high and hence it is desirable to have a server which can perform the function of file/ print sharing for the network users and provide reliability, and better availability of data. The networking operating system options are Microsoft SBS(Small Busincss Server) and Novell Intranet ware. Servers also help in hosting the company website, to provide information on the web for prornotional/marketing purposes and the related software is typically bundled in the NOS (Networking O/S). This website needs to be very visual for attracting customers, online for 24 hours-a-day, seven days a week as the SMBs (Small and Medium Business) are becoming global in operations.

After networking the departments and having Company's website, what next? How does SMB network its branch offices and other locations with customers and suppliers? Is there an opportunity that can be reaped at this stage for SMBs to be having a strategic business advantage? The answer to all these questions look to be E-Business, which is fast emerging as a strategic and necessary business tool. Simply put, E-businсss is using the Internet for remaking the conventional business interactions across the Supplier Business-Customer value chain. This will result in enhancement of computing technology and Internet to connect businesses directly to key constituents' employees, customers and suppliers. *(Foil 4)*

The benefits are multifold in this approach as entering into E-business clearly enables tighter interaction of the organisation with customers, suppliers and employees as well as penetrate new markets by doing business on the internet.

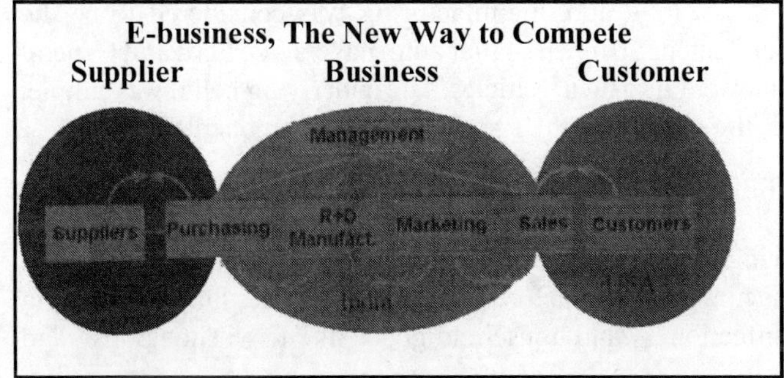

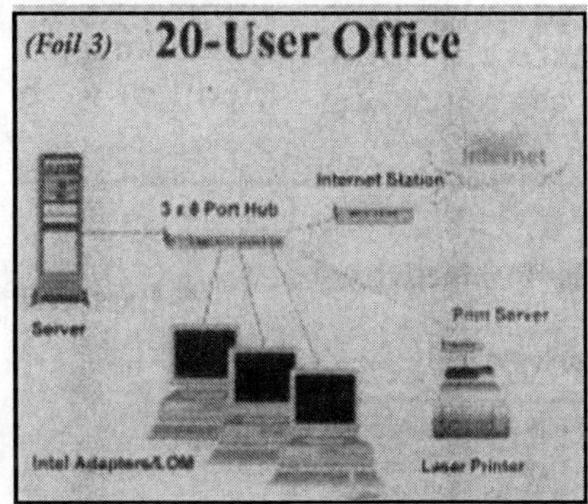

A number of Indian SMBs are already conducting business on the internet and making inroads into newer markets and this is clearly a huge business opportunity for Indian SMBs to leapfrog to 21century.

The E-business is proven to reduce cost of sales, enhance productivity further and aid SMBs to reach out to newer markets. This roadmap to E-busincss is simple once the organisation is networked and having Internet presence. *(Foil 5)*

In a nutshell Indian SMBs now have a unique opportunity to compete in a global economy by deploying networking technology steps leading to E-business which are easy-to-install and use, easy to grow with the organisation and very cost effective.

The responsibility lies with the SMB decision makers to react quickly and reap the benefits falling which our SMBs are likely to become less competitive and profitable in the global, liberalised economic scenario.

E-manufacturing: Not Science Fiction

The World Wide Web (www) enabled factory will be the marketer's dream and the production manager's nightmare. Tomorrow, customers won't surf a company's site just for information or even order placement. They will actually be custom-building online their next car, computer, music system, or even home furniture. In fact, in a truly networked environment, the customer will be able to bid for the best bargains from the manufacturer's vendors, part-cutting into the company's profit margins.

To be able to manufacture to thousands of different orders and still meet the quality and delivery deadlines, the production man will have to create a wired factory. ERP would be a bare minimum, but it must be layered on top of the web so that remote customer orders automatically translate into partpurchase orders (also trigger a job order) at the concerned vendors. To do so, the wired factory will probably rely an internet devices that come with pre-loaded and management-approved links to websites, including those of suppliers, dealers, and associates. Remotely-hosted software programs will keep track of operations within and outside the factory, reducing cost, increasing compatibility, and reducing time-to-market.

Manufacturing: Network Efficiencies

Buzzword for tomorrow: collaborative manufacturing. Tomorrow's winning product will be designed, developed, and manufactured across networked units.

If boardrooms are where corporate strategies are conceived, then it's the shopfloor where they are hammered, chiselled, and assembled to shape. Not long ago, manufacturing was considered to be the single-most important activity that a company performed, So much so that auto makers like Ford and General Motors chose to self-make all the components that went into their vehicles. The underlying belief was simple: if you don't make it, you can't control the price, the quality, or the supply of those components.

But trying to do everything yourself, manufacturers have now realised, is not just expensive, but also inefficient. In fact, growing consolidation in vendor base and increasing parity in terms of technology are forcing companles to question their manufacturing strategies. The issue is not so much of how and where to make, as whether to make or outsource. And it is not just manufacture-intensive industries that are debating the issue. For instance, Sara Leewhich sells confectionery and household goods like Kiwi shoe polish and

Brylcreem-announced two years ago that it would divest all its manufacturing operations. Instead, it would focus solely on marketing and brand-building.

In the near future, most big car makers — Ford, General Motors, DaimlerChrysler, and Toyota — and even pharmaceutical companies will increasingly want to take the Sara Lee route. The drivers of change are, of course, consumers. Besieged by competition and diversity of global consumer preferences, companies are discovering that there's more value-addition in product development, brand management and marketing than in manufacturing. From mass production, the shift will be to mass customisation.

So, does all that mean the end of manufacturing? Hardly. If anything, manufacturing as a function will become even more critical. Global competition, demanding consumers, changing value equations, fragmented and niche markets will put further pressure on shop-floor efficiency and flexibility. That, in turn, would usher in an era of collaborative manufacturing: an era where "spot markets" or product manufacturing will emerge. Therefore, instead of relying on its vendor network, an OEM could source a component from the most competitive supplier. So, if your bearings supplier ditches you, and you have 2,000 cars that need to be shipped out in two days, no problem. Call the bearings manufacturer in Mumbai who'll have the requisite numbers sent to your factory ASAP.

But for all that to happen, the factory of today will have to virtually reinvent itself.

Lean and Agile

The modern economy owes much to the system of mass production first popularised by Henry Ford. To this day, machines are built to a very specific brief: to, say, cut or stamp continuously. But the machines of future will be designed to perform differently. The sheer variety of products, a smaller but a more dispersed customer base, shorter delivery lead times, and just-intime supply would mean that instead of churning out the same product in three shifts, the machine would need to make five or six different products a day. For example, a body press shop would need to make small cars (of different colours each) in the morning, sedans (with customised interiors) in the afternoon, and may be sports vehicles in the evening — all without compromising on the quality and economy. Similarly, a paint shop would need systems that allow mass customisation.

The machines would also need a higher degree of intelligence so that human failure (the biggest reason for poor quality) can be minimised. In the factory of the future, almost all work will be done by artificial intelligence (robotic systems) and the only human being present will be the supervisor.

Yet, that kind of a scenario in India (except in hitech industries) may not happen at all. Since skilled labour is cheap and aplenty, companies would want to avoid low-end automation like using a robotic arm to load a component onto the machine. Instead, automation would be used in high precision jobs.

Tiered, but Integrated

The most important raw material that flows through an organisation's value chain is not goods, but information. Information about market demand, supplies, production schedules, bottlenecks, delivery, and cost. Leveraging that information ensures production of parts that meet the customer specifications in terms of model, quantity, and delivery schedules. Typically, such a seamless integration of information flow does not happen in real life because the number of participants in the supply-chain are several and each one of them uses different IT systems.

To survive, the wired factory of tomorrow will need complete connectivity *(See e-Manufacturing. Not Science Fiction).* The Original Equipment Manufacturer's (OEM) shift from production to mere assembly will push cost and quality pressures further upstream. Instead of supplying discrete parts, the vendors would need to send in fully built up modules, say, the entire chassis, wheel and brake assembly. To be able to meet the OEM's quality, cost, and delivery targets, the vendors will need to work closely and crossshare capabilities. Quality systems will have to become more robust and product development capabilities will need to be enhanced. In fact, in more ways than one, the shopfloor of tomorrow will have to mirror the imperative of the corner-room.

✱ ✱ ✱

27

SUCCESS STRATEGY

Although, every success strategy is different, one hasto find the approach that works for him. But almost all successful people share more than just a few of these characteristics. The characteristics into a success strategy are:

THE TO-DO LIST

- Take a do it now hustle approach to life.
- Have a character base that fosters long-term success,
- Evaluate risks, and take the best ones.
- Be a time miser,
- Communicate effectively, verbally and non-verbally.
- Have a thick skin.
- Be an optimist, and a good finder.
- Learn to be obedient so that you learn to lead others. Know that courage upholds all other qualities.
- Be intolerant of immoral behaviour.
- Develop a sense of humour.
- Form winning habit.

The successful people without exception ambitiously dissatisfied with the satus quo. They have specific objectives in mind, get busy seeking them, and work hard. *They hustle*.

Another factor is *character*. Character is the ability to carry out a good resolution long after the excitement of the moment has passed.

Risk-taking is yet another feature of success. One has to evaluate risks, and take the best ones.

One has to use *time* appropriately, productively. More effective work-habits to realise goods yield maximum benefits from their time.

Effective *communication* does make a difference and influence in the process.

The way the successful ones handle crificism is a big part of their success. Cultivate *a thick skin.* One need to incorporete *obedience* into their success strategy. Learn to obey before leading.

Courage is yet another characteristic of success. *Courage* uphold all other traits.

Intolerance is part of a workable success strategy. Be intolerant of immoral, unethical or illegal behaviour or event.

Persons with a good sense of humour don't take themselves overly seriously. Develop a *sense of humour.*

Winning hebits are the best friends in business. Timeliness, commitment, courteous, conscientious, promptness and going the extra mile are all habits that lead to success. Good habits must be grabbed firmly and with a strong commitment.

Now, take the success strategy to find audit out the varience of success.

THE SUCCESS STRATEGY AUDIT

Does your success strategy have the right mix? Or is it too feckless to succeed? Take our quiz to find out.

(1) Do you appreciate that where you are is a part of the process of getting where you want to be? Yes No

(2) Do you have the ability to carry out a good resolution long after the initial excitement has passed? Yes No

(3) Can you put aside apprehensions of rejection and failure, and take risks to achieve a higher goal? Yes No

(4) Do you make and use to do lists, and use your time to accomplish your goals in an efficient manner? Yes No

(5) Do you ensure that your body language doesn't contradict what you convey, verbally or in writing? Yes No

(6) Have you developed a thick skin to deal with the barbs that will, inevitably, come your way? Yes No

(7) Do you recognise that obedience is one of the first principles of leadership? Yes No

(8) Do you realise that you should be intolerant of certain things even while having an open mind? Yes No

(9) Are you a pleasant, optimistic person, who usually leaves a positive impact on others? Yes No

(10) Do you have good work habits, such as arriving at work and completing assignments on time? Yes No

THE SCORE

Give yourself 10 points for every Yes, and 0 for every No.

TOTAL [ ]

THE RATING

0–30	You would do well to give serious thought to your success strategy.
40–70	There are some vital ingredients you need to add to your success strategy.
80–100	Cheers! You have all it takes to make a success of yourself.

SUCCESS STORIES

Himatsinga Siede Ltd

Business Focus

100% Export of Silk to Germany, Italy and other European countries.

Vital Statistics

Rs. 60 crores turnover, 400 employees, ISO 90002 certified production and export unit. One of the top five exporters for Silk production from India.

Challenge

As a part of its ISO 9002 quality certification programme which was essential for Himatsinga to bag a number of prestigious orders from highly quality European market, the organisation automated the entire organisation. This called in for implementing a system that needed to be stable, robust and fault tolerant as their International clients demands for quality matched with their expectation for timely deliveries.

Solution

Every single operation from material procurement, design, planning, production, marketing, accounting, and even administration was computerised. The company went in for a network consisting of 60 HP Vectra Intel Pentium based PC running on Microsoft AEs popular windows 95 operating system. The network was supported by two HP NerServers in the factory taking care of the Designs and Production departments. The power scalability and high fault-tolerance of the Servers running on Microsoft Windows NT operating system helps the design and production departments to deliver high quality products in time.

In the corporate office all accounting, documentation and administration work are done on a separate Windows NT based network running on an HP Netserver with an Intel Pentium based Pentium processor. Using Microsoft Exchange server all inter office commuications are being implemented through E Mail which has cut down communication bills notably. Understanding that speed and robustness of the network is very important to the organisation Aes growth the MIS department redesigned the network with every desktop having a Fast Ethernet adapter connected through three Fast Ethernet hubs which are supported on the backbone through two Fast Ethernet switches.

Result

Himatsingka Siede group improved its productivity by cutting down excess consumption of raw products for production of garments. The design department with help of the fast Intel based PCs and Nedgraphics software managed to produce faster designs which in turn helped the production cut down the time needed for production. As information was available at hand management was able to take decisions faster. The communication costs came down by twenty per cent because of the e-mail system based on Microsoft exchange.

Quote

"I would not be exaggerating if I say that the backbone of our silk exports is the network of computers used in our factory and offices." Mohan Rao, President.

Yokogawa Bluestar

Business Focus

Industrial Process Automation

Vital Statistics

Rs. 150 crore company

8 branch offices

Challenge

An Indo Japanese venture Yokogawa Bluestar has 8 branch sales offices all over India and has its head office, factory and a software development center in Bangalore. Industrial process automation being a high tech area different offices, factory and the parent company in Tokyo had to be in constant touch with each other. The traditional ways of communications like faxes, telephone calls and courier were employed. The management in September 1997 felt a need to cut down communication costs without bringing down the productivity of the organisation. To cut down one crore rupees plus annual communications costs the management decided to implement an E-mail based communication system.

Solution

All the 11 offices in India were connected through VSNL (Videsh Sanchar Nigam Ltd.) E-mail service by November 1997. In the first phase of E-mail; deployment roughly 170 employes within the organisation were provided with their own E-mail addresses and were encouraged to use E-mail instead of faxes or lengthy telephone calls. Every office had a dedicated E-mail server based on a Intel Pentium processor based PC. The remote login software used by the servers updated the mail boxes of every employee every thirty minutes. All documentation including confidential financial data, technical diagrams ctc. which were previously couriered between offices were also send through E-mail.

Results

In the first four months starting from November 1997, the communication cost came down by more than 25%. The finance and accounting department estimates the money saved to be to the rune of twenty lakhs. As the total investment in to the E-mail system including the hardware, VSNL charges and other miscellaneous cost for all the offices put together was less than eight lakhs there has been a 100% return of investment within the first phase. The management estimates that they will be able to cut down the communication costs fifty percent once every employee starts using the E-mail.

Quote

"Usage of e-mail within the organisation has not only cut down our communication expenses, but also have boosted our productivity considerably." — Lekshmy Sekhar, Deputy Manager, Finance.

✱ ✱ ✱

28

Technology — The Competitive Weapon

Viewed as the systematic organisation of know-how, technique and production methods adopted in the manufacture of products and use of processes, Technology is one of the intangible factors in a production system, an essential input as important as manpower or financial resources — a Competitive Weapon. It is a fact well accepted that measures directed at stimulating industrial development need to consider not only locational and financial factors but also technical factors impacting on the viability of projects assisted. This is necessary as all initiatives directed under the umbrella of technology and innovation also increase the innovative capacity and productivity of industrial firms at all levels. Yet, transfer of technology alone is not sufficient to increase the level of productivity. What is equally important is the building up of Technical Capacity — the entrepreneur's intrinsic knowledge and skill to absorb and understand new technologies. This entails the creation of a 'Technological Environment' which involves continuous and sustainable efforts at promotion of technological research and innovations, perception of the need for technological change, creation of an awareness of the availability of new technologies through information, transfer of technology, evaluation of appropriate technologies and finally its selection, acquisition, adoption and implementation.

Issues Facing Small Enterprises Today

The opening of the Indian economy has led to the entry of superior, technologically more advanced products into the domestic market. This is accompanied by the dismantling of global trade barriers, offering ample opportunities for Indian industries to enter the newly emerging global markets. The SSIs in India are today confronted with the dual challenge of competing on the home front with internationally recognised brands and increased pressure of competition from technologically superior and environment friendly products in the international market. No longer can they rely on their low-cost low-overheads production strategies, as the market is gradually shifting from price competitiveness to quality competitiveness. Stringent environmental laws are likely to be enforced with greater vigil in the coming years. It is here that the crucial role of appropriate technology gains importance. Technological progress in communication, computers, robotics and other fields offers significant opportunities to SSIs. Yet the application of new technologies in small enterprises is not without constraints. Shortage of skilled workers (underdevelopment of technical capacity), high cost and complexity of new technology, inaccessibility to information sources coupled with limited access to training, are some of the dampers to the acquisition of appropriate technology. A structured policy framework has to be evolved for channelising technology flows into the small-scale sector, but the option for adopting a superior technology is best left to the small enterprises themselves, though it needs to be backed up with adequate institutional support.

The Potentiality of Small Enterprises

It is paradoxical that while technological obsolescence is one of the major threats faced by small firms in the emerging global economy, it is the small enterprises which have shown a greater potential to upgrade technology due to their inherent qualities of flexibility and adaptability. Flexible manufacturing processes

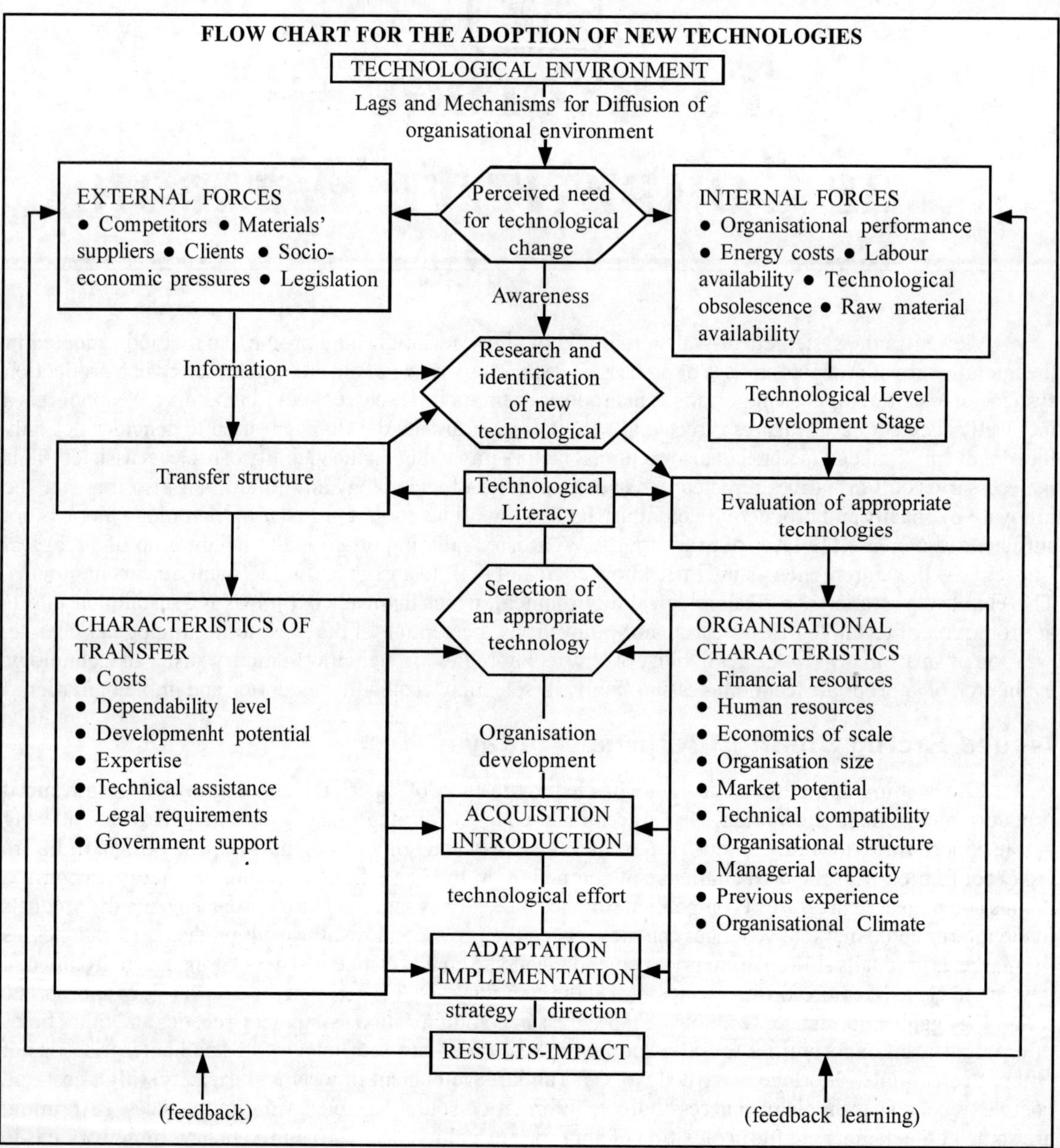

enable small firms to quickly switch over to new markets and diversify into differentiated products with state-of-the-art manufacturing processes. Again upgradation of locally developed technologies and bleding them with imported technologies is easier. Thus both 'product innovation' and 'process innovation' is simultaneously and quickly feasible for SSIs. The creation of the complete 'Technological Environment', can make technical progress sustainable through *(i)* the invention and innovation of technological equipment (the hardware) and *(ii)* develooment of human resources (the software). While both are equally important the latter is of greater relevance to SSIs.

Manpower in small and tiny enterprises is better placed for development of special skills either on its own or through collaborations with research institutions or through linkages with large enterprises as trainces. Transfer of knowledge between universities/research institutions and small firms could take place through consultancy, contract activities, exchange of students as trainees, etc. All this helps to increase the receptiveness of small enterprises to transfer of technology and builds up the necessary technical capacity which must precede diffusion and adoption of new technology.

Transfer of Technology — International Experience

As seen in the last issue the creation of a complete "Technological Environment" must precede the diffusion and adoption of new technology. Though the ultimate option for selection and adoption of new or upgraded technology remains largely with the enterprises themselves, the creation of the necessary infrastructure for the transfer, acquisition and adoption of new technologies still remains in the hands of the governing authorities. Broadly the SSIs have three options for acquiring and adopting modern technology. *(i)* Transfer of technology from abroad *(ii)* Adaptation and modification of imported technology and *(iii)* Innovation and development of locally suited technology.

Transfer of Imported Technology

An upgraded technology in the production process can be transferred from an advanced country to industries (particularly SSIs) in the developing regions through intergovernmental agreements or through non-governmental or nodal agencies or as part of technical collaboration or joint ventures with Multinational Corporations. This is considered the simplest and hence more conducive to prevailing conditions of unskilled manpower and lack of infrastructure in the developing countries.

Adaptation and Modification of Imported Technology

While complete transfer of technology is said to discourage innovations, the localization of imported technology is the method that clubs transfer with innovations. This mode of technology transfer is particularly important to SSIs as it is not only less costly than imported technology but also because it sharpens the entrepreneurial ability to innovate.

Innovation and Development of Technology

Innovations can be for both the 'process' or the 'product.' The classic example of success of traditional industries through innovation is the Italian 'Industrial District' concept, which concentrates on a whole production cycle in a given area, creating an environment which stimulates innovation and change.

Access to Capital — A Major Constraint

One of the most important constraints of technology upgradation among small enterprises is the lack of capital. In many countries, governments have entered into arrangements with UNDP and other donors like Development Banks and Bilateral Donors to address the issue of capital. What is equally important is the creation of an atmosphere wherein the small enterprises are not discriminated against in terms of cost of capital and ease of access. Venture capital companies are best suited for financing new innovative and rapidly growing small companies. These companies offer a complete package of financial and non-financial services which include development of innovative business ideas — often high technology based -into a product or service, value addition to the company by active participation and higher risks assumption with the expectations of higher rewards. In this way Venture Capital firms have a long-term orientation and have thus been indispensable in the developed countries for nurturing the growth of hi-tech industries.

Innovations through Institutional Support

In an environment of liberalisation and deregulation assistance and support from Chambers of Commerce and Industry Associations is crucial for small scale units going in for superior technology. These bodies often act as conduits for transmission of vital industry related information relating to research and technology. R&D work undertaken by industry in the private sector is also geared to the needs of the manufacturing sectors. Partnerships, networking and technology broking have emerged as other mechanisms of technology transfer which have made the process of transfer more rapid and effective.

A new form of institutional support which has been successful in USA, Canada and Japan is the formation of **"Business Incubators."** These are intended to nurture innovative technology firms in their initial stages, by reducing their working capital requirements, by providing them with centralised services, easy access to seed capital, physical infrastructure, management and consultancy services, etc. The United Nations Fund for Science and Technology Development (UNF STD) has introduced the business incubation process into many developing countries, with the association of local consultancy groups.

In Korea, the Korea Technology Banking Corporation (KTB) is the answer to the growing SSI demand for competitive technology. The Bank takes an equity position in new high-tech enterprises and provides conditional loans for the process of innovation, commercialisation of R&D and training. KTB's activities range from start-up support to creating value addition for its client's products, disseminating knowledge of new technologies, rendering assistance for trade in technology and providing capital and management know-how required to sustain growth.

Technology promotion has become a major constituent in the small-scale industry development strategy of Philippines catalyzed by the growing interest in export. For the effective provision of technological services to small enterprises, the Ministry of Industry is implementing the Technological Services Delivery System (TSDS) in collaboration with UNIDO. This system provides a link between small enterprises and Technology Research Institutes (TRIs). It covers three types of services; plant level consultancy, in-plant technical training and technical information dissemination.

In China, a series of pragmatic measures have been adopted to promote technological innovations. Requisite infrastructure is being provided in specially set up "Technology Development Areas" with Government assistance. These facilitate joint foreign ventures and mobility of technologists and scientists. The Programme of Technology Incubation Centres (TICs) is also being actively pursued in China. A particularly noteworthy programme initiated in China since 1986 is the "Spark" programme which aims at revitalising the rural economy through the application of Technology. The term "Spark" is taken from a Chinese proverb "A single spark can start a Prairie fire", implying that even modest efforts at technological improvements in the rural economy would result in substantial gains for the rural entrepreneurs yielding sizeable returns in terms of rural productivity.

The rapid growth of technological innovations, has resulted in a growing trend towards more specialisation which has strengthened the role of small enterprises. But the role itself needs to undergo a transformation, through re-orientation and retraining. Within the small-scale sector, what is required to be further developed is a system of interlinked production, information exchange and combined marketing strategies.

* * *

29

ENTERPRISE MOBILITY

The continual need for organisations to excel has led to the advent of a new business process transformation. This latest shift is being driven by mobile technologies that are enabling workers to be in constant contact with customers, business partners and critical company information anywhere and anytime. Just as the Internet has changed the way companies do business, mobility is now becoming the next competitive frontier.

The increasing availability of high speed wireless data networks and practical mobile devices and applications has allowed a growing number of companies to embrace mobility to improve efficiency. As we speak, mobile technology is helping:

- Salespersons to retrieve customer data and place sales orders;
- Field support personnel to check spare parts and access client service history;
- Operations managers to track inventory and status of goods in transit; and
- Business executives to make decisions while on the go.

In short, businesses are leveraging mobile technology in all areas of operations to reduce cost, increase revenue, improve customer service and create new channels to market.

Yet despite the acknowledged value of mobility, building the right mobile strategy for sustainable competitive advantage is not an easy task. Organisations wishing to benefit from mobility must possess not only a thorough understanding of their own business, but a good grasp of mobile technologies and issues surrounding mobile solution deployment.

Fiction: Only a select group of businesses can capitalise on the benefits of mobility.

Mobility can benefit all types of organisations by giving them instantaneity and flexibility.

Organisations large and small are tapping into the benefits of mobile enterprise solutions. The key to a successful mobile initiative lies with careful technical and business planning. IDC recommends businesses take into consideration the following elements:

Business Considerations

Mobility audit

Investigate business processes that can be made more efficient with mobile technology. Proof-of-concept and trials can be improved through a thorough understanding of the business requirements and potential mobile solutions.

Option evaluation and standardisation

Compare each solution in terms of performance, ease of installation and use, upgrade path, and cost. Companies should also standardise for ease of management, future expansion and greater purchasing power.

Cost and benefit analysis

Consider both 'soft' and 'hard' benefits when performing the analysis, which needs to be revisited regularly even after the project is rolled out because factors do change.

User education and change management

Do not underestimate the value of user training as it is highly critical and should be done well before the project goes live. Because it is inevitable that some business processes will change, or new ones will be added with the introduction of mobile solutions, change of management will also be a key to success.

Work Goes Mobile

Mobility has fundamentally changed the workplace. At Nokia, we believe it will continue to do so. It gives people the freedom to work on their own terms: when they want, how they want and from wherever they happen to be. Enabling them to get more done in less time and facilitating a more collaborative environment.

As a global leader in mobile communications, Nokia is ideally positioned to help companies mobilise key applications beyond voice and simple messaging — for example, e-mail, sales force automation and customer relationship management tools — on mobile devices.

When it comes to mobility, Nokia meets both the competitive demands of companies and the diverse needs of the people who work for them. To this end, we offer:

(1) Business devices and enhancements that integrate voice, messaging, e-mail, intranet and Internet access, and more.

(2) Application mobility that brings support for industry leading business applications to our devices to increase employees' interactions with colleagues, partners and customers, while providing them access to key company information.

(3) Secure connectivity software and gateways that provide reliable connections from many mobile devices and control access to enterprise networks to ensure the integrity of the network and the content that flows in and out of it.

(4) An expanded enterprise Nokia service and support offering that includes deployment and professional services for everything from our mobile devices to gateways.

Finding the right solution for your enterprise

Experience has led us to understand that within any enterprise, the need for mobility varies. And because there is no one size fits all solution, we offer our customers a choice.

Technical Considerations

Mobile devices and wireless technologies

Select the appropriate devices (e.g., voice-centric versus data centric smart phones and laptops) with the wireless technologies (e.g., cellular versus wireless LAN and wireless broadband) that suit mobile workers' needs. A combination of devices and wireless technologies may be required.

Mobile infrastructure integration

Alleviate back end legacy system complexity through mobile middle ware and create an integrated environment in which existing infrastructure is extended to mobile users.

Mobile applications and management

Prioritise business functions and applications that need to be mobilised, and ensure a single view of administration, including asset management, software distribution and upgrade, and data backup and recovery on mobile devices.

Security

Mitigate security risks through both technology, at the device and corporate network levels, and appropriate user policy that only allows the right groups of mobile employees to access the right information while out of the office. Physical security measures dealing with device loss or theft should also be considered.

Fact: You can mix and match technologies to custom-create a mobile solution that matches the needs of your workforce.

Wireless technology can deliver both 'hard' and 'soft' benefits

On the other hand, implementing mobile solutions is not always challenge free. IDC's studies have consistently shown that the top three inhibitors regularly mentioned by decision makers of mobile enterprises are:

- Security, including the threat of hacking and absence of appropriate internal policy;
- Upfront and on going solution costs, and ensuing difficulty in justifying investments; and
- Lack of mobile technology standards.

Although these challenges are common across companies of all sizes, their extents do vary rather significantly. For example, cost and investment justification tend to be a greater issue among smaller firms, while larger businesses are more likely concerned with the lack of mobile solution standards, which in turn can lead to management and integration problems.

Asia Pacific decision makers are not alone, however. IDC global research has indicated that these three factors also top the wireless barrier list in North America and Western Europe. The good news is industry players have recognised these challenges and have been working to address them, providing increasingly standardbased, affordable and secure mobile solutions.

Mobility delivers both 'hard' or easily quantifiable benefits, such as increased sales and reduced operational costs, as well as 'soft' benefits that are not readily measured in fiscal terms, such as timely access to information and improved business productivity. IDC has found that difficulty in quantifying the 'soft' benefits is contributing to companies' inability to meaningfully justify their mobile investments, and that assistance from experienced vendors in this regard can go a long way.

Fiction: Implementing an enterprise mobility solution typically involves re-engineering the internal processes of your business.

A similar IDC study conducted in the United States last year also reveals the same trends. While e-mail and personal information management (PIM) have become the dominant enterprise wireless solutions among American companies, future adoption will be concentrated around CRM, salesforce and workforce automation. Another common trend found in both the Australian and U.S. markets is that enterprise mobility projects tend to be initiated by line-of-business users, rather than by the IT department.

Companies in all industries are benefiting from mobile technology. However, IDC has found that organisations in the following verticals are at the forefront of the mobile enterprise movement: Banking, insurance and financial services (including brokerage and trading houses); Professional services (e.g., accountants and engineering consultants); Retail and wholesale; and Government and education.

The notion of going mobile is not limited to large businesses and multinational corporations. Smaller firms with few employees are also reaping the benefits. Real estate agents and graphic design companies in Australia, for instance, are equipping themselves with mobile solutions to get ahead of competition.

Fiction: Wireless technology only delivers 'soft' benefits that cannot be quantified.

Drivers & Challenges

IDC research shows that organisations with enterprise mobility solutions share common drivers, Regardless of their industry verticals, sizes and geographical locations, they often cite a similar set of factors that encourage them to embrace mobile technology.

These factors include the need to:

- Improve business productivity and workforce efficiency;
- Have timely access to critical information for decision making;
- Cut costs; and
- Enhance customer relationships and satisfaction.

While mobile solutions tend to be first rolled out to field and sales personnel and the travelling executive, these benefits are not limited to 'road warriors' and occasional travellers. Commuters and office-bound workers, commuting to and from the office and going from meeting to meeting, are just as mobile and will also greatly benefit from the technology. Mobility allows everyone to be more productive by enabling them to be location and time independent.

Fact: One in five of the globle workforce are mobile workers.

Fiction: Mobile workers are a specialised group who are few and far between.

Going Mobile: Mobility Value Chain

Unlike wireless voice, enterprise mobility goes beyond wireless carriers and mobile handsets to include a host of other high-tech players. Since corporate applications are mobilised, IT infrastructure and business application vendors are part and parcel of the enterprise mobility spectrum, as are network equipment suppliers and systems integrators. Business consultants have also jumped on the bandwagon, bringing their business process expertise to the equation.

Despite their differing backgrounds, these industry players are collaborating with an aim to make mobile solutions simpler for businesses. The rise of Internet protocol technology and convergence — merging voice and data, IT and telecom, and wireline and wireless — are also blurring the demarcations between these vendors. Major market factors driving enterprise mobility developments are summarised in Figure 1. It is critical that companies considering a mobile solution rollout think holistically across this value chain.

Fiction: For the majority of businesses in Asia Pacific, telecom services account for a fraction of the overall technology budget.

Fact: One-quarter of Asia Pacific companies spend at least 70% of their technology budgets on telecom services.

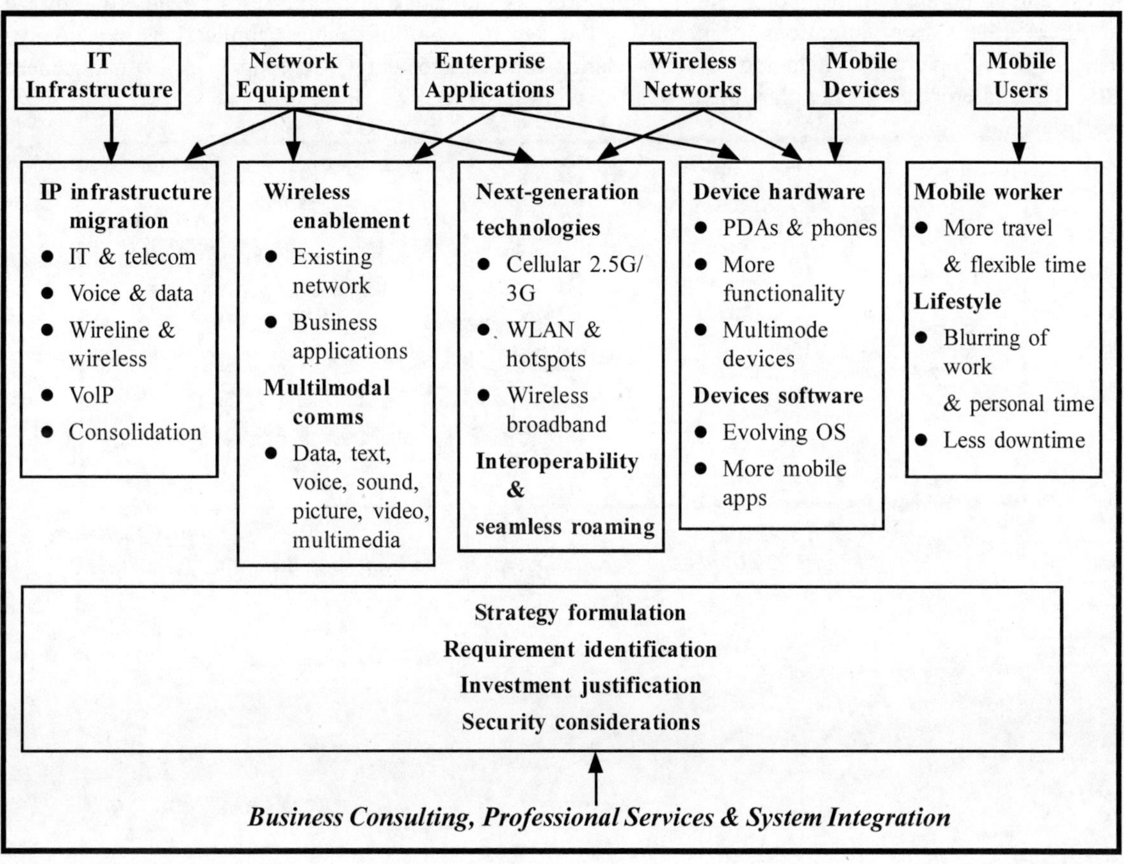

Fig. 29.1: Enterprise Mobility Value Chain

Going Mobile : Mobility Readiness

IDC's on-going research shows that mobile phone usage in Asia Pacific will enjoy very strong growth, with the number of users rising from just over 530 million last year to nearly 850 million by 2008. That growth, along with the rapid rise of other related technologies such as wireless LAN, wireless broadband and handheld devices, is puffing the region in a prime position to take advantage of enterprise mobility. In fact, in more mature countries like Australia, enterprise mobility has already become a reality.

An IDC study conducted in 2004 reveals that about one-third of Australian companies either have implemented or were in the process of implementing an enterprise mobility solution. While most of the mobile applications today remain concentrated around the 'first wave' of horizontal applications, with Internet access and corporate e-mail topping the list, study results indicate that businesses are ready to embrace mobility further. Strong intentions for mobilising the 'second wave' of business applications that involve critical business operations, including customer relationship management (CRM), supply chain management (SCM) and enterprise resource planning (ERP), are witnessed (see Fig. 2).

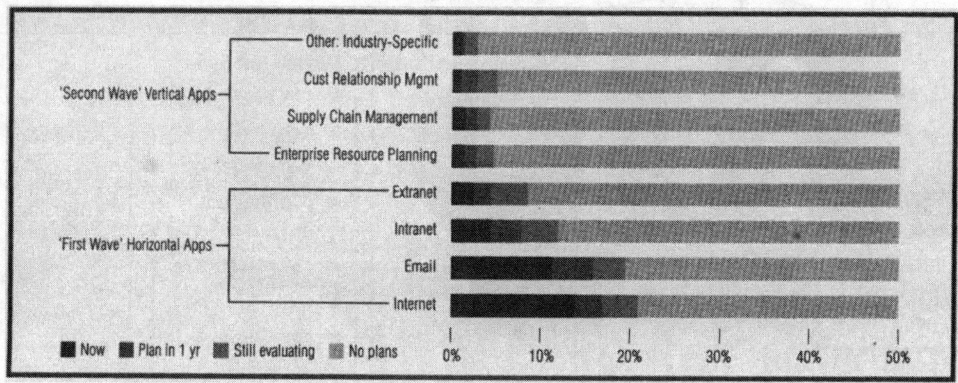

Source : *2004*

Fig. 29.2: Adoption of Mobile Enterprise Applications in Australia

* * *

30

THE SWOT ANALYSIS

A turnaround involves managing a series of changes, some minor and other major. Managing change involves tactful handling of people, so that resistance may be successfully overcome. Change creates a fear of the unknown — among empoyees. Proper communication helps a great deal in achieving a smooth and successful changeover.

(1) Improving Public Image: Public image should be improved so that more competent employees will come and work for the company. Similarly, better suppliers should be willing to do business with the company, better dealers should come forward to sell its wares. A good public image, thus, helps a great deal in raising resources, in attracting talent, and in marketing products and services.

(2) Restoring Investor Confidence: Investor confidence in the future success of the company is essential. If investors are sufficiently enthused, they can extend, they can extend a helping hand by participating in rights issues of equity shares and debentures. A good image among the investing public helps in building a strong company, particularly after completing the turnaround process.

When evaluating business opportunities, you could apply the SWOT analysis more rigorously. This is a method which compels you to think or reason out systematically and analytically, the important facts of:

Strengths	Weaknesses
Opportunities	Threats

Strengths and weaknesses are always related to the individual or an organisation interested in a business. Opportunities and threats are usually related to the outside environment.

(a) Now, let us consider the Example 5 on Balloons, Inc. and apply SWOT analysis. The strengths and weaknesses of a particular individual, as identified by himself or herself, could be as under:

Strengths	**Weaknesses**
Capacity to put in hardwork	Poor communication Skills
Good understanding of market	Losing temper quickly
Tenacity to complete work in spite of problems and hurdles	Deficiency in skills to operate gas cylinder and valve.
Willingness to take calculated risks	

(b) The Opportunities and Threats, as perceived by the same individual could be as under:

Opportunities	**Threats**
Large number of children to come to festival	Unexpected competition
Aluminium bolloons are novelty	Disturbances during festival due to rain or other unforseeable events.
Dealers available to give helium cylinder, valve and balloons	
Many people are not yet familiar with these new balloons	

(c) With this analysis, it will now be possible for the individual to assess the implications of all the four factors — strengths, weaknesses, opportunities and threats — in a total and integrated way. He or she can, thus, arrive at a reasoned decision on converting this opportunity to a business or not. It should be emphasized that these analyses will be different when undertaken by different individuals.

If you try to identify each of the above associated with each opportunity, it would enhance your reasoning process. Often, it helps to ask a friend to assist in recognizing the weaknesses and threats as you may be too excited about the idea to notice. This is called the role of the devil's advocate in some circles. Once you have a fair and exhaustive list of each, you can then weigh the strengths and opportunities against the weaknesses and threats and see if the positives outweigh the negatives. It also enables you to think of ways to overcome the risks or threats.

A brief summary of corporate analysis, based on strengths, weaknesses, opportunities and threats associated with turnaround companies is commonly known as a SWOT analysis. Strengths and weaknesses are primarily internal to the organisation, whereas opportunities and threats are related to the external environ in which these turnaround companies operate.

THE SWOT ANALYSIS

More opportunities & less threats	Chaotic (Disinvestment)		High Investment Situation
Balanced opportunities & threats	Medium Investment Situation		
Less opportunities & more threats	Disastrous (Disinvestment)		Complacent (Disinvestment)
Less strength More weaknesses	Balanced strengths & weaknesses		More strengths Less weaknesses

What we are presenting here is an overview of SWOT analysis of typical turnaround companies. All these features need not be present in every company, and some companies may have very peculiar features which may not find a reference here. The SWOT analysis is a powerful too to assess the internal and external situation of any particular company. Investors can use the SWOT analysis for investment and disinvestment decisions with the help of the chart.

High Investment Situations: Companies with growing strengths and opportunities are ideal for investment. The strength inherent in a business and the encouraging opportunities in the environment provide an excellent backdrop for success.

Medium Investment Situations: Companies with a balanced portfolio of strengths and weaknesses on one side and opportunities and threats on the other side, can be considered for investment only if the management is dynamic and experienced in nature. A dynamic management team will be able to build on its strengths over a period of time, exploiting the available opportunities to the full extent.

Disinvestment Situations: There are three types of such situations.

Disastrous Situations: Practically no worthwhile strengths and no real opportunities. Has only weaknesses and threats. Very difficult to survive.

- **Chaotic Situations:** High level of opportunities, but bogged down by serious internal weaknesses. Management is tempted by opportunities and launches new projects and products. Due to a lack of internal strengths, they fail one after the other.
- **Complacent Situations:** Has some internal strengths, but hurt by a lack of adequate opportunities. Slowly, the strengths evaporate and the company becomes a shadow of its past. You should get out of such disinvestment situations as fast as you can.

Steps

The following steps are involved in finding and evaluating business opportunities:

(1) Recognise opportunities/trends/ideas.

(2) Use methods such as Brainstorming and Attribute listing for generating ideas.

(3) Determine trends and implications:
   - demographic
   - economic
   - socio-demographic
   - socio-economic
   - socio-cultural
   - psychological

(4) Identify opportunities inferred by these trends.

(5) Consider ideas to become business opportunities.

(6) Evaluate business opportunities.

(7) Correlate opportunities to personal concerns or constraints.

(8) Use SWOT analysis techniques for a rigorous evaluation of business opportunities.

(9) Create a personal opportunities file.

(10) Guard your business ideas.

✱ ✱ ✱

31

Enterprise Risk Management: Practical Implementation Ideas

Introduce

One of the most critical challenges for management today is determining how much risk the business is prepared to accept as it strives to create value. Yet, research consistently indicates that six of ten senior executives "lack confidence" that their company's risk management practices identify and manage all potentially significant business risks.

With the heightened focus on risk management, it has become increasingly clear that traditional approaches do not adequately identify, evaluate and manage risk. Traditional approaches tend to be fragmented, treating risks as disparate and compartmentalized. These risk management approaches often limit the focus to managuncertainties around physical and financial assets.

Because they focus largely on loss prevention, rather than adding value, traditional approaches do not provide the framework most organizations need to redefine the risk management value proposition in this rapidly changing world.

Under enterprise risk management (ERM), the focus is on integrating risk management with existing management processes, identifying future events that can have both positive and negative effects, and evaluating effective strategies for managing the organization's exposure to those possible future events. ERM transforms risk management to a proactive, continuous, value-based, broadly focused and process-driven activity.

A New Approach to Risk Management

ERM differs from traditional risk management approaches in terms of focus, objective, scope, emphasis and application. It aligns strategy, people, processes, technology and knowledge. The emphasis is on strategy, and the application is enterprisewide.

Under an ERM approach, managements attention is directed to the uncertainties around the enterprise's entire asset portfolio, including its intangibles such as customer assets, employees and supplier assets, and such organizational assets as its differentiating strategies, distinctive products and brands, and innovative processes and systems. This expanded focus is important in this era where market capitalizations significantly exceed balance sheet values and many companies desire to focus on protecting their reputation from unacceptable risks relating to potential future events.

	Risk Management	*Business Risk Management*	*Enterprise Risk Management*
Focus	Financial, hazard risks and internal controls	Business risks and internal controls, taksing a risk-by-risk approach	Business risks and internal controls, taking and entity-level view of risk
Objective	Protect enterprise value	Protect enterprise value	Protect and enhance enterprise value
Scope	Treasury, insurance and operations involved	Business managers accountable (risk-by-risk)	Applied across the enterprise at every level and unit
Emphasis	Financial and operations	Management	Strategy-setting
Application	Selected risk areas, units and processes	Selected risk areas, units and processes	Enterprisewide to all sources of value

Fig. 31.1: ERM Approach

The COSO Enterprise Risk Management – Integrated Framework, issued in September 2004, defines ERM in broad terms that underscore some fundamental concepts and provides a common language as well as guidance on how to effectively manage risks across the enterprise. Like its internal control counterpart, the COSO ERM framework is presented as a three-dimensional matrix. It includes four categories of objectives across the top: strategic, operations, reporting and compliance. Eight components of enterprise risk management are shown across the face of the cube. Finally, the entity, its divisions and business units are depicted as the third dimension of the matrix along the side.

This ERM framework does not replace the internal control framework. Instead, it incorporates it. As a result, businesses may decide to implement ERM to address their internal control needs and to move towards a more robust risk management process.

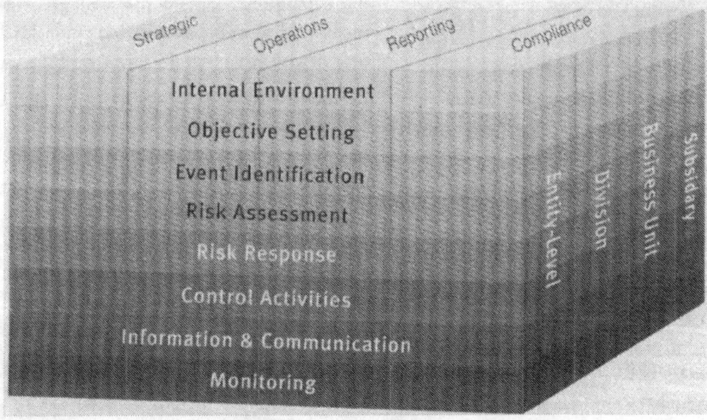

Fig. 31. 2 : ERM Framework

Why Implement ERM?

ERM provides a company with the process it needs to become more anticipatory and effective at evaluating, embracing and managing the uncertainties it faces as it creates sustainable value for stakeholders. It helps an organization manage its risks to protect and enhance enterprise value in three ways. First, it helps to establish sustainable competitive advantage. Second, it optimizes the cost of managing risk. Third, it helps management improve business performance.

These contributions redefine the value proposition of risk management to a business, One way to think about the contribution of ERM to the success of a business is to take a value dynamics approach. just as potential future events can affect the value of tangible physical and financial assets, so also can they affect the value of key intangible assets. This is the essence of what ERM contributes to the organization: the elevation of risk management to a strategic level by broadening the application and focus of the risk management process to all sources of value, not just physical and financial ones.

ERM transitions risk management from "avoiding and hedging bets" to a differentiating skill for protecting and enhancing enterprise value as management seeks to make the best bets in the pursuit of new opportunities for growth and returns. ERM invigorates opportunity-seeking behavior by helping managers develop the confidence that they truly understand the risks and have the capabilities at hand within the organization to manage those risks.

Five Steps to Implementing ERM

For organizations choosing to broaden their focus to ERM, there are five practical steps for implementation. While the following steps provide a simplified view of the task of implementing ERM, the implementation process does not occur overnight and, for certain, is not easy to accomplish. ERM is a journey and these steps are a starting point.

STEP 1: *Conduct an enterprise risk assessment (ERA) to assess and prioritize the critical risks.*

An ERA identifies and prioritizes the organization's risks and provides quality inputs for purposes of formulating effective risk responses, including information about the current state of capabilities around managing the priority risks. If an organization has not identified and prioritized its risks, ERM becomes a tough sell because the value proposition can only be generic. Using the entity's priority risks to identify gaps provides the basis for improving the specificity of the ERM value proposition. The message: Avoid endless dialogues about ERM. Get started by conducting an ERA to understand your risks.

STEP 2: *Articulate the risk management vision and support it with a compelling value proposition,*

This step provides the economic justification for going forward. The "risk management vision" is a shared view of the role of risk management in the organization and the capabilities desired to manage its key risks. To be useful, this vision must be grounded in specific capabilities that must be developed to improve risk management performance and achieve management's selected goals and objectives.

"Risk management capabilities" include the policies processes, competencies, reporting, methodologies and technology required to execute the organization's response to managing its priority risks. They also consist of what we cat("ERM infrastructure," To illustrate:

Item A: Defining the specific capabilities around managing the priority risks begins with prioritizing the critical risks and determining the current state of capabilities around managing those risks. (See Step 1 with regards to conducting an ERA). Once the current state of capabilities is determined for each of the key risks, the desired state is assessed with the objective of identifying gaps and advancing the maturity of risk management capabilities to close those gaps.

Item B: ERM infrastructure consists of the policies, processes, organizational oversight and reporting in place to instill the appropriate discipline around continuously improving risk management capabilities. Examples of elements of ERM infrastructure include, among other things, an overall risk management policy, an enterprisewide risk assessment process, presence of risk management on the Board and CEO agenda, a chartered risk committee, clarity of risk management roles and responsibilities, dashboard and other risk reporting, and proprietary tools that portray a portfolio view of risks.

Here is the message: The greater the gap between the current state and the desired state of the organization's risk management capabilities (Item A), the greater the need for ERM infrastructure (Item B) to facilitate the advancement of those risk management capabilities over time. A working group of senior executives should be empowered to articulate the role of risk management in the organization and define relevant goals and objectives for the *enterprise as* a whole and its business units.

STEP 3: *Advance the risk management capability of the organization for one or two priority risks.*

This step focuses the organization on improving its risk management capability in an area where management knows improvements are needed. Like any other initiative, ERM must begin somewhere. *There are* many possible starting points. Examples include:

- Compliance with the Clause 49 requirements or the Sarbanes-Oxley Act (specifically Sections 404 and 302).
- Risks other than financial reporting risk (for example, one or two. priority financial or operational risks, operationat risk in a financial institution, other regulatory compliance risks and/or governance reform issues, etc.).
- Evaluating enterprisewide risk assessment results to identify priority areas. (in other words, migration to ERM begins with first selecting the priority risks and assessing the current state of risk management capabilities addressing those risks, as discussed in Step 1.)
- Integration of ERM with the management and operating processes that matter (for example, strategic management, annual business planning, new product launch or channel expansion, quality initiatives, performance measurement and assessment, capital expenditure planning, etc.).

Many public companies in India may begin their evolution to ERM with Clause 49 compliance because the first-year compliance investment is significant and a company cannot have sound governance without transparency in its financial reporting. A strong focus on reliable financial reporting is a good foundation on which to build ERM capabilities, Regardless of where an organization begins its journey, the focus of ERM is the same: to advance the maturity of risk management capabilities for the organization's priority business risks.

STEP 4: *Evaluate the existing ERM infrastructure capability and develop a strategy for advancing it.*

It takes discipline to advance the capabilities around managing the critical risks. The policies, processes, organization and reporting that instill that discipline are called "ERM infrastructure." We have asserted that the purpose of ERM is to eliminate significant gaps between the current state and the desired state of the organization's capabilities around managing its key risks. We provided some examples of ERM infrastructure above when discussing Step 2. Other examples include a common risk language and other frameworks, knowledge sharing to identify best practices, common training, a chief risk officer (or equivalent executive), definition of risk appetite and risk tolerances, integration of risk responses with business plans and supporting technology.

ERM infrastructure facilitates three very important things with respect to ERM implementation. First, it establishes factbased understanding about the enterprise's risks and risk management capabilities. Second, it ensures there is ownership over the critical risks. Finally, it drives closure of gaps.

ERM infrastructure is not one-size-fits-all, What works for one organization might not work for another. The elements of ERM infrastructure vary according to the techniques and toots deployed to implement the eight ERM components (see the COSO ERM framework introduced on page 2), the breadth of the objectives addressed, the organization's culture and the extent of coverage desired across the organization's operating units. Management should decide the elements of ERM infrastructure needed according to these and other appropriate factors.

STEP 5: *Advance the risk management capabilities for key risks.*

This step begins with selecting the enterprise's priority risks. After the first four steps are completed, it will often be necessary to update the ERA for change. Once the priority risks are defined, based on the updated ERA, management must determine the current state of the capabilities for managing each risk and then assess the desired state with the objective of advancing the maturity of the capabilities around managing those risks. This has already been accomplished for one or two priority risks (see Step 3). Now management broadens the focus to other priority risks.

Risk management capabilities must be designed and advanced, consistent with an organization's finite resources. For each priority risk, management evaluates the relative maturity of the enterprise's risk management capabilities. From there, management needs to make a conscious decision: How much added capability do we need to continually achieve our business objectives? Further, what are the expected costs and benefits of increasing risk management capabilities? The goal is to identify the organization's most pressing exposures and uncertainties and to focus the improvement of capabilities for managing those exposures and uncertainties. The ERM infrastructure that management has chosen to put in place drives progress towards this goal.

Companies in the early stages of developing their ERM infrastructure often lay the foundation with a common language, a risk management oversight structure and an enterprisewide risk assessment process. Some companies have applied ERM in specific business units. And a few companies have evolved towards more advanced stages, such as the management of market and credit risks in financial institutions and the management of compliance risks in other industries.

Wherever a company stands with respect to developing its risk management, directors and executive management would benefit from a dialogue around how capable they want the entity's risk management to be with respect to each of its priority risks. The capability maturity model provides a scale for evaluating the maturity of an organization's risk management capabilities. The model provides five states for rating the maturity or capability of any process, ranging from "initial" to "optimizing."

The capability maturity model, shown above is a powerful tool for evaluating sustainability. Using this model, management rates the enterprise's capabilities in key risk areas, identifies gaps based on the level of capability desired in specific areas, and shifts the dialogue on operating metrics to incorporate appropriate emphasis on process maturity. The ERM infrastructure ensures that the rating process is fact-based and conducted with integrity by the participating risk owners. The model provides a valuable framework for facilitating substantive dialogue among directors, management and others regarding the capability of the

Continum	Capability Attributes	Method of Achievement
Optimizing	(Continuous Feedback) Risk management a source of competitive advantage	● Increased emphasis on exploiting opportunities ● "Best of class" processes ● Knowledge accumulated and shared
Managed	(Quantitative) Risks measured/managed quantitatively and aggregated enterprisewide	● Rigorous measurement methodologies/analysis ● Intensive debate on risk/ reward trade-off issues
Defined	(Qualitative/Quantitative) Policies, process and standards defined and institutionalized	● Process uniformly applied across the firm ● Remaining elements of infrastructure ● Rigorous methodologies
Repeatable	(Intuitive) Process established and repeating: reliance on people continues	● Common language ● Quality people assigned ● Defined tasks ● Initial infrastructure elements
Initial	(*Ad Hoc*/Chaotic) Dependent on heroics; institutional capability lacking	● Undefined tasks ● Relies on initiative ● "Just do it" ● Reliance on key people

Process Evolution

Source : Adapted from the Carnegie Mellon University Software Engineering Institute, 1994

Fig. 31.3 : Process Evaluation

organization's processes as compared to the critical risk areas identified in their risk assessments. Armed with this tool, Boards and management are able to satisfy themselves that risk management improvements are directed to the areas of greatest concern and exposure. The focus is then directed to implementing those improvements according to management's plan over time. Again, the ERM infrastructure provides oversight to ensure that improvements are on schedule.

Managing the ERM Journey

Companies evolving towards ERM should keep in mind that it is a journey, not a destination. ERM can potentially represent a sea change in organizational attitude and behavior. As with any significant change, the adoption of ERM is fundamentally a process of building awareness, developing buy-in and ultimately driving the acceptance of ownership throughout the organization. Change enablement is, therefore, a significant aspect of an ERM initiative because everyone's perspective about risk varies.

To help ensure success, keep the following in mind when implementing ERM:

- Develop a compelling business case linking the ERM agenda to real priority business needs, garner support from the top and manage progress against milestones over time.

- Obtain agreement on risk management objectives and the necessary ERM infrastructure, consider relevant cultural issues and focus on enterprisewide application.
- Implement an effective enterprise-wide risk assessment process early.
- Clarify process ownership issues: who decides, who designs, who builds and who monitors?
- Integrate risk management with the business planning process.
- Don't forget the true purpose of ERM infrastructure be sure to define the future state goal of the capabilities around managing the critical risks and contrast it with the current state.
- Use the COSO ERM components as a framework against which to benchmark ERM requirements.

Properly implemented, ERM can help organizations pursue strategic growth opportunities with greater speed, skill and confidence. Opportunity-seeking behavior is invigorated if managers have the confidence that (1) they understand the risks they are taking on and (2) the organization's risk taking is aligned with its core competencies and risk appetite. Markets will differentiate competing organizations by the quality and extent - real or perceived - of their risk management capabilities.

Transaction Advisors blend practical business, financial and commercial exertise to assist on complex mergers, acquisitions and other corporate reorganizations, both domestically and abroad. We understand the dynamics of transactions. This experitise is used to find exposures, and negotiate appropriate warranties and indemnities. We partner with you through the entire deal continuum from pre-investment to investment through to assisting in exit strategy.

Pre-investment	*Investment*	*Exit*
– Key investment issues – Desktop reviews – Sell side reviews – Industry reviews – Promoter background checks	– Financial due diligence and compliance review – Review of critical processes and information systems – Business plan analysis – Environmental diligence – Closing review	– Internal audit – Detailed operations review and risk assessment – Investment management and periodic investor reviews – Follow-on acquisitions, spinoffs and divestitures – Pre-exit diligence

Our Approach: We focus on the business, financials, operatinons and projections to identify key transaction risks, as shown below. Our combination of global and local specialists utilize in-depth industry knowledge and market know-how to identify the comprehensive key transaction risks and concern areas (value destroyers) along with potential upsides (value enhancers).

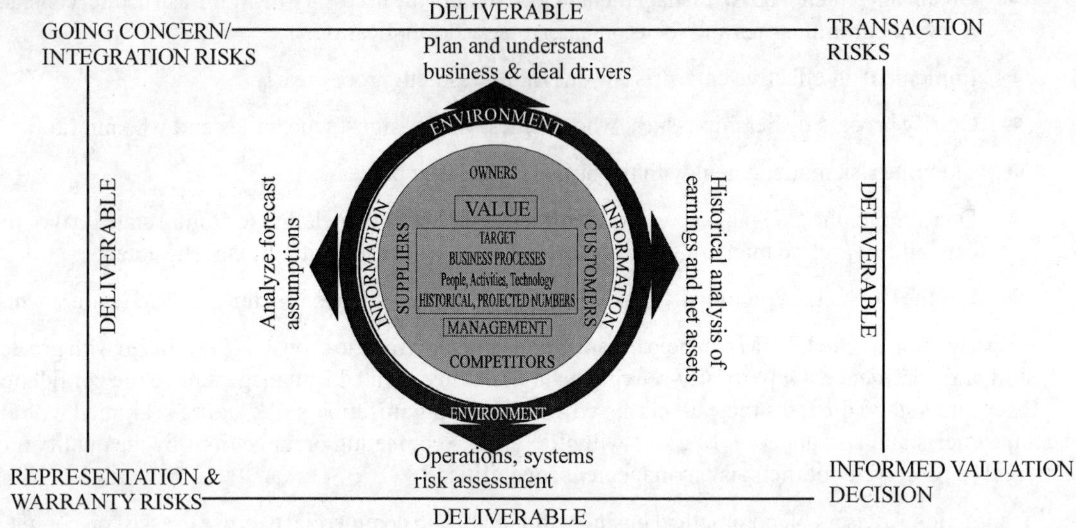

Fig. 31.4 : Key Transaction Risks

⬢ ⬢ ⬢

APPENDIX

Innovate in Business Processes

Globalisation and technological advance during the last two decades has necessitated that the organisations and entrepreneurs might need to change thier business processes. First, existing business processes may not be designed to handle the new economic order. Therefore, there is a need to re-think and redesign the business. Secondly, the business processes of most organisations are a legacy of the past and are not designed to include Information Technology (IT) as a central, crucial element. At the same time, quality has emerged as a key element in the competitive process.

The outlines of the 21st century management model are already clear. Decision-making will be more peer based; the tools of creativity will be widely distributed in organisations. Ideas will compete on an equal footing. Strategies will be built from the bottom up. Power will be a function of competence rather than of position. In terms of the future of management, we're at the beginning of what will be a fairly long journey You can see some of the pieces starting to come together, but we're not there yet,

To become inspired management innovators, today's executives must learn how to think explicitly about the management orthodoxies that bound their thinking-the habits, dogmas, and conceits they've never taken the trouble to challenge. For example, many people believe that it takes a crisis to change a large organisation, and when we look at the evidence this seems to be the case.

These changes have necessitated the acquisition of new skills, adoption of new business processes, innovative technology and innovative management practices by the entrepreneurs for continued success.

Quality Initiatives

Quality is conformance with requirements as stated by the customers:

- In case where requirements are not explicitly stated by the customer, it becomes the responsibility of the supplier of products / services to understand the implied requirements and conform to the same. Definition of "Quality" keeps on changing with changing the needs of customers. Thus quality is a moving target and to have competitive edge, the product or service supplied must match contemporary requirements.

Quality Management System (OMS) helps:

- determine what is required to be done;

- converts this into clear and unequivocal instructions;
- confirm that it is followed;
- check that everyone in the organisation has knowledge, ability and will to do the job;
- provide equipment and procedures to enable the work to be done;
- check that the job has been done correctly.

Various initiatives are being taken by different organisations to improve their quality of products/ services for building organisational competitiveness. Some of the important initiatives include:

Benchmarking

Benchmarking process, which is simple to apply and does not require advance and high degree of sophisticated techniques, provides an external stimulus to encourage a reflective environment of continuous learning in the organisation. Benchmarking, a viable approach for improving business effectiveness, means adopting the best practices of other organisations for better performance.

Benchmarking helps in:

- providing breakthrough insight by examining superior management practices;
- inspiring people by demonstrating; and
- setting objective targets by highlighting the gaps to improve the organisation's competitive position and its learning abilities.

Business Process Re-engineering (BPR)

Re-engineering is the fundamental rethinking and radical redesign of business processes to achieve dramatic improvements in critical, contemporary measures of performance, such as cost, quality, service, and speed. Re-engineering an organisation, which involves going back to the basics and inventing a better way of doing work, means tossing aside the old system and starting new ones. It also means abandoning long -established procedures and looking fresh at the work required to create an organisation's product or service and deliver value to the customer.

Re-Engineering Tools					
Total Category	*Preparation*	*Identification*	*Vision*	*Solution*	*Transformation*
Project Management	✓	✓	✓	✓	✓
Coordination	✓	✓	✓	✓	✓
Modelling		✓	✓	✓	✓
Business Process Analysis		✓	✓	✓	✓
System Development			✓	✓	
Human Resources		✓	✓	✓	✓
Analysis & Design					

Source : The Re-engineering Handbook, by Ramond L. Manganelli and Mark M. Klein

Smartsizing

Sizing or smartsizing, the doctrine of core competency of business organisations, relates to reshuffling business portfolio with a view to having competitive advantage. Organisations identify their fundamental strengths and discontinue businesses where they do not have competitive advantages. These bundle of skills and fundamental strengths have come to be known as "core competence". Following six strategies facilitate smartsizing:

Vision of growth : The objective of resizing is to ensure that growth is achieved and that it is not merely a cost cutting exercise.

Decision making process : There has to be a consensus for the disinvestment decisions from the top management.

Managing managers: The managers who take investment decision should be rewarded suitably and they should also be retrained to manage the new business.

Communication: Top management should communicate with their employees about the sizing changes in the organisation.

Innovation: The process of disinvestment should be done innovatively so as to retain profitable part of the unit.

Journey, not a Destination: The opportunity cost should be constantly evaluated, even of the continuing profitable business.

Total Quality Management (TQM)

TQM is organisationwide programme that integrates all functions and processes of the business such that all aspects of the business are aimed at maximising customer satisfaction through continuous improvements. TQM is the mother of all systems and its adoption help organisations to carve out niche areas of competency in a highly competitive business environment. Customer satisfaction is another core area where TQM has helped to bring about substantial improvement.

Standardisation

Standardisation, in terms of the organisational competitiveness, is the process of making standard of quality management and quality assurance by adopting the International Organisation for Standards (ISO) quality management norms. ISO certification usually require:

- ISO assessment — reviewing the organisation's quality system and procedures;
- Quality assurance and policy manual preparation- compiling the specific quality -- oriented techniques and policies to be followed;
- Training of employees in ISO;
- Documentation of work instructions – documenting each new work procedure; and
- Registration audit – having quality system reviewed by a special "registrar" who audits the organisation's quality efforts.

The involvement of employees and customers are the two unique factors of TOM implementation. Employee education and training coupled with application of work management concepts help in creating a new work culture cutting across the entire spectrum of the staff.

How Re-engineering Meshes with TCM

THE PROCESSES RE-ENGINEERED	Vendor Integration	Vendor Rationalisation and Development	Manufacturing	Sales Forecasting Integration with Procurement	Use of Media	Process Automation
THE METHODS USED	Alternative Material Use	Strategic Sourcing	Total Productive Maintenance	Enterprise Resource Planning	Align Media Buying to Measurable Parameters	Redeployment of Manpower
THE COSTS ATTACKED	Material Sourcing	Inventory Management	Work-In-Progress Inventory	Distribution Network Management	Media and Promotions	Spares Management
	Vendor Conversion	Vendor Management	Energy and Fuel	Finished Goods Inventory	Trade Discounts and Commissions	Labour

Total Cost Management (TCM)

TCM is a management planning and control system adopted by business organisations to enable them in enhancing their competitiveness. TCM involves the following:

- Identifying and measuring the cost of resources consumed in performing the significant activities of the organisation ;
- Determining the efficiency and effectiveness of the activities performed ; and
- Identifying, evaluating and implementing the most appropriate methodologies to enhance the competitiveness of the organisation with a view to achieving long term leadership.

TCM Tools

There are various TCM tools which are applied in managing strategy such as ;

- customer/market segment profitability;
- channel profitability analysis;
- target cost management;
- product line profitability management;
- vendor cost analysis; and
- total cost of buying.

The five principles for building organisational competitiveness through Total Cost Management (TCM) are:

(i) The first rule organisations should keep in view is that "to price first and then cost"- in times of high demand, organisations should enhance productive capacity and during the period of lean demand, reduce capacity and lower head count.

(ii) The second principle is value management and marketing valuebased pricing should dominate cost based pricing.

(iii) Third principle is to sell to segmented markets and not to mass markets - organisations should seek and seize revenue advantages rather than worry about cost disadvantages.

(iv) The fourth principle is to save the product for most valuable customer — "first come, first served" principle does not serve relationship management where decisions are based on knowledge and riot on supposition.

(v) The fifth principle is to exploit and leverage each product's value cycle – maximise value of products in markets overtime.

THE TCM CORPORATION'S COST-MAP

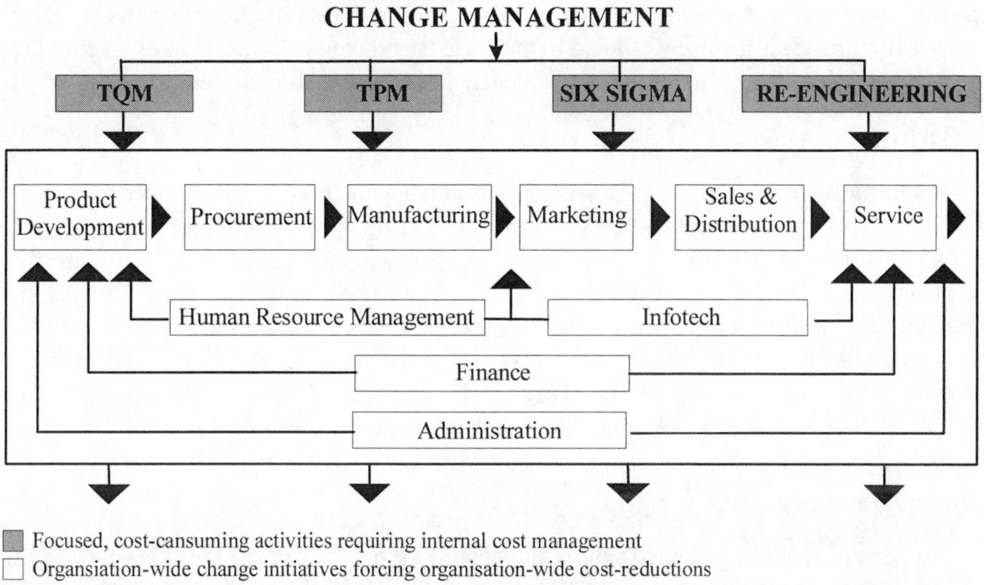

CHANGE MANAGEMENT

TQM TPM SIX SIGMA RE-ENGINEERING

Product Development | Procurement | Manufacturing | Marketing | Sales & Distribution | Service

Human Resource Management

Infotech

Finance

Administration

Focused, cost-cansuming activities requiring internal cost management

Organsiation-wide change initiatives forcing organisation-wide cost-reductions

Customer Relationship Management (CRM)

Customer Relationship Management (CRM) solutions unlock potential revenue by capturing valuable data and turning it into required knowledge to understand, predict and leverage consumer behaviour patterns thereby enabling organisations to build and retain customer loyalty.

The first aspect of CRM is Operational, i.e. data generated by operational systems such as sales order processing, credit agreements, etc. or transaction based data which is gathered at all points of customer contacts. For instance, a banker, at a click of a button, would know the details about the customer he is dealing with.

Other aspect of CRM is Analytical which converts operational data into knowledge by studying and analysing behaviour patterns thereby bringing out future opportunities of value creation. It provides details of specific customer's interests in a particular product, his preference, etc. Thus in the case of the example of the banker, such analysis can help position the sale of the product to the customer who is most likely to buy, rather than dealing with his routine enquiry.

Business Process Outsourcing (BPO)

At present Business Process Outsourcing (BPO) is creating ripples in various service segments. BPO is the long term contracting of non-care business processes to outside service providers. Non-core business processes are those which are fundamental to all businesses, but are not unique to the particular organisation. These could include billing and collection, order entry, human resources administration, training, procurement, tax compliance, internal audit, customer relations, "backoffice" functions etc. Outsourcing noncore processes helps the organisation to focus on their areas of core-competence. Although cost savings may be a major motivator, BPO is seen as a vital management tool to direct strategy. No doubt, determining what is the "core competency" of an organisation is a difficult task; yet, outsourcing has gained importance.

According to management consultancy, Price Waterhouse Coopers, "because of increased global competition, (companies) face constant pressure to improve performance. Adopting BPO gives them access to best-practice processes precisely tailored to their needs and requirements, thereby freeing them to focus their strategic energies in improving core functions.... and gain that all important competitive edge".

Six Sigma

Another important initiative organisations are adopting to improve performance relates to Six Sigma. Implementing Six Sigma improves processes, maximizes business performance, and adds to the bottom line, resulting in gaining competitive edge. Six Sigma is a statistical measure of variability, typically in a given process, and a business performance target specifically focused on critical customer specifications. In manufacturing, for instance, Six Sigma could measure the number of defects in a subassembly. Compared to the estimated 6,000 defects per million which occur in most companies, Six Sigma aims to limit the defects to 3.4 per million. In other words, it aims at virtually defect-free performance, thereby adding to competitive advantage and improved profit performance. Recognizing. the powerful nature of this tool, service organisations including financial institutions have also adopted it widely.

SIX SIGMA FUNDAS

- Strong customer-oriented approach that relies on data to create more efficient processes or refine existing processes
- Under the prescribed specifications there cannot be more than 3.4 defects (defined as anything that does not add value to the end customer), per million opportunities
- You can apply it to anything, from making a movie to manufacturing truck tyres!!
- It needs the unstinted support of organisational leaders, and emphasises teamwork and lifelong evolution of practices and processes.

(1) Meaning

Six Sigma is derived from statistics and used to define the. process capability. It is a strategy used to manage defect free manufacturing and error free business process. The term defect or error refer to anything that dissatisfies the customer. So the strategy which seeks to identify and remove the causes of defects and errors in the business processes is termed as six sigma. It is used by the designated experts within the organization by way of well defined and laid down quality measurement and statistical tools.

(2) Methodology

The methodology of six sigma was developed by Bill Smith and practiced in Motorola in 1986 by combining quality Improvement methods like TOM, Zero Defects & Quality Control etc. It is based on the basic assumptions that the organization is committed to make continuous efforts for stability. The performance results can be predicted and the process is controllable, measurable and improvable. It focuses on strong leadership support and objective decisions based on statistical data for achieving measurable and achievable returns or performance. The ultimate goal is to improve the quality and quantity of all business processes. It has following 2 key methods:

DMAIC:

D Define the project goals and customer (internal and external) deliverables

M Measure the process to determine current performance

A Analyze and determine the root cause(s) of the defects

I Improve the process by eliminating defects

C Control future process performance

DMAIC should be used when a product or process is in existence, but is not meeting customer specification or is not performing adequately.

DMADV:

D Define the project goals and customer (internal and external) deliverables

M Measure and determine customer needs and specifications

A Analyze and process options to meet the customer needs

D Design (detailed) the process to meet the customer needs

V Verify the design performance and ability to meet customer needs

DMADV should be used when a product or process is not in existence and one needs to be developed or the existing product or process exists and has been optimized (using either DMAIC or not) and still does not meet the level of customer specification or six sigma level.

HOW IT'S DONE

Jack Welch's directive that his GE managers could wriggle out of six Sigma training at the cost of losing their promotion only goes to show how important it is to enforce this practice from the top. The people involved in six Sigma execution are, a) master black belts who are well versed in the rules of the game, b) black belts (technically oriented individuals involved in the process of organisational change and development) and c) green belts (employees who lead six sigma project teams).

P Ramesh, General Manager – Corporate Quality, CSC India lists the high-level steps involved in implementing Six Sigma in an organisation:

- Identify business goals from customer requirements
- Assess the current level of performance to determine the gaps
- Identify improvement projects and prioritise
- Form Six Sigma improvement teams, comprising stakeholders, for each project

- Equip the Six Sigma improvement teams with Six Sigma training on methodologies and tools
- Allocate Six Sigma specialist to support and guide the teams, sponsor to champion the project
- Track progress of Six Sigma teams through management reviews and resolve issues
- Audit completed Six Sigma projects to ensure they have achieved the goals
- Reward and recognise Six Sigma teams

Not a Perfect System

For all its wonders, Six Sigma is not invulnerable to weaknesses. "A common criticism against Six Sigma is its heavy focus on rigour and discipline related to methodology. There are occasions when Six Sigma demands exhaustive data collection that can be painstaking and formidable. On account of these there is a tendency for Six Sigma projects to take longer time for completion than desired," says Ramesh. Experts say that given its current form, defining the problem is not very easy. Also the fact that only traditional brainstorming for coming Up with potential solutions to obtain solutions is another weakness in the methodology.

The solution to this is probably to integrate Six Sigma with other tools and techniques such as Lean, I-Triz, Taguchi Techniques, etc. Managers need to be absolutely clear whether they're ready to go the distance to execute six Sigma in their organisations. Thomas says, "Why Six Sigma? What is there in it for me? Such questions or similar ones need to be addressed by customised training, involving the right people and selecting the right project the first time to show that it works across functions."

Software Matters

As the time frame for making decisions decreases and the amount of information at hand continues to increase, companies must deploy the tools to enable their people to succeed: tools to help turn the noise of constant information into the music of knowledge.

Software has the unique ability to amplify people's efforts, capitalizing on their skills and knowledge while providing the flexibility that helps companies adapt to change. Software is a key component of any peopleready business. While organizational structure, a clear understanding of priorities, and engaged and effective leadership are prerequisites for a people-ready business, providing people with the right information at the right time-and the tools to act on that information-is key to turning business culcture into business results.

Software provides the infrastructure, the foundation for the most important systems of any business. Software also makes the difference in how useful those systems are. Software captures the relationships, intellectual property, and processes that underlay a business, linking the ways that customers interact with employees and connecting the line-ofbusiness applications that they depend on with various other systems and information.

Strategic Human Resource Management

Trends like globalisation and technological innovation are changing the way organisations are managed. Organisations today are grappling with revolutionary trends to compete. In the organisations that have successfully responded to these changes, new modes of organising and managing have emerged. The fact that employees today are central to gaining competitive advantage has led to the emergence of Strategic

Human Resource Management (SHRM) which links HRM practices to the strategic goals and objectives in order to build organisational competitiveness and develop corporate culture that foster innovation and flexibility.

Spatial Data Engineering (SDE)

The cutting edge of spatial data engineering (SDE) combines multiple applications to fine tune management, rounting of networks, georeferencing and projection. SDE capabilities married with business analytics and data mining provide powerful business intelligence solutions, which will help the industry immensely.*

The uses are almost limitless to the corporates. Enterprise Performance Management (EPM). Enterprise Performance Management (EPM) is a tope management need to-day.

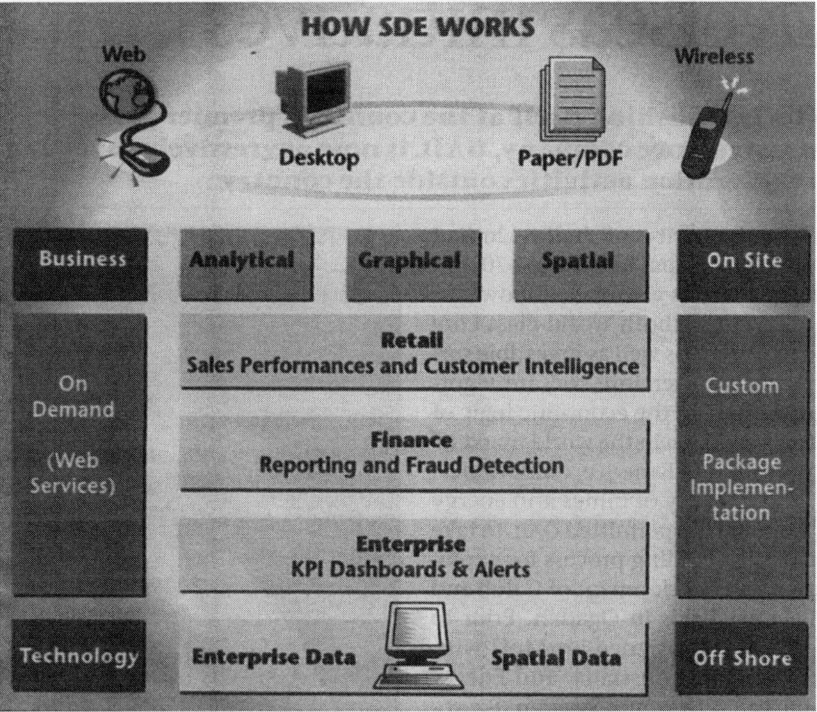

It allows the management to query the sales database and produced spatial analytical views for value, quantity and growth of sales, as well as penetration index and market potential - fight from territory level to that of the wholesale stockists.

The combination of GIS and effective data mining has been useful in giving the top management an accurate view of our best as well worst performing markets/products right down to the stockists' level. Since all this data is online, it is available at the click of a button.

Mapping businesses includes:

- creating intuitive spatial decision support interfaces by leveraging BI and GIs;
- integrating enterprise data with geographic data for analytics with a location context;

Geographic Information System

- managing assets and facilities for utilities;
- GSM-cell based tracking (alternative to GPS) for cost-effective fleet management;
- offering real-time location based services (LBS) for wireles subscribers, etc.

In the future more and more companies wish to mine their existing data and then combine with smart analysis to make their business decisions.

Seven' Ways to Avoid the Growth Traps

So, your startup has become a success and is all set for the growth phase. Good luck, but take care to avoid the following traps.

Underestimating The Cash Burn Rate

Here's an all too familiar scenario: Projected revenues start taking off in year five, but it's only year three, the company is still losing money and it only has 12 months worth of cash in the kitty. Remember: Growth is great, but only if you can survive long enough to watch it kick in. Until then, keep your belt tightened, temper those sales forecasts and make sure customers pay on time.

Misallocating Capital

Once you've raised some cash, spending it is all too easy. Too many growing companies end up investing in nonproductive assets, from costly marketing campaigns to fancy new office furniture, while the software they're selling is still infested with bugs. Best bet: Put a formal system in place whereby any expenditure over a certain amount requires clearance by at least two key people.

Going On An Acquisition Spree

Market share is a good thing, and making an acquisition (or perhaps even forming an alliance or joint venture) can be a way of grabbing it. Shooting stars Cisco Systems and Google successfully inhaled scads of targets in the last decade. But then, those behemoths also used their richly priced shares as currency, making the prices they paid seem a lot more attractive. Sadly, mergers and acquisitions on the whole tend to destroy value, be it because the buyer overpaid or the integration flopped. Tread cautiously.

Forgetting Rules Of Good Customer Service

The first rule is obvious: Don't be so fixated on winning the next customer that you forget about the ones who already paid and, with any luck, will put in the good word with their friends. But there's another, less intuitive rule: Don't be afraid to fire bad customers. These scourges demand lots of service but spend little- or worse, end up not paying at all.

Refusing To Delegate Authority

Sooner than later, a company will grow beyond the core management team's ability to micromanage it. But learning to let go is harder than 11 ii sounds. "There are lots of people that start companies and do very well, says Paul Marshall, professor of management at Harvard Business School. "But they haven't had to share decision making authority and responsibility, and they find that hard to do.

Relinquishing Too Much Equity Too Soon

True, most small businesses fail because they are undercapitabsed. But selling off a healthy chunk of ownership and control - either to a venture capital firm or in a public offering - isn't always the answer to fast cash.

Pocketing A Few Perks

It's tough running a business, and no one works harder than you. Still, you have to battle the urge to put precious growth capital for that imported car. Investors won't like it — and employees may doubt your commitment to making their financial dreams (read: stock options) come true.

Conclusion

Coping with the changes that a globalised market has brought, will be the biggest challenge that Indian public sector banks have to face. In the emerging financial landscape, quality of service will command a premium. Building competitiveness would be the only route to survival and growth and towards this end, the banks may well adopt some of the above mentioned emerging strategies. How well and effectively such initiatives are implemented will be critical in deciding the competitive position of Indian public sector banks. However, such efforts will remain just as concept until human resources translate them into reality. Thus, entrepreneurs will have to focus on increasingly aligning their HRM practices to corporate strategy.

Those running businesses, however, have to deliver success: grow revenue and profits, satisfy customers and stakeholders, and successfully navigate the perpetual winds of change. For each business-and for every employee-the particulars may differ, but the outcomes that drive business success tend to remain the same creating loyal and profitable customer relationships, inventing and enhancing products or services, managing a business in the most efficient way possible, and building highvalue connections with partners and suppliers. The emphasis may vary, but every business must focus on these outcomes. Whether closing a sale, designing the next great product, or discovering a way to squeeze inefficiency out of the supply chain, success depends on the people in a company.

Rarely in business does total victory or complete catastrophe stem from a single decision. Rather, success or failure is based on the cumulative impact of a myriad of decisions and actions by a broad range of people.

Are the systems, tools, and culture of the business enabling people to make better decisions? Does the business get its people the right information so they can delight customers, create new products, or work with business partners, whether they are at a desk or on a cell phone thousands of miles away? Does the business culture help break down barriers so people can work more easily with each other'? With partners? With customers? Are the right priorities, organisation, motivation, and leadership in place to drive success'? Does the technology that supports your business adapt to change so that your people don't have to? In short, is your business people-ready?

Even though many ot today's tasks are automated, people remain the heart of any business. People develop relationships and close. deals. People make insights. Ad improve products. People work together to make the thousands of small decisions that collectively add up to success. Finding, developing, and retaining the right people is a crucial and increasingly difficult task for today's businesses.

HOW THE STATE MUST ORCHESTRATE REFORMS

	The first Generation		*Second Generation*	
Main Objectives	◆ Crisis management: reducing inflation and restoring growth		◆ Improving social condilions and competitiveness, maintaining macro-economic stability	
Instruments	◆ Drastic budget cuts ◆ Tax reform ◆ Price Liberalisation ◆ Trade and foreign Investment liberalisation	◆ Deregulation ◆ Social funds ◆ Autonomous contracting agencies ◆ Partial privatisation	◆ Civil services reform ◆ Labour reform ◆ Restructuring of social ministry ◆ Judiciary reform	◆ Modernising of the legislature ◆ Upgrading regulatory capacity ◆ Improved tax collection
Actors	◆ Presidency ◆ Economic cabinet ◆ Central bank	◆ Multi-lateral FIs ◆ Private financial groups ◆ Foreign portfolio investors	◆ Presidency and Cabinet ◆ Legislature ◆ Civil service ◆ Judiciary ◆ Unions	◆ Political parties ◆ Media ◆ State and local govts. ◆ Private sector ◆ Multilateral FIs
Main Challenge	◆ Macro-economic management by an insulated technocratic elite		◆ Institutional development highly dependent on middle management in the Public sector	

Direct Tax Code 2010 For Small Co.s

Small-scale & Medium Industries (SMEs) are an important and crucial segment of the Indian industry sector. The India government has accorded high priority to this sector as it plays a vital role in balanced and sustainable economic growth. In the current context of rapid economic development, one must view taxation benefits in relation to the need for increasing investment in small-scale medium and ancillary industries.

Here are few key proposals of the Direct Tax Code, 2010, (DTC)

Income-expense Model

In terms of the DTC, besides the presumptive and special taxation regimes for specified businesses, the profits from all other businesses will be equal to gross earnings from the business minus the amount of allowable deduction.

Gross earnings from the business

All accruals and receipts from business, besides those derived from business assets, make up the gross earnings of the business of the tax payer. For instance, profit on sale of an undertaking under a slump sale; advance or security deposit on long-term lease of business asset; or reimbursement of any expenditure etc.

Allowable deduction

Generally, all operating expenses incurred essentially for business purposes are deductible from gross total income. The requisite for deductibility of expenses is that expenses must be wholly and exclusively incurred for business purposes; and incurred or paid during the previous year and supported by pertinent papers and records.

Expenses of a personal and capital name, remuneration payable to a "non working participant". Any unascertained liabilities etc., are not deductible.

Expenditure incurred by way of land revenue, local rates or municipal taxes, sales tax, duty, cess, fees, bonus or commission to employees, leave encashment is deducible in the financial year in which the liability arose only if paid in the financial year or by the due date of filing the return of tax bases for that financial year. Otherwise it will be allowed in the financial year in which it is actually paid.

Expenditure incurred by way of interest on loans or borrowings from permitted financial institutions is deductible in the year of accrual or payment, whichever is later.

Depreciation on business capital assets (including acquired by the lessee under financial lease) is calculated on the declining balance method and is based on the "block of assets". The `block of assets' concept suggests aggregation of all assets with the same depreciation rate into a common block for calculation of depreciation. Depreciation is computed at varying rates as prescribed and in the year of purchase, is available for the full year if an asset is used for more than 180 days. In other cases, depreciation is allowed at halt the normal rates.

Besides depreciation, a manufacturer or producer of an article or thing is allowed initial depreciation on new machinery and plant (except 'office appliances' and assets not installed in office premises, guest house of any other residential premises) at the rate of 20% of the original cost of the asset for the full year if the asset is used for more than 180 days. In other cases, initial depreciation is allowed at half the normal rates.

Deferred revenue expenditure by way of, i.e., non-compete fee, premium paid on lease or rental asset, amount paid to an employee under voluntary retirement scheme, expenses incurred by an Indian company wholly and exclusively, preliminary expenditure, etc., will be allowed deduction in six financial year starting the year of actual payment, or year of business reorganisation, or year of start of business, extension of business or set up of new business, as the case may be.

Tax Holidays

The DTC has grandfathered, though restrictive, the tax holiday to all special Economic Zone units for the unexpired period out of 15 years, including new such units that start operations on or before 31st March, 2014. The tax holiday will be computed on the lines discussed in the above model with two exceptions namely: capital expenditure and expenditure incurred prior to the start of business.

Unfortunately, there is no exception for SEZ units from MAT. Absence of MAT exemption under DTC would mean that SEZ units would need to pay a minimum tax of 20% on book profits.

Business Reorganisation

It covers transactions between two or more residents involved in amalgamation or de-merger. Reorganisation, ordinarily being tax neutral is subject to 'test of continuity of business' and other conditions as are necessary to prevent abuse of the Code.

The successor of business will pass the 'test of continuity of business' if he : i) continuously holds at least 75% of the book value of the fixed assets of the predecessor acquired through business reorganisation for at least five financial years immediately succeeding the year in which the business reorganisation takes place ii) continues the business of the predecessor for at least five financial years immediately succeeding the financial year in which the business reorganisation takes place; and iii) meets such other conditions as may be prescribed to ensure the revival of the business of the predecessor or to ensure that the business reorganisation is for genuine business purpose.

In the case of de-merger, the resulting company must issue only its equity shares to the shareholders of the de-merged company on a proportionate basis to avail of tax exemption and benefit of carry forward of unabsorbed tax losses.

Tips on time management for Entrepreneurs

1. Keep your to-do list short. Do not go beyond 6-8 things to do. When you finish ticking each item on the list, you will have a feeling of accomplishment.
2. At the end of the day, organise your desk and e-mails so that you do not waste time next morning.
3. Identify time wasters – internet, e-mails, forwards, phone calls — before planning you day.
4. Learn to prioritise. Complete most important tasks first.
5. When you have identified and prioritised your tasks, set a time limit & stick to it
6. Take regular breaks to get back focus. It gets difficult to concentrate when you are at something for too long.
7. Keep business and family separate when at work, concentrate on it.
8. Partner with a virtual assistant for administrative tasks that can be delegated. This would let you spend more time in attending to clients.
9. There are a number of tasks which are repetitive. Develop a routine around them to be more productive.
10. Allow time between tasks to re-evaluate priorities.

✱ ✱ ✱